The New History of England

General Editors
A.G. Dickens and Norman Gash

9

The New History of England

1 J.R. Lander   Government and Community*
England 1450–1509

2 G.R. Elton   Reform and Reformation*
England 1509–1558

3 Patrick Collinson   Queen and Realm
England 1558–1603

4 Derek Hirst   Authority and Conflict
England 1603–1658

5 J.R. Jones   Country and Court*
England 1658–1714

6 W.A. Speck   Stability and Strife*
England 1714–1760

7 Ian R. Christie   Wars and Revolutions*
Britain 1760–1815

8 Norman Gash   Aristocracy and People*
Britain 1815–1865

9 E.J. Feuchtwanger   Democracy and Empire*
Britain 1865–1914

10 Max Beloff   Wars and Welfare*
Britain 1914–1945

* Already published

Democracy and Empire

Empire

Britain 1865–1914

E.J. Feuchtwanger

Edward Arnold

© E.J. Feuchtwanger 1985

First published in Great Britain 1985 by
Edward Arnold (Publishers) Ltd, 41 Bedford Square, London WC1B 3DQ

Edward Arnold (Australia) Pty Ltd, 80 Waverley Road, Caulfield East, Victoria
3145, Australia

Edward Arnold, 300 North Charles Street, Baltimore, Maryland 21201, USA

British Library Cataloguing in Publication Data

Feuchtwanger, E.J.
  Democracy and empire: Britain, 1865–1914.—
  (The New History of England; 9)
  1. Great Britain — History — Victoria, 1837–1901
  2. Great Britain — History — 20th century
  I. Title   II. Series
  941.081   DA560

  ISBN 0–7131–6161–2
  ISBN 0–7131–6162–0 Pbk

Text set in 11/12 pt Baskerville Compugraphic
by Colset Private Ltd, Singapore
Printed and bound by Richard Clay (The Chaucer Press) Ltd, Bungay, Suffolk.

Contents

Preface   vii

Introduction: Political Stability and Social Change   1
1 Parliamentary Reform and the Structure of Politics 1865–1868   27
2 The Gladstone Ministry 1868–1874   55
3 Disraeli in Power 1874–1880   84
4 The 1880s: Victorian Confidence Falters   112
5 Ireland Transforms British Politics 1880–1886   147
6 Salisbury Consolidates the Conservative Ascendancy 1886–1895   192
7 The End of Isolation, the Boer War and Tariff Reform 1885–1905   223
8 The Liberals in Power 1905–1914   273
9 Foreign Policy before 1914 and British Society on the Eve of War   346

Bibliography   372

Tables   385

Index   387

Preface

The plan of this book is broadly chronological. The principal exceptions are the introduction, chapter 4 and sections IV to IX of the final chapter; these are devoted mainly to economic and social developments which by their nature defy chronological treatment.

Like other contributors in this series I owe a great debt to the many historians who in the past and more recently have written on this period and these topics. My particular gratitude is due to Professor Norman Gash for performing his task as editor so thoroughly and so helpfully; I also had the advantage that his *Aristocracy and People: Britain 1815–1865* was already published when I started to write this volume which follows it. My thanks are due to my colleagues at Southampton, Professors Paul Smith and F.C. Mather, for many useful hints, to Dr A.J. Hanna, for transcripts from the Balfour and Chamberlain Papers, and to Miss Ethel Drus, for books from her library. The University of Southampton enabled me to make a start on the book through a period of leave in 1981 and I am indebted to the staff of the University Library for their unfailing assistance. Mary Gribble, my secretary, turned my illegible manuscript into typescript. Last but not least, my wife and children put up with my frequent retreats into the nineteenth century.

E.J. Feuchtwanger
Southampton, August 1984

Introduction: Political Stability and Social Change

I

In the autumn of the year 1865 there began in Britain a period of considerable political turmoil which within two years led to the passage of the second Reform Bill, one of the major milestones in nineteenth-century English history. The turmoil was precipitated by the death in office of the Prime Minister Lord Palmerston, who had been the dominant figure in British politics for at least a decade. His closing years in power had been a time of inertia and relative calm in domestic affairs, which were to contrast markedly with the swifter moving and more unpredictable events that followed. The departure of Palmerston is therefore a convenient dividing line between two volumes of a mainly political history of England. Much the most striking event of 1865 was the end of the American Civil War; the year also saw some important moves towards the unification of Germany under Prussia. Subsequent developments in America and Germany were to have profound repercussions on Britain's position in the world. Soon there was to be growing alarm about the relative decline in Britain's pre-eminence as the workshop of the world and her loss of power and status in the international system. For the moment, however, the mid-Victorian mood of confidence prevailed unimpaired.

Faith in the political institutions of the country was a substantial element in the optimism of the Victorians and in the 50 years up to 1914 this faith was on balance to prove itself justified. In this period major social, cultural and economic changes were gradually to undermine many of the ideas and beliefs of the mid-Victorian age, but the political structure of the country would show great resilience.

If stability is a blessing for any society, then the British political system continued to make its contribution to it, in spite of many changes in its detailed operation. In the middle 1860s politics was dominated by the long battle over the extension of the franchise. The settlement of 1867 lasted only half as long as the previous reform of

1

1832; the two Reform Bills of 1867 and 1884 each increased the electorate by about 80 per cent, whereas that of 1832 had added only about 50 per cent. By 1869 about one in three of adult males had the vote in Great Britain; by 1886 the figures were about two in three in England and Wales and three in five in Scotland. It was, however, itself a sign of stability that most of those who were pressing for reform in the 1860s regarded a change in the method of electing the House of Commons as their first priority. Most of the parliamentary political leaders of the time, except the total opponents of reform on the right and the extreme left-wing opponents of gradualism, were confident that a widening of the franchise would assist social and political stability and that the parliamentary system would survive the change fundamentally unharmed. Their confidence was not diminished by the broad philosophical debate about representative government and democracy which took place in the 1860s, ranging from J.S. Mill's *Considerations on Representative Government*, published in 1861, and the *Essays on Reform* of 1867 to innumerable speeches and articles. Many of the classical problems of mass participation in government – the dangers of the tyranny of numbers, the possible threat to property from giving the lion's share of power to those without it, the fear of allowing the most numerous class to predominate, the chances of reasoned argument prevailing in a democracy – were thoroughly debated in the context of parliamentary reform. In the end faith in the adaptability of the existing system much outweighed fear about the future. At the height of the Reform Bill debates in May 1867, Robert Lowe, the most prominent parliamentary opponent of the Bill, said: 'What I am surprised at even with fresh proofs of it accumulating daily before my eyes is, that you, the gentlemen of England – you with your ancestors behind you and your posterity before you – with your great estates, with your titles, with your honours, with your heavy stake in the well-being of this land, with an amount of material prosperity, happiness, dignity, and honour which you have enjoyed for the last 200 years, such as never before fell to the lot of any class in the world – that you wildly fling all these away without, as far as I can see, the shadow of an equivalent.'

Yet a majority of the gentlemen of England allowed the reform of 1867 to pass. As a result the House of Commons gradually ceased to be the aristocratic assembly Robert Lowe conceived himself as addressing. In 1865 it was still possible to trace a family relationship between more than half of the members of the House and the heads of the 30 most important aristocratic families. Leaders of reform like John Bright spoke out against aristocratic government; moderates like Gladstone professed themselves supporters of it. All this would have been an anachronism by 1914, but the change was more one of form than of substance. On the eve of the First World War Westminster had still not been taken over by the working classes, who for at least a generation had constituted the majority of the electorate. Established élites were still in control, even if most of them no longer belonged to the older aristocracy in a formal sense. Widening political participation had been absorbed by the system, both by containment and response. Parliamentary reform, with its milestones of 1832, 1867 and 1884, providing the key to other reforms, can be neatly fitted into a Whig interpretation of history, with a sophisticated governing class responding with wisdom to change and progress. The historical reality was more messy, but it accords even less comfortably with a Marxist-type interpretation of a relentlessly advancing proletariat.

The two major existing political parties, the Conservatives and Liberals, continued to play an important role in the political socialization of new voters. It was not until the 1880s that the idea of a separate working-class party, which had been the consequence of democratic advance in many other European countries, made any substantial headway in Britain. The liberal creed of individual dignity based on equality before the law remained in harmony with the outlook and aspirations of the most politically conscious section of the working class, the skilled artisan, who was proud of his independence but also aware of what separated him from even the lowest rungs of the middle class, the growing army of white-collar workers. Often he was a nonconformist and his political outlook was shaped more by his religious beliefs than by class-consciousness. Even more remarkably, Toryism continued to appeal to a sizeable part of the working-class electorate, particularly in areas like Lancashire and London. The appeal was based on a mixture of patriotism, deference, religious affiliation and a record of practical reform which bolstered the Tory image of caring paternalism in contrast to the harshness of economic liberalism. The adaptation of the political parties to wider political participation entailed changes in the political system. Governments could rely on tighter party discipline and acquired more grip on the procedure of the House of Commons. They were thus increasingly able to control the content and progress of legislation and the balance between executive and legislature shifted in favour of the former. These developments met up with and were complementary to the rapid expansion of State activity and of bureaucracy, a process that had been going on throughout the nineteenth century. The demand for legislation went up by leaps and bounds and governments were progressively more able to meet it. The widening of political participation was itself aided by and linked with the growth of communications, transport, urbanization and the dissemination of news. The removal of 'taxes on knowledge', culminating in the abolition of the paper duties in the 1861 budget, had given a great stimulus to the metropolitan and the provincial press. Politics became more national and less local and community-based. Deferential ties to landlords or employers, often reinforced by religious allegiance, became weaker and the nationwide criteria of social and economic class became more important as determinants of political affiliation. This in turn made it more difficult for the established parties, particularly for the Liberals, to maintain their support across the classes and the way was open for a separate party of Labour, but up to 1914 it functioned in the main as an adjunct to and not as a replacement for the Liberal Party.

In her external relations the 1860s marked for Britain the beginning of the end of a period when 'splendid isolation' could be an appropriate description of her situation. In terms of power the world was still Eurocentric and in Europe the power of Britain was such that a position of detachment could normally be maintained. That power was, however, insufficient to make any specific intervention in Europe an easily available option, as had been demonstrated in the case of Poland and Schleswig-Holstein in 1864, though British policy had played a major role in the process of Italian unification slightly earlier. Britain's world-wide imperial position brought her here and there into conflict with major powers outside Europe, mostly in the Near East and Levant; the long border between Canada and the United States was also, intermittently, a security problem. An era was about to dawn when Britain's multitudinous world-wide involvements would increasingly limit her freedom of manoeuvre by involving her in Great-Power rivalries. The cultivation of the British imperial domain was in consequence pursued more actively as part of public policy and became a major matter of political controversy. In 1868 Charles Dilke, a rising Liberal politician about to be elected to the House of Commons, published *Greater Britain*, in which he emphasized the significance of the cultural bonds that united the English-speaking peoples the world over, including the United States. It was an indication of a revival of interest in Empire and in imperialism as an ideology.

An essential ingredient in the imperialist ideology, when it came to full flower, was the feeling of the undisputed superiority of the civilization of which England was herself regarded as the most advanced and successful part. In the 1860s confidence in this superiority was as yet unshaken and its economic foundations were still beyond question. In the late 1850s Thomas Tooke, a contemporary statistician, had written of the 'solidity and vastness of amelioration in the state of Great Britain' since 1840. The amelioration continued apace in the 1860s: financial crises, like that of 1866, were swiftly overcome and the economy had never been as thriving as it was in the early 1870s. In January 1866, the Tory *Quarterly Review* declared: 'Our wealth is overflowing, our commercial prospects are unclouded, save by the excess of our own activity and nothing seems likely to disturb either the peace of Europe or the profound contentment which this island is enjoying.' In 1914 it would have been unlikely that an informed commentator would commit himself to such a statement.

II

In 1865 England was powerful and confident, but beneath the surface forces were already at work foreshadowing the very different conditions of the twentieth century. Amongst the most significant of these forces were shifts in the structure of the population and of the family, changes in the position of women, the advent of compulsory popular education, and the clash between organized religion and scientific secularism. At the beginning of the period the rapid population increase which had accompanied the Industrial Revolution was still continuing and even at its end showed only moderate signs of faltering. Between 1861 and 1871 the increase amounted to 13.5 per cent; between 1871 and 1881 it rose to 14.5 per cent; even in the decade 1901–11 it was still 11 per cent, scarcely less than what it had been 50 years earlier in the decade 1851–61. There was, however, a perceptible change in the manner in which this continued population increase came about. Up to the 1870s birth and death rates had been at a high level for some time; they then began to fall simultaneously, but the excess of births over deaths was only gradually getting smaller. This change has been termed the demographic transition, to distinguish it from the previous phase of population explosion. Well into the 1870s the crude birth rate remained above 35 per thousand, but it was below 25 per thousand by 1914. The fall looks even more dramatic when expressed as a rate per thousand women aged between 15 and 44: it dropped from more than 150 to less than 100 between the 1860s and 1914. It has been estimated that mid-Victorian couples had on average five or six children per marriage, while those married between 1900 and 1909 had only three or four. The connection between this trend and the change in the position of women during this half-century is obvious, particularly in view of the increasing life expectancy that was also being experienced. Women were concerned with child bearing and infant care for a progressively decreasing proportion of their adult lives and an increasing percentage were completing their families by the time they were 30. Death rates decreased steadily during the period from 22 per thousand in 1871–5, to 19.4 in 1881–5, to 16.1 in 1901–5 and to 14.3 in 1911–15. The fall in infant mortality was much more dramatic: it was still at 149 per thousand for infants up to one year in 1890–2, a figure hardly different from what it had been mid-century; it then dropped to 110 per thousand in 1910–12. In children aged 1–4 mortality had begun to fall by the 1870s and in the 40 years up to 1907 dropped by a third. These improvements were not due so much to specific medical advances, except for smallpox vaccination, as to higher standards of nutrition and better conditions of public health. The impact of infectious diseases like typhus, typhoid, scarlet fever, smallpox and above all tuberculosis was progressively reduced. A major cause of the sharp drop in infant mortality at the turn of the century may well have been the availability of cleaner milk. Even as late as 1911 the infant mortality among unskilled workers was twice as high as in the upper and middle classes and informed contemporary opinion put much of the blame for this on the employment of women. Average life expectancy for those born between 1838 and 1854 were 39.9 for males and 41.9 for females; for those born between 1901–12 it was 51.5 and 55.4 respectively. In the 1860s Britain was still a fast-expanding community with a high proportion of young people, but by 1914 the number of young people had already begun to decline: those under 15 formed 36.3 per cent of the population in 1861, but only 30.8 per cent in 1901. The great rise in the proportion of over-65s in the population however, was still to come. As yet there was no reduction in the proportion of the economically active age-groups between 15 and 65. From a demographic point of view the years after the middle 1870s therefore saw the beginning of a gradual change from a population explosion of unprecedented intensity and duration which had gone on since the middle of the eighteenth century, to a more stable situation, which by the 1930s looked like threatening a population decline. The social implications of this change were widespread and profound: smaller families, greater emancipation for women, different attitudes to children, higher material aspirations, and altered economic perspectives. Scarcely any facet of social life remained unaffected.

The fall in fertility was deliberately brought about through more widespread use of birth control methods of all kinds; the decline in the number of marriages, mainly due to postponement of marriage, was only a minor contributory factor and was probably itself the result of the same pressures that made for family limitation within marriage. In most of the advanced countries of Europe a phase of explosive population growth was followed in the later nineteenth century by a slow-down, due to the deliberate control of fertility. Such control was the almost inevitable concomitant of falling child mortality, although the link is not equally close everywhere and at all times. Methods of contraception became more developed, better known and more widely available, and the will to use them spread through all classes of society. In 1877 Charles Bradlaugh and Annie Besant were accused of reissuing a pamphlet on birth control, Charles Knowlton's *The Fruits of Philosophy*, which had first been published in the 1830s and previously been the subject of prosecution. The Bradlaugh – Besant trial was a key event in stimulating knowledge and debate on a hitherto forbidden subject. The accused were found guilty, though the conviction was quashed on appeal, the press was entirely hostile - and the pamphlet itself highly misleading; nevertheless sales shot up from 700 a year to 125,000 in three months. The economic advantages of smaller families and fewer children became more evident for a variety of reasons. The development of education and factory legislation made the employment of children more difficult. The interruption in economic progress after 1873, known as the Great Depression, may have dampened the optimism of many; among the better-off material aspirations and expectations were growing; even the poor, who naturally found it most difficult to acquire the knowledge and means of birth control, were becoming more aware that large families were one of the major causes of poverty, a fact noted by social investigators like Rowntree at the turn of the century. Women seized the opportunity to free themselves from excessive child-bearing as far-reaching changes in the moral climate made contraception more acceptable. The grim Malthusian doctrine about the inevitability of conflict between the pressure of population and the finite nature of resources had already lost much of its cogency by the 1850s and 1860s; the facts of rapid population growth in combination with rising living standards were clear evidence against Malthus. Falling birth and death rates and the slowing down of natural increase further weakened the doctrine and with it the structure of orthodox economic thought in which it held so important a place. The way was open for a new concept of poverty which regarded it no longer as an inevitable consequence of 'the niggardliness of nature', to use J.S. Mill's phrase, but as the product of the injustice of society. Nevertheless advocates of family limitation often still used Malthusian arguments.

Migration, both external and internal continued to have an important impact on the structure of the British population during this half-century. Some 10 per cent of the natural increase in England and Wales was lost through net emigration between 1871 and 1911; in Scotland the loss was much higher. There were peaks of emigration

in the 1880s and just before 1914, and the hope of economic betterment, particularly at moments when at home the rise in living standards appeared to be faltering, was clearly one of the main motives.
Most emigrants went to the United States and to the British Empire;
the flow towards the Empire, particularly Canada, became predominant in the latter part of the period. Emigration was still seen as a
possible cure for poverty and for unemployment, which itself became
recognized as a distinct problem by the 1880s. This view that emigration would be beneficial was often counterbalanced by fears that the
outflow would weaken the country and in combination with the
inflow of racially inferior elements contribute to that 'national
deterioration' which was so much debated by the beginning of the
new century. There was a heavy preponderance of men among overseas emigrants and this contributed to the excess of women over men
in the population.

The internal migration from rural to urban areas, which had been
one of the principal features of the Industrial Revolution, continued
apace during these 50 years. The number of towns in England and
Wales with a population of over 50,000 doubled from 37 to 75
between 1871 and 1901 and the proportion of the population living in
them rose from 36.5 per cent to nearly 45 per cent. Growth was
particularly rapid in medium-sized towns of 50,000 to 200,000 inhabitants, like Leicester, Nottingham and Hull. The six great English
conurbations of Greater London, the West Midlands, South East
Lancashire, West Yorkshire, Merseyside and Tyneside did not grow
quite so rapidly but the percentage of the English population living in
them rose from 39 to 44 in the same 30 years. If it had not been for the
work of the great public health pioneers like Sir Edwin Chadwick and
Sir John Simon in earlier years the herding together of great multi-
tudes in cities would have pushed up mortality rates to even higher
levels. The counterpart of the drift into the towns was rural
depopulation, but it is statistically more difficult to pin down. It is
reckoned that between 1871 and 1901 the rural part of the population
declined from 38 per cent to 23 per cent and every decade in the later
nineteenth century between 650,000 and 850,000 people left the
countryside. Many of the problems of late Victorian society could still
be seen as arising from the relentless process of urbanization: the
country dweller, even if poor, was healthy and close to the balance of
nature, '. . . in spite of their poverty and the worry and anxiety
attending it, they were not unhappy and, though poor, there was
nothing sordid about their lives', wrote Flora Thompson about the
inhabitants of Lark Rise in the 1890s, while a writer on the health of
urban life at the same time described city dwellers as 'neurotic,
dyspeptic, pale and undersized in adult state'. Between 1865 and

1914 Britain's two major industrial rivals, the United States and Germany, were increasing their populations much faster than Britain, the former mainly through large-scale immigration, the latter through political unification and the forces it unleashed. In the degree of urbanization Britain remained well ahead of her rivals up to 1914. By comparison with France British urbanization was still overwhelming: in 1891 nearly 32 per cent of the population of England and Wales lived in cities of over 100,000 inhabitants while only 12 per cent did in France.

III

A high natural increase in the population and falling mortality rates for both adults and children had already earlier in the nineteenth century begun to change the typical family structure. The family was becoming a more stable, long-term institution, in which both partners could hope to survive well beyond the child-bearing age of the female. It was the normal expectation that most of the children born would survive; they would know and live with their parents during their formative years and often know even their grandparents. It was rare for a family to comprise less than six members, four of them children. This pattern was the norm until at least the end of the century and only then began to change gradually towards the present-day nuclear family, with the more affluent classes leading the way. For the working classes their large families meant that a balance had to be struck between sending their children into employment at an early age to contribute to the family budget and the need and desire for education. The census of 1851 included household returns in which children between 3 and 15 were classified either as scholars or unemployed or as undescribed. Even though the figures may well exaggerate the extent of schooling that was going on, they show that between the ages of 5 to 9 the percentage of boys listed as scholars rose from 50 to over 62 per cent while the equivalent percentage for girls rose from over 46 to over 58. Most of working-class education took place up to the age of 10; after that the percentage of those in employment rose rapidly to over 48 for boys aged 13. Being a scholar did not mean full-time attendance all the year round; many children in rural areas helped in the fields, particularly at harvest time, and girls were occupied in child-minding. Between the ages of 10 and 14 37 per cent of boys and 22 per cent of girls were described as gainfully occupied in 1851. The overall figure was 30 per cent but had fallen to 17 per cent in 1901, most of them aged 13 and 14, and by 1911 only 2 per cent of children between 10 and 13 were occupied. Even in the mid-Victorian period child labour, on the abuses of which so much attention has been focused, was for the majority at most intermittent or in a domestic context. In 1865 most parents still had to make their own choice of how much education to provide for their children and had to pay for it. By 1914 elementary education was free and compulsory up to 14, although half the children still left between 12 and 14 for various reasons. Yet even in 1865 the majority of children received some schooling and the Elementary Education Act of 1870, the most important piece of educational legislation of the period, was not so much a revolution as a milestone in a long drawn-out transformation.

For a number of reasons the 1860s were a time when there was much heart-searching about education. Alarm about the loss of industrial and technological leadership, which formed so persistent a theme for the next half-century, was just beginning to be heard and educational deficiencies in comparison with other countries were among the shortcomings receiving attention. Prussia, whose educational system had often been praised, was winning spectacular victories on the battlefields. The protracted struggle about the extension of the franchise in the mid-1860s occasioned much debate over the ability of those about to be given the vote to exercise it sensibly, and again educational improvement was seen as the key to progress. The concern about the inadequacies of education expressed itself in a context in which the main purpose of schooling was still regarded as equipping pupils for the station in life to which it had pleased God to call them rather than offering them a ladder to social advancement. Thomas Wright, a journeyman engineer, writing in 1867 'on the habits and customs of the working classes' had no hesitation in saying that 'considering that the children of the working classes must under the most favourable circumstances leave school at 14 years of age, and many of them much earlier, it is a mistake to attempt to extend their school studies beyond the plain foundations of reading, writing, and arithmetic.' Each of the three enquiries into the state of education whose reports appeared in the 1860s looked at schools intended for different social classes: the Newcastle Commission on Popular Education, reporting in 1861, concerned itself with the schools provided for the children of the independent poor, namely those children whose parents were not expected to pay more than a minimum fee but who were not compelled under existing legislation to go to reformatory or industrial schools. Most of the schools for the independent poor were provided by the National Society for

Promoting the Education of the Poor in the Principles of the Established Church, some 6,000 schools; another 1,500 were provided by the mainly nonconformist British and Foreign Schools Society. Both these societies were in receipt of State aid and by the 1860s the amount of education grant was second only to defence as a charge on the national budget, constituting about a fifth of civil expenditure. It was the size of this burden on the taxpaper that helped to make education so much of a public preoccupation at this time. The Taunton Commission on Endowed Schools, reporting in 1868, was set up to enquire into schools for the middle classes. As a rough rule the Commissioners assumed that they were concerned with the education of children whose parents were above that six-sevenths of the population who were regarded as the labouring classes. The proportion of six-sevenths was still used as a guideline in determining educational need when under the Elementary Education Act of 1870 school boards came to be set up in areas where provision was deemed to be inadequate. Lastly the Clarendon Commission, reporting in 1867, looked at the seven long-established and well known public schools, Eton, Harrow, Winchester, Westminster, Rugby, Charterhouse and Shrewsbury, which were expected to educate the children of the upper classes. In practice the social structure of England and Wales was far too complex by the 1860s to enable the schools to be so neatly divided according to the social background of their pupils.

The Clarendon Commission's recommendations were concerned with a widening of the curriculum and with the administration of the seven public schools, but the reforms associated with the names of Dr Arnold and other reforming headmasters such as Thring of Uppingham had already been in progress for a generation and the middle years of the century had seen many new foundations, such as Marlborough and Wellington. By the last third of the century the public schools, revived and much more numerous, were the normal means of education for the sons of the aristocracy, landed gentry and upper middle classes. It was still the case that two prime ministers of the 1860s from very different social backgrounds, Russell and Disraeli, had both been privately educated. Russell after a brief sojourn at Westminster was educated by a clergyman along with other sons of the high aristocracy; Disraeli, for reasons unknown, escaped being sent to Winchester like his younger brothers and went to a Unitarian clergyman. Such educational histories were, however, becoming rarer among leading men and to have attended a major public school was becoming as important as having been to Oxford or Cambridge. This now more clearly marked out educational route through the public schools inevitably increased the distance between those who took it and those who did not. In the eighteenth century the

sons of local tradesmen had sat alongside the offspring of the aristocracy at Eton or Winchester, but it was no longer so. Dr Moberly, the
Headmaster of Winchester, said in his evidence to the Clarendon
Commissioners: 'Every school of this size has a definite character,
and gives a peculiar stamp to its pupils; and I could, with more or less
distinctness, characterize the pupils of the public schools of England
by the particular stamp or mint-mark they bear'.

   The Taunton Commission looked at a much wider range of
schools, 942 in all, a sample of all types of secondary schools lying
between elementary schools on the one hand and the seven public
schools investigated by Clarendon and his colleagues on the other.
Many, including Matthew Arnold, regarded this as the weakest part
of the whole educational system, with the middle classes who patron-
ized it lagging far behind their continental equivalents. Secondary
education of this type was provided by all kinds of endowed grammar
schools, often very ancient, some very decrepit, others so successful
that they had moved into public-school rank. There were proprietary
day schools founded within the last 30 or 40 years such as University
College School or King's College School and also private boarding
schools like Cheltenham or Malvern. There were some schools like
the foundations of Nathaniel Woodard seeking to provide a public-
school education, including a strong Anglican orientation, on a more
modest scale. These schools provided education for the middle classes
who could not quite afford the leading public schools. The whole of
this sector was without any public supervision, except that, where
there were endowments, these had come within the purview of the
Charity Commission, which was established in 1853. The abuses
which Dickens tried to expose with Dotheboys Hall could and did
occur. The recommendations of the Taunton Commission were far-
reaching and owed a good deal to the work done by Matthew Arnold,
who had made an intensive study of continental secondary education
for the commissioners. They would have liked to regularize the
immense diversity of this educational sector into a threefold hierarchy, corresponding to the social standing of the pupils and their
parents and their respective aspirations, but also serving as a means of
reaching the highest rungs of the educational ladder. There were to be
four boarding schools of the highest grade for every million inhabitants and one of the second grade for every 100,000, and a day school
of the third grade for every town. So ambitious a scheme would have
required a degree of government interference hardly in keeping with
the spirit of the times. Woodard feared that the religious purpose of
his schools would be lost. Thring and others feared that their own
reformed and successful schools would be artificially distinguished
from the Clarendon Seven and lumped together with a lot of inferior

establishments. He started what became the Headmasters' Conference to organize opposition to the Taunton proposals.

As a result of such criticism the Endowed Schools Act of 1869 had only the limited purpose of improving the application of existing endowments. An Endowed Schools Commission was appointed to draw up reorganization schemes for endowments more than 50 years old and more recent ones where this was asked for. Parents could withdraw their children from religious instruction and teachers did not have to be in holy orders. Decaying old grammar schools like Oundle or Sedbergh were enabled to graduate into the ranks of public schools, while others, like Sherborne or Repton, where that process was already under way, could carry it further. To meet the requirements of the endowment, separate day schools for the sons of local tradesmen and artisans, the third grade of the Taunton Commission, were often established. A major gap remained in English secondary education, in comparison with Scotland and many continental countries, for no general network of cheap and easily accessible secondary schools came into existence at this stage. Although some of the bigger school boards began to enter the field by the 1880s, the gap was not really closed until the Education Act of 1902.

The future of the schools investigated by the Clarendon and Taunton Commissions was of great significance for the development of the élites in English society, but the most urgent concern in the 1860s was with that part of the child population, allegedly six-sevenths, which lay outside their enquiries. Whereas the Newcastle Commission had been reassuring, claiming that only 120,000 out of over 2,600,000 children between the age of 3 and 15 received no education, most of those with the closest knowledge of this situation, the school inspectors, regarded these figures as over-optimistic both quantitatively and qualitatively. Since 1862 the government's grants to voluntary schools, mainly the National and the British schools, had been governed by the famous Revised Code and were based on achievements mostly in the three 'R's (reading, writing and arithmetic), as assessed by the school inspectorate. This system of 'payment by results' was called by Matthew Arnold, because of its narrowing effects, 'the heaviest blow dealt at civilization and improvement in my time'. There was an increasing tendency for lower middle-class parents, small farmers and businessmen, shopkeepers, foremen and overseers to patronize National and British schools for their children. Their view of education was often narrow and they, like most working-class parents, did not want their children to go beyond a good grounding in the three 'R's. 'Too much schooling oftener mars a man of business than makes him' was a common opinion and many businessmen of considerable affluence were self-made and had little education. School managers were tempted to charge higher fees and move their schools up-market. They forgot that their schools were originally established for the education of the poor. In 1864 the Education Department issued instructions to make ineligible for grant the children of parents in certain occupations who were capable of paying more than ninepence a week, but the inspectors found these instructions difficult to enforce. If it was one of the objects of the Revised Code to limit expenditure it certainly failed, for in 1869 the central government spending on schools was back where it had been in 1861. The fact was that there was a great need among the lower middle classes and the better-off sections of the working classes for good elementary education. More money went to places where schooling was already reasonably good; slum areas of big cities and parts of the countryside lacking patronage were comparatively neglected. An inspector commenting in 1869 on the situation in Manchester and Liverpool said that the class 'which lies between paupers and criminals on the one hand and skilled working men on the other hand . . . finds the provision made, whether by voluntary effort or by the State . . . wholly insufficient'. Ragged schools, which had come into existence in the 1830s, could not fill the gap; in the 1860s, when the Ragged School Union was at its most active, it assisted 200 schools claiming an average total attendance of 20,000 pupils.

It was thus left to the Elementary Education Act of 1870 to fill the gap in the education of the children of what were sometimes called 'the dangerous classes'. The school boards established under this Act did gradually provide more educational opportunities for that broad band of children whose parents were below the level of the skilled and respectable working classes, but who did not fall into the net of remedial measures provided by law for the children of the criminal or destitute. The period of grace which the Act allowed the voluntary system before calling for the establishment of school boards greatly stimulated denominational effort in building new schools and improving existing ones. Once the school boards were in existence, particularly in the big towns, they took compulsory powers, so that by 1873 40 per cent, and by 1876 50 per cent of the population was under compulsory powers, 84 per cent in boroughs. The majority of schools were still voluntary schools – 14,000 out of over 17,000 in 1880 – but it was a steadily declining majority. The feeling that the voluntary system could not in the long run compete with the board schools was one of the motives behind the further Education Act the Conservatives passed in 1876. Even many Tory squires and parsons now felt that more general powers to compel attendance were necessary to keep voluntary schools in rural areas in business. The 1876 Act used the principle of indirect compulsion by forbidding the employment of children under 10 and making the possession of a certificate of attainment or of attendance a condition for the employment of children between 10 and 14. A Liberal Act of 1880 developed the network of compulsion further. A new education code introduced in 1875 raised the standard in the obligatory three 'R's and encouraged the teaching of a broader range of subjects, such as history, geography and elementary science. The bigger urban boards began to establish so-called Higher Grade Schools, providing a kind of secondary education; children from the lower echelons of the middle class rubbed shoulders with working-class children in such schools.

Both quantitatively and qualitatively big strides forward were thus made, but many shortcomings remained. The educational system as a whole reflected the hierarchy of social classes and elementary education was in the main provided for the working classes. There were the beginnings of a meritocratic ladder, but it worked only for a small minority. A network of schools charging different levels of fees came into existence in the big cities, but those from the poorest homes tended to be kept segregated in the cheapest and least favoured schools. Artisan parents did not have to worry too much that their children would pick up lice from classmates coming out of the slums. There was still much truancy and evasion of the complex regulations for compulsion; it was not until 1891 that the virtual abolition of fees supplied an essential prop to the enforcement of attendance. The system could initially hardly cope with the growing influx of poor and ignorant children and much of the learning remained of the mechanical kind encouraged by the Revised Code of 1862. The actual proportion of pupils who qualified for grant even in the three 'R's remained at 25 per cent in 1880. Yet Thomas Hardy tells us of Tess of the d'Urbervilles, probably born in the late 1860s:

> Between the mother [of Tess], with her fast perishing lumber of superstitions, folklore, dialect, and orally transmitted ballads, and the daughter, with her trained National teachings, and Standard Knowledge under an infinitely Revised Code, there was a gap of two hundred years as ordinarily understood. When they were together the Jacobean and the Victorian ages were juxtaposed.

IV

While the gradual introduction of compulsory education had thus a profound impact on working-class life in the later Victorian period, it was among the middle and upper classes that changes in the position of women showed themselves most clearly. Long before the demographic shifts had made their impact intrepid individuals had made assaults on specific sectors of the great bastion of male supremacy and female inequality, from Mary Wollstonecraft in the late eighteenth century through Caroline Norton to Barbara Leigh Smith and Florence Nightingale in the 1850s. Minor reforms had been made in the massive inequality of women before the law, over the custody of infants in 1839 and over divorce in 1857. The passage of the Marriage and Divorce Act of 1857 had cut across a simultaneous attempt to deal with married women's property. If it was right to protect a woman's property when she had been injured by her husband's adultery and misconduct, there was no need, so it was still argued, to give a woman who was safely married any right of disposing over property independent of her husband. To do so would have, in the words of the *Saturday Review*, 'set at defiance the commonsense of mankind and would revolutionize society. There is besides a smack of selfish independence about it which rather jars with poetical notions of wedlock.' Twenty-five years later sentiment had sufficiently changed to make possible the passage of an effective Married Women's Property Act. The cause of female advancement was even more clearly symbolized in the demand for women's votes, which in organized form first appeared in the 1860s. During the debates on parliamentary reform in 1866 a petition for female suffrage signed by 1,500 women was presented and in the following year an amendment in favour of substituting 'person' for 'man' in the Reform Bill then before the House was defeated by 196 to 73. Leading these moves was John Stuart Mill, for long an advocate of women's rights; his book on *The Subjection of Women*, published in 1869, became a bible for feminists the world over. The failure to include women's votes in the 1867 parliamentary reform led to the foundation of the National Society for Women's Suffrage and thenceforth the cause was constantly but not prominently on the political agenda. Its parliamentary supporters were mostly on the left of the Liberal party.

Another cause which brought the legal and social aspects of women's rights to public attention from the late 1860s onwards was the campaign for the repeal of the Contagious Diseases Acts. These Acts had been quietly slipped on to the statute book in the 1860s; they were designed to combat sexually transmitted diseases through the control of prostitutes, mainly by subjecting them to periodic medical examination, and they owed a good deal to continental models. The operation of the Acts was confined to garrison towns and to naval dockyards, but there was an influential body of opinion that wanted to extend them. The crusade against the Acts was led by Mrs Josephine Butler, the prototype of the fearless, dedicated, principled Victorian reformer. In the House of Commons James Stansfeld, a Liberal Radical, became the champion of this cause and finally achieved the repeal of the Acts in 1886. The core of Josephine Butler's campaign against the Acts was an attack on the dual standard of sexual morality, by which women were condemned, treated as outcasts and subjected to humiliating treatment, while the men who used their services retained their reputation and respectability. Society condoned a great deal of sexual licence in men while the slightest transgression lost a woman her reputation:

> Adultery it is not fit
> Or safe, for women, to commit

as the poet Arthur Hugh Clough put it. The counterpart to the 'fallen woman' was the pure woman, the guardian of the hearth who was not defiled by any suspicion of sexual desire. The mirror-image of public prurience was the easy availability of pornographic material. These Victorian attitudes to sex were closely interlinked with class: purity and delicacy were attributes of middle-class ladies, for whom work was not fitting and sex was not a matter for pleasure, but had no application to working-class women nor to the large army of mostly female domestic servants. The campaign against the Contagious Diseases Acts, the 'Safe Harlots Protection Acts' as some called them, attracted a good deal of working-class support, not least because the prostitutes affected by the Acts were generally working-class, while the higher class of kept women, mistresses or fashionable courtesans were left undisturbed. The mostly middle-class suffragists, on the other hand, tended to steer clear of Josephine Butler's campaign in spite of its feminist emphasis, because they did not want to get mixed up with so unsavoury a subject as prostitution. In fact the campaign was by no means out of step with the prevailing repressive and prurient public attitude to sex, for it was always stressed that by licensing prostitution the Acts condoned an evil that should never be tolerated.

In a long drawn-out process of women's emancipation the battles against discriminatory laws were of practical but of even greater symbolic importance. Battles and victories owed much to the general advance of women, mostly middle-class women, out of their domestic role, but they also blazed a trail for this advance. In the most active

age-groups there was a surplus of women of around 10 per cent, yet
the opportunities for employment for unmarried middle-class women
were very limited. The usual fate of such women was to become a
governess; in Victorian fiction she is more often than not stereotyped
as a sad and vulnerable figure. Perhaps the most famous example is
Jane Eyre; Charlotte Brontë was a governess only briefly but,
according to Mrs Gaskell, had decided views on the subject:

> She said that none but those who had been in the position of a governess could
> ever realize the dark side of 'respectable' human nature; under no great tempta-
> tion to crime, but daily giving way to selfishness and ill-temper, till its conduct
> towards those dependent on it sometimes amounts to a tyranny of which one
> would rather be the victim than the inflicter . . .

George Eliot, herself a great champion of women's rights, makes the
beautiful Gwendolen Harleth, the heroine of *Daniel Deronda*, exclaim
when threatened with becoming a governess: '. . . I don't see that it
would be pleasanter to be looked down on in a bishop's family than in
any other . . . I would rather emigrate than be a governess'.

It was therefore natural that in an age of widening educational
opportunities for men, and when the professions were becoming more
organized and institutionalized, women should become part of this
movement. The 1860s were a time of significant early advances for
the women's cause often in the face of deeply entrenched attitudes of
hostility. Miss Buss and Miss Beale had emerged in the 1850s as
pioneers of girls' secondary education at the North London
Collegiate School and at Cheltenham College. Both of them gave
evidence to the Taunton Commission in 1865, along with Emily
Davies, another pioneer of female education. Women had almost
never before appeared before such a committee and even these
intrepid ladies were highly nervous, but this made a good impression
with the Commissioners. 'We were all so much struck by their perfect
womanliness. Why there were tears in Miss Buss's eyes!' said one of
them. The Taunton report was encouraging for girls' education and
condemned the indifference of parents towards it. 'The appropriation
of almost all the educational endowments of the country to the
education of boys is felt by a large and increasing number both of men
and women to be cruel injustice.'

Advances in girls' secondary could not be separated from women's
progress in higher education. The University Extension Movement
flourished largely because it met the desire of middle-class women to
break out of the narrow domestic horizons conventionally prescribed
for them. In 1867 James Stuart, the Cambridge don who was to
become a principal protagonist of the movement, went to Liverpool,
at the request of Mrs Butler and of Miss Clough, sister of the poet and

later the first Principal of Newnham, to lecture on Astronomy. It was still regarded as improper for young ladies to question or be questioned by a young man and Stuart therefore distributed printed questions and offered to correct written answers. He expected 30 and got 300. The Cambridge Local Examinations system facilitated the admission of women to public examinations; from this it became possible to press forward to the foundation of a women's college. At first it was located at Hitchin in Hertfordshire, but in 1870 it moved to Girton. The distance of two miles which separated it from Cambridge itself was felt to be the minimum required to save the University from upheaval, but not long afterwards a few female students were accommodated in a house in the city, the modest beginnings of Newnham. A few years later Oxford followed, with Somerville and Lady Margaret Hall.

In the meantime the battle to open more of the middle-class employment market to women was proceeding. Florence Nightingale had turned nursing into a trained profession fit for ladies. Pioneers like Elizabeth Garrett and Sophia Jex-Blake had prised open the entry into the medical profession for women, though here the results were more symbolic than real. In 1881 there were 25 female medical doctors of all kinds, and in 1901 there were still only 212, whereas the number of male doctors had risen from 15,000 to 22,000. Other professions were even more difficult for women to enter: in the law there were 100 female clerks in 1881 and 367 in 1901, compared with 25,000 and 34,000 men respectively and there were no women barristers or solicitors. The employment of women was very much a question of class. The great expansion of female employment was in the lower middle-class white-collar occupations, such as clerks and shop assistants. The Post Office, for example, had taken on women for the first time in the Savings Bank Department in 1872 and had to dismiss them again because of male opposition; but by 1881 there were 2,000 in the telegraph service. By 1911 the General Post Office employed nearly 35,000 women in the telephone and telegraph service and as counter clerks. Working-class women had always been in employment above all as domestic servants. In 1881 44 per cent of all female employment was still in domestic service but 20 years later the percentage was down to 40. Teaching had long employed many women; the numbers rose from 80,000 in 1861 to 150,000 in 1891.

In the industrial employment of women the battle had always been for its limitation, often against the opposition of men and women, both in the numbers of hours worked and in the exclusion of women from dangerous or socially objectionable occupations, like underground work in the pits. As late as 1887 regulations made to exclude women from certain mining work considered injurious to health aroused vigorous protests from the women involved. They were supported by the women's suffrage movement and a deputation of them went to see the Home Secretary accompanied by Mrs Fawcett, the leading suffragist. When the Home Secretary said that he had been advised by a medical officer that lifting heavy hammers was bad for women of child-bearing age, a member of the deputation called out 'I ha'had 14 children, sir, and I never was better in my life'. The crux of the matter was the much lower pay received by women in working-class and lower middle-class occupations compared with men: in most areas of employment women received scarcely half of what men were paid. In the world of trade unions the women's cause had an uphill battle; the work of Emma Patterson bore fruit only after her death, in the formation of the Women's Trade Union League in 1889.

V

The restriction of women to 'separate spheres' was mainly a middle-class phenomenon and it was mainly progressive reformers from the middle classes who started to break down these restrictions. The great demographic changes described earlier had to make themselves broadly felt before the position of women in all classes could be transformed profoundly. The coming of the demographic transition was in its turn intimately connected with the process of urbanization and secularization. The decline in the power and influence of organized religion was one of the most striking developments of the half-century before 1914 but in the 1860s it had scarcely begun. The famous census on religious worship of 1851 had reported over seven million persons attending a place of worship on a Sunday and just over half of them were Anglicans. Over five million who could have attended did not do so. The Church of England was delicately poised between vigour and decline. It was still much the largest of the denominations, but with so many giving their allegiance to other denominations or apparently outside the reach of organized religion, the claim to be the national Church was open to attack. In the Church of England energies were as much taken up by the continuing conflict between the parties within the Church as by the defence of the Church from outside attacks. High, Low and Broad Church were in a state of considerable polarization and the frequent resort to legal proceedings did not encourage a spirit of conciliation. The High Church party was not synonymous with the Oxford Movement, now in its second generation, but it still owed much of its vigour and influence to the infusion of spirit of some 30 years previously. The younger generation of Tractarians were generally known as Ritualists, because of their emphasis on formal liturgical ceremonies. These attracted much hostility among Evangelicals and Low Churchmen and became the object of a number of court cases. Ritualists felt the shadow of martyrdom falling on them and became in the main enemies of establishment. More moderate High Churchmen like Gladstone also felt uneasiness about secular and lay interference in matters of doctrine and Church discipline. Politically the Ritualists were a thorn in the flesh to Tories, because it made the mobilization of Anglicanism as an electoral force difficult. Disraeli, himself hardly a sectarian churchman, felt increasing animosity against the High Church party, which was heartily reciprocated. All this was to have political repercussions during the Eastern Crisis in the mid-1870s. The Low Church had been in the ascendant in the Palmerston years. Palmerston, of whom it was said that 'he does not know, in theology, Moses from Sydney Smith', made most of his ecclesiastical appointments from that section, often on the advice of the famous Evangelical Lord Shaftesbury and the Queen sometimes protested against them as being unscholarly. She and the Prince Consort favoured moderate Low Churchmen. The average energetic and strenuous, but none too dogmatic Victorian cleric was most likely a Low Churchman; Trollope's Dr Proudie, 'who bore with the idolatry of Rome, tolerated even the infidelity of Socinianism, and was hand in glove with the Presbyterian Synods of Scotland and Ulster', and evidently appointed to the Bishopric of Barchester by Palmerston, was perhaps a little too tolerant for a Low Churchman, while in his chaplain Mr Slope, who 'in doctrine like his patron, is tolerant of dissent' but whose 'soul trembles in agony at the iniquities of the Puseyites', Trollope drew a caricature of the cleric low not only in churchmanship but in cunning.

The Broad Church was less of a party than a number of influential individuals, lay as well as clerical, but it stirred up as much if not more controversy than the Ritualists. These liberal Anglicans wanted to make Christianity compatible with two major developments which might otherwise turn an increasing number of the best minds away from it altogether. On the one hand there was the school of scientific biblical criticism, mainly German, and to a lesser extent the German philosophers from Kant onwards. The other threat to faith came from the theory of evolution, enunciated most fully by Darwin in *The Origin of Species* in 1859; it endangered belief in the literal inspiration of the Bible, central to much of Protestant Christianity. In 1860 a number of liberal churchmen published *Essays and Reviews*, a book in which they tried to demonstrate that the Church could come to terms with these challenges. Benjamin Jowett and Mark Pattison, both notable Oxford figures, were the inspirers and among the contributors to the book. Pattison was generally taken to be the model for Mr Casaubon in *Middlemarch*; George Eliot herself had translated D.F. Strauss's *Leben Jesu*, one of the key works of German biblical criticism, and had become a prey to religious doubt. The two beneficed clergy among the contributors to *Essays and Reviews* were prosecuted, but acquitted on appeal to the Judicial Committee of the Privy Council in 1864. In the following year the same body also acquitted Bishop Colenso of Natal, who had questioned the literal accuracy of the Bible. These decisions greatly agitated the High Church party, while not really alleviating the sense of persecution among Broad Churchmen. High Anglicans began to have doubts again about the Establishment and certainly wanted a reform of the judicial system for ecclesiastical cases. In the Colenso case Gladstone claimed that 'this sentence of the Privy Council amounts to the utter destruction of the supremacy in South Africa by the Crown itself'. *Essays and Reviews* and the Colenso case kept minds astir for years. There were many gradations of view among Broad Churchmen: Frederick Temple, for example, the Headmaster of Rugby and another of the contributors to *Essays and Reviews*, found his way back to acceptable orthodoxy sufficiently to be made Bishop of Exeter by Gladstone in 1869 and eventually became Archbishop of Canterbury. A.P. Stanley, the Broad Church Dean of Westminster, to whom Disraeli is supposed to have said 'Remember, Mr Dean, no dogma, no dean', was well qualified to be a bishop, but too much of a marked man to be made one. The growth of religious doubt, although it affected the Church of England most of all, was a problem for all Christian denominations; therefore evangelical churchmen could sometimes be found fighting alongside dissenters against what was regarded as insidious subversion by liberal doctrines. The great mid-Victorian agnostics, from George Eliot to T.H. Huxley, were in fact as representative of their age as the believers. Most of them thought that morality could be upheld without the prop of the Christian religion. Their high-minded optimism was often based on a refusal to contemplate the deeper abysses of the human condition. This limitation of vision, partly deliberate, partly unconscious, was a characteristic which they shared with that majority of their countrymen who had retained their faith, but which set them apart from some of their leading contemporaries on the continent.

The often bitter fighting among churchmen was a distraction from what was widely recognized as perhaps the most urgent problem facing the Church of England as well as the nonconformists: the apathy among the working classes towards religion, at any rate in any organized form, revealed by the census of 1851. Between that date and 1871 the Church of England increased its number of churches by more than 10 per cent, though neither the numbers of buildings nor of the clergy kept pace with the growth of population. The custom of charging pewrents was still widespread and only gradually declined in the closing decades of the century. It segregated the moneyed and respectable members of the congregation and therefore constituted a barrier to working-class attendance at church. Shortcomings in facilities were, however, not the main reason why the Church had difficulty in approaching those at the lower end of the social hier-archy. A former costermonger told Henry Mayhew, the observer of the London poor, 'the costers somehow mix up being religious with being respectable, and so they have a queer sort of feeling about it. It's a mystery to them.' F.D. Maurice, Charles Kingsley and other Christian Socialists were trying to bridge this gulf. The problem was acute in large urban areas and increasing urbanization was aggravating it. The parish organization of the Church of England, which in rural areas still worked well in drawing all the people into its net, was much less well adapted to urban conditions and particularly to the poorer areas of large towns. Anglicans began to adopt the revivalist approach of the dissenters and the use of missions and settlements, sponsored in many cases by Oxford and Cambridge colleges and the public schools. Even so it is unlikely that the hold of the Church on the poorer classes was any greater in the 1870s than it had been in the 1850s.

On the face of it, the nonconformists should have been better placed to cope with the religious need of the urban poor, but it was not necessarily so. They had men like the Baptist minister Charles Spurgeon, thought to be the greatest preacher of the age, who could draw large congregations running into tens of thousands. Observers were uncertain, however, whether he was mainly preaching to the converted rather than attracting the otherwise apathetic working classes. In the 1870s the American evangelists, Moody and Sankey, enthused large audiences by impressive congregational singing, in a new revivalist wave, but again opinion was divided on their success in appealing to previously impervious sections of the population. The older dissenting denominations, Baptists, Congregationalists, Unitarians, Presbyterians and Quakers, now represented so much of the wealth and leadership in the provincial towns where they were strong that it was no easier for them to approach the poor than it was for the Church of England. Apart from the Primitive Methodists, who flourished in a few towns and in some agricultural and mining areas, the original Wesleyan Methodist Connection was probably the most successful of the nonconformists in holding congregations in the big manufacturing centres in spite of their traditional political conservatism and in spite of the growing worldly success of many of their members.

The sects themselves were becoming more organized as denominations, with centralized bureaucratic institutions controlling their various activities, such as missions and training of ministers. This was particularly true of the Congregationalists and Baptist, but even the various Methodist sects, in spite of the pride they took in their original revivalist inspiration, did not escape it. After the 1860s centralization proceeded rapidly: for example, the Baptist Union established augmentation and annuity funds in the 1870s and in 1873 adopted a new constitution strengthening the central organization against the local churches. In theology the hard edges of Calvinist doctrine had long been softened and literal preaching of the Bible had given way to a more eclectic and liberal approach. The great nonconformist preachers of the later Victorian period took scriptural texts as pegs on which to hang their own interpretations of doctrine and experience. Dr Clifford, the famous Baptist divine, wrote in 1888: 'systems of doctrine are trifles light as air to souls that see God face to face in immediate fellowship with the Eternal Spirit'. In its own way nonconformity was changing under the impact of the general challenges to the Christian faith that also faced the Church of England. Politically it remained tied to the Liberal Party and later passed some of its ethos on to the Labour Party. It continued to inspire some of the particular causes, from temperance to disestablishment, within the Liberal movement; but both organizational and doctrinal developments were weakening the cutting edge of its radicalism. As dissenting grievances were one by one dismantled, religious nonconformism became for many individuals a less important determinant of their political choice.

The spread of religious doubt and secularism were perhaps the most important among all the agents of change in late Victorian England. J.A. Froude, the historian, had himself experienced the great Victorian crisis of faith. The hero of his novel *Nemesis of Faith*, published in 1849, is an Anglican priest who moves from Tractarianism to Catholicism and yet finds his faith crumbling – his 'new faith fabric had been reared upon the clouds of sudden violent feeling, and no air castle was ever of more unabiding growth; doubt soon sapped it, and remorse, not for what he had done, but for what he had not done; and amidst the wasted ruins of his life . . . he sank down into the barren waste . . .' Froude became the biographer and hero-worshipper of Carlyle, gloomiest and most negative of Victorian critics, yet he could also write: 'in every department of life – in its business and its pleasures, in its beliefs and in its theories, in its material developments and in its spiritual convictions – we thank God that we are not like our fathers.' Froude was among the small minority most fully aware of philosophical and theological doubt, yet he still shared the faith in progress of mid-Victorian Britain. The vast majority of Englishmen were unaffected by doubt or cultural pessimism and expected their country to remain in the van of human progress.

1 Parliamentary Reform and the Structure of Politics 1865–1868

I

When Palmerston died of a chill on 18 October 1865, two days before his eight-first birthday, it was felt to be the end of an era. Coming away from the funeral, Sir Charles Wood, soon to become the first Viscount Halifax and a colleague of Palmerston's in many Whig cabinets, remarked: 'our quiet days are over; no more peace for us.' Parliamentary reform was the most important domestic political question becalmed by Palmerston's longevity. Since the great Reform Act of 1832 massive changes in the size and distribution of the population had produced growing inconsistencies in the representative system. Such illogicalities constituted an argument for reform quite apart from any desire to distribute the franchise more widely and from 1850 onwards there had been attempts by successive governments to legislate, but absence of strong public pressure had rendered them abortive. In July 1865 Palmerston fought his last general election and did not mention reform in his nomination address; eight years earlier, in the general election of 1857, he had at least made an ambiguous reference to it. Most of the members elected in the Palmerstonian majority of 1865 had similarly ignored parliamentary reform in their election addresses. Yet, reluctant though Whigs, moderate Liberals and Palmerston himself were to tackle the question, it would not lie down. In the interval between the election and Palmerston's death a possible reform bill in the next session of parliament was under discussion in the cabinet and elsewhere. The extent of enfranchisement proposed by such a bill could become a divisive issue in the heterogeneous Liberal Party. There was much talk of a realignment of parties, possibly after Palmerston's departure, a fusion of Whigs, moderate Liberals and Conservatives. For many years the Conservatives had offered little opposition to Lord Palmerston's government and many Tory back-benchers probably preferred him to their own leaders, Lord Derby and Benjamin Disraeli, particularly the latter. These two men had led the Conservatives for some 15 years, one in the Lords, the other in the Commons. Their followers had for most of the 20 years since the great Tory split of 1846 formed the largest and most coherent grouping in the House of Commons, but it was a party never quite large enough to sustain a majority government. Facing them was an amalgam of Whigs, middle-of-the-road Liberals, Radicals of various persuasions and loosely connected groups of Irish members. Amongst the leaders of this amalgam members of the Whig aristocracy were still prominent, men like Lord John Russell, now first Earl Russell, son of the sixth Duke of Bedford, the fourth Earl of Clarendon, a member of the Villiers family, and George Leveson-Gower, second Earl Granville and a member of the family whose principal title was the Dukedom of Sutherland. Also among the leaders were a few survivors of the Peelite group, the free-trading Tories who had remained loyal to Sir Robert Peel after 1846; the most important of these was William Ewart Gladstone, Chancellor of the Exchequer under Palmerston. The Whig-Liberal Party had been for most of the time since 1846 the party of government, but even when its position seemed most secure, as after the greatest of Palmerston's election victories in 1857, its lack of cohesion was such as to cause Palmerston to fall from power less than a year after his triumph at the polls.

Conservatives and right-wing Liberals often had more in common than the latter had with their formal allies the Radicals. The veteran John Bright, first elected to Parliament in 1843, was, after the death of Richard Cobden in 1865, the most conspicuous leader of the Liberal Left. The Radicals had received important reinforcements in the election of July 1865, not so much in members as in personalities. John Stuart Mill, perhaps the most prestigious living philosopher of representative government, Thomas Hughes, Christian Socialist and author of *Tom Brown's School Days*, and Henry Fawcett, the blind economist, were among a number of gifted left-wing Liberals who first entered the House of Commons at this time. Outside Parliament some of the trade union leaders of the 1860s, men like Robert Applegarth and George Odger, attached as much importance to political activity as they did to the improvement of social and economic conditions through the work of their unions. A number of foreign causes, Garibaldi and the Risorgimento, Poland, above all the American Civil War, had roused them and their followers and had created a network of institutional and informal links between organized and politically aware members of the working classes, parliamentary Radicals, middle-class intellectuals and journalists.

This loose connection was by 1865 turning its attention to parliamentary reform again, after some years when this cause had seemed without immediate prospects of realization. Symptomatic of this revival of interest was the foundation in April 1864 of the National Reform Union, based in Manchester. It was a predominantly middle-class body, which included among its members some prominent Radical MPs, such as Peter Taylor, T.B. Potter and Henry Fawcett, as well as intellectuals like T.H. Green and Thorold Rogers. Its original programme advocated the ballot, namely secret instead of the customary open voting, a redistribution of seats according to population and property, triennial Parliaments and a franchise in counties and boroughs for every male person, householder or lodger, rated or liable to be rated for the relief of the poor. Mention of manhood suffrage was carefully avoided. At about the same time, in the spring of 1864, parliamentary reform was arousing attention again in the world of the London labour movement and its various organizations, much stimulated by Gladstone's famous statement in the House of Commons that 'every man who is not presumably incapacitated by some consideration of personal unfitness or of political danger, is morally entitled to come within the pale of the constitution.' The eventual outcome was the foundation, in February 1865, of the Reform League, a body mainly of working-class reformers. Its declared objective was manhood suffrage. This could, however, be taken to mean the vote for every adult male who through a permanent residence qualified for inclusion in the electoral register. The door was therefore left open to compromise with other reformers, among them Bright, who were not prepared to go all the way to manhood suffrage. The Reform League and the Reform Union became the most prominent promoters of parliamentary reform but the existence of this extra-parliamentary reform movement was by no means a major factor in the decision of the new Russell government to introduce a reform bill in the session of 1866.

The choice of Russell to succeed Palmerston was almost inevitable. As an ex-Prime Minister and the greatest living embodiment of Whiggism his claims could hardly be passed over. The composition of his long-standing feud with Palmerston in 1859 had been a major element in producing the political stability of the last few years. Russell's return to the highest office after an interval of over 13 years and at the age of 73 was not calculated to arouse enthusiasm. Even in his hey-day he had a reputation for poor judgement, lack of tact and administrative incompetence. With Russell in the Lords, Gladstone became leader of the House of Commons as well as remaining Chancellor of the Exchequer; he was clearly the second man in the government. Both Russell and Gladstone were in favour of committing the government to parliamentary reform. For the new Prime Minister it was the last opportunity to crown his life's work, which he had begun with the introduction of the first reform bill in 1831. Gladstone had for long displayed reluctance to support further parliamentary reform but the signs of greater social harmony in recent years and the sense of responsibility displayed by many sections of the working classes had convinced him, like many others among the political classes, that the arguments for further enfranchisement were now irresistible. His public if cautious endorsement of this position had more than anything else marked him out as a possible future leader of Liberalism. In the long evening of Palmerstonian inertia the Radical movement increasingly placed their faith in Gladstone as the one leading member of the government sympathetic to their aims.

Russell and Gladstone were faced with a delicate problem of political balance in keeping the far-flung Liberal connection united after the removal of Palmerston. Clarendon, another pillar of Whiggism, who had just returned to the Foreign Office, wrote of the party as 'a great bundle of sticks . . . now unloosed . . . nobody to tie them up'. The nature and extent of parliamentary reform was part of this problem. A group of anti-reform Liberals had shown its hand earlier in the year and its most articulate spokesman was Robert Lowe, an ex-minister whose utilitarian, Benthamite liberalism was strongly élitist. Russell and Gladstone had also to be mindful of keeping the strengthened Radical group loyal to the government. The offer of a cabinet post to Bright would have been too contentious; W.E. Forster, a middle-of-the-road Radical and member for Bradford, was in fact brought into the government as Under Secretary for the colonies. He made his acceptance conditional on the introduction of a reform bill without the delaying device of a committee of enquiry, a procedure favoured by some of the Whig members of the cabinet. Thus the government became increasingly committed to legislate on the franchise, in spite of all pressures from within and without to delay and prevaricate. Only the shape and extent of the bill remained wide open.

There were matters other than parliamentary reform that clamoured for public attention in the late autumn of 1865. Fierce controversy surrounded Governor Eyre, who had suppressed a native insurrection in Jamaica with what was widely held to be excessive cruelty. On one side were ranged all those of liberal conscience who were concerned for the rights of the underdog and in this instance particularly for the black man: radicals of various persuasions, the Anti-Slavery Society, and Exeter Hall, the headquarters of nonconformity. On the other side were the defenders of law and order, those who believed in the words of the conservative *Saturday Review*, that to the Radicals, 'every rebel is a hero or victim, and a guardian of law and order, even when he acts in self-defence, is guilty of lawless violence.' A number of prosecutions mounted against Governor Eyre failed and in 1874 the new Disraeli government granted him a pension. Nearer home the cattle plague, or rinderpest, which had begun to spread in the summer of 1865, was causing great alarm to land owners and farmers. Such was the urgency of the situation that a bill providing for the slaughter of diseased animals was given precedence over other business at the beginning of the parliamentary session in February 1866. The debate produced a clash between Lowe and the Radicals, in the persons of Bright and J.S. Mill, over the compensation to be paid for animals compulsorily slaughtered. Bright and Mill regarded this as an enforced payment by taxpayers, many of them poor, to the privileged landed interest. Lowe called Bright's speech 'a specimen of a manufacture with which we are unhappily and through his own agency too familiar – the manufacture of grievances'; while Mill thought that the aristocracy 'in as much as they enjoyed the highest honours and advantages, ought to be willing to bear the brunt of the inconveniences and evils which fall on the country generally'. It all sounded like a dress rehearsal for the reform bill debates. The Conservatives could pose as the detached bystanders contemplating the deep gulf between the Liberal factions.

Amid all these preoccupations the shape of the proposed reform bill continued to engage the cabinet's attention. On becoming Prime Minister again, Russell had instructed the Poor Law Board to ascertain the numbers of ratepayers in parliamentary boroughs at each one-pound level from £10 down to £6, and the numbers in the counties at £12, £15 and £20. When these statistics appeared to show that the proportion of working-class voters on the borough electoral rolls was more than double what it had been supposed, the right wing of the cabinet once more argued strongly for delay and a commission of enquiry. The question whether the vote should be based on a rental or rating qualification remained unresolved almost right up to the publication of the bill in March 1866. At the same figure a rental qualification would enfranchise more people than a rating one, for the rateable value allowed deductions for repair and maintenance from the gross estimated rental value. If personal payment of rates was required for inclusion in the electoral register, as had been the case since 1832 and was implied by a rating qualification, this would tend to limit the extent of the enfranchisement. It would exclude from the vote the so-called compounders, those who included an amount for rates in the payment of rent to their landlords. The custom of compounding was, however, subject to many local variations and so was the assessment of rateable values and the compilation of rate books. The original decision of the cabinet in 1865 was for a rating qualification, but when the information supplied by the Poor Law Board showed the erratic inequalities between different

localities that would be perpetuated, it was decided, against the opposition of most Whig ministers, to switch to a rental qualification.
Another thorny problem was whether the franchise bill should be
accompanied by a bill for the redistribution of seats. If the two bills
were before Parliament at the same time, MPs whose seats were to be
redistributed out of existence would be more likely to oppose the
whole package and an early election on the new franchise and
constituencies could hardly be avoided. If redistribution were held
over it might later take a more radical form in a House elected under
the new franchise. Bright, who had all along pressed the cabinet to
adopt a rental qualification, was also in favour of a single-barrelled
franchise bill. Russell and Gladstone had, however, to avoid carefully
any appearance of following the dictates of Bright if they were to keep
the loyalty of the right wing of the cabinet and the party.

When the bill was finally made public in March 1866 it was based
on a £7 rental qualification in the boroughs and £14 in the counties
and it was not accompanied by a redistribution bill. Although it was
the product of last-minute shifts and changes, it could nevertheless be
regarded as representing a broad consensus of what seemed acceptable, not merely within the Liberal Party but beyond it. It was
assumed that the respectable, stable sections of the working class
would be enfranchised, while those below them, the residuum as it
was often called, would continue to be excluded. Moderate opinion
demanded that no one class should be able to swamp the electorate
and the proponents of the bill felt confident that they could argue that
under their proposals the working classes would not preponderate.
Since the statistics provided by the Poor Law Board showed that over
a quarter of the electorate was already working-class under the
existing franchise, it was not a very convincing argument. The *Law
Times* published figures relating to the fairly typical borough of
Preston. On the existing £10 franchise over 2,500 men had the vote,
of whom 800, but possibly far more, were reckoned to be working-
class. If the qualification dropped to £8 another 1,050, all working-
class, would be enfranchised, thus giving the working class a clear
majority; with a £6 franchise the working class would have a 4 to 1,
with household suffrage a 6 to 1 majority. It was also calculated that
houses rated at £10 and above accounted for three-quarters of the
value of all rents paid at Preston; the renters of such properties had
2,860 votes; yet those who paid only one quarter of the value of all
rents, for houses valued at less than £10, would have more than
9,500 votes.

Such figures and arguments were eagerly seized upon by opponents of the bill within the Liberal Party. Any hopes the government
might have had that its proposals would command widespread assent

were quickly dashed. The Whigs in the cabinet might have been induced reluctantly to accept to bill, but the same pressures did not operate on the anti-reform Liberals outside the government, some of them disappointed office seekers. Lord Elcho had, in addition to Robert Lowe, emerged as their leading figure. Heir to the earldom of of Wemyss and extensive estates, particularly in Scotland, he regarded himself as a moderate Liberal and promoter of social harmony between classes, but he was also a strong individualist and believer in *laissez-faire* economics, who feared democracy, the rule of numbers and the tyranny of trade unions over workers. The group round Elcho and Lowe was shortly to be christened the political Cave of Adullam by Bright, where 'everyone that was in distress and everyone that was discontented foregathered'. It was in the Cave of Adullam that David took refuge from Saul and gathered other malcontents around him.

Given the signs of opposition from within the Liberal party, the Conservatives had to show their hand. Their long truce with the Liberals had been shaken by the death of Palmerston, and they were also a 'hungry party', for too long excluded from the fruits of office. Lord Derby, elderly and prostrated by gout, might have been prepared to let the reform question be settled moderately and by consent, but in fact his conduct in the next two years showed his zest for power little diminished. Disraeli's position as leader was insecure and dependent on Derby. Many Tories distrusted him as much as ever and much of this distrust stemmed from the sterile manoeuvres by which he had attempted over many years to attach various factions and groups, from Irish Catholics to British Radicals, to the Tory cause. More recently the apparently hopeless position of his party had often made him politically apathetic, but the death of Palmerston and the signs of disarray among Liberals had given him fresh hope. When he perceived that his followers were in fact looking for a strong lead against reform, it was not difficult to respond and persuade Derby to do likewise. The Conservative line therefore became one of outright opposition to the government's bill and there was much concerting of tactics with the Adullamites. Thus the government found itself from the outset supported mainly by the Radical wing of their own party. Bright was not happy with the bill, but he knew as well as anybody that it probably did as much as would be swallowed by the existing House of Commons. Remarking that beggars could not be choosers, he approved it as payment on account. Once it had become clear that the government's bill was capable of being destroyed, Tories and anti-reform Liberals succeeded in forcing the cabinet to produce a redistribution bill to accompany the franchise legislation – the very step it had hoped to avoid. The redistribution bill, with its rather arbitrary grouping of small boroughs into single constituencies, was manifestly open to attack and, as expected, compounded the government's difficulties. On top of this, in early May, a financial crisis of major proportions broke when the City banking house of Overend, Gurney and Company failed. Gladstone had to suspend the Bank Charter Act and the bank rate rose to 10 per cent. It was to prove the beginning of an economic depression which sharpened social discontent in the country and thereby influenced the climate in which debate about reform was carried on over the next 15 months. Abroad war clouds were gathering between Austria and Prussia, adding to the sense of crisis. On 18 June the government was defeated by 11 votes on a wrecking amendment to substitute a rating for a rental qualification in the boroughs. About 40 Liberals had voted against their own side. The government now felt unable to go on, but rather than dissolve Parliament and have an election, as many of the Liberal left wanted, Russell and his colleagues decided to resign.

Many cross-currents and complexities had produced this astonishing reversal of party fortunes. Barely a year earlier, the Liberal coalition had won a convincing electoral triumph and the Conservatives were left more than ever dispirited. In both parties there had been a widespread disposition to settle the reform question along moderate lines. Yet among Liberals Gladstone proved unable to build on this disposition and found himself increasingly bracketed with Bright as a 'dangerous' man. Among Tories the exhilaration of seeing the opposition divided and the prospect of ditching 'Gladstone and Democracy' soon proved more attractive than solving the reform question by consent. Disraeli cleverly exploited this mood and for the first time the duel between him and Gladstone assumed a central place in politics.

The parliamentary debates on reform and the public arguments surrounding them were for the most part conducted on a high intellectual plane. Lowe's polemics against reform were based mainly on utilitarian arguments. He accused Gladstone in particular of having advocated the granting of the franchise on '*a priori* rights', such as 'formed the terror and ridicule of that grotesque tragedy, the French Revolution'. On this basis there would be no resting place short of universal suffrage. In Lowe's view, a sound parliamentary assembly and good government were paramount considerations and required a restricted franchise. This laid him open to the counter-argument by the reformers that the exclusion of large numbers of respectable citizens from the political process deprived government of the essential element of legitimacy. In fact the debates themselves and above all the eventual failure of Russell's bill contributed not inconsiderably to raising the level of public agitation, which had initially been low. If the House of Commons was not prepared to pass so limited a measure, what hope was there of progress except under the threat of violence? In his first major speech on the bill, on 13 March 1866, Lowe had been unwise enough to say 'if you want venality, if you want ignorance, if you want drunkenness and the facility for being intimidated, or if, on the other hand, you want impulsive, unreflecting, and violent people, where do you look for them in constituencies? Do you go to the top or the bottom?' Much applauded as this speech was by anti-reform opinion, these remarks were to rebound on the speaker. The reformers made the most of them and Bright told an audience in Birmingham: 'let us arouse the spirit of the people against these slanderers of a great and noble nation'. Lowe's powerful oratory was, however, the stimulus for Gladstone's equally powerful counter-rhetoric which made him appear much more democratic than he was and which caused unease among Whigs and moderate Liberals. As quotable as Lowe's remarks about venality were Gladstone's when objecting 'to the whole mode of dealing with this question of statistics, as adopted by honourable members. . . . They seem as if they were engaged in ascertaining the numbers of an invading army; but the persons to whom their remarks apply are our fellow-subjects, our fellow-Christians, our own flesh and blood, who have been lauded to the skies for their good conduct'. How could one, with such an argument, stop short of full democracy? But what most MPs still wanted was a balance of classes; the working classes should be represented, but should not preponderate by virtue of numbers.

II

It would have been in the logic of events if the fall of the Russell government had produced a coalition of Conservatives and moderate Liberals, the long-heralded realignment of parties. Such a government might either have turned its back on the reform question for a while or it might in due course have promoted a bill establishing the desired balance of classes. There were two main reasons for the failure of a coalition to come about. One was the excessive price, in terms of cabinet places, demanded by the Adullamites for their co-operation. The Peelites had, in 1853, been able to exact such a price, but the Adullamites had much less talent and experience to draw on and were less cohesive. The other reason was the reluctance of Derby and

Disraeli to be relegated. Disraeli was playing for high stakes. A broad-based and effective Whig – Conservative fusion would have left him, widely distrusted as he was, with much reduced scope, just at a moment when he had scored a more substantial success in destroying Liberal unity than at any time during nearly 20 years as a Tory leader. Disraeli had to give the appearance of wanting a coalition, but when the possibility of fusion was finally dashed he could not but feel relieved. It was a decisive moment not only in the evolution of the reform question but in the development of the party system. The dividing line between the parties remained where it had been. The third Conservative minority government since 1852, with Derby as Prime Minister and Disraeli as leader in the Commons, was, as it turned out, much less able and willing to play the card of resistance than a Whig – Tory coalition would have been. As so often in poli-tics, personalities played an essential rôle in these developments.

The Radicals in Parliament had been helpless and shocked specta-tors of these events. Bright had tried to persuade Russell and Gladstone to dissolve Parliament: 'A general election for reform and for a reform government would bring an immense force of popular feeling into the field and I do not believe in your being beaten.' The cabinet could not agree to a dissolution and the formation of a Tory government seemed to mark a severe setback for the cause of reform. It was the moment when the extra-parliamentary reform movement, particularly the Reform League, with its mainly London-based trade union connections, was bound, willy-nilly, to take action. The League's position had been uncomfortable while the Bill was before the House of Commons. The moderate leaders, men like Edmond Beales, the league's barrister president, and George Howell, the trade unionist secretary, had led their organization into supporting the Bill, while not giving up manhood suffrage as the ultimate objec-tive. This had been too much for the more militant element; for example, the old Chartist leader Ernest Jones had resigned rather than support 'a measure which is a deliberate insult to the working class, and will deprive them of the little political power they possess'. Now that even this Bill had gone down to defeat and the Tories had formed a government, the Reform League leaders had to move if they were to stay in control of the movement. With demonstrations and meetings already occurring here and there, they decided to hold a national demonstration on 23 July, to which provincial branches and other organizations would be invited. Because of the expected size of the crowd it was to be held in Hyde Park. Five days before it was due to take place Sir Richard Mayne, the Metropolitan Commissioner of Police, informed Beales that it would be prohibited. The Reform League regarded this prohibition as illegal and an interference with the lawful right of assembly. In this it had the support of Bright, though, significantly, he was reluctant to have his view made public. Beales hesitated to go ahead in defiance of the authorities, but a majority of his executive decided to persevere.

On the day a cordon of police guarded the park gates. Beales and other officials then led a procession to Trafalgar Square, where they addressed the crowd. The mob left behind in Park Lane began to skirmish with the police and as the excitement rose and truncheons were used, the park railings gave way. Disorder and riots in and around the park went on for two more days and troops had to be called in. Negotiations took place between the League officials headed by Beales and the Home Secretary, Spencer Walpole, during which the latter was alleged to have burst into tears.

The Hyde Park riots caused some alarm and anger, but only a minority regarded them as the beginnings of a revolution. *The Times* said: 'As to the working classes of London having any sympathy with all this nonsense, no one who is really acquainted with them will credit it for a moment'. The League leaders were desperately anxious to stay within the law, but they challenged the government's view of what the law was. They were as frightened as anybody by the violence they could not control and embarrassed by the ruffianly elements that infiltrated their demonstrations. Nevertheless, the Reform League emerged from these events with its expectations raised from their low level at the fall of the Russell government. They realized that they commanded a sizeable constituency in the metropolis and elsewhere.

John Bright, however, could still evoke a much greater response and remained 'the constitutional monarch' of the whole reform movement. He had never endorsed the League's aim of manhood suffrage and did not believe that the vote should be given to the 'residuum'; he supported the League in its struggle for freedom of assembly and contributed to a defence fund for those arrested; but he was not prepared to come to London to take part in any demonstrations and carefully distanced himself from any violence. The Hyde Park riots, however, convinced him that among the working classes a demand for reform had been aroused which the parliamentary parties would resist at their peril. He decided that the time had come to embark upon his own reform crusade, the second of his career. He began in August in Birmingham, his own constituency, and enormous meetings, said to have been attended by crowds of over 100,000, took place throughout the autumn in the great provincial cities, Manchester, Leeds, Glasgow. Bright's theme was 'Let us trust the nation' and he stressed that an extension of the franchise was in the interest of the middle as well as the working classes. It was as the reforming champion of this union of classes against an entrenched aristocracy that Bright appeared once more, as he had done throughout the middle years of the century. The Liberal Party was the essential vehicle for Bright's broader objectives of establishing a society which guaranteed full equality before the law for all citizens whatever their religious denomination, and which did away with all aristocratic privilege. When the Liberals were still in power trying to pass a reform bill, he could only attack the resisters in his own party. Now his full assault on the enemy, the aristocratic Tories, could be unleashed. Bright thus became the spearhead of a broad movement of agitation throughout the country in the autumn and winter of 1866–7, into which were swept all the divergent strands, working men, militant trade unionists, respectable provincial manufacturers, Reform League and Reform Union.

The agitation contributed to a climate of opinion, reaching from the Queen downwards, that held it was time the reform question was settled. There was, however, also a considerable risk that the agitation might have the opposite effect. London mobs on the rampage and Bright on provincial platforms strengthened conservative feelings in both parties. Any reform, Derby's as well as Russell's, would have to be passed by a House of Commons elected on the existing franchise. Now that Derby was Prime Minister, the possibility of dissolving Parliament and holding an election was in his hands. If the electorate was sufficiently frightened, it might prefer Derby to a Liberal Party largely in hock to Bright. The pressure built up by the extra-parliamentary reform movement was thus a double-edged weapon and could have only a limited influence on the decisions of the parliamentary politicians.

III

For Derby and Disraeli there were, on balance, strong arguments in favour of introducing a reform bill of their own. In their previous period of office as a minority government, in 1858–9, they had attempted to consolidate their position, unsuccessfully as it turned out, by bringing in such a bill. If they opted for total inactivity on the reform front, the Liberals, whose disunity on reform had after all been on points of detail, might well find a way, at the opening of the next session of parliament in 1867, of recovering their unity sufficiently to turn the Tories out. The prospect of heading a third short-lived caretaker government did not appeal to Derby, let alone Disraeli, and there was no need, after their success in destroying Liberal unity, to contemplate it, but to introduce another Tory reform bill also had its dangers, for its details might well destroy Conservative unity. There was, however, a way of avoiding this difficulty, by first introducing a few reform resolutions stating broad principles and leaving details open as long as possible. Another possibility was to proceed by a commission of enquiry, a proposal which some of the Adullamites had been trying to press on the Russell government and which might therefore appeal to them. Derby and Disraeli picked their way through these and other options pragmatically, determined to avoid an early defeat, intent on maximizing the disarray in the Liberal camp and circumventing possible disagreements in their own ranks. The Hyde Park riots and Bright's monster meetings were only at the margin of their considerations and posed almost greater problems for the Liberal leaders. The Queen's view, that a moderate reform should be quickly passed by agreement between the parties, in order to end the dangerous social disharmony in the country, was natural from someone in her position. Derby used the royal views in arguments with his colleagues when it suited him. Nevertheless, Derby's decision, taken in September 1866, to choose reform rather than inactivity had a momentum of its own and without it the temper of the popular movement might have become uglier.

If it was to go for reform, the Conservative cabinet had to decide on a level of enfranchisement that distinguished its prescription from the Liberal proposals it had succeeded in destroying in June 1866. It was generally accepted that the next layer of voters in the boroughs, below the £10 householder enfranchised in 1832, was solidly Liberal, particularly in large cities. Only by going even further down the social scale could the Tories hope to tap additional support. It was such considerations that led ministers to toy with 'rated residential suffrage' or household suffrage. By the beginning of the parliamentary session in February 1867 ministers were agreed that household suffrage, based on personal payment of rates, thus excluding the compounder, should be the basis of their scheme. Lengthy residence qualifications and various types of plural voting would counterbalance this enfranchisement. No sooner had the cabinet reached these decisions than its unity was broken by the threatened resignation of General Peel, the Secretary of State for War and younger brother of the former Conservative Prime Minister; and then, more seriously, by the growing opposition of Lord Cranborne, the Secretary of State for India. Known until 1865 as Lord Robert Cecil, Cranborne was soon to become the third Marquis of Salisbury and eventually, in 1885, Prime Minister. A frequent contributor to the

Quarterly Review, he was a highly articulate opponent of democracy, the shortcomings and disappointments of which he predicted with considerable prescience. Cranborne was prepared to see some enfranchisement of the working classes and the arrival of a contingent of working-class representatives in the House of Commons, but he was strongly opposed to giving these classes a preponderance among the electorate. He would have welcomed a coalition with the Adullamites after the fall of Russell and was suspicious of Disraeli, though not at this stage hostile. At a crucial cabinet meeting on 23 February, Disraeli put before his colleagues statistics collected by Dudley Baxter, the distinguished Conservative statistician, designed to calm fears about household suffrage. When Cranborne studied these statistics more closely he became particularly concerned about the situation in small boroughs, such as his own constituency of Stamford, where Baxter seemed to have underestimated the level of enfranchisement under the proposed bill. Carnarvon, the Colonial Secretary and a fellow High Churchman, shared Cranborne's doubts. An emergency cabinet had to be called on 25 February which was presented with the threat of Cranborne's and Carnarvon's resignations. With only minutes to spare before Disraeli was due to appear in the House to give an outline of the government's Bill, the cabinet abandoned household suffrage. Instead, a rating franchise of £6 in the boroughs and £20 in the counties was proposed.

The Conservative government was now in deep crisis. The new proposals, quickly dubbed the Ten Minutes Bill because of their rapid birth, pleased no one. Not even the denizens of the Cave of Adullam could be expected to support something so similar to the Bill of the previous year, in opposition to which they had destroyed the unity of their party. The ball was back at Gladstone's feet. His position since leaving office had been difficult. He had to keep his distance from the Radicals, with their excessive expectations of him, and placate Whigs and right-wing Liberals, who were highly suspicious of him. When the parliamentary session of 1867 began he had played a waiting game, giving the impression that he would support any reasonable Tory propositions on reform, avoiding the appearance of snatching prematurely at office and power, hoping nevertheless that sooner or later he would have the opportunity of reuniting the Liberal Party and turning the Tories out. Such a moment seemed now to have arrived.

The only way Disraeli could avoid defeat was to drop the Ten Minutes Bill and revert to the original bill clearly based on household suffrage. The risks were great: Cranborne, Carnarvon, Peel and possibly others would resign; the safeguards and counterpoises in the bill might be whittled away on its passage through the House, particularly as on occasion Radical votes might have to be relied on. The alternative, however, was humiliating defeat by Gladstone, the return of a Liberal government and in due course a reform bill not only more thorough-going than last year's, but tailored, particularly in its provision of parliamentary seats, to Liberal needs. Derby and Disraeli detected clear signs that the majority of their followers now preferred the risks of a household suffrage bill to a triumph by Gladstone and that only a small minority would follow Cranborne, Carnarvon and Peel. The three opposing ministers were allowed to resign. It was fortunate for the Tories and Disraeli that Cranborne neither had the personal qualities to lead the Conservative dissidents nor was the parliamentary situation favourable to the organization of a revolt. In the cabinet reshuffle caused by the three resignations two Tory dukes, Marlborough and Richmond, both potentially hostile to Disraeli, and Henry Corry, the father of Disraeli's private secretary Monty, entered the cabinet. The Conservative government was thus committed to household suffrage, counter-balanced by such safe-guards as the House of Commons would accept. Disraeli had prob-ably come to the conclusion that whatever new electorate emerged the Conservative Party could live with it and that the old methods of electoral manipulation would remain largely effective. Lord Derby seems to have thought the same. On 10 March 1867, while the bill was still being considered in cabinet, his son Lord Stanley noted in his journal: '. . . talk with Ld D. whom I find bent on remaining in power at whatever cost, and ready to make the largest concessions with that object'. In spite of his obvious tactical flexibility and oppor-tunism Disraeli, greatly helped by Derby's unremitting support, managed to keep all but a few Tories loyal and reassured.

A successful counterattack from Gladstone was, however, still very much on the cards. In early April he made a strong effort either to remould the bill or kill it and the government with it. He moved an instruction designed to confer the vote on all above a certain fixed line, by entering all those above the line in the rate books, while those below it would be relieved of liability to personal rating. It was known, though not explicitly stated, that £5 was the limit Gladstone had in mind. This was entirely consistent with the aim which he had declared throughout the reform crisis, of enfranchising the morally sound, stable working class, while excluding the so-called 'residuum'. It was an aim which should have commanded wide-spread support not only in Gladstone's own party but among Tories.

Yet, paradoxically, the tactical situation in the House and the suspicions surrounding his own personality were such that Gladstone failed miserably to get his way. A few days after he had made the instruction known at a party meeting, the 'tea-room revolt' forced him to withdraw it again. The majority of the 50 or so tea-room rebels were moderate, left-of-centre Liberals who did not want to abandon the household suffrage principle, even if restricted, for an apparently more restrictive fixed-line franchise. A few days later, on 12 April, Gladstone was defeated on a series of amendments which he had substituted for the instruction. On this occasion a different but even larger number of Liberals either voted for the government or abstained. Only a few were radical tea-roomers who hoped to get virtually unrestricted household suffrage from Disraeli; about 20 were Adullamites motivated by deep distrust of Gladstone; the remainder went against their own side from a variety of motives, such as reluctance to exacerbate the party struggle at such a moment for fear of a dissolution. The vote, which the government won by a majority of 21, was generally regarded as decisive. Disraeli had pulled out all the stops to win. He had published a letter to his followers in *The Times* warning them against a 'party attack' dictated 'by a candidate for power' who forgot that he 'has had his innings'. After the vote Disraeli was acclaimed at the Carlton Club; on his return home Mary-Anne received him with champagne and a Fortnum and Mason pie, which elicited his well known remark 'why, my dear, you are more like a mistress than a wife'. Gladstone called it 'a smash perhaps without example' and on 17 April renounced the day-to-day leadership of the Liberal Party in the House.

Even after these triumphs and disasters the final issue remained in doubt. The general drift of events in the House of Commons was towards the dismantling of the restrictive safeguards surrounding household suffrage. Not all the changes, however, were in the nature of nasty medicine to be swallowed by Conservatives. The lowering of the county occupation franchise from £50 to £12, for example, was, on balance, regarded as working in the interests of the Tory Party. Some Liberal amendments designed to maintain or extend the 'contamination' of county electorates by potentially radical borough voters, long a matter of concern for Conservatives, were defeated. All this helped to keep Conservative defections to a minimum.

The major restriction on the borough franchise which remained in the bill was the exclusion of the compounder, who did not personally pay his rates. This principle was not acceptable to many Liberals, including Gladstone, for it created an entirely illogical division between voters and non-voters. Disraeli had wanted to deal with this problem, as with others, in a conciliatory fashion. This was made more difficult for him by the government's poor showing over the Reform League's Hyde Park demonstration of 6 May 1867. Once again the Home Secretary, Spencer Walpole, had been ill-advised enough to issue a proclamation declaring the use of the park for such a purpose illegal, without having either the means or the intention of enforcing such a prohibition. The League's successful defiance of the government led to the Home Secretary's resignation. This was not the moment when Disraeli could show any weakness or appear to appease the left. When 9 May, an amendment was moved designed to help the enfranchisement of compounders, Disraeli moved a counter-amendment and made it a matter of confidence. The government won this division by 66 votes, the largest majority of the Reform Bill votes. Gladstone's loss of control over his party and especially over its right wing was re-emphasized, but he was thus relieved of any need to pay regard to the Liberal anti-reformers. Two days after the division he addressed a 'monster deputation' from the Reform Union and made it clear that he was now no longer bound by his proposal of a £5 fixed-line franchise.

Gladstone's leftward turn freed Disraeli from the danger of being out-flanked on the right. The way was open to the solution of the difficult compounder problem by the acceptance of Hodgkinson's amendment a few days later. This amendment was designed simply to abolish the custom of compounding by proposing that no person other than the occupier should be rated to parochial rates in a parliamentary borough. At a stroke another half million men might now be enfranchised and whatever the subsequent difficulties of implementation, the change has always rightly been seen as the most decisive breach of the original safeguards in the bill. Disraeli justified his change of front on the enfranchisement of the compounder in these words: 'I waited till the question was put when, having revolved everything in my mind, I felt that the critical moment had arrived when, without in the least degree receding from our principle and position of a rating and residential franchise, we might take a step which would destroy the present agitation and extinguish Gladstone and Company.' Disraeli had little difficulty in getting his cabinet colleagues to endorse his move. He also accepted an amendment providing for a £10 lodger franchise, another major change.

In the meantime the redistribution bills were undergoing revision. Initially the English bill was restricted to the reallocation of 30 seats. Partly with the connivance of Disraeli this was later extended to 45 seats. Birmingham, Leeds, Liverpool and Manchester were turned into three-member constituencies; the one important change made to the bill in the House of Lords was the introduction of the limited vote in such constituencies, namely that every elector should have one less vote than the available number of seats. It was hoped that this would help the Tories to win at least one of the three seats. Disraeli managed to appoint a boundary commission very favourable to the Tories and the removal from the Conservative bastions in the counties, strengthened through redistribution, of potentially radical urbanized electors proceeded apace. This was often to bring a double benefit to the Conservative Party, for it was such suburban areas that led the drift of middle-class voters from Liberalism to Conservatism in years to come.

IV

The exact size of the enfranchisement accomplished in 1867 will never be precisely known. Dudley Baxter calculated that the total United Kingdom electorate increased by over 1.1 million, or 82.5 per cent, between 1866 and 1868, the English borough electorate by 670,000, or 134 per cent. Contemporary opinion was in no doubt that it was a large enfranchisement and Carlyle's image of shooting Niagara expressed a widespread feeling. It was and has remained a matter for astonishment that it should have been done by a Conservative government. From his lugubrious perspective Carlyle expressed this sentiment, too: 'Nay have not I a kind of secret satisfaction . . . that other jugglers, of an unconscious and deeper type, having sold their poor mother's body for a mess of official pottage, this clever conscious juggler steps in, "Soft you, my honourable friends; I will weigh out the corpse of your mother (mother of mine she never was, but only Stepmother and milk-cow); – and you sha'nt have the pottage, not yours, you observe, but mine!" '

A matter of much dispute among historians is the degree of importance to be attached to the public agitation for reform. It was itself a complex movement, ranging from 'the cream of the middle-class politicians of Yorkshire and Lancashire – . . . the self-made men of industry, . . . who can subscribe £1,000 for a purpose', who attended a Reform League banquet in Manchester in November 1866, to militant elements around the League and the London Trades Council interested in mobilizing working-class power as an end in itself. As the reform crisis lurched forward, the extra-parliamentary movement as a whole contributed to the feeling that it had better be brought to a conclusion sooner than later. There were other elements of unrest that also contributed to the feeling: the occasional violence surrounding trade unionism and the rise of Fenianism in Ireland and England. The extra-parliamentary reform movement had its influence above all within the Liberal Party, where it alarmed and in the last resort weakened the Whigs, where it lent power to the elbow of Bright and where it made it increasingly necessary for Gladstone to look to the future in which the forces represented by the movement would loom larger in the Liberal spectrum. On the other hand the public agitation often had a counter-productive effect: it strengthened the forces of resistance in all parties and made it more difficult for them to retreat; it made it easier for all anti-reformers to don the mantle of moderation. The final verdict must be that the public reform movement did not do much more than act the part of the chorus in this play.

The personalities of Gladstone and Disraeli were central to the reform crisis, which in turn had a decisive impact upon their careers. Gladstone seemed initially to experience failure in his first test as a parliamentary manager in supreme command. As opposition leader he found the Party slipping even further from his control. This débâcle occurred because his zealous personality, deep moral convictions and strongly profiled High Anglicanism did not strike a chord with the worldly gentlemen who made up much of the Liberal Party. These handicaps of Gladstone's leadership became something of an advantage once the Conservatives had made certain of a far-reaching bill. By May 1867 right-wing Liberalism had lost and Gladstone, as the major Liberal parliamentary politician with a large following out of doors, was well set for the leadership. It mattered little that the real Gladstone was rather different from the image of the People's William revered by such large numbers.

Disraeli's aim in the two years during which parliamentary reform dominated politics did not differ greatly from Gladstone's. He did not in principle object to changes in the system of representation, especially as it was a Conservative article of faith that the Party was at a disadvantage under the existing system. He did not contemplate, any more than Gladstone, a decisive transformation, creating major shifts of power and a new style of politics. But this basic attitude was subject to overriding tactical necessities. In the first phase of the crisis, the session of 1866, the opportunities created by the first major split in the Liberal coalition in years had to be fully exploited. This meant taking up a restrictive position towards reform, if not one of outright hostility. Once these tactics had achieved more than hoped-for success in the fall of the Russell government, the position changed. From June 1866 Disraeli had to continue to maintain the division in the Liberal ranks, but it was not in his interest, nor in Derby's, to amalgamate with the Adullamites or with a wider Whig grouping, or even to get into too much dependence on such forces. In the session of 1867 Disraeli practised the tactics he had used so often since he became leader of his Party, the attempt to link up with any available group to

secure a majority. Previously these tactics had done little but earn him
suspicion, but this time they were triumphantly successful. He may
well have been fortified in his confidence that tactical flexibility would
bring long-term party advantage by the contemporary examples of
Napoleon III and Bismarck. In France and Germany a wide franchise
was being used to outflank the mostly liberal middle classes by
appealing to the more conservative classes below them. The majority
of Disraeli's followers felt that his course in 1867 was for the good of
the Party, but there was a minority, of whom Cranborne remained
the most notable, who thought him guilty of betrayal. Whereas
Gladstone managed to snatch victory from the jaws of defeat, for
Disraeli the sequel to triumph on reform was disaster at the polls.
After a brief moment of glory, when following the retirement of
Derby he became Prime Minister in 1868, the Tory defeat in the
general election of 1868 virtually put him back where he had been for
20 years. His hold on the leadership became insecure again, Derby
was no longer there to support him and the feeling that he had been
guilty of betrayal in 1867 became more widespread.

Myth soon enveloped the rôles of both Gladstone and Disraeli in
the passage of the second Reform Bill. The predominant Whig interpretation of history managed fairly quickly to explain away the fact
that the measure had been passed under a Conservative government.
It did this by making Gladstone the driving force behind it, who had
compelled a minority Tory cabinet to do his bidding. There was an
element of truth in this, for it was by concentrating the minds of his
followers on the humiliation of Gladstone that Disraeli succeeded in
driving them along behind the bill. Gratitude to Gladstone for having
given the vote to the working man was a factor in the rhetoric, at any
rate, of the 1868 election. Disraeli had a more difficult task, for he had
to create the myth that what was a piece of shrewd tactics and 'dishing
the Whigs' was in fact deliberate, long-term policy, consistent with
his own past principles, and in the essential interests of the Conservative Party. He started to claim that he had 'educated' his party and
that what he had done with the Reform Bill was consistent with his
life-long convictions on the relationship of classes. In October 1867 he
declared at Edinburgh: 'I have always looked on the interests of the
labouring classes as essentially the most conservative interests of
the country. The rights of labour have been to me always as sacred as
the rights of property'. Disraeli could make such claims with some
plausibility, but in practice he was slow to cultivate the newly enfranchised voters and his encouragement to those in his party who were
trying to do so was decidedly cautious. Popular appearances and platform oratory were not really congenial to him and he knew that he
could not compete with Gladstone in that sphere. The linking of

Disraeli and Tory democracy was as yet tenuous.

The electoral arrangements introduced by the legislation of 1867 lasted only 17 years, until the further radical changes of the third Reform Bill of 1884. Even in the intervening period there was at least one important additional change, the introduction of the secret ballot in 1872. The second Reform Bill did not anywhere create the conditions of fully-fledged democracy on the basis of one man, one vote. It did, however, establish nearly 100 constituencies, about a quarter of the total, where, in 1881, the number of electors per member exceeded 6,000. There survived nearly 140 constituencies in which the number of electors per member did not exceed 2,000. Over much of the country the representative system changed only marginally and the political pyramid which rested upon it, with Parliament and cabinet at the apex, remained therefore essentially what it had been between 1832 and 1867.

The large boroughs with something like a mass electorate did, however, form the breeding ground for experiments that were in due course to become universal and transform the political system. Extra-parliamentary party organization in its modern form is characterized by three major institutions. At the constituency level there are party associations which make the formal claim of being representative of the members of the party in the constituency and this in turn legitimates them to select the party's candidate. Secondly, at the national level these constituency associations come together in federations, which in turn gives rise to a claim that these national federations are legitimate bodies to play a part in the formulation of party policies and the selection of party leaders. Thirdly, an enlarged central party bureaucracy comes into existence to enable the party leaders to mobilize, manipulate and control the party. After 1867 entirely unsystematic and unpremeditated moves towards all three of these institutions occurred in both major parties. In the Conservative Party they owed more to central initiatives, while in the Liberal Party they arose more from local necessities. Both parties were, particularly in the constituencies, carrying on developments which had been in progress at least since 1832.

On the Tory side it was a group of younger politicians of the second rank, some of them actively committed to giving the party a more popular base, who, in 1867, began to promote a movement for the formation of Conservative working-men's associations and clubs in borough constituencies. Such bodies came into being alongside and overlapping with existing Conservative and Constitutional associations. In the same year a national federation of these organizations was started and acquired the name of National Union of Conservative and Constitutional Associations. Disraeli and other party leaders

gave only lukewarm and reluctant support to these initiatives. They
were in potential conflict with other local and regional bodies; they
were in general confined to boroughs, while in the counties the traditional forms of electoral management under the control of local magnates went on undisturbed. In retrospect it turned out to be a decisive
step when Disraeli appointed John Gorst, one of the young Tory
politicians associated with the movement of working-men's associations, as party agent in 1870, on the retirement of the previous agent
of many years standing, Markham Spofforth. Disraeli was beginning
to wake up from the political doldrums in which the defeat of 1868 had
left him. Gorst operated from a Central Conservative Office in
London, the beginnings of party bureaucracy distinct from the parliamentary whips. He made the National Union into the central
federation of constituency Conservative associations and housed it
alongside his own office. In the localities working-men's clubs and
similar bodies became linked with or absorbed by the main associations; Disraeli himself did not approve of party organizations divided
along class lines, when he was portraying the Tory party as the
national party capable of uniting all classes. Gorst thus created a
system of party organization in the early 1870s in which the three
main features of comprehensive constituency association, a central
federation of these and a central party bureaucracy were all present,
at least in embryo.

The best-known development on the Liberal side was the rise of the
Birmingham caucus, so-called mostly by its opponents, who wanted
to discredit it by evoking associations with American politics. The
Birmingham Liberal Association was founded in 1865 and reorganized
for the election of 1868. It was distinguished by an elaborate
machinery built from the ward level upwards, designed to give the
rank-and-file member a say in the affairs of the association and ultimately in the selection of candidates. In practice it was, like other
organizations, subject to the iron law of oligarchies, but by showing at
least a façade of popular participation it enabled Joseph Chamberlain, soon to become the most important figure on the Radical wing of
the liberal party, and others to claim that it should become the model
for the organization of Liberalism in all large towns. The promoters
of the Birmingham caucus were in fact among the principal figures of
advanced Liberalism after 1868; in particular, the agitation of the
National Education League against the Education Act of 1870 spread
their influence. The caucus also showed that it controlled its voters so
tightly that it could win all three seats at Birmingham in 1868, in spite
of the limited vote introduced by the Bill. In each ward voters were
instructed which two of the three Liberal candidates they should
support. This procedure could, however, go disastrously wrong if the

overall level of party support fell below expectations: thus at Leeds in 1874 the Liberals got 54 per cent of the vote, but only one of three seats. But Liberal associations in other large towns did not necessarily follow the Birmingham example. The problem was how to pull the diverse strands of Liberalism sufficiently together to select acceptable candidates and to present a united front at elections, particularly where there was a strong Tory challenge. Before the 1860s a straight Whig – Radical compromise was normally made, and a constituency association, usually dominated by locally influential moderate or right-wing Liberals, selected the candidates. Now a widening political spectrum had to be covered. The continuing Whig landed influence, the increasingly right-wing urban oligarchies, the newly enfranchised working men, sometimes still organized in branches of the Reform League, advanced Liberals of differing persuasions, with various special interests or 'faddists', such as the United Kingdom Alliance, pressing for temperance, or the Liberation Society, pressing for disestablishment – all these had to be accommodated. Otherwise they might, if the worst came to the worst, throw their weight behind 'spoiling' candidatures. To span this wide spectrum, at least for electoral purposes, was the main object of Liberal associations in places like Manchester, Leeds or Sheffield. Even if they originally owed little to the Birmingham model, there was a tendency for them, since they had to look representative, to approximate to it. Everywhere there were local peculiarities, for instance the influence of important liberal notables like the Baines family at Leeds or the Leader family at Sheffield, both controlling important newspapers. The effort to keep the Liberal 'broad church' united at least for elections did not always succeed. At Bradford W.E. Forster and Edward Miall, the founder of the Liberation Society, were both elected in 1868. After 1870 Forster, as the principal author of the Education Act, became anathema to most nonconformists. When Miall retired, the question of his successor and the continuance of Forster as candidate tore the Bradford Liberal Association apart. In 1877 the National Liberal Federation was founded, mainly by the Birmingham men, though other Radical leaders like Sir Charles Dilke also played a part. In due course most of the Liberal associations in large boroughs affiliated to the National Liberal Federation and modelled their constitutions on that of Birmingham. The aims of those who promoted the federation went, however, far beyond the objective of an organizational tidying-up. They wanted to capture the whole of the Liberal Party for the Radical cause and programme and reduce to naught what remained of Whig and right-wing power and influence in the party. The origins and purposes of the National Liberation Federation were therefore very different from those of its Tory counterpart.

The Liberals were slower than the Conservatives in developing anything like a central party bureaucracy at the disposal of the party leader. As with the Tories, most of the work of central party management rested traditionally with the chief whip, but in the Liberal Party the party agent remained a very subordinate figure. Only when in 1886 Frederick Schnadhorst, the secretary of the National Liberal Federation, moved to London after the breach with Chamberlain over Irish Home Rule did the Liberal Party acquire someone who played a role comparable to Gorst's in the early 1870s. The diversity of the party, the existence of many national organizations within the spectrum of Liberal politics, as well as Gladstone's inspirational leadership, reduced the scope and the need for central organization. In the 1868 election, for example, what remained of the Reform League entered, through its secretary George Howell, into a close relationship with the Liberal whips. The kind of work that Howell and his colleagues did for the Liberal whips in supplying information, sorting out candidatures and getting working men through Reform League branches to support the Liberal Party, was not unlike the work done by Gorst and his organization on the Conservative side between 1870 and 1874.

The development of extra-parliamentary organization after the second Reform Bill was of considerable long-term significance for the evolution of the political system. There is, however, little evidence that it contributed very directly to the greater cohesion and delineation of parties that undoubtedly occurred. This greater sense of party identity was due to the involvement of larger numbers of people in the political process; to the fact that these larger masses could be moved through issues and personalities, while the possibilities of direct manipulation receded; that the issues and personalities were becoming to a greater extent national rather than local; that two strongly contrasting political leaders moved to the centre of the stage; and that members felt tied to their constituents through issues and personalities and less through their own personal influence. During the passage of The Irish Church Disestablishment Bill in 1869 Disraeli spoke of a mechanical majority when on a succession of votes the Liberals mustered their full strength and the entire majority they had obtained in the election of 1868. But the Liberals were exceptionally united on this issue and the election had given them a clear mandate for it, while Conservative opposition was uncertain. In the next session there was much cross-voting on the Education Act, with Tories joining moderate Liberals in sustaining the government against Radicals and nonconformists. In the session of 1873 the Liberal government was actually defeated on the Irish University Bill by a combination of Conservatives, Catholics and Radicals. Thus it would be impossible to claim that party discipline was as yet rigid and automatic. Nevertheless there was less of a sense of fragmentation, such as had prevailed in the 1850s, when Whigs, Tories, Radicals, Peelites, Irish Brigaders were often plying their separate trades, when Disraeli was always casting about for allies and Palmerston found himself suddenly defeated only a year after handsomely winning a general election. Between 1868 and 1885 governments only left office when they were defeated at the polls. Disraeli's resignation in December 1868, after the election results were declared, but before meeting parliament, was a portent for the future. In general the extension of the franchise in 1867 further strengthened the sense of obligation among members of Parliament to those who had elected them and for most of the time the best way of heeding this sense was to support the national leaders and national policies on whose behalf most members claimed to be presenting themselves to the electorate. This benefited party cohesion.

Expectations or fears that the social composition of the parliamentary parties would change rapidly after 1867 proved to be unfounded. The parliamentary Liberal Party moved only slowly away from its predominantly Anglican, land-owning and professional character. The business element had been significant at least since 1832 and from it was drawn a section of the Radical MPs whose political impact was far greater than their numbers. The succession from Cobden and Bright to Joseph Chamberlain, who entered the House in 1876, was a change of generations and not of social class. There was a tendency for the business and nonconformist element to become gradually more conservative and Radical employers like Samuel Morley, member for Bristol, A.J. Mundella, member for Sheffield, or Peter Taylor, member for Leicester, were not in due course adequately replaced. Radical intellectuals and academics, who had received reinforcement in the election of 1865, continued to play a role in promoting reforms and supplying a link with the world of labour. John Stuart Mill, perhaps the most conspicuous of them, was in fact defeated in 1868 at Westminster, against the general trend; it was an early indication of the movement to the right of middle-class electors in constituencies of the suburban type. The first two working-class members, Thomas Burt and Alexander Macdonald, entered the House as Liberals in the election of 1874. Significantly, they were miners whose closely knit communities were in a few areas able to exert decisive influence on local Liberal associations in the selection of candidates. Macdonald was, however, elected for Stafford, where there were no miners, but Burt sat for Morpeth, where there were many. It was this kind of lib-labism, mostly sustained by the miners, that formed the one concrete development coming out of the efforts to promote labour representation after 1867. At the other end of the Liberal Party, the genuinely Whig element, never numerically very large, undoubtedly suffered a loss in the proportionate importance of its electoral base and perhaps an even bigger loss in expectations and morale. Nevertheless, given the large measure of continuity in the make-up of the parliamentary Liberal Party, it is not surprising that Whigs of unquestioned purity should still be found well represented at the highest levels of the party.

The Conservative Party had for long suffered from the fact that in its parliamentary ranks members of the landed interest predominated. There was a small professional element, some of them lawyers, some of them members of the squirearchy who had turned into something like professional politicians and provided the Tories with some of their all too scarce front-bench material. Sir Stafford Northcote and Sir John Pakington were examples of the latter, Lord Cairns of the former species. Representatives of the business and commercial world were a small minority in the Party. These classes, although generally Liberal in their party-political allegiance, were, however, even in the 1850s becoming more conservative in disposition. After 1867 more men from such social backgrounds began to make an appearance on the Tory benches and were given increasing attention by the party leaders because they provided a link with spheres of the national life that could not be ignored. W.H. Smith was perhaps ultimately the most successful of these men. He was a Wesleyan who became an Anglican: he stood as a Palmerstonian Liberal against John Stuart Mill at Westminster in 1865 and defeated him as a Conservative in 1868. The creation of his newsagents business had made him into a national figure, but did not save him from whispers of 'the bookstall man' when he joined the Carlton Club. With the Conservatives as with the Liberals, the parliamentary party was slow to mirror the social shifts among their respective voters.

Between the second and third Reform Bills, however, nonconformity and dissent still supplied much of the rank and file of the Liberal Party. The late 1860s were perhaps the heyday of nonconformism as a political force. Lord Salisbury called the dissenting chapels 'earthworks and blockhouses for the maintenance of an untiring guerrilla' and dissenting ministers 'ready-made electioneering agents'. Nonconformity spanned a wide social spectrum, from the wealthy manufacturers, some of whom were the leaders of the various movements, to the craftsman, artisan and small shopkeeper. It was in that portion of the working classes often called the labour aristocracy, admittedly an imprecise concept, that political awareness and activism went hand in hand with the nonconformist conscience. Lower down in the social scale, among that two-fifths of the population rated as non-churchgoing in 1851, this kind of outlook would be rarer, one of the reasons why Disraeli and other Tories felt that a large enfranchisement would not necessarily work against them. It was assumed in mid-Victorian Britain that the middle classes, another very imprecise concept, were in general predominantly Liberal. The decline of this predominance after 1868 is most clearly evident in the suburban areas surrounding London and in middle-class areas of London itself. In 1868 Westminster and Middlesex fell to the Tories, in 1874 suburban Surrey, Kent and Essex and the City itself followed, and in 1880 there was little reversal of these developments in spite of the decisive overall Liberal victory.

Gradual shifts in voting habits of this kind did not alter the fact that after 1867 the solid basis of Conservative electoral support continued to be the agricultural vote in England. About three-quarters of English county seats were still held by the Tories in the three elections of 1868, 1874 and 1880. The provisions of the 1867 legislation designed to help Conservatives in such areas seem to have been effective in counteracting the increasing urbanization of the country. Here, as well as in many of the smaller boroughs the traditional methods of electioneering were left largely untouched. Influence remained the major factor determining the allegiance of voters; influence could have its basis in natural deference, in corrupt practices of various kinds, in intimidation open or implied, or in a combination of these. It was a normal expectation that employees should follow the political lead of their employers. This was most natural in the case of the landed estate and those who worked on it, but it extended equally to many industrial employers and their workforce. The introduction of the secret ballot in 1872 changed these habits and expectations only gradually in the ensuing two general elections. The Conservatives, even more than the Liberals, therefore operated on two levels: the old world of electioneering, based on local men of influence, gently prodded from the centre by the whips and their associates; the new world of Gorst's organization: attempts to compete with the Liberals and Gladstone by platform oratory and building up a stake in the Press.

The balance of the constitution as a whole was little altered by the events of 1867, but the sense of greater party identity which prevailed from the late 1860s onwards markedly reduced the opportunities for exercising political discretion that still rested with the monarchy. The death of the Prince Consort and the seclusion of the widowed Queen had already reduced the extent to which these opportunities were utilized. After 1868 there were no occasions when the monarchy could influence the composition of ministries in the way it had done in the 1850s. Behind the scenes the Queen became increasingly a fierce partisan; it was the result partly of genuine political conviction, partly of her growing antipathy to Gladstone and friendship for Disraeli, deftly exploited by the latter. These feelings could only to a limited extent be translated into action. In 1880 the Queen would dearly have loved to avoid having to call on Gladstone to form a government, but she was unable to do so. Her opinions still carried weight; a Prime Minister like Disraeli who had her on his side could derive much advantage from the fact, while her relentless hostility became a heavy burden for Gladstone. Nevertheless, the monarchy in its public face became more fully a constitutional monarchy after 1867 than it had been before. Thus the second Reform Bill, remarkable in its genesis and far-reaching in its provisions, nonetheless took its place in the continuous web of English history.

2 The Gladstone Ministry 1868–1874

I

In February 1868 Disraeli succeeded the ailing Derby as Prime Minister. Russell had announced his retirement from politics two months previously and Gladstone could reasonably expect to hold the highest office in the not too distant future, provided he could assert his leadership of the Liberals and they could win the next election. In March Gladstone announced his intention of moving resolutions in favour of ending the Anglican establishment in Ireland. At the beginning of May the first of these resolutions was passed with a majority of 65, putting the government on short notice to quit and showing that Gladstone was now in control of his party. Disraeli managed to persuade the Queen and his colleagues against an immediate resignation and in favour of a dissolution only when the new registers should be ready. Gladstone did not move a vote of censure, for his party, still licking their wounds from the previous two years, were not ready for an immediate election on the old franchise. The new registers were going to be available by November, somewhat earlier than expected. Thus the stage was set for an election in the late autumn, with the disestablishment of the Irish Church as the principal theme.

The theme was not new and its reappearance at this time not surprising. The Irish Church had figured prominently in the politics of the 1830s. Disraeli had, in 1844, diagnosed 'an alien Church' as one of the fundamental ills of Ireland. Gladstone had increasingly convinced himself that an Anglican Established Church in Ireland was no longer defensible and had made his conviction public at least since 1865. At about the same time the problem of Ireland was forcing itself once again upon the attention of the people of England. After a period of relative calm, when Irish aspirations were mainly represented by a constitutional party at Westminster, the Irish 'Brigade', nationalism in Ireland again assumed a revolutionary form. Fenianism was born, committed to a republican democratic Ireland, and a new secret society, the Brotherhood, later named the Irish

Republican Brotherhood, began to make many recruits from the late 1850s onward. A new and important factor in these developments was the support this movement now received from the many Irish immigrants who had escaped to the United States from the effects of the famine. The public in England was first woken up to this recrudescence of the Irish problem in 1866 by a Fenian raid across the Canadian border and by a Fenian rising in Ireland in March 1867. These events added to the sense of violence and insecurity engendered by the great reform agitation. The Fenian rising in 1867 was a pathetic affair and speedily crushed; it evoked little sympathy in Ireland, but the widespread arrests which followed its suppression fanned nationalist feeling for several years and made its contribution to the rise of a new Home Rule movement by 1870. Even closer to home was the successful release of several Fenian prisoners in Manchester in September 1867, involving the death of a policeman, and the Clerkenwell explosion in December 1867, when the attempt to blow up the prison wall killed a number of innocent people. Ireland was squarely back on the agenda. A Royal Commission on the revenues and administration of the Church of Ireland was sitting and its report was being awaited. Disraeli toyed with a plan of concurrent endowment of all three major denominations in Ireland, Anglican, Presbyterian and Roman Catholic, and the possible grant of a charter to a Catholic university in Dublin. He was in touch with Cardinal Manning on these plans. All these Conservative initiatives became a dead letter the moment Gladstone took up the disestablishment of the Irish Church.

Thus religious and ecclesiastical issues bulked large in the 1868 election. The allegiance of nonconformists to the Liberal Party was once more strengthened. Affluence and respectability made the remaining vestiges of second-class citizenship, revolving round Church rates, endowed school trusteeships and other educational issues, even more intolerable for dissenters. Anglicans saw highly organized nonconformist attacks on comparatively minor targets as the thin end of a wedge directed against the establishment itself. Disestablishment was indeed the avowed object of the Liberation Society and of many dissenters, though neither defenders or opponents of the establishment could realistically believe that it lay just round the corner. The Liberation Society had its counterpart in the Church Institution, known from 1871 as the Church Defence Institution, and the Conservatives made the most of its support in 1868. The proposal to disestablish the Irish Church also raised again the Catholic question, which only in the recent past had shown itself capable of arousing strong popular emotions. The position of the Papacy, locked in battle with the new Italian national State, the ultramontane influence in the Catholic Church, and the relationship between the Irish Catholic Church and subversive Irish nationalism, as many saw it, these were matters of immediate moment in 1868. Among the lower strata of the working class hostility to the Catholic Irish, the principal immigrant community of the period, was rife, for the unskilled Irish labourers were rivals in the employment market.

In Irish Church disestablishment Gladstone had thus found a cause which reunited not only the parliamentary Liberal Party, but made the most of his support in the country for the forthcoming election. A remarkable combination of dissenters with Irish and even English Catholics formed behind him. For a leader of such a combination Gladstone's position as a High Anglican ex-Tory, neither Radical nor Whig, was decidedly ambiguous. His conversion to the cause of full civic equality for members of all denominations was, however, not in question. For some years he had been in correspondence and in personal contact with moderate leaders of dissent, in particular with the two prominent Congregationalists Newman Hall and Henry Allon. He had laboured hard to resolve the most pressing of the nonconformist grievances, the question of Church rates. He was convinced that the Church of England could only hope to retain its privileged position if it made concessions in matters where manifest justice demanded it. On the other hand his commitment to the Church never wavered and set a limit to the extent of understanding he could ever achieve with dissenters. Many of the latter, however, now preferred to avert their eyes from these limits and to see in Gladstone the man who could lead them into a bright future.

It was difficult for Disraeli to trump Gladstone in policy or personality in the 1868 election. Disraeli had highly idiosyncratic views on race and religion, but in ecclesiastical politics he was very much at sea. His strategy, in so far as he had one, was to mobilize Protestant anti-Catholic feeling. It was not a forlorn hope, considering the long history of popular anti-Catholicism in Victorian England. As it was, an exceptional amount of Church patronage came his way in the run-up to the election. He thought it a great coup when he appointed Canon McNeile, a famous and fierce evangelical preacher from Liverpool, to the Deanery of Ripon, only to be told by Conservative agents and election managers that McNeile's appointment was damaging the Party's prospects, because it was alienating clergy and laity at the other wing of the Church of England. He became more cautious in his Church appointments. The most important vacancy he had to fill was the see of Canterbury. Tait was not his own first choice; he was a moderate evangelical favoured by the Queen, who in the past had been criticized for not condemning the authors of *Essays and Reviews* sufficiently strongly and who was firmly opposed to the

Ritualists. Disraeli could not, in fact, through his Church appointments or in any other manner construct an effective answer to the
Liberal challenge on the Irish Church. The Protestant 'cry' sounded
uncertainly in 1868 except in Lancashire, and Disraeli, who had so
often in the past tried to ally himself with Irish Catholics, was not the
man to sound it.

The Irish Church was not the only issue in the 1868 election, any
more than it would be in a modern election. The enlargement of the
franchise did not immediately alter the fact that a large number of
seats were left uncontested, about a third in 1868, declining to about
one-sixth by 1880, but this decline owed a good deal to a marked
increase of contests in Ireland, due to the rise of a Home Rule party. It
was a grave Tory handicap in 1868 that Conservatives left far more
seats uncontested than the Liberals. The theme that appeared most
widely in election addresses and speeches, apart from the Irish
Church, was the need for making elementary education generally
available, highlighted in Lowe's phrase 'we must educate our masters'. What he actually said, in July 1867 was: 'I believe it will be
absolutely necessary that we should prevail on our future masters to
learn their letters.' The claims of administrative reform, impressed
upon the public mind ever since the Crimean War were still much
discussed, especially the introduction of more meritocratic principles
in the selection of public servants. Gladstone himself continued to
emphasize the importance of curbing public expenditure, a policy
which had built up his public reputation in the 1850s; the attack on
'Tory extravagance', which was followed by many Liberal candidates, was given point by the unexpectedly large expenditure caused
by the Abyssinian War of 1867. Beyond these specific questions there
was a general appeal to the newly enfranchised working-class electors,
but it was a matter which appeared 'dark' to even the most experienced election managers.

The light which the election results threw upon this matter was less
clear than the overall outcome. The Liberals ended up with a majority
of about 110, as against 70 in 1865. Their most striking success was
perhaps in Wales, where this election marked a revolt from a long-
standing Anglican gentry and landlord ascendancy. The rise of
greater Welsh national and cultural consciousness had been evident
for some time. The Liberation Society became very active electorally
in Wales in the 1860s and the extension of the franchise greatly
increased the scope for such efforts. In Merthyr Tydfil the electorate
increased ten-fold and Henry Richard, prominent liberationist and
also secretary of the Peace Society, topped the poll. H.A. Bruce,
about to become Home Secretary in Gladstone's government, was
pushed into third place; he was a churchman, a great local employer

and opponent of trade unionism. Radical Liberals won some other contests in Wales of equally symbolic significance. The Liberal ascendancy was further strengthened in Scotland and Ireland, though in the latter country it was soon to be swallowed up into a new Home Rule movement. In England the over-all change was not great, with the Liberals advancing in the big boroughs and the Conservatives profiting, as expected, from the new £12 occupation franchise in the counties. The bright spot for the Tories was Lancashire, where they won 22 out of 33 seats, against 12 out of 27 in 1865. Gladstone was defeated in southwest Lancashire, whither he had come 'unmuzzled' only three years before from Oxford, and had to take refuge in Greenwich. Anti-Catholic feeling, aroused by the presence of large numbers of Irish immigrants, was undoubtedly a major ingredient in the Lancashire results; on several occasions during the campaign there had been inter-sectarian violence, caused by the inflammatory speeches of an itinerant ultra-Protestant agitator, William Murphy. Even in Lancashire the Tories did not necessarily, in terms of votes, improve their position as a result of the arrival of an extended urban working-class electorate, but the existence of a substantial Tory element in it meant that they suffered no damage. Nationally the continued predominance of Liberals in large boroughs concealed the existence, in terms of votes, of what contemporaries were beginning to call 'a Tory democracy'. Amid the Conservative débâcle of 1868 there was thus some justification for Disraeli's reform policy.

II

Gladstone, who upon receiving the Queen's commission remarked 'my mission is to pacify Ireland', formed a cabinet which reflected the traditional balance of elements in the parliamentary Liberal Party rather than the new Liberal electorate. Whigs occupied many of the leading positions: Clarendon was at the Foreign Office, Granville at the Colonial Office; Spencer was Irish Viceroy, Kimberley and Hartington were in the cabinet. Gladstone, who still had to labour against Whig suspicions and in any case believed in the governing mission of the aristocracy, could hardly do otherwise. On the other hand John Bright, whose presence in a Liberal cabinet was out of the question in Palmerston's day, now became President of the Board of Trade. Forster, probably the minister nearest to the Radical wing of the party in the previous Liberal government, was given the important office of Vice-President of Committee of Council for Education and attained cabinet status in 1870, when the Education Bill was passing through Parliament. Given the nature of elections this incoming government was no more than its predecessors saddled with a programme. The only certainty was that there would be legislation on the Irish Church. What turned out to be one of the most extensive reform programmes of the nineteenth century, undertaken by this ministry, was thus the product of a variety of influences. Gladstone himself was the driving force behind the Irish legislation; in some areas such as education or army reform there was a wide consensus that action was needed; trade union legislation was brought in as a consequence of a royal commission reporting; licensing legislation and the ballot were expected to come from a Liberal government. Gladstone had a very delicate sense of the independence of individual ministers, but once a policy or bill had been adopted by the cabinet he considered it his duty as Prime Minister to throw his formidable parliamentary abilities behind the policy or bill if this support was needed.

The Irish Church Disestablishment and Irish Land Bills were the work of Gladstone, not merely in principle, but in detail. He showed his great command of detail in personally conducting most of the consultations necessary, in drafting these bills and piloting them through the House of Commons. Both had implications for the rest of the United Kingdom, which were the cause of most of the opposition he had to circumvent. On the Irish Church the verdict of the electorate had settled the two major questions of principle, disestablishment and disendowment. Even among Conservatives there were some who thought disestablishment inevitable and High Churchmen often had only tepid sympathies for the Irish Church, because of its strongly evangelical flavour. Uncompromising defenders of the Irish Church, in England or Ireland, had to put their faith in the House of Lords or even the Queen; or concentrate on a rearguard action over the terms of disendowment. Even so there was much room left for bitter controversy, which concerned mainly the terms of the disendowment, the compensation for the disestablished Church and its clergy, and the disposal of the surplus revenue remaining after the compensation had been allowed for. It was also proposed to abolish the *Regium Donum* to the Presbyterian bodies of Ireland and the famous grant to the Catholic Seminary at Maynooth, compensation for these to be paid out of the funds of the Irish Church. The Conservatives were unable to achieve any major modifications of Gladstone's scheme in the Commons and any hopes that Disraeli claimed to have of dividing the Liberal majority failed to materialize.

The battle shifted to the House of Lords where the Conservative peers were divided: many wanted outright resistance, not only because they wished to save as much as possible for the Irish Church, but because they refused to have the principle established that the Lords should give way to the clearly expressed will of a broadly elected House of Commons. This conflict was to flare up at intervals over the next 40 years, during which time the Upper House became progressively more one-sidedly Conservative, and ended in the curtailment of the powers of the second chamber. At a crucial moment in the passage of the Irish Church Bill through the Lords, John Bright raised the issue of the future of the House in an open letter to his constituents: 'In harmony with the nation they may go on for a long time; but throwing themselves athwart its course, they may meet with accidents not pleasant for them to think of.' Such threats from a member of the government did not help the forces of compromise which were hard at work, led by the Queen and Archbishop Tait. The Tory peers were not sufficiently united to secure the rejection of the bill on second reading, but they amended the disendowment clauses out of recognition in committee. In July 1869 the clash between the two Houses came to a head dramatically on the Lords' amendments. A possible dissolution of Parliament, in which the future of the House of Lords would have been bound to be an issue, loomed in the background. Discussions between the party leaders finally produced a compromise which substantially preserved Gladstone's original scheme.

Supporters of the Anglo-Irish ascendancy feared that the destruction, as they saw it, of the Irish Church was the thin end of a very wide wedge and in the long run these fears proved justified. Immediately, Gladstone tried to alleviate the grievances of the Irish majority in two other respects, the problem of land tenure and of higher education. On neither count was he as successful as in the case of the Irish Church in finding a solution. His Irish Land Act of 1870 did not adequately protect the Irish peasant against the evils of eviction and rack-renting and he had to have a second bite at the cherry in 1881. The Irish University Bill of 1873 did not even reach the statute book and its defeat marks a stage in the decline of Gladstone's government. The Land Act of 1870 was again the product of the Prime Minister's own initiative as well as detailed preparation although he knew less about the land problem than about the Irish Church. The Irish peasant felt that he had proprietorial rights in the land he farmed, but according to the strict, English-made law of the land he was only a rent-paying tenant. To give him some security of tenure a curtailment of the full property rights of the landlord was inevitable. It was on this point that opposition to Gladstone's bill, considerable within his own cabinet, focused. If it was possible to tamper with the prerogatives of landowners in Ireland, so some of Gladstone's landowning Whig colleagues argued, it would not be long before the position of the landowning aristocracy was undermined in England. Once the bill was before Parliament it did not encounter a great deal of opposition and it passed before the curious alliance of the party of British nonconformism with Irish Catholicism came to an end.

III

Gladstone's preoccupation with Ireland did not seriously impair the flow of his government's reforming legislation. In its broad tenor this legislation kept within the limits set by the canons of *laissez-faire* to the sphere of the State. Nevertheless this great spate of activity was bound to create the impression and expectation of widened responsibilities of government, which in due course eased the transition to a more collectivist view of the State. When Disraeli, at a time when Gladstone's ministry was already in decline, accused ministers of having 'harassed every trade, worried every profession, and assailed or menaced every class, institution, and species of property in the country', he was not speaking as extravagantly as even some of his own supporters thought, but articulating a feeling that the government now had a finger in every pie. Gladstone and his colleagues, however, were still so firmly convinced that they were the normal party of government that the electoral consequences of their numerous enactments caused them little concern.

The Education Act of 1870 was of all the legislative measures of the Gladstone government the one which had the greatest potential impact and the widest consequences in the long run. Its basic principle of building on existing voluntary effort in elementary education makes it fit into the philosophy of limited State action, but in a more fundamental way it implied an extension of the responsibilities of the State in a vital sphere. For more than a generation the State had in fact become increasingly involved in education, but the fear that this might pose dangers to freedom, reduce voluntary effort and place too heavy a burden on the taxpayer had been one of the factors inhibiting educational progress. Between 1866 and 1868 education was, apart from parliamentary reform, one of the main preoccupations in domestic policy of the Derby-Disraeli government. Some Conservative ministers, notably Stanley and Sir John Pakington, the First

Lord of the Admiralty, were keen on educational reform, but in general the attitude of the Tory Party was ambiguous. Many thought of education chiefly in terms of social control or their main concern was the maintenance of the Anglican ascendancy in this field. In spite of much discussion and the introduction of an actual bill in 1868, which soon had to be withdrawn, the Conservative government was unable to achieve anything substantial.

Conservative inaction further roused the expectation that the Liberals would move on education when they came into office. Education Aid Societies had been founded in 1864 at Manchester and 1867 at Birmingham, to improve local provision, and it was the latter which became the National Education League in January 1869. The original circular inviting support for the League stated as its object the universal provision of 'unsectarian' and free education, with the State or local authorities having the power to compel attendance. The word 'unsectarian' was carefully chosen to avoid 'secular', with its connotation of an anti-religious bias. Compulsory, free and secular education was, however, the aim of the inner core of the League's leaders. They included George Dixon, the Anglican member for Birmingham and sometime Mayor of the city, Joseph Chamberlain, a Unitarian, and his close associate Jesse Collings, William Harris, a leading spirit of the 'Caucus', and J.T. Bunce, the editor of the *Birmingham Daily Post*. Some of those who joined the League did not fully share all the League's objectives. This was true, for example, of R.W. Dale, the famous Birmingham Congregationalist minister, who did not believe that rate-aided schools should be free. The Central Nonconformist Committee, of which Dale and the Birmingham Unitarian minister Crosskey were secretaries, organized the dissenting opposition to the 1870 act as much as the League did; but the League, with its more extreme and clear-cut programme, pulled most nonconformists along with it into opposition against the Gladstone government and after 1870 Chamberlain used it to mount a general attack from the Left against the Liberal Party and government.

All this lay as yet in the future and for the moment the National Education League saw itself in the line of descent from the Anti-Corn Law League and the Reform League as the leading promoter of Radical Liberal policies. A rival body, the National Education Union, came into existence in Manchester in November 1869 with the object of 'judiciously supplementing the present system of denominational education'. The list of its sponsors was studded with the names of archbishops, dukes and lesser peers, and it stood in the paternalist tradition of promoting 'the education of the poor'. It was mainly Anglican, but included nonconformist supporters of denominational education, such as Edward Baines, the proprietor of the *Leeds*

Mercury and a leading voluntarist. The voluntarists were mainly non-conformists and had in the past been opposed to all State involvement in education and still preferred to see it limited.

Forster laid his scheme before the cabinet in October 1869. He stated as his object 'to supplement the present voluntary system – that is to fill up its gaps at least cost of public money, with least loss of voluntary co-operation, and with most aid from the parents'. He explicitly condemned the proposals of the League, as likely to undermine the existing schools, entail great public expense and 'drive out of the field most of those who care for education'. The school board was the instrument which Forster's bill proposed to establish to fill the gaps. England and Wales (the Act did not apply to Scotland or Ireland) were to be divided into school districts, of which London was one; if in a district the provision was, in the view of the Education Department, not 'efficient and suitable', then, after a period of grace, a school board would have to be set up. In boroughs the council, and elsewhere the ratepayers could, by a majority, demand the establishment of a board. These boards, with 5 to 15 members according to the size of the district, had extensive powers to establish schools, they could require local authorities to raise a rate in aid of the board schools and they could take power to enforce attendance. By a later amendment school boards were to be elected by cumulative voting: every voter had as many votes as there were seats on the board, but he could cast them all for one candidate. This would help the representation of minorities. Originally the secret ballot was also provided for, but was rejected by the House of Lords. The problem of religious instruction in board schools presented a major problem and Forster hoped to deal with it by allowing a kind of local option. Each school board was to decide what kind of religious instruction was to be given in its schools. A conscience clause would give those parents who did not wish their children to receive the religious instruction provided the chance of withdrawing them. Forster hoped by these proposals 'to canter over' the religious difficulty, as he rather injudiciously put it. The cabinet, in which the Education Department was represented by de Grey, the Lord President of the Council, approved the bill without giving very serious consideration to the political damage it might do to the Liberal Party.

Initially the bill was well received, but it soon ran into strong opposition, mainly from the nonconformists. Their deep-seated fear was that the denominational schools, where the Anglican preponderance was so marked, would not only be preserved indefinitely, but that their hold on elementary education would actually be strengthened. Just before the second-reading debate on the bill, in March 1870, Gladstone met a delegation consisting of 46 MPs and 400

members of the Education League, led by Joseph Chamberlain. It
was the first meeting between the two men and Chamberlain put the
League's views in forthright, even threatening terms. As controversy
engulfed the Education Bill, Gladstone threw the full weight of his
great parliamentary authority behind it, even though its religious
provisions were not greatly to his taste; the Irish Land Bill, however,
remained his own and the government's first priority.

When the Education Bill resumed its parliamentary progress in
June 1870, two major amendments were accepted by the government
to meet the objections of the nonconformists. One was the famous
Cowper-Temple clause that in publicly provided schools 'no religious
catechism or religious formulary which is distinctive of any particular
denomination shall be taught'. The clause did not inhibit the teacher
from putting his own views and following his own conscience, the
point of Disraeli's remark in the debates, 'you are inventing and
establishing a new sacerdotal class'. The arrival of a new form of
religion, 'Cowper-Temple religion', was widely feared. Anglicans
and Roman Catholics, for whom their catechism was an integral part
of religion, saw cause for concern. The second major change in the
bill accepted by the government was a time-table conscience clause,
as opposed to the simple conscience clause initially proposed, by
which in publicly aided schools religious instruction had to take place
before or after the main body of instruction. The withdrawal of children from religious lessons would thus become a more realistic possibility. Many additional concessions were made to nonconformist
views: the grant to denominational schools to come from the central
government only, not from local rates as well, as originally envisaged;
school boards to be elected by the whole body of ratepayers instead of
by town councils or parish vestries; building grants to voluntary
schools to cease after six months, instead of a year.

These concessions did not satisfy those nonconformists committed
to free, secular and compulsory education, nor did they greatly pacify
more moderate dissenters. The government was, however, always
able to command a majority, partly made up of Liberals and sometimes of Tories as well, and the opponents of the bill lost all hope of
stopping it. It was this that made Edward Miall, Forster's uneasy
companion in the representation of Bradford, yet a strong opponent
of the Bill, declare that he and his supporters had been made to pass
through the valley of humiliation and that they were 'once bit, twice
shy', to which Gladstone replied impetuously that he hoped 'my
honourable friend will not continue that support to the government
one moment longer than he deems it consistent with his sense of duty
and right'. The wounds of the Liberal Party went deep. Clause 25,
under which the school boards could pay the fees of poor children out

of the rates, the focus of subsequent agitation against the Act, passed, however, without discussion or division. By withdrawing the original proposal that school boards could use local rates to subsidize denominational schools the government appeared to have given way on a point which touched the dissenting community closely and it was not noticed that clause 25 in effect reinstated the principle which was so deeply abhorred.

Even politically moderate nonconformists were thus left with a grievance which the National Education League could exploit. Its policy in the next few years proceeded on the parallel lines of making the most of the opportunities offered by the Act while attacking it fiercely for having failed to establish free compulsory secular education, and for giving the Anglican ascendancy in elementary education a new lease of life. There was pressure by the League to set up school boards wherever possible. School board elections were hotly contested, not always successfully, for it required careful organization of the voters to prevail under the cumulative voting system. Even in Birmingham itself, where the Education League undoubtedly commanded a majority and the Liberal Party was highly organized, the nominees of the League headed by Chamberlain only secured 6 out of 15 seats. Boards, like the Birmingham one, then became battlegrounds between nonconformists and churchmen. In some extreme cases, for example at Sheffield in 1872 and 1873, there was a move to refuse the payment of rates and incur martyrdom. In 1872 the National Education League had come out with a set of demands more uncompromising than before: school boards should be established everywhere and should control all existing schools; denominations should be confined to providing religious instruction in out-of-school hours.

It was, however, becoming apparent that many ordinary nonconformist Liberal voters had only a limited interest in education and that the Education League was comparable to pressure groups like the United Kingdom Alliance or the Lord's Day Observance Society rather than a broadly supported movement like the Anti-Corn Law League. It could make no dent in the unity of the Liberal cabinet on the education question. John Bright, for example, always concerned for the Liberal Party's survival as a united body, declared in 1870 that the 1870 Act 'was the worst Act passed by a Liberal government since 1832', but he rejoined Gladstone's government in 1873, having had to leave it three years earlier for health reasons. In 1873 Forster brought in an amending act to transfer the responsibility for paying the fees of needy children from the school boards to the Boards of Guardians and making them compulsory. This was entirely unsatisfactory to the League, because it was anticipated that payments to voluntary schools from this source would now become even bigger. In June 1873 the League threatened to run a separate candidate at the second Bath by-election of that year and only withdrew him after receiving assurances from the official Liberal candidate that he supported school boards and compulsion and was against the payment of fees by Guardians. Following the London School Board, most of the big urban boards interpreted the Cowper-Temple clause as meaning 'that no attempt must be made to attach children to any denomination' and there was also a prohibition on 'detaching' them from any denomination. This was not the interpretation that Gladstone and others had given during the parliamentary debates, but the straightforward Bible-teaching which was given in most board schools proved generally acceptable and helped in due course to reduce nonconformist opposition to the Act. Chamberlain, now increasingly in association with Charles Dilke and John Morley, seeing the limits of education as a means of 'smashing up that whited sepulchre called the Liberal Party', was feeling his way towards an organization wider in scope than a single-issue pressure group, a process that was to end in the formation of the National Liberal Federation.

The main legislative enactment of the Gladstone government in the field of university education was the abolition of religious tests for teaching fellowships at Oxford and Cambridge. It was the culmination of a process by which the two older universities had gradually been opened to non-Anglicans. Cambridge, with its more scientific and mathematical orientation, was already attracting a fair number of nonconformist students. The full admission of dissenters into the teaching body at Oxford and Cambridge had become one of the symbolic causes of nonconformist equality, not unlike Church rates. In the 1860s a number of bills had been brought forward to end the need to subscribe to the 39 Articles that kept dissenters from teaching posts. Theological liberals and political liberals from academic and public life combined to forward this cause, but this was an issue on which Gladstone himself was reluctant to follow. In 1866, when he had already ceased to represent the University of Oxford, he still voted against a bill to open fellowships at Oxford and Cambridge to non-Anglicans and it was not until 1871 that he was persuaded to make such a bill a government measure. The Education Act of 1870 and the abolition of university tests showed up the religious fissures in the Liberal coalition that had been pulled together by the cause of Irish Church disestablishment in 1868. There was alienation between the government and much of nonconformity; but there was also lack of sympathy between Gladstone, the earnest, zealous High Churchman , who found it difficult to accept the interventions of an increasingly secular State in the affairs of the Church, and Whigs of worldly disposition, who were often anti-clerical, opposed to dogmatism and in favour of firm control of the Church by the State; and there were differences also between Gladstone and many members of the Liberal intelligentsia who wanted to align the Church with what they saw as the mainstream of enlightened and progressive opinion.

III

The abolition of privileges, the removal of barriers to advancement by merit and the establishment of full civic equality were part of the philosophy of Gladstonian Liberalism and consequently the government took further steps to make merit and expertise rather than patronage the basis of recruitment to the public service. Moves in this direction had begun in the 1850s, first in the recruitments of the Indian Civil Service. Gladstone himself had initiated the Trevelyan-Northcote inquiry and the Civil Service Commission had been set up. The Crimean War produced much criticism of the system of aristocratic patronage; the growing complexity and diversity of public administration, in the civil as much as in the military service, called for more professionalism. The opportunities for attracting candidates of ability into the public service were, however, still considerably circumscribed. The examinations conducted by the Civil Service Commission were of a fairly elementary kind and heads of government departments still had discretion to nominate for vacancies or to limit competition to nominated candidates. In the 1868 election campaign Gladstone declared himself in favour of open competition, but it was Robert Lowe, as Chancellor of the Exchequer, who pressed the Prime Minister and his cabinet colleagues to move forward decisively. The result was an order-in-council of June 1870 which laid down open competitive examinations as the normal mode of entry into all Departments of State except the Foreign and Home Offices and gave the Treasury control of all recruitment procedures. When Lowe moved to the Home Office in 1873 that department also fell into line.

The civil service was divided into a higher and a lower grade, corresponding to steps in the educational ladder and therefore in the hierarchy of social classes. In the upper grade would be the small number of superior officers in each department. They would be an élite, having, in Lowe's words, 'the best education that England affords: the education of public schools and colleges and such things, which gives a sort of freemasonry among men which is not very easy to describe, but which everybody feels . . .'. In 1877, in a strong field, there were among the 11 candidates selected, one Etonian, one Haileyburian, two Harrovians, and three Wykehamists, and 9 of the 11 had been to Oxford or Cambridge and the tenth to Trinity College, Dublin. Most of the work in government departments would be done by subordinate clerks from the lower-grade entry. Candidates for the lower grade could choose subjects from a list including bookkeeping, indexing, copying, as well as geography, English history, and the three 'R's. This entry was thus open to the products of elementary schools, lower middle-class and bright working-class boys, especially those who had moved on to some of the higher standards increasingly available after 1875. Statistics about the 221 clerks appointed in 1885 showed that 95 had been educated in National, British, Wesleyan or Board schools; only 12 came from superior schools such as Dulwich or the City of London School. Lowe, in spite of his meritocratic ideas, saw no chance in practice of civil servants moving from the lower to the upper grade and the two-fold division of the civil service was confirmed by the Playfair Commission in 1874. After 1870 the Treasury under Lowe worked hard to get departments to adopt the new procedures and make them uniform. Only the Foreign Office held out; Granville, who had become Foreign Secretary after Clarendon's death, reported that his men wanted to preserve themselves from 'adulteration' and that he was afraid to 'throw the machine out of gear'.

The fight against privilege and the pursuit of meritocracy came up against a special case in the officer corps of the army. The system of purchasing commissions underpinned the close association between the ruling classes and the officers of the army. It was not only that the land-owning classes were well represented in the officer corps; there were also many serving or former army officers among members of Parliament. A period of temporary service in the army, facilitated by the purchase of commissions, followed by entry into Parliament, was a common experience for members of the leading political families. Purchasing a commission in the army was a way in which members of the middle classes arrived to wealth could imitate and graduate into the ruling classes, just as they could through the purchase of land. There were in fact many middle-class officers, particularly in regiments requiring professional expertise like the engineers or the artillery, where purchase did not operate and where the social composition of the officer corps was more like that of the navy. When commissions were not subject to purchase, they were often awarded through patronage. Nevertheless the image of the army officer was aristocratic and those who opposed abolition of purchase saw in this a bulwark of the constitution. In 1856 Palmerston, defending the purchase system in the House of Commons said: '. . . if the connection between the army and the higher classes of society were dissolved, then the army would present a dangerous and unconstitutional appearance. It was only when the army was un-connected with those whose property gave them an interest in the country, and was commanded by the unprincipled military adventurers, that it ever became formidable to the liberties of the nation.' Palmerston was speaking at a moment when failures in the Crimea had brought administration by well-connected amateurs under strong attack, particularly in the military sphere. Thus the demand for more meritocracy and greater professionalism in the military sphere touched a particularly sensitive nerve and during the next decade the controversy never died down.

The appointment of Cardwell, who for many years after 1846 had been one of the leaders of the Peelite faction, as Secretary of State for War in Gladstone's government was something of a surprise, but he had acquired considerable experience of military matters by sitting on commissions of enquiry. He came into office with carefully thought-out proposals of military reorganization and it soon became apparent that without abolishing purchase of commissions regimental reorganization would be very difficult. There was in fact a considerable weight of professional opinion among army officers that purchase should go. A memorandum from Lieutenant Evelyn Baring, later Lord Cromer, and at this time serving in the Topographical and Statistical Department of the War Office, argued that purchase blocked the promotion of the most suitable and competent officers, that abolition would not damage the regimental *esprit de corps* and that it would favour the aristocratic at the expense of the wealthy among officers.

Military reorganization was given further urgency by the Franco–Prussian war and Cardwell came forward, for the session of 1871, with an Army Regulation Bill, the centrepiece of which was the abolition of purchase. Disraeli initially gave this bill his support, but soon opposition sprang up. Particularly on the Tory side there were members who were or had been army officers and were generally referred to as 'the Colonels', who opposed abolition as such or were trying to secure better terms of compensation. In the debates on the committee stage of the Army Regulation Bill the opponents of abolition put down a long series of 'obstructionist' motions. It was a novel use of parliamentary tactics, soon to be imitated on a larger scale. The government was in an uneasy position in arguing the case for the bill: on the one hand it tried to calm fears that the aristocratic composition of the officer corps would disappear and that compensation would be inadequate; on the other it had to argue that the bill was a blow against privilege and that compensation would not be excessive. In the end most of the Radicals who had had qualms about the bill were whipped into line, the bill passed the Commons, only to have its purchase clauses struck out by the Lords.

It was then that the government decided to circumvent the parliamentary blockage by asking the Queen to abolish purchase by Royal Warrant. Renewed fierce outcries from both ends of the political spectrum followed. Some Radicals like Fawcett feared that this was a use of the royal prerogative which would set a precedent and undermine the supremacy of Parliament. Gladstone was attacked as the 'imperious minister'. In fact the Prime Minister had initially had misgivings about Cardwell's reforms and the abolition of purchase in particular, but the fierce opposition encountered by the bill made him feel increasingly that there was 'folly, faction, and the selfishness of class'. He voiced similar sentiments in a public speech to his constituents at Greenwich. It was a theme which was to recur with increasing frequency in his public and private discourse.

The abolition of purchase was a necessary prelude to the reorganization of the army which Cardwell carried out in the next two years. In itself the importance of abolition can easily be overestimated. Factors other than the purchase system, such as family traditions, education, the expense of the military life and habit, ensured that the officer corps retained its aristocratic image and its close association with the ruling classes. Nevertheless, promotion for the able and competent became easier. Professionalism had not left the army untouched even before 1870 and the development of military education at Woolwich, Sandhurst and the Staff College, Camberley, made for further progress. At the other end of army recruitment, there were moves to weaken the image of soldiering as an occupation fit only for the dregs of the community. In 1869 flogging in the army in peacetime was abolished. Overall, the effectiveness of the army for fighting small colonial wars improved, but when 30 years later the Boer War exposed some of its weaknesses in larger operations, the criticisms still had a familiar ring about them.

IV

By 1871 the Gladstone government appeared to many of its supporters to have lost momentum and sense of direction. When it was
first elected Walter Bagehot considered the Liberal majority
'unequalled . . . in earnest cohesiveness, incomparable . . . in
debating efficiency . . . still greater because it is the only first-rate
political force left'. Little more than two years later by-elections were
beginning to go against the government and, quite apart from disappointment on specific matters, like that of the nonconformists over the
Education Act, working-class voters appeared to have become disenchanted. Gladstone defending his record pointed out that three of his
major measures, the Irish Land Act, the Education Act, and the
Ballot Bill, which had been introduced but was yet to pass, were of
direct benefit to the working classes. Henry Fawcett, who had frequently criticized the government for its shortcomings from the
Radical side, thought disillusionment of the working classes with the
Liberal government would only be overcome if Liberal principles
were truly made to prevail. 'Let the Ministry resolve never to sanction any infringement of religious equality; let them carry out
economy with rigid impartiality; let them be influenced in their
choice of men by no other considerations than those of merit', and he
warned, 'There is unfortunately a growing tendency among the
working classes to rely upon State help, and they are constantly
asking the government to relieve them from misfortunes which they
have brought upon themselves, and from which they can alone be
rescued by the exercise of increased prudence and sagacity.' It was
the dilemma of Liberalism that it could remove legal hindrances to
equality but that its total commitment to individualism and repugnance for collectivism deprived it of any prescription for dealing with
economic and social hindrances to equality.

This became very evident in the Liberal government's handling of
the trade union question. There was indeed much ambivalence in the
approach of politicians and public men of all persuasions to trade
unions. There was much talk of the 'monstrous tyranny exercised by
the trades unions', but also a disposition to exploit their great political
potential. The antagonism to them was rationalized by the argument
that since wages, like everything else, were governed by market
forces, it was an illusion of the working classes to think that unions
could help them; moreover their operation damaged the competitiveness of industry and, as Robert Lowe put it 'threaten some
branches of manufactures with extinction, and seriously limit the
diffusion of others'. Hostility to unionism had received an impetus
from the Sheffield outrages; endemic violence against non-union men

in the Sheffield cutlery trades had culminated in the blowing up of a workman's house in October 1866. In January 1867 the Court of Queen's Bench heard an appeal in the case of Hornby v Close, in which the Boilermakers' Society had proceeded against the treasurer of their Bradford branch for wrongfully withholding the sum of £24. The Lord Chief Justice and three other judges decided that the Society could not sue under the Friendly Societies Act of 1855, for while it was not criminal, it was illegal as being in restraint of trade. This left the unions legally in a very exposed position. On top of this the trade depression which began in 1866 was making the economic climate adverse to unionism.

The Conservative government's solution to the trade union problem was the appointment, in February 1867, of a royal commission to enquire into the Sheffield outrages in particular and trade unionism in general. The government refused to appoint a trade unionist to the commission; it would have been an innovation to have a working man on such a body. Two of its members were, however, favourable to the point of view of the unions; Thomas Hughes, who was appointed as an MP and Frederic Harrison who was appointed on the advice of the London Trades Council. Harrison, a barrister, and Professor E.S. Beesly were the two most prominent middle-class intellectuals trying to advance the cause of labour at this time and both were adherents of the Comtean Positivist philosophy. The junta, the group of London union leaders regarded by the Webbs, perhaps with some exaggeration, as the 'inner cabinet' of the labour movement, devoted much effort to making a case, before the commission, for the unions as organizations of respectability, to counteract the impression left by the Sheffield outrages and similar incidents; they also had to frustrate attempts by the employers to influence the commission against a legalization of unionism. In 1869 the commission produced a majority and a minority report, the latter signed by Harrison, Hughes and the Earl of Lichfield. Both reports recommended legalization of the unions, but the majority report proposed to give the Registrar of Friendly Societies power to reject 'objectionable' clauses in a union's rules, mostly of the kind that could be seen to be in restraint of trade. The minority report recommended that unions should be registered by the Registrar of Friendly Societies but that he should have no powers to tamper with their rules.

It was not until the session of 1871 that Bruce, the Home Secretary, put forward the government's own proposals in a bill. While it gave full legal status to the unions, its third clause, comprehensively prohibiting violence, threats, intimidation, molestation and obstruction, immediately aroused great apprehension among trade union leaders. It was intended only to restate the law as it then stood, but unionists feared that it could make their operations virtually impossible. At a time when it was quite normal for employers to recruit alternative labour if their own work force went on strike, the unions considered the right to picket a matter of life and death. The government was not prepared, however, to make any further concessions, beyond incorporating the contentious third clause in a separate Criminal Law Amendment Act, against which the unions mounted a steady campaign over the next few years. This campaign was led by the Trades Union Congress, which had first met in 1868 in Manchester. It was one of many attempts to give the unions, with their great diversity and local autonomy, a national forum. The junta had at first boycotted it, because it feared the Congress would be dominated by elements hostile to its policy of respectability. Many trade unionists regarded the efforts to secure legal recognition as futile and wanted to have as little as possible to do with the law. George Potter and his newspaper *The Beehive* had for long been the focus of opposition to the junta. Subsequently there was a reconciliation and from 1871 the Trades Union Congress and its Parliamentary Committee, whose secretary was George Howell, formerly of the Reform League, continued to put pressure on the government to change the law, but without success.

At the grassroots, the early 1870s, a time of economic boom, witnessed a rapid growth of unionism, reaching beyond the ranks of the skilled and permanently employed who had formed the bulk of trade union membership in the middle years of the century. Workers who had previously proved difficult to organize, like the dockers, gasworkers and builders, now formed unions. Improvements in literacy and communication, through the growth of the press, may well have been among the causes; the 'residuum', which had so often seemed a frightening impenetrable mass, was becoming aware of conditions elsewhere and seeking to imitate them. The most striking development was the arrival of unionism among agricultural labourers. It was for the most part a spontaneous development, but the movement acquired a nation-wide organization through the energy and ability of Joseph Arch, originally the organizer of an agricultural workers' union in Warwickshire. Arch's National Agricultural Labourers Union, which pursued an active policy of strikes, had over 80,000 members at its peak in 1874; and in some areas there were independent unions not affiliated to it. Thereafter it rapidly declined under the impact of the agricultural depression. Many of the newly formed unions of the early 1870s also faded away again as a result of the general economic slump which began in 1873 and even the older established craft unions suffered a loss of members. The Trades Union Congress of 1874 probably represented a membership of nearly 1.2 millions, but by the end of the decade fewer than half were left.

Nevertheless there was, two decades after the demise of Chartism, a labour movement, but much of the working class was not within it. In the wake of the Paris Commune the organs of respectable opinion congratulated themselves that the English labour movement was not likely to go in the same direction and take to the barricades. The *Quarterly Review*, writing about the International Working Men's Association, the first International, said in January 1872: '. . . the secretary of that body, who assumes to direct it and to speak and write in its name, is a mischievous, hot-headed, and intemperate German, named Karl Marx . . . many of his English colleagues are disgusted at his virulence and resist his imperious behaviour, and altogether refuse to be dragged through the mire and blood which have no repugnant qualities for him . . .'. The *Quarterly* was undoubtedly right that the association of a number of British labour leaders with the International was mainly formal and that they had no clear sense of its wider objectives. Yet there had to be new political aims, particularly when the immediate effects of the wider franchise of 1867 proved to be disappointing. The obvious next step was to press for greater labour representation. This was the purpose of the Labour Representation League, founded in 1869, with which most of the prominent London labour leaders were associated. It was an uneasy compromise between those who hoped to build up a genuinely independent Labour Group in the House of Commons and those who saw no further than the formation of yet another pressure group within the Liberal Party. On the practical level the League was defeated by the fact that any parliamentary candidature required a great deal of money and the trade unions were not at this stage prepared to lay out such sums for political objectives. Moreover, candidatures which were not the result of an agreement with other interests in the Liberal Party, often caused the seat to go to the Tories. This was the result, for example, of George Odger's candidature at Southwark in 1870. In the later 1870s the Labour Representation League faded into insignificance.

For those in left-wing and labour politics who were not content to work within the existing party system republicanism became the fashionable political cause. It was capable of being combined with almost any of the other nostrums of the Left and therefore had many factions. At the simplest level there was dissatisfaction with the Queen, because of her failure to carry out the ceremonial functions of the monarchy. This dissatisfaction was aggravated by the high cost of the civil list and the periodic demands made for various members of the royal family. Fifty-three MPs opposed the allowance of £15,000 proposed for Prince Arthur, later Duke of Connaught, on his coming of age. At a more ideological level, republicanism held natural attractions for all believers in reason as the key to social arrangements, from John Stuart Mill through positivists like Beesly and Harrison, atheists like Charles Bradlaugh, to the more extreme adherents of social revolution. The Land and Labour League, founded in 1869 and avowedly republican, had far-reaching social changes, such as nationalization of land, suppression of private banks of issue, a progressive property tax and reduction of the hours of work among its programme.

Dilke was the most prominent rising politician associated with republicanism and his speeches gave the cause considerable publicity. Most public and private comment was fiercely hostile, yet the government was clearly troubled. Gladstone wrote to Granville: 'We have arrived at a great crisis of Royalty: only it is a crisis which may be overlooked, because the issue is in a remote future. Not the less is it true that this in all likelihood is the last opportunity to be given us of effecting what is requisite.' Gladstone was probably thinking of his difficulties in finding employment for the Prince of Wales, a matter on which he had expended a great deal of effort, thereby incurring that mounting hostility of the Queen which was to dog him for the rest of his political life. The Prince was about to fall victim to a severe attack of typhoid, which nearly killed him. His recovery and his appearance, with his mother, at a thanksgiving service in St Paul's in February 1872 swept away the royal unpopularity at a stroke and scuppered republicanism as a popular cause. It could not have served as a vehicle for a broad movement of the left, in the way that socialism later served. The fact that for a short while so many radical groups espoused it showed that for the moment there was little coherence, and, in the boom of the early 70s, little urgency on the left.

V

Labour as a pressure group was new, the size of its following difficult to assess, and its party allegiance not firmly fixed. The characteristics of the temperance movement stood in most respects in sharp contrast. It was long established and part and parcel of the prevailing social ethos of individual responsibility, self-help and self-improvement. Its political spearhead, the United Kingdom Alliance, was well integrated into the network of nonconformist causes and into liberal radical politics; Tory temperance men were fairly rare and support for the Conservative Party was mainly used as a threat by the Alliance against Liberals unwilling to promise them sufficient commitment. When the Alliance adopted prohibition as its policy in the 1850s there had been potential conflict between it and the *laissez-faire*, free-trading doctrines of Liberalism. This conflict seemed for a moment to become real when Gladstone with the Cobden treaty of 1860 freed the wine trade. But the general moral consonance between much of Liberalism and the temperance movement prevented such conflicts from becoming serious. The Alliance had thrown its might behind the permissive bill, the proposal for a local option or popular veto on the sale and production of intoxicating liquor. Such an exercise in decentralization and local autonomy had its own attractions for Liberals and even others. In the 60s the Alliance had steadily gained in influence and resources and the support for its permissive bill among Liberal MPs had grown, even if there was at times resentment at its blackmailing tactics in the constituencies. After 1867 there was a general expectation of new licensing legislation, just as there was of education legislation. The new voters had to be weaned from the dangers of alcohol as much as they had to be educated. Even a Conservative government might have legislated along law and order lines, for drunkenness as a social problem worried Conservatives as much as Liberals. Many Liberals were aware, however, that there were great political risks in drink legislation. Gladstone wrote to Manning, who was promoting temperance among Catholics: 'I wish well to as much restraint in the liquor traffic as the public will bear without offensive distinction between classes'.

It was unfortunate for the government that it fell to Bruce, the Home Secretary, one of the less able ministers, to devise and take charge of the proposed new Liberal licensing law in the session of 1871. It was a very complicated measure, giving magistrates responsibility for almost all drink retailing; supporters of the local option were given a sop in the proposal that a three-fifths majority of rate-payers could in certain circumstances reduce the number of licenses granted by the magistrates and curtail closing hours. The bill fell between two stools, pleasing neither the temperance interest nor the drink trade. The latter was for the first time in its entirety, from publicans to brewers, aroused unequivocally against the Liberals, whereas previously many in the trade had, like the business community as a whole, supported them. Bruce's bill was pilloried as an attack on property rights at a moment when all men of property, great or small, were alarmed by events across the Channel. The outrage of an offended vested interest was not counterbalanced by support for the government from the temperance movement. The United Kingdom Alliance stuck doggedly to its all-or-nothing attitude; their eccentric but fearless parliamentary spokesman Wilfrid Lawson announced that he would persevere with the permissive bill. In the overcrowded session of 1871 Bruce's bill did not even get a second reading, but a less controversial bill restricting opening hours passed in 1872. At least as important as the alignment of the drink trade with the Tories was the fact that the Conservative Party was now able to appear as the champion of the working man who enjoyed his pint of beer and to identify itself with that long libertarian tradition of robust enjoyment which among the lower working-class strata was more prevalent than the earnest quest for self-improvement. The demon drink may have been the undoing of many a poor family, but the public house was the centre of much working-class life. The passage of the 1872 licensing law provoked a good deal of minor rioting, much of it inspired by the sentiment that there was one law for the rich and another for the poor.

R.C.K. Ensor, whose account of this period has become a classic of historiography, saw in the positive and permanent shift of the publicans and brewers to the Tory Party an important and long-term change of electoral forces against the Liberal Party. This view seemed to be born out by Gladstone's own opinion, expressed in a letter to his brother after the defeat of 1874: 'We have been borne down in a torrent of gin and beer.' The Liberal leader was perhaps thinking particularly of his own campaign at Greenwich and the fact that he had been pushed into second place by the Tory distiller Boord. To the Queen he wrote: 'the most powerful operative cause has been the combined and costly action of the publicans except in the North where from their more masculine character the people are not so easily managed.' Gladstone was, however, hardly a dispassionate observer of his own defeat and it would be difficult to isolate the licensing question from the other factors weakening the Liberal hold on working-class voters at this time.

VI

The evident disarray into which the Gladstone government had fallen by 1872 was the signal for Disraeli to come out of his shell and assert himself politically. Since the defeat of 1868 there had been little scope either for the Conservative Party or Disraeli personally to take any clear initiative. The Liberal government pre-empted much of the political debate by its legislation, and most of the major bills offered the Tories little opportunity for decisive opposition. As for organized labour and the working classes in general, a more collectivist stance, such as might have satisfied them, was not much easier to adopt for Conservatives than it was for Liberals. The orthodoxies of political economy were so pervasive that few Tories could escape them. On some questions they might even take a harsher line than Liberals, for instance poor relief. It was axiomatic for Tories that the rate burden had become intolerable and that more of it should be shifted on to the central exchequer, but much of it was attributable to poor relief. Thus few Conservatives were prepared to see the penal character of the English poor relief system eased, though humanitarian and paternalist sentiment sometimes softened such attitudes.

Disraeli himself was sympathetic to a Tory social reform programme and in the General Preface to the 1870 edition of his novels he had remarked: 'Their [i.e. the novels] economic principles were not unsound but they looked upon the health and knowledge of the multitude as not the least precious part of the wealth of nations.' He was thus in no mood to go back on his past professions of concern for the lower classes, while affirming the orthodoxy of his economic principles. There was, however, much dissatisfaction with his leadership among all levels of the party. The 'betrayal' of 1867 still rankled and his continued addiction to literature, made manifest by the publication of *Lothair* in 1870 did not help. In 1870 there had been a serious possibility that Salisbury, Disraeli's most formidable enemy in the Party, might have become the Conservative leader in the House of Lords and in January 1872 prominent Tories met in conclave at Burghley House to consider the possibility of Derby becoming leader of the Party. Disraeli was, however, far too formidable a politician to be seriously endangered by such machinations. His low-key performance as leader of the Opposition up to 1872 was no doubt partly due to old age, ill health and discouragement; but he also realized that his best policy was to give Gladstone enough rope to hang himself.

By early 1872 Disraeli judged that the time was ripe to go over to the attack and he allowed preparations to go ahead for a visit to Manchester, with a speech in the Free Trade Hall, the enemy's citadel in symbolic terms, as the centre-piece of a great Conservative demonstration. Gorst at the Conservative Central Office had long wanted to organize such a demonstration, but had up to this time found leading Lancashire Tories, including possibly Lord Derby, lukewarm to Disraeli and some of his former cabinet colleagues. Now the atmosphere changed and the working men of Lancashire, a majority of whom had voted Tory in 1868, would demonstrate that 'the Tory democracy' was a reality. So it proved to be and Disraeli's triumphant reception in Manchester in April 1872 put an end to all doubts about his leadership. The Free Trade Hall speech, together

with a speech Disraeli made in June 1872 to a meeting of the National
Union of Conservative Associations at the Crystal Palace, constitute
a kind of Conservative manifesto and have often been regarded as the
beginning of modern Conservatism. Disraeli was not much given to
public oratory of this kind; his strength as a speaker and writer lay in
the drawing of wide perspectives, as well as in the use of vivid language and invective. He was weak on and almost impatient of detail;
on those occasions he would have been unwise, in any case, to commit
himself to specific policies and measures. The speeches are naturally
much influenced by issues of the moment; thus in the Free Trade Hall
speech he emphasized public health, because it was under discussion
in Parliament. His comments on social reform were altogether neither lengthy nor detailed. He nodded approvingly in the direction of
the nine-hour movement, for he knew that trade union leaders were
involved in it; this was well within the Conservative tradition, while
on the other hand it would have been impossible to say anything at
this juncture about trade union legislation. Disraeli was at his most
sweeping and impressive in condemning the Liberal Party for having
tried 'with so much ability and acumen to disintegrate the Empire of
England'; he thus by contrast associated the Conservative Party with
the maintenance and consolidation of empire. Here he was proclaiming a permanent feature of modern Conservatism. Disraeli's
defence of the constitution, the monarchy, the Church, the House of
Lords, was in traditional mould, but the recent dalliance of the liberal
Left with republicanism made it easy for him to call the Liberals the
'cosmopolitan' party and claim that the Conservatives were the
'national' party. In the mood of the moment it was also not difficult to
accuse Gladstone of weakness in foreign policy. Ever since the dramatic events of the Franco–Prussian war there had been a feeling of
impotence in the country, aggravated by the government's conciliatory stance in matters such as the abrogation of the Black Sea clauses
of the Treaty of Paris and the *Alabama* claims. The constitution, the
Empire, social reform and national honour – this was the Conservative programme which Disraeli sketched with broad strokes of the
brush in his speeches. At least one of the merits of this programme
was the clear alternative it offered the voter to the Liberal devices of
equality of opportunity, self-improvement, retrenchment and international understanding.

   Disraeli was beginning to believe in the disintegration of the
Liberal Party, but he knew the process required time. In the meantime minor misjudgements and mishaps further weakened the government and the tale of Liberal by-election losses continued. In March
1873 came defeat in the House of Commons. Gladstone attempted to
crown his mission of pacifying Ireland by dealing with another long-

standing grievance, the lack of a university open to Catholics. The Irish hierarchy, up to this time well disposed towards the Liberal government, wanted a denominational university, but there was no hope of getting such a proposal through Parliament. The relationship between Irish Catholics and the other religious groups supporting the Liberal Party was becoming very difficult; a major reason for this was the promulgation of the Vatican Decrees of 1870, with their uncompromising restatement of Catholic dogma, including papal infallibility. Gladstone put forward a scheme for a teaching and examining university, into which existing denominational colleges would be combined, but theology, moral philosophy and history would be excluded from the curriculum. In spite of the support of Manning the Irish bishops broke with Gladstone over this and radical supporters of secular education also found the scheme unacceptable. Irish members combined with the Conservative Opposition and a few Radicals to defeat the government by three votes. Gladstone resigned, but Disraeli refused to take office. He argued that a chance combination of groups, between whom there was no co-operation, in a matter which should not have been treated as one of confidence, carried no obligation to take office. He was in fact being advised that the Conservative reaction in the country needed more time to mature; a Conservative minority government would not be in a position, for technical reasons, to dissolve Parliament quickly and the country would therefore have time to forget the failings of the Liberal government. Since Gladstone was not prepared to ask for a dissolution himself he had to resume office. At the end of the parliamentary session he carried out a reconstruction of his government, in which the two ministers who had proved themselves particularly accident-prone, Bruce and Lowe, changed offices. Shortly afterwards John Bright's return to the cabinet appeared to be an important accession of strength, for his name still held unrivalled appeal for all men of radical views. It looked as if the damage which the Liberal Party might suffer as a result of the disaffection of National Education Leaguers or trade unionists would be limited.

Gladstone himself took over the Exchequer from Lowe and combined it with the premiership. This may well have been one of the reasons that precipitated his decision, in January 1874, not to face the House of Commons again for another session and to dissolve Parliament. There was uncertainty about whether, having thus assumed a new office, he would have to seek re-election at Greenwich. The opposition was bound to make the most of any legal doubts that existed and might seek to remove him from the House at the opening of the 1874 session. Another reason for this surprising timing of the election was disagreement in the cabinet over the naval and military estimates. In Gladstone's view the high level of this expenditure deprived the government of the one card it could have played with credibility if it carried on, economy and cuts in taxation. It was in fact such an 'economical' policy to be pursued in the future that he decided to make the centre of his appeal to the country. He held on to the hope of abolishing the income tax. It was on this policy that he had made his public reputation some 20 years earlier.

Gladstone's timing of the dissolution did at least achieve surprise. Disraeli had hurriedly to concoct a letter to his electors in the county of Buckingham, in reply to Gladstone's address to the voters in the borough of Greenwich. Disraeli could only counter the prospect of a cut in taxation held out by Gladstone with a lame 'me-too'. For the rest Disraeli again emphasized Conservative concern for the welfare of the people; promised less 'harassing legislation' and more energy in foreign policy, drew attention to the threats to the constitution from the Left of the Liberal Party and ended by an affirmation of empire. These addresses, taking the place of the more elaborate party manifestos of a more recent period, had probably no more or less effect on the outcome of the election than their modern counterparts. Disraeli and his advisers felt confident that a Conservative reaction was in progress; but even so expert an electioneer as Gorst was only prepared to predict a majority of three, with an advantage of over 80 seats in England almost entirely wiped out by a continued Liberal preponderance in the rest of the United Kingdom. Gladstone did not see the prospects very differently: even counting in the Irish Home Rulers, he doubted whether 'we should command a full half of the House of Commons'.

In the event the result was much more decisive. The Tories had an advantage of at least 110 seats in England. They advanced in all categories of English seats, but most decisively in the larger boroughs, where they had previously been so weak. They also improved their position in Scotland and to a small extent in Wales. In Ireland the Tories lost slightly, but most of those elected for formerly Liberal seats were now pledged to Isaac Butt's new Home Rule Party. The recrudescence of a separate Irish party was to have its full impact only after the 1880 election. The underlying cause of the Liberal defeat was the simultaneous loss of working and middle-class voters. The working classes were disappointed, because Liberal reform, for all its achievements, had not really changed their lot. The middle classes were alarmed not merely by what the Liberal Party had done, but by events such as the Paris Commune, which seemed to portend threats to all property and security in the future. The alienation of particular groups of Liberal activists meant that the Liberal Party could probably not realize its full voting potential, while the improvements in the

Conservative organization in urban areas had the opposite effect in the Tory camp. The Conservative Party had not won such a victory since 1841. For Gladstone the defeat was personally wounding. Five years earlier he had embarked upon a crusade and his government had transformed and modernized the framework for many aspects of life in the country. In the last year or two his crusade had faltered and now the election confirmed that many voters preferred a quiet life to his calls for high moral endeavour.

3 Disraeli in Power 1874–1880

I

'Power has come to me too late', Disraeli said, but he nevertheless enjoyed it. Not for him the pretence, so common among politicians of the Victorian age, that office and power was something one did not seek, but had thrust upon one. His style as Prime Minister was very different from that of his predecessor. He could not compete with his rival in grasp of detail or powers of work, but he may well have excelled him in his ability to direct the strategy of events and to impose his will where it really mattered. In spite of old age and ill health Disraeli could be completely the master of his government, but he did not always exercise this mastery energetically. In the business of government he believed there was a high road upon which he was determined to travel: foreign affairs, imperial questions, the fundamental conflicts and decisions of the national community at home, the disposition of the personalities in the great political and social world at whose apex he stood. He was not inclined to dissipate his flagging energies upon the minor progress of legislation and matters which did not come up to his standard of importance could arouse the flippant side of his tongue. Disraeli, like all prime ministers at the formation of their governments, had his choice of colleagues largely predetermined for him. It was from the mixture of Tory grandees and Conservative men of affairs who had previously held office that he had in the main to form his cabinet. The one major question-mark was whether he would be able to include Salisbury, his implacable enemy, who had said so many bitter things about him. Disraeli was nothing if not magnanimous and was prepared to forgive and forget. The brilliance of the Conservative victory had so vindicated Disraeli that Salisbury could find little reason for staying out and took the India Office. There was one surprise appointment, the translation of R.A. Cross, a Lancashire banker who had never held office before, to the Home Office. It was a gesture to Lancashire Conservatism and Cross was to be the minister responsible for much of Conservative domestic legislation.

Cross recorded his disappointment when he found that Disraeli had no grand design for legislative reform on coming into office, in spite of all he had said about his concern for the welfare of the people. Not only was Disraeli disinclined and ill-equipped to hatch such a design, he knew that his victory owed much to a desire in the country for a quiet life and he was not disposed to repeat his adversary's mistake of alarming all and sundry by his restlessness. When on one occasion Cross pressed him to do something about the government of London, he wrote back: 'We came in on the principle of not harassing the country . . .' What Disraeli was prepared to do, and in this he interpreted correctly the feelings of most of his followers, was to deal with problems on which government action had become inescapable. In doing so he was keen to appeal to important groups of voters, such as the trade unionists, whose normal allegiance to the Liberals had been shaken. He and his ministers were prepared to amend recent Liberal reforms in the light of Conservative interests and ideas, as they did with elementary education, and make some advances in the process. They were not motivated by any clear social philosophy and proceeded cautiously and empirically. They were as reluctant as any Liberal to embark upon State intervention or collectivism. Disraeli in particular was sensitive to public opinion and anxious to placate outraged humanitarian sentiment, as in the case of the Plimsoll agitation against 'coffin ships'. He did not wish his government to acquire a reactionary, or in the jargon of the time 'retrograde' appearance. Anything that was done could not be allowed to put an undue burden on the public revenue or to go against the Tory aim of reducing local taxation. In spite of these limited and cautious objectives the achievements of Conservative social reform were not inconsiderable.

The first session of the Conservative Parliament saw action on licensing and factory legislation and on the labour laws. Cross introduced an Intoxicating Liquors Bill, which clearly fell into the category of measures designed to correct Liberal legislation in accordance with Conservative ideas. Hours of licensing were extended, a step which Cross defended with the argument, now frequently made against the temperance movement, that excessive drinking could not be attacked in isolation, but could only be cured by general changes in the physical and moral situation of the working classes. Factory legislation had always been well within the Tory tradition and the conflict between it and doctrinaire political economy had long ago been fought and decided. In the election of 1874 many Conservative candidates, particularly in Lancashire and Yorkshire, had openly supported the Nine Hour Movement. Cross brought in a bill which did not meet the full demands of the movement but nevertheless won general acceptance.

On the labour laws the government, again represented by Cross, seemed to prevaricate and appointed a royal commission. There was little sign that Tory opinion as a whole wanted to change the law from where the Liberals had left it, but some of the Conservative borough members had given pledges during the election to the trade unionists. When the royal commission reported in 1875 it recommended changes in the Master and Servant Act, but hardly any in the Criminal Law Amendment Act. This report was signed, among others, by Thomas Hughes, a long-standing friend of the unions. Alexander Macdonald, one of two working-class members who had entered the House in 1874, gave a dissenting opinion that the Criminal Law Amendment Act should be repealed. Cross, with the full backing of Disraeli, but against the initial opposition of other members of the cabinet, decided to meet virtually in full the demands of the Parliamentary Committee of the TUC, in two bills, one now significantly named Employers and Workmen instead of Master and Servants Bill, the other a Conspiracy and Protection of Property Bill. Here was a case of Disraeli personally taking the opportunity to placate an important section of the electorate, knowing he could do so with little trouble, since his authority was at its height and industrial employers of labour were still a small minority in the parliamentary Conservative Party. This was much the most important part of Conservative domestic legislation, although from the amount of contemporary controversy and attention it generated it would hardly have seemed so. It was something the Liberals had been unable and unwilling to do. Such is the nature of politics, however, that the labour laws brought the Conservative Party little advantage, apart from their propaganda value. For the moment all legal grievances of the labour movement had been removed; the result was that the trade union establishment could return in comfort to their normal close relationship with the Liberal party.

In the clamour it provoked social reform legislation was far eclipsed in the session of 1874 by a recrudescence of religious politics. Even before the Disraeli ministry had taken office Tait, the Archbishop of Canterbury, was proposing action against ritualism, the catholicizing practices of the extreme High Churchmen. Disraeli and Cairns, the Lord Chancellor, helped unofficially to prepare a bill, which they hoped would deal with this potentially explosive issue without causing the government too much embarrassment. The bill was introduced in the Lords by the Archbishop as a private members' bill, but when it reached the Commons Gladstone moved to the attack. The ex-Prime Minister had attended the House only intermittently after his fall from power and had let it be known that he was looking forward to early retirement from the leadership of the Liberal Party. The Public

Worship Regulation Bill brought him back in full cry, fearful of what such an attempt at legally enforced uniformity would ultimately do to the Established Church. On such an occasion Gladstone was unrivalled as an orator, but parliamentary and public opinion was running strongly against him. Disraeli could not resist the temptation to catch the tide of aroused Protestantism and threw the full authority of his government behind the Archbishop's bill, a step which up to then he had carefully avoided. The High Church party was outraged and it had at least three powerful representatives in the cabinet, Gathorne Hardy, Carnarvon and above all Salisbury. Disraeli came near to weakening his government at the outset, particularly when he referred to Salisbury ill-advisedly as 'a great master of jibes and flouts and jeers'. Gorst warned him that from an electoral point of view there was 'great danger of our government being broken up by the High Church Party, as Gladstone's was by the dissenters'. The storm blew over, but the mutual antipathy between Disraeli and High Churchmen went deeper than ever.

In the session of 1875 Disraeli's authority was virtually unchallenged. Gladstone had carried out his threat to lay down the Liberal leadership, though significantly he did not resign his seat in the House. He set to work on a pamphlet about the Vatican decrees of 1870 and the doctrine of papal infallibility. When it was published it helped to repair his damaged relationship with the nonconformists and many, who believed that his retirement was not genuine, thought that this was its main objective. Nevertheless the Liberal Party was obliged to choose a new leader in the House of Commons. In many ways Forster was the obvious choice, but his Education Act had still not been forgiven and his candidature looked like precipitating a bitter battle. He withdrew and Hartington, a future Duke of Devonshire and head of the Cavendish family, became Liberal leader in the Commons. '. . . the Whigs were dished; now they are Cavendished' was a joke Disraeli reported to Lady Chesterfield. The Liberal Party was now led by two Whigs of the purest vintage, Granville and Hartington.

Apart from the labour laws, a mixed fare of cautious social legislation was put forward in 1875, dealing with artisan's dwellings, public health, Friendly Societies, pure food and drugs, merchant shipping and pollution of rivers; the last two became law only in 1876. The Friendly Societies Bill well illustrates that Conservative ministers were no less reluctant than any member of the Manchester School to countenance more than a minimum of State intervention. For the working classes the Friendly Societies were a form of self-help that covered many of the needs now catered for by the modern Welfare State. In many ways they were still the most important working-class organization of the period, with an estimated membership of about four million, many times that of the trade unions. They ranged from local clubs, whose main purpose was social, through the large affiliated societies, such as the Odd Fellows and Foresters, to what were purely insurance bodies, like the Hearts of Oak and the Royal Standard, located in London and catering for members at the upper end of the working class and above. The Gladstone government had set up a royal commission on the Friendly Societies, chiefly because their financial stability and actuarial soundness often gave rise to concern. When Bruce, as Home Secretary, asked Northcote to become chairman of the royal commission he told him that Tidd Pratt, the Registrar for Friendly Societies, believed that only 25 out of some 20,000 societies were free from considerable risks of failure. When it fell to Northcote to legislate, he was most anxious to ensure that the registration of societies and the publication of standard actuarial tables by the government should not imply any responsibility by the State for failures: 'my leading idea is, that we should leave all kinds of societies to work as freely as possible, and the people to exercise their own judgement at embarking in any of them, provided we can secure to every man a fair opportunity of ascertaining what manner of society he is about to invest in, and can educate him sufficiently to enable him to discern between the good and the bad.' Yet even this cautious aim, to make available information only, was almost too much for Cross, who as Home Secretary was also involved.

The Artisans Dwellings Act, arguably the most ambitious item in the corpus of Tory social legislation, apart from the labour laws, was typical of permissive legislation, 'the characteristic of a free people', as Disraeli put it, and therefore fitted in well with the fear of too much interventionism. An attempt had already been made in 1868, in the Torrens Act passed with the help of the then Conservative government, to deal with the problem of slum clearance. The Cross Act empowered municipal councils to draw up improvement schemes for districts certified as unhealthy by a medical officer, it gave them powers of compulsory purchase and enabled them to obtain cheap loans from the Public Works Loan Commissioners. The weakness of the scheme was that it depended entirely upon initiatives being taken by local authorities and medical officers in circumstances that made it unlikely that they would act. The operation would be costly in expenditure falling ultimately on the rates and would often result in at least a short-term loss of rateable value, while rehousing of the displaced inhabitants would cause great problems. In 1879 Cross himself introduced an amending act to deal with the burden of excessive compensation costs, but even then the legislation proved largely inef-

fective. By 1881 only 10 out of 87 English and Welsh towns in which
the act applied had taken any action under it. Nevertheless, the Act of
1875 ushers in a period when increasing attention was given to
housing as a key factor in the social problems of the urban working
classes. Joseph Chamberlain, who became mayor of Birmingham in
1876, made use of the legislation of 1875 in his own slum clearance
schemes and on that level enjoyed good relations with the Conservative ministers involved, Cross and Sclater-Booth. Octavia Hill,
whose activities as housing reformer helped to establish the whole
problem as a major national concern, was consulted by Cross in the
preparation of his Act.

Ministerial and official determination to stay on a non-interventionist course made itself felt even more on the merchant shipping
question. In this case the government had to pay heed to the emotional campaign against 'coffin ships' and for a load line conducted
for a number of years by Samuel Plimsoll, the Liberal member for
Derby, and the considerable impact it had made on public opinion.
On the other hand the officials of the Board of Trade, headed by
Farrer, the Permanent Secretary, were hostile to Plimsoll and his
campaign. There were also one or two important shipping employers
on the Tory benches, notably Bates, of Plymouth, and MacIver, of
Birkenhead, who, while hardly enamoured of Plimsoll, preferred
some government regulation to letting the villains of the trade steal a
march on the respectable owners. The shipping interest was well
represented in the House as a whole and resentful of any interference
with its affairs. Following a royal commission, a Merchant Shipping
Bill was introduced pinning liability on the owner for damage to
persons and property caused by unseaworthiness. It came under
attack from both Plimsoll and his friends and the shipping interest
and Adderley, the incompetent President of the Board of Trade,
found himself unable to cope with the opposition. Disraeli had to give
the matter his personal attention, but the Merchant Shipping Bill
began to compete for parliamentary time with an Agricultural Holdings Bill, in which the Prime Minister had a great interest. This was
another permissive bill, designed to secure to tenants the benefit of
unexhausted improvements, and Disraeli considered it of major
importance, in that it showed that the party of landowners also cared
for the tenant farmers. It was decided to give this bill priority and
withdraw the Merchant Shipping Bill. This provoked a famous parliamentary incident, when Samuel Plimsoll shook his fist at Disraeli.
A temporary Unseaworthy Ships Bill was introduced to calm the
storm and a clause providing for a load line fixed by the owner was
accepted in committee. The provisions of this Bill were made permanent by a Merchant Shipping Act passed in the session of 1876, but in

the end the government's determination not to provide the compulsion demanded by Plimsoll prevailed. Even under pressure the Conservative government was therefore not prepared to depart too much from the precepts of political economy; but Disraeli was certainly concerned to avoid any appearance of reaction or to get too far out of step with widely professed humanitarian sentiments.

The most important piece of domestic legislation in the session of 1876 was the Education Act, of which Sandon was the principal author. From a Tory point of view legislation had become necessary, as we have seen, by the pressure which the spread of school boards imposed upon the voluntary schools. In education the voluntary principle, the equivalent to *laissez-faire* in the economic sphere, had already been abandoned to such an extent that few now argued against the use of indirect compulsion, the extension of which was the act's main objective. To Tories the use of indirect compulsion was much preferable to the spread of school boards into more small and rural communities, where, in Sandon's words, 'they afford the platform and the notoriety specially needed by the political dissenting ministers (many of them, to my mind, the most active and effective revolutionary agents of the day)'. In this case Conservative concern for the survival of the voluntary schools and for religious education and fear of the school boards could conveniently be made to serve the cause of educational progress by forcing more children, particularly in rural areas, to attend school. It could be argued that refraining from direct compulsion, but making it disadvantageous to keep children away from school, was in essence similar to the permissive principle, so dear to many Conservatives as well as Liberals. The passage of the bill was marked by an intervention from Disraeli when he nearly refused to accept an amendment providing for the dissolution of unnecessary school boards, which was one of the principal sops to the Tory squirearchy. He suspected that this was a move by 'the sacerdotal party' and relented only under pressure from his colleagues. It was perhaps again an example of his anxiety not to let his administration appear 'retrograde'. He seems to have felt that the whole controversy in the end redounded to the credit of the government, because all supporters of religious instruction in primary education would be in favour of what the bill was trying to do.

After 1876 the flow of Conservative domestic legislation declined. Cross carried out a consolidation of the Factory Acts, but attempts to deal with the question of industrial accidents and injuries, which was becoming one of the main legislative demands of the labour movement, failed. Further attempts to deal with the safety of the merchant seamen also came to naught. The need to deal with London's water supply compelled Cross to produce a scheme for buying out the existing private water companies. His regard for the rights of property were such that he was forced to offer terms of compensation which were widely regarded as excessive. The share speculation which resulted and the whiff of scandal surrounding it was one of the reasons why Lord Beaconsfield – the title conferred on Disraeli in August 1876 – decided on a dissolution of Parliament in March 1880. A common jibe was that the Conservatives 'came in on beer and went out on water'. Such a decline into futility was not particularly surprising, since there had never been anything resembling the vigorous pursuit of a deliberate policy. 'Mr Disraeli, himself, if he has enough of his old energy left, will be quite sure to flirt with the democratic Conservatives, and to recommend taking the wind out of the Liberal sails by proposing concessions to the working class which Lord Hartington at least would be very unlikely to approve' wrote Walter Bagehot in *The Economist* in July 1875 but his suspicions were unjustified. From the summer of 1876 such energy as Disraeli still had was absorbed by foreign policy.

There was never any possibility in practice that the Conservative Party any more than the Liberal Party could have maintained and enlarged its working-class following simply by promoting a large programme of reform legislation. Bagehot, in the same article, recommended a policy of leaning 'on the moderates of both sides of the House, and to reduce to a minimum the influence of the democrats, whether Radical or Tory'. Even Gorst, who was such a genuine Tory democrat, believed the way to consolidate the party's urban working-class vote was to build up a committed cadre of middle-class leaders. The gradual drift of the middle class and of all owners of property from the Liberals to the Conservatives was no less important to the Tory party than the size of its working-class support. In any case, mild social reform was less important than other matters in stimulating electoral support. In 1875 the case of the Tichborne claimant caused greater popular excitement than the social reform legislation passing through Parliament. An imposter laid claim to titles and estates and attracted much sympathy among the lower classes. Such an exhibition of sentimentality and deep-seated suspicion of the established order on the part of the masses made many among the political classes fearful of the implications of advancing democracy and uncertain how to cope with it. Throughout the long-drawn-out Eastern Crisis Disraeli and the Conservative Party as a whole assumed that their robust maintenance of British interests commanded as much or more working-class support than Gladstone's call for justice for the Bulgars. They knew that 'bad trade', causing increasing distress to the poorer classes, from 1877 onwards, would not be electorally helpful to whichever party was in power. The damage would be more serious if the government pretended, by taking action to relieve hardship, that it had some responsibility in the matter, when according to the best economic opinion it was as impotent about 'bad trade' as it was about the weather. 'About distress; beware of another *coup manqué* . . .'. Northcote warned Beaconsfield in December 1878, '. . . We have bad trade, and our workmen themselves aggravate the misfortune by their disputes with the employers of labour. We want peace and confidence, and then we may hope for a return of better times. If there were deeper causes at work we must take care not to encourage the idea that they are to be met by national subscriptions . . . .'

One remedy that was being discussed and which would have been well within Tory traditions was protection. But a full return to protection was so far removed from the realms of practical politics that the terms reciprocity or fair trade were coming into vogue. It was a more plausible argument that the weapon of a retaliatory tariff should be used against those countries that placed fiscal barriers in the way of British trade. The depression was particularly severe in agriculture and proved to be the beginning of a long-term decline of that industry. Nothing could touch the electoral bastions of the Tory party more closely, but even here Disraeli could hold out no hope of action: 'Those who talk of negotiating treaties of reciprocity – have they the materials for negotiating treaties of reciprocity? You have lost the opportunity. I do not want to enter into the argument, at the present moment, whether this was wise or not; but the policy which was long ago abandoned you cannot resume', he said in the House of Lords in the spring of 1879. The depression, with its contracting effect on the income from all forms of taxation, made the government even more reluctant to undertake anything that might result in higher expenditure. Pressure on the revenue also arose from the cost of the foreign and imperial policies of the government. As Gladstone mounted his great attack on 'Beaconsfieldism' in the run-up to the 1880 election, he eagerly seized on this point and on the general disturbance to trade caused by the Prime Minister's adventurous policies. It was in these terms that the electoral debate was conducted and such achievements as the government had accomplished in improving 'the condition of the people' were all but forgotten.

II

Not surprisingly Disraeli preferred the high road of foreign and imperial

affairs to the 'suet-pudding legislation' for social reform. In his Free
Trade Hall speech in 1872 he had expressed his 'confident conviction
that there never was a moment in our history when the power of
England was so great and her resources so vast and inexhaustible'. It
was an argument not without substance, for the great transformation
that had just been accomplished on the continent of Europe could be
seen as giving Britain new opportunities for exercising influence. The
heyday of British influence in European affairs, the consequence of
the Napoleonic Wars and the Vienna settlement, had long since
passed. In his final years Palmerston, in European affairs, looked like
an emperor without clothes and his failures produced a general consensus that non-intervention was the only possible policy. The
opinions of Cobden and Bright, who in January 1865 called the
balance of power 'a foul idol', gained greater respectability. The three
men in immediate charge of British foreign policy after Palmerston's
death, Clarendon, Stanley and Granville, were, in their different
ways, well suited to carrying on a policy of non-intervention or inacti-
in Europe. Even Disraeli, temperamentally hardly inclined to inactivity in foreign policy, at this time supported 'systematic non-
interference' in Europe, though he significantly attributed this policy
not to England's apathy, but to her being 'the metropolis of a great
maritime empire'. It was in fact the growing burden of empire, particularly in North America, that made a policy of non-intervention in
Europe inescapable. The upheaval of the American Civil War had
already limited the ability of Britain to make her voice decisively
heard in Europe. The victory of the North created a situation in
which the only realistic policy for Britain in the longer run was to
avoid any challenge to the United States in the future. After resuming
office in 1868, Clarendon wrote to the Queen about Britain's treaty
obligations in Europe: 'It seems to be the duty of your Majesty's
Government to bear in mind how widely different are the circumstances of this country now to when those treaties were concluded,
and that, if their execution were to lead us into war in Europe, we
should find ourselves immediately called upon to defend Canada
from American invasion and our commerce from American pri-
vateers.' Realism therefore dictated the resort to arbitration which
the Gladstone government brought to a successful conclusion in 1872,
but without gaining much credit from the public. The eastern side of
Britain's imperial position had always been a major preoccupation of
British foreign policy, mainly in the form of the perennial Eastern
Question. The opening of the Suez Canal in 1869 and Russia's active
policy in Asia added further complications. When Disraeli spoke in
1872, the Liberal faith in an unchallenged, informal, free-trade
empire had been badly shaken and he thought the time ripe for

reverting to a more positive notion of empire as a source of strength to be defended against all comers. From this position of strength, argued Disraeli, buttressed by her overseas empire, England could assert herself in Europe, where, with the French hegemony broken, a more favourable balance of power existed.

The new balance of power in Europe had been established while Britain was in her post-Palmerstonian phase of passivity. Stanley took over the Foreign Office in 1866 on the day of the Battle of Sadowa. In a ministerial statement in the House of Lords a few days later he was at pains to stress that a Conservative government was in no way warlike, was in favour of peace and non-intervention and that the war in Bohemia was one 'in which the interests of this country are very remotely, if at all, involved'. This set the tone for the British attitude to the whole chain of events that culminated in the Franco–Prussian War of 1870. Clarendon died three weeks before it broke out and when Granville took over the Foreign Office, Hammond, the Permanent Under Secretary, made the frequently quoted remark that he had never known 'so great a lull in foreign affairs'. Gladstone and Granville were unable to influence the events flowing to and from Sedan any more than Derby and Stanley had been able to influence those surrounding Sadowa. They concentrated their efforts on securing the neutrality of Belgium, as much to preserve British self-esteem as for any other reason. Gladstone himself was in fact more of an activist in foreign policy than the other men who had conducted British foreign policy since Palmerston. His brand of international idealism did not mean passivity and in the wake of the Franco–Prussian war he was very active on two issues, Alsace–Lorraine and the abrogation by Russia of the Black Sea clauses of the Treaty of Paris. In the former case, 'this violent laceration and transfer . . . the beginning of a new series of European complications', as he put it, he achieved nothing. In the latter case he managed to assemble the London Conference which gave at least a semblance of international consent to Russia's unilateral action. The cataclysmic events of 1870 and 1871 might well, as Disraeli saw, give Britain the opportunity for a more assertive policy in Europe. They were, however, alarming in themselves and the demonstration of British impotence which they afforded could not but redound to the discredit of the government of the day.

Public opinion was even more unfair to the Gladstone government over the Treaty of Washington of 1871, the agreement of arbitration on the *Alabama* claims. Here international morality, or at any rate concern for peaceful procedures in conflicts between nations, and long-term British interests definitely coincided. The claims were for compensation for the damage done to Federal shipping by the

Confederate commerce raider Alabama, which escaped from Birkenhead in 1862. The resort to arbitration was not a nostrum of Gladstone's, but was embedded in a long tradition of Anglo-American relations and had been envisaged by the previous government as a way of dealing with claims arising out of the Civil War. American public opinion and American politicians were often in a difficult anti-British mood and brought into the negotiation their vast claims for indirect damage suffered. American opinion had for long favoured the annexation of Canada and the submission of these indirect claims could lead, in the American view, to the acquisition of Canada in exchange for the claims. There were much scepticism in Britain about the possibility of hanging on to a self-governing colony like Canada, which in the last resort could not be defended, but the British government was in honour bound to stand by the Canadians as long as they wished to remain independent of the United States. The indirect claims were still part of the American case before the tribunal of arbitration, and there was the possibility that British public opinion might force the government to renounce the Treaty of Washington. The forces of compromise were strong on both sides and the indirect claims were by agreement withdrawn from the consideration of the arbitrators. The sum of 15.5 million dollars awarded against Britain still struck much of public opinion as outrageously large, and in relation to the value of British exports to the United States, about $90 million annually between 1875 and 1879, it was in fact considerable. The Opposition had given the government consistent support over the *Alabama* question and Northcote had been one of the British negotiators of the Treaty of Washington. Nevertheless the course of events strengthened the feeling that decline and impotence had overtaken Britain and the government was given the blame. The arbitration ushered in a period when the threat of war was removed from Anglo-American relations and when there was renewed friction, over Venezuela, at the end of the century, war had ceased to be a possible way of resolving it. The government's handling of the *Alabama* problem could be criticized in detail, but morally and strategically the $15.5 million cheque, which, cancelled, was displayed in the Foreign Secretary's room, had not been too high a price to pay.

Anglo-American relations were a sphere where the Gladstonian view of international relations had validity, but unfortunately in the Europe of Bismarck it was at a discount. There were thus deeper reasons for the public dissatisfaction with the government's foreign policy which Disraeli and the Conservatives could exploit. His return to office in 1874 gave Disraeli his first chance to exercise personal control over foreign policy, for there had been few opportunities during his brief premiership in 1868. He was, however, running in harness with Derby, the former Lord Stanley, who had succeeded his father as fifteenth earl in 1869. Derby's caution amounting at times to a neurosis of indecision counterbalanced his chief's activism. Disraeli was tied to him both personally and politically and could not ride roughshod over him. The Conservative premier had no detailed knowledge or experience of foreign affairs and his pronouncements had been, as those on home affairs, percipient but broad-brush. The most marked characteristic of Disraeli's perspective on Britain's international position was his interest in the colonial Empire in the East and Asia. This interest was rooted in his deeply ingrained romanticism; England is 'really more an Asiatic Power than a European', he had said in 1866 and this is what he was thinking of when he spoke in 1872 of 'new establishments belonging to her, teeming with wealth and population, which will, in due time, exercise their influence over the distribution of power'. He had little time for a self-governing colony like Canada: in September 1866 he wrote to Derby: 'We must seriously consider our Canadian position, which is most illegitimate. An army maintained in a colony which does not permit us even to govern it! What an anomaly!' Disraeli was able to indulge in some personal diplomacy in the cause of Britain's Eastern Empire when he purchased the Khedive's shares in the Suez Canal Company in November 1875. Britain had opposed the building of the canal, preferring to rely on her control of the route round the Cape. Once the canal had been built, the maintenance of free passage and the prevention of exclusive control by another power had become a national interest. By purchasing the shares of the Khedive, the British government did not acquire control of the canal, but it prevented a strengthening of the French interest in it and deepened the British involvement in Egypt. The conferment of the title of Empress of India on the Queen was another example of the importance Disraeli attached to the British position in Asia. Such a step had been discussed ever since the Mutiny and the timing was not of Disraeli's choosing, but forced on him by the Queen; but the Prime Minister was prepared to brave considerable opposition to accomplish what could be of no more than symbolic significance.

III

The great set-piece of Disraeli's foreign policy was the crisis which began in the Balkans in 1875. Here Disraeli's desire to play a more assertive role in Europe and his vision of eastern empire combined with the traditional national interest in the exclusion of Russia from Constantinople and the Straits of the Dardanelles. The generally accepted view was that the containment of Russia could only be accomplished by the maintenance of the Ottoman Empire and that it was worthwhile to face great difficulties in order to keep the sick man of Europe alive. The collapse of Turkey and the division of the spoils between the Great Powers of Europe would pose even greater difficulties and might precipitate a European war. The new element in the recrudescence of the Eastern Question at this time was the autonomous action of the Balkan nationalities. Nationalism, which had just brought about the unification of Italy and Germany, had spread to the Balkans. This was not a development which any of the Great Powers caused or could control, though they tried to exploit it. Russia and Austria–Hungary were the two neighbouring empires most closely concerned. When insurrection first broke out in Herzegovina and Bosnia in July 1875, neither empire was initially keen on intervention, let alone on a collapse of Turkish rule. Both at Vienna and St Petersburg there were, however, divided counsels and annexationist elements, and the local agents of the two powers often followed a course of their own. Russia and Austria–Hungary were rivals in the Balkans and eventually their rivalry was a major element in the outbreak of a general European war; between 1875 and 1878 their rivalry was, however, veiled by agreement most of the time, either on non-intervention or on mutual annexations. The other European powers were more indirectly involved. Germany was guided by considerations of the general European power balance, the desire to keep France isolated, and reluctance to choose between Vienna and St Petersburg, both her allies in the Three Emperors' League. Britain's interest was initially well served by a policy of non-intervention, provided this was observed by all the powers, particularly Russia and Austria–Hungary. Such a policy also fitted in with the personal inclinations of the two men most closely involved in making it: Derby, who wanted to avoid any wider crisis arising from the insurrections; and Elliot, the British ambassador in Constantinople, who did not want the Porte's sovereignty to be infringed. For most of those who came to oppose the government's Turkish policy Elliot became a scapegoat, because it was alleged that his sympathies were entirely on the side of his host government. Even Disraeli came to feel that Elliot had misled him and he was removed; in fact Elliot was very active in the early stages of the crisis impressing on the Turks the need for reform of their administration in the Balkan provinces.

Until the spring of 1876 Disraeli had only intermittently intervened in the conduct of British policy towards the crisis. He was aware of

Derby's chronic indecision and of the temperamental gulf that separated him from his Foreign Secretary, but found it difficult to admit it
to himself. He was irritated by Britain's diplomatic isolation and the
lack of weight she carried in the counsels of Europe, matters which
had drawn his fire when they had become evident under the previous
government. He had no plans for the future of the Turkish Empire in
Europe. He was quite prepared for territorial modifications, provided they were carried out with the full agreement of Britain and
provided that vital British interests, such as the freedom of Constantinople and the Straits from control by another power, were safeguarded. He attached little importance to the Balkan nationalities
and their claims; it was a realistic recognition of the fact that national
independence in an area of interlocking national and religious blocs
surrounded by major powers would not mean much. This was the
background to the British refusal to become associated with the Berlin
Memorandum in May 1876, perhaps the first major British initiative
in the crisis. The Memorandum, addressed by Austria, Germany
and Russia to the Sultan, contained somwhat peremptory demands
for reform in the Balkans. Disraeli was offended by the method rather
than the substance of what the three northern courts were doing: 'It is
almost a mockery for them to talk of a desire, that the powers should
''act in concert'' and then exclude France, Italy, and England from
their deliberations, and ask us by telegraph to say yes or no to propositions, which we have never heard discussed', he wrote in a memorandum for the cabinet. There was little dissent from this assessment
and by this assertion of independence the British government made
its voice better heard in the management of the Near-Eastern crisis.
The rejection of the Berlin Memorandum and the despatch of a naval
squadron to Besika Bay seemed to make a welcome change from the
impotence of previous British policy and was generally applauded.
When the three powers withdrew the Berlin Memorandum in June
1876 the British government seemed to have scored a definite success.

The Berlin Memorandum coincided not only with the overthrow of
one Turkish government, but also with the spread of insurrection into
Bulgaria. News of atrocities committed in Bulgaria, particularly by
irregular forces, Circassians and bashi-bazuks, reached England in
late June 1876 and was carried mainly in the liberal *Daily News*. The
government and Disraeli personally poured cold water on these
reports; the Prime Minister declared in the House that their 'object is
to create a cry against the government'. When by early July he was
forced to admit that 'proceedings of an atrocious character' had
occurred, he was still inclined to belittle them. He let fall the unfortunate sentence that he doubted 'that torture has been practised on a
great scale among an oriental people who seldom, I believe, resort to

torture, but generally terminate their connection with culprits in a more expeditious manner'. It raised a laugh, but was not meant to do so. This phrase and a later reference to 'coffee-house babble' were hostages to fortune Disraeli came to regret. He complained that he had not been fully informed by Elliot and the Foreign Office, but the way he dealt with the atrocity reports was very characteristic of his attitude. He knew that atrocities on both sides were bound to be committed in such a situation; he felt that to enlarge upon them was a hypocritical attack on him and his policies by his enemies in the press and the country and that the only consequence would be to inhibit him and his government from maintaining the interests and the prestige of the nation. It might have been wiser if he had recognized that the moral sensibilities of a significant part of the nation were genuinely roused. He thus contributed to the rise of the bitter domestic controversy which complicated the conduct of British foreign policy over the next two years.

The controversy was relatively muted before Parliament rose for the summer recess in August 1876, because the Opposition found little to quarrel with in the policy of non-intervention, which had been given additional emphasis by the rejection of the Berlin Memorandum. Gladstone made his only intervention in a debate in the House of Commons on 31 July. He mildly rebuked the government for having cut adrift from the continental powers, but hardly any of the other Opposition speakers echoed this criticism. The atrocities did not figure prominently in Gladstone's intervention, though he wanted an enquiry. The atrocities were discussed on two subsequent occasions before Parliament adjourned and caused rather greater heart-searchings, but at this stage they had not yet become the focus of an organized agitation in the country.

In August 1876 further details of the atrocities, especially from MacGahan, the strongly anti-Turk correspondent of the *Daily News*, arrived in London. They were up to a point corroborated by the reports of Walter Baring, a Second Secretary at the Constantinople embassy, who had been sent to conduct an official investigation. The campaign about the Bulgarian events was now taken up by the press generally, including *The Times*. Thus far it had been mainly men like the Oxford historian E.A. Freeman and the High Anglican Canon Liddon of St Paul's who had tried to stir the public conscience about the situation in the Balkans and after the end of the parliamentary session a group of Radical MPs kept a watching brief on the position. Now the campaign spread to the provinces and the nonconformist conscience became involved. A key figure was W.T. Stead, at this time the obscure editor of the *Northern Echo* at Darlington. His paper reprinted the *Daily News* reports and he organized a series of public meetings in the north. Much the most important event in the unfolding of the atrocities campaign was Gladstone's decision to lend it his support. He was moved from the cautious position he had maintained while Parliament was still sitting by the evidence which had since been piling up about the depths of the horrors in Bulgaria. Even more compelling to Gladstone were the signs that the masses were stirred by growing moral indignation. Gladstone had withdrawn from the Liberal leadership when his link with the moral sensibilities of the ordinary people of England appeared to have snapped. The news which now reached him of working men's demonstrations and public meetings against Turkish atrocities and the British government's policy showed him the possibility of reestablishing the bond. He knew that his support for the atrocity campaign must have profound consequences for the Liberal Party and for his own position towards it; there would be advantages as well as anomalies and embarrassments, but this kind of moral leadership from a position of detachment was his unique contribution to politics. 'Good ends can rarely be attained in politics without passion: and there is now, the first time for a good many years, a virtuous passion', he wrote to Granville when he had started writing his pamphlet *Bulgarian Horrors and the Question of the East* at the end of August 1876. Within a week he had finished it; when Disraeli, now Earl of Beaconsfield, received his unsolicited copy his characteristic comment to Derby was: 'The document is passionate and not strong; vindictive and ill-written – that of course. Indeed in that respect, of all the Bulgarian horrors, perhaps the greatest.' It was an anti-Turkish diatribe, but beneath its rhetoric of 'bag and baggage' lay concealed the fact that Gladstone was not advocating the expulsion of Turkey from Europe. At one point he remarks that 'the responsibility of silence, at least for one who was among the authors of the Crimean War' was 'too great to be borne'. For Gladstone the campaign upon which he now entered was undoubtedly an expiation of the guilt he had always felt about his involvement in the Crimean War.

To some of its participants the agitation seemed like an intervention from God and it was certainly unprecedented in its force and intensity. Much of the passion came, as with Gladstone, from feelings of guilt about the British role in propping up an immoral regime for so long; this combined with the high moral sensibility of the Victorian age that had given rise to campaigns like the anti-slavery movement and, on a lesser scale, the Governor Eyre controversy. The nonconformists were the backbone of the agitation: the identification with peoples oppressed for their religion was easily made and there was little in all the circumstances of the Eastern Question that could make a nonconformist doubt where his duty lay. To men like Edward

Miall, champion of the Liberation Society, the atrocity campaign came like a moment of blessed renewal. Many of the causes for which they had fought for so long, like disestablishment, might now reach their goal. The reconciliation with the Liberal Party, symbolized by Gladstone's support for the agitation, came as a great relief. To Gladstone the stirrings of the nonconformist conscience were confirmation of his conviction that the moral instincts of the masses were superior to those of the 'classes', whose moral sensibilities were blunted by their material interests. 'The superiority of the popular judgement in politics . . . is . . . due mainly to moral causes, to a greater mental integrity, which, again, is greatly owing to the comparative absence of the more subtle agencies of temptation', he wrote in 1878. Gladstone's personality was eminently suited to be the prophet of nonconformist morality and this union, only now fully consummated, was to have profound consequences for the Liberal Party and British politics. It was hardly surprising that many nonconformists, in the fervour with which they welcomed Gladstone's leadership of the atrocity campaign, overlooked the fact that he always carefully limited and reserved his exact position on foreign policy in the Near East; and that he no more than previously shared causes like disestablishment.

The other main religious group which figured prominently in the atrocity campaign were High Churchmen and more particularly Anglo-Catholics. Freeman, a moderate High Anglican, Canon Liddon and his close associate Malcolm MacColl, who played a key role in getting Gladstone involved, were not only among the launchers of the campaign, but were also among its most fanatical and sometimes virulent advocates. For some lay High Anglicans like the Marquess of Bath, commitment to the anti-Turkish position took precedence over their normal political Conservatism. In the case of Lord Carnarvon, the Colonial Secretary, it led to his resignation from the cabinet in January 1878, an event which Liddon sought to celebrate by having his portrait put in the Bodleian. The central reason for the High Anglican espousal of the anti-Turkish cause was their sympathy and ecumenical affinity with the Greek Orthodox subjects of the Ottoman Empire in the Balkans. Resentment over the Public Worship Regulation Act and hatred of Disraeli, the Jew, sometimes added venom to the feelings of Anglo-Catholics. The Church of England as a whole supported the government in its policy of upholding the national interest, as they saw it, in the Near East. Among Low Churchmen there was often strong antagonism to the atrocity agitation. Magee, who had been appointed Bishop of Peterborough from the 'Low' Church of Ireland by Disraeli in 1868, and who is chiefly remembered for his remark during the licensing debates that he preferred England free to England sober, wrote in September 1876: 'I doubt if the whole history of democracy, rife as it is with instances of passionate injustice, supplies a grosser one than the cry against the Ministry of the last three weeks'. For the majority of the Anglican clergy their patriotism and political Conservatism went hand in hand with support for the government's policy.

Rarely has a question of foreign policy stirred the country so profoundly and split it so deeply. The antagonisms aroused took on a momentum of their own, because the question went to the roots of philosophical attitudes and political behaviour, and at the extremes slid into hysteria. Broadly, the metropolis, clubland and the upper classes were pro-Turk, the provinces and Radicals anti-Turk. To this there were many exceptions. For some Radicals like Joseph Cowen, the member for Newcastle, fear of Russia outweighed all other considerations. Dilke, who was an imperialist as well as a Radical, held similar views. Joseph Chamberlain cared little for the Eastern Question in itself, but was quite prepared to use the stir on the left of the political spectrum to advance his particular brand of Radical Liberalism. The veteran John Bright hovered uneasily on the fringe of the agitation, restrained by his non-interventionism. Many of the prominent working-class leaders, men like George Holyoake, George Howell and Henry Broadhurst, marched at the side of Gladstone and for them, as for nonconformity, the atrocity campaign marked their full reconciliation with the Liberal Party. Others like George Potter, still in control of the important working-class newspaper *The Beehive*, became anti-Gladstonian, seeing in the agitation an emotional distraction from the real working-class interest. He was influenced by the attitude of the positivist friends of the trade unions, Beesly and Harrison, who were repelled by the religious revivalism and pro-Russianism of the atrocity agitators. Working-class opinion was undoubtedly divided: where the nonconformist influence was strong the tide flowed for Gladstone, but elsewhere robustly patriotic popular Toryism may well have been in the ascendant. There was always a suspicion that the atrocity campaign itself was more a middle than a working-class movement.

Suspicion of emotionalism and ridicule inspired by the spectacle of high-minded indignation in full flood motivated many of the intellectual critics of the atrocity campaigners. 'I know of no more contemptible or disgusting spectacle in the world than excited Britons, headed by idiotic Bishops, roaring to belligerents: "We stand aghast at cutting throats, burning houses, and outrages worse than death . . . how can men with immortal souls dare to scandalize us",' wrote Fitzjames Stephen. The controversy over the Eastern Question marks indeed a watershed in intellectual attitudes. Individualist, anti-Statist Liberals were for the most part anti-Turk, men like Goldwin Smith, Henry Fawcett or Herbert Spencer. Some of the younger intellectual leaders from the universities who were increasingly concerned about the realities of power and empire and were later to become Liberal imperialists, men like Alfred Milner and Herbert Asquith from Jowett's Balliol, distanced themselves from the agitation against Disraeli's foreign policy. Jowett himself, the initiator of much Liberal reform, could no longer share what he regarded as Gladstone's self-delusion; fear of enthusiasm and irresponsibility outweighed his normal liberalism. Matthew Arnold, himself one of 'the lights of liberalism', was perhaps predictably opposed to the atrocity campaign; it smacked too much of the 'hebraic philistinism' of nonconformity which he had just castigated in *Culture and Anarchy*. Less predictably, Carlyle sympathized with the atrocity agitation. He saw in Russia a strong autocratic power and the upsurge of feeling about Turkish oppression seemed to him evidence for the morality behind the mammon for which he was always looking. The reactions of the leaders of thought cannot be brought down to a common denominator, but the intensity of the passions stirred made them, like many ordinary men, re-examine the bases of their beliefs.

The peak of the atrocity campaign in September 1876 came at an awkward time for the government. Serbia and Montenegro had declared war on Turkey, but by the end of August Serbia had been defeated and was compelled to sue for an armistice. It now had to be the main aim of the British government to prevent Russia from intervening unilaterally and profiting from the situation. Derby's and Disraeli's style was cramped by the state of British public opinion and this was only too evident in St Petersburg and elsewhere. Disraeli was determined to avoid any appearance of being deflected by the popular agitation, but in practice he knew that the possibility of deterring Russia was limited. In addition there was a growing divergence between him and Derby, who was reluctant to go along with the naval and military moves Disraeli was initiating to lend credibility to the British position. The divisions within the government were paralleled by those within the Liberal Party. The fact that the government gave the appearance of not bowing to the pressure of public opinion made Gladstone feel that he had to go on with his campaign, even if there was a note of caution in his actual foreign policy pronouncements. In December he spoke at a National Conference on the Eastern Question in St James's Hall; among his fellow speakers were Freeman and Liddon, the former in particularly bigoted and virulent vein, and in a much publicized gesture Gladstone helped Mme Novikov, the prominent advocate of the Russian case, from the platform. Granville and particularly Hartington were markedly unenthusiastic about these proceedings and the latter remarked that if Gladstone 'goes on much further, nothing can prevent a break-up of the party'.

In the meantime the Powers had agreed to send representatives to Constantinople to discuss a Balkans settlement and the British emissary to this conference was Lord Salisbury. Participation in the conference by Britain represented a considerable departure from the principle of non-intervention and respect for Turkish sovereignty which, on the surface at any rate, had prevailed since the rejection of the Berlin Memorandum. Salisbury, whose influence on Disraeli and the cabinet was growing, was 'convinced that the old policy – wise enough in its time – of defending English interests by sustaining the Ottoman dynasty had become impracticable'; the possibility of territorial partition was increasingly contemplated, even by Disraeli. The Constantinople Conference failed, because the Porte refused to accept its programme of internal reform and change in the Balkans. A portion of the British cabinet would have been prepared to go along with an international effort to coerce the Turks into acceptance, but Disraeli and Derby were not. Disraeli feared that such intervention would be a cover for a Russian takeover; Derby always favoured inaction and the line of least disturbance. Salisbury was anti-Turk, much more concerned for the Christians in the Balkans than Disraeli and inclined to give the Russians the benefit of the doubt. He was not convinced of the strategic importance of Turkey as the key to India, but even he did not want to see Russia in Constantinople.

After the failure of the Constantinople Conference Ignatiev, Russia's influential pan-Slav ambassador at the Porte, travelled round Europe and produced another agreed reform programme, the so-called London Protocol. The British government went along with it, but was still not prepared to coerce the Turks, who again refused to accept such a programme. The Russians were, however, preparing the ground for their own military intervention, for the failure of all these international efforts at least ensured that none of the other Great Powers would in the end be in a position to stop Russia from acting. Most important was the fact that the Tzar's government had secretly squared the Austrians; the Habsburg Empire was, in return for its neutrality, to obtain ample compensation from a Russo–Turkish war. It is arguable that but for the state of public opinion the British government could have acted more firmly to prevent the outbreak of this war. There is no evidence that Disraeli was secretly undermining the efforts at Turkish reform or looking for a war with Russia. Such suspicions, harboured by the atrocity agitators and to a large extent by Gladstone himself, were unfounded. Disraeli was not wedded to the status quo in the Near East; 'all the Turks may be in the Propontis, so far as I am concerned', he had written to Derby at one stage. Rightly or wrongly he regarded it as incompatible with the British national interest that Russia should control Constantinople and the Straits and about this he remained adamant. He spoke to his cabinet about 'the two policies now in conflict; the Imperial Policy of England, and the Policy of Crusade'. Nevertheless when Russia declared war on Turkey on 24 April 1877 British neutrality was not in doubt.

In the meantime, in February, Parliament had reassembled. The focus of British public sentiment was therefore transferred from the atrocity agitation in the country to the House of Commons. Within the parliamentary Liberal Party, opposition to or reservations about the 'atrocitarians' was considerable and embraced the two leaders Hartington and Granville. The disunity of the Liberal Party was perhaps most evident when shortly after the outbreak of the Russo-Turkish War, Gladstone insisted, against the advice of most of the other leading Liberals, on moving five resolutions, the burden of which was that all moral and material support should be withheld from the Porte until it gave good government to its Christian peoples. Northcote's comment on this to the Queen was: 'There is a general impression that Mr Gladstone has become so much excited by a morbid idea that he is partly responsible for the Bulgarian outrages, on account of his support of the Crimean War, that he does not know what he is doing.' By this time the Queen, herself a violent partisan, needed no persuading that Gladstone was a madman. In the vote on the first of the resolutions the government had a majority of 131 and had thus nothing to fear from its divided opponents. The lack of firm support which Gladstone encountered among his parliamentary colleagues was one of the reasons for his decision to accept the invitation from Chamberlain to address the inaugural meeting of the National Liberal Federation a fortnight later. Chamberlain cared little for the Bulgars and Gladstone not much more for the Birmingham caucus, but each hoped to extract advantage from the occasion. Gladstone's suspicions of the Prime Minister were at their most feverish: 'I have watched very closely his strange and at first sight inexplicable proceedings on this Eastern Question: and I believe their fountain head to be race antipathy, that aversion which the Jews, with a few honourable exceptions, are showing so vindictively towards the Eastern Christians. Though he has been baptized, his Jew feelings are the most radical and the most real, and so far respectable, portion of his profoundly falsified nature.' Gladstone's decision to appear at Birmingham was received with distaste by Hartington and Granville.

The disunity of the Liberal Party aggravated the disunity of the cabinet, though it was more concealed from the public. Even before the war broke out, ministers had strongly disagreed about the recall of

Elliot from Constantinople; he was replaced by Layard, the excavator of Nineveh. Once the war had broken out, it was a question of what limit Britain should set to Russian aims, for it was universally assumed that the Turks would be beaten; and by what methods Russia should be made to conform to British requirements. A gulf now opened between Disraeli and his Foreign Secretary. The Prime Minister had at various times hoped to reach agreement with Russia and had not on the whole interfered with Salisbury's efforts to do so at Constantinople. He believed, however, that an understanding with Russia must be based on a position of strength. Derby essentially believed in appeasing Russia and building on relationships with those Russian policy-makers who were in favour of a peaceful solution of differences with Britain. Lord and Lady Derby worked closely with Shuvalov, the Russian ambassador in London, who was a strong opponent of pan-Slavism, and went to the length of keeping him informed of divisions in the cabinet. Yet Disraeli was unwilling to lose Derby, because of the electoral damage his resignation would do to the Conservative Party, particularly in Lancashire. Salisbury often backed Derby, but he was at the same time critical of the Foreign Secretary's passivity and indecision. The 'third lord' who often found himself in opposition to Disraeli was Carnarvon, whose attitude was almost wholly determined by his concern, as a High Anglican, for the Christians in the Balkans.

The Russo–Turkish war had its ups and downs. After initial victories the Russians were held up outside Plevna for four months. This show of strength by the sick man of Europe on his death-bed was perhaps as decisive for the ultimate survival of the Ottoman Empire as anything the British government did. By the end of 1877 the Turkish army was, however, in a state of collapse, but the Russians were also militarily exhausted. The crunch of the crisis, which but for Plevna might have been reached earlier, therefore came at a time when the British government was in a much better position to act firmly. The atrocity campaign had lost much of its sting, or was at any rate counterbalanced by a strong popular tide of Russophobia and jingoism. There is a story, probably apocryphal, that Disraeli went incognito to hear the great MacDermott sing his famous music-hall song with the refrain 'We don't want to fight; But by jingo if we do, We've got the men, we've got the ships, we've got the money too', in order to assure himself of the state of popular feeling. Even for some of the nonconformist rank and file their patriotism began to prevail over the line preached by their leaders. At least as important was the fact that under the impact of an imminent Russian occupation of Constantinople the differences in the cabinet were resolving themselves. Salisbury, the key figure, was coming down on the side of firmness and against Derby's vacillations. The Foreign Secretary had tried to convince Salisbury that the Prime Minister was hankering for war: 'He believes thoroughly in "prestige" as all foreigners do, and would think it (quite sincerely) in the interests of the country to spend 200 millions on a war if the result was to make foreign States think more highly of us as a military power.' It was a revealing statement, not least for its categorization of Disraeli as a foreigner. Salisbury and the cabinet thought more weighty matters were at stake and in the first few months of 1878 consistently acted with firmness. With the aid of parliamentary credits, movements of fleets through the Straits and of troops to the Mediterranean Russian gains were kept in bounds without war. Russia had imposed the Treaty of San Stefano on Turkey, incorporating the pan-Slavist aim of a large, independent Bulgaria. Neither Britain nor Austria–Hungary could accept this and Russia was finally compelled to submit the Near-Eastern settlement to revision by a European congress. In March Derby, who had come close to a nervous breakdown, finally resigned and was succeeded by Salisbury, who was to control British foreign policy for much of the rest of the century.

It was mainly Salisbury who prepared the Congress of Berlin, though the general feeling that it was Disraeli's triumph was largely justified. The integrity of the Ottoman Empire had been saved once more, this time without war. It was, however, no longer the Ottoman Empire that Palmerston had expended so much effort in propping up. It was almost entirely an Asiatic power now, but it was still effective in keeping Russia out of the Mediterranean. Parts of the Big Bulgaria created by San Stefano were returned to Turkey. Important by-products for Britain were the acquisition of Cyprus and the declaration that she might in future pass ships through the Straits without reference to the Sultan. Britain acquired prestige in Europe that was somewhat out of line with her real means of action. Nevertheless the balance drawn at this time between the British and Russian position in the Near East proved to be even more enduring than the actual territorial settlement of 1878.

Disraeli's return from Berlin bringing 'peace with honour' was so palpable a triumph that the temptation to cash in on it by calling a general election was obvious. There was a good deal of speculation about a dissolution of Parliament and even a discussion in the cabinet. Leading Tories in urban constituencies, for example A.B. Forwood, a pillar of Liverpool Conservatism, thought it was a favourable moment for their party. But premature ending of a Parliament, in which the government of the day had a secure majority, was against normal practice. And ministers were very conscious of the difficulties the trade depression was creating: taxation was bringing in less revenue and votes of credit for naval and military moves were increasing expenditure. For all this blame would be heaped upon the government. Disraeli himself showed that he was alive to the connection between foreign policy and economic well-being. At a banquet to celebrate the conferment of the freedom of the City of London on himself and Lord Salisbury in August 1878 he said: 'I hope . . . that . . . our conversation will be no longer of wars and rumours of war . . . and that in the future it will be on the revival of industry and the arts of civilization, that I shall have to address – periodically – the chief magistrate of the greatest city in the world.'

IV

It could not have been anticipated in that moment of triumph that the foreign and imperial policy of the Conservative government was itself about to suffer serious reverses. Ironically, Disraeli bore little personal responsibility for what occurred in South Africa and Afghanistan, yet these setbacks made plausible Gladstone's attack on 'Beaconsfieldism', a conflation of all the sins and vices of an arrogant policy abroad. Imperial and colonial policy, in the narrower sense and as distinct from foreign policy, had not been much different under the Conservative government from what it was under Gladstone's government. In the heyday of non-intervention the Tory government of 1866–8 had fought the Abyssinian war and had made the most of its success, while the Liberal Opposition attacked the cost. Gladstone had acted similarly with the Ashantee War of 1873 and wrote to Granville, in considering the prospects for an election in January 1874: 'The conduct of the Ashantee campaign does much credit to the ministers concerned: but all they can do, all that fortune can do in this direction, is to save us from a specified danger. The Ashantee War might have been our death, it cannot be our life, any more than the Abyssinian War could prolong the existence of the last government'. In the 1870s the time had not yet arrived when competition for territory and for trade, protectionism and a general sharpening of international rivalries were acting as a direct spur to colonial expansion. The evolution of events was still in the main the product of local circumstances, of the men in control on the spot and long established attitudes and policies of the Colonial Office at home.

Disraeli had perhaps some responsibility for the disasters that befell in Afghanistan, for he had made Lytton, another romantic novelist with ambitious visions, Viceroy of India. The despatch of a British mission to Kabul was Lytton's own initiative and came about in spite of the home government's instructions. Carnarvon as Colonial Secretary was responsible for South Africa and Disraeli left him largely to his own devices. Carnarvon had been responsible for the federation of Canada, for which he received much credit, and tried to put the same federal principles into action in South Africa. He had appointed Sir Bartle Frere to the post of Governor of the Cape Colony and Frere promoted the expansionist policies that produced the Zulu War. In September 1878, when the simultaneous threat of trouble in South Africa and on the northwest frontier caused him grave irritation, Disraeli wrote to Lady Bradford: '. . . if anything annoys me more than another, it is our Cape affairs, where every day brings forth a new blunder of Twitters.' This was the nickname for Carnarvon, who by then had been succeeded by Hicks Beach. The great disaster of the Zulu War was the defeat of Lord Chelmsford at Isandhlwana in January 1879, made doubly humiliating by the death of the Prince Imperial, the son of Napoleon III. The subsequent defeat of the Zulus had scarcely began to assuage the public's discontent when disaster struck in Afghanistan. The British mission which had been successfully established at Kabul under Sir Louis Cavagnari, was massacred in September 1879. At a time when the next general election could be at most 18 months away, such disasters made a perfect background to the Liberal counterattack on the government.

In this counterattack Gladstone took a prominent personal part. Disraeli's triumph at Berlin left him with a sense of accounts still to be settled. Personal relations between the two men were as bad as they had ever been: Gladstone called the Cyprus convention 'an insane covenant', to which Disraeli replied that he would not pretend to be a judge of insanity and called his adversary 'a sophisticated rhetorician, inebriated with the exuberance of his own verbosity'. Gladstone was not the leader of the Liberal Party and enjoyed therefore greater freedom of expression than he would have done if he had not laid down the leadership in 1875. He had decided not to stand again at Greenwich at the next election and many constituencies were competing for his candidature. In January 1879 he chose Midlothian, the Scottish county seat stretching round the environs of Edinburgh. The seat was normally Tory held and the current member was Lord Dalkeith, eldest son of the Duke of Buccleuch, whose interests were pervasive in the constituency. W.P. Adam, the Liberal chief whip, encouraged Gladstone's candidature, forecast a Liberal victory and a beneficial effect throughout Scotland. Lord Rosebery also played his part in getting Gladstone to Midlothian; the young, brilliant and immensely wealthy Scottish nobleman became a personal friend of the Gladstones, but it was a friendship that did not always run smooth, personally or politically. The powerful Rosebery interest was thrown into the scales against the Buccleuch interest in Midlothian. Gladstone waxed eloquent against the creation of 'faggot' or fictitious votes by his opponents, but he did not know that his supporters were also creating them to deny any advantage to Dalkeith. Thus Midlothian had many of the characteristics of an old-fashioned contest between rival aristocratic magnates using time-hallowed methods of corruption.

Gladstone's use of Midlothian as a platform from which to put his case to the nation in anticipation of a general election, while not perhaps entirely new, was nevertheless modern. It took the use of the public platform outside Parliament by a leading political figure a step further: by making a series of connected speeches, developing a coherent series of themes, over a period of two weeks and under conditions of maximum publicity Gladstone was breaking fresh ground. His opponents felt that such relentless exposure to 'drenching rhetoric', as Disraeli called it, verged on the unconstitutional. The first Midlothian campaign began on 24 November 1879 and ended a fortnight later. Gladstone reckoned that he had addressed over 85,000 people and *The Times* printed about as many words of his speeches. The central theme of the speeches, from which much of the rest radiates, was the enunciation of 'the right principles of foreign policy'. Gladstone put forward six of these principles: 'to foster the strength of the Empire by just legislation and economy at home'; 'to preserve to the nations of the world . . . the blessings of peace'; 'to strive to cultivate and maintain . . . the concert of Europe'; 'avoid needless and entangling engagements'; 'to acknowledge the equal rights of all nations'; and 'the foreign policy of England should always be inspired by the love of freedom'. There would be no clearer contrast with Disraeli's policy of assertion and prestige than these six principles. He brought them home to his audience in many a memorable flight of oratory. Speaking of the indivisibility of justice he said: 'Remember the rights of the savage, as we call him. Remember that the happiness of his humble home, remember that the sanctity of life in the hill village of Afghanistan among the winter snows, is as inviolable in the eye of Almighty God as can be your own.' Although the moral appeal was uppermost, Gladstone did not neglect to involve the material interests of his audiences. It was not difficult to point out the connection between financial extravagance and a foreign policy motivated by hunger for prestige. He showed how the surplus built up by his government had been dissipated by the high expenditure, mainly military, of the Tory government. 'What is even worse than mis-management of finance is destruction or disparagement of the sound and healthy rules which the wisdom of a long series of finance ministers, of an excellent finance department, and of many Parliaments had gradually and laboriously built up, to prevent abuse, to secure public control, to work by degrees upon the public debt of the country and to take care that the people shall not be unduly burdened.'

The first Midlothian campaign took place at a time when a dissolution of Parliament, while it could not be far distant, had not been announced. Gladstone felt that no opportunity should be missed 'of stirring the country' and that it was 'good policy to join on the proceedings of 1876–9 by a continuous process to the dissolution'. Disraeli's own verdict was this: 'hard times' was the cry against us. The suffering want a change – no matter what, they are sick of waiting . . .'. The political reversal of 1880 was itself the indicator of a sea-change in the general atmosphere, of which the economic down-turn was one of several causes.

4   The 1880s: Victorian Confidence Falters

I

The 'Great Depression' which began in 1873 and lasted till 1896 may be largely a myth conjured up by economic historians. What is beyond dispute is that the year 1873 marked the end of one of the most frantic booms of the nineteenth century both in the international and the British economy. For Britain it did not end with a traumatic financial crash, such as was experienced particularly in Austria and the United States. In the City of London there was no panic comparable to that of 1866, although there were a number of important business and banking failures in the next few years. What was meant by 'hard times' and 'distress' was a slackening of business activity and profits accompanied by a prolonged drop in prices, and unemployment – although the word itself was hardly yet established in the vocabulary and there were no reliable statistics for it. All this was not a new phenomenon, but it seemed more prolonged than in previous slumps, for by the end of the 1870s there were only slight signs of a recovery. A renewed down-turn in the middle 1880s reinforced the feeling that the Golden Age was a thing of the past. A special case of hardship was agriculture, which at the beginning of the 1870s still employed nearly half as many people as all the manufacturing industries including textiles taken together and produced about four-fifths of the food consumed in the country. From 1873 onwards there was a series of bad harvests of which that of 1879 was the worst. In previous years farmers had usually been compensated for poor crops by high prices, but now the opening up of the British market to cheap grain imports mainly from North America produced a combination of bad harvests and low prices. It was widely believed that the malaise of agriculture in the late 1870s was a principal reason for the prolongation of the general slump.

The inability of the economy to recover rapidly, unprecedented since the 1840s, led to the belief that a secular turning point had been reached in the material fortunes of the country. It had long been feared and anticipated that Britain's unique industrial advantage could not last. Up to the middle of the nineteenth century Britain's industrial revolution and export trade had been overwhelmingly concentrated in textiles. The proportion of the occupied population employed in textile and clothing manufacture fell from 21.4 per cent in 1851 to 17.8 per cent in 1871; while those employed in other manufacturing industry and in transport rose from 15.4 per cent to 18.7 per cent in the same period. The proportion of British exports consisting of textiles fell from 63 to 56 per cent and those consisting of metal and engineering products rose from 18 to 21 per cent in those years. It was not an overwhelming shift, but undoubtedly more of the British industrial effort went into equipping other countries to become eventual rivals. This was particularly evident in the building of railways, in which British engineers and equipment played a prominent part the world over. Up to 1914 textile engineering was the largest single branch of engineering in Britain; its exports again largely went to equip other countries, in the first instance the next generation of advanced economies, to compete with Britain in the area where the foundation of her early pre-eminence had lain. In theory it had always been accepted albeit reluctantly by many devotees of free trade that the very success of British trade in the phase that followed the early concentration on textiles must in due course end the British quasi-monopoly of industrialism. As early as 1851 *The Economist*, looking at the United States, had written: 'From the relative progress of the two countries within the last 60 years, it may be inferred that the superiority of the United States to England is ultimately as certain as the next eclipse.' When the end of the Civil War fully released the dynamic force of the American economy, there was nevertheless alarm; the German economy was also about to enter a dynamic phase, but this was not yet fully noticed in Britain at the end of the 1870s.

Another manifestation of Britain's long success story as an industrial nation was paradoxically causing alarm in the depression of the 1870s, the tendency of exports to grow less rapidly than in the past and to cover a smaller portion of the cost of imports. There was a jump in the adverse balance of visible trade in the later 1870s. Much of this adverse balance had always been covered by receipts from shipping; there was now a steep rise in the income from foreign investments, the fruit of past success. In 1850 British foreign holdings amounted to about £225 million pounds; in 1875 they were in the region of £1,000 million and by 1885 they were half as much again. Britain was in fact becoming a rentier nation and the heyday of the City of London as the hub of international finance now dawned and lasted till the First World War. In the wake of the financial collapse of

1873 a number of foreign governments defaulted and it was therefore hardly surprising that the positive side of the British invisible trade surplus was less in the contemporary eye than the plight of despoiled holders of foreign bonds. The largest group among them were the holders of Turkish bonds and their plight figured much in the debate over the Eastern Question, with many accusations levelled against the government that it was acting on their behalf. Carriages were laid up, servants dismissed and seaside resorts like Bournemouth, only recently become fashionable, were feeling the pinch. All this was merely a temporary hiccup; the steadily ascending curve of British overseas investment was an indication of the wealth of the country, as yet unrivalled elsewhere.

The role played by foreign investment income in financing Britain's deficit on external trade also illustrated the extent to which the British economy had now become part of a world-wide economy and was therefore inevitably exposed to the fluctuations of that world economy. In 1870 British visible trade amounted to over £17 per head of population, while in France it was only just over £6, in Germany over £5 and in the USA over £4. Ten years later the figures were less than £20, over £9, £6.50 and over £6 respectively. Alarm was naturally felt when the British share of the trade, and particularly the export side of it, no longer increased as dramatically as it had done in the middle of the century. Much of the reduction in the annual rate of increase in trade was a reduction in value rather than volume, due to the general fall in prices after 1873. Nevertheless the perception that Britain was experiencing difficulties and hindrances to her trade on a greater scale than hitherto was not without justification. The metal and engineering industries were now in the van of industrial progress. Steel, manufactured by new processes such as Bessemer and Gilchrist-Thomas, was playing an increasingly important role. In this area Britain never, or only briefly, enjoyed the unique advantage over other countries that she had had in textiles, and by the 1880s the United States and Germany were advancing at least as rapidly or more so and protecting themselves with tariffs. In 1885 a Royal Commission on the Depression in Trade and Industry was appointed; through the evidence given to it there runs the complaint that the British metallurgical industries were increasingly finding it too difficult to export to markets like Germany, which now had their own industries protected by tariffs, and were also facing growing competition in neutral markets. Chambers of Commerce and employers' organizations were liable to ascribe such loss of competitiveness as they were prepared to admit to the operation of the Factory Acts and the activities of trade unions. The gloom was probably overdone: the decline in iron and steel exports was not drastic and only to be expected; machinery exports were still increasing and textile exports were shifting from the more developed economies to the less developed, particularly to India and the Far East. The increasing importance of the Indian and imperial markets generally was beginning to provide a justification for the Disraelian rather than the Gladstonian version of imperial policy.

Much of the gloom among businessmen about the depression of the late 1870s was caused by falling prices, leading to reduced profits and, it was feared, declining investment. The falling prices did, however, effect a considerable redistribution of the national income in favour of wage earners. There was, of course, also a good deal of wage cutting and high unemployment, but the real wages of those in work undoubtedly rose. The scope for redistribution of income from the higher to the lower income groups was, to be sure, large. In 1868 Dudley Baxter, fresh from his statistical labours on the Reform Bill, had published comprehensive and careful estimates of the national income for the previous year. For England and Wales he put the income per head at £32 and for every person with a separate income at £68; for the United Kingdom as a whole the respective figures were £27 and £59. He also estimated, however, that less than 10 per cent of all income receivers were getting more than half the total national income. Thus Baxter's averages mean that in the 1860s the incomes of the majority of the population were scarcely sufficient to provide an adequate subsistence; with a theoretically equal distribution they would just about have provided an existence of bare comfort for everyone. Between 1860 and 1890 real wages rose by at least half, largely because of the fall in prices, and the distribution of income was becoming a little less unequal.

Agriculture was the one area in the nation's economic life where decline was indisputable. Up to the 1870s it had survived remarkably well as an industry. With its large units it was by international standards very efficient. Just as the uneven distribution of the national income as a whole helped to ensure a high rate of investment and growth in the economy in general, so the concentration of landholding helped to produce high investment in agriculture and up-to-date methods of farming. The ownership of land was certainly highly concentrated, with almost half the area of England and Wales owned by a little over 4,000 persons; 900 landlords owned estates of over 10,000 acres each. At the other end of the tripartite rural hierarchy of owners, tenant farmers and labourers, the wages of the agricultural workers had risen considerably in the early 1870s, mainly as a result of the remarkable upsurge of trade unionism under the guidance of Joseph Arch. Within a few years money wages rose by as much as a third on average: after 1875 they fell back again, though not as drastically as the number of trade union members. The agricultural labourer profited, as did the industrial worker, from the decline in prices so that his real wage kept up reasonably well even after the agricultural depression had struck. The owners of land were, however, hit by the full force of it and never recovered. By 1885 it was estimated that there had been a fall in land values of 8 per cent, a fall in income of 7 per cent and a drop in rent of nearly 10 per cent. These declines continued, reaching over 20 per cent by the early 1890s. The fall in prices, the corollary of the rise in real wages in the economy as a whole, was particularly marked in grain products; but much less pronounced in meat and dairy products; evidence again of the gradual improvement in the diet of the population in general. The amount of land under arable cultivation gradually decreased, while pasture increased; the adaptation to changes in demand was slower than it should have been, particularly in the grain-farming areas of southern England. The number of hired agricultural workers decreased from nearly a million in 1871 to 860,000 in 1891. The writing was on the wall for the landed aristocracy as a political force. The Royal Commission on the Depression in Trade was told that between 1879 and 1884 there had been a decline of £150 million in the capital value of land. As an industry, agriculture recovered somewhat from the very bad years at the end of the 1870s and the gradual shift from arable farming helped to restore its income. Its importance in the national economy declined very considerably; its contribution to the national income in 1871 was estimated at over 17 per cent; by 1911 it was down to less than 7 per cent.

II

The Royal Commission on Agriculture which reported in 1882 found it difficult to discern what was happening and much blame was put on a succession of bad harvests. It was even more difficult for contemporaries to see clearly the changes that were affecting the industrial economy. The effect of the depression and of the gloom and bafflement engendered by it was, however, to concentrate minds wonderfully and to accelerate the questioning of long-established orthodoxies. Urbanization, the aggravation of social problems in large towns, growing awareness of poverty as a problem, the expansion of central and local government, doubts about the natural harmony of individual interests, fears of the newly arisen political power of the masses, all these and many other factors had for some time agitated perceptive and far-seeing minds; the economic malaise of the late 1870s supplied a focus to such perceptions and gave them general currency. The growth of religious doubt, on the one hand, and the unchallenged prestige of natural science, on the other, made this a time when the application of scientific method to the social life of man seemed to be the way to progress. Auguste Comte, Herbert Spencer and Charles Darwin were for many the prophets of the moment. Political economy had always made a strong claim to be a social science and had been widely regarded as the central science of man. Even before the onset of the slump of the 1870s the economics of Adam Smith, David Ricardo and John Stuart Mill, which were still exercising so powerful an influence, were being re-examined and revised. The reassessment was directed at the theoretical framework the classical economists had created; it also consisted of a more historical pragmatic approach to the understanding of economic phenomena. On the theoretical level such classical concepts as the labour theory of value, free markets and perfect competition, nationally and internationally, the wage fund theory and the natural harmony of interests came under attack. One of the implications of this theoretical revision was that the classical wholly negative view of economic regulation by the State or other bodies could no longer be sustained. The historical approach, based on the view that the abstractions of economic theory are unreal, divorced from the historical circumstances in which they operate, worked in the same direction: it created greater awareness of the unique nature of English industrialism and of the fact that the classical economic theories had arisen from this very special experience.

Some of those changed perspectives were already implicit in the writings of John Stuart Mill, not least in the importance he attached to the political roots of the economic circumstances of society. After him the work of developing economics as a branch of knowledge was largely carried on by academic economists like Stanley Jevons and Alfred Marshall and economic historians like W.J. Ashley and W. Cunningham. Their work took account of the changes in the real world. A rigid wage fund theory was adapted to cope with evidence of a gradual rise of real wages combined with a rapid rise of the population. The free market account of the accumulation of capital and the rôle of the entrepreneur was modified to accommodate the evidence of increasing concentration and the growth in the size of productive units. The impact of economic fluctuations focused attention on a problem that meant little to the classical economists, with their assumption of an equilibrium that would always automatically restore itself. There were signs that the State might have to take on responsibilities beyond keeping the ring, for example in education and the protection of industries against unfair competition; in some other countries, whose economic success was being watched with increasing apprehension, it was doing so. Along with the theoretical adaptations the science of political economy was having to make, there went a feeling among its practitioners that the days of its pre-eminence were over. 'The controversies which we now have in Political Economy, although they offer a capital exercise for the logical faculties, are not of the same thrilling importance as those of earlier days; the great work has been done', said Robert Lowe at the Centenary dinner of the Political Economy Club in 1876.

In the wider field of social science, where Lowe was perhaps looking for more exciting discoveries, there was also a perceptible move away from the individualism that had been for so long dominant. In itself the faith in social science as a means of solving human problems implied a recognition that the social environment was as much the key to the individual man's destiny as his own independent action. In the 1880s the debate about the shape of the future and the path to be followed towards it was focused round the polarities of individualism and collectivism. Individualism was still powerful and the very challenge to it which now arose sharpened its defence. This polarization in the realm of ideas hardly did justice to what was going on in the real world: the State had never in practice confined itself to keeping law and order at home and defending the country against its foreign enemies. It was a question of degree and undoubtedly there was truth in the perception that the combination of evangelical religion and utilitarian philosophy for which the individual had been the starting point was losing its force. By 1880 the Idealist philosophy of T.H. Green was fashionable and cast a spell upon many young men who were soon to be in positions of power and influence. Green was a committed Liberal; his neo-Hegelian position was always tempered by thoroughly English notions of balance. In a famous lecture delivered in 1880 on 'Liberal Legislation and the Freedom of Contract' he said that individual rights were not absolute in themselves, but means to an end: 'That end is what I call freedom in the positive sense: in other words, the liberation of the powers of all men equally for contributions to a common good. No one has a right to do what he will with his own in such a way as to contravene this end.' Green used such arguments to justify the legislation of the Gladstone governments on education, licensing and public health; there was no politician he admired more than Bright and he was strongly imbued with the moralism of Victorian political philosophy. Nevertheless Green's philosophy and vocabulary provided a rationale for collectivist action going much beyond what Gladstonian Liberalism had up to now contemplated. Arnold Toynbee, his acolyte, put it thus: 'First, that where individual rights conflict with the interests of the community, there the State ought to interfere; and, second, that where the people are unable to provide a thing for themselves, and that thing is of *primary social importance*, then again the State should interfere and provide it for them.' After Toynbee's early death in 1883, the pioneer settlement in the East End of London, Toynbee Hall, was to be named after him; it attracted a steady stream of volunteers from the universities, some of them to gain high distinction in later life, in whom the Idealist philosophy of Green and his successors had inspired the urge to minister to the poor.

The collectivist implications of that philosophy did not have their full impact in terms of practical politics until later, perhaps not until 1906, but immediately they fuelled the intellectual and political controversy round the polarities of collectivism and individualism. The latter was far from being a spent force; even if its evangelical and utilitarian sources were weaker, individualism was now regarded as firmly rooted in the theory of evolution, and as having therefore all the authority of natural science behind it. Herbert Spencer was still the most prestigious Social Darwinist of the period and in his best known work of political philosophy, *The Man versus the State*, published in 1884, he reiterated the case for individual freedom and against State intervention, based on evolutionary theories, in uncompromising form. Social Darwinism was to prove janus-faced; it could be used to give the State a very positive role both in domestic and foreign affairs, in safeguarding the nation in its struggle for survival against other nations. Yet in the hands of Spencer and other lesser men Social Darwinism justified individualistic liberalism often in so extreme a form that even the government's role in education, which the Liberal Party itself had advanced so much, was called in question.

III

In the controversies of the 1880s the terms collectivism and socialism were often used interchangeably. Socialism was a name given to any form of public action designed to deal with social evils. Even Lord Salisbury was prepared to say 'It is our duty to do all we can to find the remedies and even if we are called socialists, in attempting to do it, we shall be reconciled if we can find these remedies, knowing that we are undertaking no new principle but pursuing the long and healthy tradition of English legislation.' It was, however, a measure of the depth of the crisis, of which the 'Great Depression' was the outward and visible manifestation, that socialism in a more specific and far-reaching sense was now experiencing a revival in Britain. The socialist revival drew on the rich vein of social criticism that had always run alongside the confidence and faith in progress of the Victorian age. Carlyle, Dickens, Matthew Arnold, Ruskin and William Morris were merely the most prominent of the many critics of industrial, competitive society, even though their distaste had only a few common denominators and they did not offer much in the way of a coherent counter-doctrine. Ruskin and Morris, the one tenuously and the other closely connected with the socialist revival, had both come to their political views from their artistic and aesthetic preoccupations. Since the early 1870s Ruskin had been publishing *Fors Clavigera: Letters to the Workmen and Labourers of Great Britain*, full of passionate, if cloudy, denunciations: '. . . the guilty Thieves of Europe, the real sources of all deadly war in it, are the Capitalists – that is to say, people who live by percentages on the labour of others; instead of by fair wages for their own.' He had long advocated against the prevailing notion of Economic Man, on which the classical school of economists had based all their wisdom, the ideas of intrinsic wealth, divorced from money and exchange values, and of social justice independent of competition. Morris had been much influenced by Ruskin in his belief in the unity of art and work and in his protest against the degradation of labour in contemporary society. The Eastern Question had brought him into active politics in the middle 1870s and into contact with advanced radicalism and some of the leaders of labour. There was in his vision of the good society a strong element of withdrawal into an imaginary utopia, a kind of children's paradise, but his loathing of the alienation imposed upon workers by the meaningless grind in the factory and 'his hatred for modern civilization' made him look by the early 1880s for a fundamental transformation of society in a socialist direction. He found in the Democratic Federation an organization which he hoped would further his aims. It had been started in June 1881 and its leading spirit was H.M. Hyndman, a figure in the long line of peculiarly English radicals, in whom utter devotion to a cause and fierce eccentric independence combined with gentlemanly breeding. Hyndman's family came from the West Indian planter aristocracy; he was a product of Eton and Trinity College, Cambridge and had played cricket against W.G. Grace. He was an imperialist and at times a Tory Radical; he had a long interview with Disraeli shortly before the latter's death. He managed to combine this with an interest in native welfare in the colonies, the state of Ireland and in a wide range of radical ideas and policies, but he was also strongly anti-Gladstonian and highly sceptical of the Liberal Party and mainstream radicalism.

The Democratic Federation was founded as an alternative to the National Liberal Federation, which was already regarded by those on the far Left as too middle-class and compromised by its acceptance of capitalism. Its initial programme evoked echoes of Chartism with its demands for universal suffrage and equal electoral districts and it was also an attempt to revive the idea of a separate Labour Party, now that the Labour Representation League was moribund. The ideas of Henry George the American single-taxer bulked large; his book *Progress and Poverty* had appeared just at a moment when the agricultural depression made his prescriptions seem highly relevant. The land question was also at the root of Irish problems and much of the energy of the Democratic Federation was taken up in its first year by opposition to the Liberal government's use of coercion in Ireland. Links with Parnell and hostility to Gladstone soon lost the Democratic Federation the support of many traditional working-class radicals and this enabled Hyndman to move the organization in a more positively socialist direction, signified by the change of name to Social-Democratic Federation in 1883. The nationalization of all the means of production became part of the programme. Hyndman himself had been converted to socialism in 1880, largely as a result of reading Marx's *Das Kapital*. He had popularized the Marxist arguments in two chapters of his *England for All*, but with only an indirect acknowledgement to their originator; his relations with Marx and later Engels were always strained. Hyndman took some basic Marxist concepts, like the theory of surplus value and the class struggle, and grafted them in a rather rough and ready way on to some of the prevailing traditions of British radicalism.

In the longer term the importance of Hyndman and the SDF lay in the fact that they introduced the Marxist strand into the ideas of the British Left. In the short term the discrepancy between ambitions and realities was marked. The SDF had hardly any base among the working class and in the trade unions. It suffered from the sectarianism and cliquishness common on the extremes of politics and Hyndman's domineering personality did not help. In 1884 William Morris and others left and founded the Socialist League but it was in turn to tear itself apart a few years later between supporters of parliamentary action and anarchists. Morris believed that cataclysmic events would usher in a new, simpler society, more akin to the Middle Ages, in which strong and genuine feelings would sweep away current hypocrisies. He castigated 'the political opportunism and State

Socialism of the SDF'; parliaments and elections were to him a path
to corruption. In his vision of the new society, *News from Nowhere*,
which appeared in 1890, he says looking back from the twenty-first
century, with Utopia realized, to his own time '. . . we can see that
the great motive-power of the change was a longing for freedom and
equality, akin if you please to the unreasonable passion of the lover; a
sickness of heart that rejected with loathing the aimless solitary life of
the well-to-do educated men of that time.' William Morris for all his
gifts, reputation and attractive personality, could not save the
Socialist League as an organization and the SDF proved to have the
greater staying power. The romantic utopianism of Morris remained
a potent influence and ethical socialism, which owed much to him,
went on playing a more important part in the British socialist tradition than Marxism.

Hyndman's organization was itself uneasily poised between the
ambition to become a new party of labour and the expectation of
imminent revolution, between immediate political demands, such as
the eight-hour day, and Marxist-socialist dogma. In the 1885 general
election, candidates were put up in Hampstead and Kensington and
received 27 and 32 votes respectively. The fact that these candidatures
had been supported with funds coming indirectly from Conservative
sources, the so-called Tory gold scandal, added discredit to ridicule.
On the other hand John Burns, an important recruit to the Federation, did much better at Nottingham by polling nearly 600 votes.
Hyndman expected revolution by 1889, the centenary of the French
Revolution, and the renewed deepening of the depression and rise of
unemployment in the middle 1880s gave at least a little substance to
his hopes. In February 1886 there was a great demonstration of the
unemployed in London which produced what was, in the opinion of
The Times, the worst riot within living memory, worse in some
respects than the Hyde Park riots in 1866. The SDF was competing
for the favours of the mob with the Fair Trade League, which enjoyed
some Conservative support at this time. The League speakers attacked
Hyndman for his 'socialistic nonsense' and called him a middle-class
man who dabbled on the stock exchange, while Hyndman and Burns
warned the crowd that the Fair Trade League was advocating higher
food prices for the benefit of capitalists. The SDF speakers attempted
to tread the narrow path between inflaming the mob and keeping
some control of it. Burns asked 'When we give the word for a rising,
will you join us?', but according to the SDF's own report he added:
'Then go home quietly, and the signal will be given if the government
does not act.' Smashing of windows in clubland and looting of shops
in the West End followed. For two more days London was in the grip
of panic and fear about mob violence. Charges of seditious conspiracy

were brought against Hyndman, Burns and others, but they were acquitted. More demonstrations and disorders in the capital and elsewhere followed over the next two years, the most conspicuous of them Bloody Sunday, the demonstrations and riots of 13 November 1887 in London. These events made public opinion much more aware of socialism and the personalities and organizations promoting it, but they also showed how remote from reality the revolutionary expectations of the far Left were.

In the meantime another socialist body had appeared on the scene, the Fabian Society, whose staying power and influence were to be greater than those of the SDF. It had its origins in the same amalgam of aspirations for social change, a new way of life, revolt against bourgeois conventions, free thought, free love and romantic utopianism as many of the older small groups of the far Left. The Fellowship of the New Life from which it hived off drew much of its membership from young men and women who had recently come to London to work mostly in lower middle-class occupations, were personally and socially insecure and in consequence often suffered identity crises. The novelist George Gissing called them a 'a class of young men distinctive of our time – well educated, fairly well bred, *but without money.*' This description fits some of the famous recruits of the Fabian Society, men like George Bernard Shaw and Sidney Webb. It was they, and others like Graham Wallas and Sydney Olivier, who gave the Fabians their distinctive orientation. The study of Marx was their starting point, but they modified many of his economic doctrines: for example, they preferred Jevons's marginal utility theory of value to Marx's labour theory of value; to them surplus value arose not only from the ownership of capital, but also of land and of skills. The class struggle remained, but in a non-revolutionary form; there was not much concern with raising working-class consciousness. The ethical socialism derived from Ruskin, Morris and from the Christian Socialist tradition was brushed aside by Webb and those who thought like him; on the other hand the utilitarian tradition from Bentham to Mill and the positivism of Comte and his English followers was highly relevant to Fabianism of this variety, and so was the statism of T.H. Green. What emerged therefore was a reformist creed, based on an empirical and scientific study of social problems. It did not rely specifically on the working class or trade unions, but on 'canons of moral judgement accepted generally'. Hence the Fabians could work through any political organization or party and their strategy was one of 'permeation', of getting their ideas and prescriptions accepted by those who had the power to put them into practice. Membership of the Fabian Society overlapped with many of the other groups on the far Left, particularly the SDF. As the Society became more clearly reformist, with a strong tendency towards empirical social engineering, many who were more inclined to revolutionary purity or fundamental ethical change left. On the other hand as the Fabians focused on immediate, practical but limited objectives it became possible for people of very divergent fundamental views to unite in pursuing them. It may be open to question to what extent Fabianism was socialism, but the pragmatic advocacy of collectivist remedies was precisely what made it so influential. Reformers of the Fabian variety tended to be marked by another characteristic intellectual and spiritual configuration of the time, the combination of religious agnosticism, ethical idealism and faith in science. This combination has often been called 'secular evangelicalism'. Many of those who shared it had an evangelical upbringing which left them with deeply rooted moral convictions and an active social conscience. Their education had exposed them to the apparent conflict between science and religion and had deprived them of their religious faith. Their moralism was thus left without its religious anchor, but this only redoubled their zeal for social betterment.

The socialist revival remained on the fringe of politics in the 1880s, but the educated public became well aware of its existence and even the Queen wrote of the '*momentary* triumph of Socialism and disgrace to the capital' after the riots of February 1886. One of the reasons why socialism could not escape being noticed was its international character; indeed its British adherents were much influenced by what went on abroad, particularly in Germany. Respectable opinion might still congratulate itself on the fact that the great mass of the British people remained unshaken in its loyalty to existing political parties and institutions. The divisions in the Liberal Party, especially after the Home Rule crisis of 1886, and the ideological weaknesses of Liberal radicalism did, however, create opportunities particularly for tactically flexible socialists like the Fabians, which they were not slow to exploit. The limit to these opportunities was set by the predominantly middle-class composition of the socialist societies and their lack of support in the trade union movement. The SDF tried to strengthen its links with the workers by supporting strikes in various parts of the country, but Hyndman always considered 'the trade union fetish' as the 'chief drawback to our progress'. He felt that it was only a self-seeking aristocracy of labour that was organized in unions and he had nothing but contempt for the trade union leaders, 'the most stodgy-brained, dull-witted, and slow-going time servers in the country'. Among the organizers of what came to be called the New Unionism there were members of the SDF, men like John Burns and Tom Mann, and also individual members of the Fabian Society. The great mass of the working class, whether organized or not, and the trade union establishment remained obstinately loyal to Gladstone and the Liberal Party; the Tory Party could also count on a sizeable working-class vote and a few union leaders, like John Mawdsley of the Lancashire Cotton Spinners, were Tories. Socialism in the 1880s was mainly a form of social criticism and it was only in the 1890s that it began to appear as an organized force in parliamentary politics. Socialism, however, had a future, unlike the republicanism of the early 1870s which had proved a dead end.

IV

Poverty and how to deal with it – this was the great problem that made many turn towards socialism and also bulked large in the Radical programmes of the 1880s. The shift from classical economics made it possible to take a more optimistic view of alleviating poverty. Much of what the dismal science had taught could no longer be regarded as gospel, neither the iron law of wages nor the inevitability of much of the population having to eke out their lives at bare subsistence level. It followed that attempts to raise the living standards of those at the bottom of the economic heap were no longer condemned to futility. The shift from individualism in the wider field of social science and philosophy, in conjunction with the changing views of the economic process, made it difficult to attribute poverty simply to faults of character, such as indolence, improvidence and fecklessness. If poverty was the result of social malfunctioning it had to be tackled by social action; charity or appeals to self-improvement were no longer enough. Notwithstanding the concern about the decline of agriculture and the condition of the agricultural labourer, the poverty that was getting most of the attention in the 1880s was urban. This was a reflection not only of the growing urbanization of the country, but also of the much greater difficulty the traditional institutions for coping with poverty, like the Poor Law, encountered in the great cities. Here the contrast between rich and poor was at its starkest; it inspired guilt and fear among the better-off and aroused the emotions of the reformers and would-be revolutionaries. In the cities, above all in London, the biggest city in the world, an alarming gulf had developed between the prosperous and the poor, which divided even the working classes themselves. The urban population was segregating itself into different housing areas; many of the more prosperous were moving into the suburbs. As we have seen, the building of railways frequently had the effect of destroying a great deal of poorer housing and forcing the displaced inhabitants into even more unwholesome slums. Slum clearance under the Torrens Act of 1868 or the Artisans' Dwelling Act promoted by Cross in 1875 often meant 'shovelling' the poor into denser heaps next door. It was hoped that the railways, by providing workmen's trains and cheaper fares, would themselves help to disperse the working population, but certainly in London such hopes were largely disappointed. The sheer size of the city and the peculiar nature of the London labour market made it necessary for the lowest paid in particular to hang on to whatever habitation they could secure in the centre or the East End. Thus the conditions which Henry Mayhew had described in *London Labour and the London Poor*, and Dickens had translated into fiction in characters like Fagin, persisted. Here lived the 'residuum' which figured so much in the debates on electoral reform. Normally it was an object of curiosity and charity, but every now and again, as in 1866 or 1886, it erupted and struck fear into the minds of the respectable classes.

In the 1880s the London poor and their degrading conditions of life became news as never before. The serious newspapers and periodicals were constantly preoccupied with the problem and it was also grist to the mill of popular and sensational journalism. The *Daily News*, the paper that had first drawn public attention to the Bulgarian Atrocities, ran a regular column by the popular journalist George Sims describing in lurid colours, and not without a similar element of titillation, the hardly less atrocious sufferings of the 'London heathen'. The pamphlet which did for London's poor what Gladstone had done for the oppressed Bulgars, was *The Bitter Cry of Outcast London*; it appeared in the autumn of 1883 and its author was almost certainly Andrew Mearns, the secretary of the London Congregational Union. His purpose was to call for an effort to evangelize the slum-dwellers of London, who had become separated by a widening gulf from the churches and the chapels, but the real impact of his pamphlet came from the detailed descriptions of the horrors of London tenements, peopled by 'one-roomed helots', 'reeking with poisonous and mal-odorous gases arising from the accumulations of sewerage and refuse'. Public attention was now focused firmly on housing; to some extent this was a diversion from the problem of poverty, for it concentrated on symptoms rather than causes. In November 1883 Lord Salisbury entered the fray with an article on 'Labourers' and Artisans' Dwellings' in the *National Review*. He argued that *laissez-faire* had not in the past stood in the way of legislation on housing, in fact the Torrens and Cross Acts had demolished thousands of working-class dwellings; his specific recommendation was for government loans at low rates of interest and he called for more information. Mild as these suggestions were, there was an immediate howl of 'socialism' in many quarters; the *Manchester Guardian* called Salisbury's proposals 'State Socialism pure and simple, and the same arguments which are used to justify the housing of a class at the expense of the community might be used to justify it being fed and clothed in the same way'. Joseph Chamberlain had also gone into print on the housing question and his proposals became part of his Radical Programme. On the one hand his suggestion of taxing the large ground landlords, in line with Henry George's ideas, was far-reaching; on the other hand he was if anything more cautious than Salisbury in the treatment of State intervention in housing.

Early in 1884, on Salisbury's initiative, a Royal Commission on the Housing of the Working Classes was appointed. Salisbury and Cross from the Tories, Dilke, Broadhurst and Jesse Collings from the Liberals, and Cardinal Manning and the Prince of Wales were among those who served on it. Much of the evidence given before the Commission and its report issued in 1885 show the continuing strength of traditional notions about the poor and poverty and reluctance to weaken individual self-reliance by any public action. These traditional notions still inspired the Charity Organization Society, which since its foundation in 1869 had become the most influential body dealing with poverty, particularly in London, and whose representatives gave evidence before the Commission. The Society's approach to the poor was unsullied by any idea that overall reduction of poverty might be a feasible goal and it totally accepted the Poor Law's less-eligibility principle. It distinguished clearly between the deserving and the undeserving poor and in principle help was given only to the former. This help was rendered in such a way that 'habits of providence and self-reliance' were in no way weakened. Within these limits the Society had established a system of district committees and casework administered through paid officers that undoubtedly constituted an advance in the treatment of the poor. Octavia Hill was closely associated with the Charity Organization Society; she was the grand-daughter of Dr Southwood Smith, the public health reformer, and Ruskin had advanced her the money for her first experiment in managed housing in 1865. Although the number of people accommodated in her properties hardly exceeded 4,000, they were mostly drawn from the very poor who were not reached by other model housing companies. She established a personal relationship with her tenants and prided herself on the fact that, without demolition or rehousing, she produced improvement on a self-financing basis. Octavia Hill was totally opposed to State or municipal interference and suspicious even of the type of aid through low interest rates advocated by Salisbury. In her evidence before the Royal Commission on Housing she said: '. . . I do not think that any rate or State-supported scheme could ever meet the requirements of the case, because if you once assume that it is your duty to provide houses for the poor at a price that they assume they can pay, it will just be a rate-in-aid of wages like the old Poor Law system, and if the labour market is in an unsatisfactory state, wages will simply fall . . . the effect of various forms of pauperization on the poor of London is something awful . . .'. A similar note ran through the evidence given by Lord Shaftesbury.

The Commission amassed a great deal of information about wages, rent and housing, particularly in London, the most coherent evidence on poverty until Charles Booth's survey a few years later. It put the wages of casual workers, like costermongers and hawkers at an average of 10 to 12s. a week, of dockers at 8 to 9s. a week, at its highest 12 to 18s. Booth defined poverty as an income of less than 18 to 24s. for a moderate size family. Eighty-eight per cent of the London working class paid more than a fifth of their income in rent, and 46 per cent between a quarter and half. The Commission did not look at the problem of poverty as such, nor did it deal with the more contingent causes of urban population pressure, such as the drift from agricultural employment. The stress was firmly on overcrowding rather than sanitation, as it had been in previous housing legislation. Thus one of its main recommendations, apart from the strengthening of existing legislation and powers of sanitary inspection, was the removal of control over lodging houses from the parish vestries, whose main aim was to keep the rates down, to the Metropolitan Board of Works. Another recommendation was that the sites of some London prisons should be used for the development of working-class housing. The recommendations formed the basis of the Housing of the Working Classes Act of 1885, passed by the Conservatives after their return to office in June of that year. It was a typical example of Tory social reform, or what was now generally called Tory democracy.

Collectivism of this kind was opposed by a number of organizations committed to the individualist position, the best-known among them the Liberty and Property Defence League. The ideological inspiration was largely taken from Herbert Spencer and the network of membership and contacts of the League and other bodies of a similar orientation was widespread in politics, journalism and academic life. Lord Elcho of Adullamite fame, since 1883 the Earl of Wemyss, was a leading light of the League and frequently attacked Salisbury on the housing issue and Torrens, the Liberal MP who had promoted the

Act of 1868, was a member of the League's committee. A number of publicists in the cause of individualism were connected with the LPDL, among them Thomas MacKay, a vice-chairman of the Charity Organization Society, and W.L. Mallock, who later became one of the most active Conservative writers against socialism. In the higher ranks of politics Goschen and the Duke of Argyll took a doctrinaire anti-collectivist line. Goschen as a member of the Royal Commission on Housing added a separate memorandum to its final report opposing the plan to sell the prison lands in London below market value; Argyll resigned from the Gladstone government in 1881 over what he considered the confiscatory clauses of the Irish Land Act. Principled individualism was almost stronger in the Liberal Party, both on its Whig and Radical wings, than it was among Conservatives, where the paternalist tradition was still alive. Henry Fawcett, who died in 1884, and Auberon Herbert were prominent advocates of individualism on the left of the Liberal Party. Charles Bradlaugh was also a strong individualist. His debate on this issue with Hyndman in 1884 seemed to symbolize a change of generations on the far Left in British politics.

V

Imperialism offered another way of transcending the social and economic pressures of the 1880s. It was not a new sentiment, for it held a central place in the great foreign policy debate between Disraeli and Gladstone, and its pedigree then continued back through Palmerston. There was, however, a perceptible change in the nature of imperialism in the 1880s. The earlier debate had been about national power and how it should be asserted; now the focus was on imperial possessions, how they should be acquired, developed and protected and what contribution they might make to national power. Geographically, interest shifted from Europe to Asia, to the overseas territories inhabited by people of British stock and above all to Africa. The new imperialism was a response to threats rather than a sign of undiminished confidence: apprehension of economic decline, concern for markets, rivalry with other imperial nations. Historians have coined the term 'informal empire' for the spread of British influence in the heyday of free trade; now there was less scope for 'informality' or 'absence of mind' in matters of empire and a more conscious cultivation of imperialism, as practice and ideology, was required. It was often laced with a strong dose of Social Darwinism and with racial theories of doubtful validity. Sir Charles Dilke, in his book *Greater Britain*, published in 1860, and the historian J.A. Froude were early advocates of the new imperialism. The classic statement in the 1880s came from J.R. Seeley, the Regius Professor of Modern History at Cambridge, in his lectures on *The Expansion of England*, delivered in 1881 and published in book form in 1883. 'Will the English race, which is divided by so many oceans, making a full use of modern scientific inventions, devise some organization like that of the United States, under which full liberty and solid union may be reconciled with unbounded territorial extension? And secondly shall we succeed in solving a still harder problem? Shall we discover some satisfactory way of governing India . . .?' Seeley sought answers to these questions in history; the survival of the country was possible only as a World State, something other countries like the United States and Russia, perhaps even Germany, could realize in their large compact territories.

He was writing before the scramble for Africa was fully under way and adding yet more urgency to the maintenance of Britain's stake. The acquisition of territory in Africa might be expensive and bring little in the way of immediate returns, but the advocates of expansion were looking to the future. In 1893 Rosebery as Foreign Secretary was justifying the acquisition of Uganda in these words: 'we are engaged at the present moment . . . in "pegging out claims for the future". We have to consider, not what we want, but what we shall want in the future . . . . We should, in my opinion, grossly fail in the task that has been laid upon us if we shrink from responsibilities and decline to take our share in a partition of the world which we have not forced on, but which has been forced upon us . . . .' Although the new imperialism arose from a sense of being threatened, it soon developed many-sided positive arguments. The civilizing mission, the white man's burden, was one prominent strand; the world-wide unity of the British race another. The connection between imperialism and the view of life as a struggle was obvious; the argument that abdication from empire meant racial suicide was often heard. Social Darwinism could be both inward and outward looking. In its classic statement, by Herbert Spencer, it had been inward-looking, justifying free competition and individualism at home and a Cobdenite view of international relations. Now it was more often outward looking; groups, nations, races were struggling for existence and the weaker deserved to go to the wall. There was a clear connection between the state of the nation at home and its ability to compete abroad. Not only did social and economic pressures at home, contracting markets, loss of competitiveness, render cultivation of empire necessary, it was also a healthy domestic condition of the nation that made successful pursuit of empire possible. An ideology of imperialism could hardly fail to develop a dimension of social imperialism. Cecil Rhodes, after seeing conditions in the East End of London in 1895 remarked: 'The Empire . . . is a bread and butter question. If you want to avoid civil war, you must become imperialists.' At its crudest, social imperialism was a way of diverting the attention of the masses from their real grievances to the pursuit of national glory abroad, but many high-minded progressive imperialists embraced the synthesis of social reform and empire with complete intellectual honesty. It was in this way that rising Liberal politicians like Asquith and Haldane, Fabians like Shaw and the Webbs, progressive colonial administrators like Alfred Milner and perhaps most prominently Joseph Chamberlain could regard progress at home and imperial expansion abroad as complementary. Theories about the racial basis of empire, the civilizing mission of the white man, the unity and superiority of the Anglo-Saxon race, found their counterpart in theories about the social health of the population at home. In their more extreme version these took the form of the pseudo-science of eugenics; a less strident version was a cult of national efficiency, which some leading politicians like Rosebery were increasingly in the habit of proclaiming.

The 1880s saw an intensification of the debate about empire, but it was not until the later 1890s and the approach of the Boer War that it was to reach its full force. Part of this debate was the argument about free trade versus protection; calls for fair trade or reciprocity were made in many quarters and a National Fair Trade League was established. It had considerable support in the Conservative Party, but the more prominent Tory leaders were cautious and non-committal in their attitude. It was again only after the Boer War that this question became a central political issue. In the 1880s free trade was still so firmly entrenched that a major departure from it was not practical politics; but with nations like the United States and Germany building up their industries behind high tariff barriers and, particularly Germany, becoming a serious competitor in third markets, the feeling was growing that Britain should look to her imperial markets, where she had an in-built advantage. Imperialism as an ideology was thus closely linked to the many immediate economic and social problems Britain was experiencing; it also influenced the pragmatic day-to-day conduct of foreign and imperial relations.

VI

Industrialization and urbanization, the harbingers of a new civilization of which Britain was the pioneer, had excited awe and admiration and been taken as proof positive of progress. Social critics, from Dickens to Carlyle and from Ruskin to Matthew Arnold had stressed the ambivalence of these achievements. The palpable economic and social problems of the 1880s increased the unease about the urban, industrial way of life and roused the nostalgia, never far below the surface, for the older, simpler ways of an idealized rural England. New faith in industrial progress and the beneficence of the machine age had declined by the 1880s from the heights that had been celebrated 30 years earlier in the Great Exhibition. In the British love–hate relationship with industrialism awareness of the 'dark, satanic' face of industry was growing again, but this went somewhat incongruously with the anxiety about the loss of competitiveness and the rise of trading rivals. The ambivalence of attitudes to industry, technological progress and the making of money is reflected in the shifting composition and outlook of the élites in the British body politic. The decline of the traditionally predominant landed aristocracy was in many ways obvious: it had for long been a major political theme and the sudden onset of agricultural depression seemed to reinforce it. There were certainly examples of political families among the aristocracy finding their ability to play their accustomed role curtailed by falling rent rolls. On the other hand many members of the aristocracy had long since begun the process of broadening their economic interests, through share-holdings and directorships. This movement was facilitated by the increasing use of the joint-stock form of company. W.S. Gilbert's definition of limited liability was that 'some seven men form an association (if possible, all Peers and Baronets)'. The branching out from agriculture into industry and commerce was made easier by the fact that the running of large agricultural estates had been a commercial enterprise in Britain for a long time and in many cases, where landed estates had mining interests or other industrial undertakings attached, had been virtually indistinguishable from industrial activity.

The obverse side of the commercialization of the landed classes was the assimilation of the successful business man and entrepreneur into the ranks of the traditional aristocracy and his conversion to their values. It was a well-worn mechanism that had functioned even in the eighteenth century and had been helped in the nineteenth century by integrative institutions like the public schools. It did not always function smoothly and great antagonisms arose in the days of the Anti-Corn Law League or in the wake of the Crimean War. Mutual distaste was not entirely dead in the 1880s and was one of the causes of the tensions that arose in the Conservative Party in the early years of the decade. Lord Randolph Churchill's dismissive remarks about the owners of 'vineries and pineries' and the tedium Lord Salisbury experienced in his rare contacts with provincial party leaders are vivid illustrations of continuing antipathies. Nonetheless, the Tory Party was becoming another integrative institution in which the upper bourgeoisie and the aristocracy were moulded into a homogeneous upper class. Paradoxically the aristocracy, in spite of its clear political decline and the economic difficulties it was undergoing in the agricultural sector, did not suffer a commensurate loss of confidence. Aristocratic values and life styles were still admired and imitated; from the ranks of those successful in business and commerce there was a steady stream of recruits for the life of the country gentleman. The English country house continued to function with scarcely diminished glory: the agricultural depression forced some families to sell up, but there was little difficulty in finding buyers from among more recently arrived dynasties in business and commerce and new houses on a grand scale were still being built.

Some of the greatest fortunes in the land had not been made in industry but came from finance even at the height of the Industrial Revolution. Of the 60 millionaires who died in the period 1880 to 1899 and whose wealth was not landed, 13 came from banking, merchant banking and stockbroking, 12 from brewing and distilling, but only 9 from iron and steel, shipbuilding and engineering. For the period 1900–19, of the 101 non-landed millionaires who died, 30 came from the financial sectors, 10 from brewing and distilling and only 8 from iron and steel, shipbuilding and engineering. In the whole period between 1809 and 1914 only one Manchester cotton manufacturer left an estate of more than one million. The size to which a fortune could grow was more limited in manufacturing than it was in finance; moreover most British manufacturers did not extend their major investments beyond their own firms, while it was easier for those in finance to have a spread of interests and this was further facilitated by the increasing number of limited liability public companies. Well known families in banking and finance, the Barings, Rothschilds, Lloyds, Gurneys and others, found assimilation to the aristocracy easy even if they were not Anglicans, and they had a dynastic approach to their wealth, similar to the relationship of the great landed families to their estates. The same was to some extent true of the brewers, families like the Charringtons, Whitbreads and Meux. Most of the financial wealth came from the City of London and some of the brewing wealth was also London-based. Manufacturers and industrialists were inevitably more provincial; in such families those in the second and third generation were more likely to retreat from active connection with the family business and to use their inherited wealth in rentier fashion to become leisured country gentlemen or to underpin a career outside the business world. This could be evidence of a decline of the entrepreneurial spirit, but it was also a way of letting in fresh blood. In any case the self-made entrepreneur, with a nonconformist background, had never been as typical of an earlier phase of the Industrial Revolution as has often been supposed.

Among the upper ranks of British society there always had been a considerable degree of social mobility and there was clear evidence for it in the period after 1880. It is symbolized by the suddenness with which, around 1885, territorial titles, principally peerages, but also baronetcies, became available to men of substance even if their wealth did not derive from land. Disraeli was still reluctant during his last period in office to grant such titles to provincial supporters, however wealthy, if they did not own land. Thus Andrew Barclay Walker, the great Liverpool brewing magnate, who left about three million when he died in 1893, was several times Mayor of Liverpool and gave the Walker Art Gallery to the city, was suggested for a baronetcy in 1874, after having been host to the Duke of Edinburgh. Comparison was made with Sir William Brown, a Liberal donor of the Liverpool City Library, who was made a baronet in 1863; significantly Brown was a merchant banker, partly London-based and the Brown family turned to Liberal Unionism in 1886. Lord Sandon, Liverpool's aristocratic Tory MP, anxious though he was to secure recognition for Walker from his own Government, had to point out that a baronetcy would 'socially' hardly do. Walker had to content himself with a knighthood in 1877, but was advanced to a baronetcy by the Salisbury Government in 1886.

Social mobility among the élites in British society also encompassed the professional classes. When Matthew Arnold was conducting his investigations into continental educational systems on behalf of the Taunton Commission in 1866, he found that the professions did not anywhere share the outlook of the upper class as much as they did in England; though he also noted that in England the professions were 'separate, to a degree unknown on the Continent, from the commercial and industrial class with which in social standing they are naturally on a level'. In the mid-nineteenth century most professions had established their standing by acquiring governing bodies, often with a royal charter, which to a greater or lesser degree could regulate entry by defining qualifications and by setting examinations for the acquisition of such qualifications. This movement was still going on: for example the Royal Institute of British Architects, the Institute of

Chartered Accountants and the Surveyors' Institution were all set up in the 1880s; the Medical Act of 1886 created a conjoint qualification and in engineering qualifying examinations were introduced in 1898.

The numbers of professional men were still increasing much faster than the general population, though no longer as fast as in the middle of the century. Since 1841 the census had listed various professional occupations, gradually adding categories and refinements, but there is naturally much uncertainty about the definitions used. Nevertheless, the general picture of a rapid increase in the size of the professional classes is correct: between 1841 and 1881 those who listed themselves in professional occupations, exclusive of teachers, increased by 103 per cent and there was another increase of 50 per cent by 1911. The increase was, however, much slower in the older professions, the law, medicine and particularly the Church. It was, however, just these older professions whose status was closest to the upper classes: ministers of religion were clearly a special case; barristers had long enjoyed high status, solicitors, especially in London, had risen more recently; doctors were still fighting their way in. When Lister received a peerage in 1897 it was for his scientific work, and not as a doctor. It was a matter for fine judgement which part of the whole spectrum of the professional classes was within striking distance of the upper classes. It depended mainly on education and income. As for education, the public schools again performed a vital function in amalgamating the upper reaches of the professions with the other strata at the top of society. Much of the demand for public school education, which produced such a notable increase in the number of schools, came from the professional classes. Incomes in the professional classes varied very widely and there were many different opinions about their level. In the law very high salaries were paid to judges, £5,000 a year to puisne judges and £8,000 to the Chief Justice of the Queen's Bench. Few QCs earned as much as this and for junior barristers £500 to £1,200 was regarded as normal. Solicitors did not make as much, but often had opportunities to engage in profitable investments. As for doctors, in London and other great towns they could make £2,000 and more and really distinguished doctors could make a great deal more; but for the average General Practitioner elsewhere £500 or £600 was about the average. In the Church incomes were naturally much lower; only a very small proportion of benefices were worth more than £1,000 annually and the majority lay between £100 and £400. It was therefore only the upper ranks of the professions that had the wherewithal to meet other sections of the upper classes on something like equal terms.

VII

By the 1880s the public-school ethos of the later nineteenth century had burst into full flower and was having its impact upon all sections of the upper classes. The aim of the schools was to produce English gentlemen; the academic education they offered was still predominantly based on the classics, but the building of character was regarded as at least as important as academic achievement. Dr Arnold's vision of turning boys into Christian gentlemen, manly and virtuous, had in the course of time, at other schools and through other men, undergone developments reflecting the manifold changes in the general environment and the clientele of the schools. The cult of organized games and athleticism had become pervasive and sometimes obsessive and had become a prime element in character-building. The different varieties of football played in the older public schools were rough and sometimes brutal and formed part of the unsupervised leisure activities of the boys. The codification of the rules of football and cricket was one of the points at which developments within the public schools, increasingly separated from the rest of society by their role in the formation of an élite, fed back into the lives of the mass of the people; football in particular was about to take a central place in the leisure time of the urban working class. The growing place of sport in public school life was partly the result of changing religious sensibilities, a turn from an emphasis on moral earnestness and a Christian code of inner discipline to a more extrovert, 'muscular' Christianity. Thomas Hughes in *Tom Brown's Schooldays* purports to depict Arnold's Rugby, but the revered Doctor would not have recognized the place as entirely true to his ideals. Organized games fulfilled an essential function in bringing the lives of boys in a boarding school effectively under the control of the authorities. Gone were the days when boys outside the classroom were largely left to their own devices, a system to which even Dr Arnold had still subscribed, although it had been his central purpose to ensure that this freedom should not be abused in licentious and brutal behaviour. In the public school of the later nineteenth century the day was almost entirely organized from morning to night, in the classroom or on the playing field and neither idle hands or thoughts were allowed to stray into mischief. It was a totally formative experience and few of those who underwent it, even the small minority who rebelled against it, escaped being indelibly marked by it.

Not far removed from sport and athleticism was the inculcation of a patriotic and even martial spirit. The schools were training not merely a national but an imperial governing class and their playing fields were preparing boys for the work of imperial expansion and administration. A college song from Marlborough, a school particularly strongly influenced by athleticism, proclaimed: 'Be strong, Elevens to bowl and shoot, Be strong, O Regiment of the foot, with ball of skin or lead or leather, Stand for the Commonwealth together'. Most of the schools had cadet or rifle corps; a Christian soldier like General Gordon was a hero figure. It was, however, only after the Boer War that the importance of military training was fully recognized in the public schools and officer training corps incorporated in the reserve system created by Haldane's army reforms.

Not even its own custodians always accepted the public-school ethos uncritically. Excessive concentration on games and competition for sporting success could produce philistinism or straightforward ignorance and headmasters and others tried from time to time to redress the balance. Some put down the failures in the Boer War to the amateurism and lack of seriousness inculcated by the mentality of the playing field. In his poem 'The Islanders', published in January 1902, Kipling voiced his feeling of the British imperial mission betrayed: 'Then ye returned to your trinkets; then ye contented your souls. With the flannelled fools at the wicket or the muddied oafs at the goals'. From the Clarendon Commission onwards there was pressure on the public schools to broaden their curriculum and in particular to increase and improve their science teaching. This was an uphill struggle, for it continued to be strongly and sincerely held that the classics educated the whole man, while science imparted merely information, which at best was at a lower utilitarian level and at worst was quickly forgotten. There were practical difficulties about providing more science teaching: ultimately the schools had to cater for the wishes of fee-paying parents, who wanted their sons to receive an education fit for gentlemen and could see little relevance in having them exposed to such 'stinks'; moreover good science teachers were difficult to find, especially as the salaries offered to them and even to modern language teachers were much lower than those acceptable for classics dons. Yet leading engineers and scientists like Brunel and Lyon Playfair sent their sons to public schools. Again some headmasters did not share the view that science had little educative value. F.W. Sanderson who, after a period as an assistant master at Dulwich, became headmaster of Oundle in 1892, was a notable example. Oundle was the kind of local grammar school that had come under investigation by the Taunton Commission, but which in the end was left to its own devices. Soon the attempt was made to elevate it into a public school, by developing a 'second grade modern school' to which the local tradesmen could continue to send their children, while the grammar school was to be 'composed exclusively of the sons of gentlemen, almost all being boarders'. The attempt to turn Oundle into a public school had not been completely successful by the time Sanderson took over. He gave it a distinctive character by giving science and technical education, as well as languages, history, art, music and handicrafts their full place in the curriculum. He wanted every boy to develop his potential and was thus a pioneer of modern educational principles.

After 1902 the development of State secondary education under the Balfour Act put increasing pressure on all public schools to broaden their curriculum and make provision for scientific education on a level with other fields of knowledge. Even this did not alter their basic orientation: their products were equipped to act as self-confident leaders in all walks of life, a quality sometimes denounced as 'well-bred arrogance'; they were given a general training of the mind, but were taught to regard the amateur with character as superior to the expert with knowledge. The ideals which inspired the public schools were naturally far removed from those of the counting house; money-making, profit, industry and production had no place in their ethos. When the sons of northern, provincial industrial and commercial dynasties began to arrive in southern public schools the intention of their parents was to emancipate them from their origins, their accents and their cousinage. Many such families, Hornbys from Blackburn, Birleys from Manchester, Bibbys and Holts from Liverpool, were, particularly the Anglicans, already gentrified for two or three generations; often they had built themselves houses in the country, had become Tories if they had not always been, were magistrates and held commissions in the Volunteers. Sending their sons away to a major boarding school, instead of to the local grammar school, meant that they were becoming yet more fully part of a nation-wide, homogeneous upper class. In a maturing industrial economy and with so many second or third-generation industrial and commercial dynasties among their clientele it was only natural that public schools should not look to production and profit as their foremost ideal.

VIII

When alarm was expressed about Britain's loss of economic leadership the public schools were not, apart from their excessive concentration on the classics, singled out for blame. In Germany, which in educational matters was so often taken as a model, the gymnasia also provided a predominantly classical education and the eagerness of the bourgeoisie to embrace the values of a much more feudal-military aristocracy was even greater than in Britain. A more common target for criticism was the British failure to provide enough scientific education and technical training in general and the narrow base of university education especially in England. James Bryce complained in 1885 that Germany with a population of 45 million had over 24,000 university students while in England and Wales with 27 million there were only 5,500. Britain certainly could not boast institutions comparable to the German *Technische Hochschule*; but there was a wide variety of establishments, from Mechanics Institutes and learned societies to the prestigious Royal Institution, from professional colleges to institutions with the claim of being almost fully-fledged civic universities, like Owen's College, Manchester. There were the chartered Universities of London, a great examining machine with affiliated colleges, and of Durham, and both were granting degrees in science. But many of these colleges had never fulfilled the hopes reposed in them and were struggling financially and in student numbers. Gladstone had appointed a Royal Commission on Scientific Instruction in 1870, which recommended a greater scientific element in school-leaving examinations and more science professors and research at Oxford and Cambridge and other universities. Fifteen years later the Royal Commission on the Trade Depression was still pointing to the superiority of American and German university education, particularly in science.

By the 1880s, however, the tide was turning. New civic institutions of higher education, with a strong scientific and technical element, were being founded at Leeds, Newcastle, Birmingham, Bristol and Liverpool. The initiative often came from leading local industrial or commercial magnates, with representatives from the aristocracy and gentry with local connections taking a part in the founding committees and governing bodies. Long-standing suspicions, between Anglicans and dissenters, and between the protagonists of the old classical and religious curriculum and the advocates of scientific and secular culture, were now less in evidence. It was another milestone when in 1880 the Victoria University of Manchester, with Owens College as its first constituent college, was granted a charter by the Privy Council. For a time it was to play a role in Lancashire and Yorkshire as a federal university similar to that played by the University of London elsewhere.

Another impulse to the spread of higher education came from the University Extension Movement at Cambridge and later at Oxford. Ideas for making the benefits of what the two older universities had to offer available to a wider public outside their walls were first mooted in the 1850s and in the 1870s both universities set up organizations for providing extension lectures. The motive was not merely that the spread of education should be undertaken as good in itself, but that under-privileged groups such as members of the working classes and women should be helped. The object of helping the working classes was slow in being achieved and it was only a generation later that organizations like the Workers' Educational Association managed to establish an effective link between the older universities and working men who saw in education a tool of emancipation. The University Extension Movement did, however, make an immediate contribution to the expansion of higher education by linking up with local colleges and Mechanics' Institutes and stimulating the establishment of new extension colleges. At Nottingham, Sheffield, Reading and elsewhere they became the starting point for future university colleges and universities.

Such institutions and most of the existing older ones could not thrive to the fullest extent as long as they were dependent on private or local sources of finance. The fears about Britain's industrial decline were again a strong lever for eventually prising support from the central government. In 1887 the Hartley Institution at Southampton, which was planning to turn itself into a university college, called a meeting of similar colleges to press the government for a grant of £50,000 to English university colleges. Various speakers drew attention to the world-wide competition from more educated foreigners. In 1889 the Treasury at last provided £15,000 for distribution to the colleges and set up a committee of distinguished men to supervise the disbursement of the grant, a University Grants Committee in embryo. At this time a Technical Instruction Act was also passed to enable the county and county borough councils, established under the Act of 1888, to levy a rate for technical education. The Technical Education Committee of the London County Council under Sidney Webb became a powerful organ for promoting technical education. Through it various institutions of the Polytechnic type, including the Regent Street Polytechnic refounded in 1882 by Quintin Hogg, were aided and new ones established. The Webbs, together with Haldane, became leading influences in British university development in the 1890s and in the new century; the establishment of the London School of Economics and of Imperial College, the British Charlottenburg, owed much to them.

Thus there was much progress in higher education and particularly in scientific and technical education, though it came late and exhibited a typically British diversity of institutions and methods. The spur was not only fear of the loss of industrial supremacy, but also faith in education as an engine of progress. In spite of the expansion of opportunities the criticism was never stilled, before 1914, that what Britain was doing was too little and too late in comparison with her competitors. It was true that Britain had lost the lead in some newer technologies like chemicals and electricity. A close examination of the electrical industry shows, however, that it is very difficult to establish a link between the fact that Britain was slower in adopting or manu-facturing electricity and electrical devices in their various forms and the slow development of higher education or the hostility to produc-tive industry and loss of entrepreneurial spirit among the upper classes. For a variety of reasons, some of them demographic, the British economy was growing more slowly than that of Germany or the USA in the 1880s and after, and the more rapid adoption of electricity would at best have made only a marginal contribution to more rapid growth. Gas was much cheaper in Britain than in the United States and the adoption of electricity for lighting was therefore bound to be slower. Urbanization was advanced much earlier in Britain than in the USA or Germany and was no longer going on as explosively as in those countries; house-building was therefore proceeding relatively more slowly towards the end of the century and the additional benefits to be reaped from urban electric tramways and underground railways was more limited. Urban and suburban railway networks based on steam were already largely constructed by the 1870s and 1880s in Britain. An extensive underground electric railway network was in fact built in London before 1914, but the economic returns were not very good. This was in spite of the fact that London's population was still growing more rapidly than that of the country as a whole and that the number of passengers carried by the London transport system grew about eight-fold between 1881 and 1915. It was perhaps unfortunate for electric transport that almost as soon as it arrived it began to face competition from the internal combustion engine. British industrialists were conservative, but there was often good reason for their conservatism. It did not necessarily always pay to scrap well-functioning plant for new technology. Undoubtedly Britain was slow in developing a capacity for manufac-turing electrical machinery, but under conditions of free trade this was not too much of a disadvantage.

In the chemical industry the British failure to develop a large-scale dye-stuff industry was serious and the Germans eventually took 80 per cent of the market. Originally Britain, with its large use of dye-stuffs in the textile industry, had a considerable lead. Some of the scientists who had established that lead had turned into entrepre-neurs, but by the 1870s most of these had retired and a few had returned to Germany, whence they had come in the hey-day of British industrial supremacy. Subsequently British industrialists were slow to see the importance of developing synthetic dye-stuffs and of the research required to do so. Here lack of scientific education and the tendency to rest on one's laurels made themselves felt. Other factors were, however, also at work, for example the state of the patent law, which enabled foreign manufacturers to take out British patents with the sole object of preventing the exploitation of the process in the British market. Thus Britain suffered some disabilities as a result of being a more mature industrial nation, but loss of entrepreneurial spirit and nostalgia for a pre-industrial past were perhaps over-estimated both by contemporaries and subsequent generations as causes of national decline.

IX

If there was national decline it was relative and not absolute; feared as a prospect for the future rather than experienced as a contemporary reality. Trade depression and growing awareness of poverty as a social problem had not seriously dented faith in progress. For those in work real wages were still rising and leisure was increasing. The working week for a growing number of the manually employed now finished around Saturday lunchtime. This left great scope for leisure and recreation in a form appropriate to urban dwellers who have to spend their working lives in factories. It was therefore not a paradox that England, as the first country to experience a high degree of urbanization, was now to give the world many of the organized sports of modern times. Association Football is the most obvious case in point. The game took on its modern regulated form mainly from the varieties of it played in the leading public schools. Written rules were formulated, clubs were formed and the Football Association formed in London in the 1860s gradually came to be recognized as the leading authority in the game. Football clubs were initially mostly middle-class, formed by old boys of schools where they had played the game. As a working-class sport, clubs were being organized with their base in churches or chapels, in public houses or at the workplace. The setting-up of a works team was a way in which, at a time of increasing impersonalization of employment and growing distance between employers and men, a sense of loyalty to the firm could be maintained. West Ham United, set up in 1895, was an example of a team established in a paternalistic effort to improve industrial relations in one of the largest Thames shipyards. Football rapidly became the most popular spectator sport: whereas in the 1870s only one or two games a year were estimated to have been attended by more than 10,000, by the 1880s the number had risen well into two figures. More organized competition between clubs, with the Football League being founded in 1888, soon sent the numbers up further: in 1897 a cup final crowd first exceeded 50,000. The sport became at least partly professionalized, to which there was in Association Football less resistance than in cricket or rugby. In the early 1900s there were some 4,000 to 5,000 professional players, though at the time of the 1909 budget the Football Association still claimed to be speaking for over 300,000 amateur players organized in 12,000 clubs. It was noted that the great football crowds were increasingly working-class in make-up and no other sport became so much part of working-class culture in all its aspects, spectators, professional players and attendant features like gambling. Thus the professionalization of the sport made for class separation, yet it could also make a contribution to social harmony: the organization and business aspect of the clubs brought the classes together and support for the home team fostered local loyalties.

Municipal parks, public baths and libraries, and other amenities made their appearance more and more frequently as part of the civic culture at this time and were another way in which the urban environment, now accepted, in spite of bouts of rural nostalgia, as the common lot of most Britons, could be improved. The concern for reform was shifting from the basic necessities, such as public health, sewage, water and housing, to the improvement of the quality of life. Following the example of Chamberlain's 'municipal socialism', municipalities were often responsible for introducing such amenities, but much was also achieved as a result of private philanthropy. In either case it was often the leading industrial and commercial families in the larger cities who took the initiative, in a combination of local pride, paternalism and social concern. In the public library movement, for example, which acquired great momentum after 1880, municipal support and private philanthropy came strikingly together. Since 1855 towns with over 5,000 inhabitants had been allowed to levy a penny rate for libraries, but the considerable capital expense involved in establishing new libraries made private benefactions essential. Sir William Brown at Liverpool had become one of the first to use his wealth for this purpose, with a gift of £40,000 in 1863; many others followed, among them W.H. Wills, the British tobacco manufacturer and in 1906 the first nonconformist peer, and later Andrew Carnegie, the Scottish steel magnate. The public library movement testified to the continuing strength of the progressive faith,

because libraries were not only amenities but more significantly bea-
cons of enlightenment. As Gladstone himself put it: 'These libraries,
these gymnasia, these museums, this system of public education, they
are all instruments with which a war is carried on. War against what?
War against ignorance, war against brutality.' Faith in the possibility
of improving the quality of life in an urban environment showed itself
in many other ways. Sir Titus Salt had become in the 1850s the
pioneer of the New Model employers. Influenced by Ruskin and by
Disraeli's picture of Trafford of Woodgate as the ideal employer he
built the model village of Saltaire near Bradford for his work force.
Others followed suit, the Ripley family, also at Bradford, the Akroyds
at Halifax, Samuel Morley, later W.H. Lever at Port Sunlight and
the Cadburys at Bourneville. Towards the end of the century
Ebenezer Howard advocated the building of garden cities, and
Letchworth became an example of his ideas. Neither new-model
employers nor garden cities became the norm, but even as isolated
cases they set standards and raised expectations.

Continuing faith in progress, improvement, education and
enlightenment indicate that the economic uncertainties of the 1880s
did not seriously undermine Victorian confidence. Some were fearful
and a few hoped that the future would bring great social upheavals,
with the masses, herded together in the slums of great cities and
moved by new religions like socialism rising up to smash the existing
order. There were indeed many developments that lent colour to such
a vision and it is not difficult to discern the trends that were putting
class above religious and community ties as the determining factor in
social and political relations. The corollary of the consolidation of a
homogeneous upper class was its increasing separation from those
below it, in particular the growing distance between the industrial
employer and his workforce. It was a physical as well as a psycho-
logical distance, with the employers moving into segregated residential quarters of cities or out into the country. Amongst the workforce
the experience of working in a large factory, which in an earlier phase
of the industrial revolution had been confined to a few industries like
textiles, was becoming more the rule. In such circumstances and as a
result of technological developments, skill differentials among
workers were becoming less significant. It was comparatively easy to
pick up the skills required for any industrial employment and in a
number of industries the apprenticeship system was breaking down.
The concept of a labour aristocracy, always difficult to pin down, was
also becoming less significant. The level of prosperity in a working-
class household was in any case not simply determined by the earning
power of the bread winner, but many other factors, such as the size of
the family, the number of earners within it and the skill and prudence

exercised in the management of its affairs. To the extent that there was a labour aristocracy its role was not that ascribed to it by Friedrich Engels, when towards the end of his life he felt increasingly frustrated by the failure of the British working class to live up to Marxist revolutionary expectations. The labour aristocracy had never been so much an emollient of the class struggle as an incubator of political consciousness and provider of political activists. It may, however, also be true that politically conscious active members of the upper echelons of the working classes helped to steer events in a reformist rather than a revolutionary direction.

Even if in the 1880s the trends were towards a more class-based society, the evolution was slow and it was towards a structure with many layers rather than a simple polarization of capital and labour. As it was, religious and community loyalties were still very strong and regional variations very great. In Lancashire the existence of large, modern textile factories, with relatively advanced industrial relations, helped to foster a loyalty to the employer and the firm. The workforce took its political colour from the employer, even after the introduction of the secret ballot made the exercise of direct pressure difficult. Deference is often given as an explanation for the existence of a large Tory working-class vote, particularly in Lancashire, but deferential habits of behaviour were equally effective in maintaining the ability of the Liberal Party to appeal across class lines. Deference was a compound of feelings of solidarity and clannishness, encouraged by paternalism, and genuine respect for one's betters; but into it there also want less admirable sentiments, such as snobbery and the lack of confidence felt by the poor in the presence of the more successful; and an undercurrent of fear and coercion was not absent. In the West Riding of Yorkshire a more primitive textile industry, more exposed to market fluctuations, kept an existing tradition of radicalism going and facilitated an early rise of an independent political labour interest. Everywhere the cleavage between church and chapel was still of overriding importance. A city like Liverpool, with its deep sectarian divisions and large Irish population, had a wholly distinctive social and political profile. London was a case *sui generis*: much of the manual employment was either connected with its huge port or was in small firms producing luxuries for the wealthy; there was also a rapidly increasing class of white-collar workers employed in what was the largest concentration of commerce and finance in the world. In complete contrast the tightly-knit mining communities of the coalfields, varying again in their economic circumstances, furnished the most stable basis for working-class Liberalism. In many such communities the marriage between Liberalism and nonconformity, particularly Methodism, was still intact and embraced owners and men. Solidarity and trade unionism did not inevitably connect with class consciousness and the miners, in defending their economic interest, did not necessarily challenge the social order. The special ethnic, religious and cultural situation of Scotland and Wales added yet another dimension. With the extension of the franchise, the Liberal and Conservative Parties had to develop machinery and techniques to organize this diversity for their own political ends. This was the endeavour of politicians like Joseph Chamberlain, and party organisers like Gorst. Britain retained her distinctive political culture and the day of class-parties comparable to the German Social Democrats was slow in dawning.

The 1880s saw dramatic developments in the parliamentary parties which are the theme of the next chapter. These events are largely autonomous, independent of the evolution at the grass roots, and were the result of the interplay of parliamentary forces and personalities. Nevertheless it would be unreal to separate artificially the drama of high politics from either the slow-burning changes in the cities, the countryside, the factories and the boardrooms, or from the movement of ideas and perceptions.

5 Ireland Transforms British Politics 1880–1886

I

During the first Midlothian campaign Gladstone had challenged Disraeli to dissolve Parliament and had pointed out that in his experience, stretching over half a century, parliaments had never lasted beyond six sessions. Nonetheless, the Parliament of 1874 assembled for a seventh session in February 1880, but within a month a dissolution was announced. The main reason why ministers reversed their decision to soldier on was the impression, mistaken as it turned out, that Tory electoral fortunes were on the mend. After performing reasonably in two by-elections at the beginning of the year, the Conservatives scored a real triumph after the reassembly of Parliament by taking a normally Liberal seat at Southwark. Skene, Gorst's incompetent successor at the Conservative Central Office, advised Disraeli strongly to dissolve immediately rather than wait until the autumn.

Not much had been heard from the Prime Minister since Gladstone's pilgrimage of passion to Midlothian and as a peer he was not expected to take part in the election campaign. His sole incursion into the battle was an attempt to turn the state of Ireland into an issue and it made little impact. Other leading Conservatives could not match the Liberal front bench in rhetorical power and energy. Gladstone embarked upon a second Midlothian campaign and kept the themes of 'Beaconsfieldism' firmly in the forefront of the public mind. It was a backward-looking election: the past sins of the government's foreign policy, the resulting financial extravagance and the depression of trade were the staple diet of Liberal speeches; the Conservatives harked back to peace with honour and perceived signs of an economic recovery. Little was said on either side about future legislation. The Liberals made a commitment to put the county franchise on the same basis as the borough franchise and only a few on the Right of the Party, notably Lowe and Goschen, refused to endorse this commitment. The Liberals also undertook to relax the laws of settlement and entail. They had considerable hopes of driving a wedge between

landlords and tenant farmers, normally united in support of the
Tories. The Farmers' Alliance, a pressure group of tenant farmers
loosely attached to the Liberal Party, was active in many constituencies and received pledges from about 60 candidates, nearly all of them
Liberals.

A new and controversial feature of this election was the intervention of the National Liberal Federation. After the Liberal victory
Chamberlain claimed that the federation had fought in 67 boroughs,
in 60 of them successfully, and had won seats in 10 county
constituencies. Chamberlain's claims were not universally accepted
and many on the Right of the Liberal Party saw in the Federation a
divisive force. The advocates of the Federation claimed that it was in
fact an instrument for bringing order into the diversity of Liberal
interest groups and opinions. When the National Liberal Federation
was being blamed for the loss of the Southwark by-election,
Gladstone disagreed and felt that what had operated was a 'counter-
feit' of the Birmingham organization, 'mobile sections . . . *dub* themselves representatives of Ward A, Ward B and so on . . . and then go
through a mischievous farce in *choosing* candidates'. Other parts of the
Liberal organization, such as the Central Liberal Association and
London Ward Associations not affiliated to the NLF, were working
well in 1880; the activists, whose alienation had damaged the party in
1874, were now enthusiastically back in the fold. In contrast the
Conservative organization had decayed after Gorst's departure,
though the Tories were, like most election losers, inclined to impute
too much of their misfortune to faulty organization.

The result of the election amounted to an almost exact reversal of
the 1874 election. The Liberals now had that majority of about 50
over Conservatives and Home Rulers that the Tories had had over
the other two parties in 1874. The Liberals did particularly well in
Yorkshire, where they had always been strong, Lancashire, where
they wiped out the Tory gains not only 1874 but also of 1868, and in
the Midlands. They also did well in Wales, where the Tories were left
with only two seats, and in Scotland. The Conservatives further
improved their position in the Home Counties and held their own in
London. This was further evidence of the secular drift of the suburban middle classes into the Tory camp; in London Beaconsfieldism
had always been popular, not only among the well-to-do, but also
among the working classes. The agricultural depression and the split
in the farming interest weakened the Conservative position in the
counties but not drastically. The reversal of votes was not as great as
that of seats; there was evidence that in large urban constituencies the
Conservatives were not quite pushed back to the position of 1868 and
that Tory democracy had some substance to it. The Liberal victory

and its size came as a surprise to many, for most of the metropolitan press was expecting the government narrowly to survive. Disraeli had been sufficiently confident of victory to allow the Queen to depart for a holiday in Baden-Baden; when he telegraphed news of his defeat her comment to Ponsonby, her private secretary, was 'this is a terrible telegram'.

On her return the Queen had to face the problem of Disraeli's successor. The Liberal victory was Gladstone's and there was never much doubt that he must be her eventual choice. It was, however, both constitutionally proper and only courteous that Granville and Hartington, the two formal leaders of the Party, should be consulted and given the opportunity to form a government. Disraeli advised the Queen to send for Hartington, although he was the junior of the two. Herbert Gladstone later thought it had been an attempt to keep his father out of office, for Disraeli knew that Hartington was much less likely to make way for Gladstone than Granville. There were no doubt many, both on the right and on the left of the Liberal Party, who would have been glad to seize this opportunity to rid themselves of an overpowering and ageing leader, had this been possible. Both Hartington and Granville made it clear to the Queen that they saw no alternative to Gladstone as head of the government and she had to bow to the inevitable. Gladstone's protestations that he would not be Prime Minister for long were genuine enough: he wanted to settle accounts with Beaconsfieldism and this was the one clear mandate the election had given.

Gladstone put together a cabinet very much in the traditional mould. Many of the leading posts went to Whigs: Granville was again Foreign Secretary, Hartington went to the India Office, Spencer became Lord President and Kimberley returned to the Colonial Office. Gladstone, lifted back into office by popular forces, felt that this was a proper and necessary obeisance to the traditional balance of forces in the Party. He was more reluctant to accept the claims of the Radical wing and of the representatives of the National Liberal Federation. His intention to apply 'Peel's rule', that no one should be admitted to cabinet office who had not previously held junior office, would have kept both Chamberlain and Dilke out of the cabinet. It was an indication of the enhanced status of the Radicals and of the close personal ties between the two Radical leaders that Gladstone was forced to break the rule, if indeed it can be said to have existed, and appoint Chamberlain as President of the Board of Trade, with a seat in the cabinet. Dilke was the more likely candidate for cabinet office, but his espousal of republicanism would have made it difficult to get the Queen's consent to an appointment that would have brought him into personal contact with her. Dilke was made Under Secretary at the Foreign Office, an important position since the Foreign Secretary was in the House of Lords. Chamberlain and Dilke had seen the National Liberal Federation as a means of remodelling the Liberal Party along new lines; their entry into Gladstone's cabinet meant that they were now accepting the rules of the game of Liberal politics as traditionally played. John Bright, still the doyen of the Left but remote from the new-model Radicalism of Chamberlain and Dilke, also entered the cabinet, as Chancellor of the Duchy of Lancaster.

It was a much more factionalized cabinet than Gladstone's first administration had been, but this was only one of the reasons for the rough passage it experienced in the next five years. Another was the sheer pressure of events that crowded in upon it, Egypt, the Sudan, South Africa, Afghanistan, the Bradlaugh case, but above all Ireland. If it is the test of successful statesmanship to achieve some mastery over uncovenanted events, then Gladstone's second ministry did not pass it with flying colours. The succession of crises through which this government passed aggravated but also concealed its lack of a domestic programme. This time there was no accumulation of important departmental measures waiting for their place in the parliamentary queue as there had been in 1868. Not only the various crises, but also the log-jam in the parliamentary machine, caused largely by Irish obstruction, would have made the passage of any legislative programme difficult. Reforms which might have been approved by a broad consensus in the Liberal Party were postponed: for example local government reform which could have been part of a pattern of devolution helpful in the Irish situation, a new system of government for London, or a revision of the land laws to which the Party was pledged. On the other hand the extension of the county franchise, to which the Party was also committed, but which had to wait until the session of 1884, was a massive political achievement by any standards. The Irish Land Act of 1881 was also a great parliamentary feat and made a major contribution to the solution of the Irish agrarian problem. For all its shortcomings and in spite of the crises that beset it, the second Gladstone government was therefore by no means barren of success.

II

The reversal of Beaconsfieldism was the most obvious immediate task for the government, but it conflicted with the principle of continuity in foreign policy. Once burdened with the responsibilities of office the Liberals had to practise continuity to a much greater extent than the pronouncements of Gladstone and others in Opposition would have led one to expect. There was, however, a distinct change of approach. Dedication to the Concert of Europe and to the public law of Europe played a very real rôle in the conduct of foreign policy by Gladstone and Granville. Recording a conversation with Granville in September 1880 about carrying out the Treaty of Berlin, Gladstone wrote: 'Our policy thus was only as follows: to require what Europe had decided, and to require it through the agency of Europe.' Unfortunately it was not an easy policy to pursue when all the other Great Powers of Europe acted on a meticulous calculation of their advantage and neither Gladstone nor Granville were always competent in pursuing it. After five years of Liberal government, Salisbury's verdict was 'They have at least achieved their long-desired "Concert of Europe". They have succeeded in uniting the Continent of Europe – against England.' The reversal of 'forward' policies proved easiest in the case of Afghanistan. Lytton was recalled, a withdrawal to Kandahar was ordered and the construction of the strategic railway to Quetta was suspended. General Roberts's brilliant feat of arms in relieving Kandahar facilitated the evacuation of this remaining British position in Afghanistan. It had looked in 1879 as if Russia and Britain between them had succeeded in demolishing Afghanistan as a buffer state. Fortunately for the Gladstone government the emergence of a strong Afghan ruler, Abdurrahman, resurrected a viable independent state and thus lent credibility to the British policy of withdrawal. Nevertheless the Russian policy of expansion in Central Asia went on relentlessly.

A simple reversal of Disraeli's and Salisbury's Turkish policy was not possible for Gladstone and his colleagues. They withdrew the British military consuls from Asia Minor; but they could not give up Cyprus, and the integrity of Constantinople remained a vital British interest, as did the possibility of sending the navy into the Black Sea. Gladstone and Granville went out of their way to work in concert with the other Powers in forcing the Turks to make territorial concessions to Greece and Montenegro, as provided by the Treaty of Berlin, but this invocation of the Concert of Europe was little more than window-dressing. The reality was that Bismarck was already at work behind the scenes activating the Three Emperors' League. The German Chancellor had an increasing interest in keeping Britain isolated. Mainly for reasons of domestic German politics, his dislike of English Liberalism was strong. The diplomatic, commercial and political course to which he had committed himself since 1879 was in many ways the antithesis of Gladstonianism. He was to become an increasingly formidable, though initially largely hidden foe of the foreign and imperial policy operated by Gladstone and Granville in the Near East, Egypt and South Africa.

III

In dealing with South Africa the Gladstone government faced not only the problem of how far it could make a break with previous policy but also the more fundamental question whether the rising nationalism of a subject people should be met with coercion or conciliation. In the Midlothian campaign Gladstone had used the epithet 'insane' in referring to the annexation of the Transvaal. He had created the strong expectation among Liberals at home as well as among Kruger and his fellow citizens in the Transvaal that the policy of the previous government would be reversed and its most conspicuous agent, Sir Bartle Frere, recalled. Yet the policy of confederation in South Africa which had been so forcefully applied by Carnarvon was also Kimberley's in his previous tenure of the Colonial Office in the first Gladstone government. It seemed from the vantage point of London a way of meeting the conflicting requirements of the South African situation: the safeguarding of the British strategic interest in the Cape, the humanitarian concern for the native races against oppression by the Boers, and the overriding concern to achieve these objectives at an economical cost. Gladstone and Kimberley were persuaded that confederation should be given another chance.

It soon became apparent, however, that confederation was not acceptable in the Transvaal and stood in danger of putting the Afrikaners in the Orange Free State and even in the Cape Colony itself against British imperial control. Its failure and disappointment at Gladstone's inability to stick to the policy he appeared to have advocated in opposition led to the Boer revolt in December 1880. This development took the cabinet by surprise; it was at the time heavily occupied by developments in Ireland and had given little attention to South Africa. As soon as the rebellion started Kimberley began to have doubts whether suppression was a feasible policy and the cost worth while. By January 1881 the cabinet was turning away from coercion in South Africa and allowing Kimberley to start negotiations with the Boers. Unfortunately the Liberal government was no better served by its agents in South Africa than the Conservatives had been. Major-General Sir George Colley went on pursuing punitive action against the Boers with conspicuous lack of success and did little to put out peace feelers, in spite of instructions from London. At the end of February 1881 he blundered into a major defeat at Majuba Hill; his death in the action made him into a national hero.

Majuba evoked strong sentiments of revenge, from the Queen downwards, occasioned bitter attacks against ministers and complicated the pursuit of conciliation. The Radicals in the cabinet kept up the pressure for an agreement with the Boers and eventually the Pretoria Convention was signed. The Transvaal became an independent republic again, but under British suzerainty. It was not the end of the matter, not even for the Gladstone government. Relations with the Boer republic remained turbulent, revolving round the interpretation of the Pretoria Convention and the control of Bechuanaland. The London Convention of 1884 went as far as it was possible to go in reverting to the mid-Victorian position, when the Boers had been allowed to go their own way in the interior of southern Africa, while the British maintained their interests along the coast. But such a solution was no longer possible in the 1880s, even before the appearance of the Germans in southwest Africa and the discovery of gold on the Rand injected yet further complications into the area. For the Gladstone government the dilemma in South Africa was that the avoidance of all 'forward' or expansionist moves was not practicable. It was part of a wider dilemma of Gladstonian imperial policy: unless Britain was to retreat positively from her empire, something that was never in Gladstone's mind and would not have been at all realistic, the only alternative was an active defence of the British imperial position not excluding, where necessary, its extension.

IV

This inescapable logic asserted itself even more strikingly in the case of Egypt. Here was a classic case of informal empire, latterly exercised by France and Britain in collaboration. Even Disraeli's government had never contemplated the occupation of Egypt, sometimes put forward as an alternative to or compensation for maintaining Turkey. 'As for compensation to England by having Egypt and Crete, this is moonshine. If Constantinople is Russian, they would only be an expensive encumbrance', Disraeli had written to Derby in October 1876. In August 1877 Gladstone had, more characteristically, warned, in an article in *The Nineteenth Century*, against a territorial occupation of Egypt. It was therefore one of the ironies of history that five years later his government should initiate this occupation, which was to last for over 70 years. The parlous state of Egyptian finances had forced the Powers, led by Britain and France, into greater involvement in Egyptian affairs in the 1870s. This foreign interference was itself the main cause of the revolt against the Khedive, nourished by complex xenophobic and nationalist motives, which resulted in the crises that confronted the Gladstone government. Gladstone's inclination was again to invoke the Concert of Europe. As late as June 1882, when the crisis had already progressed a long way, he wrote to Granville: 'the more I reflect the more I feel unprepared to take any *measure* with regard to the Suez Canal singlehanded, or in union with France, apart from any reference to the authority of Europe.' Three weeks later, by which time a British naval bombardment of Alexandria had already taken place and the cabinet had just decided on the despatch of an expeditionary force under Sir Garnet Wolseley, Gladstone said in the House of Commons: 'we shall look during the time that remains to us to the co-operation of civilized Europe, if it be in any case open to us. But if every chance of co-operation is exhausted, the work will be undertaken by the single power of England.'

Thus step by step the Liberal government was driven towards the occupation of Egypt, sealed by Wolseley's victory at Tel-el-Kebir on 13 September 1882. There had again been much divided counsel in the cabinet, intertwined with and overshadowed by the simultaneous divisions on Ireland. The air was thick with threats of resignation, including Gladstone's own. It was, however, remarkable that the two Radical leaders, Chamberlain and Dilke, this time moved over to the 'forward' party led by Hartington. Dilke had all along been much more in favour of a decisive policy of intervention. His interest in imperial development had helped to mark him out for the post he held at the Foreign Office. Chamberlain had at first fully supported Gladstone on Egypt, but by June 1882 he had become an interventionist. He had never, as his attitude over the Bulgarian atrocities had shown, been an instinctive sympathizer with a moralizing foreign policy. Now he convinced himself that Arabi, the leader of the Egyptian revolt, was a dangerous adventurer and not a genuine nationalist and he was concerned for the security of the Suez Canal and the British trade passing through it. He was also conscious of the fact that weakness over Egypt was damaging a government already low in public esteem. Chamberlain was, however, careful in choosing the ground for justifying his pro-intervention stance in public, for he was still very dependent on his 'Little Englander' Radical support nor as yet seriously at odds with its outlook. The only Radical who resigned from the cabinet in 1882 over Egypt was Bright, still a name to conjure with, but no longer with enough of a following to split the Liberal Party.

The victory of Tel-el-Kebir was popular among all but the most committed Little Englanders and even Gladstone was in high spirits. He wrote a note of congratulation to Cardwell in retirement, for the army reforms of the previous Liberal government had made no small contribution to this feat of arms. Wolseley, an advocate of these reforms and that rare bird among army officers, a Liberal, was the hero of the hour. The occupation of Egypt was regarded as temporary and on this all sections of the Liberal cabinet were for the moment agreed. Egypt would be helped to re-establish her own effective government; British interests would thus be safeguarded and withdrawal would then follow. It was easier said than done. It proved very difficult to resurrect a properly functioning self-government in Egypt after the collapse of the Arabi revolt and Britain got ever more deeply sucked in. The career of Sir Evelyn Baring, later Lord Cromer, as Consul-General started in 1883. Soon the formidable complication of the revolt in the Sudan, led by the Mahdi, the self-proclaimed Messiah, was added to the burden of Egypt. By 1884 the state of Egyptian finances became a major and constant preoccupation of the British government. The British occupation of Egypt had broken the *entente* between the two liberal powers of Western Europe, France and Britain, a situation which suited Bismarck well and which he had always had in mind in encouraging British involvement in the Nile valley. The Gladstone government had been forced into a position completely at variance with its professed principles.

V

Ireland confronted Gladstone and the Liberal Party in a much more pressing and politically menacing way with some of the same harsh choices that were so difficult to make in foreign and imperial policy. The balance between conciliation and coercion, and already looming in the distance, the choice between the maintenance and the relinquishment of empire, these were the issues in Ireland as in South

Africa and Egypt. But the intensity of the struggle was much greater: Ireland was on the doorstep, an integral part of the United Kingdom linked into many of the religious and ethnic conflicts of the country as a whole and directly represented at Westminster by a strong phalanx of nationalists led by a man of political genius. Matters had moved a long way since Gladstone had tried to solve the Irish problem during his first administration. The failure of this great effort of conciliation had produced the beginnings of a new Home Rule movement. Under Isaac Butt it was conservative both in its aims and methods. Butt wanted federalism, an Ireland that would take its autonomous place in a great British imperial federation. His party was a loose grouping, quickly put together before the election of 1874. Many of its candidates were Liberals who had, under pressure from the Home Rule League and faced with an election held for the first time with a secret ballot, hastily taken a Home Rule pledge. Members of the landed gentry and the professional classes still predominated. This parliamentary group, lacking cohesion though it nominally comprised nearly 60 members, was unable to make any significant impact in the 1874 Parliament, during which Ireland received little attention. Isaac Butt believed that respectable behaviour would increase Irish influence and sympathized with Disraeli's imperial policy. A few Home Rulers thought that rougher tactics might well secure Ireland a better hearing, notably J.G. Biggar, a lower-middle-class Belfast merchant and convert to Catholicism. Biggar used and developed the methods of parliamentary obstruction first employed by the 'colonels' opposing the abolition of purchase of commissions. In 1875 he was joined by Charles Stewart Parnell, returned at a by-election in County Neath. Parnell had an unlikely background for a leader of Irish nationalism. He was a Protestant, a landowner and country gentleman, a member of the Anglo-Irish ascendancy with an English education. His strong anti-English feelings were in part derived from his mother, an American heiress; they were reinforced during his student days at Cambridge. Parnell was a man of little intellectual cultivation; he drifted into politics almost inadvertently and to begin with was painfully inarticulate. There was always a gulf between him and his followers. Yet he became a leader of extraordinary power: he had charisma and great tactical skill and sensitivity.

In the late 1870s the time was ripe for the various elements of the Irish situation, the agrarian problem, revolutionary nationalism and a foothold at Westminster, to come together and the moment found its man in Parnell. The Fenians and their organization, the Irish Republican Brotherhood, had, in spite of the support they enjoyed among Irish-Americans, reached a dead end. Their concern for revolutionary purity was cutting them off from any practical action. The emergence of Parnell on the parliamentary side, committed not only to more rigorous tactics but to more far-reaching aims, not excluding ultimately Irish independence, made it possible for the revolutionaries and their Irish-American allies to contemplate a 'New Departure'. This was the idea that, for the time being at any rate, revolutionary nationalism and constitutional action for Home Rule could travel along the same road. This coming together of previously incompatible forces was made at once easier and more urgent by the exacerbation of rural distress in Ireland. Here the lead was taken by Michael Davitt, who was to become an important link between Irish nationalism and left-wing forces in Great Britain. In 1879 Davitt founded the Irish National Land League, to defend the Irish peasantry against landlords, eviction and starvation, and in the longer run to secure 'the land of Ireland for the people of Ireland'. Parnell became president of the Land League. The general election of 1880 changed the balance in the Home Rule Party at Westminster so that Parnell became its chairman. He could count on the allegiance of 24 members at the outset and another 15 became increasingly committed to him out of a total of some 60. In social composition the parliamentary party had also moved away from the almost exclusive predominance of the landed gentry and there were now more small tradesmen and tenant farmers. Parnell was at the beginning of his career as the uncrowned King of Ireland, but there was a good deal of ambivalence in his position. He had simultaneously to lead a violent agrarian revolt and a parliamentary party, while keeping the support of nationalist revolutionaries, particularly in America. He needed the desperate pressure of a half-starving peasantry behind him, but he could not risk precipitating them into an outright conflict with superior British force; only at Westminister could he obtain alleviation for the plight of the Irish peasant and eventually self-government for Ireland and his great tactical skill found its fullest outlet in the House of Commons; once self-government was granted the tides of history could be relied on to secure full independence and an Irish republic. Parnell's balancing act to cope with these conflicting pressures was a *tour de force*.

The full extent of the Irish crisis and the new alignments in Irish nationalism were not appreciated in England in 1880, Disraeli's election manifesto notwithstanding. Gladstone had paid his first and only visit to Ireland in 1877, but it was mainly a progress round the mansions of Whig noblemen. There was little support in Ireland for his crusade on the Bulgarian Atrocities; the Irish hierarchy supported the Disraeli line, as did Manning and Wiseman in England. Among nonconformist Radicals in the Liberal Party there was not much sympathy for the home rule position and occasional resentment of the attempts by the Home Rule Confederation of Great Britain to extract pledges from members of Parliament and candidates. By 1879, when Parnell had already become the leading Home Rule personality in the House of Commons, Chamberlain and Dilke tried to construct an understanding with him. Parnell was far too cautious and suspicious to enter into anything like a formal alliance, but Irish land reform was an issue on which Home Rulers and Radicals could unite. Thus there were some links between the Parnellites and sections of British radicalism, including its trade union element; but other Radicals resented the disturbance caused by Irish nationalism and on the Right of the Party the Irish problem was seen above all in law and order terms. It was mainly this aspect of the problem which turned the Gladstone government's attention to Ireland: in 1877 there had been 963 evictions and 236 outrages; by 1880 there were over 2,000 evictions and more than 2,500 outrages.

The Liberal government's first measure was a conciliatory gesture, a Compensation for Disturbance Bill to compensate certain classes of evicted tenants out of the Irish Church surplus. It was rejected by the House of Lords, Disraeli calling it 'a reconnaissance against property', and produced the first ministerial resignation. By the autumn the cabinet was deeply divided over the correct balance between conciliation and coercion. Forster, now Chief Secretary for Ireland, retained some vestiges of his former attitudes, but was by now remote from nearly all sections of radicalism in the Party. The officials at Dublin Castle had convinced him that the maintenance of law and order should be the first priority. The cabinet came under increasing pressure from him to sanction a new Coercion Bill; Gladstone resisted, Chamberlain threatened to resign, but in the end they all had to agree to the introduction of such a bill. On the positive side, to meet Irish grievances, Gladstone proposed a scheme of Grand Committees of the House of Commons for the three parts of the United Kingdom, with the double purpose of defeating obstruction and going some way towards devolved government, 'what is styled (*in bonam partem*) "Local Govenment", and (*in malam*) "Home Rule" '. These proposals, pointers to the future, were too bold for the moderate section of the cabinet, but there was agreement, or at any rate acquiescence, that there should be legislation on land. Some wanted to develop a system of land purchase; on the insistence of Bright there had been purchase clauses in the 1870 Land Act, known as Bright's clauses, but they had remained almost a dead letter. When the recommendations of the Bessborough Commission on Irish land became known, it was decided to concentrate once more on the three 'F's, fair rents, free sale and fixity of tenure. This was the basis of the 1881 Land Act, a measure of great complexity and many shortcomings, but which did in the end achieve a considerable easement of the pressures in the Irish countryside. The Radicals in the government were reconciled to coercion by this simultaneous adoption of a more positive approach to the Irish problem.

The government's treatment of Ireland proceeded along these parallel lines of coercion and conciliation for most of the year 1881. The Coercion Bill, which was so far-reaching that 'it practically enabled the Viceroy to lock up anybody he pleased, and to detain him as long as he pleased', ran, not unnaturally, into fierce opposition from the Irish Nationalists. Obstruction reached uprecedented levels; they spoke, as Gladstone described it, 'sometimes rising to the level of mediocrity, and more often grovelling amidst mere trash in unbounded profusion'. A 41-hour sitting at the end of January 1881 was only brought to an end by the Speaker putting the question. Formal powers to close debate were given to the Speaker the following year and became part of the normal rules of the House in 1887. The closure was an important step in the process by which the government took increasing control of the business of the House. For at least 50 years Parliament had experienced growing pressure of business; it had come to be seen as a legislative machine and achievements of goverments were measured in terms of legislative output. The consolidation of parties after 1867 had given the government greater control over legislation than had been the case in mid-century; but only from the 1880s was the executive increasingly in a position to draft a legislative time-table comprising several major measures a year. The balance of power was thus tilted against the legislature and towards the executive; the ground was prepared for an enlargement of State activity by legislation.

Once the Land Act was on the statute book the question was whether it would work and whether the Land League would allow it to work. By the autumn of 1881 it seemed increasingly to ministers that Parnell and his associates were bent on outright defiance of the existing order. In fact Parnell grasped at an early stage that the Land Act would work and would, in due course, cut the ground from under the Land League; but since he had allowed it to pass, avoiding the extremes of obstruction and even giving it some assistance, he was now, in the execution of his balancing act, required to lean towards the violent and revolutionary side. In October 1881 Gladstone accused Parnell publicly of trying to frustrate the Land Act and threatened that 'the resources of civilization are not exhausted'. Parnell replied by attacking him as 'this masquerading knight errant, this pretending champion of the rights of every other nation except those of the Irish nation'. A few days later Parnell was arrested and lodged in Kilmainham gaol. This was what he may well have been

seeking, for it endowed him with a martyr's crown while absolving
him from responsibility for the decline of the Land League. On the
other hand during his incarceration the secret societies, an endemic
feature of the Irish scene, began to lead the perpetration of violence
and there was a growing danger that Parnell would lose control of
forces he had so far successfully harnessed to his chariot. This was also
a danger to the government and to the continuing success of the Land
Act. It was gradually perceived in London that no useful purpose was
served by Parnell's sojourn in prison.

Thus the way was opened for the negotiations that led to the so-
called Kilmainham 'treaty'. The opening moves and some of the
subsequent exchanges were conducted through the curious, raffish
figure of Captain O'Shea, the husband of Parnell's mistress. Leading
ministers knew something of the Parnell–O'Shea triangle, which is
perhaps why they took some note of what O'Shea and Mrs O'Shea
had to say. After first approaching Gladstone without eliciting an
immediate response, O'Shea addressed himself to Chamberlain as a
'Minister without political pedantry' and asked the pertinent questions 'how the Liberal Party is to get in at the next election, and at the
one after, and so on against the Irish vote? And if by any chance it did
get in how on earth is it to get on? Why is the government in such a
mess?' The understanding reached with Parnell was that some of the
most obvious gaps in the Land Act would be plugged, notably the
question of arrears of rents. In return Parnell declared that this
would, in his judgement, 'be regarded by the country as a practical
settlement of the Land Question' and 'would I feel sure enable us to
cooperate cordially for the future with the Liberal Party in forwarding
Liberal principles and measures of general reform'. By implication
there would be no more Coercion Acts and there would be no reason
for keeping Parnell, Dillon and other leaders in prison.

Forster resigned over Kilmainham. Chamberlain expected to succeed him, but Gladstone appointed Lord Frederick Cavendish,
brother of Hartington and husband of Mrs Gladstone's niece. It was
one of the many examples of the imperfect sympathies that existed
between the Prime Minister and the Radical leader. Cavendish was
murdered in Phoenix Park immediately after his arrival in Dublin.
The terrorists belonged to a secret society and Parnell was himself so
shaken that he wrote to Gladstone offering to retire from politics; but
in the event the Phoenix Park murders did not in fact seriously disrupt
the programme of appeasement envisaged in the Kilmainham 'treaty'.
The summer of 1882 marks the end of a phase in Irish affairs. The
agrarian unrest died down, though sporadic outrages continued.
Parnell could now put Home Rule in the forefront of his objectives
and the Land League was replaced by the Irish National League. He

knew that when the Liberal government carried out its pledge to extend the county franchise his position and leverage at Westminster would be greatly strengthened.

For two years Ireland had imparted to British politics a degree of drama and bitterness rarely surpassed. For Liberals it was a heart-rending and deeply divisive matter, made no easier to endure by the simultaneous eruption of other great issues. Again and again the party looked like breaking up and was only held together by the massive presence of Gladstone. This was the more remarkable in that the Prime Minister was, particularly on Ireland, himself a strong partisan. On the Right, among the Whigs and moderate Liberals predominant in the Cabinet, there was little sympathy for Irish nationalism or even much recognition of its fundamental legitimacy. Attitudes were tinged with racial contempt. On the other hand there was much concern for the Anglo-Irish ascendancy and its future. Measures like the Land Act constituted an interference with the rights of property, sacred to Liberals, which was very difficult for many members of the Party to swallow. All this had deep implications for the rest of the country, where the attack on property and particularly on landowners was already at the centre of public debate. It was on this issue that the Duke of Argyll, one of Gladstone's closest friends in politics, resigned in April 1881.

On the Left of the Liberal Party Ireland was an agonizing problem: instinctive sympathy for the underdog clashed with the outrage felt over Parnell's affront to the whole Liberal movement and to law and order. In principle Chamberlain and Dilke were against coercion and for conciliation, yet Chamberlain even more than Dilke at crucial moments supported coercion and the arrest of Parnell. 'Parnell is doing his best to make Irish legislation unpopular with English Radicals. The workmen do not like to see law set at defiance and a dissolution on the ''justice to Ireland'' cry would under present circumstances be a hazardous operation', wrote Chamberlain to Dilke in October 1880. Bright, the veteran Radical, also continued to support conciliation in principle whilst becoming increasingly embittered with Parnell. On the other hand there were Radicals who remained in all circumstances opposed to coercion and were guided by the view that injustice and repression was at the root of the Irish problem and that the same enemy confronted them in Ireland and in England. Typical of this attitude were the views of John Morley, at this time editor of the *Pall Mall Gazette*. With Chamberlain and Dilke he made up a triumvirate of advanced Radical leaders and he was the philosopher and intellectual mentor of the group. After the passing of the Coercion Act of 1881 he declared that 'the leaders of the party of progress have lost their title for a long time to come to talk their old languages, or to appeal to the deep and generous commonplaces of law and freedom.' Morley thus became separated from time to time from his close friend Chamberlain, whom he admired as a man of action. In 1883 he entered the House of Commons and soon became a leading political figure himself; gradually the political gulf between him and Chamberlain widened. Morley's consistent opposition to coercion in Ireland was shared by many politically conscious working-class radicals and by a minority of parliamentary Radicals, but among them there were such well known figures as Joseph Cowen, Sir Wilfrid Lawson, Charles Bradlaugh and Henry Labouchere. In the Liberal cabinet those who wanted to tread the path of conciliation on Ireland were, in spite of their numerical inferiority, quite powerful; not only because the Prime Minister was with them, but because the combination of a section of Radicals in the Commons with the Parnellites constituted a formidable threat. Thus the Phoenix Park murders did not get the better of the forces of conciliation, and for a while the condition of Ireland became calmer.

VI

If Ireland, Egypt and South Africa were not enough to explain the frustrations of the Liberal majority of 1880, there was yet another bog into which the government stumbled. The Bradlaugh case was a less substantial problem in itself than the future of important countries, but almost equally potent in disorganizing the parliamentary timetable and disorientating the supporters of the government. Charles Bradlaugh was a leading advocate of three causes highly abhorrent to the vast majority of his fellow-citizens, atheism, republicanism and birth control. He was a strongly principled freethinker prepared to endure persecution and hardship for his beliefs. His attacks on the monarchy were often vitriolic; in his *Impeachment of the House of Brunswick* he wrote: 'I loathe these small German breast-bestarred wanderers. . . . In their own land they vegetate . . . Here we pay them highly to marry and perpetuate a pauper prince race.' His advocacy, in collaboration with Mrs Annie Besant, of birth control was put down by his attackers to an addiction for free love; in fact it was part and parcel of his radicalism, a neo-Malthusian recognition that family limitation was necessary for an improvement in the condition of the people. In his challenge to some of the most dearly held values of the age Bradlaugh as a person exhibited many of the strenuous, puritanical virtues of his contemporaries.

Bradlaugh had been contesting Northampton in general elections and by-elections since 1868, in competition with moderate Liberals and Tories, and eventually won one of the seats in 1880. He hoped to be allowed to make an affirmation, instead of taking the customary oath when the new Parliament met; this procedure was accepted in courts of law under legislation which Bradlaugh had himself helped to get on to the statute book. The Speaker refused to make a ruling himself and the House appointed a select committee. By the casting vote of its chairman Spencer Walpole, who had clashed with Bradlaugh over the Hyde Park riots of 1867, it rejected the claim to affirm. Bradlaugh, who had no intention of provoking a prolonged struggle, then prepared to take the oath. On the day he was to do so, *The Times* published a letter from him, stating that his duty to his constituents compelled him 'to submit to a form less solemn to me than affirmation' and would force him 'to repeat words which I have scores of times declared are to me sounds conveying no clear and definite meaning'. The letter, seen by many as deliberately provocative, caused a considerable stir. When Bradlaugh advanced to the Table to take the oath, Sir Henry Drummond Wolff objected. Thus the Bradlaugh Case and the Fourth Party were born together.

The latter title was bestowed, initially in jest, upon the quartet of Tory freelances, Wolff, Lord Randolph Churchill, Gorst and A.J. Balfour, who came together in attacking the Liberals as well as their own front bench. Wolff was a much-travelled, suave and witty minor diplomat. Lord Randolph Churchill, son of the Duke of Marlborough, had entered the House in 1874 for the family borough of Woodstock, but had up to this moment scarcely made a mark. Gorst had fallen out with the Tory Party establishment, as he saw the work he had done for the 1874 election decay and his advice brushed aside. After he had entered the House as member for Chatham in 1875 his hopes for rapid political advancement were disappointed. The defeat of 1880 was a kind of back-hand vindication for Gorst and he was soon re-engaged to advise on organization though he refused to return as full-time party agent. The fourth member of the quartet, Arthur Balfour, stood somewhat apart from the other three. Nicknamed Clara, his languid bearing concealed a steely determination. He had a trained philosophical mind and had just published *A Defence of Philosophical Doubt*. He did not share to the full the revulsion from Bradlaugh's views which the other three felt and took little part in the Bradlaugh case. Nevertheless there were strong ties of personal and political friendship between all four in the first few years of the 1880 Parliament; Balfour's particular importance was that through him there lay a ready line of communication to his uncle, Lord Salisbury. The Bradlaugh case saw the Fourth Party in action for the first time and henceforth these four men were to have no mean influence on the course of parliamentary events and on the internal politics of the Conservative Opposition.

The key to the development of the Bradlaugh case was that the Liberal government could not rely on its normal majority. When Wolff moved to bar Bradlaugh, Gladstone could not simply oppose, for he was advised by his whips that he would be defeated. Instead he had to propose a second select committee. In spite of the committee's equivocal report, Bradlaugh was eventually allowed to affirm and take his seat, but not before having been briefly confined to the Clock Tower after one of his abortive attempts to gain entry to the House. In March 1881 he was unseated as a result of legal proceedings brought against him, but promptly re-elected at Northampton. There followed a further forcible ejection, a vote of expulsion, another re-election and again expulsion. The most significant effort to resolve the long-running dispute was made in the spring of 1883, when the cabinet decided to introduce an Affirmation Bill. By this time by-election losses had whittled down the Liberal majority and the great majority of Irish Home Rulers was opposed to Bradlaugh, so that in spite of only a few Liberal defections, but a rather larger number of abstentions, the Bill was narrowly defeated. Bradlaugh was re-elected for Northampton for the third time in 1884, making it clear beyond a shadow of doubt that the electors would not take upon themselves the burden of resolving the case. At the beginning of the 1886 Parliament the Speaker at last allowed Bradlaugh to take the oath and an Affirmation Act passed in 1888 created a general right to affirm for anyone objecting to the oath on grounds of religious belief or because he had no religious belief.

The Bradlaugh case was sheer agony for the Liberal Party. Liberalism meant nothing if it did not mean that the rights of citizens should not be subject to any religious tests. The views of Bradlaugh were, however, so repugnant that even for many Liberals, nonconformist as well as anglican, the preservation of a Christian Parliament against atheist defilement outweighed all other considerations. The wish was often expressed that Gladstone, if he had to support Bradlaugh's right to take his seat, should dissociate himself in the clearest terms from Bradlaugh's views. To talk of an alliance between Gladstone and Bradlaugh was too tempting a way of making political capital for all opponents of Liberalism. Gladstone himself found the Bradlaugh case 'the one thing above all others which is genuinely disagreeable and distasteful'. He knew only too well where his ultimate duty lay, but for a long time he fought shy of bringing legislation to resolve the issue. The Affirmation Bill of 1883 was taken up by the cabinet in his absence, but he became an enthusiastic advocate of it. His speech on the second reading was generally considered to be one of his finest and, circulated in pamphlet form, gradually helped persuade many Liberals that they must support Bradlaugh's right to take his seat.

The Bradlaugh case further soured the troubled relationship between Liberals and Irish Nationalists. In the early stages Parnell personally supported Bradlaugh, 'declaring that he was disgusted with some of the bigoted sentiments he had heard expressed'. In his own beliefs he was probably close to agnosticism, while Bradlaugh had sympathized with fenianism as early as 1867. The Irish Catholic Church was, however, solidly anti-Bradlaugh and so were most of the Home Rulers at Westminster, including many of the Parnellites. Parnell increasingly kept his silence and by 1883, for tactical reasons, opposed the Affirmation Bill. In the execution of his finally calculated balancing act it would have been imprudent for him to get out of step with the Catholic Church. As for the Catholic Church in England, it was overwhelmingly anti-Bradlaugh. Cardinal Manning published a number of articles on the Bradlaugh case, under titles such as 'Without God, No Commonwealth'. Cardinal Newman, on the other hand, refused to be associated with the campaign against the Affirmation Bill, conscious as he was of the long Catholic struggle against civil disabilities. For Catholics, as for many nonconformist Radicals, the Bradlaugh case posed a dilemma between their interest, as a minority, in religious toleration and their concern for a Christian basis of society.

VII

Bradlaugh and all the other 'specialities', as Gladstone called them, that crossed the path of the Liberal government largely account for the dearth of domestic reform legislation in the first four sessions of the 1880 Parliament. One step had, however, long been on the Liberal agenda, household suffrage in the counties. In itself it was a change of the machinery rather than of the substance of politics, but like all previous reform bills it was bound to precipitate a prolonged and complex crisis, probably involving a clash between the two Houses of Parliament. It could therefore not be undertaken until the decks had been properly cleared. Yet even the Radicals, frustrated as they were by 1883, for the most part agreed that it should have priority over other reforms, for it would shift the balance of power decisively to the left. At a deeper level the difficulty about reform legislation in the early 1880s was the large gap between the new problems, challenges and ideas discussed earlier in these pages and what the existing political, institutional and social structures could in practice deliver. The proliferation of royal commissions at this time, on agriculture, on the depression of trade, on working-class housing, was evidence of a degree of bafflement. It would be a long time before some of the social problems, now appearing on the horizon and being reflected upon by the men of ideas, were to produce attempts at governmental solutions.

Not that the early years of the 1880 Parliament were entirely barren of domestic reform. Employers' liability was a cause for which the trade unions had already fought a long parliamentary battle. The doctrine of 'common employment' had for a generation made it impossible for workmen to obtain compensation for injuries received through negligence of their fellow workmen. The Board of Trade, Chamberlain's department, was mainly responsible for the Employers' Liability Act of 1880. It had its shortcomings, in that the doctrine of common employment was not abolished and it continued to be possible through subsequent judicial decisions for employers to force their workmen to contract out of the Act by offering private insurance schemes. Nevertheless the 1880 Act represented a major interference with the freedom of contract and was an example of that creeping extension of State activity which was still so widely disliked. Men of property were outraged, on both sides of the House. Knowles, a Tory and Lancashire mine owner, declared: '. . . I believe this is the most revolutionary measure ever brought into this House against the trading community of the country'. The mavericks of the Fourth Party took a line of their own on employers' liability, accusing the government of going insufficiently far to safeguard the working popu-lation from the consequences of industrial injury. Lord Randolph Churchill and his three friends took this stand not so much because they had worked out a programme of Tory democracy, but because they were less inhibited by considerations of economic rectitude than their leaders and had a kind of aristocratic contempt for that growing species, the Tory businessman. Lord Randolph, with his caustic wit, had already dubbed the two venerable Tory statesmen, R.A. Cross and W.H. Smith, 'Marshall and Snelgrove'.

Among other lesser bills the Corrupt Practices Bill, passed in 1883 was probably the most important. Its key provision was the stipula-tion of maximum expenses for various types of constituencies, with somewhat larger allowances in far-flung county constituencies than in boroughs. Spending was to be closely audited and made through a single election agent. The bill was precipitated by revelations of serious corruption in the election of 1880, in spite of the secret ballot and so much previous corrupt practices legislation. The Act of 1883 within a few more years transformed electoral practices and the last vestiges of Eatanswill, the symbol of corrupt electioneering created by Dickens, disappeared.

In December 1882, Gladstone, celebrating the fiftieth anniversary of his entry into the House of Commons, reconstructed his government. Dilke was brought into the cabinet as President of the Local Government Board, a sop to the Radicals. The anniversary, as well as a prolonged stay in Cannes for health reasons, early in 1883, strengthened anticipation of Gladstone's imminent retirement. Manoeuvring for the succession, in the Prime Minister's absence, complicated preparations for the Queen's speech. When their hopes of major legislation were again disappointed, the Radicals stepped up their rhetoric. Chamberlain, after an attack on him by Lord Salisbury in his native Birmingham in March 1883, made the famous rejoinder: 'Lord Salisbury constitutes himself the spokesman of a class – of the class to which he himself belongs, who toil not neither do they spin . . .'. In June, at celebrations of Bright's jubilee as member for the city, Chamberlain's keynote was 'every day the country is becoming more radical and more democratic'. Some lighthearted remarks about the absence of high officials and representatives of royalty, and nobody missing them, drew the displeasure of the Queen. 'A Cabinet Minister or indeed any Minister, should not hold such dangerous and improper language', she wrote to Gladstone. The rebuking of Chamberlain and his defence from the strictures of the Queen was to be an on-going task for Gladstone, as the battle for the reform of the franchise flared up. In Tory and Whig eyes Chamberlain was 'Robespierre revealed'; in fact the class war rhetoric covered lack of action and a programme that was far from revolutionary.

VIII

Fortunately for the Liberals, the Conservatives were almost as much in disarray in 1883. The Tory malaise was the result of frustration at their inability to topple the government in spite of all its crises and divisions; and of fear what the future would hold after franchise extension. The scapegoat for these frustrations was Northcote, an eminently decent and respectable political workhorse, who had found his appropriate niche as a lieutenant of Disraeli, but lacked the steel to be a leader in his own right. A personal reverence for Gladstone – he had first called him 'the Grand Old Man' – going back to their Oxford connection in the 1850s, did not help him to play his difficult role as leader of the Opposition. The escapades of the Fourth Party sprang from Northcote's failures and from the consequent dissatisfaction of the Tory rank and file. For a time the cleavage between the Fourth Party men and Northcote was mainly tactical and every now and then covered up by professions of loyalty from them, even if in private they were increasingly contemptuous of 'the Goat'. After Disraeli's death in April 1881, the leadership of the Tory Party was vested in the dual control of Northcote and Salisbury. Those Tories who were dissatisfied with the performance of their party now had a ready-made target in the shortcomings of dual control and particularly Northcote's part in it.

Churchill was rising rapidly as the new star on the Tory horizon. He was the Conservative answer to Gladstone, combining great parliamentary skill with rousing platform oratory, and all this before the age of 35. In the House he could bait Gladstone like no-one else, until the great man was sitting on the edge of the bench, clasping his legs beneath his knees and calling out angrily 'No, No!' and then rising to his feet to give a needlessly lengthy reply. The platform oratory, which Gladstone more than any other man had made part of the political coinage, was now turned by Churchill, often in much cruder form, against the Liberals. His enthusiastic audiences would encourage him with shouts of 'Give it 'em hot, Randy!'.

As a result of populist performances of this kind Churchill came to be linked with Tory democracy and in retrospect type-cast by many historians as the archetypal Tory democrat. In fact Churchill used the term but rarely and when he did so he was usually only referring to a mass electorate voting Tory. In 1885, when there was universal household suffrage and he was challenging Bright's seat at Birmingham, he attempted a public definition: 'The Tory Democracy is a democracy which has embraced the principles of the Tory Party. It is a democracy which believes that a hereditary monarchy and hereditary House of Lords are the strongest fortifications which the wisdom of man, illuminated by the experience of centuries, can possibly devise for the protection of democratic freedom'. Churchill was therefore a firm believer in the traditional pillars of Toryism, the monarchy, the Constitution and the Church. Never swerving from these unalterable convictions he was prepared to be flexible and unorthodox on specific issues, above all if this served his other over-riding priority, the disorganization of the Liberals and their eventual defeat at the polls. He had first-hand knowledge of Ireland to a greater degree than most of his fellow-politicians, but his views were not particularly profound. He opposed coercion, cultivated friendly relations with Irish Nationalist MPs, but was strong on law and order and blamed the party leaders for not supporting Salisbury's hard line on Ireland in 1882. In his Edinburgh speeches at the end of 1883 he urged that the Tory reply to the demand for Irish self-government should be 'an unchanging, an unchangeable and a unanimous "No" '. He supported Egyptian nationalism and opposed an indefinite occupation of Egypt, and in this was at odds with most Conservative opinion. He flirted with fair trade or tariff reform and it was Chamberlain who went around answering him. In the Edinburgh speeches he opposed franchise reform, at a time when the general Tory line was to accept it in principle and at any rate in public, and only changed his stance when reform became inevitable. Churchill was a populist, but his interest in change and reform as an end in itself was limited.

Churchill's meteoric rise had an unsettling effect on a party fearful for its future and saddled with an unresolved leadership problem. At the end of March and early April 1883 two letters appeared in *The Times* challenging the choice of Northcote to unveil a Beaconsfield statue in Parliament Square. In May Churchill published an article in the *Fortnightly* analysing the future of Conservative policy and calling for a leader on whom 'Elijah's Mantle' could descend. It could be seen as a call for Lord Salisbury to assume sole charge, but it was also widely interpreted as an attempt by Churchill to push his own claims. From the autumn of 1883 till the summer of 1884 the in-fighting in the Tory Party revolved to a large extent round the party organization. Lord Randolph's choice of the National Union of Conservative Associations as a battleground for reforming the party was clearly influenced by his perception of the role played by the National Liberal Federation in the Liberal Party. Gorst, Churchill's associate in this battle, knew the Conservative organization better than anyone else; his recurring complaint was that it was in the hands of a narrow aristocratic clique, 'the old identity', who knew nothing about the urban constituencies where the future of the Tory Party had to be built. In 1882 he had once more resigned from his position in the central organization. With the drift of the middle classes into the party, local party organizations in big provincial cities were now often dominated by a new breed of wealthy men, risen to eminence in business and commerce, who in the past would have been more likely to have made their political home in the Liberal Party. Such men wanted to have influence in the party or at least a channel of communication to the party leaders. Churchill and Gorst could use pressures of this kind in their efforts to recast the party organization and they received a good deal of support from prominent provincial Tories. The particular object of their attack was the Central Committee of whips and party managers and its chairman Edward Stanhope; their professed aim was to supersede oligarchical control exercised by this committee and replace it by democratic control exercised through the National Union.

Throughout the battle Salisbury and Northcote, while prepared to make concessions on details, maintained steadily that 'the parliamentary leaders must be held responsible for the direction of the political action of the party'. The two Tory leaders worked loyally together to maintain this position, but Salisbury would have been less than human if he had not welcomed the gradual weakening of Northcote's position. Taken in conjunction with recurring disagreements over franchise extension, Egypt, Churchill's support for leasehold enfranchisement and other matters in 1884, the threat to the unity of the Conservative Party seemed at times as real as the possible break-up of the Liberal Party. Churchill and Gorst suspected that Northcote's ultimate aim was to pull the Whigs into the Tory fold; Northcote and others feared 'a rapprochement between the Tory Democrats and the Radical Democrats'. The Tory organization battle was rather suddenly composed in July 1884. The chief concession made by the party leaders was the disbandment of the Central Committee; otherwise there was, apart from the recognition of the Primrose League, little constitutional change. The National Union reverted to its place alongside the Conservative Central Office as the officially recognized federation of constituency associations. Churchill was more than ever acknowledged as one of the leading men in the party, a remarkable achievement for one who had never held even junior office.

IX

In the meantime Gladstone had, ahead of the session of 1884, taken vital decisions about the extension of the franchise. The Liberal bill was to apply equally to the whole of the United Kingdom including Ireland. Any differential treatment of Ireland would mean that the

Parnellites and other Irish factions would do their utmost to block the bill. The application of household suffrage to Ireland would make it virtually certain that a nationalist party greatly enlarged would appear at Westminster. Gladstone also decided to introduce the Franchise Bill first, separately from redistribution. This was what Chamberlain had demanded and it had been endorsed by the annual conference of the National Liberal Federation at Leeds. The advantage was that it would be a simpler measure, more likely to be passed by the Commons. Once on the statute book, the Franchise Act would create a strong motivation to pass a Redistribution Bill, for an election on an extended franchise but on the old constituencies would be extremely damaging to the Conservative Party. Franchise first would also cut out many Irish complications, for example whether there should be a reallocation of seats in favour of Ulster.

The fact that 'franchise first' was a policy which pleased the Radicals and alarmed Tories and moderate Liberals made it likely that it would lead to Whig resignations from the cabinet and to eventual rejection by the Lords. Gladstone managed to prevent Hartington, who feared the consequences of the bill in Ireland, from resigning and to circumvent the opposition of other members of his cabinet; it was no part of his purpose to allow the Lords to force him into an election, but he probably calculated that after a rejection of the Franchise Bill by the Lords strong forces for compromise would begin to operate. His main concern therefore was to make sure of large majorities for the bill in the Commons in order to weaken the opposition of the Lords. This meant above all securing the support of Irish Nationalist members, not only by including Ireland in the bill, but by letting it be understood that redistribution, when it came, would not involve a reduction in the number of Irish seats, absolutely or relatively. Ireland was thus to be treated equally in all respects except in the number of seats, where she would continue to have preferential treatment. The claims of Ulster were deliberately played down in the pursuit of nationalist support, thus foreshadowing the failure to safeguard Ulster in the Home Rule Bill of 1886. Ulster members and Irish Liberals who supported the Gladstone government figured prominently among those who advocated proportional representation, which they saw as a means of securing minority interests in Ireland.

The main provisions of the Franchise Bill which Gladstone introduced at the end of February 1884 were simple. The household £10 occupation and lodger qualifications applying in the boroughs were extended to the counties; the £12 rateable value franchise established in the counties in 1867 was reduced to £10 and the £50 tenant franchise, the Chandos clause of the 1832 Act, was abolished. It was household, not manhood suffrage, a difference that was fundamental to the electoral and political conditions prevailing until the end of the First World War. The passage of the Bill was both helped and hindered by the simultaneous flare-up of Egyptian business. The Mahdi's revolt had engulfed the Sudan, in January 1884 Gordon had been sent to evacuate the Sudan, and the financial affairs of Egypt, with their damaging effect on British diplomatic relations particularly with France, were constantly on the agenda. On Egypt the government was simultaneously assailed by the right and the left wing. The right wing was led by Goschen and Forster. The former had refused government office in 1880 because he could not accept the commitment to franchise extension. He was by now hardly more than a nominal Liberal, but with a wide reputation for 'soundness', possibly a major figure in the eventuality of a party realignment. Forster's attitude to imperial questions had always been coloured by humanitarian anti-slave trade sentiment, but by 1884 his main motivation had become thirst for revenge and unsatisfied ambition, following his exclusion from the cabinet in 1882. In the Gladstone camp his attitude was regarded as particularly 'nasty' and for Gladstone 'Forsterism' was a word for an unpleasant species of renegade liberalism. On the Left of the Liberal Party some Radicals carried their revulsion from the government's Egyptian imbroglio into the division lobby, but few Liberal MPs wanted to face an election on Egypt, on which the government was vulnerable and unpopular. Gladstone used the interlocking of issues astutely to survive on Egypt and pass the Franchise Bill. By the end of June 1884 it received its third reading with scarcely a change and without a division; amendments to introduce proportional representation and to admit women householders to the vote were rejected. In the Commons not many Tories had attacked the equalization of town and country franchises on principle.

Early in July 1884 the House of Lords, while ready to accept the principle of further enfranchisement, declined to give the Franchise Bill a second reading unless it was accompanied by a Redistribution Bill. This was the tactical ground chosen by Salisbury to make the Conservative stand. Compromise was in the air right up to the end; as it was, the government defeat in the Lords was by only 59 votes. After the vote in the Lords Gladstone announced that the Franchise Bill would be reintroduced in a special autumn session of Parliament. The way was now open for three months of political campaigning in which the future of the House of Lords even more than the franchise would be the point at issue. It was what Chamberlain and other Radicals had always wanted and they set out to make the most of the opportunity. For Chamberlain himself, however, events hardly came up to expectations. At many of the numerous Liberal meetings and demonstrations up and down the country he roused his audiences against the House of Lords: 'We will never be the only race in the civilized world subservient to the insolent pretensions of a hereditary caste.' In the autumn the Aston Park riot weakened Chamberlain's public standing. This occurred when a Radical mob invaded a Tory meeting, held on Chamberlain's home ground and addressed by Sir Stafford Northcote and Lord Randolph Churchill. Chamberlain was blamed for the issue of forged tickets and on the reassembly of Parliament rebutted a vote of censure with some difficulty. The 'peers versus people' campaign did not put new wind into the sails of the long-frustrated Radical wing of the Liberal Party and Gladstone was the real beneficiary. It was demonstrated once again that his hold on the public at large was unrivalled, that only he could keep the Liberal factions together and bring a complicated parliamentary battle involving both Houses and possibly the Crown to a successful conclusion. On the other side of the party divide Salisbury, having composed his quarrel with Lord Randolph Churchill, also showed that he had judged the balance between all-out resistance and compromise shrewdly. He could not deliver the total rejection of franchise extension, which many Tories undoubtedly would have liked, but he could make sure that the redistribution scheme would be acceptable to his party.

The divide between the leaders of the major parties was in fact not wide. Gladstone wanted to see a third reform scheme, including franchise extension and redistribution, enacted. Salisbury was prepared to accept this provided the redistribution did not put the Conservative Party at a disadvantage. Increasingly the nature of the redistribution scheme became the central issue. The implications which various possible schemes of redrawing constituencies had for the two main parties were not seen very differently in 1884 than they had been in 1866. In spite of the fact that they were enfranchising the agricultural worker the Liberals still felt that the urban areas were the bulwark of their electoral strength. By the same token, the Tories wanted to keep agricultural bastions as uncontaminated as possible by urban electors. Whigs, whose reluctance about franchise extension matched that of many Tories, wanted to retain as far as possible the traditional system of two-member constituencies, for it was through the custom of splitting the representation of such constituencies with left-wing Liberals that they had been able to maintain their strength in the liberal Party. The idea of equal electoral districts or single-member constituencies surfaced from time to time in the debate and discussions about redistribution. Salisbury, in an article in the *National Review* in October 1884, considered it one of the ways in which Tory requirements on redistribution might be satisfied. Equal electoral districts with single members proved in fact the key to a settlement when the time for direct talks between the party leaders finally came in November 1884, after the House of Commons had passed the Franchise Bill a second time in the specially summoned autumn session.

Gladstone, Salisbury and Dilke were the chief protagonists at the Downing Street talks which settled redistribution, although Hartington, Granville and Northcote were also present. Never before had the details of a measure yet to be introduced in Parliament been discussed between the leaders of the major parties beforehand. Gladstone found it a pleasure to deal with 'so acute a man' as Salisbury, but was surprised at his lack of respect for tradition. The main points of the agreement arrived at were the adoption of single-member constituencies of roughly equal size as the norm of representation; boroughs which were double-member constituencies and qualified for two members according to population were to retain the status quo – this was probably a concession to Gladstone's personal preference for retaining historical communities; boroughs with less than 15,000 inhabitants would be disfranchised and those with less than 50,000 would be reduced to one member. A number of specific deals about constituency boundaries were made between Dilke and Salisbury, who met regularly as members of the Royal Commission on Housing, but the main business of drawing up boundaries was to be left to the three boundary commissions for England, Scotland and Wales. Their main instructions were to have regard 'to the pursuits of the population'. The question of university representation nearly caused a last-minute breakdown of the inter-party agreement, but it did not prove difficult to persuade Gladstone that, whatever the views of his Radical colleagues, this should continue. In its final shape the settlement owed more to Conservative than to Liberal views, but in going for equal electoral districts the Tories had appropriated a traditional Radical device. They did so because on the one hand it helped to segregate rural and urban voters, on the other hand it would help them to capitalize on their strength in suburban and middle-class areas of big cities. Salisbury had probably become convinced that it was worth taking a gamble on Tory democracy and that there were many Tory supporters among the industrial proletariat.

Once there was agreement between the party leaders on redistribution the passage of the bill embodying the scheme was largely assured; the work of the boundary commissions went ahead efficiently and with little party acrimony. The parliamentary reform of 1884–5 was, in equalizing the borough and county franchise, less controversial than the legislation of 1867 and 1832, but the recasting of the constituencies was more radical and longer lasting. To this day the single-member constituency electing a member by bare plurality remains, with all its far-reaching consequences for the political system as a whole, characteristic of Britain. Household rather than manhood suffrage remained the order of the day until 1918. Registration procedure had been changed in 1878 in boroughs, so as to make the preliminary lists of electors more accurate and therefore lessen the scope for vexatious objections by the parties. The Act of 1878 was now extended to the counties, as was one promoted by Dilke in 1878 to lengthen the hours of polling, important for allowing working-class electors to record their vote. Nevertheless there was no fundamental change in the system of registration; it still put the lower class of voters, who might frequently change their place of residence, at a considerable disadvantage. This continued to be reflected in the striking difference in the proportion of electors registered in the affluent as against the poorer constituencies in large cities. Much plural voting survived, not only through the university seats, but through the surviving property franchises, which continued to provide a considerable proportion of electors in county divisions. The extent to which the electoral system fell short of realizing the principle of one man, one vote had much bearing on the prospects of the political parties until the First World War.

X

The enactment of reform was a triumph for Gladstone, but the immediate consequence was that speculation about his retirement revived strongly. An end-of-term atmosphere enveloped his government, for it was plain that as soon as the various bills connected with parliamentary reform would have passed into law in the early months of 1885 there would have to be an appeal to the new constituencies. At the beginning of February the news of Gordon's death reached London; he had been under siege at Khartoum and the force to relieve him arrived just too late. It was the most terrible blow to the government and the Prime Minister since the Phoenix Park murders. The government had been determined to pull out of the Sudan, but 'Chinese' Gordon was an odd choice for the task of evacuation. There had been a press campaign for his appointment and Gladstone had agreed to it reluctantly. He and his colleagues soon realized they had given a hostage to fortune; only a month after Gordon's appointment Gladstone was saying that he must win or lose by him. The immediate

result of Gordon's death, however, was that for the moment
Gladstone's retirement was again postponed. He could hardly end his
illustrious career at a moment when he was under hysterical attack
from much of the press and the public.

In three public speeches in January 1885 Chamberlain fired the
opening shots in the campaign that was intended to make his brand of
radicalism prevail in the Liberal Party and perhaps enable him personally to become Gladstone's successor. The groundwork for the
prescription he was offering had been laid over the previous two years
in a series of articles in the *Fortnightly Review*, which were about to be
published in pamphlet form as *The Radical Programme* in preparation
for the forthcoming election. Events were to decree that these proposals never became official Liberal Party policy in 1885 and hence
the term 'unauthorized programme', used in the autumn campaign
by Goschen as a counterattack from the opposite wing of the party,
became attached to them. Chamberlain hardly wrote any of *The
Radical Programme* himself, but it owed much to his initiative and
formed the substance of his speeches in 1885. The very existence of
the programme shows that Radicals like Chamberlain and Dilke were
committed to a new concept of politics. They assumed that the masses
in the democratic age wanted reforms to improve their living conditions and deal with their grievances; these had to be embodied in a
coherent programme, which had to supersede the separate causes or
'fads' that up to now inspired the Liberal movement, be they
temperance or the Bulgarian Atrocities. In the National Liberal
Federation the organizational structure had already been created to
carry such a programme to the people and to help shape it in the
future.

The element that figured most prominently in the Radical Programme were proposals about land: the power of local authorities to
acquire it, the tenure and taxation of it and the provision of allotments. It was ironical that urban politicians like Chamberlain should
have been so much concerned with essentially rural problems, but it
was not entirely surprising in view of the fact that the agricultural
labourer had the vote for the first time and that land reform ideas had
such a wide currency on the far Left. Moreover some of the proposals,
such as compulsory powers of purchase, related to urban slum
clearance and owed a good deal to Chamberlain's own 'municipal
socialism' at Birmingham. The slogan 'free land' encompassed the
land proposals of the Radical programme; 'free schools' was the
slogan for the demand, simple in itself, that elementary education
should be free. By implication this demand raised the difficult
problem of the future of denominational schools. If these were to
remain under Church control, then free education would raise the

spectre of Clause 25, the nonconformist grievance about paying rates or taxes to Church schools. If it meant free board school education, then it constituted an attack on the future of the Church schools. In spite of Chamberlain's disavowal this was what it was often taken to mean and it may well have backfired electorally. Other points in the Radical programme related to the further progress of democracy in the system of government, in local government through the establishment of elected county councils, in central government through payment of members and, rather vaguely, through reform of the House of Lords. The programme identified what was to prove one of the most potent engines of future change in demanding graduated taxation, but it was traditional in supporting the old nonconformist cause of disestablishment.

In his public utterances Chamberlain did not always commit himself to every detail of the Radical Programme and it was often the manner as much as the substance of what he said that carried the challenge not only to Tories and men of property, but also to the right wing of his own party. In his first speech of the year 1885 Chamberlain had used the phrase 'what ransom will property pay for the security which it enjoys?' and this was much held against him. All this 'Jacobin' rhetoric could not disguise the fact that the Radical Programme hardly went much beyond traditional liberalism in its specific demands and was new mainly in its sweep and coherence. It assumed an ultimate harmony of classes and a willingness on the part of the wealthier members of the community to pay a 'ransom' to ensure the contentment of their poorer brethren. Gladstone deprecated the Radical Programme as 'constructionism', for it contrasted with his way of leading the Liberal 'broad church' through inspirational causes; it was also often attacked as 'collectivist' and 'socialistic'. Yet it hardly foreshadowed the kind of social reforms a Liberal government eventually carried after 1906 and it has been called one of the outstanding dead ends in British political history. Some of its demands, like elected county councils and free elementary schools, were only a few years later carried by a Conservative government with the support of Chamberlain.

The first broadsides fired by Chamberlain on behalf of the Radical Programme in January 1885 may, amongst other things, have been designed to stake out his position in the plot that appeared at that moment to be going on to install Hartington as Prime Minister. Gladstone soon overcame the nervous prostration and insomnia that afflicted him in the first two or three weeks of 1885 and the crisis of Gordon's death restored his powers miraculously. With Granville he was able to bring the harassing problem of Egyptian finances to an international agreement, though it proved hardly satisfactory in the long run. Then the problem of Russian expansion on the Afghan border once more reached flash-point when a Russian army defeated the Afghans at Pendjeh. This time the government had no option but to present a firm front and Gladstone, to some extent against his inclination, had to strike a patriotic Palmerstonian pose. The speech he made on moving a vote of credit for possible hostilities in Central Asia received universal approbation and thus by early May the government which had been so greatly abused for its alleged weakness abroad could claim to have successfully asserted the national interest. The situation seemed again propitious for Gladstone's retirement and for once Mrs Gladstone, normally reluctant to move from the centre of affairs, was reconciled and beginning to pack.

This time it was Ireland again that looked like breaking up the Liberal Party and made it impossible for Gladstone to give up, or, in another interpretation, gave him an excuse for staying. The prospect of a greatly enlarged Parnellite party in the new Parliament had for long cast its shadow over all political calculations. Chamberlain had in the winter of 1884/5 put out renewed feelers to Parnell to revive something like the Kilmainham alliance, after a period when relations between Irish nationalists and British Radicals had become distinctly cool. He had proposed a scheme of devolution for Ireland, a Central Board to replace Dublin Castle, with subordinate County Boards, which was, however, to stop well short of Irish independence or even a fully-fledged Irish Parliament. Chamberlain later claimed that he had been misled into thinking that Parnell accepted his scheme as a final solution of the Irish problem, for Captain O'Shea, once more the intermediary, had failed to pass on the letters in which Parnell made it clear that he was at most prepared to look on the Central Board proposal as an interim step. It is hardly likely that Chamberlain did not know this but throughout the early months of 1885 the Parnellite alliance was a prize he was determined to pursue.

Chamberlain was not the only political leader to fish in Irish waters. In advance of the vote of censure on the government's policy in the Sudan on 28 February 1885, the Tory chief whip, presumably with the agreement of his leaders, had had an interview with Parnell at the latter's request. The Irish leader sought information on the Conservative attitude to redistribution and the number of Irish seats, in the event of a change of government, and was assured that the Tories would stand by the Downing Street agreements. The question which now moved to the centre of Irish affairs was the renewal of the Crimes Act, passed for three years in 1882. Lord Spencer, the Irish Viceroy, whose views carried much weight with Gladstone, was convinced that the government must retain some special powers, given the tenuous state of law and order in Ireland, and the Prime Minister reluctantly agreed. Chamberlain, Dilke and Gladstone himself wanted a more positive approach. The negotiations over the Central Board scheme were still going on and Chamberlain hoped to bring them to a successful conclusion with the aid of Cardinal Manning and his influence on the Irish hierarchy. Spencer and others were averse to granting the Irish anything so far-reaching as a national elected body and there were also disagreements in the cabinet about the desirability of promoting a land purchase scheme for Ireland. Throughout May 1885 Chamberlain and Dilke were threatening resignation. On the other hand Parnell was increasingly given reason to expect that if the Tories were to form a government they would not renew coercion in Ireland. Late at night on 8 June 1885 the government was defeated by a majority of 12 on the budget. The Parnellites had voted with the Tories and over 70 Liberals, mostly on the Left of the party, did not vote. Next morning the government, having teetered on the brink of disintegration and defeat for months, decided to resign. Especially for Chamberlain and Dilke it was a matter for relief, for they would now be free to campaign for their Radical Programme and Irish policy free from the restraints of office.

XI

The situation now had similarities with both 1873, when Disraeli refused to take office after Gladstone's defeat on the Irish University Bill, and with Peel's short-lived government of 1835. As in 1873, there were genuine doubts whether it would be to the advantage of the Tories to take office as a minority government, thus allowing the voters to forget the shortcomings of their predecessors. It could be argued, as in 1873, that there was nothing in the parliamentary defeat to compel the resignation of the government. Unlike 1873, the arguments in favour of taking office prevailed among Conservatives this time and after a fortnight of negotiation Gladstone's undertakings about securing current business in the House were considered sufficient. There would have to be at least several months of minority government, for the process of redrawing the constituencies would not be completed until well into the autumn. The similarity with Peel's situation 50 years earlier lies in the fact that this Conservative caretaker government, almost equally short-lived as that of 1835, enabled Salisbury, like Peel, to consolidate his leadership of the party.

Northcote's claims to the premiership were finally set aside, but he was relegated with some dignity, assuming the position of First Lord of the Treasury, clearly designated as the second man in the team and having an earldom conferred on him. Churchill at the India Office had limited scope for making trouble. Salisbury clearly demonstrated that he was in command and thus began 17 years as party leader, during which he served as Prime Minister longer than anyone since Liverpool. He was a most unlikely man to preside over the political fortunes of Britain in an age of mass electorates and advancing democracy. His scepticism about the political wisdom of the masses was on record; in his younger days it had amounted to neurotic fear. He was an intensely private man who had only gradually accustomed himself to leaving Hatfield on the speech-making forays which his prominent role demanded. His skill as a political operator was to show itself to the full in the momentous crisis which now unfolded.

One of the first decisions which the Conservative government took was not to renew coercion in Ireland. They also decided to introduce an Irish Land Purchase Act, known as Ashbourne's Act, after the new Lord Chancellor of Ireland, the first of a succession of Conservative Irish land purchase measures. It was part of the policy which later became known as 'Killing home rule with kindness' and in the longer run land purchase undoubtedly helped to draw the sting of Irish agrarian grievances. Some members of the Tory cabinet, notably Churchill and Carnarvon, now Irish Viceroy, wanted to go further in dealing with the Irish problem and in doing so cementing the tacit alliance with Parnell that had brought the Tories to power. Salisbury had never had much sympathy with Irish nationalism and saw it as the main task of the party to support those elements in Ireland, Anglo-Irish landlords and protestant Ulster, that upheld the Union. He was, however, prepared to give his colleagues some room for manoeuvre and it was thus that Carnarvon had his secret meeting with Parnell in an empty house in Mayfair on 1 August 1885. No commitments of any kind arose out of this meeting or other contacts; when Parnell revealed the secret the following year and claimed that he had been offered Home Rule by Carnarvon, his aim was to embarrass the Conservatives. Salisbury was well aware that even the slightest suspicion of a conciliatory policy towards Irish nationalism would upset many sections of his party at a time when his hold on it was not yet secure. On the other hand Salisbury had no intention of throwing away the advantage the Tories would reap, particularly in borough elections, from a decision by Parnell to instruct Irish voters in Great Britain to support the Conservatives. There were at least several reasons why Parnell might well give such an instruction. He might judge that this could be the best way of keeping the two major parties as closely balanced as possible, thus making the most of his own bargaining power. Moreover, the Conservatives controlled the House of Lords and had therefore a better chance of getting an Irish Home Rule Bill on to the statute book than the Liberals. In addition there was one issue on which Irish Catholics and Anglican Tories saw eye to eye: both were opposed to the 'free school' plank in the Radical programme. Salisbury therefore had to tread a delicate path between keeping his lines open to Parnell and staying in the mainstream of Tory opposition to nationalism. In October 1885 he made an election speech at Newport which was suitably ambiguous, mentioning both 'the integrity of empire' and the 'prosperity, contentment and happiness' of the Irish people.

Ireland was, however, by no means the predominant issue in the summer and autumn of 1885. More preoccupying was the question in what shape and under what leadership the Liberal party would contest the election. The continuing divisions in the Liberal cabinet, in the closing stages mainly on Ireland, ensured that Gladstone would stay as leader, at least through the election campaign. Soon after the fall of the government, the attempt to reach an understanding between Chamberlain and Parnell along the lines of the central board scheme collapsed. Chamberlain had placed a great deal of faith in the alliance with the Nationalists as a means of capturing both Gladstone and the party as a whole; the humiliating rebuff he now received, with the Nationalist newspaper *United Ireland* openly attacking him, may well have determined him never to put any trust in Parnell again. But just as Chamberlain was discarding an Irish solution as a major plank in the Liberal election programme, Gladstone became increasingly convinced that Ireland would be the dominant issue after the election, and he hinted to the principal figures in the party that only a big Irish crisis would induce him to postpone his retirement after the election.

In the autumn election campaign he was back in his old role as the mediator between the right and the left wing of the Liberal Party. Public salvoes from Hartington and Chamberlain staked out the positions of the two wings; Gladstone's own pronouncements clung carefully to the centre. The Liberal broad church was in fact no more nor less divided than for many years previously and everybody found it desirable to go on sheltering under the Gladstonian umbrella. On Ireland Hartington and Chamberlain took much the same line, a clear 'no' to Parnell's public demand for an Irish national Parliament, and thus moved much closer together than had been the case before the Liberal government fell. Gladstone himself remained studiously vague in his public pronouncements on Ireland and left himself every room for manoeuvre; he refused to enter a bidding auction for the support of Parnell. As the election drew nearer there were many indications that Chamberlain's campaign, in particular 'free schools' and disestablishment in England, Scotland and Wales, was antagonizing moderate voters. On the Conservative side the demand for protection or 'fair trade' was heard a good deal, but it was far too divisive an issue to receive any official endorsement; the Salisbury government's method of defusing it had been the appointment of the Royal Commission on the Depression of Trade. Just before the voting began Parnell issued his manifesto instructing Irish voters in Great Britain to vote against the Liberal candidates. How much weight this carried remains a matter for debate; it is probable that the pressure of the Catholic Church, led by Cardinal Manning, to oppose the advocates of secular education was at least as effective and that local factors were often decisive. Liberal pundits reckoned after the election that the Parnell manifesto cost them at least 20 borough seats, but this may well have been an alibi for their unexpectedly poor performance in the boroughs. It is indisputable that the Parnell manifesto made it that much more difficult after the election to bring the Liberal Party into an alliance with the Irish Nationalists.

Parnell achieved his aim of holding the balance between the British parties with almost mathematical accuracy. 335 Liberals, 249 Conservatives and 86 Irish Nationalists were elected. The radical changes in the electoral system make it difficult to compare this election with previous ones. Undoubtedly the general contemporary judgement that the Liberals had done well in rural and badly in urban constituencies was correct. The enfranchisement of the rural worker had opened for the Liberal Party a new reservoir of electoral support. It is impossible to discover whether the motivation behind the Liberal surge in counties was gratitude for the enfranchisement, the impact of the land proposals, particularly 'three acres and a cow', in the Radical Programme; or long-standing class antagonism now free to express itself and perhaps accentuated by the agricultural depression. Economic depression, sharp again in 1885, may well have been the main cause for the relative Liberal slump in cities; Gladstone attributed it to this cause and the fair trade cry. 'Fair Trade + Parnell + Church + Chamberlain have damaged us a good deal in the boroughs . . . I place the *causae damni* in what I think their order of importance.' Chamberlain was perhaps the greatest loser: the gulf was large between his earlier expectations that his type of radicalism would take over the Liberal Party and the situation on the morrow of the election. In Ireland politics was sectarianized: the Parnellites carried all but the University seats outside Ulster, while all Liberals failed in Ulster.

The result of the 1885 election, with its potential for stalemate, pitched the political world into a welter of calculations and manoeuvres.

The Westminster parliamentary system, placed in an intractable situation, largely turned in on itself and became almost totally preoccupied with finding a method of functioning again. A large number of permutations were conceivable: there could be an understanding between the two main parties to settle the Irish issue by agreement, but there could also be a pact to proceed with other agreed policies, such as the reform of parliamentary procedure, while ignoring Ireland. Many Liberals were so disenchanted with Parnell and the Nationalists that they were not in a mood to back a policy of concessions to Ireland. Various party realignments could be envisaged: a Tory–Whig coalition, or a centrist coalition, perhaps dominated by the two maverick figures on either side, Chamberlain and Churchill, and with the existing leaders Gladstone and Salisbury relegated in one form or another. Another obvious possibility was a Liberal–Parnellite alliance united on offering self-government to Ireland. All these possibilities were explored by the leading political figures and by lesser men, sometimes tentatively, sometimes definitely, secretly or openly. Gladstone's conviction that an Irish crisis was inescapable seemed to have been borne out by events. His preference was for keeping the Tories in office and letting them produce an Irish settlement, with Liberal support. Failing this he would take up the Irish cause himself; this was how he had led the Liberal Party in 1868 and again in 1876. Both alternatives would keep him at the forefront of the stage. Salisbury had never shown much inclination to embark upon a large-scale enterprise of remedial legislation for Ireland and the risks to his party and his own position were far too great. Gladstone and Salisbury remained in control of their parties and their attitudes ultimately prevailed.

Gladstone played his cards with consummate skill, revealing nothing of his intentions before the meeting of the new Parliament at the end of January 1886. His hand was all but forced by the Hawarden 'Kite', the revelation by his son Herbert, an ardent Home Ruler, to Wemyss Reid, the editor of the liberal *Leeds Mercury* that his father had been converted to Home Rule. The 'Kite' had been flown to counteract the apparent intention of Chamberlain, Dilke and their associates to keep the Tories in office, shelving both Ireland and Gladstone. The 'Kite' made it that much easier for the Conservative cabinet to decide to have nothing to do with an Irish settlement and to reject Gladstone's offer of support in such an enterprise. On the other hand Salisbury found it difficult to unite his cabinet on a positively pro-Union, anti-nationalist policy, including if necessary coercion. Churchill, Hicks Beach, Chancellor of the Exchequer and Leader of the House, and Carnarvon were still casting about for alternatives; Churchill would have preferred collaboration with a Liberal section around Chamberlain and a Tory reconstruction enhancing his own power at the expense of Salisbury. Thus the government was unable, on the reassembly of Parliament, to present a forthright Irish policy until too late and lost the opportunity of forcing Gladstone to declare himself. Salisbury's defeat at the end of January 1886 was more humiliating than it need have been. Nevertheless the Tory leader, now firmly in control of his party, was confident that events would soon turn his way. Over 70 Liberals, including John Bright, had abstained in the division, on a 'three acres and a cow' amendment, that defeated Salisbury, and 18 including Hartington had voted with the government.

XII

Gladstone entered upon the difficult task of forming his third government with considerable buoyancy. He had reasserted control over his party, yet had kept his hands unfettered apart from an unspecific commitment to present an Irish policy without coercion or repression. To those whom he offered a position in his cabinet he read a statement that he proposed 'to examine whether it is or is not practicable to comply with the desire widely prevalent in Ireland . . . for the establishment . . . for a legislative body . . . to deal with Irish as distinguished from imperial affairs . . .'. Hartington refused to join the new ministry on these terms, but Chamberlain did. The circumstances and manner of his appointment to the Local Government Board showed, however, that he came in clearly as a subordinate and that his position in this third Gladstone ministry was tenuous. His bargaining power had been much reduced not only by the election results: his closest associate Dilke had seen his career shattered by a divorce scandal and the rift with Morley was all but complete. In a surprise move Gladstone appointed Morley to the key post of Chief Secretary for Ireland and thus made him into one of his principal lieutenants for the remainder of his term as Liberal leader.

By contrast, Chamberlain stayed in the third Gladstone government only a few weeks: when the outlines of Gladstone's Irish settlement had become clear, he resigned, together with Trevelyan, another Radical who had become deeply alienated from Irish nationalism. It would have been difficult to foresee that this was in fact the first step towards Chamberlain's permanent separation from the

Liberal Party. There has been much speculation about Chamberlain's motives. His proclaimed objections to Gladstone's proposals are hardly sufficient reason for his separation from the Liberal leader now, when previously he had always gone to great length to stay under the great man's umbrella and when he himself had put forward Irish proposals not so very different from those put on the table now. Chamberlain had many reservations about Home Rule, but so did others who remained in the Liberal cabinet; his probable calculation was that Gladstone was bound to fail and that by separating from him at this stage he would best be able to regain a leading position in a radicalized Liberal Party. Gladstone declared later: 'Nothing in this whole affair gave me greater satisfaction than Chamberlain's resignation'; he was released from the necessity of fighting for his Irish bills inch by inch against a determined opponent inside his own cabinet.

There were to be two Irish bills, one to set up a separate legislature in Dublin, the other a Land Purchase Bill to buy out the Irish landlords. Gladstone felt that if the new system of governing Ireland was to have a chance of succeeding a further large step towards solving the agrarian question must be taken. The Irish legislature was to be unicameral but with two orders, which, on demand, could be required to vote separately. The first order was to consist of 28 Irish representative peers and 75 members elected on a £75 franchise. This first order could veto the proposals of the second, popularly elected order, for three years. A considerable safeguard was thus built in for the minorities of Ireland, above all the landowners. The Irish legislature could not deal with certain subjects, such as defence, foreign affairs and international trade, which were reserved for Westminster, from whence all Irish members would be removed. The disappearance of the obstructive Irish from the House of Commons was one of the attractions of the bill for many, particularly on the Left of the Liberal Party. Chamberlain made this one of his chief points of objection, on the ground that without Irish representation at Westminster, final separation would become inevitable. Moreover, since Ireland would contribute one-fifteenth of the imperial revenue, there would be taxation without representation. In the original draft of the bill there were powers for the Irish legislature to impose a tariff. This was alarming to many including again Chamberlain, particularly at a time of economic depression, and was eventually dropped. Under the Land Purchase Bill landlords would be bought out at 20 years' purchase of their rental, while tenants could secure 100 per cent loans at low interest to buy. The operation would be financed by a large loan from the British treasury. This aspect ran into opposition from all quarters; particularly the Radicals found it difficult to stomach that the British taxpayer should incur a large debt in order to put money into the pockets of landlords.

The Home Rule Bill made no separate provision for Ulster, in spite of the clear indication in the election of 1885 that the politics of the province were now dominated by fear of rule from Dublin. There were severe sectarian riots in Belfast in 1886. Lord Randolph Churchill was the first major politician to exploit Ulster sentiment with a visit to the province in February 1886, when he coined the slogan 'Ulster will fight, and Ulster will be right'. Churchill did not normally sympathize with Ulster Tories, but it suited him at that particular moment to 'play the Orange card'. The moderate Irish unionists who had considerable influence on his views were by now much alarmed by the gathering pace of Home Rule policy. Gladstone felt that Ulster could not be allowed a veto over Irish policy and that the minority safeguards in his bill afforded sufficient protection.

Gladstone's proposals were conservative and the fact that Parnell accepted them was an indication of the extent to which the Irish leader was now committed to constitutional progress. There was also an air of unreality about the whole enterprise, for even if the bills passed the House of Commons it was certain that the Lords would reject them. Nevertheless a great wave of hostility met Gladstone when his scheme became public. Perhaps the most fundamental emotion aroused was fear that a separate, hostile Ireland, supported by other hostile powers, might in the future hold a dagger to the throat of England. The disintegration of the British Empire would have begun. 'That a powerful nation should (except under the force of crushing defeat) assent to an arrangement which would decrease its resources and authority must inevitably appear to all the world to be . . . such a sign either of declining strength or declining spirit as would in a short time provoke the aggression of rivals and enemies', wrote A.V. Dicey, the well-known constitutional lawyer and supporter of Unionism. There was a great sense of outraged property: if Irish landlords, protestants, Ulster could all be thrown to the wolves in order to appease a violent agitation from below, nothing would be safe. There was the traditional contempt for the Irish and the feeling that the interests of England and her Empire must take precedence over those of Ireland. A small country mainly populated by an ignorant peasantry held in thrall by an obscurantist Church should not be allowed to turn in on itself, but was better governed by a great and enlightened nation from without. On the other side of the divide, the broader argument in favour of Home Rule was based on justice, in Gladstone's case strongly tinged by his religious beliefs. A union of hearts and minds would end the unhappy relationship between the two countries. On a more restricted level the manifestation of Irish feeling in the 1885 election, with the nationalists sweeping the board outside Ulster, could not be brushed aside by anyone who attached importance to the popular will; many on the Radical wing of the Liberal Party, who had been alienated by the antics of the Parnellites and particularly the injunction to vote Tory in November 1885, were nevertheless now persuaded by the argument that the clearly expressed will of the Irish people should not be thwarted. Among the intellectual and academic community the same attitudes that had caused many to frown on Gladstone's Bulgarian Atrocity campaign now led them into opposition to Home Rule. Men like Leslie Stephen, Goldwin Smith and Henry Sidgwick, all Liberals in their day, were now, with different emphases, opponents of Home Rule.

Public clamour about Home Rule was perhaps disproportionate to what was at stake since there was so little immediate likelihood of the bills becoming law; it was the opinion-makers rather than the general public who were in a state of excitement. The destinies of the Westminster world were, however, closely affected by the fortunes of Home Rule and the two months between the introduction of the Home Rule Bill in April 1886 and its defeat in June were filled with feverish political activity. When Parliament reconvened after the Easter recess at the end of April the shadow of another general election, which was bound to come fairly soon whether the Home Rule Bill passed or not, loomed over all calculations and manoeuvres. Gladstone sought to consolidate his hold on the left of centre in the mainstream of British politics; in an address to the electors of Midlothian on 1 May he said: 'The adverse host, then, consists of class and the dependants of class . . . this formidable army is . . . the same . . . that has fought in every one of the great political battles of the last 60 years, and has been defeated . . .'. Five days later the General Committee of the National Liberal Federation overwhelmingly endorsed Gladstone and Home Rule. The instrument which Chamberlain had created had repudiated him. Gladstone was winning the battle for the hearts and minds of Radicals in the country: not only the National Liberal Federation, local and regional Liberal and Radical associations and clubs backed him, but also the principal figures in the traditional Liberal auxiliaries like the Liberation Society, the United Kingdom Alliance and the Peace Society, even if the organizations themselves maintained a nominal neutrality on Home Rule. The same was true of most of the Radical and nonconformist press.

The battle was on for most of May for the vote of Radical MPs, who constituted something like half the total number of Liberals returned in 1885 and would make up an even larger proportion after the inevitable defection of right-wingers on Home Rule. Chamberlain and Gladstone manoeuvred for advantage, the former demanding concessions, such as the retention of Irish MPs at Westminster, the latter appearing to make some, and neither wishing to accept the blame for a split. Churchill's comment on these manoeuvres sums them up neatly: 'Gladstone is pretending to make up to Joe in order to pass his Bill; and Joe is pretending to make up to Gladstone in order to throw out his Bill. Diamond cut diamond.' At the end of May Chamberlain managed to rally around 50 members to vote against the second reading of the Home Rule Bill, due a week later, but only about 30 of these could be regarded as Radicals, the rest being Hartingtonians. A letter from Bright, now a convinced opponent of Home Rule, had a strong influence on the Radicals in the group. Hartington was the leader of all moderate and right-wing Liberals and Whigs who opposed Home Rule and at least until the middle of May 1886 cherished the hope that he could recapture the Liberal Party for a policy of moderate Irish reforms falling short of the establishment of a separate legislature in Dublin. If Gladstone had been less successful in retaining control of the bulk of the Liberal Party, a 'Palmerstonian' Liberal government led by Hartington would have been a distinct possibility. Chamberlain was increasingly driven into collaboration with the Hartingtonians but had to take care that these links with Whigs and through them with Tories did not damage what remained of his popular base.

In the meantime Lord Salisbury was working to consolidate his position on the Right of the political spectrum, just as Gladstone was doing on the Left. He did so in a typically relaxed fashion, returning to London only in early April after a month on the Riviera. He had meetings with Hartington, the beginning of the eventual Conservative–Liberal Unionist alliance, and found him sympathetic to deal with. He was irritated, however, by the continuing emotional attachment of Whigs to the Liberal Party and the caution which Liberal opponents of Home Rule approached any collaboration with Tories. Salisbury made his strongest bid for the support of all right-wing opponents of Home Rule in a public speech on 15 May, in which he compared the Irish with the Hottentots in their incapacity for self-government, advised them to emigrate to Manitoba to solve their economic woes and called for 20 years' 'resolute government' in Ireland. Such language, 'manacles and Manitoba' Morley called it, from 'the master of jibes and jeers' was perhaps not surprising, but Salisbury had a definite purpose in mind in appearing so reactionary. He was trying to reassure all those who had been alarmed by the previous Tory flirtation with Irish nationalism and feared another *volte-face*. He was also trying to counteract Hartington's attempt, then at its height, to recreate Liberal unity around himself; by tarring all opposition to Home Rule with the brush of reaction, Salisbury was making it difficult for Hartington, already seen in association with Tories, to become the rallying point for a wide section of Liberals. A 'Palmerstonian' Liberal government under Hartington would have suited Salisbury no more than it would have Gladstone. As for Churchill he was at this stage acting as Salisbury's loyal lieutenant; he had much contact with Chamberlain and other Liberal dissidents and in the longer run still had his eye on a reconstruction of the Conservative Party in his own image.

The Home Rule Bill was defeated on 8 June by a vote of 341 to 311. Over 90 Liberals voted against the Bill, less than a third of them followers of Chamberlain. Two days later the cabinet decided to dissolve Parliament. It had been a factor of importance in the evolving situation that since early April there had been in existence an understanding in principle that Conservatives would not put up candidates in opposition to Liberals who declared against Home Rule, in return for a rather vague commitment by the Liberal Unionist leaders to instruct their sympathizers to vote against Home Rule Liberals. This compact certainly strengthened the resolution of Liberal Unionist MPs who were under pressure from Gladstonian constituency associations. Salisbury hoped that an early election would consolidate the parliamentary split in the Liberal Party into an electoral split, which would prove more irreversible. In the event the Unionist electoral compact worked remarkably well, in spite of much local bitterness. The efforts by the Conservative Party managers to prevent their men from opposing Liberal Unionists failed in only three cases in the election of 1886; 16 anti-Home Rule Liberals did not stand again; probably in some cases because they would have been opposed by Tories. Nevertheless the general election of 1886 confirmed the existence of a separate Liberal Unionist Party of about 78. They were mainly Whigs and moderate Liberals, but included a group of about 20 Radicals, most of them followers of Chamberlain, who retained his base in and around Birmingham.

On the Liberal side Gladstone strongly advised his colleagues to go for an immediate dissolution rather than resignation; he put great store by the fact the Irish vote would this time go to the Liberals and that the Liberal masses were enthusiastic for Home Rule. Schnadhorst, the organizer of the National Liberal Federation, gave an optimistic assessment of Liberal prospects based on similar arguments. In the event the Liberals suffered losses as a result of four main causes: the Liberal-Unionist electoral compact; the large number of uncontested seats, over 150, three-quarters of which returned Conservative or Liberal Unionist members; disillusion among rural voters, first-time Liberals in 1885; differential abstention by voters – in a low turn-out far more Liberals than Conservatives abstained. Liberals maintained their position tolerably well in Scotland and in Wales, where Liberal Unionists fared badly, and their losses were less marked in working-class areas than elsewhere. Thus previous trends were generally confirmed: the Liberals still had a majority of the working-class vote, were predominant on the Celtic fringe, but the middle classes and suburbia were more firmly Tory than before. In terms of seats the Liberal losses, 143, were the most marked since 1832. In the new Parliament there were 316 Tories, 191 Liberals, 85 Parnellites and 78 Liberal Unionists. The future was as uncertain as ever; the obstacles to a whole-hearted alliance between Conservatives and Liberal-Unionist were still great, many minds were still set on a Liberal reunion, and no calculations could be made without taking into account the presence of the 85 Irish Nationalists.

Nevertheless, much of great importance for the future of British politics had occurred. Gladstone, whose retirement had been a probability throughout 1885, was firmly back in control of the Liberal Party and was to remain there for another eight years. It was no longer the broad church it had been for over 50 years. The departure of most Whigs and many on the right of the party lay in the logic of events; Home Rule was the occasion rather than the underlying cause of their apostasy from Liberalism. Men like Hartington or Goschen could, however, have remained within the Liberal fold with no greater discomfort than Harcourt and Rosebery. Gladstone was thus left with a party more radical than ever before and this hardly accorded with his inclinations. Even the Radical wing of the party was gravely weakened by the loss of Chamberlain, more seriously than the relatively small number of followers he took with him would suggest. The Radicals left in the Liberal Party were, in spite of their numerical ascendancy, unable to adapt the party quickly enough to the developing concerns of the working class. Chamberlain might have helped the process of adaptation; his unauthorized programme was itself insufficient, but he had energy and an eye for the material needs of the masses. Home Rule and Gladstone's continued leadership were not solely responsible for the Liberal Party's difficulties in accommodating the demands of labour, but they much aggravated these difficulties.

Gladstone's success in asserting his leadership exacted a high price. Even the cause of Ireland was not necessarily served by 'the old man in a hurry' who had taken it up against all the odds. More modest Irish reforms, including elected local government bodies, soon to be established in the rest of the United Kingdom, might well have been of greater practical benefit than the national autonomy which was not immediately attainable. Chamberlain's failure was greater than Gladstone's, for in spite of many tactical successes he completely failed to convert the majority of Liberal Radicals to his way of thinking and found himself isolated. As time went on Liberal reunion became more not less difficult; his growing association with the Tories put his political base, even in Birmingham, in jeopardy. None of the substantive reasons for Chamberlain's course, concern for imperial integrity, fear of Irish tariffs, distrust of Parnell, can entirely explain his conduct. He was a ruthlessly ambitious man whose instinct when cornered was to fight back viciously; this drove him step by step into outright opposition to Gladstone and his former party. The great gainers from the events of 1885 and 1886 were the Conservatives and Salisbury. Contrary to expectations, and prognostications, they inherited a long period in office, helped by Gladstone's untimely dissolution in 1886. Within the Conservative Party Salisbury managed to retain control and to move nearer to his goal of making it a party of resistance. It was perhaps the most surprising outcome of a crisis second to none for drama and swift reversals.

6   Salisbury Consolidates the Conservative Ascendancy 1886–1895

I

The party realignment of 1886 made Ireland into the touchstone and yardstick of British politics. The supporters of the Union were on one side of the political divide, the advocates of Irish autonomy on the other. It was, however, hardly likely that Ireland, an issue essentially extraneous to the persistent problems and divisions of British society, could for long crowd out other more pressing matters. The Conservative hold on power was tenuous and to consolidate it a choice had to be made. Either there had to be a programme of Tory democracy, or 'stealing the Whigs' clothes while they were bathing', a swimming with the tide of radical reform, which was thought to be still running strongly. This was Churchill's prescription. Salisbury's view was quite different: everything should be done to encourage the conservative mood of resistance which the country had just shown in refusing to give way to the demands of Irish nationalism; reform by legislation could only be forced down the throats of Tory supporters in small doses, otherwise their morale would be irretrievably damaged.

Salisbury's hope of establishing a broadly based government of resistance could not be immediately realized, because the Liberal Unionists refused to take part in a coalition. Salisbury offered to serve under Hartington, making only the one significant condition that Chamberlain should not be included in the cabinet. Hartington had to refuse: he would have had to preside over a predominantly Tory government and many of his Liberal Unionist colleagues preferred to keep the option of Liberal reunion open. Thus a purely Conservative administration was formed, which had to rely for its survival on Liberal Unionist support. Inevitably Lord Randolph Churchill, in many ways a more popular Tory leader than the Prime Minister himself, was a central figure in the government, as Leader of the House of Commons and Chancellor of the Exchequer. During the five months that he remained a member of the cabinet conflict between him and most of his colleagues over almost the whole range of domestic and foreign policy virtually never ceased. In part it was a campaign of self-advancement by a man who saw himself clearly marked out for leadership. It is impossible to account for Lord Randolph's impatient and often erratic course except through the state of his health: the disease which was eventually to kill him, general paralysis of the insane probably caused by syphilis, was increasingly evident and must have made him aware that the time left to him was short. If he had a general political concept, it was to put reform unionism in place of Salisbury's resistance unionism, and to bring about a further restructuring of unionism, with himself and probably Chamberlain at the centre of it. In spite of his impatience, excitability and frequent downright rudeness, he still displayed much tactical skill and retained his hard-hitting style as a platform orator. On Ireland Churchill was now a relatively orthodox anti-Home Ruler, but he still had not given up hope of a lesser step towards devolution. On foreign policy he was for the moment almost Gladstonian, opposing the anti-Russian stance of Salisbury and the cabinet over the current crisis in Bulgaria, anxious to avoid expensive commitments, never averse to crossing swords with his old bugbear Northcote, who as Earl of Iddesleigh was now in charge of the Foreign Office. In domestic affairs Churchill put forward a wide-ranging programme of reforms in the so-called Dartford manifesto, a speech delivered on 2 October 1886: elected local government, extension of elementary education, reduction of taxation and expenditure, allotments, easement of land transfer, tithe and railway rates reform. Churchill afterwards claimed that he had cleared the speech with Salisbury and that it was in substance similar to what Salisbury had himself said a year earlier at Newport. Nevertheless it was felt that Churchill had spoken as if he was the head of the government and that he had virtually appropriated the Liberal or even the Radical programme. Increasingly over the next two months he seemed to be forcing the government to capitulate to his ideas, often using the threat that otherwise Chamberlain might be forced to return to the Liberal fold.

The breach came over local government and the budget. On the former Churchill, in agreement with Chamberlain, claimed that new elected bodies should have control over the poor law – 'rather like leaving the cat in charge of the cream jug', was Salisbury's comment; and that any non-elected element on these bodies should be kept to a minimum. This was just the kind of medicine Salisbury was unwilling to force down the throats of his reluctant followers among the Tory gentry. On the budget Churchill envisaged a scheme of lowering income tax and making relatively large grants to local government, all this to be paid for by various savings and increased estate duties and indirect taxation. It was to be a popular budget, though in fact fairly orthodox and Churchill's colleagues did not greatly demur. The traditional clash between the Treasury and the two major spending departments, the Admiralty and the War Office, soon occurred and Churchill acted overbearingly. When he threatened to resign, almost a routine step in such circumstances, Salisbury took him at his word. The immediate ground for the breach was, from the Prime Minister's point of view, well chosen, for 'the classical annual resignation of a Chancellor of the Exchequer against his colleagues in the Army and Navy', as Chamberlain called it, was not likely to enable Churchill to mobilize a wide measure of support. He began instead to experience the disfavour which Tories traditionally reserve for rockers of the boat, particularly at a time when the boat's position was so obviously insecure.

Salisbury for a second time offered to step down in favour of Hartington, but given the embattled mood of the Tory party at this moment of danger it was hardly surprising that the Liberal Unionist leader felt unable to accept. Hartington did, however, give his approval to the appointment of Goschen to succeed Churchill as Chancellor of the Exchequer and the Conservative–Liberal Unionist alliance was thus perceptibly strengthened. Goschen's doctrinaire liberalism descended from Robert Lowe; he believed that the 'new democracy' required an authoritative élite to direct it and he was equally averse to Radical and to Tory populism. In the reconstruction of the ministry Salisbury resumed control of the Foreign Office and W.H. Smith became Leader of the House of Commons.

Another year was to elapse before the Conservative–Liberal Unionist alliance could feel securely established in power. The joker in the pack was Chamberlain; although he did not command enough parliamentary votes to bring the government down, he remained a central figure in potential party realignments. His immediate reaction to Churchill's resignation was to play the card of Liberal reunion: '. . . we Liberals are agreed upon 99 points of our programme; we only disagree upon one . . .'. Two months of abortive 'round table' negotiations with Gladstone and other Liberal leaders followed; the stumbling block to an agreement remained Gladstone's determination to exact the subordination of Chamberlain to Home Rule and his leadership. Hartingtonian and Chamberlainite Liberal Unionists were greatly concerned about the gradual erosion of their electoral base; in order to retain what was left of it they had to be seen exerting pressure on the Conservative government in the direction of domestic reform and an Irish policy not based purely on repression. By the end of the parliamentary session of 1887 it had became clear that a 'National Party' of the centre around Chamberlain and

Churchill, the object of dinner-table gossip and press speculation for the past two years, was not a runner. The erratic Churchill was rapidly fading as a major figure, though his famous remark, 'I forgot Goschen' may well be apocryphal. Chamberlain had to make his bed with the Tories and now accepted a temporary diplomatic appointment in Washington from the government. Salisbury had obtained something like the party of resistance he had always wanted.

II

Throughout the Parliament of 1886 Ireland remained, in spite of the fact that it was of marginal concern to the British electorate, at the forefront of politics. A royal commission on the Irish land question, under Lord Cowper, was appointed. The recrudescence of agrarian distress forced the government to act and like its predecessors it had to strike a balance between repression and coercion. The situation was aggravated by a new Irish campaign of agitation, the 'Plan of Campaign'; tenants were to adopt trade union tactics of collective bargaining to force the landlords to accept levels of rent even lower than those judicially fixed under the Land Act of 1881. The Plan of Campaign soon unleashed the familiar chain of eviction and violence in the Irish countryside. Parnell played a less prominent role in this act of the Irish drama. His alliance with Gladstone and the need to make the Home Rule cause as popular as possible with the British electorate compelled him to restrain Irish violence as far as possible. Illness and his liaison with Mrs O'Shea, now a marriage in all but law, forced him to take a back seat and to confine himself to playing his part as parliamentary leader. In September 1886 he introduced a Tenants' Relief Bill, which was seen by the government as little more than an attempt to make them break their undertakings to the Irish landlords and drive a wedge between Tories and Liberal Unionists. It was ominous for the government that Chamberlain abstained on this bill, while the Hartingtonians voted with the Conservatives against it. Strategically Ireland might be the cement of unionism, but tactically it retained great power to divide.

In March 1887 Hicks Beach, the Chief Secretary for Ireland, was forced to resign for reasons of health and was succeeded by Arthur Balfour, the Prime Minister's nephew. 'It seems like breaking a butterfly to extend Mr Arthur Balfour on the rack of Irish politics', was the comment of the *Freeman's Journal*. In fact Balfour, in his resolute pursuit of coercion and conciliation during the next four and a half years, proved to be one of the few British politicians to have enhanced his reputation over the affairs of Ireland. The government now introduced a stiffened Crimes Act, which outraged the Liberal Opposition and the Irish Nationalists, but was reluctantly accepted by all but a handful of Liberal Unionists. To sweeten the bitter pill of coercion for the more liberal elements in the Unionist alliance a new Land Act was introduced; it was similar to the proposals made by Parnell in the previous session and then rejected by the government. It provided for the revision of judicial rents, fixed under the 1881 Act for a term of 15 years, in line with falling prices. This constant interference with market forces in favour of the tenant and against the landlord came hard to many Conservatives, including Salisbury. To redress the balance again the cabinet decided to proscribe the Irish National League under the Crimes Act. It was on this decision that Chamberlain and a few of his adherents voted with Gladstone; it was no more than a gesture, for the Radical Unionist leader reaffirmed his commitment to keep the government in office. In particular the Crimes Bill faced heavy obstruction in the House of Commons and new rules of procedure had to be adopted, enabling the Speaker to apply the guillotine more frequently. Ever since the great influx of Parnellites in 1885 further reform of parliamentary procedure had figured prominently in the various discussions about party realignment.

Since Ireland remained so much in the forefront of the party battle, the government was eager to present Irish nationalism in the blackest possible colours before the bar of public opinion. As accompaniment to the passage of the Crimes Bill through Parliament *The Times* published a series of articles entitled 'Parnellism and Crime', purporting to show that Parnell had approved the use of violence and had in particular condoned the Phoenix Park murders of 1882. It seems only too likely that there had been collusion between *The Times* and the government in the preparation of these articles and the government certainly did all it could to exploit them. Salisbury told the Primrose League in April 1887: 'What do you think will be the position of Mr Gladstone going to the country when the electors have thoroughly realized that he accepts in political brotherhood men upon whom the presumption of conniving at assassination rests . . .?' It proved treacherous ground for the Prime Minister to take his stand on. It never seemed very likely that a man as cautious as Parnell would have committed himself on paper in the way the letters published in *The Times* showed. Parnell was dissuaded from bringing an immediate libel action against *The Times* by doubts about the impartiality of an English jury, but also by the anxieties of his Liberal allies, who feared that a court case might yet unearth damaging evidence about the Land League. In 1888 an inconclusive libel action brought against *The Times* by one of his colleagues compelled Parnell to reopen the matter. The government responded by setting up a special commission to inquire into the charges and allegations. It was a way of dealing with the affair which stacked the cards against Parnell, for the whole Irish nationalist movement was, as it were, put on trial; 'a revolutionary tribunal for the trial of political opponents', Lord Randolph Churchill called it. The government involved itself even more deeply by allowing the Attorney-General, Sir Richard Webster, to represent *The Times* before the commission.

The great moment of drama in the long sittings of the commission came in February 1889. Richard Pigott, the seedy journalist from whom *The Times* had obtained the letters allegedly written by Parnell, was forced to admit that they were forgeries; he fled the country and when cornered by the police in a Madrid hotel, blew his brains out. Parnell was vindicated; a crowd cheered him in the Strand when he left the law courts and the Liberals in the House of Commons gave him an ovation. He seems to have recognized that this might be a moment of reconciliation, for an unusual note of propitiation crept into his public pronouncements at this time: 'It is legitimate and right that we, being the smaller country, should endeavour to conciliate you in every possible way, and yield to you, and agree to such safeguards as you think necessary . . .'. Parnell's apotheosis gave the whole cause of the Liberal Party a lift and in December 1889 Gladstone received him at Hawarden.

Within days of Parnell's visit to Hawarden, Captain O'Shea filed a divorce suit against him. The fuse was lit that was to blow Parnell and Parnellism sky high and inflict grave damage on the Home Rule cause and the Liberal Party. There were probably political and personal reasons why O'Shea decided to strike only now over a liaison the existence of which he must have known for many years and from which he had not scrupled to draw political benefits. These benefits had ceased to flow since 1886 and O'Shea's evidence before the Special Commission had revealed the depth of hostility to Parnell which now motivated him. The personal reasons were pecuniary. O'Shea was chronically short of money and may have hoped to be bought off. There is no concrete evidence that either the government or Chamberlain conspired with O'Shea in the divorce suit, but it is possible that he was given help with his legal costs, to ensure that he would not be bought off. Throughout 1890 Parnell himself assured both his Irish colleagues and the English Liberal leaders that the divorce suit could not harm him; perhaps he believed that O'Shea would be bought off in the end. When the suit was heard in November 1890 it was undefended, because Parnell wanted to be free to marry Mrs O'Shea. The revelations of an apparently long-running sordid story of adultery had a devastating impact on British public opinion.

It was inevitable that Gladstone and his colleagues, mindful not only of public opinion in general, but of the susceptibilities of their large nonconformist following in particular, should now feel that they could continue to pursue Home Rule in alliance with the Irish Nationalist party only if Parnell ceased to be leader. Only if Parnell resigned, at least for the time being, could Gladstone himself retain the leadership of the Liberal Party, 'based as it has been mainly upon the prosecution of the Irish cause'. It made a bad situation worse confounded that the views of Gladstone and the Liberal leaders could not be conveyed to Parnell and the Irish parliamentary party before they formally re-elected him leader on 25 November 1890. When immediately afterwards the Liberal demand for Parnell's withdrawal was made public, it looked like an English ultimatum. At the beginning of December, after bitter wranglings two-thirds of the Irish Parliamentary Party reversed their previous decision and repudiated their leader. Parnell fought on, proud and defiant, until his death in October 1891. He rejected all efforts to construct a temporary *modus vivendi*; his conduct in this tragic closing phase, while it may have helped to establish his myth as an Irish hero, did nothing to mitigate the blow to the Home Rule cause in Britain. In Ireland Parnell's leadership was under challenge even before the divorce case, for it was exercised more and more fitfully and from a position of increasing aloofness. After the divorce scandal had broken, the Church turned against him and in 1891 his candidates were defeated in three bitterly fought by-elections. These events left a legacy of divisions in the Irish parliamentary party which could not be overcome for a decade. The rejection of Parnell's leadership by a majority of the party in December 1890 had formally restored the Home Rule alliance with the Liberals, but could not undo the damage done to the cause. During the session of 1890 the morale of the Unionists in the House of Commons had dropped very low and the government on several occasions scored very low majorities. The failure of the Special Commission to spike Parnell's guns was one reason for this malaise. Another was the mismanagement of parliamentary business by the Leader of the House, W.H. Smith, whose health was failing. Now party fortunes were reversed and by 1891 there was no longer any likelihood that Salisbury might be forced into a dissolution of Parliament at a moment not of his own choosing.

The Irish problem was never isolated from the many other issues that stirred the British political scene. The Crimes Act of 1887 aroused the wrath of all Radicals and when the inevitable clashes and bloodshed occurred, first at Mitchelstown in County Cork, Gladstone roused his followers with the cry 'Remember Mitchelstown'. Balfour earned himself the sobriquet 'Bloody Balfour', but his vigorous defence of the forces of law and order in turn fortified the conservative mood wherever it was to be found. The big demonstrations initiated by the Social Democratic Federation in November 1887, which produced 'Bloody Sunday' and the Trafalgar Square riots, were a protest against the imprisonment of William O'Brien, one of the leaders of the Plan of Campaign, but they broadened into a general protest against distress and unemployment. Ireland combined with domestic issues in offering the Liberal Unionists, especially Chamberlain's small band of followers, opportunities for emphasizing their separate identity, through their concern for conciliatory and constructive policies.

III

It was fortunate for the Salisbury government that the volume of Irish business, still accompanied by much parliamentary obstruction, made it impossible to legislate too much. Only two major reforms were carried out in the six years it held office, the establishment of elected county councils in 1888 and the introduction of free elementary education in 1891. Both these major changes had long been obvious planks in the Radical programme, but they could be equally well justified from the point of view of Conservative resistance. Once democracy had progressed as far as it had done since 1884 in central government, the extension of it in local government could be seen to be well in accordance with Conservative traditions of decentralization and local accountability. Although Salisbury was not slow to point out to Chamberlain how much 'we have acceded to your views', the Local Government Bill did not contain some items which the Radical Unionist leader would have wanted, for example lower tiers of democratically elected district and parish councils. Nevertheless, it was a sweeping measure to transfer the local government functions of quarter sessions to elected county councils; only a third of these bodies would be made up of co-opted aldermen and these need not be magistrates. Salisbury feared that the country gentlemen would revolt against the proposals. He tried to point out that the squirearchy had already been dethroned by having most of its powers transferred to the central government and that the new bodies were likely to attract the same sort of people as were serving on quarter sessions. Another carrot for the country gentlemen was the prospect that under the new dispensation there would be more support from the central exchequer for local expenditure. In the event the Act of 1888 did not drastically change the kind of persons who put themselves forward to deal with local affairs.

The exception was London. The inclusion of the metropolis in the bill was virtually inevitable, for the inadequacy of the institutional structure for governing the world's largest city had long been obvious and there had been a succession of abortive legislative proposals to deal with it. The pressure for change came mainly from the Radical side and a London Municipal Reform League had been in existence since 1881. The obstacle to change came mainly from the existing institutions, above all the City Corporation and the Metropolitan Board of Works. By 1888 the Board of Works was facing accusations of corruption and the outcry about the London slums had further increased the pressure for reform. Even so, the 1888 Act kept the changes in London to a minimum: the Board of Works was abolished and in its area of operation the London County Council was established, analogous to the county councils in the rest of England; the City Corporation was left untouched, and so were the numerous smaller vestries and district boards. Eleven years later, in 1899, another Conservative government, fortified by its dislike of the London County Council, was to replace these smaller authorities with 28 metropolitan borough councils, thus still leaving the capital with a somewhat anomalous and divided structure of local government. Nevertheless the London County Council proved to be a focus of left-wing opinion and policy and the Progressive Party which emerged in the first LCC elections in 1889 was undoubtedly an important injection of energy and initiative into the politics of the Left.

The introduction of free elementary education, or 'assisted' education, as Salisbury preferred to call it, looked on the surface like the kind of left-wing outflanking manoeuvre that the Prime Minister had always set his face against. 'The duty of sending your children to school is not a natural duty like that of feeding them – it is an artificial duty invented within the last 60 years', wrote Salisbury to Cranbrook, who as Lord President of the Council was in charge of education. The compulsory attendance of children at school, which the Conservatives had taken their share in introducing, was therefore putting a new complexion on the problem of school fees. The fees were very difficult to collect from poor parents; it added yet another problem to the growing financial difficulties the voluntary schools were facing. It was a problem many of them tried to evade by charging fees sufficiently high to exclude the poorer children altogether; the eventual consequence of such a policy would, however, be that denominational education would become inaccessible to a large part of the population. Concern for the future of the Church schools was strong in the Conservative Party and in the course of the election campaign of 1885 the first Salisbury government had promised to appoint a royal commission, mainly to inquire into their position. This commission, under R.A., now Viscount Cross, produced a majority and two minority reports in 1888 and the question of free education was one of the main points on which there were different shades of opinion.

Salisbury became convinced that if the Liberals returned to power they would legislate for free education, combined with popular control of all schools, in essence the programme which Chamberlain had put forward in 1885. In November 1889 he startled his colleagues by publicly advocating free education as a logical consequence of compulsion. Another year and a half elapsed before the broad and vague suggestions which Salisbury had tossed out were enshrined in a bill. The complexities of the case were formidable: there was the cost, on which particularly Goschen as Chancellor of the Exchequer wanted to set a limit; the problems caused by the fact that there was a wide variation of fees charged, not necessarily related to the standard of education achieved; and above all by Salisbury's determination not to go the whole hog towards a State scheme of free elementary education. When the bill was passing through Parliament the Liberals naturally pressed the case for public control, but with Chamberlain on their side the government had little difficulty in rebutting it. When the Liberals returned to power in 1892 further legislation on free education had in fact been pre-empted. On the other hand the provision under the 1891 Act, under which, after a year's grace, school boards could be instituted if a deficiency of free places was established, was fully exploited by the Liberals after 1892. A considerable relaxation of the system of payment by results had also emerged from the recommendations of the Cross Commission. Taken together, the work of the Salisbury government in elementary education did not amount to a fundamental revision of the system established in 1870, but nevertheless to a considerable acceleration in its development.

IV

In education and local government the Tory cabinet had purloined some conspicuous garments from the Liberal wardrobe and fitted them comfortably round Conservative shoulders. Together with the more dramatic developments around the Irish question and Salisbury's skilful handling of foreign affairs these achievements had helped to consolidate the Unionist alliance and establish it much more securely in office than could have been anticipated in the early months of the 1886 Parliament. All this compounded the problems which the Liberal Party experienced in recovering from the fiasco of 1886 and in adapting itself to new social, economic and political pressures. Questions of leadership and of policy were inextricably intertwined. Gladstone's decision to remain in politics was declared to rest entirely on the need to press on with the Home Rule cause and unless they were prepared to face a further upheaval in the party situation the Liberals had to stand by Home Rule. Making a virtue of necessity Gladstone and others declared that until Home Rule was achieved the path to other reforming legislation was blocked. Home Rule could further be represented as a cause that established a system of priorities in the chaos of competing Liberal and Radical causes. In the years after 1886 there was thus a massive Liberal campaign to persuade their own followers and the nation as a whole that Ireland was the question 'upon which, in truth, all other questions of the highest order now substantially turn'. When Gladstone bade his followers to 'remember Mitchelstown' abuse was poured upon him and he was blamed for 'Bloody Sunday' in Trafalgar Square. His reply to such accusations was that those who blocked a settlement in Ireland bore a heavy responsibility for raising the spirit of revolution in England. The commitment to Home Rule was itself open to doubt and different interpretations; the land purchase proposals of 1886 had not been welcomed by many loyal Liberals and the extent to which Irish members should be allowed to vote at Westminster continued to cause differences of view even among the Liberal leaders. Rosebery spoke for those who wanted to make Irish Home Rule part of a general scheme of federation for the United Kingdom. Relations with the Irish Nationalist Party did not always run smooth; for example the support for free publicly controlled education among many Radicals was not generally shared by Roman Catholics. In spite of all difficulties the split in the Irish parliamentary party in 1891 and Parnell's attack on his former allies, Gladstone managed to maintain the priority of Home Rule among Liberal causes without revealing precisely how he would implement it.

None of this could still the argument about the future orientation and programme of the Liberal Party. The events of 1886 had freed the National Liberal Federation from the overwhelming dominance of Chamberlain and Birmingham and had made it easier for the rank and file of Liberal activists to use its annual meeting as a forum for airing an abundance of radical ideas. The leading figures of the parliamentary Liberal Party were increasingly in the habit of attending; Gladstone came in three consecutive years from 1887 and again to the famous Newcastle conference of 1891. As he had foreseen in 1886, the departure of Whigs and right-wing Liberals had left the field to the Radicals and he and his colleagues had to recognize the fact. The Celtic fringe was also more dominant in the party. There was a compact body of some 30 Welsh Liberal MPs, who organized themselves into a group and their two joint secretaries were renamed whips in 1888. Their leader Stuart Rendel was one of the close friends of Gladstone's old age; Tom Ellis, influential and widely popular, became Liberal chief whip in 1894; and in 1890 the group acquired the young David Lloyd George, member for Carnarvon Boroughs, who believed in pushing Welsh concerns regardless of the feelings of the Liberal front bench. The Welsh group had less than half the strength of the Scottish Liberals in the Commons, yet it managed to get Welsh disestablishment lodged in the Liberal programme ahead of Scottish disestablishment. Scottish Liberalism was more diffuse and divided, with strong Whig elements, not all of which had defected to Liberal Unionism; the Church of Scotland was an indigenous growth and the case for disestablishment was therefore less clear-cut. Gladstone himself was always somewhat reluctant about disestablishment and had blamed Chamberlain for raising it in the election of 1885. He refused to vote for a Welsh disestablishment bill in 1889; but the following year he voted for a Scottish disestablishment motion and this may well have contributed to the diminution of his majority at Midlothian in 1892.

In the House of Commons 70 Radical MPs now made up about a third of the parliamentary party and after 1889 employed their own whips. In the long run it was of no less significance that there was also a group of young Liberal MPs who combined an interest in social questions with a willingness to contemplate collectivist remedies, and whose idealism was untainted by utopianism. Among them were H.H. Asquith, R.B. Haldane and Sir Edward Grey, all of them destined to rise high in the party; they also included Arthur Acland, son of Sir Thomas Acland, a close friend of Gladstone's in his younger days, R.C. Munro-Ferguson, Rosebery's private secretary in 1886 and 1892, and more peripherally Sydney Buxton, scion of a famous Quaker family, and Tom Ellis, the Welsh politician. They

came from professional or aristocratic backgrounds and were clearly
marked out for promotion, most of them receiving office in
Gladstone's last ministry. They set themselves the task of converting
the leadership and their links were particularly with Rosebery and
Morley. They were an obvious target for Fabian tactics of permeation
and they had also links with the Progressives on the LCC; where the
NLF was provincial they were metropolitan. The main influence of
this group lay in the future, with the coming of Liberal Imperialism
and the New Liberalism, but they were already making an impact on
Liberal policy particularly in the area of labour questions.

   The relationship with labour and the working classes was in fact to
prove the crucial issue for the future of the Liberal Party. It was a
problem both of men and measures. If the party was to retain the
loyalty of the most active and politically conscious elements in the
labour movement it had to find room for them as parliamentary
candidates. This was proving very difficult. The Corrupt Practices
Act of 1883 had made elections cheaper, but they were still very
expensive. The move of the middle classes away from Liberalism had
made party organizations in the constituencies financially weak and
often altogether moribund. The popular, democratically controlled
caucus pioneered at Birmingham 20 years earlier had largely become
a chimera and local organizations were often in the hands of
unrepresentative cliques. In these circumstances the wealthy candidate of good social standing had an overwhelming advantage over a
manual worker without resources. Furthermore it was often argued
that working men did not really want one of themselves to represent
them in Parliament. However, there was a Labour Electoral Association to promote working men as candidates. The Liberal whips had a
long-standing policy of helping suitable working-class candidates.
Gladstone had himself donated money for this purpose and proclaimed the urgency of increased labour representation at the
Newcastle conference in 1891. In spite of all efforts little was
achieved. The fact was that the Liberal whips and organizers like
Schnadhorst had more important priorities; they wanted more working-class candidates, but not too many. It was of critical importance
in the establishment of an independent Labour Party that in the late
1880s and early 1890s men like Keir Hardie, Ramsay MacDonald and
Arthur Henderson experienced rebuffs at the hands of local Liberal
associations and decided that their future lay elsewhere.

   The Liberal Party was equally slow and indecisive in adapting to
the demands of labour in measures as it was in men. The eight-hour
day was the proposal that raised the most acute dilemma for the
Liberals. Organized labour was itself divided on the question; some
in the TUC were in favour of a universal limitation of hours, others

were against legislation and preferred to rely on collective bargaining. Even among miners there was no unanimity, since in some areas an eight-hour day had already been improved upon. Left-wingers within the labour movement, like George Lansbury, and Fabians like Sidney Webb tried to commit the National Liberal Federation to an eight-hour day. Most Liberal employers opposed the demand, including influential men like Alfred Illingworth the Yorkshire textile manufacturer, and Sir James Kitson, the Leeds iron and steel magnate, who as President of the NLF had done much to bring it over to Gladstone in 1886. Parliamentary leaders like John Morley, who had sympathy for social reform, nevertheless had ideological scruples about State-imposed limitation of hours. By the time the National Liberal Federation met at Newcastle the eight-hour question had not been resolved. The particular importance of this meeting arose from the circumstances: a general election could not be far off and the trough in which the Home Rule cause and the whole Party seemed to be wallowing made it imperative to satisfy as many aspirations among Liberals as possible. 'Omnibus' resolutions embodying a large number of proposals had been passed at previous conferences. This time Gladstone gave a general endorsement to the resolutions as representing the desires of the Party, which he could probably have avoided only by staying away. He must have been well aware of the need to offer Liberals of all persuasions a full 'bill of fare' to give the faltering Home Rule cause as much impetus as possible. His speech at Newcastle was selective in the emphasis he put on the policies which had emerged from the conference. Thus the Newcastle programme was born, a prescription for the old rather than the new Liberalism. Irish Home Rule, disestablishment in Wales and Scotland, the local veto on sale of intoxicating liquors, land reforms, abolition of primogeniture and entail; elective parish and district councils; public control of denominational schools; extension of employers' liability; further moves towards 'one man one vote'. In later years, in times of Liberal travail, the programme was often regarded as a liability for the Party.

V

The years after the great political crisis of 1886 were the first period when the ideas and organizations of the far Left, usually lumped together under the label of socialism, were making an impact beyond the rather inbred world of their devotees. In London, where any popular movement was always likely to receive great publicity and to have an immediate impact on political opinion, the riotous outbreaks of 1886 and 1887 were not repeated, partly because of stricter enforcement of public order. In 1888 and 1889 a number of strikes were, however, equally effective in keeping the social question in the public mind. The strike of the Bryant and May match girls in 1888 was on a small scale, but it aroused much publicity and sympathy and involved figures of the far Left like Mrs Annie Besant, now a Fabian socialist. The gas workers' and dockers' strikes of 1889 were on a much larger scale; particularly the latter, accompanied by colourful street demonstrations, evoked much middle-class support and was settled through the mediation of Cardinal Manning, whose Irish co-religionists were numerous among the strikers. Socialist union leaders like Will Thorne, Tom Mann, John Burns and Ben Tillett sprang into prominence. The main result was that the dockers got the sixpence an hour they were demanding, 'the full round orb of the dockers' tanner', and eightpence for overtime. Gladstone regarded the outcome as a real social advance.

These events were a manifestation of the 'new unionism', a label later attached by the Webbs, which dramatizes and also distorts complex developments. A temporary upswing in the trade cycle in the closing years of the 1880s undoubtedly put fresh wind into the sails of trade unionism and swept many of the less skilled and less securely employed workers into the net. The spread of unionism among the lower ranks of labour had been reversed in the late 1870s, though it had never died away completely, but the upsurge of the late 1880s was also ephemeral in many areas. Conditions varied greatly from one industry to another; the whole movement was a reflection of the growth of employment in large impersonal units, where there was a tendency for skill differentials to become obscured. The dock industry was particularly affected by the contrast between the relatively skilled and regularly employed stevedores and lightermen and large numbers of unskilled casual workers. In the coalfields there was a marked differentiation between those areas producing mainly for the home market and those producing for export, where sliding wage-scales were often in operation. It was an important step when in 1889 most of the regional mining unions came together in the Miners Federation of Great Britain. The development of unionism was also much affected by the attitude of employers, the degree to which they were prepared to grant recognition to unions and the extent to which they were themselves organized. The numerical increase in trade union membership was certainly dramatic: at the 1889 Trades Union

Congress 885,000 members had been represented, in 1890 the number jumped to nearly 1 ½ million, it then dropped back again to 900,000, but then steadily recovered. Movements of such magnitude were clearly determined mainly by trade conditions rather than by the spread of new doctrines like socialism among the workers. Neither socialism nor the absence of the 'friendly society' side of trade unionism were necessarily characteristic of this great expansion. Nevertheless a new generation of working-class activists now appeared in the labour movement, many of them socialists, who challenged the economic and political notions of the old TUC establishment. It was symbolic of the change in generations and attitudes when Henry Broadhurst resigned as secretary of the TUC's Parliamentary Committee in 1890. Politically he was totally identified with the Liberal Party and had held junior office in 1886; ideologically he was committed to the market economy and self-help; and the trade union movement in which he played so prominent a role mainly represented the skilled regularly employed artisans, perhaps never more than 10 per cent of the workforce, for whom it provided a variety of welfare benefits.

As Broadhurst represented the older unionism and the Lib-Lab orientation in politics, so James Keir Hardie, one of his fiercest attackers, represented the new generation of socialist activists who regarded the Liberals with growing scepticism. Hardie had himself been slow to move away from the advanced Radical section of Liberalism and he continued to support much of that section's programme even after he had lost all faith in the Liberal Party as such. All his life he remained a strong advocate of temperance, a course almost more deeply embedded in Liberalism than any. His socialism was ethical and romantic, but also pragmatic, an affair of the heart rather than of the mind. He never made a systematic intellectual assessment of Marxism; the prediction that inevitable nemesis would overtake capitalism as the class-consciousness of the workers matured appealed to him, but he took little interest in the whole body of Marxist economic analysis. The cloth-cap image, which has clung to him because of his defiant entry into the House of Commons in 1892, does not really fit; far from being a typical working man, he was a sensitive, romantic bohemian, with touches of eccentricity which included a penchant for spiritualism. A decisive moment in his career came with his candidature in the Mid-Lanarkshire by-election of 1888. He tried to secure adoption by the local Liberal Association, but he can hardly have seriously thought that he would get it. Already he had begun to move away from conventional Liberal Radicalism, largely under the impact of his experiences in the Lanarkshire coalfield in the severe depression of 1887. He had already, at the trade union congress of

1887, fired a broadside against Broadhurst for his class-collaborationism and his refusal to support the miners' eight-hour day. In the Mid-Lanarkshire by-election he tried to construct a broad left-wing base of support which would allow him if necessary to act independently of the local Liberals. He appealed to Scottish Home Rule sentiment; he set up links with these elements in the Irish nationalist movement who valued their connection with Labour above their alliance with the Liberals. He courted the crofters, with their grievances about the alienation of the Highlands; they had succeeded, by running separate candidates in the 1885 election, in extorting legislation from the Liberal government of 1886. Hardie emphasized in his campaign that Labour must stand on its own feet and called himself the 'Labour and Home Rule' candidate. He refused Liberal offers to make him withdraw; he was taunted with the smear that he was a Tory pawn, particularly as one of his principal financial backers, H.H. Champion, had been involved in the 'Tory Gold' scandal of 1885. In the event Keir Hardie suffered a humiliating defeat, polling only just over 8 per cent of the vote. The Mid-Lanarkshire by-election was not only a milestone in Keir Hardie's move towards an independent party of Labour, but epitomized the state of left-wing politics; dissatisfaction with the Liberals among working-class activists, but continuing loyalty of the mass of Liberal voters to Gladstone and his party. The fact that a good deal of working-class support went to the Tories and the nature of the electoral system sharpened the dilemmas of the Left.

Mid-Lanarkshire did not mark a final breach between Keir Hardie and the Liberal Party. His message was that Labour needed its own programme and representation. 'If the Liberal Party desired to prevent a split, let it adopt the programme of the Labour Party', he wrote in 1888. At successive meetings of the Trades Union Congress he put forward his views; he remained in the minority, but the great influx of 'new unionists' ensured him a better hearing. The eight-hour day became the centrepiece of an independent Labour programme, above all because it was regarded as an antidote to unemployment. Lack of secure and regular employment was only just being recognized and defined as a separate phenomenon and the term 'unemployment' was coming into use. It was a matter of the greatest concern to those lower ranks of the working classes who were now being unionized; yet the Liberal Party and those in the Labour movement who remained tied to it found it difficult to accept a statutory limitation of hours. The idea of an independent Labour programme and representation soon found support in many parts of the country, particularly in the north of England. Here the journalist Robert Blatchford became associated with it and his popular socialist journalism, in the *Workman's Times* and above all *The Clarion*, some of it reappearing in a widely-read penny edition *Merrie England*, did more than anything else to spread the gospel of socialism among ordinary working men and women.

Keir Hardie had in the meantime transferred himself from Scotland to London. The Scottish Labour Party, into which he had put most of his effort after his failure at Mid-Lanark, was a step ahead of England in that it represented at least an effort at country-wide co-ordination. In practice it was an umbrella organization embracing a motley array of radicals, trades councils, single-taxers and land leaguers and was riven by political and personal rivalries. Early in 1890 Keir Hardie received an unexpected invitation to stand as a Labour candidate in the London East End constituency of West Ham and not surprisingly he seized the opportunity. There was a strong local base for a Labour candidature, for Labour candidates had done well in elections to the municipal council, the Board of Guardians and the School Board and many dockers were among the voters. There was never any attempt at a deal with the Liberals at West Ham, but Hardie made the broadest possible appeal to the whole Liberal electorate. Foremost among the social questions which he highlighted was unemployment, while socialism, on the other hand, scarcely received a mention. The strength of Hardie's support was such that the official Liberal candidate, a working man emphasizing his proletarian credentials, withdrew immediately before polling day in the general election of July 1892. Thus Hardie had a straight fight with a Unionist and won with 57 per cent of the vote.

Hardie was the only genuinely independent Labour member elected in 1892. The other two nominal Labour members of 1892 Parliament, J. Havelock Wilson, who sat for Middlesbrough, and John Burns, elected at Battersea, were soon indistinguishable from Lib–Labs. Ben Tillett had come a respectable third at Bradford in a three-cornered contest. The results of the 1892 election were therefore hardly a boost for the idea of separate Labour representation. In London developments pointed in the direction of a continued collaboration of the various sections of the Left under the Liberal umbrella. The Progressive Party on the London County Council brought together Liberals, Radicals, members of the SDF and Fabians. There was so much work to do, after years of neglect, that men of widely differing views could collaborate in practice. It was ideal ground for Fabian tactics and Sidney Webb's prescriptions in particular had much influence on the municipal socialism of the LCC. John Burns was a member of the Progressive group on the LCC and had no difficulty in mending his fences with the Liberals after his election at Battersea. Hardie, on the other hand, went out of his way to antagonize the Liberals by campaigning against John Morley at Newcastle, where voting took place a few days later than in West Ham, because of Morley's opposition to the eight-hour day. In the subsequent ministerial by-election caused by Morley's appointment as Chief Secretary for Ireland, Hardie even advised voters to support the Unionist candidate. In the Commons Hardie, having caused a sensation by his mode of entry, 'yellow tweed trousers, serge jacket and vest, and soft tweed cap', became a somewhat isolated and not very effective figure.

Nevertheless, and in spite of the paltry results in 1892, the idea of independent Labour representation was sufficiently well established to bring about the co-ordination at national level that had hitherto been lacking. The foundation of the Independent Labour Party in January 1893 was the result of many efforts and influences. It was significant that it took place at Bradford, for most of the 120 delegates came from the industrial north of England and from Scotland and the London-based SDF had as a national body refused to co-operate in calling the conference. Many individual members and whole branches of the SDF were, however, represented and Bernard Shaw was one of the two London Fabian representatives. He made a valuable contribution to the discussions and quickly saw that here was something more substantial than the SDF, whom he regarded as armchair revolutionaries; but his expectations for the party about to be born were not very high. The new party avoided the term 'socialist' in its name, but its programme was entirely compatible with the basic doctrines of socialism, as well as containing many of the Radical demands of the moment, above all the eight-hour day. The ILP had firmer roots in the working class and a greater potential for converting the trade unions from their Liberal orientation than the existing organizations of the radical Left.

VI

As the end of the 1886 Parliament drew nearer, the main political parties were still chiefly preoccupied with fighting each other rather than with the threat from the left-wing fringe. As the shock of Parnell's fall and its aftermath receded the Liberals recovered somewhat and the Newcastle programme, whatever its shortcomings in the longer run, gave them at least a standard around which all sections of the Party could rally. The Conservatives had strengthened themselves through the elevation of A.J. Balfour to the leadership of the

House of Commons; on the accession of Hartington to the Dukedom of Devonshire Chamberlain had become leader of the hard-pressed Liberal Unionists. Both parties were paying much attention to their electoral machinery, but whereas Schnadhorst had long outlived the reputation for electoral wizardry which he had once had, the Tories had found in Captain Middleton an exceptionally successful party organizer. His advice and that of the other Conservative and Liberal Unionist whips and party managers was responsible for the choice of the election date, July 1892. In the election campaign Irish Home Rule inevitably bulked large, even though the electorate was clearly fatigued with it, Unionists even more than Liberals. A Tory commentator described the apathetic attitude of the working man: 'The Irish are a bad lot: if Home Rule will keep them quiet, let them have Home Rule.' There were some new angles on the Irish question. The Ulster problem was more strongly emphasized by Unionists than before. It could be claimed that far from bringing about a union of hearts, as Liberals hoped, Home Rule might produce civil war in Ireland. Nonconformist supporters of Gladstone were made to feel uneasy by the appeals of their co-religionists in Ulster against separation. It was plain to see that the anti-Parnellite majority of the Irish Nationalist Party was much influenced by the Irish hierarchy; nonconformists could therefore be warned against a priest-ridden Ireland, if Home Rule was successful. Joseph Chamberlain was undoubtedly an asset for Unionism in any attempt to detach the nonconformist vote from Gladstone. The Unionist answer to Home Rule was constructive Unionism, linked with the name of Balfour. In Ireland as in the rest of the country the Unionists claimed to be the 'party of performance', while the Liberals were merely the 'party of promise'.

For the Liberals, Home Rule, linked with Gladstone's leadership, venerable and selfless in pursuit of justice, continued to serve as a kind of figleaf to cover the chaos of other Liberal causes, most of them enumerated in the Newcastle programme, without any clear priorities between them. There was a good deal of competition between the parties for the rural vote, the loss of which, it was felt in the Liberal Party, had been a major factor in the defeat of 1886. Neither party was committed to the eight-hour day, the litmus test of sympathy for the demands of urban labour, so it was left to individual candidates to define their position. The 'fair trade' cry had been sounded from Tory platforms in the previous two elections and Salisbury gave it some cautious, carefully qualified support on the eve of the election.

Nobody had a more difficult position to defend in this election than Joseph Chamberlain. He had to make it appear that the government's progressive record in domestic legislation was due to the pressure he had steadily exerted. Just before the election Salisbury had to warn Chamberlain against pursuing this line too avidly during the campaign, because it would scare off many Conservative voters: 'If you say that the Tories have given in on all the points on which you have differed from them in 1885 – you give them an uncomfortable feeling that they have deserted their colours and changed their coats.' The most important new proposal Chamberlain now put forward was for old age pensions and he continued to demand improved industrial accident insurance. One remarkable feature of the election results was Chamberlain's ability, amid a general weakening of the Liberal Unionist position, to maintain and even strengthen his 'duchy' in the West Midlands. It confirmed him as the leader of Liberal Unionism and principal ally of the Tories.

For the Liberals the outcome of the 1892 election was if anything an even greater blow than their defeat in 1886 and was ample reason for the disappointment and even despair that seized Gladstone as he received the results while staying with Rosebery at Dalmeny. His presence in politics since 1886 had rested on the assumption that the Home Rule cause would be vindicated and now his great career threatened to end in anti-climax. With Home Rule hardly likely to reach port the tensions in the Gladstonian party would come increasingly to the fore. The election campaign itself had shown that economic issues and class divisions formed more of the substance of political competition than ever before. Nevertheless Gladstone was well aware that he could hardly avoid taking office as Prime Minister for a fourth time. Salisbury for his part determined to meet Parliament before resigning, in order not to give the election results any appearance of decisiveness. In the new House there were 273 Liberals, 81 Irish Nationalists, and one Independent Labour member, facing 268 Conservatives and 47 Liberal Unionists. A Liberal government would therefore have a majority of 40, dependent on the Irish. It suited Salisbury personally that in such a situation the House of Lords might well have a decisive role to play.

VII

In contemplating the formation of his last government Gladstone seems at first to have toyed with the idea that he might be able to perform a holding operation in Ireland, since with such a small majority in the Commons he had no chance of forcing a full-scale

Home Rule Bill through the House of Lords. It quickly became evident that without an immediate Home Rule Bill a Liberal government could not survive. The Irish were still divided between anti-Parnellite and Parnellite factions, although the latter had only 8 or 9 members in the House. They could not afford to strike any deal with the Liberals that would not give them the pure milk of Home Rule. All that Gladstone and his cabinet colleagues could do therefore was to consider a programme of British bills that might accompany the Irish measure, but this programme would have to be light enough to avoid a log-jam of parliamentary business. If the House of Lords rejected not only Irish Home Rule but also the fare of British bills emanating from a Liberal government, then at least a powerful case would be built up against the peers as obstacles to the popular will.

Gladstone's fourth and last cabinet was not inferior in ability to those he had constructed over the previous quarter of a century. The major political figures in it were Morley, back as Chief Secretary for Ireland, Harcourt at the Treasury and Rosebery at the Foreign Office. The latter was a most reluctant recruit, barely recovered from the death of his wife in November 1890. His presence in the government was considered essential, for he had a great public reputation, was a fine orator and many of the bright young men of the party looked to him for leadership. It was not yet widely recognized that he was moody and, every possible advantage of birth and wealth having been showered upon him, he lacked the ultimate spur of ambition. Morley was the minister most totally committed to Home Rule, while Harcourt pressed most strongly for an attractive British programme to supplement Home Rule. Harcourt and Rosebery, on the other hand, clashed over imperial policy, with Rosebery as the champion of Liberal imperialism and Harcourt the opponent of jingoism; they were also rivals for Gladstone's succession. From the rising younger generation of Liberal MPs Asquith went straight into the cabinet as Home Secretary. It was a remarkable achievement for a man barely 40 years of age and not born to the purple: he came of Yorkshire nonconformist stock, but it was a background that he had already cast well behind him. His brilliant second marriage to Margot Tennant completed his acclimatization to the metropolitan world of high politics and society. Arthur Acland entered the cabinet as Vice-President for Education and Edward Grey became Under Secretary for Foreign Affairs. This accumulation of ability, significant for the revival of the Liberal Party over a decade later, could not compensate for the weakness of its present position: an inadequate majority, a Prime Minister well in his eighties and manifold divisions among the other leading men.

Another Irish Home Rule Bill was the labour of Sisyphus imposed upon Gladstone and his colleagues. Only Morley and one or two others were eager and anxious that a bill should pass before Gladstone was finally compelled by failing health to retire. Harcourt and Rosebery often occupied an 'ostentatious position apart from the rest' on what they called 'the English bench' during the long cabinet discussions on Home Rule, a protest against the amount of energy and time devoted to the Irish cause. The main principles of the second Home Rule Bill were proposed by Gladstone himself: this time 81 Irish members were to be left at Westminster, but allowed to vote only on Irish and imperial affairs. On the Committee stage, however, full voting rights were conceded to the Irish members remaining at Westminster. If the bill had become law Ireland would not only have secured a separate Parliament in Dublin, but retained the ability to obstruct the business of the rest of the Kingdom as well as to make and unmake British governments. Again it was seen that it was virtually impossible to superimpose a federal system upon British constitutional arrangements. The financial settlement between London and Dublin was a very complex matter and on the Committee stage the Government recast the bill to provide an impartial tribunal to settle financial disputes between the two countries. In the Commons the bill occupied 85 sessions, an indication of the extent to which it deprived the Liberals of the chance of passing other legislation. Gladstone still showed much of his old parliamentary skill and mastery of detail, although he was plagued by failing eyesight and deafness. The Home Rule Bill had a second-reading majority of 43 in April 1893, and a third-reading majority of only 34 in September; within a week the Lords had rejected it by 419 votes to 41 and the majority included all the bishops.

The consequences of Gladstone's heroic and doomed last effort to enact Home Rule were somewhat intangible. To have made the attempt may have helped to keep a constitutional Irish Nationalist Party in existence as an ally of the Liberals; events in Ireland had in any case defused a situation that had been potentially revolutionary in the 1880s. In the longer run the memory of the obstruction that the House of Lords had placed in the path of a Liberal government, not only on Home Rule, may have contributed to the eventual curtailment of the upper chamber's powers. For the moment the Lords had, however, spoken for the majority of the non-Irish people of the United Kingdom and Salisbury, as leader of the Unionist peers, emphasized this point robustly. He and his fellow peers enjoyed a good deal of popularity.

The time apparently wasted on Home Rule caused much bitterness among Liberal Radicals. Gladstone's intention to accompany Home Rule with a programme of English bills had produced a clutch of measures ranging from electoral registration and the local veto to the Welsh Church, but most of these had to be dropped because of the parliamentary battle on Home Rule. The only major one that survived was the Parish Councils Bill promoted by H.H. Fowler, the President of the Local Government Board. Even this was much weakened by the limits imposed on the spending power of parish councils, but at least it did something to meet the long-standing Liberal desire to introduce elective local government below the level of county councils. It was a portent for the future that the vote was now given to married women, and that women qualified to vote could also be elected. The Employers' Liability Bill, which was in the charge of Asquith and was again a long-standing Liberal concern, had to be dropped because the House of Lords insisted on inserting a 'contracting out' clause.

Gladstone had briefly entertained the notion of an election on the 'peers versus people' issue immediately after the failure of the Home Rule Bill, but when he revived it early in 1894, while staying in Biarritz to recuperate, his colleagues, expecting his imminent resignation rather than another prolonged battle under his leadership, were in no mood to listen. The Liberal Party was in no shape, financial or political, to fight another election. In the meantime Gladstone had also become involved in a battle over increased naval estimates, for there was now formidable pressure, both from public opinion and the Board of Admiralty, for increased naval expenditure. The demand was for the maintenance of the two-power standard, namely that the Royal Navy should be the equal of the next two most powerful navies put together. For the moment these were the French and Russian navies. The Prime Minister saw this as a manifestation of jingoism: 'I shall not break to pieces the continuous action of my political life, nor trample on the tradition received from every colleague who has ever been my teacher. Above all I cannot and will not add to the perils and the coming calamities of Europe by an act of militarism which will be found to involve a policy, and which has less excuse than the militarism of Germany, France or Russia. England's providential part is to help peace.' When Gladstone's resignation was finally confirmed at the end of February 1894, it came from a combination of failing health, inability to mount another major battle against the House of Lords, and a feeling that he was 'a survival', out of tune with many currents in Liberal politics. The most distressing feature to Gladstone about his resignation was the Queen's evident relief at his departure. He wrote about the three interviews he had with her during the week of his resignation: 'Substantially then the proceeding was brief though the interviews were eked out with secondary matter. The same brevity perhaps prevails in settling a tradesman's bill, when it reaches over many years.' Gladstone never returned to the House of Commons after his resignation, but he kept his seat and this was enough to produce speculation from time to time that he might be staging a comeback.

VIII

If the Queen had asked Gladstone's advice about his successor, he would have proposed Spencer, a compromise between the rivals Rosebery and Harcourt, and a supporter of Home Rule. Her own preference was for Rosebery and this accorded with the views of most of the members of the cabinet, though perhaps less with feelings in the parliamentary Liberal Party. Morley, having in the past supported Harcourt as a successor to Gladstone, had increasingly, though hardly consistently, moved to back Rosebery. He was not rewarded with the Foreign Office, which he coveted; this went to Kimberley. Thus both the Prime Minister and the Foreign Secretary were peers; otherwise there were no major changes in the cabinet. Morley, confined to his 'Irish back kitchen', was thenceforth a much diminished political figure.

Rosebery was as reluctant to become Prime Minister as he had been to become Foreign Secretary and was entering upon a wasting inheritance. Another general election could not be very distant. The weak Liberal position was aggravated now by deep divisions in the cabinet: Harcourt never forgave Rosebery. The conflict between the Prime Minister and the Leader of the House of Commons coincided with the division between imperialists and Little Englanders. Rosebery was in a weaker position to conduct foreign policy than he had been playing an independent hand as Foreign Secretary under Gladstone; he and Kimberley spent a lot of their energy circumventing Harcourt. If this was not enough to fray the nerves of a man as sensitive and moody as Rosebery, he also had in public to proclaim a domestic policy for which he had little stomach. On his first appearance as Prime Minister in the House of Lords he said that '. . . before Irish Home Rule is conceded by the Imperial Parliament England, as the predominant member of the partnership of the Three Kingdoms, will have to be convinced of its justice and equity.' This admission very nearly caused disaster at the outset and he had to back-pedal furiously in a public speech a few days later. In October 1894 he declared in ringing tones in a speech at Bradford that the next election would be fought on the House of Lords. The only action he could take, however, was to propose a resolution, to be passed by the Commons, deploring the Lords' mutilation and rejection of bills. The Cabinet refused to follow him even in this mild gesture. For all his pains the attacks on the House of Lords did the Liberals little good, for by-elections, which had been reasonably reassuring since Rosebery took over, began to go against them and to whittle away further the same Liberal majority, now only just over 20, in the Commons. For the parliamentary session of 1895 the government had to take up again some of the items of the Newcastle programme that up to now had been crowded out by Home Rule, partly to satisfy restive Liberal supporters, partly to build up the case against the Lords further, a process which came to be called 'filling the cup' or 'ploughing the sands'. There were proposals for Welsh disestablishment, another Local Veto Bill to control the liquor trade, one man, one vote and gestures about agricultural distress and trades disputes. Welsh disestablishment was the most important and controversial of the bills. There had been strong pressure for it by Welsh Liberals since the beginning of this Parliament: a Suspensory Bill freezing the situation failed to pass in 1893 and four Welsh members, including the young Lloyd George, renounced the Liberal whip when the government did not produce a Disestablishment Bill in 1894. The bill of 1895 had not passed the Commons when the Rosebery government fell in June.

The position of parliamentary frustration which Rosebery inherited from Gladstone did not prevent the many able Liberal departmental ministers from achieving a good deal of improvement through administrative reform. Asquith at the Home Office greatly strengthened the factory inspectorate and, introduced in the session of 1895 an important consolidating Factories and Workshops Bill which was completed, with his help, by the incoming Conservative ministry. It was a pity that Asquith's name was tarnished for many working-class people by his connection with the Featherstone incident in 1893, when two miners were killed in a violent colliery dispute in Yorkshire. The government also improved the condition of its own employees in naval and military establishments, both in raising wages and shortening hours, although the strong feelings of many Liberals, including Gladstone and Morley, prevented any general limitation of hours by statute. Acland at the Board of Education was motivated by strong radical sentiments and although he could not legislate carried out considerable educational advances in his short period of office.

Harcourt's budget of 1894 proved to be the most important act of escape from the legislative impotence of the Liberal régime. The

demonstration that the House of Lords could by convention not muti-
late finance bills was itself a pointer to the future. The Chancellor of
the Exchequer was helped in his preparation of the budget by Sir
Alfred Milner, who more than anyone else personified the related
strands of Liberal imperialism, social reform and national efficiency.
The main innovation of the budget was the introduction of death
duties on the consolidated value of an estate, in place of the various
imposts that had previously existed on the passing of different forms
of property. The tax was to be graduated according to the size of the
estate, not according to the receipts of a particular beneficiary,
although for the moment the highest rate of tax was only 8 per cent on
estates of over one million. It was the thin end of a very wide wedge,
though increasingly blunted by avoidance, and also introduced the
principle that the State could tax capital and spend it as income. The
statistics on wealth distribution improved considerably from this
date. Harcourt also increased the income tax by a penny and put
sixpence on a gallon of spirits and a barrel of beer. All this was
required to pay for the increased naval estimates. Both Gladstone,
who had still been Prime Minister while the budget was being prepared, but was nevertheless surprised by its content, and Rosebery,
the incoming Prime Minister, were opposed to the budget, particularly by its implications for landed wealth. Gladstone called the new
estate duty 'too violent . . . by far the most Radical measure of my
life-time'. Rosebery complained of the 'horizontal division of parties'
and drift of property away from the Liberals and pointed out, more
mundanely, that contributions to party funds would suffer. Characteristically he did not carry his opposition to the budget proposals
beyond complaints; had he done so, his government might well have
foundered at the outset.

 Only a year later a death wish had come upon it. The Irish and the
Scottish were dissatisfied; the more radical Welsh members, like
Lloyd George, doubted the government's sincerity on the Disestablishment Bill and lost interest in its survival. The cabinet was alarmed
that Gladstone, who told Spencer that 'there is some flavour in the
Welsh bill that is rather too sharp for my taste', might return to
the House and vote against some of its clauses. There was, however,
no particular premonition of defeat when in a thin house on a Friday
the government lost the customary vote of a reduction of the minister's salary by £100 on the army estimates. The minister under
attack was Campbell-Bannerman, a universally popular man, who a
little earlier had nearly become Speaker of the House. He had just
announced the successful conclusion of months of negotiations
leading to the resignation of the Duke of Cambridge, the Queen's
cousin, as Commander-in-Chief of the army; aged 76, he had for long

been an obstacle to change. The slightly spurious charge against Campbell-Bannerman was that the supply of cordite for the army was inadequate and the adverse vote was, even with the Government's small nominal majority, only due to a ruse. It should have been quite possible to reverse this vote and 'rehabilitate' Campbell-Bannerman, though there was the possibility of defeat on Welsh disestablishment not many days away. The will to power and survival had, however, been thoroughly sapped in the Rosebery government and for once the Prime Minister and the Chancellor of the Exchequer were agreed that they could not go on. Advice from the Chief Whip and from Robert Hudson, Schnadhorst's successor as secretary of the Liberal Central Office, that it would be better electorally to hang on 'by hook or by crook' was ignored. The absence of anything other than the 'worn out and effete' Newcastle programme as an election manifesto made it easier to decide on resignation rather than a dissolution of Parliament. Thus for the third time in less than a decade an election would be fought upon ground and at a time not propitious for the Liberal Party. This, coming on top of the many obvious weaknesses of the Liberal Party in programmes, personalities and electoral base, accounts for the lack of success since 1886 and for the further decade in the wilderness that was yet to come.

IX

The stage was now set for the formation of a full coalition government of Conservatives and Liberal Unionists. The election of 1892 and three years of Liberal government had increasingly convinced both partners in the Unionist alliance that their parliamentary and electoral collaboration would have to blossom into a cabinet coalition when the time came. Salisbury was slow to come to this conclusion, for the differences in outlook and temperament between himself and Joseph Chamberlain, undoubtedly the most important Liberal Unionist, were deep. Salisbury was in politics to preserve existing institutions and remained profoundly suspicious of democracy, the placing of 'individual rights, and liberties . . . at the mercy of a mere numerical majority'. The years of the Liberal government, when the House of Lords could, usually with popular acclaim, thwart Liberal legislation, presented a situation which suited Salisbury's political style very well. Whereas Salisbury believed that the threat of socialism had little staying power, Chamberlain took it seriously and wanted to reinforce it by the kind of class collaboration that had always been a specific feature of Birmingham. In practice Salisbury and Chamberlain found cooperation usually not too difficult. During the years of Unionist opposition Chamberlain's interest in empire advanced apace and on this there were no differences between him and the Tories. Many motives and policies came together in Chamberlain's imperialism: he was anxious to cast off all vestiges of his past Little Englandism, to make Unionism into a great national party and to brand Liberalism as neglectful of the national interest; he was impressed by the economic arguments for imperial development as an antidote to economic depression, although he did not as yet consider fair trade or protection practical politics; imperial federation, the unity of the Anglo-Saxon race, as well as expansion of the new African empire all appealed to him. Whatever the differences between the former Radical and his Conservative allies, there is little doubt that during these years Chamberlain had become increasingly the *arriviste* who had arrived and who was prepared to accept the place Society now offered him.

Right up to the fall of the Rosebery government the Unionist alliance, though basically intact, had been disturbed by minor tensions. Disagreements flared up over the allocation of parliamentary seats. Conservatives resented Chamberlain's support for Harcourt's death duties and Welsh disestablishment and blamed him for the continued survival of the Rosebery government. The Liberal Unionist leader in his turn was alarmed by attacks on him in Tory journals and complained indirectly to Salisbury. The Tory leader showed little sympathy: '. . . he means to shape his political life on the Birmingham view of Church and squire . . . if he will put that philosophy in the lumber room for the present, as Pitt did his views on reform, or Canning and Castlereagh their views on Catholic emancipation, this little breeze will very speedily be forgotten.' Only two months later, Salisbury, having received the Queen's commission, proceeded with great speed to form his coalition government. The most significant appointment was that of Joseph Chamberlain as Colonial Secretary. It was what he wanted, in preference to some major domestic office, such as the Home Office or the Treasury, which he could have had. He had clearly become convinced that his ability to promote social reforms would always be limited by the reluctance of his Tory allies to support them and he insisted only on the appointment of a small expert committee on old age pensions. It turned out that from the Colonial Office he was able to play a very major role, which would have much impact on the conduct of foreign policy, once again in Salisbury's hands.

Within three weeks of the formation of the Unionist government the general election began. The Liberals fought it from a position of weakness. Excluding Ireland and the universities they allowed 110 Unionists to be returned unopposed, as against 40 in 1892; while only 11 seats were not fought by the Unionists. They had no coherent programme: Rosebery emphasized the House of Lords issue, Harcourt was mainly associated with his Local Veto Bill and Morley with the moribund cause of Home Rule. 'Bible, beer and bad trade' worked against the Liberals. Nevertheless the magnitude of the Unionist victory came as a surprise: there were in the new House of Commons 340 Tories and 71 Liberal Unionists opposing 177 Liberals and 82 Irish nationalists. Harcourt and Morley lost their seats, the latter because of the intervention of an ILP candidate. This holocaust is put in perspective by the much smaller shift of votes, a swing of approximately 3 per cent to the Unionists in Great Britain. The Liberal Party remained a powerful electoral force even in adverse circumstances. The threat to its left flank was still marginal. This was the first election fought by the Independent Labour Party, which put up 28 candidates; there were also four SDF candidates. These 32 candidates polled 44,000 votes, only about 1 per cent of the total vote, and Keir Hardie lost his seat.

The cause of independent Labour representation had seen its fortunes fluctuate during the years of Liberal government. Disillusion with the Liberal failure to achieve substantial legislative reforms brought even many of the London Fabians to the view that it was time to switch from permeation to the promotion of Labour candidates with the help of the trade unions. This was the gist of Shaw's article 'To Your Tents, Oh Israel!' in the *Fortnightly Review* of November 1893, later issued as a tract '*A Plan of Campaign for Labour*'. ILP candidates achieved some striking near-misses in by-elections and successes in local elections. Especially in Yorkshire and Lancashire the ILP had many active local branches and the journalism of Blatchford spread the socialist gospel with considerable effectiveness. The difficulties which Labour personalities continued to experience when they tried to get nomination by Liberal associations confirmed the trend to separate candidatures. Against this the effort to convert the unions to independent Labour representation faltered. John Burns, now committed to the Liberal Party, joined with John Mawdsley, the Tory general secretary of the important Cotton Spinners Association, to prepare new standing orders for the TUC: these introduced the card vote, giving greater power to the big unions; they excluded trades councils from sending delegates, and this was the way many socialists and independent labour supporters got to the Congress; and they excluded as delegates all those who were not working at a trade or were not paid officials of a union. These standing orders were adopted at the Trades Union Congress of 1895, when the dismal showing of Independent Labour in the general election was already known. Keir Hardie and others like him were thus excluded from the Congress. The Webbs now reverted to the view that the ILP was a wrecking party and had committed suicide.

To many observers the result of the election of 1895 seemed the end of an epoch. On the eve of it Salisbury had called for an end to 'the kind of muffled civil war in which the country had lived for more than a generation'. This is exactly what the outcome seemed to him to have brought about. 'The tinkering at the mechanism of the constitution is at best an evil necessity, and cannot be more than an exceptional proceeding. The Liberal Party have committed a fault in believing that for all time they were to uproot and uproot and uproot, and that no other result is to come from the political exertions of their followers. The great lesson of this election is to dissipate that doctrine to the winds', Salisbury declared. He believed that the Unionist alliance was set for 'an epoch of continuous rule'. There seemed to be less cause for the great fear with which democracy had always filled him.

7 The End of Isolation, the Boer War and Tariff Reform 1885–1905

I

Foreign rather than domestic affairs were dominant for much of the decade of Unionist government that started in 1895. Salisbury was back at the Foreign Office, but in spite of the political strength of his government, greater than it had been in his previous tenures of power, his own control of external affairs was if anything less complete than before. Partly this was the result of age and declining powers; partly it was due to the presence of Joseph Chamberlain at the Colonial Office. Salisbury had never been greatly interested in imperial expansion as such, as distinct from the maintenance of British interests as a world power and the discharge of the trust that Britain's vast imperial possessions had placed upon her. Yet it was imperialism in the forward-looking expansionist sense that often held the centre of the stage, particularly in South Africa, in the years after 1895.

Salisbury was in charge of the Foreign Office during his first ministry in 1885 and for the duration of his second ministry, except for the initial few months, when Iddesleigh was in nominal control. In the interludes of Liberal government in 1886 and after 1892 Rosebery and Kimberley held the Foreign Office. They were Liberal imperialists and there was consequently considerable continuity of foreign policy throughout the decade from 1885 to 1895. When there was major conflict over foreign policy it arose mainly within the Liberal party, between Rosebery on the one hand and Gladstone, Harcourt, Morley and other exponents of Cobdenite Little Englandism. Only during Lord Randolph Churchill's brief membership of the second Salisbury government was there as much disagreement within the Tory cabinet.

Salisbury had thus been the dominant influence in British foreign policy since 1885. It was a sphere particularly congenial to him, for in the minutiae of diplomacy his pragmatic approach and 'instinctive reverence for facts' could have full rein. With his scepticism about democracy he preferred an area of political activity that was often somewhat removed from the public gaze, but at the same time he was fearful that the impact of emotional public opinion would make the conduct of rational diplomacy virtually impossible: 'The terrible phenomenon of the time is that nations have a power of irritating each other enormously larger than they ever possessed before.' He was often criticized, particularly from the Radical and Little England wing of the Liberal Party, for his preference for secret diplomacy.

One of Salisbury's main concerns was to bring Britain out of the isolation into which the ineptitude of Gladstone and his colleagues, in spite of their theoretical devotion to the Concert of Europe, had led her. One of his nightmares was that there might be a major war between the continental powers, in which British imperial possessions would become the spoils of war. Nevertheless Salisbury did not want to go to the full length of a continental alliance and he often used Britain's parliamentary system as an excuse to avoid too deep a commitment. Most of the time he kept close to the Triple Alliance of Germany, Austria and Italy and at moments, for example in 1889, a formal alliance seemed possible. But Salisbury did not really want to pull Bismarck's chestnuts out of the fire, so that the German chancellor could have a free hand against France. Britain needed the Triple Alliance mainly in the Mediterranean, where French naval power and continuing rivalry over Egypt threatened British interests. The secret Mediterranean Agreements which Salisbury concluded with Italy and Austria were designed to counteract this danger. Salisbury at one time hoped that British troops could be withdrawn from Egypt, provided there were adequate arrangements for re-entry in case of a threat to British interests. Attempts at negotiating a convention for the evacuation of Egypt failed in 1887 and it was gradually perceived that the British occupation of Egypt was permanent. Even the Liberal government was compelled in 1893 to take a strong line when the Khedive dismissed Lord Cromer. It was one of the occasions when Rosebery and Gladstone hotly disagreed; the Prime Minister said he 'would as soon put a torch to Westminster Abbey than send additional troops to Egypt'. In spite of all the difficulties with the French in the Mediterranean and the Near East Salisbury wanted to 'keep friends with France as far as we can do it without paying too dear for it'. The Naval Defence Act of 1889 and the adoption of the two-power standard was designed to strengthen the British position in the Mediterranean and elsewhere.

Over the decade since Salisbury had become the dominant influence in British foreign policy there had been an improvement in relations with Russia. The rivalry in Central Asia, which had led even Gladstone to the brink of war at the time of the Pendjeh incident, was eased by boundary agreements in Afghanistan, though it continued at a less intense level all the way from Persia to China throughout the 1890s. Turkey, the traditional bone of contention between Russia and Britain, was decreasing in importance in British eyes, just as Egypt was increasing. By the end of his ministry in 1892 Salisbury was saying, in response to reports from naval and military intelligence, that it was no longer possible to protect Constantinople. British influence in the Ottoman Empire, which had been so strong for most of the century, declined steeply. The big change in the position of Russia came with the Franco–Russian rapprochement after 1890. In some ways, given the continuing friction with France in Africa and Indo-China, and with Russia on the Indian frontiers and in the Far East, this might have pushed Britain finally into the arms of the Triple Alliance. There were, however, also tensions with Germany and in spite of Salisbury's efforts to remove them by exchanging territory in East Africa for Heligoland in 1890 they kept recurring in Africa and the Pacific. In fact the Franco–Russian rapprochement meant that the Triple Alliance needed Britain more than she needed them, but Bismarck's successors in Berlin behaved as if Britain could be had at any time. Thus Britain remained isolated, trying to maintain good relations with all the Great Powers, but, because of the multitude of problems thrown up by her vast imperial possessions, finding it difficult in a period of growing rivalry and nationalism.

The three years during which Rosebery was principally in charge of foreign policy did not constitute an impressive record. Rosebery was more positively an imperial expansionist than Salisbury and practised what he preached, particularly in Egypt and Uganda. The opposition within the cabinet to his policies made him only more determined to pursue them, but for this reason and others he operated more erratically than Salisbury. Just before the Rosebery government fell British isolation seemed to be demonstrated by the fact that she refused to co-operate with Russia, France and Germany in compelling Japan to disgorge some of the gains from her victory against China in the war of 1894/5, which heralded her arrival as a major power. British inaction, partly the result of the paralysis which had overtaken the Liberal cabinet, proved beneficial in the long run, for Japan became an important British ally. Nevertheless, Rosebery's aim of a rapprochement with both the French–Russian alliance and the Triple Alliance had got nowhere and it was widely hoped that Salisbury would do better.

These hopes were not destined to be realized. The first crisis Salisbury had to deal with on his return of office in 1895 revolved again round the future of the Ottoman Empire. This time the main focus was on Armenia, on the insurrection that had begun there in 1890 and had flared into an uprising in 1894, and on the massacres carried out in reprisal by the Turks in August 1894, and repeatedly thereafter, especially in the autumn of 1896. The situation was now very different from what it had been over the Bulgarian Atrocities 20 years before. Sections of public opinion were again stirred by these events, but on nothing like the scale of the 1870s. Nevertheless sympathy for the Armenians was sufficient to compel action by the British government while at the same time restricting its freedom of manoeuvre. This time the British approach to the problem consisted almost entirely in efforts to impose reforms on the Sultan in co-operation with the other powers, including Russia. Salisbury could not get the consent of his cabinet in 1895 to a possible naval demonstration against the Sultan, after joint action with Russia had proved impossible.

When Turkey encountered further problems with her subject peoples in Crete and Macedonia Salisbury began to see the disintegration of the Ottoman Empire as imminent and he tried with Russia and the other powers to get some agreement about the future in the autumn of 1896. None of the Powers wanted a disturbance of the territorial *status quo* and they cared a lot less than British public opinion about what the Sultan did to his subjects. Russia had on the whole become conservative with regard to the Ottoman Empire; the Russians preferred that for the time being Constantinople and the Straits should remain in the hands of a weak Sultan. The old pro-Turkish, anti-Russian bias of British Near Eastern policy was dead and even in Tory circles there was now little sympathy for Turkey.

All this can be seen as part of a movement to bring British capabilities and commitments into a more realistic relationship in a period of growing international rivalry. A similar development had occurred in the Far East, where the entry of Japan into the power arena had, as we have seen, opened new options for British policy. The acceptance in 1896 of American pressure for arbitration in the Anglo-Venezuelan dispute about the boundary of British Guiana, another occasion when Salisbury was overruled by his cabinet, showed that Latin America was also no longer an area of high priority for the British; it indicated that, given Britain's continuing isolation from the European alliance system, it was judged prudent in London to remove possible sources of conflict with the United States. The same realization dictated British neutrality in the Spanish–American War over Cuba in 1898. But Africa was a different matter and here British policy continued to be 'forward'.

The three main African areas of British involvement in the years after 1895 were, in ascending order of importance, West Africa, the

Nile Valley and South Africa. In West Africa Britain had limited interests in Sierra Leone and Gambia, more substantial ones in the Gold Coast and a considerable stake in what later became Nigeria. In all these areas British traders came up against the French, who were establishing a vast empire stretching from the Mediterranean to the Gulf of Guinea and beyond. The clash of British and French interests became particularly acute in the Niger territories, where the Royal Niger Company, under the redoubtable figure of Sir George Goldie, had pushed far inland. When this matter reached crisis point in 1898, it revealed a wide difference of approach between Salisbury and Chamberlain and a gradual loss of control even over his own sphere of foreign policy by the ageing Prime Minister. Salisbury saw West Africa as a minor problem in a complex international situation and as a field for possible concessions to France in return for French concessions in the Nile Valley, which had bulked so large in his order of priorities for at least a decade. Chamberlain saw West Africa as part of the imperial estate which he wanted to develop; it was as an imperialist politician that he now came before the public and in that role he commanded a wide following. His style in foreign policy was the same that he had always adopted in the cut-and-thrust of domestic politics, believing in attack as the best means of defence. In comparison Salisbury now appeared almost Gladstonian. As it was, the frontier settlement on the Niger was reasonably satisfactory for Britain. The Royal Niger Company was bought out and the Crown Colony of Nigeria became, under Goldie's successor Lugard, the model for 'indirect rule', the method of government through native princes and institutions.

The Nigerian settlement came just before Anglo-French relations reached a much more serious crisis in the Fashoda incident in September 1898. 'We cannot afford to have more than a limited area of heather alight at the same time', Salisbury had pointed out. A British drive up the Nile, ending in Kitchener's victory over the Mahdist forces at Omdurman, had come up against a small French expedition under Captain Marchand which had left French Congo two years earlier. Still in the days of the Rosebery government Grey had declared that Britain would regard a foreign intrusion into the Upper Nile as an act of hostility. The pivotal importance of the British position in Egypt made it necessary to secure the Sudan, a problem that had cast its shadow since the days of the Mahdi and Gordon; the collapse of Italian power in Abyssinia in 1896 created a further reason for moving against the dervishes. The French move from the Congo was badly thought out and initially hardly troubled the British government. When it came to the confrontation at Fashoda Salisbury displayed firmness and scored something of a diplomatic triumph.

Even here there were differences of emphasis between him and more belligerent ministers like Chamberlain. Salisbury did not wish to humiliate the French, least of all goad them into war, but he was faced with a group of colleagues who considered him an appeaser.

II

South Africa had, of all foreign and imperial issues, far the greatest impact on British politics. Even those sceptical of the benefits of imperial expansion could hardly deny that British economic and strategic interests in southern Africa were substantial and were under challenge from within and without the area. The Jameson Raid formed a kind of curtain-raiser on the Unionist government's encounter with the South African problem. In the decade since the conclusion of the London Convention of 1884 the policy of virtual disengagement from the Boer republics had been entirely negated by the course of events. Gold was turning the Transvaal into the richest part of southern Africa and then into a growing challenge to British predominance in the area. The Boers, under the leadership of Kruger, became with their new wealth and importance progressively less inclined to accept British tutelage and their hand was strengthened by the German presence in southwest Africa after 1884. The rising German ambitions in the area further raised the stakes for the British, while the growth of the Uitlander community, the large number of people, mostly British, drawn into the Rand by the developing mining industry, had created a Trojan horse of formidable proportions within the Boer Republic. In 1890 Cecil Rhodes, the politically most prominent, though by no means the wealthiest of the South African mining magnates, had become Prime Minister of the Cape Colony. He personified that amalgamation of imperialism and capitalism that exists more often in myth than in the real world. His vision of a great industrial and commercial empire in southern Africa under British hegemony could not be realized unless the Transvaal with its mineral wealth took its place within it. The Uitlanders provided a ready means for putting pressure on Kruger and the British government was to provide the cover against external interference particularly from Germany. The outlines of this situation were already taking shape before Chamberlain got to the Colonial Office. Rhodes was always opposed to 'Downing Street government' and was hardly the man whom Whitehall could hope to control, but even the Liberal ministers shared his general analysis of the position in southern Africa. Chamberlain was looking for something that would be 'a feather in his cap' and was less cautious in supporting Rhodes in his intention to exploit a generally expected Uitlander uprising, but the final decision, to pre-empt the planned uprising by launching a raid into the Transvaal, was taken by Dr Jameson himself, Rhodes's commissioner in Bechuanaland. The fiasco of the raid was a serious British setback in South Africa and strengthened Kruger's determination to assert the Transvaal's complete independence. For public opinion at home the humiliation of the raid's failure was almost eclipsed by anger over the Kaiser's congratulatory telegram to Kruger, and there was general agreement that Germany must not be allowed to undermine the British position in southern Africa.

Over the next few years Chamberlain tried to rebuild this position. Sir Alfred Milner, appointed British High Commissioner in February 1897, became the chief agent of this policy. Milner, partially German by birth, had risen from relatively humble beginnings by sheer intellectual brilliance. He was a product of Jowett's Balliol, an early acolyte of the New Liberal gospel of social efficiency through social action. An encounter with the electorate as a Liberal candidate in 1885 had given him a distaste for democratic politics which was to grow steadily into contempt for the parliamentary system and its practitioners. He therefore made his career on the administrative side of public affairs, first as private secretary to Goschen, then in the financial administration of Egypt and from 1892 as Chairman of the Board of Inland Revenue. His belief in national efficiency and greatness had made him into an ardent imperialist and believer in the world-wide mission of the British race. In outlook he had much in common with Chamberlain and like him he was eventually to end up in the Unionist fold.

Milner's move to Cape Town coincided with the meetings of the House of Commons Select Committee of Inquiry into the Jameson Raid and the British South Africa Company. Chamberlain's complicity in the events leading to the raid was such that a full revelation of the facts would probably have ended his political career. The case against him was never pressed, for there was a broad political consensus, extending to most of the Liberal Party, that British control of southern Africa, including the Boer republics, was an important national interest. Chamberlain and Milner realized that for the time being the aim of tying the Transvaal into a British framework could only be pursued with patience. After a year or more of dealing with Kruger on the Uitlander problem Milner, however, became convinced that there was little hope of progress and that it might become necessary 'to work up to a crisis'. At the end of 1898 he still found it difficult to get Chamberlain's open backing for such a course.

By 1898 control of the general direction of British foreign policy was slipping away from Salisbury, weakened by ill-health and age, and Chamberlain's influence was increasing. The potential for conflict between the Foreign and the Colonial Office had been kept in check for the first two years of the coalition; Chamberlain had deferred to his chief's experience and reputation in the conduct of foreign policy, while Salisbury, always respectful of departmental autonomy, had left the internal problems of areas such as South Africa, which he regarded as a colonial matter, largely to Chamberlain. The Colonial Secretary and other ministers had, however, become increasingly concerned about Salisbury's lack of energy in pressing British interests here, there and everywhere, although it was sometimes the cabinet that prevented him from acting strongly, as in the case of the proposed naval demonstration at Constantinople in 1895. There was also much concern about Britain's continuing diplomatic isolation; Chamberlain, in spite of German machinations in South Africa, had come to the conclusion that an alliance with Germany should be actively promoted. During one of Salisbury's absences owing to illness in March 1898, he launched an initiative for a German alliance, which proved ill-judged and abortive. One of the reasons for Chamberlain's move was the situation in China, which was at this moment the centre of attention. Here again Salisbury's view of the limits of British power and of the true nature of British commercial interests proved in the long run more realistic. A policy of establishing a thorough-going colonial situation in China was, leaving aside Hong Kong, no longer practicable. It nevertheless figured in the excitable minds of men like Chamberlain; Russia was seen as the main opponent and Germany as a possible partner. In fact Germany's main interest in a British alliance, as Salisbury saw clearly, was as security against the French desire to recover Alsace-Lorraine and against a Russian threat to Germany's declining partner Austria-Hungary. It was not within Britain's power or interest to offer such security.

In the negotiations with Kruger Salisbury was often less inclined than Chamberlain to take any Boer concessions on trust and was prepared to back Milner's hard line. Chamberlain did not want to burn his fingers again, as he had done over the Jameson Raid; yet he would not let down the powerful High Commissioner who commanded such widespread support and admiration in public opinion at home and with whose ultimate aims he agreed. Chamberlain remained for a long time optimistic that the game could be won without war and he understood better than Milner how carefully the British public had to be prepared to face a war. Thus Milner, without much resistance from Salisbury or Chamberlain, dragged a divided cabinet along a path of successive confrontations with Kruger, which had to be won if loss of face was to be avoided. 'We have to act upon a moral field prepared for us by him and his jingo supporters', was how Salisbury put it. A crucial juncture was the Bloemfontein Conference at the end of May 1899, when a reluctant Milner was induced to meet Kruger. The High Commissioner was convinced that any concessions the Boer President might make to grant the Uitlanders their reasonable civic rights, particularly the franchise, would be merely a sham, designed to gain more sympathy from the Africaners in the Cape and to disarm British public opinion. It was obvious that if all Uitlanders were enfranchised they would swamp the Boers. 'It is our country you want' Kruger cried out in anguish as the conference failed. After Bloemfontein Milner's 'helots' dispatch was published, which he had sent to Chamberlain before the conference. It took its name from the phrase 'thousands of British subjects kept permanently in the position of helots'.

In the next few months a compromise on the Uitlander franchise still seemed possible and Milner was aghast at the prospect. Chamberlain himself still hoped for compromise but increasingly he and his colleagues were inclined to accept the argument that a show of force was necessary to call Kruger's bluff and avoid a war. Early in September 1899 the cabinet decided to send troop reinforcements to South Africa. Chamberlain told the cabinet that what was at stake now was 'the position of Great Britain in South Africa – and with it the estimate formed of our power and influence in our colonies and throughout the world'. In the end Kruger sent his own ultimatum in October 1899, relieving Chamberlain of making the final case for war and cutting the ground from under the feet of all but the out-and-out anti-imperialists in the Liberal Party. Britain appeared to have embarked upon another minor colonial expedition, but in fact it was the biggest war since the Crimea and its impact upon public affairs at least as great.

III

Once the Boer War had broken out and revealed itself as a conflict of unexpectedly large proportions it naturally overshadowed everything else in public life. Even in the previous four years of Unionist government domestic and Irish affairs had lacked the drama and failed to arouse the intensity of interest of previous years. Salisbury still saw little merit in chasing the elusive 'swing voter' and thereby alienating the solid core of Conservative support. Chamberlain had staged a deliberate retreat from domestic affairs; Balfour, the third of the 'quartet' of leading ministers, had no particular line to peddle except a residual interest in Irish legislation; and the Duke of Devonshire was often literally a sleeping partner. In 1896 the government introduced an Education Bill, designed to help the denominational schools, which in the previous few years of Liberal administration had been more than ever exposed to competition from the rising standards of the board schools. Many Conservatives, not least Salisbury, were eager to resume the battle, but there were limits to what the nonconformist supporters of Chamberlain could be asked to swallow. A new system of educational committees was to be set up in counties and county boroughs which eventually might absorb the school boards, while there was to be a modest increase in financial aid to voluntary schools and greater freedom for parents to opt for denominational religious instruction. In return for more financial support for the denominational schools, these would be subjected to a degree of supervision by the new education committees. The bill came under fire from both nonconformists and Anglicans and foundered under Balfour's weak parliamentary management. It was replaced by a modest measure of increased subsidies to voluntary schools in 1897. Thus Salisbury found himself partly thwarted in a matter on which he had staked some of his personal credit.

Chamberlain underwent a similar experience with Workmen's Compensation, an issue with which he had been associated since 1880. The bill was largely based on Chamberlain's ideas; although it did not apply to some important categories of workers like agricultural labourers, seamen and domestic servants, it gave less scope for 'contracting out' which had vitiated so much previous legislation. It came under strong attack from Conservative employers, led in the House of Lords by Lord Londonderry, great Irish landowner and northern coal owner. Salisbury had to remind Londonderry that it was a long Tory tradition that the claims of 'mere liberty should not be allowed to endanger the lives of citizens'. In the event the Workmen's Compensation Act of 1897 was a step forward, but more of a lawyers' paradise than Chamberlain had anticipated. Even more embarrassing for the Colonial Secretary was the failure to act on old age pensions. The subject was buried under commissions of inquiry, which jibbed at the expense and the danger to individual thrift. Eventually the high cost of the war in South Africa scuppered old age pensions, especially with so rigid an economist as Hicks Beach at the Treasury.

For the moment the internal tensions in the Unionist camp and the paucity of legislative achievement mattered little, for there was no chance of the Unionist alliance coming apart. There could never be perfect sympathy between the *grand seigneur* of Hatfield and the *arriviste* of Highbury, but their political marriage was indissoluble. The Liberal Party was in much greater disarray. The failure of Rosebery and Harcourt to collaborate or even to communicate continued to dog the party in opposition as it had done in government. They represented different facets of liberalism: Harcourt was a Gladstonian Little Englander, Rosebery a Liberal Imperialist. When Gladstone made a speech calling for action over the Armenian massacres in September 1896, Rosebery seized the occasion to resign the Liberal leadership. For the moment his desire to escape was genuine, but what he hankered after was to play a role without responsibility, with the possibility of a return to the lead never ruled out. As the only living Liberal ex-Prime Minister, after Gladstone's death in 1898, this was exactly the position he created for himself for about a decade after his resignation and it was scarcely helpful to his party and his successors.

After Rosebery it was Harcourt's turn to lead the Liberals, more by default than by acclaim, but as long as Rosebery remained in the wings, Harcourt could not lead convincingly. He was a formidable parliamentarian and had successfully disorganized the government's parliamentary programme in the session of 1896; but he was not the man to oppose the Unionists with clear Liberal policies. 'The only thing I can see', he had written to Labouchere in a previous period of Liberal opposition, 'is to go on "pegging away" in season and out of season – picking the mortar out of the Unionist joints – and then one fine day the wall falls down, and no one knows exactly why.' In theory Harcourt might have been well placed as a Gladstonian to attack the government's imperialistic policies; in practice there was a great deal of consensus and continuity. Harcourt conspicuously failed to make the most of the South Africa enquiry, perhaps because the Liberal leadership was too deeply implicated. Had not Rhodes donated £5,000 to Liberal Party funds in 1892, on condition that there would be no reversal of Egyptian policy? Harcourt's part in what came to be called the 'lying-in-state in Westminster' did nothing to strengthen his tenuous hold on the Liberal leadership. By the end of 1898 Harcourt had had enough of leading a weak and divided opposition and resigned. So did Morley, who had been acting as his deputy and who had now been commissioned to write Gladstone's biography. By a 'process of exhaustion', as *The Times* called it, the poisoned chalice of leading the parliamentary Liberal Party in the House of Commons now devolved upon Sir Henry Campbell-Bannerman. The only other alternative was Asquith. He could not afford to give up his high earnings at the bar, with which he sustained the hectic social life of his wife, but he could afford to wait: he was 46 while Campbell-Bannerman was 62 and in uncertain health. Campbell-Bannerman was enough of an anti-jingo to be acceptable to the Radicals, while he had enough of a reputation for relaxed inactivity not to disturb the Right Wing and the Liberal Imperialists. Few believed that they were choosing a future Prime Minister.

The vicissitudes of the Liberal leadership were an indication of the impotence of the party, though up to this point the Liberal by-election record was by no means catastrophic. Negative leadership and waiting on events was severely criticized by men like Sidney Webb who believed that it was the function of the Liberal Party to carry into effect a positive programme. Such arguments about the function of a party, particularly when it is in opposition, are common enough; what contributed to the particular disorientation of Liberals at this time was a sense that deep-seated changes were in progress. It looked as if politics was becoming more class-based and in this process the Liberal party was in danger of ceasing to be a national party and of becoming a party of labour. The crisis of liberalism as a philosophy, with individual emancipation giving way to collectivist action as the guiding principle, was widely discussed. The Boer War made a depressing outlook much worse. It forced the party to declare its position on an issue which caused one of the major fault lines in the Liberal body politic. Pro-Boers and Liberal Imperialists differed bitterly in public and Campbell-Bannerman found himself struggling to hold together a deeply divided party.

IV

Within a few weeks of the outbreak of hostilities it was becoming apparent that the war in South Africa was different in kind from previous colonial expeditions. Normally there were about 10,000 British troops in South Africa and it was reckoned that against them the two Boer republics could raise citizen armies of over 50,000 men. The Intelligence Department of the War Office, which had a budget of only £20,000 for its world-wide operations, put a low value on the fighting efficiency of the Boers and predicted that they would be confined to a raiding strategy, with forces of 2 to 3,000 men. Milner and Chamberlain were for long so convinced that they could call Kruger's bluff that they gave little thought to the military situation that would arise if their own bluff was called. The cabinet's decisions to send reinforcements were taken late, for ministers like Hicks Beach, the Chancellor of the Exchequer, Lansdowne, the Secretary of State for War, Balfour and not least Salisbury were reluctant to be stampeded. Luckily the Kruger ultimatum was delayed by the need to act jointly with the Orange Free State, so that the first British reinforcements arrived before the Boer invasion. The army corps sent out from England, commanded by General Sir Redvers Buller, only left after the ultimatum had been received. Its mobilization proceeded smoothly and the 25,000 reservists who had to be called to the colours under the Cardwell system responded swiftly. Wolseley, who had inspired so much of the Cardwell reforms, was supervising the mobilization as Commander-in-Chief. Years of penny-pinching had, however, left serious deficiencies of equipment, particularly of heavy guns, mounted troops and transport, and this had delayed the sailing of Buller's corps.

Buller himself seems to have realized that the initial strategy of defending northern Natal was a mistake, for which he himself would have to pay dearly. The decision to adopt this forward strategy was largely political, for it was feared that any retreat would encourage an Afrikaner rising in the Cape and swiftly make the entire British position untenable. The early British reverses were the result: the siege of Ladysmith and the failure of Buller's first attempt, at the battle of Colenso, to relieve it. The news of this reverse and of the defeats of Gatacre at Stormberg and Methuen at Magorsfontein reached London in 'Black Week', in December 1899. The British public was not accustomed to surrenders and casualties running into several hundreds or even thousands. It was at this moment that the 80-year old Queen said to Balfour: 'Please understand that there is no one depressed in *this* house; we are not interested in the possibilities of defeat; they do not exist.' Defeat was never likely, but the spectacle of one of the world's smallest nations holding the mighty British Empire at bay was galling. Buller was now replaced as Commander-in-Chief by Roberts, the veteran of Kandahar, but continued to play an important role in the war. Roberts was the most eminent of the 'Indian' ring of British generals, while Wolseley was the chief of the 'African' ring, of whom Buller was also one. The rivalry between these cliques did not assist the conduct of the South African war. Roberts was fortunate to reap the benefits of the strategic errors into which the Boers now blundered by dissipating their forces on the costly sieges of Ladysmith, Mafeking and Kimberley. The best Kruger could have hoped for from his early tactical victories was to win complete independence for the Transvaal, just as 20 years earlier, after the British defeat at Majuba, suzerainty had been won. But in 1881 a Liberal government had been in power pledged to reverse Beaconsfieldism. Now there was a Conservative government committed to imperialism, the Liberal Party was deeply divided and the spirit of Cobden, Gladstone and Bright no longer had much hold on British public opinion. Outside Britain there was much sympathy for the Boers and a great deal of fierce anti-British rhetoric. None of this turned into concrete help for the Boers. Kruger's only other option was a war of attrition, for a forward sweep into the Cape, aided by an Afrikaner rising, was now beyond Boer resources.

Soon the humiliation of the early British reverses was wiped out by a string of British victories: French's relief of Kimberley, Cronje's surrender at Paardeberg, Buller's relief of Ladysmith, the fall of Bloemfontein. These successes in the early spring of 1900 were followed two months later by further victories: the relief of Mafeking, the capture of Johannesburg and Pretoria; in October the annexation of the Orange Free State was proclaimed. Of all these events it was the relief of Mafeking that inspired the greatest enthusiasm among the British public: when the news broke, great and with few exceptions good-humoured crowds gathered spontaneously in London and other centres and spent the rest of the night in a carnival atmosphere. A new word 'mafficking' was added to the English language. Mafeking was not as much of a side-show as military historians have often made it out. Colonel Baden-Powell's force had been sent there, the place from which the Jameson Raid had been launched, in the summer of 1899 to play their part in Milner's game of bluff with Kruger. By refusing to surrender he drew off considerable Boer forces which might otherwise have raided to the south at a time when British reinforcements were not yet available and might thus have given the Boers a crucial advantage. After this early phase the siege of Mafeking became a side-show, but Baden-Powell maintained himself by all manner of enterprising and unorthodox devices, including the use of natives in active warfare. Just five days before it was relieved, Mafeking was attacked by a daring Boer raiding party led by Kruger's grandson, which made deep inroads into the town before it was defeated. The instinct of the British public to celebrate the relief of Mafeking with exceptional fervour was thus not misplaced. The popular response to the war was not so much one of aggressive jingoism, but a deep-felt desire to see national honour, pride and the superiority of things British vindicated.

By the autumn of 1900 the war seemed to be over. Kruger had fled into exile and Roberts and Buller came home, leaving Kitchener in charge. It proved a serious misjudgement. Roberts in particular knew little about South Africa, and looked upon the Boers as a traditional state: once the enemy's capital was occupied, his main armies beaten, it seemed all over. The Boers were not such an enemy: the guerilla tactics upon which they now embarked prolonged the war for another 18 months. The military misjudgement of Roberts ran in tandem with the political misjudgement of Milner and Chamberlain about Afrikaner nationalism: that it could be finally subdued and assimilated into British South Africa. The guerilla phase of the war brought burning of farmsteads from both sides, the establishment of camps for the women and children of Boer farmers and a fearful death toll from disease in these camps. The term 'concentration camp' came into use. It was deliberately readopted by the Nazis 30 years later to cover their own more sinister purposes. This phase of the South African war is now studied as the precursor of many similar guerilla campaigns all over the world, in which the struggle for the hearts and minds of a whole population becomes a central feature of the military conflict. In Britain much of the glamour with which the earlier victories had invested the imperial cause now faded. By the time the Peace of Vereeniging finally brought hostilities to a close in May 1902 the war had exacted a heavy price. There were more than a 100,000 casualties among the 365,000 imperial and 82,000 colonial troops who had fought in the war. Nearly 6,000 were killed in action and over 16,000 died of wounds or disease. It is estimated that there were over 7,000 deaths among the 87,000 soldiers who fought for the Boers; between 18,000 and 28,000 died in the concentration camps. The war cost the British taxpayer £200 million.

V

As the gravity of the war was borne in upon the public, it inevitably rallied behind the government, yet Salisbury and his team were not well equipped to conduct a war. The large cabinet had always been run with a loose rein and at this late stage in his career the Prime Minister would not have had the energy, even if he had been willing, to change matters. It was an innovation that a Defence Committee of the cabinet had been formed in 1895, of which the Duke of Devonshire became a chairman. In practice neither Lansdowne at the War Office, nor Goschen, the First Lord of the Admiralty, were willing to subordinate their departments to a cabinet committee. Thus there was no effective political direction of the preparations for war or the war itself. Both Balfour and Salisbury admitted as much publicly when responding to the thoroughly alarmed public mood after 'Black Week'. Balfour, with that lack of sensitivity for popular feeling that so much impaired his effectiveness as a political leader, tried to explain away the failure of the government to authorize reinforcements earlier by blaming public opinion: 'When the nation and the community lags behind the necessities of the case, there may be occasions when rapidity of action is denied the executive government.'

On the reassembly of Parliament there were rumours that the government might fall, to be replaced by a national government under Rosebery. Salisbury made an even more inept speech than Balfour, stressing naively the Government's ignorance of the state of Boer armaments. The Prime Minister's position in these closing years of his career was in many ways sad and ambivalent. In spite of doubts he had not opposed the drift to war, but his presence was an assurance to the national conscience that it was a just war, notwithstanding all the atrocities of the guerilla phase. Salisbury was convinced that the Boers had to be fought to a finish; the side of his character that was always prepared to meet Irish rebellion with repression was here uppermost. Yet Salisbury loathed war and he was out of sympathy with the apostles of national efficiency, who were advocating all sorts of changes in the structure of government, in national institutions and even in the national character. The glory of the British system for him was the safeguard against the abuse of power, even if this meant a loss of efficiency in fighting wars and he was not tempted, like Milner, Rosebery or Chamberlain, to cast envious glances in the direction of more authoritarian systems on the continent.

Chamberlain now became the central figure in the government. Much suspicion still surrounded his role in bringing about what Campbell-Bannerman always called 'Joe's War', but as far as majority opinion was concerned he had followed the right line between standing up to Kruger and being prepared to compromise. Again and again he effectively rallied the government's forces in the House of Commons: 'You may blame us, and perhaps rightly, that throughout this business we have been too anxious for peace. But no impartial man . . . can truly and properly blame us for having been too eager for war. Our efforts were fruitless. Our objects were reasonable . . .'. These were his words in the big debate when Parliament reassembled in January 1900. What consoled the country and seemed to lend substance to Chamberlain's vision of empire was the evidence that Canadians, Australians, New Zealanders and men of British stock from all over the Queen's dominions were rallying to the mother country. Such solidarity was heart-warming, but in fact Chamberlain's schemes of imperial development and imperial federation were making little progress.

In spite of military defeats and the exposure of administrative blunders and inefficiencies the government was in no danger, for the Opposition continued to be bitterly divided. The leaders of the pro-Boer faction were Harcourt, Morley, Labouchere, Sir Wilfrid Lawson, the veteran temperance champion, and David Lloyd George, the young Welsh Radical. Behind them was a network of radical, labour and trade union organizations. The anti-war cause proved to be a means of drawing the Left Wing of liberalism and labour closer together. Within this movement there were many divisions: there was a moderate South Africa Conciliation Committee which issued pamphlets designed to counteract the 'jingo' press; there was a more extreme Stop-the-War Committee, the leading light of which was the journalist W.T. Stead; there was a League of Liberals against Aggression and Militarism, which saw itself continuing the tradition of Fox, Lord John Russell and Gladstone. There was widespread agreement on the Left that the war was about the gold mines on the Rand and that it was being fought for the benefit of the mine owners. Some 60 to 70 Liberal MPs were unqualified pro-Boers. There was, however, never any sign that the pro-Boers could generate the kind of widespread popular support that Gladstone had aroused over the Bulgarian Atrocities. Arrayed against the pro-Boers were the Liberal Imperialists who numbered around 60 Liberal MPs among their supporters. They did not have so many extra-parliamentary organizations to draw upon as the pro-Boers, but they had personalities of heavy intellectual and political calibre. They still looked to Rosebery as their leader; one of their problems was that Rosebery was never prepared to step firmly back into the arena. In between the pro-Boers and the Limps were the moderates, among them Campbell-Bannerman, who summed up his attitude thus: 'I have never uttered a pro-Boer word: I have been anti-Joe but never pro-Kruger. And it is as clear as a pikestaff that the countries must be in form "annexed".' This was in June 1900; a few weeks later, on 25 July, the extent of the Liberal disarray was revealed when Sir Wilfrid Lawson moved an amendment to reduce Colonial Office supply: 31 Liberals voted for this amendment, 40 including Grey voted for the government, and 31 led by Campbell-Bannerman walked out.

Before the outbreak of war there had been a general expectation that the next election, which could hardly be postponed beyond the year 1901, would bring the Liberals back into office, in spite of all the difficulties over leadership and policy which were afflicting them. The 'swing of the pendulum' had on the whole proved itself since 1868 as a plausible electoral rule-of-thumb. The by-election record seemed to indicate that the Unionist defeat would be of 1892 proportions only, although there were times in 1899 when it looked as if it might turn out worse. The war reversed these prospects and when the victories of May and June 1900 seemed to indicate the virtual collapse of Boer resistance the moment appeared favourable for a dissolution of Parliament. Chamberlain and other ministers in the Commons pressed strongly for an early election. Salisbury was reluctant and felt that such a move would display a lack of 'character'. Additional international complications, arising from the Boxer Rebellion in China, enabled the Prime Minister to stall off the pressure. But the annexation of the Transvaal in August changed the situation, for now it could be argued that only a re-elected Unionist Government could bring the Boers to negotiate their final surrender. Thus Parliament was dissolved in September and the 'Khaki' election took place.

British general elections rarely revolve around a single issue and it cannot be taken for granted that the war was the sole or even universally the dominant theme of this election. Undoubtedly Chamberlain, who campaigned prominently, made the war and Britain's imperial destiny the main theme of his speeches. A good many Unionist candidates followed him, sometimes making a crude appeal along the lines 'a Liberal vote is a vote for Kruger'. Where there were Liberal pro-Boer candidates the war was much debated, but the pro-Boer faction was by no means decimated, dropping down to some 50 seats. Lawson was defeated, and Lloyd George just scraped in. Pronounced Liberal Imperialists did not necessarily fare any better. On the other hand Salisbury's own manifesto was very restrained, emphasizing merely that a divided Liberal Party could not govern effectively. The Unionists obtained over 50 per cent of the United Kingdom vote, more than in 1895, which was itself a very solid victory. On the other hand it was no overwhelming endorsement of imperialism, for the overall Unionist majority did fall by 18 seats. There was much evidence of apathy, with the total vote over a million down on 1895. This was partly accounted for by the larger number of uncontested seats, for the Liberals were this time unable to contest 143 Unionist seats excluding Ireland and the universities, as against 110 in 1895, a measure of their disorganization and division. Even in contested seats the turn-out was down. There were a good many local variations. It was the peak of urban Conservatism, with the Tories strengthening their hold on boroughs in England and Scotland. All but eight London seats went to the Conservatives; here the Liberal organization was in particular disarray and it was often possible for Conservative candidates to make an effective appeal not merely on empire but also on social reform. The Liberals gained about a dozen seats in English county constituencies: here the war and its attendant clamour may have had less impact on a more scattered and isolated population. The Conservatives did well in Scotland, but badly in Wales; in the Principality Home Rule candidates had often divided the Liberal vote in 1895, but did not do so this time. In some English constituencies like Torquay the dying embers of the anti-Ritualist campaign seem still to have made an impact. All this suggests that the term 'Khaki' election may be something of a misnomer, but on the other hand the Liberal and Labour Left entirely failed to mobilize any broad popular anti-war sentiment.

After the election there was a reconstruction of the government. Lansdowne, who had become the scapegoat for the shortcomings of the War Office, took over the Foreign Office from Salisbury. Londonderry, who had led the Tory opposition over education and workmen's compensation in 1896 and 1897, was brought into the cabinet, to reassure the Tory Party, 'some of whom were frightened of Mr Chamberlain', as Salisbury told the Queen. Chamberlain, for all the central part he played in recent events and in the election, was barely consulted in these changes. Insofar as the election was a victory for jingoism, it alarmed Salisbury. All his deep-seated fears of the vagaries of a democratic electorate, calmed in recent years, were reawakened. He was determined to maintain barriers against the high spending, populist social imperialism of Chamberlain. He went to great length to persuade Hicks Beach, 'Black Michael', the stern Gladstonian Chancellor of the Exchequer to remain in office. In times past Salisbury had hardly been a follower of the Manchester School either in domestic or foreign policy and in more recent years had often railed against the Treasury, which had increasingly become the central department of State and could lay the dead hand of parsimony on the execution of policy in many fields. But as his colleagues began to challenge his control of foreign policy since 1898 with their ambitious schemes Salisbury himself became something of a Gladstonian. Balfour, the nephew and likely successor of the Prime Minister, was more ambivalent in his views and much impressed by the need to improve national efficiency and to end Britain's diplomatic isolation. The press jeered at the reconstructed government as the 'Hotel Cecil', for Salisbury's son-in-law Selborne, a devoted acolyte of Milner, had also succeeded Goschen as First Lord of the Admiralty and his son, Lord Cranborne, had become Under Secretary at the Foreign Office. Salisbury had, however, done no more than carry out a holding operation to maintain the kind of Conservative government he believed in. The seeds of disintegration were already there.

For the moment it was the unity of the Liberal Party that was put under even greater stress by the final guerilla phase of the war in South Africa. The Gladstonian wing of the party believed that regardless of what was popular at the moment, Liberals had to stick to the principles that now and in the past had distinguished them from the Tories. War and imperialism were morally wrong, Liberal Imperialism was only 'Chamberlain wine with a Rosebery label', as John Morley put it. The Gladstonians could point to the fact that the leaders of Labour were almost entirely with them on this issue, whatever their followers might think for the moment. The Liberal Imperialists saw themselves as the great modernizers in the party who would drag it into the twentieth century with a new and interlocking programme of social reform, national efficiency and empire development. Throughout the year 1901 the battle raged, 'war to the knife and fork', as the veteran parliamentary reporter Sir Henry Lucy called it, for many of the salvoes were fired off in after-dinner speeches. It was also fought out in the press. A pro-Boer syndicate, organized by Lloyd George, bought the *Daily News* with Cadbury money and the Roseberyite editor E.T. Cook had to leave. This was counterbalanced by the fact that H.W. Massingham, an equally distinguished pro-Boer Liberal journalist, was dismissed from the *Daily Chronicle*, the main Liberal Imperialist organ. The return of Milner on leave to England in May 1901 fuelled the flames. The day after his arrival he made a speech which did not spare the feeling of Liberal pro-Boers: '. . . I do not know whether I feel more inclined to laugh or to cry when I have to listen for the hundreth time to these dear delusions, this Utopian dogmatizing, that it only required a little more time, a little more tact, a little more meekness, a little more of all those gentle virtues of which I know I am so conspicuously devoid, in order to conciliate – to conciliate what? Panoplied hatred, insensate ambitions, invincible ignorance.' Yet even Asquith, the most cautious of the Liberal Imperialist leaders, had made it clear that 'to countenance an attack on Milner would be to split the party at once into fragments'.

Returning on the same boat as Milner was Emily Hobhouse, the social reformer, a determined woman of the stamp of Florence Nightingale and Octavia Hill. She had toured the concentration camps in South Africa and she now laid the horrifying evidence she had collected before the Leader of the Opposition. Campbell-Bannerman was profoundly moved and determined to speak out. Lloyd George had already raised in the Commons the 'appalling state of things' in the camps; but had been fobbed off by St John Brodrick, the new Secretary of State for War, with the remark 'war is war'. Campbell-Bannerman now said: 'A phrase often used is that "war is war", but when one comes to ask about it one is told that no war is going on, that it is not war. When is a war not a war? When it is carried on by methods of barbarism in South Africa.' The phrase 'methods of barbarism' brought down on Campbell-Bannerman a stream of obloquy, among it Rudyard Kipling's description of him as a 'Mildly nefarious, Wildly barbarious, Beggar that kept the cordite down'. The Liberal Imperialists were up in arms and even Rosebery, from his detached position, called it a sinister event.

The Liberal Imperialist counterattack gathered pace during the summer and autumn of 1901. There were however, two major weaknesses in the Liberal Imperialist position. One was that there were too many chiefs and not enough Indians. Men like Asquith, Grey and Haldane could ultimately not afford to cast loose from the Liberal Party, because they had no other following. The second major weakness was the position of Rosebery. He still held aloof, for reasons which were a mixture between genuine reluctance to descend into the arena and the calculation that by holding himself above party he might become the catalyst for a party realignment. There was talk of a Rosebery-Chamberlain-Milner axis. As the autumn wore on Asquith, Grey and others proclaimed the Liberal Imperialist message in speeches that implied a barely disguised attack on Campbell-Bannerman's leadership. At last in December 1901, Rosebery himself came down from the mountain and made a speech at Chesterfield, where Asquith and Grey supported him on the platform. He was critical of the government's handling of South Africa and particularly of Milner; but he also said that the country would never trust the Liberals again until they broke with the Irish Nationalists, whose vindictive rejoicing at British reverses had caused widespread offence. Other relics of the Liberal past, 'the fly-blown phylacteries of obsolete policies', must also be jettisoned; 'I hope, therefore, that when you have to write on your clean slate, you will write on it a policy adapted to 1901 or 1902, and not a policy adapted to 1892 or 1885 . . .'. He proclaimed the gospel of efficiency. Rosebery's 'clean slate' speech commanded a great deal of attention; even Herbert Gladstone, now Liberal Chief Whip, was impressed. Within days Campbell-Bannerman and Rosebery met; it was a tactical move on the part of the Liberal leader who had no intention of surrendering his post to the wayward ex-Prime Minister. Only a week earlier Lloyd George, most abrasive of pro-Boers, was nearly lynched by a mob when he dared to trespass on Chamberlain's home territory at Birmingham. Early in the new year 1902 the Liberal Imperialists seemed to be moving towards an open split by setting up the Liberal League, with Rosebery as President. In the debate on the address when Parliament reassembled, the leading Liberal Imperialists did not support the party and walked out. The storm in the Liberal Party was, however, about to blow itself out. By May 1902 the war was over and the bitterness of the Liberal divisions abated.

The end of the war also gave Salisbury his release from a position which had become increasingly burdensome to him. The death of the Queen in January 1901 had snapped one of the bonds that kept him tied to his post. Without overestimating her intellectual capacity he had thoroughly respected her and he had learnt to gauge from her own instinctive and unflinching moral judgements the likely reaction of middle-class England to public events. She in return had reposed complete trust in him. For Edward VII Salisbury could not have the same respect; he had known too much of his social and sexual conduct as Prince of Wales. There was never any doubt that Arthur Balfour would succeed his uncle, even though there was some support in the press, including *The Times*, for Chamberlain. The Liberal-Unionist Colonial Secretary would not have been acceptable to large sections of the Tory Party and he had reconciled himself to the fact. Salisbury's retirement was timed to take place after the King's Coronation at the end of June 1902. The King's sudden illness from appendicitis caused the Coronation to be postponed, Salisbury's departure was delayed for a fortnight and thus occurred at a crucial moment for the Unionist Coalition. Chamberlain had just been incapacitated in a cab accident; in his absence Balfour had accepted an open vote on the Committee stage of the controversial Education Bill, on a clause to make rate-aid to denominational schools optional. The clause was deleted, as Balfour had anticipated, but Chamberlain, had he been present, might have done his utmost to retain it. It was the beginning of a process that was to lead to the disintegration and finally the electoral rout of the Unionist alliance.

As the Boer War drew to a close the pressures for educational reform had redoubled. In the general alarm about lack of national efficiency the shortcomings of the educational system were singled out as a major cause of national failure. The elementary school system remained patchy, with large differences between the schools run by the financially strong school boards in big cities and poor voluntary schools in rural areas. The denominational schools were still losing ground rapidly. There was no general system of secondary education and it was again the larger and more active school boards that had gone beyond their original brief and were making provision in this field. So were county and county borough councils under the Technical Instruction Act of 1889. A Royal Commission under James Bryce had reported on secondary education in 1895; one of its recommendations, that there should be one central authority for elementary and secondary education, was implemented in 1899 with the formation of the Board of Education. Robert Morant, one of its officials and perhaps the most creative civil servant of the period, knew that the work of school boards in secondary education was legally *ultra vires* and this was confirmed by the Cockerton Judgement in 1901. Thus was created both the need and the opportunity for a comprehensive new ordering of the educational system and especially of secondary schooling.

Salisbury was disinclined to stir yet again the hornets' nest of education by major legislation and Chamberlain, mindful of the delicate denominational balance in the Unionist coalition, was also disposed to move cautiously. Devonshire, as Lord President of the Council responsible for education in the cabinet, had always been unsympathetic to what he considered Salisbury's religious prejudice in favour of Anglican schools. He and Balfour were the ministers in charge of drafting the Education Bill and their desire for a substantial legislative achievement got the better of political caution. A major bill, affecting both elementary and secondary education, largely inspired by Morant, was the result. It swept away the school boards and made county and county borough councils the local education authorities for elementary and secondary schools, except in some areas where municipal borough and urban district councils had responsibility for elementary education only. A statutory system of secondary education was thus created, but at great political cost to the government. Chamberlain hoped to limit the political damage by avoiding any payment to denominational schools out of the rates, which he knew would enrage the nonconformists, but Morant pointed out to him that the expenditure on the Boer War made it impossible to place any additional burden for education on the central exchequer. The 'adoptive principle', that it would be left to local authorities to decide whether to use the rates to assist voluntary schools, seemed to offer a way out. Balfour, however, had become convinced that such an option would lead to endless local wrangling and both he and most Anglican Tories realized that it would put the denominational schools very much at the mercy of such local conflicts. Thus he allowed the clause to be struck out. Nonconformity as a political force, which had seemed to be dying, was at a stroke revived and the Liberal Party was given a powerful boost. The nonconformists waged a relentless campaign against the bill, led by Dr Clifford, the famous London Baptist minister. He coined the phrase 'Rome on the Rates' even though the number of Catholic schools which would benefit was a small fraction of the Anglican schools that stood to gain. By-elections began to go spectacularly against the government.

In England most of the nonconformist campaign against the Act once it was on the statute book remained in the realm of rhetoric and the Passive Resistance League which Dr Clifford promoted did not receive official Free Church support. In Wales matters were more serious. Welsh County Councils refused rate-aid to denominational schools unless they were given far-reaching control over these schools. In reply the government passed a Default Act, enabling it to withhold grant from local authorities which illegally refused to aid voluntary schools. In many Welsh villages the Anglican village school was still a symbol of that domination of Anglican squire and parson against which the principality had been in revolt ever since the 1860s, which fuelled the demand for disestablishment in Wales and was a powerful ingredient in Welsh nationalism. Preparations were made to withdraw children from Church schools in rural Wales and teach them in improvised premises. The campaign coincided with a wave of revivalism inspired by the young miner Evan Roberts, during which active membership of nonconformity increased by over 80,000. The battle over the schools in Wales never went the whole way, for only five local authorities had actually suffered penalties before the government fell in 1905.

VI

There was a direct link between the disarray into which the Unionist coalition had fallen over education and the even deeper disunity that was to afflict it over tariff reform. The Education Act may have been necessary and beneficial, but it violated one of the understandings on which the coalition was based, the maintenance of the status quo between Anglicans and nonconformists. It released Chamberlain from any reciprocal obligation to his Conservative allies. He was finding himself in a position of increasing frustration, a far cry from the pinnacle on which he stood at the time of the Khaki election. Like so many others, he diagnosed Britain's position to be in decline and under threat from external and internal causes, but none of the remedies he had devised had shown any results. His schemes for ending British isolation, mainly through a German alliance, a grand union of the Teuton and Anglo-Saxon races, had repeatedly been stillborn. Ideas of an imperial federation, or an empire Zollverein, he had first put forward in 1896; he had tried to interest colonial governments in them at the time of the Queen's Diamond Jubilee, and on several subsequent occasions, most recently at Edward VII's investiture in

January 1902. None of these initiatives, whether the emphasis was on closer economic or defence ties, had prospered. Nor had much come of Chamberlain's attempts to stimulate economic development in the colonies directly administered from Whitehall. He had since 1895 deliberately taken a back seat in domestic affairs, again as part of the compact on which the coalition rested, and the one proposal, old-age pensions, with which his name and credibility was linked, had got nowhere. Added to Chamberlain's frustration at the level of grand strategy there were now the failures of the government at the more immediate political and electoral level. In the light of its inglorious final phase more people were seeing the South African war, 'Joe's War', as a fiasco rather than a victory and the shine on the imperial idea was threatening to rub off.

In April 1902 Hicks Beach in his last budget had to impose a shilling duty on imported corn to meet high demands on the revenue arising from the war. It was unpopular and cries of 'Grinding the Poor' were heard. Balfour had hastily to deny any protectionist intent, when Sir Wilfrid Laurier, the Canadian Premier, linked the corn duty to the forthcoming Colonial Conference and the possibility of colonial preference. On 16 May 1902, just after the Education Bill had received its second reading, Chamberlain in a speech at Birmingham gave a clear hint, without directly referring to the corn duty, that imperial commercial integration was still very much on his mind. 'The days are for great Empires, not for little states', he said and old shibboleths should not stand in the way. During the Colonial Conference it became clear that no progress was likely on imperial defence, but that imperial preference was of interest to the colonial ministers, particularly to the Canadians. In the meantime Balfour had become Prime Minister, Beach had retired and had been succeeded at the Exchequer by Ritchie, an orthodox financier. By the autumn the Colonial Secretary, isolated on education, with by-elections showing evidence of the government's growing unpopularity, put the idea of colonial preference before the cabinet. Ritchie put in a strong countermemorandum stressing the importance of cheap imports for the competitiveness of British industry. He was fortified by Sir Francis Mowatt, the Permanent Secretary of the Treasury and a fanatical free trader, and by Eddie Hamilton, the Assistant Secretary and former private secretary to Gladstone. Chamberlain departed for a tour of South Africa in the winter convinced that he had won the battle in the cabinet, but in fact all the potential for a split was already there.

Chamberlain's South African tour was in itself a considerable success and was intended to be the first of a series of tours round the dominions. He returned in triumph, but the state of politics was even less to his taste than it had been before he left. Ritchie had made use of an escape clause allowing reconsideration of the previous cabinet decision in favour of colonial preference if the state of the revenue required it. Chamberlain was almost back to where he had been in 1887, a prisoner of the Tories and deprived of his normal following. He bided his time for another two months and then spoke out at Birmingham on 15 May, in a speech which is rightly regarded as a turning point in Edwardian politics. It was a declaration for the consolidation of the Empire through imperial preference. Chamberlain denied that he was a protectionist, but 'a small remnant of Little Englanders of the Manchester School' could not stand in the way of Britain and her Empire, threatened by powerful and jealous rivals. The speech was an invitation to start a debate and thus carefully avoided a challenge to cabinet unity, but that it implied such a challenge was widely perceived. It was quickly followed by speeches in the House of Commons, in which Chamberlain, replying to a taunt from Lloyd George about old age pensions, declared that tariffs could be a source of funds for that purpose, and that they would also help employment and wages in agriculture, and would prevent 'dumping' by foreign manufacturers. There could be no doubt that Chamberlain was now advocating a fundamental change in the free-trading commercial policy of the country, which for over 60 years had, it was widely believed, ensured prosperity. He was also threatening to transform the now crisis-ridden Conservative and Unionist party. It was still a party in which aristocratic, landed, Anglican elements, not least the House of Cecil, were influential, and even dominant at a time when the supporters of the party in the country were increasingly middle-class, involved in industry and commerce. Already the cabinet was under attack on the question of army reform by a group of young mostly aristocratic Unionists, dubbed 'Hughligans' after their leader Lord Hugh Cecil, amongst whom was the recently elected member for Oldham, Winston Churchill. It had riled Chamberlain that on the Education Bill Balfour and his colleagues had paid more attention to the demands of Lord Hugh Cecil and other High Anglicans than to his own nonconformist followers. Churchill and Hugh Cecil felt that if the Tory Party became protectionist it would become 'rich, materialist, and secular' and lobbies would produce corruption of an American type.

Thus a general crisis of government and party blew up rapidly, perhaps more quickly than Chamberlain had anticipated in calculating his moves. Balfour now had to take a position. Aware as he also was of the manifold challenges to Britain's supremacy, he was prepared to question dogmatic adherence to free trade, but he doubted if protection was the answer and he was certain that hardly any of it was for the moment practical politics. The position which he worked out for himself in the next few weeks, enshrined in a pamphlet *Economic Notes on Insular Free Trade* was 'retaliation'. The government should be free to make commercial treaties, irrespective of any economic doctrine, where British producers were really threatened by unfair competition. Beyond the theologies of the protection versus free trade debate Balfour was above all concerned to keep the party he had inherited from Salisbury together and to retain control of it. Balfour had no intention of surrendering to Chamberlain, but for obvious political reasons he did not want to lose him and his supporters. He was prepared to lose the dogmatic free traders Ritchie, Lord Balfour of Burleigh and Lord George Hamilton. He wanted to retain if possible the Duke of Devonshire, who was a less rigid free trader and whom the growing divisions within Unionism had once more made into a key figure.

Throughout the summer of 1903 Balfour was working skilfully to keep his contentious crew together. While he was doing it the opposing forces in the Unionist camp were organizing themselves. Spurred on by the powerful figure of Hicks Beach, now in retirement, the free traders set up the Unionist Free Food League. Chamberlain was already using a Birmingham Tariff Reform Committee to pour out a stream of propaganda; in addition the Tariff Reform League was now established. In the cabinet the point of decision was reached in September when Chamberlain and the free traders resigned, the latter having been deliberately kept in the dark about the former's resignation so as to clinch their departure. As for Chamberlain's resignation, it was on the understanding that Balfour sympathized with his point of view, but could only move in the tariff reform direction if there were clear signs that the country was being converted. Chamberlain would be in a better position to undertake the task of conversion outside the government. As a token of the ties that still bound him to the Balfour government his son Austen succeeded Ritchie as Chancellor of the Exchequer. On the other hand all the Prime Minister's efforts to retain the Duke of Devonshire failed and he resigned a fortnight after the other free traders and now became their leader. There were at least two major miscalculations in Chamberlain's strategy. His tariff reform campaign did not sweep the country; it merely made considerable headway in the Unionist Party and thereby kept it divided, while it reunited and reinvigorated the Liberal Party. The second miscalculation was that Balfour would soon have to go to the country under the tariff reform banner. In fact the Prime Minister manoeuvred endlessly to contain the divisions in his party by a finely calculated balancing act and was above all determined, not necessarily from unworthy motives, to hang on to power.

Initially the omens for Chamberlain's success were good. In the summer of 1903 he and his supporters were moving swiftly to strengthen their hold on the Conservative and Liberal Unionist party organizations. The Unionist Free Fooders had a very difficult row to hoe. Should they make common cause with the Liberals? Or would it be better to seek co-operation with the Liberal Imperialists only, thus splitting both parties? Churchill was one of the first to make a direct approach to Campbell-Bannerman in the summer of 1903 and he was soon to leave the Tory Party, but for most people traditional party loyalties were very hard to break. As for the Liberals they could hardly believe their luck. When Asquith saw *The Times* reporting Chamberlain's speech of 15 May he exclaimed: 'Wonderful news today, and it is only a question of time when we shall sweep the country.' This turned out to be an accurate prognosis, but before it could come true there was still much uncertainty and fear that the terrible Joe might after all succeed in persuading the nation to his way of thinking. Campbell-Bannerman was too wily a politician to exploit Unionist divisions prematurely; in the summer of 1903 he played it quietly to allow these divisions to mature.

In the autumn of 1903, Chamberlain embarked on his campaign to convert the country to tariff reform. Again the imperial theme was central to his message, 'the realization of the greatest ideal which has ever inspired statesmen in any country or in any age – the creation of an Empire such as the world has never seen'. He had, however, also to sell the imperial ideal to his audiences in terms of material advantage and this led him into a much broader protectionist argument. He told his working-class listeners that what undercut their products and threatened their employment were the lower wages being paid by foreign manufacturers and the absence of any social welfare or health and safety provisions abroad. To safeguard their own higher standards they needed protective tariffs. He poured scorn on the free trade argument that productive resources, which because of cheaper foreign imports could no longer be employed in one industry, could move into another; this might benefit the middle-class consumer or the recipient of foreign investment income, but not the working man displaced from his job. He varied his theme to appeal to local interests; he included agriculture among the industries that would benefit from tariffs, even though its interest was in protection and not in imperial preference. He stressed the usefulness of tariffs in paying for social reform. He always came back to the argument that tariff reform was about the survival of Britain and her Empire as a powerful force in the world. Looking into the future he said that if nothing was done 'in the course of another generation, this will be much less an industrial country, inhabited by skilful artisans, than a distributive country with a smaller population consisting of rich consumers on the one hand, and people engaged in the work of distribution on the other . . . we may be richer, yet weaker.' Chamberlain faced the problem that his campaign had to work within a short time-scale determined by the political configuration of the moment, but that he was proposing remedies for long-term problems. The ideological implications of his programme, if followed to their logical conclusion, were wide and they led away from Britain's traditional liberal society to a more collectivist, perhaps more authoritarian future. On the Liberal side, Asquith emerged as the most diligent platform orator to make the case against Chamberlain. He had a lawyer's command of facts and figures, not always Joe's strongest point. He stressed the importance of the 'cheap loaf' for the working man, the threat to real wages and to competitiveness from a rise in real costs.

Would tariff reform have been the answer to the problem of Britain's industrial and economic decline and helped her remodernization? The evidence for this decline was seen in statistics such as that Britain's share of world manufacturing production had slipped from over 30 per cent to less than 20 per cent since 1870 and that the United States had overtaken her in the early 1880s and Germany around 1900. Even more serious, from the point of view of naval and military strength, was the fact that Britain had been overtaken as the world's leading pig-iron and steel producer by the United States some time ago and by Germany more recently. Against such rivals, with large domestic resources and markets, acquired through processes of unification, only a similar unification of the British Empire would suffice. Some of the more logical 'whole hog' tariff reformers were prepared to contemplate a situation where eventually the centres of manufacturing might be dispersed to other parts of an autarchic Empire. This concept of a cohesive Empire was, however, the least realistic aspect of tariff reform, for even before 1914 the trends were the other way, towards decentralization and self-government. Only from the point of view of defence was the Empire still a unity, provided the mother country continued to be able and willing to shoulder the burden.

There remains the question whether tariffs, preferential, retaliatory or plain protective, could have produced a modernization or regeneration of industry, and to this there can be no conclusive answer. In the period between 1900 and 1914 British exports to the Empire were, even without preferential tariffs, becoming more important as a share of total British exports. The industries from which these additional exports came were, however, traditional ones like textiles and iron goods. It seems probable therefore that tariffs would have provided a further cushion for these older industries rather than have led to the growth of newer industries like chemicals and electricals, the area in which Britain was lagging behind her competitors. Protective tariffs could have been used along with other measures to stimulate investment in such high-technology industries, but such a degree of interventionism was never likely before 1914 nor would it necessarily have been successful. There were also weaknesses in the free trade arguments. Under the open commercial system the huge and increasing British investments abroad undoubtedly made a growing contribution to the British balance of payments. The gulf between the City and its financial institutions and manufacturing industry was, however, one of the reasons why too much of this outflow went into safe rather than growth investment and the income from it was obviously very unevenly distributed.

It remains remarkable that such highly technical questions, to which even now historians can give no clear answer, should for years on end have formed the staple diet of political debate. It was a tribute to the powerful and fiercely controversial personality of Chamberlain, but he had clearly hoped to win the debate more swiftly and more conclusively. In the winter of 1903 he seemed to be riding on the crest of a wave. Tariff reformers won three by-elections in December 1903 and if Balfour had held an election then he might well have won. Such a victory might, however, have delivered him into the hands of Chamberlain. There were also reasons of national interest, in foreign and defence affairs, why he should have heeded the advice of Fisher, the First Sea Lord, to hang on like grim death. After this Chamberlain, in spite of his growing control of central and constituency party organization and the large sums of money put at the disposal of the Tariff Reform League, was never in such a strong position again. The by-election record early in 1904 showed that Chamberlain was failing in his campaign to persuade the mass electorate to accept tariff reform.

Balfour hung on through the parliamentary sessions of 1904 and 1905. The Free Fooders, over 60 MPs at one time, were a dwindling band, but still sufficiently numerous to be able to threaten to bring the government down. On the other hand Balfour was determined to avoid a complete take-over of the party by the tariff reformers. He believed that this would not help the party electorally nor did it accord with his ideas about the nature of the party. He believed that representatives of the traditional governing classes like himself still had a major role to play. As it was he still commanded the loyalty of a group of Unionist MPs at least equal in size to the Tariff Reform 'Whole Hoggers', though the dividing line between the two groups, given Balfour's own vaguely defined position on tariffs, was naturally difficult to draw. In a division in February 1904, from which the Prime

Minister was absent owing to illness, 26 Unionist Free Traders voted against the government. A month later 112 tariff reform MPs forced the government to withdraw an amendment which confirmed Balfour's position on retaliation, but seemed to them to go too much against the line taken by Chamberlain. As the Unionist electoral position disintegrated, Balfour's authority in the party paradoxically increased, for back benchers were now frightened of an election. By the autumn Chamberlain and his son Austen were making another attempt to force Balfour off his intermediate position, arguing that the government's by-election defeats would end if there was a whole-hearted acceptance of tariff reform. Instead the Prime Minister came out with a 'double election' pledge: if the Unionists won the next election a colonial conference would be held to discuss imperial preference; if this was accepted a second election would be held to get the approval of the British electorate. It was yet another stalling device. In January 1905 Balfour, in response to a taunt by Morley, outlined his intermediate position once more, 'on half a sheet of notepaper'. A month later Chamberlain and the Prime Minister met; Balfour pointed out again that 'the prejudice against a small tax on food is not the fad of a few imperfectly informed theorists: it is a deep-rooted prejudice affecting the large mass of voters, especially the poorest class . . .'. Matters had moved ominously close to a breach. In the House of Commons the government on one occasion blocked a vote which would have revealed the split among its followers, on another Balfour and his supporters abstained by ostentatiously leaving the Chamber. These were humiliating tactics, but Balfour was determined not to be driven off his central position by either the tariff reformers or the free traders and he managed to hold to this line until he resigned in December 1905.

VII

The reasons for Balfour's prolonged rearguard action, ingenious, but scarcely dignified, and electorally disastrous, lay in the critical state of Britain's international position and her defences. The long-running dispute about whether and how to end British isolation had not been resolved when Salisbury handed over the Foreign Office to Lansdowne in November 1900, but by the time Balfour left office in December 1905 something like a diplomatic revolution had taken place. The

Boer War had produced a great deal of hostility to Britain in the press and public opinion of many countries and thus seemed to emphasize the dangers of isolation. The anti-British tone of the German press particularly riled British public opinion, but the Germans never showed any serious signs of abandoning their neutrality and the Kaiser plied his uncle, the Prince of Wales, with well-meant, if tactless advice on the conduct of the war in South Africa. Thus the possibility of an Anglo-German alliance remained alive and Chamberlain and others continued to advocate it in public.

The Boxer Rebellion, which in June 1900 led to the siege of foreign legations in Peking, brought international attention back to China. In the Far East the main protagonist that Britain had to fear was Russia and the continuing problem of containing her there and all along her long southern border from Turkey to Tibet put fresh life into the German alliance project. Lansdowne was endeavouring in the early weeks of 1901 to bring about a British-German-Japanese tripartite alliance in the Far East. It proved abortive, for the Germans made it clear that in case of war with Russia in the Far East they would remain neutral. The Germans still persisted in the mistaken belief that it was the British who would have to make most of the running if there was to be an alliance, yet in May 1901 it seemed close to a conclusion, this time in the shape of a global understanding. Most members of the cabinet, including even Chamberlain, got cold feet about the extent of the commitment, but Balfour and Lord George Hamilton, at the India Office, were attracted by such a positive end to isolation. Once more Salisbury criticized the whole project fundamentally, pointing out that isolation had not historically been a danger to Britain and was not now. He again used the argument that in Britain no government could guarantee the observance of such far-reaching undertakings; on the German side he thought that 'a defensive alliance with England would excite bitter murmurs in every rank of German society – if we may trust the indications of German sentiment, which we have had an opportunity of witnessing during the last two years.' Public opinion in both countries was indeed making the conclusion of an Anglo-German alliance increasingly difficult and it was significant that so sensitive a political weathervane as Chamberlain was beginning to lose his enthusiasm for the project. By 1902 the advocates of a German alliance no longer had much influence and the configuration that might have made it possible was passing. The building of a big ocean-going navy soon made Germany the most menacing of all the major powers from a British point of view; old enmities, with Russia and France, abated and Japan became the first ally to end British isolation.

The alliance with Japan was the result of the failure to enlist the collaboration of Germany in the Far East and the simultaneous inability of either Britain or Japan to set limits to Russian ambitions in China. The naval situation was also a contributory factor: Selborne, the First Lord of the Admiralty, had been warning the cabinet in a series of memoranda that the two-navy standard on a global scale had ceased to be realistic and that in the Far East alone Britain was merely one, and by no means the strongest, of a number of naval powers. Salisbury was still opposed to the Japanese alliance, believing that it would allow a Japanese government to invoke the *casus foederis* through its own possibly aggressive actions, but this was the last occasion on which he produced a major memorandum for the cabinet. Balfour was also unhappy about the Japanese alliance, but for the opposite reason: he still hankered after the world-wide end to isolation that would have been implicit in a German alliance. The Japanese alliance was in fact the kind of limited arrangement that fitted in well with traditional policies, yet it was widely noticed that it did represent the formal ending of 'splendid isolation'.

When Balfour took over as Prime Minister the possibility of a German alliance was receding, but attempts to settle differences and improve relations with the two antagonists of long standing, France and Russia, had not progressed far. In the wake of the Anglo-Japanese treaty little could be done about Russia. A counterpoise to Russia in the Far East had been found, but fears about the Russian threat to India were at their height. The building of the Trans-Siberian railway and other lines in the Caucasus and Central Asia had much increased the Russian ability to concentrate troops for attacks in a southerly direction. Curzon, the Indian Viceroy since 1898, wanted to meet the Russian threat with a forward policy in Afghanistan, Persia and Tibet and railed incessantly against the parsimonious attitude of ministers at home which made such a policy too difficult to follow. Balfour himself was much impressed with the need to give a high priority to the defence of India, but on the whole he wanted as far as possible to avoid conflict with Russia. 'There is really nothing in the way of territory which Russia possesses and we desire', he wrote late in 1903. It required the defeat of Russia by the Japanese before real improvements in Anglo-Russian relations could take place and by that time the Balfour government was about to leave office.

The improvement of Anglo-French relations was susceptible to more immediate treatment. As anti-German feeling rose, so did Francophilia, from the King downwards; it was shared by many influential members of the Foreign Office and Chamberlain was now coming round to the view that there should be an accommodation with France. At the end of 1902 a revolt against the Sultan of Morocco presented an opportunity to open up the question of the French and the British stake in that country. British policy-makers were aware of the weakness of Britain's position in the Mediterranean and were by now very conscious of the dangers of over-commitment. This opened the way to a broader deal: Egypt, where France was weak, to be recognized as a British sphere, Morocco where Britain was weak, as a French preserve. This was the heart of the agreement concluded in April 1904, which has come to be known as the *entente cordiale*. It was not an alliance, but a removal of sources of friction. Some of the lesser of these, for example, the Newfoundland fisheries, proved difficult to settle until the outbreak of the Russo–Japanese War in February 1904 gave a fillip to the negotiations. Sentiment also helped to bring about the agreement: the King's visit to Paris in May 1903 was a great success, Cambon, the French ambassader in London, was a great Anglophile. On both sides the *entente cordiale* was the result not of a major initiative but of pragmatic and tentative responses to changing realities.

The major international crisis, with which the conclusion of the *entente cordiale* coincided, was the Russo-Japanese war. The Dogger Bank incident in October 1904, when a Russian fleet sank two Hull trawlers having mistaken a British fishing fleet for Japanese, for a moment brought Britain and Russia to the brink of war and much alarmed the French; throughout this period Britain and Japan were allies. In 1905 the Germans decided to put the Moroccan under-standing between Britain and France to the test by pressing their own interests in Morocco, signalled by the Kaiser's visit to Tangier in March. It was not a well thought-out step, though at that moment the Russian defeats in the Far East and the outbreak of revolution at home had created a favourable situation for Germany in Europe. The Germans were working to clinch an alliance with the hard-pressed Russians. The ups and downs of the Moroccan affair caused some misunderstandings between London and Paris but in the end the German pressure strengthened the *entente cordiale* rather than weakened it.

Lansdowne and Balfour continued the policy begun under Salisbury of dismantling causes of friction with another great power, the United States. From an industrial and commercial point of view America was now a far greater rival than France and at least as much of a threat as Germany. But whereas strategic analysis, secret and open, and public opinion increasingly came to regard Germany as a potential menace, the opposite development occurred with regard to the United States. It became an accepted principle of British foreign policy that it was not possible to challenge American supremacy in the western hemisphere and that a general understanding with the

United States was desirable. The Admiralty was rather quicker to come to this conclusion than the War Office, who went on solemnly drawing up plans for war with the United States. Russia and the United States were, after all, the only two great powers with whom the British Empire had a common land frontier. The feeling that the United States could no longer be regarded as a potential enemy rested on sentiment and a perception of intentions. Public opinion in both was not always well disposed to the other: in the Spanish–US War in 1898 there had been a good deal of sympathy with Spain and in the Boer War some American opinions, for example, Irish Americans, were pro-Boer. All this never affected the neutrality of both governments. The official recognition that America could not be opposed in the western hemisphere and that one might as well get out of harm's way had led Britain to renounce her rights to share in the construction of a canal across the Central American isthmus without demanding any *quid pro quo*. The Hay-Pauncefote Treaty of November 1901, which enabled the United States to go ahead with the building of the Panama Canal, had been eagerly sought by Lansdowne in the hope that it would turn America into a friendly power. In the next few years Britain tried increasingly to enlist the help of the US in the Far East and by 1905 Theodore Roosevelt was talking of the identity of interests between the two countries in that part of the world. In August 1905 the Anglo-Japanese alliance was renewed for 10 years; it was to operate in case of attack by one power, Britain recognized Japanese preponderance in Korea and Japan guaranteed India and adjoining territories. At the moment when Balfour and Lansdowne left office in December 1905, three major transformations in Britain's international position had just been confirmed: the formal alliance with Japan, the *entente cordiale* and the friendly relationship with Washington. It meant that the world-wide British imperial position was no longer so grossly overextended and it counterbalanced the anxieties about German naval expansion.

VIII

Britain's diplomatic revolution was accompanied by far-reaching changes in the machinery by which the government dealt with questions of defence and strategy. Up to the time of the Boer War there was hardly any such machinery, apart from that Defence Committee of the Cabinet under the Duke of Devonshire which proved so inadequate to the task. Britain's secure international position had meant that overall problems of foreign policy and strategy could be left with the cabinet, while specific questions like colonial or coastal defence were left to relatively minor departmental committees. The growth of international rivalry, the arrival of larger navies and armies, as well as the increasing technical complexity of defence matters were beginning to change the problem of decision-making well before the Boer War, but Salisbury had taken little interest in these affairs. The war, and the deep public alarm about the inadequacies it revealed, changed things radically. It gave rise to a spate of inquiries, the most important of them the Royal Commission on the South African War under Lord Elgin, reporting in 1903, and the War Office Reconstitution Committee under Lord Esher reporting in 1904, both of them initiated by Balfour. Unlike Salisbury Balfour had a strong interest in strategy and the rapid changes in Britain's international environment clearly made a coherent approach to the interlocking problems of foreign policy and defence necessary. The desire to see these developments brought to fruition was another motive behind Balfour's reluctance to relinquish power. He and many of the government's service advisers felt these matters would not be safe in the hands of the Radicals.

Balfour's first step towards improving the machinery of defence planning was the reconstitution of the Cabinet Defence Committee and its renaming as Committee of Imperial Defence in December 1902. It remained under the chairmanship of Devonshire, but the Prime Minister always attended and it became in due course closely associated with that office. The two service ministers were members, as they had been of the previous committee, but it was a new departure that their senior professional advisers, the First Sea Lord and the Commander in Chief, and the Directors of Naval and Military Intelligence were also members. The next major step arose from a recommendation of the Esher Committee, which although concerned with the reform of the administration and direction of the army, had also turned its attention to the problem of co-ordinating its proposed new structure for the control of the army with the overall planning of defence. Esher and his colleagues, among them Admiral Fisher, suggested that the CID should be given a permanent naval and military staff, a Defence Committee Department, not far removed from a ministry of defence. There was still reluctance to accept something so ambitious, with a nomenclature that smacked of continental, militaristic arrangements: but a permanent secretariat under Sir George Clarke, a well-established defence administrator, was set up. The CID had in future a flexible membership, with the Prime Minister as the only 'ex officio' member. A standing cabinet committee of this kind, with a membership reaching beyond the circle of political ministers, and with a permanent secretariat was a constitutional innovation. From the First World War onwards it became the prototype for a more formalized system of cabinet government, with a network of committees and a machinery of secretaries, civil servants and records under the control of the Prime Minister.

Under the Balfour government the CID defined Britain's role as a 'great Naval, Indian and Colonial Power'. The analysis was that the British Empire was based on maritime supremacy. The navy was unequivocally the senior service which could still guarantee the security of the mother country and her far-flung dependencies. The one major commitment which required land forces was the Indian frontier. It was the responsibility of the Indian rather than of the British Army, but it imposed a considerable burden on British military manpower. Whenever problems like the invasion of the British Isles or the security of Egypt were examined, naval supremacy in home waters or in the Mediterranean was considered sufficiently effective as a defence and the provision of bigger land forces was thought to be unnecessary. For Balfour and his colleagues there was as yet no serious German threat, but the first Moroccan crisis, just before the government fell, foreshadowed the change to a more continental strategy. The possibility of despatching an expeditionary force had to be seriously investigated. Because of its domination by the 'blue water' school, however, the soldiers disliked the CID. Thus it ceased to be used after 1905 as a forum for thrashing out the great strategic issues and became a body for the discussion of technical problems. A constitutional innovation with great potential for the future, it failed in the crucial years between 1906 and 1914 to function as an instrument for deciding grand strategy.

The Esher Committee had also recommended the setting up of an Army Board, analogous to the Board of Admiralty, with a Chief of Staff as the principal military member. There was, however, still reluctance to equip the proposed Chief of the Imperial General Staff with a fully-fledged general staff and within the army there was much opposition to the creation of a *corps d'élite* of staff officers such as existed in many continental armies. Not much came of the other army reforms advanced by Balfour's two Secretaries of State for War, St John Brodrick and Arnold-Forster. Brodrick had hoped to use the 'shriek of a nation in its agony' during the Boer War to push through a major increase in the size of the army. He even hinted that if he could not obtain the necessary number of men by voluntary recruitment the security of the country might require recourse to conscription. The scheme was attacked on all sides, with Campbell-Bannerman calling it a 'stirring up of the military spirit'. Disillusion with the South African war raised opposition to Brodrick's proposed six army corps even on the Conservative benches and difficulties of recruitment after the war caused most of the scheme to be stillborn. Arnold-Forster, who succeeded Brodrick in the great political reshuffle of September 1903, was a supporter of the 'bluewater' school and one of a small number of MPs who had for some years played the role of military pundits. His achievement as the responsible minister did not match the expectations he had raised as a critic. He was unable to impose coherence on the contending factions in the War Office and his proposal to reduce the Volunteers antagonized influential sections of his own Party. A major reform of the army, to fit in with the move towards a continental strategy, was thus left for the Liberals to accomplish.

While army reform was lagging, navy reform was proceeding briskly, mainly under the influence of Fisher, who became First Sea Lord in October 1904. British naval supremacy had been so little challenged for such a long time that the navy had become very conservative in its ways. When the nation saw 30 miles of ships at the Diamond Jubilee naval review it seemed to have little cause for disquiet. The two-power naval standard had clearly become impossible to maintain with the arrival of the Americans and the Japanese as major naval powers, but both were friendly and no threat. The creation of a big German ocean-going fleet, signalled by the German navy laws of 1898 and 1900, was a different matter and raised again, after long years of security, a threat in home waters. Alongside such profound strategic changes there were major technological developments affecting the speed and fire power of naval vessels. To respond to this new environment the Royal Navy required reforms in naval construction, disposition of ships and fleets, and in its personnel policy. As regards the latter, Fisher tried to create a more versatile, better educated officer corps recruited from wider sections of society. The sharp traditional distinction between executive naval officers and the rest meant that engineer officers, known as 'plumbers' or 'greasers', or instructors, known as 'schoolies', were looked down upon, while senior commanders would normally have very little technical knowledge. In future all officers were to have a good deal of common training at the naval colleges of Osborne and Dartmouth and gradually the cost to parents of a naval education was reduced and thus made more accessible to the less well-off. The study of the principles of naval warfare was improved by the establishment of a compulsory 'War Course' at the Royal Naval College Greenwich. Reforms in pay and living conditions on the lower deck were brought in, again largely on the initiative of Fisher.

Improvements in the fighting capacity and readiness of the reserve fleet were of great importance in increasing the effective strength of the navy in war. Fisher instituted a system of nucleus-crews to man ships in reserve, so that they could get used to them as fighting machines. The manpower for the nucleus-crews was to a large extent made available through changes in the disposition of ships. Instead of scattering a large number of sub-standard naval vessels around the world to carry out minor policing duties and show the flag, naval squadrons were concentrated, also taking into account the assumed benevolence of the US and Japanese navies and, after 1904, increasingly of the French navy. The German navy was perceived to be the major menace and the North Sea became the centre of gravity in the disposition of British fleets. Fisher believed that 'five strategic keys lock up the world', Singapore, the Cape, Alexandria, Gibraltar and Dover, and all belonged to England.

The most important of Fisher's innovations was the building of dreadnoughts, the ultimate weapon of the age. The weight of a broadside from the guns of the Dreadnought class battleships was 6,800 lbs, compared with 4,160 lbs from the heaviest battleship of the 1890s; the speed of 21 knots was 2 knots faster than any existing battleship. The *Dreadnought* was launched by Edward VII on 10 February 1906 and completed in December 1906, after a record building time of barely 15 months. All the naval reforms were highly controversial. Most of them ran into opposition from naval conservatives, but the policy of building dreadnoughts was equally attacked from the Radical wing of the Liberal Party. They argued that these powerful weapons constituted a dangerous twist in the arms race; from within the Service it was pointed out that the building of these ships would render all current naval designs out of date and negate the great margin of advantage in existing ships which Britain still possessed. In fact advances in technology made it inevitable that such ships would sooner or later be built somewhere and it was therefore as well that Britain should get in first. On the political side, Selborne presided over most of these changes until, on becoming Governor-General of South Africa in February 1905 in succession to Milner, he was succeeded by the Earl of Cawdor.

IX

In the meantime a development had occurred on the Left of British politics which was little noticed at the time, but had far-reaching consequences: the establishment of the Labour Representation Committee, soon to become the Labour Party. In the final years of the old century the attitude of trade unions and trades councils to independent Labour representation had become more favourable again. It was partly a change of generations: union leaders and officials influenced by socialist ideas were coming to the fore in the older craft unions and they had always played a role in the newer unions. Two other developments were also changing the atmosphere in the trade unions: greater organization and aggressiveness on the side of the employers and legal changes adverse to trade unionism. The greater organization of employers may have been in part a reaction to the spread of unionism in the late 1880s. In the shipping industry, where employment practices had never been good, the owners set up a Shipping Federation which compiled its own register of seamen and supplied blackleg labour where required. It succeeded in weakening the seamen's unions and led in 1893 to the formation of a body with wider aims, the National Free Labour Association. Besides supplying blackleg or non-union labour it also engaged in political lobbying. Public sympathy for trade unions, such as had been seen in the London dock strike of 1889, was short-lived and patchy. In 1896 an Employers Federation of Engineering was founded as a counterpiece to the Amalgamated Society of Engineers, which still considered itself the most prestigious of the longer-established unions. The ASE was under pressure from changes in technology and often resisted the installation of new machinery which made existing grades of skill redundant. From July 1897 there was a six-month national strike and lock-out in the engineering industry which arose out of the demand for an eight-hour day. Some employers kept their works going with labour supplied by the National Free Labour Association while the trade union movement rallied behind the engineers with financial support. The final outcome was a defeat for the engineering unions.

As for the development of the legal position of the unions, the satisfactory situation attained as a result of the Tory legislation of 1875 was perceived to have been weakened. The evolution of the doctrine of 'representative action', which first occurred in the field of company law, appeared to make it easier to hold unions legally responsible for the actions of their members and thus to make their funds liable for damages. Peaceful picketing, which had been legalized by the Conspiracy and Protection of Property Act of 1875, was again in danger, particularly through the case of Lyons *v.* Wilkins in 1898. The judges were necessarily influenced in their decisions on trade union law by the state of public opinion, particularly by the occasional outburst of violence in industrial relations. Many active trade unionists imputed class bias to the legal system, but the very uncertainty created by some judicial decisions belies this belief. Nor is there any clear evidence of a concerted employers' offensive against unionism. In many industries, for example on the railways, the employers fought stubbornly against recognizing the unions, but overall there was a drift towards recognition. Unions that had still to struggle for recognition sometimes welcomed the tendency of the law to pin liability for actions on the unions. Some union leaders also welcomed the formation of an employers' association, for they hoped that it would work towards centralized wage bargaining and militate against the autonomy of local branches. What stands out is the wide variation in conditions from industry to industry and from region to region. Nevertheless, uncertainty about the legal situation and the active political lobbying of employers' associations made it advisable for the unions to seek better access to Parliament. Some unions, notably the miners, had their sponsored Lib–Lab members already; others, like the Lancashire cotton spinners, were so politically divided between the existing parties that they preferred to let sleeping dogs lie. Most unions, however, needed little persuading that a 'better repre- sentation of the interests of Labour in the House of Commons' was desirable and a resolution calling for a special congress of unions and socialist societies to secure this objective was accepted at the 1899 Trades Union Congress by a majority of over 100,000. Significantly the resolution came from the main railway union, which was still struggling for recognition and was aware that many directors of railway companies sat in Parliament. This congress or conference convened in February 1900 at the Farringdon Street Memorial Hall in London and established the Labour Representation Committee.

The wording of the key resolution was that 'a distinct Labour Group' should be established in Parliament, 'who should have their own Whips and agree upon their policy which must embrace a readi- ness to co-operate with any party, which for the time being may be engaged in promoting legislation in the direct interest of Labour'. Added to this was the requirement that no member of the Labour group must oppose a candidate of the LRC. It was a compromise remarkable more for its negative than for its positive aspects. There was no mention of socialism, let alone of such slogans as the national- ization of the means of production, which might have smacked of Marxism. On the other hand the requirement that the men to be elected should be members of the working classes was turned down. This would have made it difficult for the socialist societies to play their role in the arrangement. A speech by John Burns, who was already well advanced in his passage to the Liberal Party, was effective in preventing the adoption of such a rule: he declared that he was tired of 'working-class boots, working-class trains, working-class houses, and working-class margarine'. The LRC was thus a compromise between trade unions mostly suspicious of socialism and the three socialist societies, the ILP, the SDF and the Fabians. The ILP was the true midwife of the committee through Keir Hardie and Ramsay MacDonald. In the late 1890s its expectations had been chastened, for it had clearly failed to become a mass party and the conversion of the trade unions was therefore the only way forward. The SDF, although counting many individual trade union leaders and officials among its members, was still dominated by Hyndman and not prepared to give up its Marxist socialism; after a year it withdrew from the LRC. The Fabians did not make much of a contribution to the establishment of the LRC; they were split over the Boer War and Ramsay MacDonald was about to resign from the society. As for the trade unions, only about a third of the members normally represented at the TUC were represented at the meeting in the Farringdon Street Memorial Hall; nearly all the miners, the cotton operatives and most of the building trade unions were among the absentees. Some of the more traditional union leaders believed that the whole enterprise was simply designed to enable the socialist societies to milk the funds of the unions.

Even in the trade union world many regarded the LRC as an ephemeral body. That it turned out differently was mainly due to the work of Ramsay MacDonald, who became the first secretary to the Committee, and to the Taff Vale decision and it was also helped along by the sense of unity created by opposition to the Boer War among Liberal Radicals and Labour. MacDonald now became the central figure in the rise of Labour as a political force. In his views he very much epitomized the progressivism of that period: his vision of socialism was of a gradual advance towards a sunlit upland, in which the ethical improvement of humanity played a central role. He did not believe in the class war as a motivating force of history. He was a fervent internationalist, who through travel had built up a wide-ranging knowledge of the world; he hated war and the pride of race that underlay so much of the imperialist sentiment of the time. He experienced religious doubt without rejecting the moral teachings of Christianity or losing a somewhat religious cast of mind. MacDonald was hardly an original thinker but he had a gift of exposition that endowed him with considerable charisma. He was a good organizer and committee man, though hypersensitive to criticism; he was rare among leading labour figures in possessing, through his wife, a private income sufficient to enable him to devote himself entirely to political work.

All of MacDonald's efforts to get more trade unions to become affiliated to the LRC would probably have prospered at best very slowly had it not been for the Taff Vale decision. After a year only 41 unions with a membership of 35,000 had affiliated to the Committee, at a time when there were nearly 1,300 unions with a membership of nearly two million. In 1901 the House of Lords handed down their decision in the Taff Vale case, followed almost immediately by another decision on appeal in the case Quinn *v.* Leathem. Both decisions meant that union funds were in future liable for damages caused by their members. In the Taff Vale case a South Wales railway had successfully sued the Amalgamated Society of Railway Servants through its officials for damages sustained through picketing in the course of a strike in August 1900. The decision was reversed by the Court of Appeal, but reinstated by the Law Lords. When the damages were finally settled in January 1903 they amounted to £23,000, so that with legal costs the railway union must have lost at least £30,000. A similar case was pending against the South Wales Miners. Taff Vale and the other related cases were much more the result of developments in the law, again mainly the doctrine of 'representative action', than they were evidence of judicial bias against the unions. Unfortunately Taff Vale seemed to bear out those in the trade union movement who believed that unions should have as little to do with the law as possible. Working-class opinion that the law was something imposed from above to the confusion of ordinary men and women was long established and deeply felt. There was, however, also a school of thought among trade union leaders that greater involvement of their organizations with the legal system would make for better central control and tighter discipline of the rank and file. Some, including Ben Tillett, the London dockers leader, had wanted to develop a system of compulsory arbitration. Such opinions were now on the retreat and Taff Vale decisively turned the unions, and with them the conduct of industrial relations, against legal interference.

Taff Vale also gave the LRC a decisive fillip. By 1903 the number of affiliated unions had risen to 127, with a membership of nearly 850,000. The Engineers and the Cotton Spinners had voted to affiliate. A parliamentary fund was set up based on a penny levy per affiliated member; over £3,000 could thus be raised, from which candidates' election expenses could be met and elected MPs would be paid £200 p.a. There were still a great many difficulties. On the one hand there was the ongoing tension between socialists, mainly in the ILP, and non-socialist trade unionists who felt that they were providing all the resources of the LRC. On the other hand there was the problem of remaining independent of the Liberals, at the very moment when the most had to be made of the radical-progressive unity in opposition to the Boer War and imperialism. Under MacDonald's guidance the LRC stressed its independence of the

Liberals, but mainly as a means to an end, to carve out a niche and bargaining position for Labour, for he saw no ideological obstacle to collaboration with Liberalism.

The electoral evidence was strengthening the bargaining position of the LRC. In the Khaki election 15 LRC candidates had been fielded, 10 of them from the ILP. Out of the total vote cast in these 15 contests the LRC candidates polled about 35 per cent. Only two members were elected, Keir Hardie at Merthyr, and Richard Bell, the secretary of the Amalgamated Society of Railway Servants, at Derby. Bell soon became indistinguishable from the Lib-Labs. By-elections showed that Labour candidates had considerable vote-getting powers and that separate Labour candidates could easily hand Liberal seats to the Tories. Thus an LRC candidate was returned for Clitheroe unopposed in July 1902: under LRC arrangements Philip Snowden, the ILP candidate, made way for a local textile union official, David Shackleton, who was a Liberal and thus able to secure the support of the Liberals; the Tories then withdrew from the contest. In March 1903 Will Crooks, a popular local trade unionist standing as an LRC candidate, won Woolwich from the Conservatives in a straight fight. In July 1903 Arthur Henderson, one of the future leaders of the Labour Party, narrowly won Barnard Castle in County Durham in a three-cornered contest. It was the most striking illustration yet of the power of the Labour vote, but the narrowness of Henderson's victory, 3,370 votes to the Conservative's 3,323 and the Liberal's 2,809, also showed that the LRC could play a purely destructive role on the Left.

Woolwich and Barnard Castle occurred while the negotiations were in progress between Herbert Gladstone, now Liberal Chief Whip, and MacDonald, with a view to establishing an electoral pact. Both sides had cards to play and dangers to face. Gladstone could offer MacDonald the inestimable boon of providing for the appearance of a sizeable Labour group in the House of Commons by facilitating a clear run for LRC candidates in a limited number of constituencies. MacDonald's cards were basically weaker, for in no way could he deliver a Labour vote and most of those who voted for Labour candidates would, in the absence of such candidates, vote Liberal anyhow. He could, however, threaten the appearance of LRC candidates who would spoil the Liberal chances and he could claim that 'the LRC can directly influence the votes of nearly a million men'. His financial resources were an attraction to Gladstone and by leaving some constituencies to the LRC the Liberals would husband their stretched resources. Both Gladstone and MacDonald faced considerable opposition to what they were doing in their respective camps and for this reason their meetings and their eventual agreement were kept secret, but they were encouraged by the identity of policies and attitudes of their respective parties. The Gladstone–MacDonald pact that emerged was no more than an understanding that both sides would use their influence in appropriate constituencies to give each other a clear run; neither side was in position to guarantee anything.

There was never much likelihood that the Balfour government might have made a bid for the labour vote in the style of Tory democracy. In the early days of the LRC and the first stages of the Taff Vale case there was little evidence that these matters had caught the attention of the average working-class voter. When in August 1901 Hardie had raised the question of protection for trade union funds Balfour had returned a flat 'no'. A little later *The Times* ran a series of articles on 'The Crisis in British Industry', which put the blame for much of the lack of British competitiveness squarely on the trade unions and their restrictive practices. Informed opinion which counted for much with ministers was clearly anti-trade union. In May 1902 the Parliamentary Committee of the TUC put all its weight behind a motion asking for legislation to restore the position of 1875. Although a few Conservative backbenchers gave support, the government replied through the Attorney-General that 'if every time a judge says something which you do not like you pass a fresh law, you may depend upon it that the law will soon be in a state of chaos'.

In May 1903 another very limited attempt to help the trade unions in their problem of liability miscarried. A bill drafted with the agreement of the Parliamentary Committee of the TUC gave unions freedom from liability only in cases where the union executive had not authorized action. This Private Member's Bill, which David Shackleton, the new LRC member for Clitheroe introduced, and from which the clauses referring to union liability had in the end to be dropped, failed by the surprisingly narrow margin of 30 votes. This perhaps convinced Balfour that some action was necessary and he appointed a Royal Commission on Trades Disputes. The TUC refused to cooperate with this commission as it included no trade unionist. The appointment of Sidney Webb as a member may have been intended as a gesture to organized labour, but failed in this purpose. The Webbs, with their contempt for the LRC and support for Liberal Imperialists, were not popular with trade union leaders at this time. The Fabian Society supported the system of compulsory arbitration and were against a direct reversal of the Taff Vale decision on unions' liability, preferring a closer legal definition of the activities which, when carried out on behalf of a trade union, were to be immune from action in the courts. Sidney Webb signed the majority report of the royal commission when it was published in 1906, recommending that trade unions should only be liable for actions of their members if these had been expressly authorized by an executive committee, the position which Shackleton's bill had sought to establish; Webb added a rider in favour of compulsory arbitration. It could be argued that by failing to act on the legal position of the unions after Taff Vale the Balfour government missed an opportunity of keeping the area of industrial relations, so vital to national efficiency, subject to a reasonable degree of control by the law.

X

The activities of the LRC and the manoeuvres of trade union leaders over Taff Vale probably had only a limited effect in swinging the large Tory working-class vote to the Liberals. The failure of the tariff reform campaign was more important and early in 1904 another issue of even greater emotive power came along, 'Chinese Slavery'. The importation of indentured Chinese coolies had been demanded by the Rand mining magnates as essential to the economic rehabilitation of South Africa in the wake of the Boer War. Milner soon became convinced by their arguments, especially as all attempts to use white men as unskilled labour had come up against insuperable obstacles from both employers and fellow workers in the mining industry. Indentured Chinese workers therefore became in Milner's view the key to South Africa's British future and he pressed his view upon a reluctant cabinet at home. Thus a Chinese Labour Ordinance was issued in February 1904: Chinese workers were to come to the Transvaal for a fixed term of years, they were to live in compounds which they could only leave on 48-hour permits, they could own no property nor have access to the courts of law, they were subject to specific penalties for offences especially defined in the ordinance, they were to work for a 60-hour week at a wage eventually fixed at two shillings an hour, and in practice they could not bring their families.

It did not take Campbell-Bannerman and the Liberal Party long to see that they had been presented with a nearly perfect weapon for attacking the Unionist government. Nothing could have been more useful in confirming the view, already widely held, that the Boer War had been a 'mine-owners' ramp'. Far better than Taff Vale 'Chinese slavery' seemed to illustrate the callous 'commodity view' of labour held by Balfour and his party and it could even be made out that British workers, already alarmed by the influx of Jewish immigrants from eastern Europe, might soon be confronted with even cheaper labour brought in from further east. The nonconformist conscience was given fresh grounds for indignation by the spectacle of Chinese men separated from their families and herded into compounds. Leo Amery, Milner's most devoted follower at home, wrote to his master: 'Every little Bethel is an anti-Chinese assembly room . . .'. Of the three Liberal Imperialist leaders, who had for so long followed the 'religio Milneriana', as Campbell-Bannerman put it, only Haldane remained loyal to the faith; especially Asquith found the temptation to make political capital out of the issue too great. When installed in office as Parliamentary Under Secretary for the Colonies early in 1906, Winston Churchill had to admit that 'Chinese slavery' was a 'terminological inexactitude', but this did not detract from its effectiveness as a political slogan.

XI

In Ireland Balfour sought to carry on the policy of constructive Unionism which he had done so much to launch in the later 1880s, but here very considerable achievements proved in the long run deceptive and failed to put Anglo-Irish relations on a permanently stable footing. In the Salisbury government Arthur Balfour's brother Gerald was Chief Secretary. He carried through the very important Irish Local Government Act of 1898, which gave Ireland a system of local government on the British model, with county councils, urban and rural district councils. In most areas the councils were dominated by the Catholic and nationalist majority who were thus trained in the skills of self-government and enabled to play a constructive role in the affairs of their country. When in 1900 Gerald Balfour handed over to George Wyndham, the economic situation of the peasantry had undoubtedly much improved and successive land purchase acts had created a peasant proprietory. There were now quite a few improving landlords who across the sectarian divide tried to do their best for their tenants. The most conspicuous example was Sir Horace Plunkett, the founder of the Irish co-operative movement. On the other hand land agitation was still going on under the aegis of William O'Brien's United Land League, founded in 1898, and it was being met by the authorities with coercion. The scale of violence was, however, not comparable to that of the 1880s. In the meantime the Irish Nationalist

Party, after years of disastrous feuds, reunited in 1900 under the Parnellite John Redmond, but constitutional nationalism was never able to recapture the vigour it possessed under Parnell. Irish national consciousness, although it appeared on the surface to be waning, was about to be revived by a cultural renaissance.

Wyndham had once been Arthur Balfour's private secretary at Dublin Castle and shared the Balfour brothers' approach to the Irish problem. He hoped in fact to solve the problem with a final and conclusive instalment of constructive Unionism. In 1903 he passed the Land Purchase Act which thereafter bore his name and went further than any previous Land Purchase Act in applying to the sale of whole estates rather than of piecemeal holdings. It was based on the ideas promoted by a Land Conference in which a number of improving landlords from the traditional Anglo-Irish ascendancy played a prominent role. The success of this co-operation between landlords and tenants, nationalists and unionists, Catholics and Protestants encouraged the notion that the time had come to settle at last, by agreement and conciliation, the problem of Irish government. Devolution proposals were worked out, largely the brainchild of Sir Anthony MacDonnell, the Under Secretary at Dublin Castle, who was a Catholic and had a brother in the Irish Parliamentary Party. MacDonnell worked with the Earl of Dunraven, one of the progressive landlords involved in the Land Conference and the promoter of an Irish Reform Association. When the devolution proposals became public a storm of suspicion blew up on all sides. The feeling at Westminster forced the resignation of Wyndham. In Ulster indignation ran especially high and the various organs of Unionism were now pulled together in an Ulster Unionist Council which was soon to become the focus for the most intransigent opposition to Home Rule. William O'Brien, the nationalist leader most deeply involved in the policy of conciliation, became isolated and virtually an outcast. The limits of constructive Unionism were clearly to be perceived and Balfour was thwarted.

XII

There was in these dying years of Unionist government yet another example of Balfour's propensity to stir up a hornets' nest by his entirely reasonable methods of dealing with long-standing problems.

As in the case of education, a judicial judgement, similarly created a need to act on the vexed question of licensing. A decision by the local magistrates at Farnham in Surrey, a place notorious for its excess number of public houses, overturned the previous legal position that no compensation was payable when a licence was withdrawn not on grounds of misconduct but for reasons of temperance. Balfour was as concerned as anyone to limit the evils of drink and felt that the Tories had a good record on licensing reform; but he had no sympathy with the fanatical temperance men who 'by some strange perversion . . . have transferred to the seller of drink the sentiments of moral reprobation which ought more properly to be reserved for the immoderate consumer'. His Licensing Act of 1904 was based on the principle that where a licence was withdrawn on the grounds of the public well-being, compensation should be paid out of a fund levied on all licence-holders. A licence to sell drink was a piece of property, for which a price had been paid and for which the holder was therefore entitled to be compensated. The withdrawal of a licence made other licences in the locality more valuable and this was the moral justification for charging them with the cost of compensation. It was an ingenious and pragmatic way of dealing with the problem which proved effective over a long period, but it could not expect to commend itself to the nonconformist temperance movement. Slogans such as 'endowing the trade' and a 'brewers' bill' were heard again. If Balfour had hoped that the storm over the Education Act was blowing itself out and that differences between politically active nonconformity and the Liberal Party, for example over Irish Home Rule, might reassert themselves, he was disappointed.

In the autumn of 1905 Balfour came to recognize that his long balancing act between tariff reformers and free traders in the Unionist Party could not be carried on into the next session of Parliament. Chamberlain and his followers wanted an election on a clear commitment to tariff reform. An appeal by the Prime Minister for party unity at the conference of the National Union of Conservative Associations, now dominated by tariff reformers, fell on deaf ears, but within a few days fresh hopes of Liberal disunity were kindled. On 23 November 1905 Campbell-Bannerman said at Stirling that 'the opportunity of making a great advance on this question of Irish Government will not be long delayed'. Two days later Rosebery felt impelled to say at Bodmin 'emphatically and explicitly and once and for all that I cannot serve under that banner'. It looked as if the Liberal Party's ability to tear itself to pieces was undiminished. In fact Rosebery was now an isolated figure. The three leading Liberal Imperialists, Asquith, Grey and Haldane agreed with Campbell-Bannerman that Irish Home Rule should remain the objective of the

Liberal Party, but that it should not have the absolute priority it had
in the Parliaments of 1886 and 1892 and that in the meantime the
Irish would have to make do with such devolution as they could get
'provided it was consistent with and led up to [the] larger policy'.
This was all that Campbell-Bannerman had meant to imply at Stirling and Rosebery's misinterpretation of it at Bodmin was felt even by
Asquith and his *confrères* to be a maladroit and irrelevant intrusion.
Nevertheless, Balfour, unable to unite his own party and scenting
disarray in the opposition, now resolved to apply the tactic of resignation and apprised the King of his intention on the afternoon of
Monday 4 December. It was a move that entirely failed to stave off or
mitigate the electoral disaster that was about to engulf the Unionist
Party. The criticism that has been levied at Balfour's long rear-guard
action should not disguise the fact that the aftermath of the Boer War
had made it very difficult to avoid electoral defeat. Too much about
that war, its conduct, the manner of its conclusion and its consequences had made for disillusionment with the imperial idea. The
Unionist Party had fought the war and even without tariff reform was
the party of Empire. It was almost inevitable that there should be
reaction against all it stood for, a reaction which was looking back to
Gladstonianism as much as it was looking forward to new prescriptions for the discontents of the moment.

8 The Liberals in Power
1905–1914

I

When Edward VII had accepted Balfour's resignation he was in no doubt that he should send for Sir Henry Campbell-Bannerman. The King had seen much of Campbell-Bannerman at Marienbad that summer and did not share the widespread tendency to underestimate the elderly Liberal leader, but it was not certain that Campbell-Bannerman would be able to form a government. The three Liberal Imperialist leaders, Asquith, Grey and Haldane, had decided among themselves that they would take office only if Campbell-Bannerman himself, while nominally Prime Minister, was relegated to the Lords and Asquith made Leader of the Commons. Unless these conditions were met all three of them would stay outside the government, thus, it was thought, fatally weakening it from the outset. This conspiracy was known to those who were party to it as the Relugas compact, for it had been hatched at Grey's fishing lodge in northern Scotland. Its existence was known to the King and to Knollys his private secretary, who had considerable sympathy with its aims. If there could not be a Conservative government, a Liberal government would only be tolerable if its dangerous Radical wing was kept in check by the Relugas conspirators holding key ministerial posts. Campbell-Bannerman quickly scented that there was an attempt to put him under pressure or possibly to replace him, at the eleventh hour, by Rosebery. If he ever felt any inclination, for reasons of age and health, to retire to the Upper House and play a mainly ornamental role, he was now stiffened in his resolve to fight back and at a crucial moment his wife gave the decisive verdict that, in spite of the risk to his health, he should lead from the Commons. Even before Balfour's resignation, Campbell-Bannerman had effectively managed to detach Asquith, whose adhesion was vital for an incoming Liberal government, from the Relugas compact. Asquith excused his abandonment of his fel-low-conspirators on the grounds that Balfour's decision to resign rather than dissolve Parliament had made the formation of an effective Liberal cabinet the overriding priority. Once armed with the royal commission, Campbell-Bannerman moved deftly to establish his complete control. Asquith accepted the Exchequer and, after considerable efforts at persuasion, Grey the Foreign Office, without any conditions. It was almost an afterthought that Haldane went to the War Office; he was the most inveterate of the Relugas intriguers and was ambitious for the Woolsack. If Asquith had been isolated in a more Radical cabinet or if Morley, as was his strong desire, had taken the Foreign Office, the British card in the international game up to 1914 might have been played rather differently.

Two other appointments in this Liberal government, which in essence was to remain in existence for nearly 10 years, are specially worthy of note: David Lloyd George entered the cabinet as President of the Board of Trade at the age of 42; and Winston Churchill, a recent convert from the Tories and less than 32 years old, became Under Secretary for the Colonies, his chief, Lord Elgin, being in the Lords. John Burns, who had moved a long way from his role as a radical Labour leader, became President of the Local Government Board, the first working man to reach the cabinet; John Morley and James Bryce, survivors from previous Liberal cabinets, got India and Ireland and Herbert Gladstone became Home Secretary. It was a strong government, though not an easy team to drive. Within 10 days of its formation, the new Prime Minister announced a dissolution of Parliament and the polling began in mid-January 1906.

The general election of 1906 still holds the record as the biggest landslide since 1832. The Unionist contingent which had numbered over 400 in the Khaki election was reduced to 157. The Liberals alone now had 400 seats, as against 184 in 1900; there were also 30 LRC members, one of the most sensational features of the election, and 83 Irish Nationalists. The Liberals thus had, for the first time since 1885, an absolute majority of 130 seats; with their allies they had a huge majority of over 350 seats. In terms of votes the result was naturally less decisive, though still impressive enough; the Liberals had nearly 50 per cent of the United Kingdom vote and the LRC nearly another five per cent, while the Unionists had dropped from over 50 per cent to 43.4 per cent. The size of this transformation startled contemporaries and has continued to be analysed by historians. Was it, as Balfour thought even before he knew the full magnitude of his party's disaster, 'the faint echo of the same movement which has produced massacres in St Petersburg, riots in Vienna and Socialist processions in Berlin'? The technical factors which had for so long favoured the Tories were now almost wholly working for their opponents. Whereas 143 Unionists had been returned unopposed in 1900 leaving aside Ireland and the universities, now there were only 3, while 27 Liberals were returned unopposed. The Gladstone–Macdonald Pact worked well: of the 45 LRC candidates in England and Wales only 6 stood in seats previously held by Liberals and 33 had straight fights with the Unionists. Compared with this relative harmony in the Liberal–Labour camp, the Unionists were divided. Apart from the dissension caused in their national organization by the tariff reform controversy there was much disarray at the constituency level. In addition to those who like Churchill had crossed the floor, nearly 100 Unionist candidates retired from political life and probably took a considerable amount of their personal support with them. Others had to change constituencies: for example Goschen, a convinced free trader, moved from the Home Counties to Lancashire. In 11 seats there were rival Unionist candidates.

An analysis of election addresses and of the campaign seems to show that tariff reform versus free trade was the most prominent issue. On the other hand it cannot be deduced from the results that tariff reform in itself was responsible for the biggest swings, except in some areas like Lancashire, where the free trade tradition was particularly strong. Tariff reform was important above all because it showed up the Unionists as a divided party, while it served as a convenient bond of unity in the Liberal and Labour camps. Many other issues, imperialism, social reform, Chinese slavery, were all connected with it. Even against Empire patriots it could be argued that tariff reform might merely create friction between the mother country and her colonies, and that the Liberal vision of an Empire freely associating under the protection of the British Navy was superior to an exploitative and coercive system run for the benefit of cosmopolitan capitalists. Nonconformists had become an active force for the Liberal Party again, mainly because of the 1902 Education Act. Yet the education issue did not stop Irish Catholics in England from voting strongly for the Liberals, because Home Rule and the recalcitrance of Ulster mattered more to them than the future of denominational schools. Taff Vale mobilized organized labour as a sectional interest against the Tories, 'Chinese slavery' aroused working-class emotions against them. Thus the Liberals benefited from an accumulation of issues to which the Unionists, through a series of tactical mistakes, had no convincing answer. Most of these issues were conventional and traditional, none more so than the debate for and against protection and free trade, where free trade represented the status quo and tariff reform meant change. Social reform, although frequently mentioned in the election campaign, appeared in rather conventional guise, mainly as a demand for old-age pensions, which the Tories were thought to have promised but never introduced. Socio-economic class had for long been becoming more important as a factor governing party allegiance, but not exceptionally so in this election. Religion remained significant as a factor structuring the vote. Commitment to free trade undoubtedly made a significant number of middle-class Tories switch their votes to the Liberals. It is thus difficult to discern in this election the social revolt that Balfour invoked perhaps as an alibi for his own miscalculations. This is also borne out by the rapidity with which, to judge from by-elections, the electoral pendulum swung against the Liberals again after 1906. Only in some areas, like working-class London or industrial Lancashire, was there a more lasting shift in electoral allegiance to the Liberals.

Nevertheless the parliamentary Liberal Party which arose out of the 1906 election was a different animal from the Gladstonian party that had allowed itself to be ousted from office more than 10 years before. There had been a fairly rapid turnover of personnel in the party during this period, perhaps accelerated by its uncertain prospects, and on top of this the number of Liberal MPs was now suddenly more than doubled. Even before 1906 there had been a decline in the business element in the party, in particular the great Liberal commercial dynasties, like the Pease or the Illingworth families, were somewhat less in evidence, partly because the Conservatives had become so clearly the party of business and commerce. Members of the same family could now be found on both sides: this was the case with the Dewars (whisky), Palmers (biscuits) and Wills (tobacco), for example. Against this, journalists, writers and academics had become more common among Liberals in the House of Commons and in 1906 a clutch of such men made their entry, among them C.F. Masterman, Hilaire Belloc, Chiozza Money, G.P. Gooch, C.P. Allen, Herbert Samuel and J.M. Robertson. The two latter eventually held government posts. There was, however, still an element of the old aristocratic, land-owning families present, slightly reinforced by defecting Unionist free-traders like Churchill. Changes in the social composition of the parliamentary Liberal Party were not directly related to the pursuit of social reform by the incoming government and even among the business section of the party there had always been some strong Radicals, but there was now less chance that departures from *laissez-faire* orthodoxy would meet with damaging resistance from the backbenches.

Some of the new Liberal MPs were associated with the New Liberalism, though the two writers most commonly identified with the term, L.T. Hobhouse and J.A. Hobson, were not in the House. The New Liberalism was an off-shoot of the progressivist movement away from individualism and towards collectivism that had its roots in Ruskin, Morris and T.H. Green. Little distinguished it from Fabian socialism; Fabians like the Webbs, Shaw, Ramsay MacDonald and Graham Wallas came together with Liberals like Hobson, Haldane and Herbert Samuel in the 1890s in groups such as the Rainbow Circle and in launching and writing for journals such as the *Progressive Review*. Imperialism, the Boer War, the Education Act of 1902 and the question to what extent one could work through a Conservative government divided them again. Protagonists of the New Liberalism like Hobson and Hobhouse never went all the way to socialism and always looked to the Liberal Party as the vehicle for their ideas, through which it would transcend the old radicalism of Gladstone, Cobden and Bright. Both Hobhouse and Hobson emphasized the ethical elements in society, which were not accounted for by the mechanisms of the market. 'Wealth is due not so much to the exertions of any assignable individual as to the general growth and energy of the community', Hobhouse wrote in the *Manchester Guardian*, under C.P. Scott the newspaper *par excellence* of the new radical Liberalism. From this sprang the reflection that capital arrogated to itself an unduly high 'economic rent' or unearned increment and that this went into the pockets of a small class. It was proper for the State to intervene to correct maldistribution of income through old age pensions and other social payments and through progressive taxation. Hobson in his economic theories identified underconsumption as a cause of trade depression and therefore of unemployment and poverty. There could be an excess of savings in the economy and there was no automatic link between savings and investment. Excessive saving arose from the concentration of wealth and resulted in a high level of capital exports. The activities of trade unions in raising wages were economically beneficial, and so was direct government intervention to alleviate poverty. Hobson's ideas in many ways foreshadow those of Keynes, but lack the rigour of the latter's economic arguments. The New Liberalism therefore created a climate of ideas that favoured government intervention to deal with the shortcomings of the market. In the election campaign of 1906 it was rarely mentioned as a slogan, though most Liberal candidates declared in favour of social reform and particularly old age pensions. For the moment, however, the specific pledges which the party had given to sectional interests like the nonconformists or the temperance organizations, and which fitted in so well with the older Radical Liberal tradition, and the intention to bring about a change of course in South Africa loomed much larger than the ideas of the New Liberalism.

II

In honouring their pledges the Liberals were bound to come up against the House of Lords. No one had seriously sought to tamper with the powers of the Upper Chamber since Gladstone and Rosebery had abortively raised the question in 1894 and 1895. It would have been unrealistic to expect the Conservative leadership not to use, in their hour of weakness, this constitutional asset, in which they outnumbered the Liberals by five to one. During the election campaign Balfour had said 'the great Unionist Party should still control, whether in power or opposition, the destinies of this great Empire', a remark often quoted against him. His opponents were bound to claim that he was using the House of Lords to obstruct the verdict of democracy in the cause of reaction, the sentiment enshrined in Lloyd George's memorable metaphor, coined in 1907: 'The House of Lords has long ceased to be the watchdog of the Constitution. It has become Mr Balfour's poodle.' In fact Balfour and his colleagues, through the selective use of the blocking power of the House of Lords, were for a time remarkably successful in frustrating the Liberal government with its huge majority and putting it, even electorally, on the defensive. It is at least arguable that if they had paired this policy of obstruction with one of reforming the Upper House, along the lines of the many schemes that were under discussion, they could have turned the tables on the Liberals and created, for the long term, a powerful constitutional mechanism against over-rapid or revolutionary change. Balfour had suffered the supreme humiliation of losing his own seat at Manchester, where he had bravely stuck it out in the heartland of free trade. He was thus absent from the House for a month at the opening of the parliamentary session of 1906 until a by-election in the City of London, his new constituency, brought him back again. During this time a challenge developed to his leadership and policies from Chamberlain and the tariff reformers, whose view still was that if tariff reform and the democratization of the Unionist party had been wholeheartedly accepted the election could have been won. Balfour and most of those not wholly committed to tariff reform put the blame on Chamberlain for dividing the party and for saddling it with an issue that turned out to be an election loser.

The cards now seemed to be stacked in favour of Chamberlain, for over 100 of the 157 Unionist MPs were tariff reformers, and he demanded not only the adoption of tariff reform as the party's official policy, but also extensive changes in the party organization. Neither he nor Balfour could, however, push their differences too far for fear of provoking a split; in particular the leadership remained outside Chamberlain's reach and this had perhaps been all along the fatal flaw in his strategy of capturing the party for tariff reform. As had been the case for three years now, yet another compromise had to be hatched, enshrined in the 'Valentine letters' exchanged by the two leaders on 14 February 1906. Chamberlain seemed, however, to have got his way more than ever before, for the party was now committed to the statement that 'Fiscal Reform is, and must remain, the first constructive work of the Unionist party', though many of Balfour's long-standing reservations also appeared again. Balfour was then unanimously re-elected leader, but there remained a strong under-current of dissatisfaction with his leadership and his dialectical style. His first speech on returning to the House, 'loose, cogitating and unhappy', was a disaster and Campbell-Bannerman tore into him with 'enough of this foolery . . . move your amendments and let us get to business'. The position between them was now reversed and, endowed with power, Campbell-Bannerman was the more effective performer. In spite of long absences, due to his wife's illness and death and his own increasingly indifferent health, he had a remarkable hold on his party and his cabinet. The large Radical tail of the party had confidence that he was instinctively with them, while the Liberal Imperialists in the cabinet found it easy to accept his fundamentally realistic and shrewd approach. Campbell-Bannerman had been underestimated so much in the past that it tended to be forgotten that as Prime Minister his control of policy was patchy and his success as party manager achieved to some extent at the price of being all things to all men. Balfour on the other hand soon achieved considerable tactical successes, in spite of his lack of forcefulness. He was helped by the fact that tariff reform, the great divisive issue, was pushed for a time into the background by more immediate controversies. The cause received a great blow when Chamberlain suffered a stroke in July 1906; by 1907 it was apparent that he would never return to active politics. There was thus no alternative to Balfour as leader.

The first great clash between the Liberals and the House of Lords came over the government's Education Bill, introduced in April 1906 as the major legislative proposal for the session. All denominational schools were now to be taken over by the local authorities; teachers were to be appointed by the authorities without any sectarian tests and not be allowed to give any denominational instruction; religious instruction was to be limited to two days a week in transferred Church schools. A few so-called 'extended facilities' schools, with denominational religious teaching allowed every day, would survive, where four-fifths of the parents requested it and where such schools were available over and above the ordinary school supply of the area. This was to assist the Roman Catholics, whom the Liberals, could not afford to antagonize. Undoubtedly this bill was specifically designed to meet the nonconformist grievances which helped so considerably to propel the Liberals back into power. It outraged the Anglicans, who felt that it endowed, 35 years after Cowper-Temple, yet another new undenominational religion, 'Birreligion', after Augustine Birrell, the minister who introduced it.

Almost straight away efforts got under way to achieve a compromise; they centred round Randall Davidson, the Archbishop of Canterbury, and the King also took a hand in them. By becoming tied up with the constitutional issue concessions on both sides were made difficult, for it was a question of who was the master now, the triumphant Liberals or the Tories, humiliated after years of ascendancy. Balfour and Lansdowne, the Leader of the Unionist peers, had earlier exchanged memoranda on how to use their unequal armies to best advantage. They agreed that they should 'not work as two separate armies', but 'cooperate in a common plan of campaign'. Balfour speculated that the more moderate Liberals, in the cabinet and in the Commons, 'will trust to the House of Lords cutting out or modifying the most outrageous provisions'. The Left Wing of the Liberal cabinet would hope to accumulate a case against the Upper House in order to appeal 'at the next election for a mandate to modify its constitution . . . I incline to advise that we should fight all points of importance very stiffly in the Commons, and should make the House of Lords the theatre of compromise. It is evident that *you* can never fight for a position *we* have surrendered . . .' On the Education Bill there was in the end no compromise and the government was forced to withdraw the Bill. There was serious talk of a dissolution of Parliament and it is possible that if the Liberals had forced the issue at this early stage, they would have won again strongly and avoided the electoral decline of the next two years. A more cautious line prevailed, mainly because the education question was of great concern to nonconformist sectarians, but would have meant little to the general electorate.

In the meantime events had taken a very different course on another question the Liberals were pledged to deal with, the problem of trade union immunities. Although opinion in the unions had moved strongly towards seeking a restoration of the full pre-Taff Vale immunity from legal prosecution and many Liberals had since 1903 supported bills designed to bring this about, the cabinet drafted a bill that did not confer on the unions this position of exceptional privilege. The royal commission set up by the previous government had recommended a separation of the benefit funds of unions from their general and strike fund, the former to be immune from action for damages. The lawyers in the cabinet, particularly Asquith, preferred to deal with the problem by restricting the law of agency in its application to the unions. Campbell-Bannerman argued in cabinet for a simple bill giving unions immunity from action for damages. Many Liberal MPs had pledged themselves to such a bill in the election; when it was brought in by the Labour group as an alternative to the government's own measure, Campbell-Bannerman decided on the spur of the moment and without consulting his colleagues to recommend its second reading, thus throwing over his own Attorney-General who had just torn it to pieces. Balfour judged it prudent not to divide against the second and third readings. Thus Lansdowne was left with no chance to resist in the Lords, although he said the bill conferred 'dangerous privileges upon one class and on one class only'. A more clearly defined legal status might have had some advantages for the unions; as it was, they preferred to remain loyal to their tradition of 'collective *laissez-faire*' and of suspicion of the law and lawyers. They recovered their immunity from legal action at the very moment when their impact on the economic life of the country and the ability to use the strike weapon had become very formidable.

If the House of Lords had destroyed the Trades Disputes Bill as well as the Education Bill there would have been a greater likelihood that the Liberal cabinet would have opted for an early general election. As it was they had to swallow the mutilation of several more bills, including an important plural voting bill designed to end the anomaly by which owners of property in several constituencies could also cast several votes. Without an election the slaughter of Liberal bills by the peers constituted no more than a process of 'filling the cup' or 'ploughing the sands', and this, it was hoped, would eventually build up so powerful a dossier against the Upper House that the electorate would insist on a curtailment of its powers. It was a weak prescription for a party which, in spite of its vast majority, found itself after only a year in office frustrated and faced by an apparent ebbing of the electoral tide. There was a marked swing to the Unionists in several by-elections, a routing of the Progressives in the LCC elections in 1907 and two Labour victories at Jarrow and Colne Valley; particularly the latter by a socialist candidate not endorsed by the LRC, Victor Grayson, caused a sensation, but in general the electoral fortunes of Labour declined in parallel with those of the Liberals.

To remove the blockage caused by the House of Lords it was, however, not only necessary to obtain an electoral mandate, which might eventually have to be used to persuade the King to threaten a creation of peers. There was also the need to offer a solution to the conflict between the two Houses and here there were two main possibilities; to alter the composition of the Upper House, mainly by reducing the hereditary element, or giving priority to a curtailment of the powers of the peers. The first solution, even if it involved some scaling down of powers, had strong conservative implications, for a reformed second chamber would be on far stronger moral and political grounds in applying the brake on the first chamber. It was not surprising therefore that in 1907 a bill was introduced by moderate Tory peers to alter drastically the composition of their House: the hereditary peers were to elect a fourth of their number to represent them and the places so vacated would be filled by the government of the day with life peers. This proposal was opposed by the more right-wing of the Tory peers as well as by the Liberal government. Campbell-Bannerman was strongly of the opinion that the first priority had to be a curtailment of the powers of the Lords, so that the will of the people as expressed through its elected representatives could prevail. Others in his cabinet, Grey for example, were not so single-minded and were at least equally concerned that the composition of the Upper Chamber should also be changed. The cabinet eventually accepted Campbell-Bannerman's scheme by which a bill passed three times by the Commons would become law without the consent of the Lords and in essence this was the solution adopted four years later. Campbell-Bannerman introduced his scheme in the form of a resolution in the House of Commons 'that the power of the other House to alter or reject bills passed by this House should be so restricted by law as to secure that within the limits of a single Parliament the final decision of the Commons shall prevail'. After a heated three-day debate, during which Churchill called the House of Lords 'a one-sided, hereditary, unprized, unrepresentative, irresponsible absentee', the Prime Minister's resolution passed with a majority of 285 in June 1907.

All this could not disguise the fact there was still no action nor was any promised in the King's speech of 1908, the last of Campbell-Bannerman's premiership. Shortly after the beginning of the parliamentary session his health finally collapsed, but owing to the absence abroad of the King his resignation was delayed until the beginning of April and only two weeks later he died. Asquith was the natural successor, as even those who, because of his Liberal Imperialist past, were disturbed by the prospect, had to admit. During Campbell-Bannerman's prolonged absences he had been the parliamentary rock on which the government rested. Asquith was succeeded at the Treasury by Lloyd George. The Welsh Radical had become a national figure through his settlement of a threatened rail strike the previous autumn, the first occasion on which a strike posed a sufficiently serious threat to the whole national economy to make intervention by the government necessary. Lloyd George's way to a settlement had been in the main by using a mixture of cajolery and persuasion on the railway directors. Up to then nearly all the railway magnates had refused recognition of the union; now they agreed to establish permanent boards of men and management to deal with wages and conditions. At the Board of Trade Lloyd George had managed to build up a reputation as an effective departmental minister while maintaining his image with the public as a hard-hitting Radical politician. He had promoted a Merchant Shipping Act which enforced substantial improvements in the conditions under which the sailors in the British merchant marine worked and which was also to apply to foreign vessels using British ports, thus seeking to prevent a loss of competitiveness by British ships. He had prepared legislation for the establishment of the Port of London Authority, to take over the management of the vast area of London's dockland, and got an important Patents Bill onto the statute book. There was a touch of protectionism about some of this legislation which earned him praises from tariff reformers. In Lloyd George a man rose to the front-rank in British politics who had no connection with the traditional British élite, nor had been assimilated to it by graduating through Oxford or Cambridge. He also had genius, an elusive quality in politics: in his case it consisted above all in an ability, amounting almost to a sixth sense, of sizing up men and manipulating them to his purposes. There was also a propensity to cut corners, combined with a certain moral laxity, that easily aroused suspicion and enmity. Until 1914 he played the role of tribune of the people, not unlike Joseph Chamberlain a generation earlier. Like his predecessor from Birmingham, the Welsh Radical also had a side to his political make-up, not immediately obvious, that tended to cross-party understandings and solutions of great national problems beyond the orthodoxies of the party system. Lloyd George was succeeded at the Board of Trade by Winston Churchill, whose recent conversion to Liberalism had proved no barrier to his rapid rise. His exceptional ability, amounting again to something like genius, was widely recognized, but it had not yet acquired much sense of direction and therefore, to many minds, smacked of personal ambition.

The formation of the Asquith cabinet did not in itself represent any major change of direction. Asquith was no more than Campbell-Bannerman a creative politician capable of setting visionary goals. He was an executant of great competence; what he lacked in comparison with Campbell-Bannerman was the generosity of instinct that reassured Radicals, but he made up for it by bringing superior ability to the support of the causes his formidable intellect had chosen to adopt. Meanwhile the pressures on the Liberal government were mounting. The peers remained as eager as ever to frustrate the

government when it was trying to meet the demands of the special
interests that had traditionally supported Liberalism. The session of
1908 was intended to give the temperance movement its due with a
Licensing Bill, the answer to Balfour's Act of 1904. The main provision in the Bill was the establishment of a fixed ratio of the number of
public houses to the population in each licensing area; holders of
surplus licences would be compensated through a levy on the trade,
but compensation payments would cease after 14 years. It was
expected that there would be at least twice as many reductions of
licences as under the 1904 Act. The Liberals had as clear a mandate
for such a measure as they had for their Education Bill, but temperance was a sectarian and not a popular cause and the powerful brewing interest was marshalled against it. Balfour thus put in operation
his tactics of fighting the Licensing Bill every inch of the way in the
Commons and finally the Lords declined to give it a second reading.

Added to the continuing Liberal frustration over the House of
Lords there was from the beginning of 1908 a renewal of the electoral
swing against the government which seemed to have abated somewhat
in the later months of 1907. The downward swing of the Liberals'
electoral support was the mirror-image of the upswing of unemployment, as the trade recession deepened in 1908. Liberals felt themselves threatened from right and left. The slump gave new impetus to
tariff reform, now accepted by Balfour as official Unionist policy; in
the Labour movement and among working-class voters it deepened
the disappointment at the meagre results of Liberal rule. It also
sharpened, by its depressing effect on the revenue, the fiscal dilemma,
the focal point of most of the conflicting pressures faced by the new
Asquith cabinet. Since going to the Exchequer in 1905, Asquith
himself had laid the groundwork for a taxation policy designed to
finance social reform, notably the old age pensions to which the
government was clearly committed, on the basis of continuing free
trade. A House of Commons Select Committee under Sir Charles
Dilke had recommended the graduation of income tax, a continua-
tion of the policy initiated by Harcourt in 1894 with his graduated
death duties. In the 1907 budget Asquith had made a start by distin-
guishing between earned and unearned income and reducing the tax
on the former from 1s to 9d on incomes under £2,000. This distinction had been anathema to orthodox public financiers brought up in
the Gladstonian school; on the other hand it fitted in well with the
tenets of the New Liberalism about redistributing wealth.

Other pressures came from the ever-increasing burden of local
rates, which played its part in the defeat of the Progressives on the
LCC in 1907. It gave new impetus to the campaign for a land value
tax, which had been a Radical cause ever since Henry George had

made it popular in the 1880s and which many Radical Liberals now saw as a counter to tariff reform. From the beginning of the 1906 Parliament a large number of Liberal and Labour MPs had organized themselves into a Land Values Group. A Land Values Bill for Scotland was brought forward by the government in 1907, but was rejected by the Lords. Even more threatening was the possible further increase in armaments expenditure. The reduction of such expenditure from the inflated level reached during the Boer War was a cause on which Gladstonian and New Liberalism were united and was part of the Liberal repudiation of Unionist imperialism. In 1907, Campbell-Bannerman wrote in the new radical journal *The Nation*, edited by H.W. Massingham, that 'the endless multiplication of the engines of war was futile and self-defeating'. Haldane managed to reduce the army estimates in 1907 and 1908 and Fisher's reorganizations had also restrained naval spending, but the *Dreadnought* building programme and the naval arms race with Germany was about to give the navy estimates a sharp upward twist and to become the subject of fierce controversy.

The potential conflict between social reform and defence spending was painful and divisive for Liberals. The additional taxation required to finance escalating public expenditure also raised fundamental political problems for them; they were still a coalition of the working and the middle classes and too much reliance on direct taxation might accelerate the drift of the latter into the Conservative fold. Not surprisingly tariff reformers thought the fiscal problems of the Liberals were not capable of solution within the canons of free trade. This impression was not dispelled by the budget of 1908 which made provision for old-age pensions. It had been prepared and was introduced by Asquith, although Lloyd George had in the meantime moved to the Exchequer. Those who had wanted pensions to be universal were disappointed. Non-contributory pensions of £13 per annum (5s. per week) for single persons of 70 and of £19.10s. for married couples were introduced, provided their income was less than £26 or £39 respectively. These cut-off points were later replaced by sliding scales, so that at an income of £26 only 3s. a week was payable, which caused Labour members to vote against the amendment, but Lloyd George had to insist on this limitation to keep the financial situation manageable. Asquith estimated that about 570,000 persons would qualify for the pensions and that the cost in a full year would be six million pounds. With the concessions made in the Old Age Pensions Bill this proved to be an immediate underestimate of over £2 million; by 1912 the government was spending £11.7 million on pensions and by 1914 £12.5 million. In spite of the current and future pressures which old-age pensions put on the public revenue Asquith also reduced the sugar duties in the 1908 budget. It was a gesture towards free trade as well as a token of the intention to reduce the burden of indirect taxation on the poorer sections of the community.

III

It was obvious to Lloyd George and his colleagues that the next budget, to be introduced in the spring of 1909 for the financial year 1909/10, would make or mar the fortunes of the Liberal government and might well furnish an instrument for circumventing the veto of the House of Lords. The possibility that the Lords might reject a budget, particularly if provisions fundamentally political in nature were 'tacked' on to its financial purpose, was being publicly and privately discussed in the autumn of 1908. Neither at this point, when the full extent of the budgetary problem was not yet clear, nor later did the Chancellor of the Exchequer actively plan to use the budget as a 'red rag' to provoke rejection by the peers. He and his colleagues hoped, on the contrary, that by giving the Lords as little excuse as possible for rejection they could use the budget to get the stalled Liberal programme under way again. In preparing his proposals Lloyd George had to overcome stiff opposition both from his permanent officials and from many of his ministerial colleagues. Sir George Murray, the Permanent Secretary of the Treasury, and Charles Hobhouse, as Financial Secretary the second political head of the department, were both orthodox Gladstonian financiers. They, and others dedicated to the traditional ways of the civil service, disliked Lloyd George's methods of work: the Chancellor did not read or write many memoranda and preferred oral communication; he tossed out unorthodox ideas with a cavalier disregard for details. Inevitably he by-passed the official hierarchy and Sir Robert Chalmers, chairman of the Inland Revenue, and Charles Masterman, the Parliamentary Secretary to the Local Government Board, became his closest associates in this phase of his career. Masterman, who after taking a First at Cambridge had gone to live in a South London slum, was a man of strong social conscience and a typical exponent of the New Liberalism. After working on the *Daily News* he became an MP in 1906 and second-in-command to the incompetent and increasingly conservative John Burns. In the cabinet Churchill was Lloyd George's closest ally; both men were agreed that social reform was the way to ensure the future of Liberalism against threats from the Right and the Left. Steady and vital, if unspectacular support was also forthcoming from the Prime Minister, for Asquith saw clearly enough that the budget presented the one real hope of saving the Liberal government from defeat. Before the end of 1908, he approved some of the basic outlines of Lloyd George's scheme, a surtax on incomes over £5,000, a capital tax on non-agricultural land and higher licence duties, features which in principle remained part of the eventual budget. At this stage a deficit of £12 million was envisaged.

Early in 1909 a considerably larger deficit began to loom as alarm grew about the apparent acceleration of the German naval building programme. The Admiralty warned the cabinet that if the existing British programme of building four capital ships annually was continued the Germans would equal or possibly outstrip the Royal Navy in the number of dreadnoughts commissioned by 1912. The Sea Lords demanded the laying down of four additional dreadnoughts at a cost of approximately £2 million each. A cabinet split threatened, with Lloyd George and Churchill fighting to keep down the naval estimates, while McKenna, the First Lord, pressed the Admiralty case, backed by Grey, Haldane and others. Asquith with great ingenuity achieved a compromise by providing for the laying down of four ships in 1909 and four more not later than 1 April 1910 if the need for them was proven. When this decision became public in March 1909 it provoked strong attacks from the Conservative Opposition, George Wyndham coining the phrase 'We want eight, and we won't wait'. On the other hand much of the heart had gone out of the Radical campaign against higher defence spending with the failure of the Hague Conference of 1907 to agree on any kind of arms limitation and the publication of the German Navy Law Amendment of 1908. The Radicals could not afford to rock the Liberal boat just when the government was embarking on further social reforms. As it was, Lloyd George was faced with an increase in the naval estimates of nearly £3 million.

Nevertheless, the row over the navy helped Lloyd George and Churchill to get the budget proposals approved by the cabinet, because it became clearer than ever that only such far-reaching measures would prevent a complete demoralization of the large Radical wing of the Liberal Party. The land value taxes were the only part of the original proposals to be modified in a major way by the cabinet. The tax on capital values was reduced from 1d to ½ d in the pound on undeveloped land, excluding agricultural land, and to a 10 per cent reversion duty on benefits to lessors at the termination of leases. The original 20 per cent tax on unearned increment was kept intact. These land taxes were estimated to bring in only half a million in the next financial year, but they would entail the valuation of land throughout the kingdom and this was to be amongst the most controversial aspects of the People's Budget. The cabinet substantially accepted Lloyd George's scheme for recasting the system of liquor licences, another effort to overcome the Lords' rejection of the Licensing Bill in 1908. There was to be a significant increase in the tax on public house licences, with the object of reducing their number while increasing the revenue. There were also to be increases in the spirit and tobacco duties, the one respect in which the budget would increase the burden of indirect taxation on the working classes, but it did not completely cancel out the benefit conferred by Asquith's reduction of the sugar duty in the previous year. On income tax the rate was to rise from 1s to 1s 2d., but earned incomes below £3,000, the bulk of the Liberal Party's middle-class supporters, were protected against the increase. There were only 25,000 incomes over £3,000.

A significant innovation, which from small beginnings became a major device for redistributing income from the better to the less well-off, was the introduction of a super tax. In the form in which the cabinet finally approved, it was to be levied at the rate of 6d. in the pound on the amount by which all incomes of over £5,000 exceeded £3,000. There were about 15,000 incomes over £5,000 and the super tax was estimated to bring in half a million. There were also increases in estate duty, stamp duty and a new tax on motor vehicle licences and petrol to establish a Road Fund. The budget was estimated to raise an additional 13.5 million, nearly 10 per cent on top of the existing revenue. Another three million from the sinking fund would be required to meet the anticipated deficit of over 16.5 million. The additional revenue would come mostly from the rich and fairly well-to-do. A new basis for raising revenue was established which remained sufficient until 1914. According to Exchequer statistics the proportion between direct and indirect taxation in 1912/13 was about 58 to 42, whereas in 1905/6 it had been nearly 50:50. Even so, Herbert Samuel calculated after the First World War that the portion of income paid in tax by those with incomes of £50 and below was reduced only from 9.1 to 8.7 per cent between 1903 and 1913; it was reduced more considerably for those with middling incomes between £200 and £2,000, and while it was increased substantially for those with higher incomes they were still paying a smaller portion of their earned incomes in tax than the large group of low income-earners.

The budget was introduced in the Commons on 29 April 1909 and quickly became the focus for fierce controversy. Initially most of the running was made by the critics of the Budget. On the Opposition side it was immediately perceived that tariff reform was under challenge and Austen Chamberlain openly accepted the challenge and declared in the second reading debate that he was ready to go to the country at any moment. Along with the Tariff Reform League a host of other organizations, from the Liberty and Property Defence League to the various bodies representing brewers and licensed victuallers, entered the lists and a Budget Protest League was formed. There was some uneasiness even among Liberals, particularly among those with business and commercial backgrounds, and it expressed itself most openly over the land taxes. The Irish Nationalists were bitter about the increased taxes on liquor and licences and 62 of them voted with the Opposition on the second reading. Nevertheless, Lloyd George and his colleagues declared themselves satisfied with the reception the budget had received from their own party and hoped that it had gone some way towards restoring Liberal morale. They were afraid, however, that the budget might fail to ignite popular enthusiasm and that support for it might be drowned out by the vociferous clamour against it. The government was heartened by four by-elections in July 1909, at which the swing against the Liberals was clearly reduced from what it was earlier in the year. A Budget League to carry the Liberal campaign to the country was now formed.

Undoubtedly much of the hue and cry against the budget presented the slightly absurd spectacle of 'rich men who won't pay for the Dreadnoughts they were clamouring for'. A turning point seemed to come with the famous Limehouse speech of Lloyd George on 30 July 1909. Among its many colourful passages the one most frequently quoted came when the Chancellor was defending his tax on minerals: '. . . when the Prime Minister and I knock at the door of these great landlords and say to them:- "Here, you know these poor fellows have been digging up royalties at the risk of their lives . . . they are broken . . . won't you give them something to keep them out of the workhouse . . ." they scowl at you and then turn their dogs onto us, and every day you can hear their bark.' It was perhaps significant that immediately after Limehouse Lord Northcliffe, the great press magnate and a sensitive barometer of public opinion, had his first meeting with Lloyd George and his mass-circulation paper, the *Daily Mail*, now declared that the agitation against the budget had fallen flat. The King remonstrated about the tone of the Limehouse speech and Asquith was clearly nervous lest his Chancellor 'rouse the suspicions and fears of the middle class'. In fact the speech was carefully calculated not only to appeal to the working classes but to rouse the resentment of the middle class against aristocracy and plutocracy. Some ducal reactions, like Beaufort's remark that he would 'like to see Winston Churchill and Lloyd George in the middle of twenty couple of dog hounds', enhanced the impression that reasonableness resided with the proponents rather than the opponents of the budget.

After Limehouse the fiercely fought land taxes passed their committee stage fairly rapidly, but attention began to focus increasingly on the question whether the House of Lords would break with a 250 year old constitutional convention and amend or even reject the budget. By August 1909 most of the Conservative press was coming out in favour of rejection, while Lloyd George and Winston Churchill were beginning to think that it was the best thing that could happen to them. Asquith was more cautious. He naturally wanted to avoid any suggestion that the Liberals were deliberately provoking rejection by the Lords and he may well have believed that the Unionist leaders would not be so reckless as to allow this to happen. In this he did perhaps not fully appreciate how difficult the position of Balfour and Lansdowne had become. There is clear evidence that soon after Limehouse and possibly even before, Balfour had made up his mind that he would have to back the rejection of the budget in the Upper House. To allow the budget simply to pass, after so long and fierce a campaign against it, would severely damage the credibility of the Unionist Party and invite a resounding electoral defeat. The tariff reformers, still much influenced by Joseph Chamberlain, saw the struggle as a clear choice between the budget and their own policy and pressed strongly for the destruction of the budget. Faced with this attitude by the most powerful section of his party, it is unlikely that Balfour could have survived as leader if he had ended up tamely acquiescing in the passage of the budget. The passage of the land tax clauses of the Finance Bill through the committee stage also convinced Balfour that the Lords would be on strong ground constitutionally in rejecting the budget. The land taxes would raise hardly any money and it was therefore clear that their real purpose was to enforce the land valuation which was blocked by the Lords' veto. The argument that the budget was itself unconstitutional by 'tacking' on to a finance bill major political changes could be made to stick. Thus the Unionist leaders convinced themselves that the decision to destroy the budget in the House of Lords was not only inevitable but also right. For this they have been severely criticized by most historians ever since. The dilemma in which they found themselves was, however, an indication of the success of the Liberal leaders in outmanoeuvring them through the budget. Balfour and Lansdowne could choose only between abject surrender, probably leading to a party split and catastrophic electoral defeat; or a step that was constitutionally dubious and unlikely to leave them electorally victorious.

The budget kept the Commons occupied for 70 parliamentary days until the beginning of November 1909. There was serious opposition from the Irish Nationalists, because the hostility in Ireland to the increased licence and spirit duties threatened their credibility as a party unless they could get concessions from the government. While the budget was still in the Commons Lloyd George spoke at Newcastle with the same provocative skill he had displayed at Limehouse: 'The Lords may decree a revolution, but the people will direct it . . . The question will be asked whether 500 men, ordinary men chosen accidentally from among the unemployed, should override the judgement – the deliberate judgement of millions of people who are engaged in the industry which makes the wealth of the country. Who made 10,000 people owners of the soil, and the rest of us trespassers in the land of our birth . . .'.

The crucial test in the House of Lords took place in the last week of November. During the debate a few Unionist peers pointed out that whatever the niceties of the constitutional argument, the House, by rejecting the budget, would be claiming the right to force an elected government to appeal to the country. Such a claim would fly in the face of a long-standing constitutional convention and could hardly be made to stick. These warning voices were not heeded and with its members swelled by a large number of 'backwoods men' the House rejected the budget by 350 to 75 votes on 30 November. This vote to all intents and purposes opened the election campaign; 15 January 1910 was fixed by the cabinet as the opening day for the polls. In a speech in the Albert Hall on 10 December Asquith set the keynote for the Liberal campaign: all the various Liberal reforms that had been thwarted by the House of Lords, education, temperance, Welsh disestablishment, land and rent reform, Irish Home Rule and more social reform against poverty, all these causes would be pushed forward again. Since the Lords' veto was the great impediment, it must go: 'The will of the people, as deliberately expressed by their representatives, must, within the limits of the lifetime of a single Parliament, be made effective.'

The truth, however, was that the cabinet failed to agree on a second-chamber strategy. Ministers were divided on whether to hold to Campbell-Bannerman's policy of 1907 giving first priority to a curtailment of the veto powers of the Lords or whether to concentrate on a reform of the composition of the second chamber. Asquith's words in the Albert Hall were generally taken to mean that the Prime Minister had secured an undertaking from the King to create a sufficient number of peers to coerce the House of Lords. In fact Asquith already knew before he made the speech that the King would be very reluctant to threaten to create the 570 peers necessary to coerce the Upper House. A few days after the speech Lord Knollys, the King's Private Secretary, confirmed the King's view that he would only be justified in threatening a large creation of peers if the 'particular project' for the 'destruction' of the House of Lords had first been approved by the electorate. There clearly was not going to be such a project on offer in the forthcoming election campaign, beyond the intention to ensure that the Lords could not in future tamper with a finance bill. Behind the problem of what to do about the second chamber there loomed the perennial question of Irish Home Rule. As soon as the Lords had rejected the budget, John Redmond, the Irish Nationalist leader, told Asquith that his party could not undertake to support the Liberals in the next Parliament unless an official declaration to bring in a Home Rule Bill was immediately made. Even more significantly, he indicated that without such a declaration he would have to advise Irish voters in the rest of the United Kingdom to vote against Liberal candidates. Thus even before the electoral battle on the budget was fully joined, a situation was building up which might well necessitate a second election fought on the House of Lords and Irish Home Rule.

In the election campaign Lloyd George, with his colourful and provocative language, played the role of keeping the more politically conscious sections of the working class loyal. Against this, Grey, the political descendant of the Whigs, went out of his way to reassure the middle classes. He pointed out that the professional man with an income of less than £2,000 paid less income tax under the People's budget than he had done under the Unionists. Even for the rich the budget had advantages, for it 'was something that staved off socialism, while tariff reform would bring socialism nearer'. Up to the New Year the Liberals had the better of the argument, not least because in Asquith, Lloyd George and Churchill they had oratorical talent which the Unionists could not match. In the final stages of the campaign the Unionists made up some lost ground and were able to focus attention more on tariff reform. They also played on fears of Germany and tried to revive something of the naval scare that had been obscured by the budget controversy. When Balfour lent his authority to the complaint that the Liberals had allowed the naval supremacy bequeathed to them by his own government to slip away the scare was taken more seriously and may well have made an impact.

The result of the first general election of 1910 left the Liberals and Conservatives very nearly level-pegging, 275 to 273 seats, there were also 40 Labour members and 82 Irish Nationalists, including 11 Independent Nationalists who had split away from the main body in offering outright opposition to the budget. The Irish Nationalists thus held the balance of power, which they could use to press for a removal of the Lords' veto to be followed by Home Rule. In Great Britain there was a swing of over 4 per cent towards the Unionists, in England alone of nearly 5 per cent. There were a good many regional variations: South-East England and the Home Counties swung heavily against the Liberals, but the swing in the working-class areas of London was much lower. Lancashire and Yorkshire remained more loyal to the Liberals and they generally fared better in urban industrial areas, as well as in Scotland and Wales. Birmingham, with its traditional loyalty to the Chamberlains and to tariff reform, experienced a swing above average against the Liberals. On the whole the Liberals held their working-class vote well and they also managed to contain Labour. They made no further concessions to Labour in allowing them straight fights, beyond those established in 1906. Labour's 40 seats won in this election must be compared with the 29 LRC members and the 24 Lib-Labs elected in 1906. There was a slight rise in the percentage of Labour votes in 1910 compared with LRC votes in 1906, but again this must be seen in the light of the disappearance of the Lib-Labs and the fact that most of the Labour candidatures were in areas where the anti-Unionist vote held up well. This election therefore confirmed the picture drawn from the by-elections of the previous year that Liberals had effectively halted any inroads into their ranks from Labour and this remained the case in the second election of 1910 and in by-elections until 1914. This achievement is rendered more striking by the fact that the turnout of voters in January 1910 reached the exceptionally high figure of 87 per cent; even in December 1910 it only dropped back to 82 per cent, largely as a result of more unopposed returns. Contemporary observers noted the north-south division in England, the two nations, already established in 1906 but less clearly visible owing to the overwhelming extent of the Liberal victory, and also the strong swing of the urban middle classes to Unionism, particularly in the south. Beatrice Webb noted 'the south country, the suburban, agricultural, residential England going Tory and tariff reform, and the north country and dense industrial populations (excluding Birmingham area) going Radical-Socialist . . .'. J.A. Hobson wrote: 'It is organized labour against the possessing and educated classes, on the one hand, against the public house and unorganized labour, on the other.'

IV

Paradoxically, the result of the election left most Liberals depressed and the Unionists somewhat elated. The position of the Asquith government was indeed very difficult. They could not even be sure of passing the budget, because the Irish Nationalists were opposed to it and would only let it go through if they were promised the removal of the Lords' veto and Home Rule. Redmond had to take a tough line with the slogan 'no veto, no budget', for Tim Healy and the Independent Nationalists stood ready to outflank him and the future of constitutional nationalism in Ireland might be in jeopardy. When it came to the Lords' veto, however, the cabinet was still not united on how to proceed and moreover their hand was fatally weakened. There could be no question now of seeking guarantees from the King about the creation of peers and there was relief in Buckingham Palace.

When on the assembly of the new Parliament Asquith had to admit that he had received no guarantees from the King about the creation of peers, the reaction of the Radicals, Labour and the Irish made it clear that the government had little chance of surviving if it took a reformist course on the future of the Upper House. It was at this stage that Asquith fell into frequent use of the phrase 'wait and see'; he meant it as a threat, but it was to haunt him ever after. For a moment the cabinet looked like disintegrating, but gradually Asquith, helped mainly by Haldane, managed to get his colleagues to agree on a procedure close to the Campbell-Bannerman plan. Three resolutions were to be introduced, as the basis for a Parliament Bill to define the powers of the Lords. Under the first the Lords would not be able to amend or reject a money bill, so certified by the Speaker of the Commons; under the second, an ordinary bill, if passed three times in successive sessions by the Commons could be presented for the royal assent without the concurrence of the Lords, provided at least two years had elapsed between the bill's introduction and final approval in the Commons; the third resolution provided for a reduction of the maximum duration of a Parliament from seven to five years. Thus any legislation in the first three years of a Parliament could become law without suffering the Lords' veto; the greater powers given to the Commons would be controlled by more frequent appeals to the voters. Grey and others still hankering after a change in the composition of the Upper House were to be pacified by a preamble in the Parliament Bill declaring the intention to reform. The cabinet also decided that if the policy outlined in the three resolutions was approved by the Commons and the House of Lords then refused to pass the Parliament Bill, they would seek an election with prior guarantees from the King about a creation of peers or possibly a referendum. Redmond was not in the end offered any concessions on the budget, but since the prospect of Home Rule outweighed even the grievances over whiskey or licence taxes the Irish Nationalists finally had to sustain the government without conditions. By the end of April 1910 the Asquith cabinet had recovered their sense of direction and had done so without suffering any resignations from their whiggish section.

In contrast the Unionist position was now less happy. Initial pleasure at having eliminated the huge Liberal majority soon gave way to the old divisions about tariff reform. Whole-Hoggers wanted to trump the Liberal combination of free trade and social reform with a strong populist appeal on protection and social reform: they were ready for far-reaching second-chamber reform and if necessary for a deal with the Irish over Home Rule. Most Tories were, however, not prepared to stake everything, the Lords, the Union, perhaps the social fabric itself, on a policy dear to some activists but of unproven electoral worth. Balfour and Lansdowne remained sceptical about tariff reform and reluctant to see the House of Lords reformed virtually out of existence.

By the end of April 1910 the Commons had passed the three 'veto' resolutions, the Parliament Bill based on them had been introduced and the government's position on seeking guarantees from the King for its passage had been made public. Finally the People's Budget completed its passage through the Commons for the second time. On 7 May Edward VII died and the expected course of events was temporarily halted. The forces of compromise immediately received fresh impetus, starting with a widely acclaimed article in the *The Observer* by J.L. Garvin, an influential figure among tariff reformers. The avoidance or at least postponement of the constitutional crisis had obvious appeal for moderate Liberals, including Asquith. The more radical ministers allowed themselves to be persuaded that it would be unwise to incur unpopularity by appearing to plunge the new monarch, George V, into partisan controversy. Lloyd George's role was crucial in enabling the cabinet to enter upon inter-party talks; the orator of Limehouse and leader of Radical Liberalism was much less committed to the conventional forms of the party battle than appeared on the surface. Agreement was thus reached on arrangements for a Constitutional Conference, to be held behind closed doors between four leaders from each of the two major parties. Asquith, Lloyd George, Augustine Birrell, the Chief Secretary for Ireland, and Crewe, Liberal leader in the Lords had altogether 21 sessions between June and November 1910 with Balfour, Lansdowne, Austen Chamberlain, as representative of the tariff reformers and Liberal Unionist, and Cawdor, former First Lord of the Admiralty. The shadow of Irish Home Rule loomed over the meetings: the Liberals could not accept any scheme that would allow the Lords' veto on Home Rule to continue and by the same token the Conservatives had to insist that

Home Rule, along with other items, such as disestablishment and the royal prerogative, should be put into a special category of constitutional legislation. Such constitutional matters would then not be subject to the normal procedures of adjusting differences between the two Houses, such as joint sittings, with which the conference was toying as a means to an agreed solution. Before the meetings were adjourned for the summer recess the Home Rule problem was not brought into the open, but it was clearly the stumbling block on which the conference finally broke up in November. 'Neither side can get over the Home Rule fence, or (to speak more exactly) the Government cannot quarrel outright with the Irish', was Austen Chamberlain's verdict.

An astonishing by-product of the conference was Lloyd George's proposal for a coalition between the parties, outlined in a memorandum written during the summer recess: '. . . the time has arrived for a truce, for bringing the resources of the two parties into joint stock in order to liquidate arrears which, if much longer neglected, may end in national impoverishment, if not insolvency.' There followed a list of topics, among them national insurance, defence, trade and imperial policy, and the land, on which Lloyd George saw an inter-party consensus as possible and of great benefit in settling long-standing national problems. One of the immediate aims that may well have motivated Lloyd George was the desire to forward his national insurance scheme, with which he was already heavily preoccupied and which he expected to be obstructed by a host of vested interests. The memorandum was known only to a few and even Asquith and Balfour only saw it in the final stages of the Constitutional Conference. Both of them seem to have regarded the proposed coalition as unlikely to come about, even if personally not adverse to it, and to have toyed with it mainly for the purpose of delaying the final breakdown of the conference. On the other hand the ideas which the tariff reformers were publicly discussing at this time, a solution of the Irish problem through federal home rule, social reform, a big navy and army reform, were not very far removed from what Lloyd George was proposing.

Two days before the Constitutional Conference formally broke down on 10 November the cabinet decided to ask for an immediate dissolution. It remained to settle the delicate problem of securing contingent guarantees from the King for the creation of peers if the Liberals won again. It was mainly due to Lord Knollys, whom George V had inherited as private secretary from his father, that the King was persuaded to give the guarantees on the understanding that they were to be kept secret and that the Parliament Bill was to be sent to the Lords before the dissolution. Knollys did not tell his master that if Asquith had resigned following a refusal of the guarantees Balfour would have been willing to take office. Such a course of events, as Knollys realized, could not have avoided dragging the monarchy into politics.

The second election campaign of 1910 was generally regarded as quieter than the first and appeared to show some apathy among the electors. A major change was that the budget was no longer an issue while the specific solution to the problem of the second chamber proposed by the Parliament Bill was now clearly before the electors. Unionist propaganda made much of the allegation that Asquith had been forced to bring the bill by Redmond, the 'dollar dictator' – so called because of the support he received from Irish Americans. Having earlier failed to support Rosebery's proposals for a reform of their Chamber, Lansdowne and his fellow Tory peers moved hurriedly to pass resolutions suggesting a reform of the House and a scheme for settling disputes between the two Houses through joint sittings and, in matters of 'great gravity', resort to a referendum. It is doubtful if these last-minute moves helped the Unionists electorally, for they received little attention in the campaign and meant a more far-reaching tampering with the constitution than the government's straightforward curtailment of the veto power. The emphasis on the use of the referendum forced Balfour into a concession which was to prove damaging to his leadership in the longer run. Asquith challenged him to answer whether the referendum was only to apply to Liberal measures like Home Rule, in which case it would be 'purely a one-sided party dodge', or whether it was also to apply to tariff reform. Balfour, after consulting only with Lansdowne among his colleagues, declared 'I have not the least objection to submit the principles of Tariff Reform to Referendum'. This may have been a necessary rejoinder to Liberal taunts and may have helped the Unionists to recover some ground in free-trading areas like Lancashire, from whence there had been pressure on Balfour to give a referendum pledge. Many Whole-Hoggers, however, were finally disillusioned with Balfour's leadership.

The results of this second election within a year showed that the political landscape had hardly changed. The two major parties remained almost exactly balanced, with 271 Liberals and 273 Unionists, the Irish Nationalists and Labour had two additional seats each, at 84 and 42 respectively, and the anti-Unionist majority remained what it had been after the January election. There was a slight overall swing to the Unionists of less than 1 per cent, after allowing for the larger number of Unionist unopposed returns; this concealed some local variations, in particular a larger swing to the Unionists in Lancashire, counterbalanced by a lesser one in the London area. Such regional variations account for the fact that within their virtually static totals each of the major parties won and lost over 20 seats. Labour ran only 56 candidates against 78 in the first election; this was not due so much to the Osborne Judgement curtailing the flow of money from the unions as to the obvious waste involved in entering three-cornered contests, in all of which Labour had failed in January. In December it was therefore easier for the leader of the party to resist the pressure of their left-wing activists for candidatures against 'the capitalist Liberals'. The issues in both elections, the House of Lords and a social reform budget, made it difficult for Labour to establish a separate identity and this helped the Liberals to limit the threat to their left flank. On the morrow of the December election there could be no doubt, as there was in January, about who had won: there could be no alternative to the Asquith government. The Prime Minister also assumed, with impeccable logic, that the Parliament Bill would now pass without any need to make public the secret guarantees given by the King. In this he was deceiving himself.

Balfour and Lansdowne still refused to acknowledge, even privately, that the stark choice they now faced was between allowing the Parliament Bill to pass, thus saving at least the two years' veto for the Lords, or a situation in which the Liberals would have a majority in both Houses and would be able to enact Irish Home Rule, Welsh disestablishment or any of their other causes without delay. Lansdowne was still putting his faith in a reform of the House of Lords which might include provision for a referendum; to many Tories it seemed within the spirit of an increasingly democratic constitution that unpopular or sectarian causes like Home Rule or disestablishment should be submitted to the people in a referendum, rather than be enacted by a parliamentary majority that had come into being for quite different reasons. Liberals were however hardly likely to accept the referendum as a constitutional device if it was only to be applied to Liberal measures at the behest of a predominantly Conservative Second Chamber.

If the Unionist leaders could thus believe that options other than the Parliament Bill were still open to them it is not surprising that they took no steps to dispel the illusion among their followers that resistance was possible. That such illusions should abound in a party emerging from its third successive defeat uncertain of its leaders and its orientation was even less surprising. It was a situation tailor-made for the advocates of resistance at any price, opponents of all compromise, addicts of political *machismo*. The more extreme tariff reformers were in a state of simmering resentment against Balfour and 'the party mandarins' who through aristocratic detachment and failure of conviction had surrendered the allegiance of the working classes patriotic at heart to the demagogues of Liberalism. An alliance was in the making between whole-hogging, social-imperialist advocates of a populist Unionism and straightforward diehards like Lord Halsbury an ex-Lord Chancellor prepared to fight every inch of the way for entrenched privilege. Even men like Lord Hugh Cecil, in the past poles apart from the Chamberlains and the tariff reformers, were now part of the alliance for resistance. Even a leader with greater authority than Balfour would have found it difficult to drive the diverse Unionist factions in their current mood meekly down the path of compromise.

The crisis over the Parliament Bill moved slowly to a climax in the spring and early summer of 1911. In the House of Commons over 900 amendments were tabled, but after only minor concessions by the government the Bill received its third reading on 15 May with a majority of 121. In the meantime Lansdowne had introduced his bill for the reform of the House of Lords in that House, but it lost much of its point when Morley, deputizing for the leader of the Liberal peers, firmly stated the government's position that the Parliament Bill would still apply to such a reformed second chamber. When the Parliament Bill reached the Lords it was amended out of recognition, roughly in line with the proposals put forward by the Unionist leaders during the Constitutional Conference. By amending the Parliament Bill in this way the House of Lords was ignoring the electorate's verdict of December 1910 and by early July 1911 the time had come for the government to remind the King of his pledge given before the election.

When the King's undertaking to create peers was made public the divisions among the Unionists came into the open. On the one side were lined up the all-out resisters, popularly known as ditchers, led by Lord Halsbury. The opposing camp became known as hedgers and comprised those who felt that it was now preferable to surrender with dignity and save what was left of the House of Lords and its powers. Lord Curzon, who had hitherto advocated outright resistance, became the most energetic organizer of the hedgers. Even now the lead given by Balfour and Lansdowne was less than clear-cut. The impression was allowed to gain ground that only a limited creation of peers, enough just to pass the bill, might be in prospect and Balfour did not regard the eventuality of another 100 peers as too disastrous. In fact the government would have had to ask for a much larger creation to make sure of passing the bill and among Asquith's papers there was a list of 250 names compiled for this purpose. Many ditchers continued to believe that the government was bluffing. The divisions in the Unionist camp became extremely bitter and old political friendships were torn apart.

Asquith had agreed to postpone the actual creation of peers until the Lords had had a final chance to pronounce upon the bill, stripped by the Commons of the Lords' earlier amendments. When he rose to announce the government's intentions in the Commons on 24 July, he was shouted down and stood at the dispatch box for half an hour, unable to make himself heard. Shouts of 'traitor', 'Let Redmond speak', 'American dollars', 'Who killed the King', filled the air. It was a demonstration staged by the supporters of the ditchers in the Lower House and it was led by Lord Hugh Cecil and F.E. Smith, the rising Tory lawyer from Liverpool, later Lord Birkenhead. Balfour did not approve of it, for it must have struck him as an example of the 'music hall' frame of mind, of which he had accused the all-out resisters. Nevertheless he did nothing to restrain it. The final act of the drama which had begun with the presentation of the people's budget nearly two and a half years previously, took place in the House of Lords from 9 to 11 August, during the hottest summer weather experienced in London for 70 years. The outcome was in doubt until the vote was taken to approve the Parliament Bill, restored again virtually to its original form by the Commons. 114 ditchers voted against; but 81 Liberal peers were joined in the government lobby by 37 Unionists led by Curzon and by 13 bishops. A creation of peers was thus avoided; the ditchers had been beaten 'by the Bishops and the Rats'.

V

Thus the final phase of the battle over the House of Lords was dominated by the divisions in the Unionist ranks, with Asquith and the Liberal government almost in the role of detached spectators. Balfour was abroad when the vote on 11 August was taken, in an unusual mood of disgust with the political scene. He began to toy with the possibility of retirement. He was aware that the crisis in the Unionist Party extended beyond policies and leaders to structure, organization and style. As is common with political parties, the successive electoral defeats had aroused strong dissatisfaction with the party organization and an organization committee had been appointed to recommend changes. In June 1911 the Chief Whip, Acland Hood, and the Principal Party Agent, Percival Hughes, were replaced by Lord Balcarres and Arthur Steel-Maitland, a tariff reformer from Birmingham. The latter was now designated Party Chairman and became a member of the Shadow Cabinet. There were many other recommendations to improve central, regional and constituency organization, but the merging of the Conservative and Liberal Unionist organizations did not take place until the following year. More fundamental problems beset the party in competing with the Liberal–Labour alliance for the ever-increasing number of working-class voters. The Unionists had nothing to fill the place the trade unions occupied in the Progressive Alliance; bodies like workingmen's clubs and organizations like the Primrose League had offered a broad spectrum of social activities through which the relationships between different socioeconomic classes could be strengthened and subtleties of deference could be cultivated. It had become more difficult to mobilize urban mass electorates in this way, especially when the middle and employing classes were solidly identified with the Tory party. Much depended on the style of the national leadership and for this reason there was now so much criticism of Balfour's aristocratic detachment and lack of the common touch.

When Balfour returned from the continent in the autumn of 1911 a campaign against his leadership had been orchestrated by Leo Maxse in the *National Review*, expressing the views of the more extreme tariff reform, imperialist sections of the party. Maxse coined the slogan 'BMG – Balfour must go', but pressure from such a quarter was hardly likely to shift the Tory leader. Nevertheless he must have decided that he could no longer lead with dignity and he announced his decision to go to his colleagues at the beginning of November. The succession lay between Austen Chamberlain and Walter Long. Chamberlain was the leader of the tariff reformers, but he was no extremist. He had been the connecting link between his stricken father and Balfour; in spite of policy differences over the referendum pledge, and even more painfully over resistance to the Parliament Bill, his friendship with the party leader had never been severed. Walter Long, a Wiltshire squire, president of organizations like the Union Defence League, to oppose Home Rule, and the Budget Protest League, was the candidate of the old land-owning section of the party. Edward Carson, the Ulster leader, and Andrew Bonar Law, a businessman from Glasgow, also entered the contest, but Carson quickly withdrew. Although most leading members of the party backed Chamberlain and considered Long lacking in competence, the two leading contenders were deadlocked. Chamberlain then offered to withdraw and induced Long to do the same. Thus the way was opened to the unanimous election of Bonar Law, whom only a handful of MPs had backed at the outset.

The process of selecting a leader in this way, with the possibility of a contested ballot, was unusual and novel for the Conservative Party; it was not even entirely clear whether what was at stake was the selection of a future Prime Minister, for in the past it had been the monarch who had made the final choice between the leaders in the Commons and in the Lords. For over a quarter of a century the Conservative leadership had been vested in the House of Cecil and now even the members of this family were divided against themselves. Bonar Law was a leader in a very different mould. He had no links with the landowning aristocracy and was not an Anglican. Born the son of a Presbyterian minister in New Brunswick whose family had come from Ulster, he had been brought up by his mother's family, wealthy members of the Scottish middle class, and had made his own way in the Glasgow iron trade. He had entered the Commons in 1900, when he was over 40, and because of his sound knowledge of trade and industry, had received rapid promotion to junior office at the Board of Trade, but he had never held Cabinet office. He was a convinced tariff reformer and Joseph Chamberlain, so similar in background, was his hero. In the last stages of the Parliament Bill crisis he had, however, become a hedger. This relative newcomer to high politics, a man of sceptical, pessimistic temperament, soon revealed the ability to give his party that populist, hard-hitting leadership that it craved.

VI

The culmination of Liberal welfare policies, Lloyd George's national insurance legislation, coincided with the climax of the constitutional crisis in 1911. It was part of the political strategy upon which Lloyd George and Churchill jointly embarked in 1908 that the financial foundations for social reform should be laid first before the main attack on the two of the major causes of poverty, unemployment and sickness, could be mounted. The long battle over the budget and the House of Lords and the two elections of 1910 brought it about that the scheme of national insurance, which Lloyd George and the men working with him had in mind, could not be introduced before 1911. Another factor which counselled delay was that the report of the Royal Commission on the Poor Law appointed in 1905 had to be awaited; majority and minority reports appeared in February 1909. The debate about poverty had advanced a good deal since the 1880s and the fresh perspectives on it had become one of the ingredients in the New Liberalism. Charles Booth and Seebohm Rowntree had developed further the scientific investigation of poverty. Charles Booth, a Liverpool businessman, a believer in individualism and politically a Conservative, was concerned to counter the sensationalized and emotional approach to poverty common in the 1880s with a more factual account. He published his first paper, on the inhabitants of the Tower Hamlets, in 1887, where, to his surprise, he had found that no less than a third of the population lived below the poverty line as he defined it. The results of the investigations he conducted between 1891 and 1903 were published in 17 volumes under the title *The Life and Labour of the People of London*. The definitions of poverty lines and categorization of classes among the lower income groups established by Booth would not pass muster by the standards of modern social survey techniques. His own remedies, for example the setting up of labour colonies, were governed by conventional economic ideas; in these colonies the lowest class of earners would be set to work on limited tasks to take them out of the competition of the labour market. Nevertheless Booth, by demonstrating the scale of poverty beyond doubt, showed that the problem could not be explained on the basis of degeneracy or inadequacy in individuals. Rowntree's study of poverty in York appeared in 1901 and was based on much more carefully defined and researched criteria of poverty. An income of 21s 8d was regarded as the minimum sufficient to maintain a five-member family. The York survey illustrated clearly the variety of conditions causing poverty and its incidence at different stages of a person's life cycle.

At the time of the Boer War the poor physical shape of many working-class volunteers for the army attracted a great deal of publicity and among the spate of inquiries into shortcomings revealed by the war there was one on 'Physical Deterioration'. There was much talk of a deterioration of the British race and Social Darwinists of various persuasions had a field day, ranging from calls for more State intervention from the Webbs to attacks on foreign immigration, demands for sterilization and better breeding, from writers like Robert Blatchford who combined fervent nationalism with socialism, H.G. Wells and Arnold White, the author of a widely read book, *Efficiency and Empire*. The detrimental impact of poverty on national efficiency was a recurring theme in the public utterances of men like Rosebery and Milner and accounts to some extent for the social reform plank in the programmes of social imperialists and tariff reformers. A programme to fight the social degradation that threatened the future of the British as an imperial race would have found an important place in the aims of a new centre party, the kind of realignment much talked about in the months before Chamberlain gave politics a different twist by opening his tariff reform campaign.

As for the remedies, the more scientific investigations of poverty now available made it easier to distinguish its various causes. Housing and old age were already firmly on the political agenda, while unemployment was gradually being more clearly analysed. There was no repetition of the violent unemployment demonstrations that had pushed the problem to the forefront of the public mind in the mid-1880s, partly because the Metropolitan Police and the Home Secretary were better prepared to forestall them, but unemployment was now seen as a persistent and endemic cause of poverty. It was becoming impossible to regard unemployment as being simply linked with social inadequacy and lack of skill, because it had become clear that even members of the so-called labour aristocracy, who were not lacking in self-reliance, were often pushed to the edge of subsistence by irregularity of employment. When the inability of the poor law to cope with cyclical industrial unemployment and the unwillingness of the respectable unemployed to accept the stigma of pauperism was recognized in the 1880s, public works came to be regarded as the chief antidote. In 1886 Chamberlain, during his brief period as President of the Local Government Board in the third Gladstone ministry, had issued a circular to local authorities urging them to schedule necessary public works for periods of depression and to provide temporary non-pauperizing employment for the deserving unemployed. This circular was reissued in subsequent years, but the limited availability of such public works and the pressure put on local rates seriously restricted the usefulness of this approach. The renewed down-swing in the trade cycle in the years between 1892 and 1895 turned attention to a number of possible remedies for unemployment: the eight-hour day, labour colonies, land settlement were all put forward as methods of alleviating the problem. The view that most of the unemployed came from the least employable sections of the working class was still strong; many of the proposed solutions amounted to a regimentation of the unemployed and the ideas for reducing the quantity of labour on the market were not soundly based.

The revival of trade from 1896 and the high level of employment during the South African war diverted attention from the unemployment problem. When it became threatening again between 1903 and 1905 it revealed the deep crisis into which the system of poor relief established in 1834 had now fallen. Less eligibility, the basic principle that conditions under which poor relief was granted should always be inferior to the lowest form of subsistence or service available, could no longer be enforced, for publicly elected authorities could hardly reproduce in their workhouses conditions which, when found outside, were condemned as degrading and harmful by public opinion. The removal of property qualifications for elections to

Boards of Guardians had brought on to many urban boards men of progressive or even socialist views. George Lansbury at Poplar had turned the workhouse into a place of tolerable comfort and those receiving outdoor relief outside the workhouse no longer had to undergo the notorious labour test of stone-breaking. This was called Poplarism and was by no means unique. Yet even with this erosion of deterrence, the Poor Law was not providing relief for the great majority of able-bodied workmen hit by temporary unemployment. Nevertheless Poor Law spending per pauper had increased by over 50 per cent between the decades 1870–80 and 1896–1906, though only about 20 per cent per head of population. The upsurge in unemployment caused by the slump of 1903–5 had again to be dealt with by distress committees; in London the Mansion House Committee on the unemployed, in abeyance since 1895, was reactivated. Although still dominated by members of the Charity Organization, some young social reformers from Toynbee Hall and from university settlements in the East End, among them William Beveridge and Percy Alden, served on it. The government was alarmed by the problem and Walter Long, as President of the Local Government Board, helped to set up joint committees of boards of guardians, borough councils and charitable associations throughout London and these sent delegates to a central committee to raise subscriptions and devise a common policy for London. This system formed the basis of the government's Unemployed Workmen Act of 1905, which provided for the setting up of similar Distress Committees in all metropolitan boroughs and urban districts of over 50,000. In London the co-ordination of relief schemes was to be the task of a Central (Unemployed) Body, on which representatives of the distress committees, the LCC and the Local Government Board were joined by co-opted experts. This was the culmination of the attempts to deal with unemployment through the provision of relief work, but it was still not an effective way of helping the able-bodied worker who was temporarily out of work. Nevertheless the Act did bring together people with expertise on the problem and helped the collection of information. Although the government had tried very hard to avoid giving an impression that legislation meant the recognition of a right to work, it was an admission that unemployment was a problem that concerned the central government.

The Aliens Act, which was passed almost simultaneously with the Unemployed Workmen Act in 1905, was also in large part a response to the unemployment problem. In some parts of the country, notably in the East End of London, anti-alienism, very often indistinguishable from anti-semitism, had become a major political issue. It was easy to link immigration, particularly the influx of a group as distinct in their cultural and religious attitudes as the Eastern European Jews escaping from Russian pogroms, with a host of indigenous problems, unemployment, sweated trades, disease and physical degradation. Hostility to the alien immigrant was being exploited politically and even Chamberlain, in his pursuit of tariff reform, was not above linking anti-alienism and protection. The attitude of the trade union movement had for a long time been ambiguous and fear of competition from immigrants was combined with expressions of brotherhood. The 1905 Act was a cautious attempt by the government to meet the demand for restrictions on immigration without appearing to flout the tradition of giving asylum to the victims of persecution.

Although social reform, apart from old-age pensions, did not figure prominently in the 1906 election, the new Liberal government was under both political and administrative pressure to move on several fronts. One of the first concrete results was the passage in the parliamentary session of 1906 of the Education (Provision of Meals) Act. The feeding of destitute school children had up to this time been left to charitable effort. In the wake of the concern about 'physical deterioration' after the Boer War, the plight of hungry underfed children attending schools received considerable publicity. Sir John Gorst, of Fourth Party fame, made the cause his own and attacked the Balfour government for inaction. Gorst, who had resigned from the Board of Education in 1902, was by this time on his way out of the Conservative Party and was fighting a last battle for Tory democracy. In response to this pressure the government issued a Relief Order instructing Boards of Guardians to feed destitute school children. The practical effect was merely to demonstrate that the Poor Law was not a proper channel for dealing with this problem. As a direct consequence a private member's bill was introduced by one of the newly elected Labour members in 1906 and the new Liberal government, unprepared with any proposal of its own, took this up. When the bill finally passed it was a modest, permissive measure, enabling them to levy a halfpenny in the pound to supplement charitable efforts. Within the next five years only 95 out of 322 education authorities in England and Wales used rate-money to provide school meals, but an important principle had been established, namely that the State could support a citizen without inflicting on him the stigma of pauperism and disenfranchisement. The right of the authorities to recover the cost of meals from parents became virtually a dead letter. By 1914 the Board of Education had acquired the power to compel local authorities to feed necessitous children. In 1907 the cause of improving the health of school children received a boost with the passage of the Education (Administrative Provisions) Act which marks the beginning of a general school health service. Medical inspection of school children had been pioneered at Bradford in the 90s by Margaret McMillan and others. The 1907 Act was the brain-child of Robert Morant who cleverly blurred the distinction between medical inspection and treatment and thus circumvented a great deal of opposition. The Act did not in fact mark as great an innovation in principle as the school meals act, for State intervention in public health matters was well established, but its immediate practical effects were greater. The need for a vast amount of medical treatment for children was uncovered; the majority of education authorities began to provide some of this treatment even if working-class parents could not afford to pay for it.

These measures to deal with children's welfare did not exhaust the Liberal government's social reform effort in the first two years of its existence. Workman's Compensation was extended and under pressure from Labour there was an abortive attempt to pass a Miners' Eight-Hour bill. The Labour Party developed a view on unemployment somewhat distinct from the Liberals and brought in an Unemployed Workmen Bill of its own in 1907, which contained a right-to-work clause. If unemployment reached 4 per cent the schemes for relief work drawn up by the local distress committees would be automatically financed from national funds. This would mean something like national action to counter the trade cycle. The bill had no answer to the question what markets there would be for the products of relief schemes and it was 'a manifesto rather than a bill'. Ramsay MacDonald earned much acclaim for his parliamentary performance in presenting this bill, while John Burns, whose appointment to the Local Government Board had been hailed as the symbol of the political arrival of the working class, was now the minister most adamantly opposed to any recognition of the 'right to work'. The bill became the focus of a 'right to work' campaign which was given impetus by the down-turn in trade beginning in 1907.

Churchill and Lloyd George saw social reform as the means to get the marooned Liberal ship moving again when they took up their new positions in the cabinet in April 1908. Just before his elevation Churchill had published a letter in *The Nation* advocating a national 'minimum standard', the organization of the labour market, labour exchanges, decasualization, the training of juveniles and 'the development of certain national industries' to counteract fluctuations of world trade. In a letter to Asquith he also proposed that the great mass of voluntary organizations of thrift and insurance that had grown up in England should be underpinned and regulated by State intervention along lines established in Germany. Churchill had at this time renewed his friendship with the Webbs and the ideas he was putting forward owed a good deal to them. The Webbs wanted, however, to go a good deal further in the direction of intervention, paternalism and even regimentation than was likely to prove acceptable to the government. They wanted to deal with unemployment outside the Poor Law, through labour organization, reformatory training, subsidized insurance and public works, supervised by a separate 'Ministry of Labour'; these recommendations formed the substance of the minority report of the Royal Commission on the Poor Law, of which Mrs Webb was a member.

Nevertheless, those ministers who were looking to social reform as a means to revive Liberal fortunes were prepared to take ideas from the Webbs as well as from any other source. They also knew that the recommendations of the royal commission were likely to make great demands on local authority finance; that this would, in view of the growing revolt of ratepayers, raise in even more acute form the problem of the balance between local and central taxation; the establishment of a sounder revenue base in the budget of 1909 was therefore crucial to the progress of social reform. But just as national taxation policy had to be carefully calculated to bring the Liberal Party political advantage, so it was with social reform. The administration of the Poor Law had imbued many generations of working-class men and women with a deep repugnance to public intervention in their lives, so that new methods and institutions had to be carefully designed to gain their confidence and support. Social reform was therefore not necessarily popular with working-class voters, beyond those who were politically conscious, and there were increasing signs that among middle-class voters, beyond those who were socially conscious, there was resentment at maintaining the workshy and feckless at public expense. A multitude of organizations, from the long-established Liberty and Property Defence League to the more recently founded Anti-Socialist Union and Middle Class Defence League, were at work fostering this resentment. Even within the Liberal cabinet such sentiments were to be found; John Burns, now a major obstacle at the Local Government Board to any innovation measures, wrote to H.G. Wells in 1910: 'The new helotry in the Servile State run by the archivists of the School of Economics means a race of paupers in a grovelling community ruled by uniformed prigs. Rely upon me saving you from this plague'. Even to those who most actively believed in social reform, like Churchill and Lloyd George, it was a question of maintaining the fine dividing line that separated social radicalism, with its continuing faith in the market and in competition, from socialism. The aim was not to abolish the market, but to spread a safety net for those least able to survive in it. Social reform and social policy, once relegated to administrators working within the confines of rigid economic theories, had now become matters of high policy and of political will.

VII

With old age pensions introduced in the spring of 1908, unemployment inevitably became the focus of attention for the active social reformers in the cabinet, for the trade depression was getting worse and in August Churchill warned his cabinet colleagues that a combination of falling employment, lower wages and rising food prices was inflicting 'a period of unusual severity' upon the working classes. Shortly after, Lloyd George left for a visit to Germany to study the German social insurance system. His mind was on the possibility of extending old age pensions through a scheme of invalidity insurance. The insurance principle was also seen as one of the major ways of dealing with unemployment, but in practice unemployment and invalidity insurance had to be enacted together, 'for it would never do to exact contributions from masters and men in successive layers', so Churchill wrote to Asquith at Christmas 1908. In retrospect both Churchill and Lloyd George claimed the credit for having introduced social insurance in Britain. In the meantime Churchill's department had been working throughout the summer on concrete programmes for dealing with unemployment. The Board of Trade now had not only a president eager for action, but officials of like mind. Hubert Llewellyn Smith, the Permanent Secretary of the Board, was a civil servant in the mould of Robert Morant and had like him had a period of residence at Toynbee Hall. In July 1908 Churchill, with the encouragement of the Webbs, appointed William Beveridge, a temporary civil servant in his department, to assist with 'work in connection with [labour] exchanges'. This young man of 29 had started his career as sub-warden of Toynbee Hall as assistant to Canon Barnett, who had been the mentor of so many of this generation of social reformers. His ideas had crystallized around the belief in the need for a scientific social policy; after a brief flirtation with socialism he had become somewhat distrustful of political democracy, but his faith in a paternalist central bureaucracy guided by scientific principles was tempered by an ambivalence which often drew him to models of social policy which relied heavily on pluralism, autonomy and individual choice. Immediately before joining the Board of

Trade Beveridge had delivered a series of lectures at Oxford on unemployment, which were published in 1909 as *Unemployment: a Problem of Industry*. He advocated a five-fold approach: labour exchanges, to promote mobility of labour and segregate the unemployable; unemployment insurance, either directly by the State or through the trade unions; the remaining three recommendations were for adjustments in wages and public works during trade depressions and reform of the Poor Law. The first two of Beveridge's proposals were the areas on which the Board of Trade now concentrated its attention.

In February 1909 Churchill announced in the Commons that he would introduce a national system of voluntary labour exchanges. The idea of a better organization of the labour market as an antidote to unemployment and casual employment was not new. Labour exchanges had been organized by local authorities, trade unions and private agencies and they had a place in the Unemployed Workmen Act of 1905. Churchill and his officials did not favour the compulsory organization of the labour market which the Webbs envisaged in the minority report of the Royal Commission. The government saw the exchanges as a means by which available workers could be put in touch with available vacancies, if both sides chose to use the service. The main criticism which had to be met came from the trade unions, who feared that the exchanges might encourage black-legging during strikes and that wages lower than those current locally might be offered. Churchill skilfully defused the anxieties of the unions. He introduced a new clause in the Labour Exchanges Bill which stipulated that no workman registered at an exchange should be prejudiced by refusing wages lower than those current in his trade or district, or by turning down a vacancy created by a trade dispute. Labour exchanges came into operation in 1910, controlled by a department in the Board of Trade of which Beveridge was the director. To staff them, men and women were recruited from outside the civil service and these included trade unionists, social reformers and people who had themselves worked in factories and workshops. It was intended above all to make the exchanges into efficient business mechanisms, designed to reduce friction in the labour market. Nevertheless the trade unions remained sceptical, especially about the effectiveness of the exchanges in reducing casual labour. There was criticism about patronage in the recruitment of staff and the local advisory committees were not notably successful in reconciling the interests of capital and labour. Respectable working men were slow to make use of the exchanges, regarding them as haunts of unemployables and blacklegs. It was not until the introduction of unemployment insurance in 1912 that the exchanges were more widely used; by 1914 there were

423 of them, registering two million workers a year.

Unemployment insurance had long been envisaged as a desirable companion-piece to labour exchanges. Beveridge and Llewellyn Smith were working on both schemes from the autumn of 1908 and the cabinet agreed about the same time that while the Board of Trade would be responsible for unemployment insurance, the Treasury would deal with sickness insurance. The unemployment insurance proposals could have been ready for legislation in the summer of 1909, but were in fact only introduced as Part II of the National Insurance Bill in May 1911. They were mainly the work of Llewellyn Smith, with Beveridge acting as a revising critic and elaborator of administrative detail. Unemployment insurance was a more daring foray into uncharted territory than the establishment of labour exchanges. The older craft unions, like the Amalgamated Society of Engineers, had been providing unemployment insurance since the middle of the previous century, but their efforts were often as much directed towards preventing unemployed workers from lowering the current wage rates as to relieving distress. Various experiments had been tried on the continent and Beveridge and Lloyd George had both been to Germany to look at the various local unemployment insurance schemes operating there. Out of these influences and considerations emerged the decision to go for a contributory scheme, with payments from workers, employers and the State. In their final form in the Act of 1911 these payments amounted to $2\frac{1}{2}$ d plus $2\frac{1}{2}$ d plus $1\frac{2}{3}$ d per week, so that after deduction of $\frac{2}{3}$ d for administrative expenses, 6d per man was available to finance benefits. It had been decided at an early stage that these benefits would have to be paid out at a flat rate; Churchill was particularly insistent that they were to be regarded as an entitlement, based on insurance, and that an inquisitorial system to debar loafers and shirkers would not be appropriate. 'We seek to substitute for the pressure of the forces of nature, operating by chance on individuals, the pressures of the laws of insurance, operating through averages with modifying and mitigating effects in individual cases', he argued. In their final form the benefits amounted to 7s. a week, payable for 15 weeks. The compulsory scheme applied only to a limited range of trades particularly exposed to cyclical fluctuations, mainly building and construction, ship building, mechanical engineering, iron founding and vehicle building. Calculations about payments and benefits had to be based on inadequate information. An unemployment rate of just under $8\frac{1}{2}$ per cent was assumed to be close to the average in all trades and on this basis the scheme would be self-sustaining after a Treasury contribution to meet initial claims.

The trade unions met the unemployment insurance proposals with considerable opposition, but were in the end bought off. They were given incentives to supplement the public scheme with their own provisions, so that weekly benefit could rise to a maximum of 12s. a week, dangerously close to the wage rates prevailing in the less well-paid trades. A sixth of the additional benefit of 5s. a week could be recovered through Treasury subsidies. The passage of unemployment insurance through Parliament proved relatively uneventful for it was largely overshadowed by the controversy over Part I of the National Insurance Bill, the sickness insurance scheme. The first contributions under the Act were paid in on 1 July 1912 and six months later the first benefits were paid out. The Labour Exchanges Office in the Board of Trade was responsible for the direction of the scheme and over $2\frac{1}{4}$ million workmen in the insured trades were covered by it, about a quarter of them through the trade unions. Only about a fifth of these had previously been insured by private schemes. Trade unions outside the insured trades made only very limited use of it. The period during which the scheme was in operation before the outbreak of war was a time of prosperity and low unemployment, only just over 2 per cent in the insured trades in 1913, and the system was therefore not fully tested before 1914. As it was limited to a few trades, it could not have dealt with cyclical unemployment over the economy as a whole, nor was it capable of dealing with the problem of casual labour. In the inter-war period unemployment insurance proved inadequate to deal with the much higher number of jobless consistently experienced, but in his report of 1942 Beveridge again recommended insurance, supported by a policy of full employment.

VIII

Invalidity, sickness or health insurance, the latter term coming to be the one more generally used, was a more ambitious and controversial scheme than unemployment insurance. Lloyd George conceived it as a way of reducing one of the great causes of poverty, ill-health in the bread-winner, thus relieving the Poor Law of another great burden. The Poor Law provided a major element in the medical services available to that five-sixths of the population living in households receiving less than £160 per annum. More than half the beds in public hospitals were in Poor Law infirmaries and these still carried the stigma of pauperism, although the Medical Relief (Disqualification Removal)

Act of 1885 had abolished disqualification from the parliamentary franchise. Voluntary hospitals provided another large element of institutional care and of out-patient facilities; their medical standards were generally high, but they were available only in large cities. There was a wide variety of charitable and provident dispensaries, usually making small charges for their services; the Charity Organization Society had been very active in setting up such dispensaries, usually requiring a regular monthly contribution from those using them. All these services were to some extent in competition with the general practitioners in working-class areas, who therefore were very concerned that such medical facilities should not be entirely free. A lot of the doctors' work was carried out on contract for the Friendly Societies, for which they received a capitation fee of around 4s. per annum. The patient who paid for his treatment through Friendly Society insurance thus had normally no choice of doctor, while on the other hand considerable tension existed between the societies and the medical profession about payment and about the terms on which patients could command the doctor's services. The medical care available to the poorer classes could hardly be described as adequate.

Lloyd George had to face three formidable vested interests in establishing health insurance by the State: the Friendly Societies, the industrial insurance companies and the medical profession. Industrial insurance companies were the providers of funeral benefits for a very large number of working-class households. Nearly 30 million policies providing on average £10 for funeral expenses were in force in 1910. The bulk of the business was done by 12 major companies of which three, the Royal Liver, the Liverpool Victoria and the Scottish Legal were collecting Friendly Societies; the remaining nine, among which the Prudential was much the largest, together collected a premium income of £20 million a year, of which a third went to the 'Pru'. This type of life insurance, for which no medical examination was required, exploited the fear of pauperism as well as the fecklessness of those sections of the working classes that were beyond the reach of Friendly Societies. The face value of policies was calculated in multiples of what was purchased by a penny a week premium. These pennies were collected by an army of 70,000 collectors, popularly known as 'the man from the Pru', the butt of many music-hall jokes. By this avenue a young working-class male could advance into the lower middle class with an income of £3 or £4 a week. Most of them were radical Liberals and there was little love lost between them and the companies for which they worked on commission; they were a constituency Lloyd George could not afford to offend. The business as a whole was very profitable, for only 37 per cent of the premium income of the nine large companies was paid to beneficiaries, while

43 per cent went in salesmen's commissions, indoor management expenses and stockholders' dividends.

Lloyd George had his first meeting with the representatives of the industrial insurance industry in August 1910 and was apparently surprised by what he learnt. It soon became clear to him that one part of his proposed scheme, widows' and orphans' pensions, would have to be jettisoned. When in January 1911 intensive planning and consultation on health insurance started, the fundamental decision was taken that there was to be a full-scale State insurance scheme, rather than an extension of Friendly Society benefits. Lloyd George had initially gained the goodwill of the Friendly Societies by assuring them they would have their place in the administration of the scheme. He now had to bribe them further by bolstering their reserves, so that the very large number of elderly people who had no previous insurance could be taken into the scheme. Many Friendly Societies were in a weak financial position anyhow and collectively the societies could not really afford to reject the liferaft which Lloyd George was offering them. In the many months of complex negotiations that went on throughout the year 1911 the Chancellor and his team were deftly playing off against each other the vested interests they had to deal with: the Friendly Societies were compelled to allow the industrial insurance companies to share in the administration of the scheme; the doctors were attracted by the panel system, under which a patient could choose his doctor, administered by the local health committees to be set up under the bill; the insurance companies, for whom medical benefits were not of major importance, were prepared to accept administration by these health committees as the price of being enabled to share in the scheme as approved societies. The major battle with the medical profession, represented by the British Medical Association, was fought after the bill was on the statute book. Lloyd George rightly suspected that the BMA was dominated by what he called 'swell doctors' and that among humble general practitioners a very different view prevailed. Under national insurance doctors in poorer areas were assured of a much more secure and also considerably higher income than before. Public sympathy was not with any direct action of doctors against what was now the law, and by January 1913 the BMA had to capitulate.

The team with whom Lloyd George worked in the preparation and establishment of health insurance included Masterman, who moved to the Home Office in 1910 and to the Treasury in 1912, Rufus Isaacs, the Attorney-General, and a number of civil servants, among whom W.J. Braithwaite was probably the most important. Braithwaite was, like Morant, a Wykehamist, and had also passed through Toynbee Hall. He knew the Friendly Society world well and understood

insurance. It was mainly due to him that the scheme came to be based
on the accumulation of a reserve like private insurance, rather than
on 'dividing out' all current contributions, a system Lloyd George
would have preferred. When the bill was introduced in May 1911 it
provided medical benefit; sickness benefit at 10s. a week for men,
7s. 6d. for women, for 13 weeks, and of 5s. for another 13 weeks, but
this was amended so that full benefits were available for 26 weeks; dis-
ability benefit of 5s. a week indefinitely, maternity benefit of 30s. and
admission to sanatoria, mainly intended for tuberculosis sufferers.
Contributions were 4d. from the employee, 3d. from the employer
and 2d. from the State.

Initially Part I of the National Insurance Bill appeared to attract no
more opposition than Part II and Austen Chamberlain welcomed it
on behalf of the Opposition. The Parliament Bill was still drawing
most of the heat and fury, but once it was out of the way, some
Conservative MPs vented their frustration on the Insurance Bill.
After the resignation of Balfour in November 1911 and a by-election
at Oldham which the Liberals lost and in which national insurance
was an issue, opposition inside and outside Parliament increased.
There was evidently political capital to be made out of the
unpopularity of stamp-licking and Lloyd George had to counter by
claiming that his scheme gave '9d. for 4d.'. On 29 November 1911
there was a great rally of domestic servants against 'stamp licking', at
which a number of titled ladies, their maids and Hilaire Belloc, no
longer a Liberal MP, appeared on the platform. This form of protest
soon fizzled out. At the other end of the political spectrum the bill had
incurred much hostility from the socialist Left, who objected to the
contributory principle as a tax on poverty. The Webbs and the
Fabian Society were also strongly opposed to 'Lloyd George's rotten
scheme of sickness insurance', mainly again because it was contributory; they consistently opposed the unconditionality of benefits. The
Labour Party in Parliament was divided, with the majority of trade
union MPs and the Chairman Ramsay MacDonald in favour of the
bill, but working to secure changes in details. MacDonald was bitter
about the challenge to his authority as Chairman that came from the
socialist Left over the Insurance Bill. Once the scheme was in full
operation, with benefits being paid out, its unpopularity quickly
subsided.

Part I of the National Insurance Act was complicated and in places
self-contradictory and its administration had to be set up with great
speed in the seven months before the collection of contributions
started on 15 July 1912. Masterman had political charge of the operation; the Chairman of the National Health Insurance Commission
was Sir Robert Morant, who now left the Board of Education.

Among the members of the insurance commissions in England, Scotland and Wales and their staffs were to be found many men of current and future distinction in politics and administration, among them John Anderson and Warren Fisher, future leading civil servants, Thomas Jones, Lloyd George's close associate, and Arthur Salter, administrator and academic. Over 12 million contributors started to buy stamps and it was calculated that upwards of 36 million people would be affected by health insurance, either directly or by having a member of their family as a contributor. Fourteen thousand out of some 20 thousand general practitioners accepted panel practice. The claims for sickness benefit particularly from women turned out to be much higher than had been anticipated. The administration of both parts of national insurance and of the labour exchanges represented a remarkable increase in the activity of the central government, an unprecedented involvement of the State in the lives of individuals and a great increase in the size of the bureaucratic machine. Patronage, corruption and interference with individual freedom constantly featured among the charges made against the new system. National insurance and labour exchanges owed their existence hardly at all to any party-political and parliamentary impulses, unlike old age pensions which had for long been a matter of public debate and recrimination between the parties. There was only a small group of social-radical Liberal MPs who were strongly interested in specific policies on unemployment and sickness. Labour pressed the 'right to work', but had hardly any concrete remedies to offer; the socialists in the Labour movement believed that unemployment would disappear along with capitalism. The Unionists never opposed the Liberal welfare measures in principle and indeed offered to better them through tariff reform, while making what political capital they could out of the difficulties and the unpopularity which the Liberal measures encountered. The small group of ministers and civil servants who were the active promoters of Liberal welfarism were, however, not merely acting from philanthrophic motives. The Poor Law was in crisis, aggravated by the slump of 1907 to 1910, and the option of doing nothing was no longer open to the central government. No deliberate, coherent decision to supersede the Poor Law was ever taken and there was no more than a distant hope that by taking major categories of poverty, like old age, unemployment and sickness, for separate treatment the Poor Law would eventually become redundant. After the passage of the National Insurance Act no further major measures of welfare came from the Liberal government.

IX

An element in the Liberal espousal of welfarism had been the desire to pre-empt socialism. The Labour Party had, however, since 1906 hardly fulfilled the hopes that ardent left-wing activists had placed in it. It had functioned mainly as a parliamentary pressure group for the trade unions and in this capacity had scored some success, most notably in determining the final shape of the Trades Disputes Act of 1906. The Coal Mines Regulation Act of 1908, which made the eight-hour day in mines statutory, was the kind of legislation on the details of which Labour MPs could make known the views of the interests they represented; Churchill's Trade Boards Act of 1909 dealing with sweated labour was a similar case.

Such parliamentary work meant little to the zealots of the Left. Membership of socialist bodies was rising after 1906; the Marxist SDF reached a membership of 12,000, the Fabians were founding new branches outside London; the number of ILP branches increased from 375 in 1906 to nearly 900 three years later with, it was said, 30,000 members; Blatchford's *Clarion* reached a circulation of 80,000 in 1908. Within the ILP, the most important component of the Labour alliance apart from the trade unions, the expectations of the rank and file were in growing conflict with the policy of working through the Labour Party. In by-elections local ILP branches often refused to abide by the rules of their affiliation to the Labour Party; yet the ILP contributed only £83 to the fund from which its elected members drew £1,400 annually. Lack of discipline among the grass roots forced MacDonald, who had been both Chairman of the ILP and Secretary of the Labour Party, Keir Hardie, Philip Snowden and Bruce Glasier to resign from the ILP's National Administrative Council in April 1909.

In spite of all the tensions that arose from the realities of Labour's position as a limited parliamentary pressure group and from the need to remain in tandem with the Liberals, the future potential of the party was still considerable and this was underlined by the decision of the miners to affiliate to the party in 1908. There was growing militancy in some coalfields, notably South Wales, where the decline in productivity, due to the need to work more difficult seams, was putting pressure on wages. In such areas there was dissatisfaction with the traditional Lib-Labism of the Miners' Federation. After a succession of ballots since 1906, the vote in 1908 went in favour of affiliation by a margin of over five to four. The importance of this affiliation may be gauged from the fact that over a third of the number counted as affiliated to the Labour Party in 1910 were miners, while only just over 2 per cent were non-trade unionists. Thirteen of the 45

Labour MPs sitting at the dissolution of the 1906 Parliament were miners. The affiliation of the miners was not welcomed by those who feared that the Labour Party would be more than ever dominated by trade union leaders who saw it as no more than an adjunct to the Liberal Party. Keir Hardie wrote at the time that control 'by Coal and Cotton . . . means more reaction' and feared that those like himself would be tricked out of their life's work 'by men who were never of us'. Individual mining Lib-Lab MPs continued in fact to behave as Liberals, to prevent the setting up of any independent Labour electoral machinery in their constituencies and virtually to flout the affiliation to the Labour Party. The Miners' Federation and most of its regional sections also failed to co-operate in setting up independent Labour organizations in the constituencies. Gradually, however, the situation changed in favour of the Labour Party, as the more militant coalfields gained influence in the Federation at the expense of the more prosperous.

There remained formidable difficulties, as was perhaps most strikingly highlighted by the Hanley by-election of July 1912. This contest, in the moderate Midlands coalfield, was precipitated by the death of Enoch Edwards, the President of the Miners' Federation, in spirit a Liberal, who had done nothing to foster a Labour organization in his constituency. The Liberals put up a candidate, a move which was felt by the national executive of the Labour Party to be an act of aggression, since formally Edwards had been a Labour member. In retaliation they put up a candidate in the concurrent by-election at Crewe, a Liberal seat. Hanley was won by the Liberals by a narrow majority, with Labour bottom of the poll with barely 12 per cent of the vote. Crewe was taken from the Liberals by the Unionists. These results showed the weakness of the Lib-Lab position in the face of Liberal determination to halt the advance of Labour, but also the danger to the Progressive Alliance from the breakdown of the MacDonald-Gladstone entente. After Hanley the Miners' Federation, under its new president Bob Smillie, moved more strongly towards the Labour Party and away from Lib-Labism.

While the affiliation of the miners, whatever difficulties it produced in the short run, was a harbinger of Labour's potential in the future, the Osborne judgement was clearly an immediate obstacle to its development. There had been previous attempts to restrict trade unions in the use of their funds for political purposes before W.V. Osborne, the secretary of the Walthamstow branch of the Amalgamated Society of Railway Servants, brought a case against his union in 1908. Many on the Left, including the Webbs, saw the move as a capitalist plot, but Osborne was both a staunch trade unionist and strong supporter of the Liberal Party and represented a substantial volume of opinion in the trade union movement. The High Court found against Osborne, but this decision was reversed by the Court of Appeal and the reversal was upheld by the Law Lords in December 1909. The Osborne judgement became a grievance for the Labour Party and its supporters in the trade union movement hardly less acute than Taff Vale had been. The loss to the party's income in the six years from 1909 to 1915 was substantial, perhaps in excess of £30,000, and Labour was prevented from gaining full advantage from the great rise in the number of trade unionists during those years. The judgement reinforced the feeling in the Labour movement against the judiciary and there was pressure on the Liberal government to reverse it, but the cabinet baulked at promising a straight reversal of a judicial decision by legislation. Instead they undertook to introduce payment of members and to restore to trade unions the power to use their funds for political purposes, provided individual members could contract out. Lloyd George provided for the payment of a salary of £400 to MPs in his 1911 budget, but he used this provision as a lever to get support from trade union MPs for the National Insurance Bill. The existence of parliamentary salaries was from now on often used in the polemics of the left wing against the parliamentary Labour Party. The Trades Disputes Act of 1913 enabled unions to raise a distinct fund for political purposes, subject to contracting out by individual members. Such a fund could not be started without a ballot of members and although in most unions ballots went in favour of establishing a political fund, substantial minorities, for example among miners and cotton workers about three out of seven, remained opposed to it and by implication to independent Labour representation.

Thus the Labour Party remained up to 1914 exposed to a variety of conflicting pressures. At one extreme were those who wanted full-blooded socialism and on the whole this view was dominant among the rank and file of the ILP. On the other hand large sections of the working class were still loyal to the Liberal Party, although in areas where Labour was well established there was a tendency to see Labour increasingly as the party for the working class, a kind of vague Labourism rather than socialism. In Parliament the Labour Party was forced into close association with the Liberals, in spite of disagreements such as that over National Insurance. MacDonald, who became Chairman of the party in the 1911 Parliament, welcomed this and friendly personal relations developed between him and many leading Liberals. From time to time there was talk of his joining a Liberal–Labour coalition. In March 1914, when a general election appeared imminent, there was a meeting between him and Lloyd George to discuss the possibility of another electoral pact. Such a pact

for a general election, which could not have been delayed beyond
1915, would, however, have been extremely difficult to negotiate.
The men and women who were the backbone of local party activity
would not have stood for it and the Liberal Party managers might well
have found it equally difficult to impose it on their own followers. In a
1915 election Labour might well have put up 150 candidates or more
and this, quite apart from other factors, might have swung the
election to the Unionists even if most of these candidates failed to
secure election. The by-election record of Labour between 1911 and
1914 was not inspiring, but neither was it disastrous. Labour lost four
seats, but three of these were in effect Lib–Lab mining seats in the
Midlands; the fourth, at Bow and Bromley, was due to the decision of
George Lansbury to resign the Labour whip and fight as a women's
suffrage candidate. In the five by-elections where Labour had fought
before, their vote increased in all but one; of the seven by-elections
where it had not fielded a candidate before, three produced a Labour
vote which was by no means a long way behind that of the other two
parties. In municipal elections Labour scored considerable successes
in many cities. Thus Labour in spite of all the debilitating tensions
afflicting it was a considerable force even under the existing restricted
franchise.

X

There is little sign that the development of the Labour Party between
1910 and 1914 was much affected by the great wave of industrial
unrest and the upsurge of trade union membership in this period. On
the other hand dissatisfaction with the performance of Labour as a
parliamentary party can have played only a marginal role in the great
strike wave and the same was true of the much publicized activity of
syndicalists. There were clear economic causes for the steep rise in the
number of days lost through strikes from 1910 to 1914, especially in
1912, and for the greatly increased number of strikes, especially in
1913. Most of the available estimates about wage rates and the cost of
living agree that after 1900 real wages were either static or in some
years declining, though there were wide regional and industrial variations and the situation may in fact have improved again from 1912
onwards. There is no doubt that from 1910 onwards there was a
cyclical upturn and unemployment having been near 8 per cent in

1908 and 1909 dropped to 3 per cent or even lower. Thus after many years when rising prices were not always fully matched by a rise in money wages, a novel and distressing experience for many categories of workers, the dissatisfaction could express itself because the fear of unemployment was much reduced. Price inflation seems to have been, by historical standards, particularly rapid in 1911–12. There also seems to have been a decline in the proportion of the national income going to manual wage-earners: it declined from 42 per cent in 1890–6 to 36 per cent in 1910–13. Even if due allowance is made for the uncertainties surrounding historical statistics, they all lend plausibility to the thesis that the industrial unrest was due to accumulated economic grievances finding a chance to express themselves. There were also more intangible factors. The distance between the working man and his master was growing, but there was also more social mobility, developments which were not necessarily incompatible. The paternalist employer personally known to his men was becoming rarer; changes in technology and financial amalgamations were making for larger and more impersonal industrial units. The physical distance between working and middle classes was getting more marked, for in the great cities they were segregated into different areas. With better chances of moving up in the social scale, the disappointment of those who remained behind was more painful. The white-collar worker distanced himself from the manual worker, but he may well have contributed to the latter's rising expectations. There may have been another factor in these rising expectations: the conspicuous consumption of the Edwardian era, which through the popular press was brought to the attention of the masses. Sir George Askwith, who as the Government's Chief Industrial Commissioner was closely concerned with the industrial unrest, mentioned this factor specifically in his report to the cabinet in 1911.

For that proportion of the work force organized in unions, about two and a half million or 17 per cent of the total in 1910, a complex system of local, regional and national procedures for negotiating wages had grown up over a generation. In several industries, cotton weaving, cotton spinning, boots and shoes, engineering, building and shipbuilding there were national procedural arrangements for negotiating wages; within these, regional and local wage rates were negotiated which varied considerably and there was a growing tendency to elect shop stewards, particularly in engineering, at the level of the firm. In some industries, such as shipbuilding, there was a move towards national wage agreements. Conciliation and arbitration was well established in many industries and the Conciliation Act of 1896 provided machinery for registering industrial conciliation boards with the Board of Trade. It was under this Act that Askwith established his role as the government's industrial trouble-shooter. This complex industrial relations machinery was put under great strain by the economic pressures and forces of instability that were impinging upon the labour scene by 1910. Conservatives had long regarded the Labour Department of the Board of Trade as the mouthpiece of Fabian socialism, dedicated to protecting the unions and to punishing capitalism. The opposite complaint was heard from the Left: the department operated a system of social control, fostered false consciousness among workers and depressed the share of wages. In fact the Labour Department worked steadily for the recognition of unions and for improvements in the legal position. On the other hand it did not, before 1906, want to see union immunities extended, but merely the existing law more fairly interpreted. Officials in the department saw it as their function to make the economic system work more smoothly and to head off any drift towards socialism.

The first major outbreak of violence in the course of the wave of industrial unrest of the four pre-war years came in the South Wales coalfield in 1910. Here militancy had been on the increase for a long time. The whole area had in the later nineteenth century experienced a massive advance of industrialism and growth of population, based on coal, iron, railways, docks and shipping. Until the end of the century nonconformity and Lib–Labism kept economic and social tensions low. In the coalfield a sliding scale which linked wages to the selling price of coal operated, supervised by a joint committee of miners' and employers' representatives. The committee's vice-chairman was William Abraham, known as 'Mabon', later first President of the South Wales Miners' Federation. He symbolized the era of class partnership and Lib–Labism, but the great lock-out of 1898 in the coalfield marked the beginning of the end of that era. Combination and cartelization, spurred on by magnates like Sir William T. Lewis and D.A. Thomas, later Lord Rhondda, increased the gulf between owners and men; the sliding scale collapsed under the strain of high labour costs, low productivity and technological inefficiency. The miners led the growth of the ILP in South Wales and were an important factor in bringing about the affiliation of the Miners' Federation to the Labour Party in 1908. The implementation of the Eight-Hour Act added to the tensions. In the autumn of 1910 a big strike movement against D.A. Thomas's Cumbrian Combine caused intense bitterness in the Welsh valleys. During rioting at Tonypandy a man died from injuries sustained in hand-to-hand fighting with the local police. It was at this point that the Home Secretary, Winston Churchill, ordered troops into the district to assist the police. Tonypandy became, like Peterloo or Tolpuddle, part of working-class mythology and the odium of having sent the troops clouded Churchill's reputation in some quarters for the remainder of his political life. The strikes against the Cumbrian Combine ended in defeat after 10 months, but produced the demand for a minimum wage, which became a focal issue in the national miners' strike of 1912.

South Wales and especially its mining communities was also an area where syndicalism made an impact. Several Welsh miners had gone to Ruskin College, which had been founded at Oxford in 1899 to provide opportunities of higher education for working-class men, and had become involved in the strike that disrupted the college in 1909. The issue was the role of education in mobilizing the working class; the dissident element at Oxford felt that Ruskin, by providing a traditional education, was propping up the existing social order. Out of the Ruskin disruption there arose the Central Labour College and the Plebs League, both of which gained much influence in South Wales, and through these organizations syndicalist ideas had a wide currency. The home of syndicalism was France and the central idea of the movement was to put economic or 'direct' action in place of the political action of the proletariat postulated by Marx. George Sorel, influenced by Henri Bergson's philosophical emphasis on the instinctual and the subconscious, saw the strike weapon and in particular the general strike as the means of producing revolutionary consciousness and the overthrow of the established order. British syndicalists were more influenced by American than by French ideas. In the United States the stress was on the creation of powerful industrial unions to oppose the growing concentration of capital through trusts and monopolies. In America the call was for centralization, whereas the French *syndicat* was to be close to the rank and file through localization. The time was judged to be ripe for another push in Britain towards the consolidation of great industrial unions, in place of the fragmented craft unions based on differentials of skill. In South Wales syndicalist ideas found their clearest expression in a document called *The Miners' Next Step* published early in 1912. This called for workers' control to be achieved by an escalating series of strikes. The workers were to be organized into one great general union to be democratically controlled by the rank and file and this would become the basis for a new social order with communal ownership for the benefit of the workers and their families. More immediate was the demand for a minimum wage of 8s a day. Even at the height of the national miners' strike over the minimum wage in 1912 the syndicalist movement in South Wales did not have the field to itself, and some of the younger leaders turned away from its anarchic tendencies and back towards political action and nationalization. After 1912 organizations like the Plebs League declined and the South Wales Miners'

Federation reverted firmly to moderate control. Even in a stronghold like South Wales the influence of syndicalism and its millenarian vision of society was always limited; nonconformism, liberalism and orthodox labourism were always at least equally strong and industrial militancy rose and fell according to economic circumstances.

Elsewhere individual activists were influenced by syndicalist ideas, for example Tom Mann, who had first come into prominence in the dock strike of 1889 and who had also involved himself in the industrial unrest in South Wales. The National Transport Workers' Federation which he founded in 1910 included dockers and seamen and through it he hoped to recapture something of the dynamic spirit that had prevailed in the trade union world 20 years earlier. In Ireland the Labour movement was just beginning to flex its muscles and unionization was spreading beyond the conservative craft unions to the unskilled. The two outstanding leaders of Irish labour, James Connolly and James Larkin, were both influenced by syndicalism, in particular the latter. The Irish Transport and General Workers Union which Larkin founded in 1908 was the kind of industrial union American syndicalists believed in. In the years from 1911 to 1914 Ireland shared fully in the industrial unrest that was sweeping the other parts of the kingdom. The climax came with the great wave of transport strikes organized by Larkin in Dublin in 1913. British trade unions showed support and solidarity and sent supplies of food to Dublin, but in the end the relentless militancy of Larkin alienated the more cautious officials of the TUC. Sympathetic strikes which Larkin tried to foment as a prelude to a general strike were seen by the Parliamentary Committee of the TUC as a senseless dissipation of effort. Thus syndicalism and 'direct action' in their various guises remained the creed of a minority of activists as several votes of the annual meetings of the TUC showed, but it had considerable impact on the course of events.

Tom Mann and his National Transport Workers' Federation had a hand in the great dockers', seamen's and railwaymen's strikes of 1911, but the central issue in these disputes was the long-standing problem of recognition of the unions by the employers. The unrest started with the seamen, who held up the new liner *Olympic* at Southampton, spread to dockers at many ports and finally involved the railways. The militancy of the rank and file took the union leaders by surprise; they had difficulty in staying in control of the situation and sometimes in getting the men to accept the agreements they had negotiated. There was again a certain amount of rioting, looting, use of troops and some bloodshed. The Shipping Federation was forced to recognize the Sailors' Union, led by Havelock Wilson, and to grant better wages and conditions. The dockers also secured considerable advances, but these proved to be inconclusive; in the following year, 1912, there was renewed conflict in London, where the Port of London Authority was now operating. When the National Transport Workers' Federation tried to turn the London dock strike into a national strike it failed and thereafter it declined. The London dock strike collapsed and the bulk of the labour in the docks continued to be hired on a casual basis.

The railways became the most important scene of industrial conflict in 1911. The settlement which Lloyd George had negotiated in 1907 to such wide acclaim proved ephemeral and the complicated scheme of conciliation boards then established in the industry did not satisfy the workers. When events were again moving towards a general railway strike in August 1911 the government had once more to intervene at the highest level. By this time political intervention entered into the calculations of both parties to the dispute and did not therefore make the task of finding a solution necessarily any easier. Moreover, opinion within the cabinet was now divided between those who were still prepared to pay a high price for conciliation, among whom Lloyd George remained the most influential, and others who wanted a firmer line against the unions. Asquith offered the unions a royal commission to inquire into their complaints, but he did so in a 'take it or leave it' manner and when they rejected his proposals, he left the room murmuring 'then your blood be on your own head'. It was again left to Lloyd George to use his formidable arts of persuasion and cajolery on both sides; this time he appealed to their patriotism by painting in lurid colours the danger of immediate war between France and Germany arising from the Moroccan crisis. The strike was called off after four days and for all practical purposes the unions got what they had long sought, recognition. Their membership rose from 116,000 in 1911 to 337,000 in 1914 and they became, along with the miners, the most powerful element in the trade union movement. Moreover, they went some way to achieving the establishment of an industrial union: in 1913, the National Union of Railwaymen was formed out of the Amalgamated Society of Railway Servants, the General Railway Workers' Union and the United Signalmen and Pointsmen's Society. The Amalgamated Society of Locomotive Engineers and Firemen (ASLEF) and the Railway Clerks continued, however, to preserve their independence jealously.

The most serious of the strikes that faced the Liberal government was the coal strike of 1912. The issue at stake was essentially the same as had brought the South Wales coalfield to a standstill in 1910, payment for working difficult seams, so-called 'abnormal places'. The Miners' Federation had received authority for strike action through a ballot of their members, on the proposal to enforce a minimum wage of 5s for adults and 2s boys. The strike over the '5 and 2' was called for 1 March 1912. Once again the government had to intervene, initially through Askwith, and then at ministerial level, with Lloyd George, Grey and Sydney Buxton accompanying the Prime Minister. After the strike had gone on for a fortnight Asquith told both sides that the government was now prepared to legislate that a statutory minimum wage should be enforceable, its level to be fixed locally by District Boards, on which employers and men would be equally represented, with a neutral chairman. This still did not satisfy the miners, who wanted the '5 and 2' specified in the bill. Lloyd George argued strongly in cabinet that this should be done, but the view prevailed that it was not Parliament's business to settle wages. The Miners' Federation again ballotted their members on the Minimum Wages Act, and although the verdict was in favour of continuing the strike it fell short of the two-thirds majority required to call a strike and the dispute was therefore called off, 'the greatest industrial strike in modern history', as some called it.

In 1913 the number of days lost in stoppages dropped back to less than a quarter of what it had been in 1912 and was on a slightly lower level than it had been in 1910 and 1911. There was no great national strike, but the number of strikes was the highest in any year before 1914 and the increase in trade union membership the biggest of that period. The growth in union membership owed something to the fact that the national insurance scheme, with the unions acting so widely as approved societies, was now fully operational. The final phase in the development of the trade union movement came in 1914 with the proposal for a Triple Alliance of miners, railwaymen and the National Transport Workers' Federation. Each of these unions had shown that they could inflict serious economic damage and compel government intervention. It had also been demonstrated that they could not escape a considerable degree of interdependence; the coal strike of 1912 had cost the railway union £94,000 for compensation to laid-off members. The main proposal for co-ordination was that the three unions should arrange to terminate their contracts at the same time. On the face of it this looked like a big step towards the syndicalist idea of a general strike. In fact the proposed alliance was much more a move by the established union leaders to pre-empt uncontrolled action from below. The tensions in the trade union movement which had just been fanned again by the contrasted reactions of militants and moderates to the Dublin transport strike showed men like Robert Smillie, of the miners, J.H. Thomas, of the railwaymen and Havelock Wilson, of the seamen, how important it was to maintain control and discipline. Difficulties about the precise terms of the alliance meant that it did not come into effect until

December 1915, by which time the war prevented it from operating in practice.

Between 1910 and 1914 trade union membership had increased from 2.5 to over 4 million and this was to form merely a base for the remarkable further expansion during the war years. Proportionately the biggest expansion was scored by the Workers' Union, a general union of men and women, whose numbers rose from 4,500 in 1910 to nearly 150,000 in 1914. The upsurge of unionization had much in common with the movement of the late 1880s, but this time it proved more permanent. In the long run the political impact of these developments was bound to be profound, but for the moment it was inconclusive. The government had been forced in a piecemeal fashion to become more and more deeply involved in industrial disputes until it had been compelled to legislate on wage rates. In the cabinet and in the Liberal Party opinion fluctuated between trying to maintain or revert to an attitude of detachment from industrial disputes and adopting a policy of enforcing 'a national minimum' across the board. In October 1911 the government set up an Industrial Council, with 12 representatives from each side of industry, under the chairmanship of Askwith. This council considered various possibilities of conciliation and arbitration and investigated the position abroad, particularly in Canada and New Zealand. Its report, issued in July 1913, favoured the existing system of voluntary agreements reached through free collective bargaining. On the employers' side there were separate memoranda proposing amendments or even repeal of the Trades Disputes Act of 1906 and the National Insurance Act of 1911, both of which were considered to have imposed serious disadvantages and burdens on British industry. By the time this report appeared the immediate pressure for action had slackened and the government lost interest in the Industrial Council.

The other two political parties found it equally difficult to come to grips with the problem of labour unrest. Among Conservatives the view was widely held that something ought to be done to limit the power of trade unions, grown inordinate through Liberal legislation like the Trades Disputes Act of 1906. Others in the Party were groping for an approach more positive than confrontation with the unions, either through more social reform or even through schemes like co-partnership or profit sharing. Tariff reformers like F.E. Smith and Austen Chamberlain wanted a combination of social reform and tougher laws on picketing and enforceability of contracts. In practice Bonar Law adopted a low profile on industrial unrest, restrained by the same considerations that had led the House of Lords to allow the passage of the Trades Disputes Act. As long as the Tories were in opposition there was no need to come out with a clear policy.

The Labour Party's difficulties in balancing between moderates and extremists were much exacerbated by the industrial unrest. To militants and syndicalists the existence of the party was itself an affront. Ben Tillett wrote of the events of 1912 '. . . Cossack methods of the Home Office forces, Parliament dumb and acquiescent, Labour Party impotent where not indifferent . . . The other lesson is that Parliament is a farce and a sham, the rich man's Duma, the employer's Tammany, the Thieves' Kitchen, and the working man's despot'. MacDonald, Henderson and other parliamentary leaders had to act as spokesmen of the labour interest in the House of Commons and did so in the great rail and coal strikes of 1911 and 1912. MacDonald was, however, also taking a leading role in the efforts at conciliation, particularly on the railways. He was just as contemptuous of the militants and syndicalists in the unions as he was of the 'impossibilists' on the political side of the movement. When troops clashed with striking workers, many trade unionists were equally contemptuous of MacDonald's role as honest broker. Even trade union leaders and officials who played a part in the incipient corporatism of the period, for example on the Industrial Council, or by accepting paid positions under the Board of Trade's Labour Department or in the National Insurance machinery, came in for a great deal of abuse. While in the long run the great expansion of trade unionism could not but enhance the potential for a political party of labour, for the moment the Labour Party could not profit from it politically.

The last phase in the evolution of Liberal social policy before the war came with the opening of Lloyd George's land campaign and the Budget of 1914. The land valuation arising from the People's Budget was still in progress and would not be completed until 1915. In the meantime the single-taxers and land nationalizers remained influential in the Liberal Party. There was a link between the concern about unemployment and a national minimum on the one hand and the land question on the other. Agricultural wages were still very low and any extension of the minimum wage principle would certainly have had to cover agriculture. If through better wages and a better utilization of land the drift into urban areas could have been halted or reversed, then the pool of urban unemployed which weakened the market for labour would have been reduced. In urban areas the problem of land values was vital in connection with taxation, housing and industrial development. In October 1913 a Land Enquiry instituted by the cabinet confirmed that low wages and poor housing were the most pressing rural problems. Lloyd George now opened his land campaign, with a promise of a Ministry of Lands and Forests responsible for land valuation, small-holdings, land purchase and the development of land-based industries. It would through land commissioners supervise questions of fair rents, tenure and a minimum income for landowners, farmers and labourers. An additional 120,000 cottages would be provided. This campaign rekindled some of the enthusiasm of Liberal Radicals, who had become unsure of their cause when national insurance encountered so much opposition and unpopularity among those whom it was intended to benefit. Lloyd George's campaign was well received in rural areas and brought the Liberals some support from traditionally Conservative farmers. The successful Liberal in the Hanley by-election, R.L. Outhwaite, was a strong land reformer and so was E.G. Hemmerde who won Northwest Norfolk. The land campaign had less impact in urban areas, but a second report of the Land Enquiry, published in April 1914 and concentrating on urban land problems, showed that again housing and low wages were crucial problems in urban areas and that rating reform was vital.

Many of these proposals and promises were dealt with in the Budget of 1914, in intention a worthy successor to the 1909 budget. Lloyd George proposed the rating of site-values, though he did not recommend a national land tax. The graduated income tax on higher earned incomes was to be increased and supertax was to start at £3,000 instead of £5,000. Death duties were also more steeply graduated. It was another powerful bid for radical support in preparation for the next election, but it seems doubtful if, even apart from slipshod preparation and parliamentary mismanagement, it could have matched the 1909 budget in saving the Liberals from defeat.

XI

The labour unrest of the pre-war years was felt to be a social phenomenon of deep significance, perhaps part of a broader international movement that might end in revolution but in its British form it lay beyond the area with which politics and politicians had traditionally concerned themselves. The campaign for female suffrage, by contrast, had a political aim of a traditional kind for which a well-tried remedy, franchise extension, was in theory available. It was the outward and visible sign of a social movement at least as profound in importance as the stirrings of the working class, but its immediate manifestations were much shallower and it therefore proved easier to resist. The pressure for women's votes had never completely subsided since John Stuart Mill moved his female suffrage amendment to the Reform Bill of 1867, but both in its slow-burning constitutional form in the nineteenth century and in its spectacular militant form in the decade before 1914 it remained predominantly a middle-class movement. Its support was thus limited, and its progress was made particularly difficult by the fact that votes for women could never be a straight party question. Its natural supporters were Liberals, but the practical problem facing the Liberal government before 1914 was that the enfranchisement of women on the same terms then existing for men would give the vote mainly to Tory supporters. In the Conservative Party leaders like Disraeli, Northcote, Salisbury and Balfour were in favour of women's suffrage, but most Tory MPs were opposed.

From 1869 women who were ratepayers and householders could vote in municipal elections, but married women were disqualified, because their property was deemed to be represented by their husbands. Legally this was called 'coverture', but the concept was weakened by the legislation enabling women to hold property independently of their spouses, most clearly by the Married Women's Property Act of 1882. By this time the suffragists, as the supporters of women's suffrage were generally called, had split over the tactical question whether to accept 'coverture' for the time being and press for the vote for unmarried women only, or whether to go all-out for putting women on an equal footing with men for the parliamentary franchise. All too frequently support for broader objectives of political emancipation would be used to relegate the women's demands and it was this attitude in men that enraged the militants before 1914. The Reform Bill of 1884 revived interest in female parliamentary suffrage, but Gladstone was opposed, declaring that the extension of the male franchise was 'a cargo as large as she can safely carry'. The enfranchisement of so many more men was, however, bound to highlight the anomaly of excluding all women from the parliamentary franchise. Developments in local government further emphasized the anomaly: suitably qualified women could vote under the County Councils Act of 1888 and married women were admitted to the vote and became eligible for election under the Parish Councils Act of 1894. Nevertheless the campaign for the parliamentary vote languished and it required the arrival of the Pankhursts to propel 'votes of women' into real prominence.

Mrs Emmeline Pankhurst and her two daughters Christabel and Sylvia were the principal leaders of the suffragettes, a term first used by the *Daily Mail* in 1906 to describe militant suffragists. Mrs Pankhurst and her husband were supporters of advanced causes and of the ILP in London and Manchester in the 1880s and 1890s. A few years after her husband's death in 1898 Mrs Pankhurst renewed her activities in the ILP in Manchester, while her young daughter Christabel worked in the North of England Society for Women's Suffrage. Labour and women's politics came together when mounting unemployment hit the female workforce in the Lancashire cotton mills in 1903. Mrs Pankhurst and her daughter founded a small group to promote political and social work for working-class women and they called it 'The Women's Social and Political Union'. In its early days the group devoted its efforts mainly to converting ILP branches to the cause of women's suffrage. The party was sympathetic, but many of its members, including influential figures like Philip Snowden, saw women's suffrage as merely one item in a general move towards adult suffrage. The WSPU on the other hand wanted the ILP to give priority to the enfranchisement of women on the existing franchise. In 1905 a private member's bill to extend the existing franchise to women was introduced; it was originally Keir Hardie's bill and the Labour leader and Mrs Pankhurst had worked together to get it launched. At this stage the WSPU was still closely associated with the ILP and was not yet clearly distinct from the National Union of Women's Suffrage Societies which had been founded in 1897 to coordinate the many existing organizations.

A new phase opened with the election of 1905. On the eve of it Christabel Pankhurst and Annie Kenney, the Lancashire mill girl who had become her faithful follower, interrupted a meeting of Sir Edward Grey in the Free Trade Hall. They were evicted, fined for assaulting a policeman and on refusing to pay the fine, imprisoned for a few days. It immediately put the WSPU in the public eye and it began to grow rapidly. For the rest of the election campaign there were no further imprisonments, but most of the principal Liberal leaders had their meetings interrupted by heckling, unfurling of banners and evictions. After the election Christabel Pankhurst moved to London and Emmeline soon followed her. The WSPU gradually detached itself from its links with the ILP and from its professed aim to work on behalf of working-class women. It ceased to support Labour at by-elections and no longer relied so much on women from the East End for its many demonstrations and marches in London. Increasingly support came from middle and upper-class women. By 1907 the annual income was over £7,000 and at a great demonstration in Hyde Park in June 1908 there were estimated to be 250,000 to 500,000 present, though many of them had come from curiosity rather than to express support. In the meantime the Pethick-Lawrences had joined the Pankhursts at the head of the movement. F.W. Lawrence was a wealthy lawyer, educated at Eton and

Cambridge, who had joined his name to his wife's maiden name on marriage; Emmeline Pethick, educated at a Quaker boarding school, was strongly committed to fighting social injustice. The Pankhursts and the Pethick-Lawrences ruled the movement like autocrats and abandoned any pretence of democracy; those who did not agree with them had to get out.

The growing size of the WSPU and the large demonstrations it managed to stage failed to move the government. Arrests, imprisonment followed by release ossified into a kind of ritual and no longer moved the public. An escalation of violence, born of frustration, followed: window-smashing and other attacks on property, imprisonment, hunger-striking and force-feeding. Liberal ministers were constant targets during the election campaign in the autumn of 1909: Churchill was horse-whipped by a lady as he got out of a railway carriage in Bristol and there were fears that Asquith might be shot at. Immediately after the election the WSPU declared a truce; it was partly the product of a realization that moderate militancy, which had imposed considerable suffering on WSPU activists, could achieve no more, partly an attempt to allow a compromise with the government to be worked out. This took the form of a Conciliation Bill, which broadly would have given the vote to women with a householder or occupation qualification and would have enfranchised about a million women, one in 13. It was drafted by an all-party committee and it was hoped that it would command wide parliamentary support. It soon became apparent, however, that Asquith was determined not to allow it beyond its second reading, which it passed by a vote of 299 to 189; Churchill and Lloyd George voted against it because they objected to the advantage which the enfranchisement of propertied women would give to the Tories. The Prime Minister's stubborn opposition to women's suffrage now became a major factor in the situation. Initially Asquith's opposition had not gone beyond a certain agnosticism, a feeling that female suffrage was unlikely to improve the quality of political life and was in any case a matter of small importance. As with many men and women, the militancy and fanaticism of the suffragettes steeled his determination not to give way to what he regarded as hysteria and unreason.

When the WSPU saw its hopes of the Conciliation Bill disappointed they broke their truce with a big demonstration on the reassembly of Parliament in November 1910. Some of the most violent scenes so far occurred on this 'Black Friday', when hundreds of police and women fought it out for hours outside the House of Commons in front of a large crowd of spectators. A few days later similar scenes occurred in Downing Street; Asquith was with difficulty spirited away in a taxi and Birrell twisted his knee. After these violent incidents the truce was resumed as the suffragists and suffragettes waited to see what would happen to their cause in the next Parliament. Asquith promised that the government would provide facilities for a new Conciliation Bill, but he carefully avoided committing himself to doing it in the next session.

The women's cause now became more than ever enmeshed in the highly complex and tense general political situation. Until the passage of the Parliament Bill in August 1911 the issue of the House of Lords dominated all political considerations and a measure like the Conciliation Bill, which in spite of all-party support also faced much opposition, had hardly any chance of passing. Once the Parliament Act was on the statute book other measures requiring to be passed under its three-session procedure, notably Home Rule, would have to have priority. Liberal and Labour objections to the limited enfranchisement envisaged in the Conciliation Bill remained; on the other hand a general Franchise Reform Bill including female suffrage would, as soon as announced, torpedo the Conciliation Bill and it would also, along with a Redistribution Bill, have to be passed under the three-sessions procedure.

The announcement by Asquith in November 1911 that the government would in the next session introduce a Franchise Bill put an end to the truce declared by the WSPU and ushered in the years of most violent militancy. The object of the Franchise Bill was to realize more nearly the 'one man, one vote' principle. It was obvious that the Conciliation Bill was now likely to fail. The government's declaration that the Franchise Bill would be so drafted that it could be amended to enfranchise women was felt to be a sham, for such an amendment had little chance of passing. In March 1912 a new Conciliation Bill was refused a second reading by a majority of 14 votes, as against the previous majority of 167 in favour of the Conciliation Bill of 1911. The growing militancy of the suffragettes may well have alienated some former supporters and contributed to the defeat. When the time came in January 1913 for the committee stage of the Franchise Bill the Speaker of the House made a surprise ruling that an amendment in favour of female suffrage was out of order. This was effectively the end of efforts to enact votes for women before 1914. The Franchise Bill was withdrawn and a more simple Plural Voting Bill, such as had been launched seven years earlier and defeated in the Lords, was substituted. This suited the electoral needs of the Liberal Party much better. Among plural voters the Conservatives had a three to one preponderance and the removal of this advantage would, according to some prognostications, give the Liberals another 30 seats.

Frustration and increasing use of violence caused tensions within the suffragette movement. In March 1912 Christabel Pankhurst fled to Paris to escape arrest at a time when her mother and other leaders of the movement were facing imprisonment. She continued to play a dominant role from afar, particularly at times when her mother was incapacitated by imprisonment and the after-effects of hunger strikes. In October 1912 the Pethick-Lawrences were unceremoniously expelled from the WSPU by Mrs Pankhurst. In order not to damage the movement to which they had devoted their best efforts for years they did not make public their differences with the Pankhursts. The Pethick-Lawrences believed in educating the public; the Pankhursts now placed their faith in dangerously escalated violence as a means of extorting female suffrage from a reluctant public.

A less dramatic divergence had in the meantime occurred within the Pankhurst family itself. Sylvia Pankhurst had remained true to the original purpose of the WSPU and was working in the East End of London among working-class women and in close association with local Labour supporters. The spotlight fell on her when George Lansbury, one of the most determined supporters of female suffrage in the Commons, resigned his seat at Bromley and Bow to fight a by-election expressly on women's suffrage. He was prompted by the refusal of his colleagues in the parliamentary Labour Party to put the government's survival at risk for the sake of women's suffrage. The by-election showed up some of the cross-currents to which the women's cause was now subjected. Sylvia Pankhurst did not see eye to eye with the organizer sent down from national WSPU head-quarters, who in her turn found it difficult to co-operate with the local Labour agent. Labour supporters regarded the WSPU as a middle-class organization committed to 'votes for ladies'. George Lansbury was an attractive candidate who had every expectation of holding the seat which he had gratuitously given up, yet he lost by nearly 10 per cent of the vote. This fiasco helped to convince the national WSPU that acts of violence, designed to frighten the public and the government into giving way, were now the correct tactic.

The final phase of the WSPU's pre-war campaign therefore took the form of a prolonged campaign of arson. The inevitable prison sentences and hunger strikes which ensued forced the government in April 1913 to rush through the Prisoners' Temporary Discharge for Ill-Health Bill, nicknamed the Cat and Mouse Act, which enabled it to release and rearrest hunger strikers. One of the more bizarre incidents occurred in June 1913, when Emily Wilding Davison threw herself in front of the King's horse at the Derby and died five days later. There was growing public hostility to the suffragettes and the WSPU became increasingly isolated from the rest of the suffrage movement. The National Union of Women's Suffrage Societies remained an important and influential body throughout the period.

Its president was Mrs Millicent Fawcett, the widow of Henry Fawcett, the Radical MP and Postmaster General in Gladstone's second cabinet. Mrs Fawcett was involved in the suffrage movement almost from its inception to its final success in 1918. She believed by 1913 that the WSPU had become a more serious obstacle to success than the anti-suffragists in the cabinet. A paranoid, anti-male mood was now prevalent in the WSPU. In 1913 Christabel Pankhurst published *The Great Scourge and How to End It* in which she contrasted the purity of womanhood with man as the polluter and carrier of venereal disease. Hostility to marriage and suggestions of lesbianism could only give substance to the impression of sexual perversion which their less delicate opponents had always sought to pin on the suffragettes.

There was thus little inducement for the Liberals to break the parliamentary stalemate on women's suffrage and it became the line of less resistance to endure the pinpricks of arson and violence. It is doubtful whether it was entirely wise. It amounted to a failure to capitalize on an issue which had a wide progressive appeal; though suffragists and suffragettes in their turn failed to align themselves clearly with the Liberals behind adult suffrage and never hesitated to embarrass those who should have been their allies. The government's inaction, however, reflected the attitude of the majority, for there was a great deal of opposition to women's suffrage among men and women of reasonable middle-of-the-road views. Before 1914 the role differentiation between the sexes remained very marked and it was not unreasonable to believe that nature had allotted separate spheres to men and women. It was taken for granted that women suffered from many physical weaknesses, and taboos embroidered by old wives' tales surrounded such phenomena as menstruation and the menopause, which were thought to disturb the female mental balance. It was thus not difficult to link anti-suffragism with soundness of view and judgement; the more extreme antics of the militant suffragettes highlighted the reasonableness of their opponents. The ridicule which began to adhere to anti-suffragism after the Great War was not discernible before 1914. The main weight of opposition to women's votes was on the Right, but it was not rare on the Left. Among Tory politicians Curzon, F.E. Smith and Lord Cromer were leading and vocal anti-suffragists; in the cabinet Lewis Harcourt, the Colonial Secretary, was the strongest opponent of female suffrage, but in addition to Asquith, Loreburn and McKenna were also hostile. A number of notable women were anti-suffragists, among them Octavia Hill, Mrs Humphry Ward, Gertrude Bell and Violet Markham. A Women's National Anti-Suffrage League was founded in 1908; it later combined with a male anti-suffrage committee to become the National League for Opposing Women's Suffrage, led by

Cromer and Curzon. It had considerable support and financial resources, though nothing like the degree of commitment enjoyed by the WSPU. The organizers and contributors were mostly rich and titled, yet it evoked some echo among the general public and drew on natural working-class male chauvinism and suspicion of middle-class do-gooders. Thus the demands of suffragists and threats of suffragettes were counterbalanced by the more diffuse presence of anti-suffragism and this issue was, like labour unrest and Ireland, left unresolved before the war broke out.

XII

The Unionist revolt over Irish Home Rule was third of the three rebellions which in the years 1911 to 1914 presaged according to George Dangerfield 'The Strange Death of Liberal England'. Home Rule and Ulster were undoubtedly the most intractable of the three from a political and constitutional point of view, but it was also the one of least concern to the English and even to the Scottish and Welsh electorates. There is an air of unreality about the hypothesis that but for the outbreak of world war the country might have been plunged into civil war over Ireland. The attitude of the Conservatives in threatening to give all-out support to Ulster's defiance of Home Rule has come in for even harsher criticism than their earlier policy of using the House of Lords to destroy the budget of 1909, but this view is also difficult to sustain. To even moderate Unionists it seemed that the Liberals had used Irish votes, in any case grossly overrepresented, to tamper with the constitution by passing the Parliament Act and were then forced to honour their part of a corrupt bargain by implementing Home Rule, an old, discredited and destructive policy, which had never been approved by the British electorate. This policy meant coercing a quarter of the population of the island of Ireland into giving up their British allegiance, a procedure which was clearly unrealistic. In these circumstances, so most Unionists felt, they could only back up Ulster's resistance.

There were admittedly many in the Unionist Party who were less concerned about Ulster and more about using it to stop Home Rule altogether. Lansdowne, with his great southern Irish estates, and the Cecil family, who had little sympathy for the bigoted Presbyterians of the northeast, were among them. For Lansdowne Unionism in the south was at least as important as Ulster. Bonar Law on the other hand, whose own roots lay in Ulster, was in the last resort prepared to accept Home Rule, provided Ulster, suitably defined, was excluded. Unionists of all shades believed that if Home Rule was clearly submitted to the British electorate, as it never had been, then the result would be a resounding Unionist victory. In the later stages of the crisis, as the Home Rule Bill neared the statute book, it became the main aim of the Unionist leaders to precipitate a general election, if necessary through the King's veto on the bill or his dismissal of his ministers. The relentless passion with which the Unionists opposed Home Rule owed something to the fact that they hoped thereby to expunge the humiliation suffered over the Lords' veto and to avoid a fourth successive general election defeat; also to the continuing difficulties in the party over tariff reform and the failure of any other coherent policies to emerge for the social and economic tensions of the age.

As for the Liberals, the cabinet began to consider at an early stage the exclusion of Ulster from a Home Rule settlement, but the restraining factor in pursuing this line was that it would undermine the position of Redmond and the parliamentary Nationalists in Ireland. As the crisis proceeded, the view that Ulster must be offered some separate deal gained ground and influential ministers like Lloyd George and above all Churchill shared it. On the other hand the violence and, as many Liberals saw it, extra-constitutional character of Unionist opposition to Home Rule, increased Liberal determination to see it through. On this even those in Labour politics who had otherwise lost their faith in the Progressive Alliance were mostly with the Liberals. Nevertheless, among all the uncompromising protagonists Asquith faced over Ireland Redmond was the man in the weakest position and his threat to defeat the Liberal government if he did not get a united Ireland was not much more than bluff. It was therefore always likely that the crisis would ultimately be settled at the expense of constitutional nationalism.

Well before the passage of the Parliament Act removed the legal barrier to Home Rule Ulster was girding its loins to resist. The fierce reactions to Wyndham's devolution proposals of 1905 had shown how sensitive Ulster Unionists were to anything that could be construed as tampering with the British connection. In the next few years closer ties were established between Ulster Unionism and Unionists in the rest of Ireland. In the south the supporters of the Union were in a much weaker situation; physical resistance was out of the question and a succession of Land Purchase Acts had, against compensation, reduced the position of the Anglo-Irish landlords to a shadow of what it once was. Nevertheless members of this Anglo-Irish ascendancy still enjoyed an influence in the British Unionist Party much more considerable than that of the Ulstermen. Sir Edward Carson, the saturnine Dublin lawyer, personified the co-operation of Irish and Ulster Unionism. He sat from 1892 as member for Dublin University; his election in 1910 as leader of the Irish Unionist group at Westminister, nearly all of whom came from Ulster, gave the anti-Home Rule cause a powerful fillip and Ulster a charismatic leader. He was one of those committed to the strategy of using Ulster to frustrate Home Rule altogether, though as he realized that this position was not fully shared by the Ulstermen nor fully backed by the southern Unionists, he modified it and was prepared to agree to a Home Rule settlement excluding Ulster. Shortly after the passage of the Parliament Act Carson addressed the first great demonstration on Ulster at which he warned that 'we must be prepared . . . the morning Home Rule passes ourselves to become responsible for the government of the Protestant province of Ulster.' The demonstration was held at Craigavon, the home of James Craig, who, behind Carson, became the great organizer of Ulster resistance to Home Rule. Steps were taken to set up a Provisional Government to take charge after the passage of a Home Rule Bill. Military drill was undertaken by Orange Lodges and Unionist Clubs and this led in January 1913 to the embodiment, by the Ulster Unionist Council, of an Ulster Volunteer Force limited to 100,000 men. In September 1912 another huge and emotional demonstration led by Curzon initiated the signing of a Solemn League and Covenant. The 471,000 men and women who eventually signed it pledged themselves to refuse the authority of a Home Rule Parliament if it was forced upon them.

In the meantime the third Home Rule Bill was introduced in April 1912, to go on the first of its three tours through Parliament. Like that of 1893 it proposed to retain a proportion of Irish members at Westminster in recognition of the fact that certain matters, defence, foreign affairs, the Royal Irish Constabulary for six years and above all control of the revenue, would still be reserved to the Imperial Parliament. Thus fears would be allayed that Ireland might be taken out of the British free trade market. It was in itself a very modest measure of self-government, but neither Redmond nor the opponents of Home Rule regarded it as more than a staging post to full separation and independence and therefore the limited nature of the bill in no way mitigated the fierceness of the battle. Bonar Law in opposing the bill asked 'do hon. Members believe that any Prime Minister could give orders to shoot down men whose only crime is that they refuse to be driven out of our community and deprived of the privilege of British citizenship?' Three months later, at a great Unionist demonstration at Blenheim he gave the pledge which has been so often criticized '. . . if an attempt were made to deprive these men of their birthright – as part of a corrupt Parliamentary bargain . . . I can imagine no length of resistance to which Ulster can go in which I should not be prepared to support them . . .'. Asquith called this a 'reckless rodomontade' which 'furnishes for the future a complete grammar of anarchy'. Parliamentary bitterness reached its peak during the first passage of the bill when Asquith announced the government's intention to reverse a defeat it had suffered on a snap division. The House had to be adjourned in disorder amid cries of 'traitor' and 'civil war'; Churchill, taunted with shouts of 'rat', waved his handkerchief at the opposition and had a book thrown at him. The Home Rule Bill completed its passage through the Commons the first time in January 1913 and was then rejected by the Lords. The second passage through the Commons and rejection by the Lords took place during the parliamentary session which lasted from March to August 1913.

The long-drawn out time-table imposed upon the Irish crisis by the requirements of the Parliament Act meant that both the forces of intransigence and of compromise could progressively muster their strengths while reserving their ultimate efforts for the final encounter. It also meant that attention was often distracted by the other great crises at home and abroad, for instance the labour unrest in 1912 and the Balkan wars in 1912 and 1913. Simultaneously with the Home Rule Bill the Liberal government was honouring another long-standing promise to its supporters on the Celtic fringe by passing the Welsh Church Disestablishment Bill under the procedure of the Parliament Act. It was no longer a matter that generated much passion in Wales or at Westminster, though it added to the sense of beleaguerment the Unionists felt since they had lost the Lords' veto. They were also afflicted by renewed dissensions in the party over tariff reform, which looked for a moment like bringing Bonar Law's leadership to a premature end. He was a strong supporter of tariff reform, believing like so many, that it was the only way of getting politics shifted from the intensifying preoccupation with wealth distribution and the class struggle 'on to other lines'. It was Canada's conclusion of a Reciprocity agreement with the USA early in 1911 that furnished tariff reformers with fresh ammunition. It was claimed that the failure to bring in imperial preference had driven the Canadians into America's arms. The shadow cabinet decided to return to the full tariff reform policy without a referendum and made its decision public in November 1912. The continuing opposition of the Unionist free traders, which had already been forcefully expressed in the inner councils of the party, now created an open furore. Lord Derby and the Lancashire Unionists threatened to support resolutions hostile to Bonar Law's line. It was at this point that the leader who had been elected only a year previously saw no option but to resign, and Lansdowne would have joined him. Law's and Lansdowne's resignation at the very moment when the first parliamentary climacteric of the Home Rule Bill was imminent would have been catastrophic for all the causes Conservatives held most dear. The two leaders were prevailed upon by an almost unanimous memorial of Unionist members to remain at their posts. Imperial preference remained the policy of the party, but without food taxes; yet without such taxes there was virtually nothing on offer for the Canadians or other members of the Empire. Tariff reform did not recover from this setback before 1914, but for most Conservatives the preservation of the Union and the defeat of the Liberals were more important.

While the Tories had their troubles over tariff reform, the Liberals were afflicted by the Marconi Scandal. Throughout 1912 there were rumours of corrupt dealings by ministers in Marconi shares. The ministers against whom accusing fingers pointed were Lloyd George, Rufus Isaacs, the Attorney-General, whose brother was also involved, Herbert Samuel, the Postmaster General and the Master of Elibank, the Liberal Chief Whip. Two Isaacs and one Samuel gave the affair distinct antisemitic overtones, especially in the comments of men like Chesterton and Belloc. The two ministers really at risk were Lloyd George and Rufus Isaacs. They had speculated in American, though not in British Marconi shares. What they did was not corrupt, but unwise and indiscreet. It was an even more serious error of judgement on their part that they gave a categorical denial to the Commons of any involvement with the British Marconi Company in October 1912, without ever mentioning their purchase of the American shares. In 1913 the Select Committee appointed to report on the affair divided on strict party lines and so did the House itself. This saved Lloyd George and Isaacs, who throughout their ordeal had been unequivocally supported by Asquith. Nevertheless the scandal weakened the authority of the government and strengthened the feeling among Unionists that in fighting such a crew almost anything was permissible.

In spite of the bitterness of the party battle there were also strong forces for compromise at work over Home Rule. In May 1912 Bonar Law had raised with the King, in characteristically blunt language, the possibility of a royal veto on Home Rule, or the dismissal of ministers, to bring about an election. It hardly endeared him to George V and from thence the King was hard at work to produce a compromise. George V was nevertheless considerably influenced by the Unionist view that the Parliament Act had created a new constitutional situation and that an issue like Home Rule could only be appropriately settled by an election and not by the automatic application of the procedure laid down in the Act. He took the threat of Ulster resistance seriously, and asked Asquith whether it was proposed 'to employ the army to suppress such disorders . . . will it be fair to the Sovereign as head of the army to subject the discipline, and indeed the loyalty of his troops, to such a strain . . .?' Already rumours were rife that many officers would prefer to resign their commissions rather than take part in the coercion of Ulster. The King nevertheless showed no disposition to step beyond a strict definition of his prerogative and Asquith pointed out that an election would hinge on many issues besides Home Rule and would therefore settle nothing, while failure to pass the Home Rule Bill might produce serious disorders in the South of Ireland.

Out of all these arguments and a succession of visits by political leaders from both parties to Balmoral in September there emerged the proposal of an inter-party conference to discuss a settlement, including the possibility of federal Home Rule throughout the United Kingdom, a solution frequently proposed since 1886. Both sides were, however, still too conscious of the restraints imposed upon them by their respective Irish allies to go into a full-scale conference. Instead there were three informal and secret meetings between Asquith and Bonar Law, at which the situation was discussed with remarkable frankness, but without achieving any substantive progress towards a settlement. Carson, who in private was much less intransigent than in public, was prepared to accept the exclusion of Ulster, but it would have to be the whole province of nine counties, including Cavan, Donegal and Monaghan with their Catholic majorities, and it would have to be in perpetuity. Redmond could not accept these conditions; the most the Prime Minister could offer was 'home rule within home rule' namely a fair degree of autonomy for Ulster under a Dublin Parliament.

In the meantime the situation was deteriorating in Ireland. The government was becoming aware that the preparations of the Ulster Volunteer Force were not bluff and that steps were being taken to import arms. All this provoked a counter-move in the south, the formation of the Irish Volunteers, the beginning of a development that was to lead to the Easter Rising and the end of the parliamentary Nationalist Party. The Irish Volunteers were quickly infiltrated by the Irish Republican Brotherhood. In the long run Ulster's resistance to Home Rule thus turned events towards the complete separation of Southern Ireland from the United Kingdom. In December 1913 royal proclamations banned the importation of arms and ammunition into Ireland. By early 1914, just before the Home Rule Bill was due to go on its third and final tour through Parliament, the possibility of civil war in Ireland, and possibly beyond, was more real than ever. The policy of the opposition of trying to force an election through the King was now no longer realistic, for George V had clearly decided against taking the advice gratuitously proffered from the Unionist side. At the same time the dangers of a split among Tories increased. On the one hand there were the diehards, many of them the same people who had fought in the last ditch over the Parliament Act. Milner was promoting a British Covenant under which the signatories pledged themselves to support 'any action that may be effective to prevent it (the Home Rule Bill) being put into operation, and more particularly to prevent the forces of the Crown being used to deprive the people of Ulster of their rights as citizens of the United Kingdom'. There were on the other hand also fears of the wider consequences if the Conservative Party too flagrantly espoused rebellion in Ulster and disobedience in the Armed Forces of the Crown. When Bonar Law and his colleagues considered the possibility of amending the Annual Army Act in such a way that the army could not be used to coerce Ulster until after a general election, Balfour cautioned Bonar Law 'that a certain number of our friends will call up visions of future labour troubles in this country, and will ask themselves whether some future Labour Ministry may not draw a perilous moral from the precedent which it is now proposed to set'. During the Balmoral talks Balfour had written '. . . I look with much misgiving upon the general loosening of the ordinary ties of social obligation . . . The behaviour of Suffragettes and Syndicalists are symptoms of this malady . . .'

The signs that the situation might soon drift into violence convinced Asquith and his friends that they would have to make further concessions. This meant putting pressure on Redmond. First he was persuaded to accept 'home rule within home rule', namely that Ulster would be granted a good deal of autonomy within the all-Ireland Parliament to be set up. He was then brought to accept the temporary exclusion of Ulster from the Home Rule Bill for three years, almost immediately lengthened to six years. Each Ulster county was to vote separately on this. It was a dangerous concession for Redmond to make, for it meant surrendering the principle of one Irish nation, but it was to a large extent a tactical move designed to throw the onus of rejection on the opposition. When Asquith announced the proposal in March in the House Carson immediately turned it down as a 'temporary stay of execution'. A week later, when the government had already initiated military moves around Ulster, Carson announced in a melodramatic gesture that he was leaving to join his compatriots in Belfast and it was widely thought that he would set up the long-planned Provisional Government, but he did not in fact do so.

The government's military measures at this juncture lacked clarity of purpose. On the face of it they were precautionary moves, designed to safeguard arms depots and lines of communication in Ulster, and to act as a deterrent to hotheads among the Ulster Volunteers. The cabinet had long been considering the arrest of the Ulster leaders as a possible option and rumours that such arrests were imminent now became more substantial. The military and naval moves were largely handled by Churchill and Jack Seely, the Secretary of State for War; both ministers were notable for pugnacity and flamboyance. Within days of Carson's rejection of the temporary exclusion proposals Churchill made a speech which was widely seen as a declaration of war on Ulster: he spoke of Carson and his associates as a 'self-elected body . . . engaged in a treasonable conspiracy' and declared that there were 'worse things than bloodshed even on an extended scale'.

A few days later there occurred the incident which has become known as the Mutiny at the Curragh. It arose when General Sir Arthur Paget, the Commander in Chief in Ireland, briefed his officers about the precautionary moves to be undertaken in Ulster. He had secured from Seely an instruction that officers whose homes were actually in the province of Ulster could apply for permission to be absent from duty during the period of operations, would be allowed to 'disappear' from Ireland, but would subsequently be reinstated. Paget painted the situation in such lurid colours, saying that he expected the country 'to be in a blaze by Saturday', that Brigadier Hubert Gough and 57 of his officers in the 3rd Cavalry Brigade took the option of dismissal rather than move north. An instruction that should never have been given had been badly mishandled. Asquith and his colleagues quickly realized that if they tried to discipline Gough and his officers further massive resignations would follow in the army and possibly the navy. Many officers had Ulster or Anglo-Irish ascendancy connections and even among those who did not there was overwhelming sympathy for the maintenance of the Union. Bonar Law was kept constantly informed of what was going on by Sir Henry Wilson, the Director of Military Operations, an Anglo-Irishman and the most inveterate of military intriguers. Field Marshal Lord Roberts, the most prestigious military figure of the time, was another Anglo-Irishman and violent opponent of Home Rule. To avoid a serious break-up of the army the reinstatement of Gough and his fellow-officers may well have been the only available course, but Seely added to the terms agreed by the cabinet further concessions which amounted virtually to a capitulation. Gough was given a document which in its final paragraph stated that the government had no intention 'to crush political opposition to the policy or principles of the Home Rule Bill'. He was able to return to Ireland in triumph and there was much bitterness among those officers who had remained loyal to the orders of the Government. It was a dangerous moment for the Asquith government, for there was outrage on the Left over the way ministers had condoned the unlawful conduct of these officers. Seely had to be sacrificed and Asquith personally assumed control of the War Office. A judicious and discreet show of force in Ulster might well have been advantageous, for Carson realized only too well that he had nothing to gain from a clash with the army nor from a civil war between Unionists and Nationalists. After the Curragh incident, however, the difficulties of coercing Ulster were only too obvious. A month later another incident, the gun-running at Larne by the Ulster Volunteers, further emphasized these difficulties; even Redmond now advised against the prosecution of the leading perpetrators, for he did not believe that Irish problems could be solved by the application of the criminal law.

There were now renewed efforts to find a settlement. A further meeting between Asquith, Bonar Law and Carson agreed that the Home Rule Bill should be accompanied by an Amending Bill incorporating agreed changes, but there was no agreement on what these changes should be. When the Amending Bill was introduced in the House of Lords in late June its main provision was the exclusion from Home Rule for six years of each Ulster county that voted to be so excluded. This was precisely the proposal already turned down by Carson in March. The Lords riposted by amending the Amending Bill to exclude all nine Ulster counties in perpetuity, but this was clearly unacceptable to the government. The time was now inexorably approaching when the Home Rule Bill would be ready for the Royal Assent and when therefore the chances of a compromise were at their best. Using the pressure of this deadline Asquith tried to reduce the differences, especially on the question of what geographical area of Ulster was to be permanently excluded from Home Rule. When the informal inter-party meetings became formal with the convening of the Buckingham Palace Conference on 21 July 1914, it was this, the area of Ulster to be excluded, which formed the substance of the discussions. Relations between the leaders, Asquith, Lloyd George, Redmond and Dillon on one side, Bonar Law, Lansdowne, Carson and Craig, were quite amicable, but 'that most damnable creation of the perverted ingenuity of man – the County of Tyrone' as Asquith put it, proved too much for them. The question of a time limit on the exclusion was not even reached before the conference broke up after three days without any agreement. Within two days of the breakdown there occurred the landing of guns at Howth by the Irish Volunteers, the Nationalist answer to the gun-running at Larne. When the

Volunteers reached Dublin, shooting broke out between a crowd and British troops in Bachelor's Walk. Three were killed and 38 injured. Redmond had only formal control of the Volunteers who took part in the gun-running and this was a portent of things to come. The breakdown of the Buckingham Palace Conference meant that Asquith had to proceed with the Amending Bill without an inter-party agreement. It now did not contain a time limit on the exclusion of Ulster and when the shooting in Bachelor's Walk hardened the mood among Nationalists, he decided to postpone it for a day or two. When he was still working on it on 30 July, with a map of Ulster and statistics of population and religion around him, he was called to see Bonar Law and Carson, who proposed that, in view of the international situation, the second reading of the Amending Bill should be postponed. Asquith welcomed this but he still saw to it that the Home Rule Bill was put on the statute book, with its operation suspended for the duration of the war. When this was done, on 15 September, the Unionists left the House in a body, described by Asquith as 'a lot of prosaic and for the most part middle-aged gentlemen, trying to look like early French revolutionists in the Tennis Court'.

When the Great War thus put Irish affairs into cold storage, Ireland was certainly set for an outbreak of violence. It is impossible to tell how far this violence would have spread and it seems likely that it would have spurred the party leaders into further efforts to find a settlement. Asquith and his colleagues had tried to deal with the Irish problem within the conventions of the British parliamentary system; Bonar Law and the Unionists had taken their stand on the fact that a representative system must take account of a minority as large and determined as the Ulstermen. Party honours were even in the battle: the government was damaged by the appearance of irresolution, but the parliamentary coalition behind it was on the whole united on this issue; the Unionists benefited from the disarray and prevarication on the government side, but it seems doubtful if Ireland could really have supplied them with a telling issue to cover up their own divisions on domestic issues in an election which they had been unable to force and which therefore still lay a year or so ahead.

9 Foreign Policy before 1914 and British Society on the Eve of War

I

The domestic events and crises which Britain experienced under the Liberals between 1905 and 1914 were momentous enough, yet in ultimate significance the conduct of foreign policy during this period was even more crucial. The course of domestic affairs was itself deeply influenced by Britain's position in the external world: the balance between spending on social reform and on defence was, for example, a problem that constantly divided Left and Right according to their different perceptions of the foreign policy environment; while the controversies about tariff reform were governed by different views about Britain's place and interests in the world. On the other hand the conduct of foreign policy was still in the hands of a fairly limited number of persons. The impact of public opinion was blunted by the claim, still widely accepted, that it fell within the sphere of the executive and that it was a matter for experts. Throughout this period Sir Edward Grey was the man who was both nominally and to a large extent effectively responsible for British foreign policy. He was at the interface between public and parliamentary pressures on the one hand and the traditional exercise of diplomacy by professionals behind closed doors on the other. Yet in many ways his control was more complete than that enjoyed by anyone in more autocratic systems, like the German or Russian. He had taken office clearly stamped as a representative of Liberal Imperialism and he had only joined the government after a more stubborn stand than was put up by his two colleagues Asquith and Haldane. In the event the past differences between Liberal Leaguers and Radicals were of less practical importance in the Liberal cabinets than many had anticipated, but they were not forgotten. At the time of the Agadir crisis in 1911 Loreburn, the Lord Chancellor, could still warn C.P. Scott that this was 'altogether an almost purely Liberal League cabinet'. Sir Edward Grey proved to be well fitted, in spite of great personal sensitivity, to weather the conflicting pressures from within the

Liberal Party to which he was exposed. A Whig by descent and attitude, he was at times radical in domestic politics. No one doubted the integrity of this high-minded Wykehamist; underneath the apparent simplicity of the country man there lurked much complexity and a formidable skill at casuistry.

The Foreign Office over which Grey presided was, apart from an enlarged Registry, no bigger than in the time of Canning. Its members were still recruited from a narrower social background than any other Whitehall department. The key officials were all very suspicious of the Liberal government, but it was just for this reason that they worked loyally with Grey, whom they regarded as the guarantor of sound policies. The Permanent Under Secretary was the most important official in the Foreign Office. The first incumbent under Grey, Sir Charles Hardinge, was a man exceptionally well connected in royal and aristocratic circles. There were few differences of policy between him and his chief. When he became Viceroy of India in 1910 he was succeeded by Sir Arthur Nicolson, who proved to be less influential, partly because Grey needed less assistance by then, partly because his pro-Ulster views alienated him from the Foreign Secretary. In the last few years before 1914 William Tyrrell, Grey's Private Secretary, was his most intimate official adviser. Another important official was Eyre Crowe, whose persistently anti-German views were cogently argued and therefore commanded respect. Grey could not help being influenced by his officials, but he was in no way clay in their hands, as his Radical critics sometimes alleged. His basic convictions largely coincided with theirs; if general political considerations demanded it he was quite capable of ignoring their advice.

Grey supported by and large the changes and adjustments in British foreign relations that had been carried out by his Conservative predecessors. He was in favour of the *entente* with France and saw it not merely as a settlement of colonial differences, but as a basic requirement of the European power balance. When Grey arrived at the Foreign Office the first Moroccan crisis was still in full swing and it was one of his first tasks to reassure the French that Lansdowne's policy of supporting them would be continued. It was at this point that the Anglo-French military conversations began. These conversations were a logical progression from the investigations that had started the previous summer under the auspices of the new Committee of Imperial Defence about the feasibility of landing British troops on the continent to assist France or Belgium in defending themselves against Germany. Grey and Campbell-Bannerman did not consider it necessary to report the military conversations to the cabinet and they did not become known to all ministers until the second Moroccan crisis in 1911. The result of the first crisis was that

Anglo-French *entente* had undergone a test and emerged strengthened and the change of government had if anything helped the process.

The possibility had long been in the air that the adjustments to Britain's international position that had produced the alliance with Japan and the *entente* with France would also lead to a better understanding with Russia. Continuing rivalries in Central Asia and the Far East had blighted these hopes in the days of Lansdowne and the demands of the Indian Government and the Commander-in-Chief Kitchener for more troops and greater investment in railways to contain possible Russian advances were still disturbing the Liberal cabinet. Russia's position had, however, radically changed as a result of her humiliating defeat in the Russo–Japanese war. Grey had for a long time been in favour of eliminating the long Anglo–Russian antagonism and he now took active steps to do so. The Convention with Russia, which was eventually concluded in August 1907, was similar to the Anglo-French *entente* in that it was not an alliance but aimed to reduce long-standing sources of imperial friction. The three areas affected were Persia, Afghanistan and Tibet. The Anglo-Russian Convention attracted considerable political criticism. On the Right a few Conservatives around Lord Curzon, whose forward policies as viceroy had been one of the obstacles to an earlier agreement, argued that too much had been given away and that vital matters like British interests in the Gulf and possible Russian pressure for access to the Mediterranean had been left undefined. On the Left many Radicals were governed by their ideological dislike of Russia. Grey had little difficulty in parrying such criticism, especially as there were clear gains from the convention in the avoidance of yet higher defence costs. For this reason Morley as Secretary of State for India had given the negotiations his strong support. In subsequent years it was mainly the Persian part of the settlement that was often attacked, because it was felt that the Russians were using their sphere of influence in Northern Persia to squash Persian liberalism. In the general Radical attack on Grey's foreign policy after the Agadir crisis in 1911, dissatisfaction over Persia was an important ingredient. In Persia, wrote H.N. Brailsford, 'we have been guilty of a treason against freedom, and in this treason our alliance with Tsardom has borne its natural fruit.'

Relations with Germany were increasingly becoming the linchpin of British foreign policy. The importance which was attached to maintenance of the Anglo–French *entente* and the conclusion of the Anglo–Russian convention was due to alarm about German power and policies. While only a few years previously a German alliance had been an option, it was now generally accepted that the main danger to British interests came from Germany. Broadly Grey shared the conclusions reached by Eyre Crowe, the Senior Clerk at the Foreign Office, in his memorandum of January 1907, that Germany was determined to play 'on the world's political stage a much larger and much more dominant part than she finds allotted to herself under the present distribution of material power' and that this conflicted with the British interest in the maintenance of the balance of power. In the next few years Anglo–German relations had many ups and downs, but all attempts at an improvement came to grief on this fundamentally adversary nature of the relationship, which found its most obvious manifestation in the naval rivalry. A real Anglo–German accommodation would only have been possible if there could have been agreement to halt the naval armaments race. There were many other elements in the Anglo–German antagonism, but these were much less compelling and frequently counterbalanced by factors that made for better understanding and more collaboration. The panic about German commercial and manufacturing rivalry was at its height in the middle 1890s, just when an Anglo–German alliance was becoming a serious possibility. In 1896 the publication of a book *Made in Germany* by E.E. Williams provided a focus for the gradually accumulating alarm about German competition in many areas of manufacturing, particularly in technologically advanced fields like chemical and electrical goods. Since then the international economy had emerged from the Great Depression and there had been a great expansion of British exports, though the British share in world trade and world manufacturing capacity was still declining. Anglo–German trade expanded enormously between 1890 and 1913: British imports from Germany more than trebled, British exports and re-exports to Germany about doubled. Britain was Germany's best customer and Germany was Britain's second-best market, after India. There was thus growing and complex interdependence. Complaints about high German tariffs and unfair competition continued from specific sections of the engineering and textile industries, especially at the time of the German tariff revision of 1902. Such complaints provided fuel for the tariff reformers in Britain, but they were nearly always balanced by counter-claims from other industries. 'Dumped' German steel hurt British steel producers who were coming up against high German tariffs, but it benefited British shipyards. British exporters still enjoyed many advantages of habit and loyalty in imperial markets and this is where the great rise in exports took place; this could be used by tariff reformers and others as an argument for preserving and developing the Empire against all comers and it could equally be used by those Germans who wanted their country to have a place in the sun. None of this could undo the fact of growing interdependence: Britain increased the exports of manufactured goods to her Empire, but Germany imported a high proportion of her growing raw material requirements from the British Empire; the adverse balance of British visible trade with Germany was compensated by British invisible earnings. Germany was a great consumer of British invisible exports, shipping, banking and insurance, though this again caused a good deal of envy in Germany. Not surprisingly support for an Anglo–German understanding was strong in the City of London. Bankers and financiers like Sir Ernest Cassell and Alfred Beit promoted organizations and publications favourable to reconciliation and their efforts were reciprocated on the German side by men like Albert Ballin, the shipping magnate and friend of the Kaiser, and the Hamburg banker Max Warburg. When specific projects like the Baghdad railway became objects of economic diplomacy, a settlement satisfactory to both sides proved in the end negotiable.

There was nothing, therefore, in Anglo–German trade relations that should have driven matters to a flash point. This still left a sense that Britain and Germany were two mighty empires destined to clash inexorably and the Social-Darwinist modes of thinking that were so prevalent fed such apprehensions. Ardent tariff reformers and imperialists, like J.L. Garvin of *The Observer* and Leo Maxse of *The National Review*, were always harping on the danger from the dynamic rise of Germany, her growing population and increasing industrial-military base. They contrasted this with the decline of Britain, ruled by effete mandarins. Their attacks on Germany were tinged with admiration and their prescriptions for the regeneration of Britain owed much to German models. Their shots were aimed as much at the domestic opposition as at the foreign foe, at the outright treachery of the Radicals and at the half-heartedness of so many Conservatives. There was a remarkable similarity in outlook between the super-patriots on both sides, but in Britain their influence on official policy was limited. At a popular level, fears and apprehensions, especially those arising from the naval arms race, were sensationalized in the press and the possibility of a German invasion was brought vividly to life in books like Erskine Childers's *The Riddle of the Sands* and William Le Queux's *The Invasion of 1910*.

The large number of Radicals, Little Englanders, disarmers and pacifists who survived from the Gladstone era or had arrived at Westminster in 1906 had to come to terms with developments which were diametrically opposed to their hopes and expectations. For a long time many of them did not see clearly the extent to which their own government was involving the country in the international power rivalry. Campbell-Bannerman's presence was reassuring; in the election campaign he had pledged himself to the pursuit of peace and the reduction of armaments. One of the first acts of the government in overseas policy, the grant of self-government in South Africa, presented a clear reversal of previous policies and the Prime Minister was given personal credit for it. Then the hopes of the peace party were pinned on the Second Hague Conference due to convene in the summer of 1907 and both Campbell-Bannerman and Grey encouraged these hopes. Even before the conference met, Bülow, the German Chancellor, made it clear that Germany was not willing to discuss disarmament. Disappointed in their major hopes, the Radicals mounted a campaign to compel the British delegation at the Hague to negotiate for the immunity from capture or destruction by belligerents of private property carried by sea during war. Even on this minor point Admiralty objections prevented the British delegation from making a stand and the Conference proved almost totally disappointing.

Shortly afterwards the naval arms race took a more serious turn with the announcement of a new German naval law and the British response to it. The debates about the naval estimates in 1908 were a foretaste of those in the following year, which form part of the history of the People's Budget. The Radicals decided to show their strength by moving an amendment to the Address in February 1908 expressing regret at the government's failure to produce proposals for reducing armaments. It was moved by Sir John Brunner, the founder, with Ludwig Mond, of what was to become Imperial Chemical Industries. He was one of the surviving Liberal business MPs who combined support for reform at home with passionate concern for arms reductions. The moderately worded amendment was defeated by 320 to 73 votes, with all the Labour members present bar one voting for it. Only a few weeks earlier 136 Liberal MPs had signed a memorial to Campbell-Bannerman calling for retrenchment in armament expenditure. The peace party were clearly under pressure and their voices were increasingly drowned by those, even in the Liberal Party, who were in favour of higher naval spending. Cobdenite Radicals of an earlier generation had always taken British maritime supremacy for granted. In the great controversies over the naval estimates of 1908 and 1909 the Radicals therefore based most of their arguments on the claim that the threat and the extent of German naval expansion was exaggerated and such claims could easily be disputed by their opponents. When anti-armament Liberals pointed an accusing finger at 'the merchants of death', the armaments manufacturers making profits out of the arms race, the argument that naval building and other defence spending provided employment was always a powerful antidote, especially for working-class voters. Up to 1910 the reductionist cause had two powerful supporters in the cabinet, Lloyd George and Churchill, who reinforced the more persistent Little

Englanders like Loreburn, the Lord Chancellor, Lewis Harcourt and Burns. Lloyd George and Churchill had, however, to accept what appeared to be the realities of the German naval programme and after the compromise about dreadnought building, which became the basis for the budget in the spring of 1909, only 28 Liberals could bring themselves to vote against the government.

The Agadir crisis of 1911 once more intensified the debate about British foreign policy and the arms race. German colonial aspirations had not in recent years been a major factor in the Anglo–German tensions and no longer occupied the place they had when the scramble for Africa was at its height. In contrast there was some irritation in the Foreign Office about French behaviour in Morocco. But when the Germans sent the *Panther* to Agadir on 1 July 1911 it was immediately seen as an attempt to smash the Anglo–French *entente*. In the ensuing crisis Grey resisted the advice of his leading officials, who were now prone to look at most international problems from the perspective of the German danger and who counselled firm British action. The cabinet was reluctant to be pushed to the brink of war, but it was of great significance that Lloyd George and Churchill now joined the ranks of those who wanted a strong line. After seeing Grey the Chancellor, due to address the Annual Bankers' Dinner at the Mansion House, delivered a warning that Britain would stand her ground as a Great Power. It caused a sensation and many saw it as a change of front in the Radical leader, but it was very much in character. A few weeks later Lloyd George used the dangers of the Moroccan crisis to help towards averting the threatened national rail strike. Lloyd George's Mansion House speech, the only overt British action in the crisis, temporarily silenced the Left, but soon the chorus of criticism against Grey's balance of power policies grew louder than ever before. Even among Conservatives, the risk of war at a time of domestic social upheaval was felt to be alarming. A Liberal Foreign Affairs Committee, joined by some 80 Liberal MPs, brought together many strands of Radicalism, led by men like Arthur Ponsonby, Sir John Brunner and Noel Buxton. Another Radical Committee to consider foreign affairs was formed under Leonard Courtney. Grey was criticized as a puppet in the hands of the Foreign Office, a narrowly selected, anti-democratic clique, which was conducting a policy of prestige in the interests of the ruling classes. To these well-worn arguments there was now added the thesis propounded by Norman Angell in his recently published book *The Great Illusion:* war was not only immoral but in an age of growing economic interdependence irrational and well-nigh impossible. To many on the Left this was a more appealing analysis than Marx's theory of inevitable war in a period of imperialist capitalism. 'Angellism' enjoyed some popularity even on the Right, among businessmen and in the City, while in contrast some financiers and businessmen with German or Jewish connections came under attack from the Germanophobe Right. Grey did not find it too difficult to disarm his critics on the Left; for one thing his personal position and often active involvement in many domestic issues, votes for women, labour unrest, was far from reactionary. In a speech in November 1911 he declared, with the sincerity he was uniquely capable of conveying, 'we have not made a single secret article of any kind since we came into office'. No one had an answer to his assertion that Britain could no longer rely on a balance of power in Europe maintaining itself without involving herself in it.

In the wake of the Agadir crisis there was in fact an attempt at relaxing Anglo–German tension and a fresh bout of negotiation. In February 1912 Haldane, a persistent advocate of an understanding with Germany, and at the same time a leading architect of the continental strategy, went to Germany. His conversations with Bethmann Hollweg were cordial, but no real progress was made with Tirpitz in halting the naval arms race. Yet in the following two years there was a better atmosphere in the Anglo–German relationship. The two governments worked well together in controlling and containing the consequences of the conflagrations in the Balkans in 1912 and 1913. The London Conference of the ambassadors of the Great Powers, which met from December 1912 to August 1913 to deal with the problems created by the war of the smaller Balkan states against Turkey, was a feather in Grey's cap and impressed even his Radical critics. There were renewed Anglo–German negotiations about the Portuguese colonies in 1913 and an Anglo–German treaty about the Baghdad railway was concluded in 1914. The Anglo–German rapprochement from 1912 onwards caused alarm in the Foreign Office because of the possible danger it posed to the *ententes* with France and Russia. If public opinion had allowed it, men like Nicolson, the Permanent Under Secretary, would have preferred to turn these *ententes* into alliances and they were afraid of the Germanophiles, the so-called 'Potsdam' party, in the cabinet. Against this Harcourt, the Colonial Secretary and one of the cabinet members most consistently pressing for British non-involvement, attacked Grey, early in 1914, for even using the term 'Triple Entente'. Grey's middle course seemed, however, in the spring and summer of 1914 to have achieved a position of relative calm in Britain's foreign relations. Nicolson wrote to Goschen, the British Ambassador in Berlin, on 5 May 1914: 'Since I have been at the Foreign Office, I have not seen such calm waters'. Many of Grey's Radical critics had been lulled into believing that since the Balkan wars 'the policy of the balance of power was exchanged for concerted action among the Powers'. Their eyes were on Ireland and they had no wish to rock the Liberal boat.

The fundamentals of Britain's international situation had, however, hardly changed. Early in 1914 the cabinet came close to a split over the naval estimates and Lloyd George, who had long ceased to side with the 'peace and retrenchment' section of the party, was nevertheless the chief protagonist against Churchill's proposals. In the end Lloyd George was persuaded by the facts and the First Lord of the Admiralty virtually got his way. Naval spending had reached £51½ million, compared with £31½ million in 1906. Agreements in peripheral areas could not end the basic Anglo–German antagonism. Britain had, in spite of all attempts to improve her relations with Germany, become more committed to the French *entente*. In order to meet the German naval threat in the North Sea, ships had been withdrawn from the Mediterranean in 1912, while the French moved their remaining battleships from Brest to Toulon. Military conversations were thus bolstered by naval arrangements and there was an exchange of letters about the latter, which, in spite of all the restrictive wording insisted on by the cabinet, were a confirmation of the *entente*. In 1914 there were moves to initiate Anglo–Russian naval talks, similar to the Anglo–French ones of 1912. When the news of this leaked out to the Germans, Grey denied all knowledge in the House of Commons. The Germans were greatly alarmed, but they were even more concerned by the growth of the Russian land armies, bolstered by increasing economic strength and railway development. This had in fact made them shift their priorities from Tirpitz's naval programme to an expansion of their armies. Austria, now Germany's one major ally, had become more than ever exposed to the force of Balkan nationalism which had won significant successes against the Turks. The coming battle lines were thus drawn in spite of the deceptive calm that prevailed until the assassination at Sarajevo on 28 June 1914 shattered it.

II

The strategic implications of Britain's involvement with the continental alliance system were far-reaching, but were never fully considered by the Liberal government as a matter of high policy. The Committee of Imperial Defence did not normally function as a body for the discussion of grand strategy, but one occasion when it did so was at a meeting during the Agadir crisis on 23 August 1911. Significantly only those ministers who knew about the military conversations with France were present; the exclusion of the others from this meeting, which seemed to them deliberate, was one of the reasons which later led Loreburn, Morley and Harcourt to press for an affirmation by the cabinet that the conversations implied no commitments. At the meeting there was a battle of the Wilsons, Sir Henry, the Director of Military Operations and Sir Arthur, the First Sea Lord. The military Wilson, for all his strong political views and capacity for intrigue, was typical of the generation of more professional military officers who had come to the fore after the Boer War and had shown up the shortcomings of military amateurism. He professed in public that a small, but well-equipped British expeditionary force could play a decisive role in a battle between the French and German armies though he would probably have preferred a larger British contribution. Plans for an expeditionary force had been around at least since the first Moroccan crisis and had been discussed in the military conversations with the French. The War Office assumed that such plans had ministerial approval, but they were only desultorily discussed by a few ministers in the know and not coordinated with the Admiralty. Sir Henry Wilson on becoming Director of Military Operations developed them further and concerted them in detail with the French. Six divisions, some 150,000 men, were to be landed in France and deployed in accordance with French strategic needs. At the CID meeting the naval Wilson opposed this continental strategy, as his predecessor Fisher had done, but the Admiralty case for coastal raids and amphibious raids was unconvincing for ministers. No formal decisions were taken, but the plans for sending an expeditionary force continued to be developed, the military talks with the French went on and Sir Henry Wilson was not sacked. The weaknesses revealed at the Admiralty led to a switch of offices between McKenna and Churchill. Under the new First Lord there was better coordination with the War Office and plans for the transport of the expeditionary force were ready by 1914. Thus the continental strategy continued by default, yet the navy was still pre-eminent, in its own estimation, in the share of resources it received and in the conduct of foreign policy. Naval thinking continued to be dominated by the big battleship and little attention was given to crucial matters like submarine warfare, torpedoes, mines, aircraft and commerce protection. The failure of the Committee for Imperial Defence to co-ordinate grand strategy stands in marked contrast to its useful work in the technical preparations for war and mobilization. Under Maurice Hankey, who became Secretary in 1912, its Secretariat and

Sub-Committees prepared a war book which in the event considerably facilitated the transition of what was still one of the world's most liberal societies from peace to war.

Haldane's army reforms were intended to underpin the formation of an expeditionary army force, but they were also shaped by the unresolved problems of army reform the Liberals inherited from their predecessors as well as by the pressures for economy in defence spending among their own followers. There were five major aspects to Haldane's work at the War Office: the reorganization of the regular army, the consolidation of the Territorial Force, the creation of an Imperial General Staff, planning for mobilization and the stabilization of the army estimates. The separate parts of the package were not original, but the concept as a whole represented a remarkable intellectual feat: to equip the nation with adequate front-line and reserve forces that could be quickly mobilized and properly deployed, but to do this without conscription and without imposing further strain on the public revenue. During the war, after he had been forced out of office because of his alleged Germanophilia, Haldane felt that he had to defend himself against the accusation that he had failed to create an army large enough to fight a continental war. To raise such an army and to introduce conscription would have been politically impossible in peacetime and it took two years of war and casualties before it could be done. Yet there was an influential and numerous compulsory service lobby which attacked Haldane's plans as inadequate. At its centre was Lord Roberts and the National Service League and many of the groups that sustained Edwardian patriotism, for example Baden-Powell's Boy Scouts, gave it support. In his plans for consolidating the auxiliary forces into a Territorial Army, his New Model, Haldane risked offending the many men of influence associated with the militia, the Yeomanry and the Volunteers, but through conciliatory tactics and much persuasion he got his way. Cadet corps were established in schools and universities and this helped greatly to cope with the high officer casualty rate when war broke out. On the army estimates Haldane had to fight a continuous battle with the Radicals in the Commons and the reductionists in the cabinet. His achievement was remarkable, for in 1914 army spending, at just under £29 million, was in fact a million pounds lower than it had been in 1905. By this time Haldane had left the War Office for the Woolsack.

III

When the final crisis that led to war began at Sarajevo Grey was at first concerned that it should be settled in a similar fashion to the Balkan flare-ups of the previous two years. Britain, as the most detached of the Great Powers, would exert her influence towards a settlement all round and would collaborate in these efforts above all with Berlin. He soon became aware that this time matters were proceeding differently. For the Austrians it was now much more a case of make or mar, either inflict a crushing defeat on Serbia and Balkan nationalism or see the Dual Monarchy severely shaken. It soon became apparent that the Germans, far from restraining their ally, had given Vienna something like a blank cheque. There was much feeling in Berlin that this might be the last opportunity to strike before Russia got too strong and that it was time for a preventive war. Little of the sense of crisis in the Foreign Office communicated itself to the general public until the Austrian ultimatum was delivered to Serbia on 23 July, the day before the Buckingham Palace Conference broke up. From this point on Grey worked desperately to avert a general European conflagration. He could not extract the full deterrent value from the British threat to participate in a general European war at the side of France and Russia, for he still had to qualify the British stand, as he always had done, with the proviso the country was 'free from engagements, and we should have to decide what British interests required us to do'. When at a late stage in the crisis, on 29 July, by which time Austria had already declared war on Serbia and Russia was ordering partial mobilization, he warned Lichnowsky, the German ambassador, that if France and Germany went to war, Britain could not 'stand aside and wait for any length of time', he was going beyond what the cabinet had authorized him to say. If Grey had been able to take a firmer stand at an earlier stage, it is by no means certain that this would have done much to avoid a general war.

The equivocation and lack of candour with which Grey had promoted the *entente* policy within the Liberal cabinet now came home to roost. On 1 August Asquith took the view, after a cabinet meeting that 'we came, every now and again, near to the parting of the ways'. Churchill had just been refused permission to go ahead with full naval mobilization. Only a few ministers, notably Morley and Burns, were for non-intervention at all costs, but many of the remainder found it very difficult to make up their minds. Lloyd George was potentially the most important of the waverers and the only man who could have led an effective peace party. Ever since his Mansion House speech during the Agadir crisis it had been clear that he could no longer be regarded as one of those Radicals who still believed in the

Gladstonian view of international relations. Nevertheless he had put faith in the efforts to improve Anglo–German relations and had still fought a rearguard action against the rise in the naval estimates early in 1914. As late as 23 July he had spoken of the improved atmosphere with Germany and the grave turn of the crisis took him by surprise. He engaged in discussions with the non-interventionists and waverers, but he knew that a general European war would very quickly involve Britain. Without leadership and inside information, the peace Radicals on the Liberal backbenches remained ineffective. Their influence had declined since 1912, their attention had been diverted by the great domestic issues and they could now do little but put their trust in Grey. Public opinion at large was confused. The assassination of the Archduke Ferdinand had provoked a surge of sympathy for Austria even in the Tory press, but once the Austrian ultimatum to Serbia had been delivered and it had become clear that Germany was not restraining Austria, the tone of the right-wing press changed. *The Times* argued that not only moral obligation but self-interest dictated British support for France. On 30 July Asquith noted 'the state of depression and paralysis' in the City, but on 2 August he remarked on the crowds cheering the King at Buckingham Palace '. . . one could hear the distant roaring as late as 1 or 1.30 in the morning. War or anything that seems likely to lead to war is always popular with the London mob'. This was before the German invasion of Belgium served as the catalyst to release patriotic emotion and the pent-up feeling against Germany, accumulated over many years of rivalry and antagonism.

A three-hour cabinet meeting on Sunday 2 August brought a decisive shift towards intervention. By this time Germany had declared war on Russia and German troops had occupied Luxemburg. A German violation of Belgium territory appeared a virtual certainty, though it was not yet totally clear whether Belgium would resist it. Most of the ministers, including Lloyd George, who still professed reluctance about British involvement, were using the Belgian case as a fig leaf to cover their move towards a British intervention in the war. It was, however, not so much Belgium as the possibility of a German attack on the French Channel coast that occupied the unusual Sunday-morning meeting of the cabinet. Grey was authorized to tell the French Ambassador and the House of Commons next day that Britain would attack if a German fleet came down the Channel to attack France. The decision was in marked contrast to the cabinet's conclusion the previous day that 'the despatch of the expeditionary force to help France is *at this moment* out of the question'. It may well be that this restraint on the Saturday helped to keep ministers united in their forward move on the Sunday. Only Burns resigned at this stage. The

Sunday morning cabinet also heard a letter from Bonar Law to Asquith offering support in any measures necessary to help France and Russia. This may well have shown the wavering ministers, if they did not know it already, that the question was not so much whether Britain would get involved or not, as under what government she would do so. If they had that morning chosen neutrality, Grey would have gone and Asquith would have followed him. When the wavering ministers lunched together after the cabinet, there was little substance left in their opposition to intervention and Morley, the only minister still to resign, called it 'a shallow affair'.

When Grey rose in the commons on Monday 3 August, he once again made the kind of speech which in its fumbling sincerity served to unite the House. As he spoke it had already become clear that German troops would invade Belgium and that the invasion would be resisted. Ministers were relieved that a clear-cut situation had arisen which absolved them of the need to quibble further about the justification for intervention, but this could not disguise the gravity of what had happened and that it was the failure of a policy. Grey more than most men realized that this war might deliver a body-blow to civilization as he knew it. He did not share the widely-held illusion that it would be a short and glorious war in which Britain's contribution would be mainly naval. His balance of power policy had failed to maintain the peace, yet there had never been a clear alternative to it. It was assumed that the German armies would defeat France if anything more quickly and thoroughly than they had done 40 years earlier. If Britain stood out, she would find herself isolated, face to face with a victorious Germany, and universally execrated for her failure to stand by her friends. Ultimately it was this assessment and the realization that the fate of France and the Low Countries involved vital British interests that pushed a pacific cabinet into war. There is no substance, in the British case, in the argument that war provided a convenient way of overcoming domestic tensions, great as these were. Asquith might privately express relief that the Irish imbroglio had been superseded, but the decisions which he and his colleagues took about war and peace were not affected by such considerations. The political, diplomatic and military decision-makers were undoubtedly influenced by the prevailing climate of opinion, in which fears about German power, apprehensions about a British decline, and the conviction that struggle and war were inevitable, figured largely; but even among Foreign Office officials like Nicolson and Crowe, who considered it vital that Britain should stand by her *entente* partners, there was no eagerness for war, merely a resigned disposition to accept the inevitable. Grey's policy in July 1914 was, by and large, passive; rather than bringing British influence actively to bear in the

preservation of peace he was content to stay on the sidelines and for
this he has been criticized. The reason for his reticence lay partly in
his assessment of the diplomatic situation and it turned out that some
of his judgements, particularly in respect of German willingness to
play a restraining role, were mistaken. He was also constrained by his
assessment of what the cabinet would be prepared to back and it was
through this mechanism that such peace and neutrality sentiment as
there was made itself felt.

The failure of a peace party in the cabinet to materialize may have
owed something to the realization that there was not enough of a tide
of public sentiment to support it. This may well have been a factor in
the decision of Lloyd George, a man whose ability to gauge the public
mood was unrivalled, to abandon any attempt to lead such a party.
The strength of patriotic sentiment could not surprise any observer of
the pre-war scene. There was never any sign that the criticism of
Grey's balance of power policies and of arms expenditure had a
popular base commensurate with the support it enjoyed among the
articulate and politically influential. Grey's critics had behind them
organizations, like the National Liberal Federation under the presi-
dency of Brunner or the Free Church Council, and they had the
backing of journalists and publicists of exceptional talent, such as
C.P. Scott and *The Manchester Guardian*, A.G. Gardiner and *The Daily
News*, H.W. Massingham and *The Nation*, J.A. Spender and *The
Westminster Gazette* and F.W. Hirst and *The Economist*. This disguised
the fact that the big battalions were on the other side. This was
obviously true of the press, where mass circulation papers, like
Northcliffe's *Daily Mail*, always took the patriotic line; brilliant
radical journalism was counter-balanced by effective publicists on the
right, men like Spenser Wilkinson, brother-in-law of Eyre Crowe and
first Chichele Professor of the History of War at Oxford, or Colonel
Repington, the defence correspondent of *The Times*. British patriotism had a broad organizational infra-structure reaching all classes:
the cadet corps in the public schools, the Navy League, the National
Service League headed by Lord Roberts, Baden-Powell's Boy Scouts,
the Boys and the Church Lads Brigades, the British Girls Patriotic
League and many more. Writers and poets like Kipling and Newbolt
expressed the patriotic mood. The masses had become insistent on
material improvements in their living standards, but they were also
patriotic and no longer receptive to the kind of moral internationalist
appeal Gladstone had made over the Bulgarian Atrocities.

IV

The outbreak of war was like the curtain falling on a play the plot of which was not yet resolved. In the political part of the action all the major protagonists had shown powers of survival but had as yet been unable to make sure of their future. On balance the Liberals had a tale of resilience rather than decline to tell in the decade up to 1914. In the elections of 1910 and in the next three and a half years the party managed to contain the threat from Labour, but could not roll it back conclusively. The Labour Party presented in 1914, both to supporters and opponents, above all a spectacle of hope disappointed. It was impossible to square the expectations of activists, who must furnish much of the proselytizing energy of a left-wing party, with the modest possibilities open to the parliamentary Labour Party, locked as it was into alliance with the Liberals. To the parliamentary leaders, above all MacDonald, the course which naturally commended itself was to build upon the Progressive Alliance. There were those, however, in the ILP and elsewhere, who were prepared to pay the price of a temporary contraction of Labour representation in Parliament for a Liberal defeat and the eventual arrival of a major socialist party of the left. It would have been a bold man who would have ventured a confident prediction in 1914 how, and how quickly, the problem of the Left in British politics would be resolved. It is unlikely that a further major change in the franchise if it had come before 1918 would have affected the problem greatly. It is improbable that the section of the working class that missed out on the vote before 1914 was drastically different from those working-class voters who were on the register. If anything it was the Conservatives who might have had a slight advantage among that part of the working class that was more swayed by deference and less susceptible to the pressures of solidarity. As between Liberal and Labour a fuller register, based on a simpler procedure for qualifying, would have made only a marginal difference.

The Conservative and Unionist Party was, however, also in an unenviable position in 1914. It was a tragedy for the party that those with the most innovative and experimental ideas put their energies into tariff reform and thereby dissipated them in internal party squabbles. Nevertheless the accession of Bonar Law to the leadership calmed the internal struggle by relentlessly attacking the enemy and succeeded in preventing a split on the extreme right. The Conservative Party remained a broad-based coalition unique to Britain. Little progress had, however, been made before the outbreak of war in sorting out a distinctive Tory reform programme and with tariff reform in suspended animation, the party was relying on Liberal disarray, especially over Home Rule and Ulster, to carry it back to power.

V

A factor that was clearly working to the disadvantage of the Liberal Party in the years up to the outbreak of war was the decline of nonconformity as a political force. On the surface the Liberal victory of 1906 had looked like a revival of that force: nearly 200 MPs of nonconformist background were elected, a far larger number than the Unionist total. It could no longer be assumed, however, that their membership of a nonconformist denomination was a significant guide to the political orientation of such Liberal MPs. Education was the major issue on which nonconformity had contributed to the Liberal victory, but even Herbert Gladstone ranked it only fifth among the causes of that victory. When the Liberal government found itself frustrated by the House of Lords over its own Education Bill, some nonconformists began to feel that it had been a mistake to get so closely involved with the Liberals and that the time had come to adopt a more neutral stance. The militant nonconformists were disenchanted with the compromises and deals which the Liberals were proposing in order to make some legislative progress on education, while others, mostly from the industrial and commercial community, were alienated by what they considered the government's drift toward 'socialism'. In the elections of 1910 the National Free Church Council, which with its many local counterparts could claim to speak for all dissenters, was more restrained in its intervention than it had been in 1906 and left the initiative mainly to the local councils. The nonconformist clergy were on the whole still strongly committed to the Liberal cause and hoped that a solution of the constitutional issue would enable further gains to be made on education and Welsh disestablishment. The laity were more divided and their vote was now as much determined by economic and ideological considerations as by their religious affiliation. George Cadbury, leading Quaker and owner of the Radical *Daily News*, questioned in his own paper whether the Free Churches should any longer contract political marriages. Nevertheless middle-class nonconformism probably helped to limit Liberal losses in many parts of the country in the 1910 elections. The number of nonconformist MPs returned went down by about a third, though they formed if anything a higher proportion of the reduced total of Liberal and Labour MPs. Since there was only a handful of dissenters among Unionist MPs, the two main political camps in Parliament remained divided on denominational lines much as before.

This could not disguise the fact that the political thrust of nonconformity was further reduced after 1910. The National Free Church Council campaigned mainly on general moral, non-political causes; for example they managed to get the Johnson–Webb world heavyweight boxing championship match cancelled in 1911, on the grounds that it was brutalizing and might raise racial tension. In Parliament nonconformists were mainly active on imperial questions, like the Congo, and in the campaign against armaments. There was now a much greater willingness on the part of organized nonconformity to collaborate with the Established Church, as both saw themselves threatened by the rising tide of religious indifference and unbelief. In spite of this, education remained a grievance for nonconformists and the redoubtable Dr Clifford was still campaigning for a new bill; but the government failed to deliver any further legislation. This again served to strengthen the detachment with which many dissenters now regarded the Liberals. One major issue remained to keep the political marriage intact, Welsh disestablishment. In England, however, this cause now raised little enthusiasm; the Liberation Society had long been in decline and disestablishment of the Church of England was no longer on the agenda. On the eve of war the Liberals and Labour were still deeply marked by their long-standing connection with religious dissent, but the former could no longer expect this connection to provide the infusion of strength it had supplied in the past. The war was about to deal a body-blow to the nonconformist hold on their members and to the nonconformist conscience and thereby it also inflicted fatal damage on political liberalism.

VI

There was a general impression in the years before 1914 that developments in the press were also to the disadvantage of the Liberal Party and reflected a decline of liberalism in the broader sense. The rise of the Liberal provincial press in the 1850s and 1860s accompanied and assisted the advance of the Gladstonian Liberal coalition and looked, particularly in retrospect, like a golden age of journalism. Papers like the *Leeds Mercury*, the *Sheffield Independent* or the *Manchester Examiner* appealed to an ever-widening circle of serious readers capable of absorbing world-wide political news, informed and sophisticated comment and long speeches by leading political figures. The Conservatives felt themselves to be at a serious disadvantage both in the metropolitan and provincial press; Disraeli himself encouraged attempts to challenge the Liberal supremacy in the press. It was universally assumed that the press, the sole available means of disseminating information, had great political influence, though the constantly fluctuating fortunes of the political parties seemed to contradict this. Gradually from the 1880s the circumstances in which the press had operated began to change. It was assumed that the universal availability of elementary education was a principal cause; in fact literacy was already widespread before 1870, so that the effects of Forster's Act, while considerable, were hardly sudden or dramatic. The rise of popular mass-circulation newspapers was as much due to technical developments in printing and distribution as to spreading literacy. Newspapers, even in the heyday of the serious political journal, had to combine the task of educating the public with the obligation to make a profit for their proprietors or at least to avoid a loss. The aim was, as J.R. Scott of the *Manchester Guardian* put it in a memorable phrase, 'to make readable righteousness remunerative'. Righteousness was, however, of major importance to the proprietors of serious penny morning daily papers in the provinces and great battles were fought over the exact political orientation of such publications. The *Leeds Mercury*, for example, in the hands of the Baines family, was considered too moderate by many Radicals and a group of them, including W.E. Forster, founded in 1857 an alternative Radical paper, the *Leeds Express*. Another famous Liberal family paper, the *Sheffield Independent* in the hands of the Leader family, was also considered insufficiently Radical by many, though no alternative materialized. Great care was taken by these and similar papers to support the leading Liberal and nonconformist causes like temperance and not to countenance what were considered vices such as betting and gambling.

Towards the end of the century righteousness was increasingly overborne by commercial considerations. The capital investment required to launch a newspaper rose dramatically: in the middle of the century it was reckoned that it cost £10–20,000 to launch a London daily, by the 1870s £100,000 was being estimated. Towards the end of the century it became possible to make a fortune out of cheap magazines and newspapers, mostly printed in London with circulations running into hundreds of thousands. Daily papers selling at only a halfpenny could be distributed from London over a wide area and subsidiary editions printed in more distant centres. Such magazines and papers had to entertain and titillate the reader rather than inform and educate him. Alfred Harmsworth and his brothers became the prototypes of the new newspaper proprietors. They built up a publishing empire through magazines of the kind pioneered by George Newnes with his *Tit-Bits*. The first of their titles was called *Answers to Correspondents*, with features such as 'What the Queen eats', 'How Madmen write' and 'An Electrical Flying Machine'. In 1894 the Harmsworth brothers bought the struggling London Conservative *Evening News* for the bargain price of £25,000. Out of this there developed in 1896 the *Daily Mail*, a halfpenny daily and the distinctive contribution of Alfred Harmsworth to popular journalism. The circulation of its opening issue was nearly 400,000 and the Boer War helped to lift it much higher. It continued to bear very much the personal imprint of Alfred Harmsworth. He was a Conservative who had tried to get into the House of Commons, but he was hardly a strong party man. It was his instinct for the reactions of the man in the street that made him successful. In 1905 Balfour, who once claimed that he never read the newspapers, recommended him for a peerage and he became Lord Northcliffe. In 1908 he bought the financially ailing *Times* from the Walter family; by 1910 Northcliffe's three London morning dailies, *The Times* the *Daily Mail* and the *Daily Mirror* accounted for some 40 per cent of the 3.6 million copies produced in London every weekday morning.

What mattered from a party-political point of view was not only that there was now a preponderance of Conservative papers among the mass circulation metropolitan press. Papers like the *Daily Mail* were largely depoliticized, but it was claimed by Radical journalists like H.W. Massingham that they encouraged acceptance of the status quo and of opinions that were safe and uncritical. Anything that might reduce vital advertising revenues had to be avoided. It came as a disappointment to Liberals that the tastes of the new mass readership did not justify their faith in rational debate and the clash of informed opinion. It may well be that in their disillusionment many Liberals overestimated the political influence of the popular newspapers. Politicians of all parties shared this overestimation of the powers of the popular press and its proprietors, even if they affected, like Asquith or Balfour, to hold them in low esteem. Others, notably Lloyd George, were open in their courting of the press and of newspaper magnates and editors. He regularly met Liberal editors and journalists and George Riddell, proprietor of the *News of the World* and Robert Donald, editor of the *Daily Chronicle* were among his close associates. His relations with the popular press helped to create around Lloyd George the aura of populism and manipulation that made him so widely suspect. The story of the *Daily News* is a good example of the buffetings to which Liberal newspapers were exposed as a result of the changing circumstances under which press and pressmen had to operate. As a penny paper it was a major Radical influence in the 1870s, but towards the end of the century it became Liberal-Imperialist. This precipitated the coup of a group of pro-Boers led by Lloyd George, helped financially by George Cadbury and others, through which the paper was returned to its Radical, nonconformist orientation. Cadbury tried to secure L.T. Hobhouse as editor, but faced with his reluctance settled on A.G. Gardiner, another famous name in the long list of Liberal journalists. The paper began to support the New Liberalism and welfare legislation; it reduced its price to a halfpenny, printed in Manchester as well as London and pushed its circulation up to 400,000. Even then it was commercially barely viable and was dependent on advertising; this made its refusal to advertise liquor and to carry betting news expensive to sustain.

The difficulties of Liberal newspapers did not prevent the Liberal Party from triumphing in 1906. Northcliffe's support for tariff reform, particularly through his Sunday paper *The Observer* under the editorship of Garvin, did not cause protection to take the Unionist Party by storm. As the example of Blatchford's *Clarion* showed, popular journalism could also be put in the service of socialism. But if politicians like Lloyd George attached so much importance to the press, it was hardly surprising that the fourth estate itself was conscious of its power. Increasingly this power was felt to reside in the proprietors and an era was about to begin when newspaper barons like Northcliffe, his brother Rothermere, or Beaverbrook, as Max Aitken already the *eminence grise* of Bonar Law, were regarded as men before whom even the most powerful of politicians should tremble.

VII

Salisbury remarked of the new popular newspapers that they were written by office boys for office boys. Mass circulation papers and magazines, particularly in the metropolis and other large cities, were indeed catering for a growing army of white-collar workers, called into existence by the bureaucratization of industry and government, and in London especially by the growth of the City and its institutions. A particular feature of office work was that it gave employment to an increasing number of women: between 1891 and 1911 the number of women employed in commerce and as clerks nearly trebled. The total number of men and women listed as employed in that category was nearly 1.2 million out of an employed population of nearly 20 million. What could be called the lower middle class extended much beyond office workers and also included shopkeepers, traders and many of those employed in the expanding service industries. The preoccupation of contemporary literature, for example of writers like George Gissing, H.G. Wells and Arnold Bennett, with this intermediate or marginal class shows how much it was felt to be real, expanding and socially significant. It was also a class whose political allegiance could not be taken for granted. Many individuals from a social stratum in which social insecurity and problems of identity were common turned into radicals. Wells himself was such a man and in his novels there are many case histories of men and women being turned into rebels by their insecure position in the social hierarchy. It was, however, just as likely that members of the lower middle class would become very conservative in their outlook and behaviour. What distinguished them above all from the classes below them were their aspirations to better themselves and their fears of failure. Clerks in private firms were looking for promotion, possibly partnership; small shopkeepers were looking for an increase in trade and financial security. The price of failure for such people was high and they could fall all the way back into the ranks of the unskilled. The increasing scale of office employment made the conditions of work of white-collar workers often as impersonal as those of their blue-collar cousins working in large factories; aspirations for personal advancement became meaningless. Similarly the small shopkeeper began to suffer competition from the multiples and the department stores. After 1900 the number of branches in food chains was doubling in each decade and in the most important grocery chains was running into several hundreds. Maypole, Lipton and Lyons and others were becoming household names and multiples were spreading in the footwear, men's clothing, haberdashery, hardware and the chemist's trades. On the whole the retailing revolution, part of increasing urbanization, did not bring advantage to the small trader. Thus the increasing opportunities for maintaining a lower middle-class style of life were matched by many new insecurities. Before the Education Act of 1902 the chances of a member of the lower middle class in Britain permanently improving his status through education did not compare favourably with those in other countries. Yet the British lower middle class faced these problems almost entirely as individuals. No major organization of the trade union type got going for white-collar workers nor did associations for small shopkeepers or independent artisan-producers make much headway. This was again a notable distinction between Britain and comparable countries like Germany. On the whole the lower middle class was content to abide by the individualist, free-market traditions that were still so strong in Britain. For security they turned inwards, to their suburban semi-detacheds, their families, sometimes to religious congregations. It was a defensive mentality, unadventurous, setting great store by respectability, while patriotism and identification with national greatness could act as compensations. All this, as well as fear of the evidently increasing power of organized labour, could make members of the lower middle class natural supporters of the Conservative party.

VIII

The rise of white-collar employment was, particularly in London, due to a considerable extent to the growing importance of financial institutions and insurance. The influence of the City of London in the world economy was undiminished in the years before 1914. It was partly the consequence of the fact that an integrated world economy, with a complex pattern of trade and payments, had become even more established than it was in the 1870 or 1880s, partly due to the fact that the United Kingdom continued to be the most important trading nation, though its relative importance as a manufacturing nation was declining, and that she was the world's greatest provider of capital for investment. After falling off somewhat in the 1890s British net investment abroad had risen immediately before 1914 to levels which were two to three times what they had been in the 1880s. The total value of British investments abroad just before 1914 was close to £4,000 million as compared with about £1,500 million in 1885. In her balance of payments Britain was in deficit with the United States and continental Europe, but in surplus with India, Australia, Japan and China. London was thus the centre of an international network of trade and settlements and was able to play this role from a position of formidable strength.

It could be argued before 1914, as it has often been since, that the economic priorities of governments were distorted by too high a regard for the interests of the City as against productive industry. Before 1914 the influence of the City on governments made itself felt mainly in the field of foreign policy and diplomacy, for example with the open door policy in China or the Middle East and ventures like the Baghdad railway. It was, however, claimed by contemporaries that there was a link between the high rate at which capital was being exported and the insufficiency of domestic investment. It was often the case that investment abroad was carried out with a rentier mentality: safe returns, possibly with a guarantee from a stable foreign government, were preferred, for example railways or public utilities. On the other hand there was no overall shortage of capital for investment at home, but there may have been difficulties in specific situations. City institutions like the stock exchange were not well adapted to lending money to the individual entrepreneur or small firm for purposes of innovation carrying a high risk. Large and well-known firms had no difficulty in raising capital publicly, if they could not finance themselves out of profits. A family firm in the hands of the third generation, which was being treated like an estate to provide a life style suitable for gentlemen, was not well equipped to attract outside capital or to look for it. Even if the export of British capital could not be blamed for the lack of domestic investment, the contrast between Britain's great international financial strength and signs of failure in her productive industries was not lost on contemporaries. In his book *Riches and Poverty*, published in 1905, Chiozza Money wrote: 'If a South African mine or a Japanese war loan offers apparent opportunities of quicker profits than putting fresh capital into British ironworks, or founding a new British industry, it is the end of South Africa or Japan which is served.' He also complained that while Britain had undoubtedly gained from being the world's money lender and from the income of the investments thus built up, this income was under the control of the few and not the many and 'whether the nation as a whole gains by this tribute depends entirely upon the wisdom and patriotism of those who receive it'.

Signs of weakness and slow-down in British manufacturing industry in comparison with the United States and Germany were much more obvious than they had been in the 1880s and the first census of production, taken in 1907, revealed some of them. The value added to the cost of materials by a worker in various British industries was on average £100, while in America it was £500. There was more than twice as much capital and horsepower for workers in American industry. The annual percentage rise in physical output per worker between 1890 and 1907 was 0.1 per cent in Britain and 2 per cent in the United States. The explanation favoured by some historians, that higher American real wages were stimulating faster innovation and mechanization, is not entirely plausible, for a similar comparison of productivity unfavourable to Britain can be made with specific industries in Germany, where real wages were lower than here. The continuing good performance by British exports was mainly in older industries like coal, textiles and ship-building. Having already failed to keep pace with her competitors in electrical manufacturing and the production of synthetic chemicals, Britain was also showing signs of lagging in the new motor industry. Some fine British cars were being made, but they were expensive vehicles produced by craftsmen; mass production of cheap cars, pioneered by Henry Ford in America, was only just being introduced, by Ford himself and by W.R. Morris, later Lord Nuffield. Even in coal mining, output per man was dropping, as a result of poorer seams being worked and lack of mechanization. The Lancashire textile industry, exporting successfully to imperial markets like India, was yet lagging in technological innovation. Ship-building, on the other hand, was still a world leader and technically as advanced as any competitor. In imperial markets, whether they were sophisticated like Canada or backward like India, British industry had an advantage over her competitors, but the same was true in countries like Argentina, where British investment was predominant.

British economic performance immediately before 1914 thus presented a very chequered picture. It was inevitable that Britain's share in total world manufacturing output or total world trade should decline as other nations became industrialized, often with British help. Nor was it possible for Britain to be in the lead in every new industry or technology. Yet there were nagging worries about the failure to innovate though the causes were multifarious. Again it was inevitable that it should be more difficult to innovate in a country where so much industry was already established, but sometimes the very solidity of British machinery and the loving care with which it was maintained was a bar to the introduction of new equipment and methods. Virtues could become vices, and the possible culprits for industrial decadence ranged from the educational system to the determination of families to retain control of their firms by restrictions on the raising of new capital. Like so much else, the debate about Britain's industrial and economic standing was in 1914 unresolved: fears of decline and decadence were widely voiced, but there was also pride that Britain, a small island with 41 million inhabitants, was still the heart of a great Empire and the centre of the world economy.

IX

In much else, British society on the eve of the Great War stood poised between the old and the new. Even outside the more directly political sphere, developments were moving that society a long way from the Victorian age into the twentieth century. Science and scientific attitudes were still undermining many accepted beliefs. A report on the work of Freud, for example, had appeared in the *Proceedings of the Society for Psychical Research* as early as 1893. The conflict between science and religion was no longer as fierce as it had been: the bitter portrait of Theobald Pontifex, as the symbol of conventional religion and morality, that Samuel Butler had painted in *The Way of All Flesh*, belonged to an earlier generation. But the decline of religion was still manifesting itself in the modification of many attitudes and the loosening of many codes of behaviour. The revolt of the suffragettes was merely the tip of the iceberg composed of changing relations between men and women, new sexual mores and altered views of marriage. It became a literary fashion to deal with such themes and major literary figures of the time, Shaw, Wells, all did so. An official recognition of a crisis in this area came with the appointment of a Royal Commission on Divorce and Matrimonial Causes, the first of its kind, in 1910. Emancipation and liberation, whether of women or of workers, inspired hope in some and fear in others. Many argued that such revolutions were inevitably linked and that socialism meant free love. Some again embraced the prospect and others were repelled by it.

Amid such uncertainties even faith in the scientific method became less sure. It had been thought that the processes of scientific analysis were beyond dispute and that they could be increasingly transferred to the arena of social and human relations. Empirical social science, as practised by the Webbs and the Fabians, had been the distinctive British contribution to the movement for social reform all over the world. These approaches still had a great deal of life left in them when the First World War broke out, but doubts were arising. Natural science itself had some of its certainties questioned through the work of Einstein and others. The ability of science to work cures in the social field was even more questioned. Masterman had graduated through the University settlement movement and had turned the evangelicalism of his background towards secular improvement. In one of his books *The Condition of England*, published in 1909, a favourite mine for quotations among historians of the period, he wrote: 'Civilization, in the early twentieth century in England, suffers no illusions as to the control of natural forces, or the exploration of natural secrets furnishing a cure either for the diseases from which it suffers in the body, or the more deep-seated maladies of the soul.'

Bibliography

Abbreviations

AHR American Historical Review
EHR English Historical Review
EconHR Economic History Review
HJ Historical Journal
JBS Journal of British Studies
IRSH International Review of Social History
VS Victorian Studies
Place of publication is London unless otherwise stated.

Bibliographies

Most of the bibliographies mentioned in volume 8 of this series are also relevant for this period. Particularly useful are H.J. Hanham (ed.), *The Bibliography of British History 1851–1914* (Oxford, 1976) and, on a smaller scale, G.R. Elton, *Modern Historians on British History 1485–1945: A Critical Bibliography 1945–1969* (1970). For the publications of subsequent years the *Annual Bibliography of British and Irish History* (Hassocks, 1976—), edited by G.R. Elton for the Royal Historical Society, and the *Annual Bulletin of Historical Literature*, published by the Historical Association, should be consulted. A classified bibliography is published in the summer issue of *Victorian Studies*.

Documents

The best collections are the two relevant volumes in the series *English Historical Documents*, edited by D.C. Douglas: vol. XII (Part 1), 1833–1874, edited by G.M. Young and W.D. Handcock (1956); and vol. XII (Part 2), 1874–1914, edited by W.D. Handcock (1977). Collections of documents on specific aspects are mentioned under the appropriate sections. There is a vast mass of documentary material for this period; it ranges from *The Letters of Queen Victoria*, series 2, 1862–1885, and series 3, 1886–1901 (edited by G.E. Buckle, 1926–32), through contemporary analyses: like W. Bagehot, *The English Constitution* (1867) and M. Ostrogorski, *Democracy and the Organisation of Political Parties* (2 vols., 1902), and contemporary descriptions like Sir H.W. Lucy's *Diaries* of the Parliaments from 1874 to 1905 (1885–1906), to pictures of country life such as Flora Thompson, *Lark Rise to Candleford* (1945) and Kilvert's *Diary* (selections edited by W. Plomer, 3 vols., rev. edn, 1977). Victorian periodicals like the *Fortnightly* or the *Quarterly* are a rich source and access to them is made easier by the *Wellesley Index to Victorian Periodicals 1824–1900*, edited by W.E. Houghton (3 vols., Toronto 1966–79). *McCalmont's Parliamentary Poll Book. British Election Results 1832–1918* (8th edn, reprinted Brighton 1971, edited by J.R. Vincent and M. Stenton) is a mine of information; Chris Cook and B. Keith, *British Historical Facts 1830–1900* (1975) is informative on cabinets, parties and much else.

General Histories

Two histories are classics in their own right: R.C.K. Ensor, *England 1870–1914* (Oxford, 1936), in the *Oxford History of England*, written by a historian who was personally involved in many events of this period as a committed Liberal; and the two concluding volumes, covering the years 1895 to 1914, in E. Halévy, *History of the English People in the Nineteenth Century*, translated by E.I. Watkin and D.A. Barker (6 vols., revised edn, 1949–52). Two works written by contemporaries from a Liberal point of view are still worth consulting: the last three volumes of Herbert Paul, *History of Modern England* (5 vols., 1904–5) and G.C. Thompson, *Public Opinion and Lord Beaconsfield 1875–1880* (2 vols., 1886). A classic analysis by a constitutional lawyer are the three works by W.I. Jennings, *Cabinet Government* (1936), *Parliament* (1939) and *Party Politics* (3 vols., Cambridge 1960–2). R.T. McKenzie, *British Political Parties* (2nd edn, 1963) and S.H. Beer, *Modern British Politics* (1965) were influential books and are still worth reading. Among more recent textbooks K. Robbins, *The Eclipse of a Great Power. Modern Britain 1870–1975* (1983) D. Read, *England 1868–1914* (1979), R. Shannon, *The Crisis of Imperialism 1865–1915* (1974) A.F. Havighurst, *Twentieth-Century Britain* (1962) and H.M. Pelling, *Modern Britain 1885–1955* (Edinburgh, 1960) should be mentioned. R. Rhodes James, *The British Revolution: British Politics 1880–1939*, vol. I: *From Gladstone to Asquith, 1880–1914* (1976) contains many shrewd insights.

Introduction

On the demographic changes of the period N.L. Tranter, *Population since the Industrial Revolution. The Case of England and Wales* (1973) and Rosalind Mitchison, *British Population Change since 1860* (1977) in the series *Studies in Economic and Social History*, give useful guidance. A number of essays in Theo Barker and Michael Drake (eds.), *Population and Society in Britain 1850–1980* (1982) illustrate the effect of population changes on social life. On the position of children and the impact of education a rather conventional picture is painted by I. Pinchbeck and M. Hewitt, *Children in English Society*, vol. II: *The 18th Century to the Children Act 1948* (1973). Anne Digby and Peter Searby, *Children, School and Society in Nineteenth-Century England* (1981) provides documents and useful commentaries. For other works on education, see below in the bibliography for chapter 2.

Ray Strachey, *'The Cause'. A Short History of the Women's Movement in Great Britain* (1928) is still useful; Richard J. Evans, *The Feminists: Women's Emancipation Movements in Europe, America and Australia 1840–1920* (1977) is a more recent comparative survey. J.L. Newton, M.P. Ryan and J.R. Walkowitz (eds.), *Sex and Class in Women's History* (1983) has a number of relevant contributions from a feminist viewpoint. A.S.G. Butler, *Portrait of Josephine Butler* (1954) and E. Moberly Bell, *Josephine Butler, Flame of Fire* (1962) are two sympathetic biographies; on prostitution, see J.R. Walkowitz, *Prostitution and Victorian Society: Women, Class and the State* (Cambridge, 1980) and Keith Neild (ed.), *Prostitution in the Victorian Age. Debates on the issue from 19th-century critical journals* (1973). Books on politics in the 1860s are listed below in the bibliography under chapter 1, and on religion and the churches under chapter 2.

1

For an understanding of politics in this period H.J. Hanham, *Elections and Party Management: Politics in the time of Disraeli and Gladstone* (1959) remains indispensable. Three books are essential for studying the passage of the second Reform Bill: F.B.

Smith, *The Making of the Second Reform Bill* (Cambridge, 1966); M. Cowling, *1867: Disraeli, Gladstone and Revolution* (Cambridge, 1967), a classic example of the 'high politics' school of historical writing; and from the perspective of popular politics Royden Harrison, *Before the Socialists* (1965). For a stimulating discussion of the issues, see also G. Himmelfarb, 'Politics and Ideology: the Reform Act of 1867', in *Victorian Minds* (1968). C. Seymour, *Electoral Reform in England and Wales* (New Haven, 1915) is still useful for details of the franchise. Important regional studies are T.J. Nossiter, *Influence, Opinion and Political Idioms in Reformed England: Case Studies from the North-East* (Hassocks, 1975) and R.J. Olney, *Lincolnshire Politics 1832–1885* (1973). For election statistics two articles by J.P.D. Dunbabin are valuable: 'Parliamentary Elections in Great Britain 1868–1900: a psephological note', *EHR* LXXXI (1966), and 'British Elections in the Nineteenth and Twentieth Century: a Regional Approach', *EHR* XCV (1980).

On the political parties three books concerned with the Conservative Party over a longer time-span are relevant to this period: Robert Blake, *The Conservative Party from Peel to Churchill* (1970), a magisterial overview; and two symposia, Lord Butler (ed.), *The Conservatives: a History from their Origins to 1965* (1977) and D. Southgate, *The Conservative Leadership 1832–1932* (1974). There is at the moment no volume to follow on from Robert Stewart, *The Foundation of the Conservative Party 1830–1867* (1978). The standard work for Conservative policy and legislation from 1866 to 1880 is Paul Smith, *Disraelian Conservatism and Social Reform* (1967); on Conservative party organization from the second to the third Reform Bill, E.J. Feuchtwanger, *Disraeli, Democracy and the Tory Party* (Oxford, 1968). R. McKenzie and A. Silver, *Angels in Marble* (1968) is interesting on the Tory working-class vote. On the Liberals J.R. Vincent, *The Formation of the Liberal Party 1857–1868* (1966, new edition Hassocks, 1980) is a seminal work. D.A. Hamer, *Liberal Politics in the Age of Gladstone and Rosebery* (Oxford, 1972) is also useful, but not entirely balanced in its emphasis. D. Southgate, *The Passing of the Whigs* (1962) is still relevant for this period. D.A. Hamer, *The Politics of Electoral Pressure* (Hassocks, 1977) gives an insight into liberalism at the grassroots; R. Spence Watson, *The National Liberal Federation 1877–1906* (1907) still has no modern equivalent; see also P. Auspos, 'Radicalism, Pressure Groups and Party Politics: from the National Education League to the National Liberal Federation' *JBS* XX (1980). For Disraeli R. Blake, *Disraeli* (1966) is the standard biography. For its rich documentation W.F. Monypenny and G.E. Buckle, *Life of Benjamin Disraeli* (6 vols., 1910–24) is still worth consulting. Among other documentary material on Disraeli two books deserve special mention: Marquis of Zetland (ed.), *Letters of Disraeli to Lady Bradford and Lady Chesterfield* (2 vols., 1929) and J.R. Vincent (ed.), *Disraeli, Derby and the Conservative Party: The Political Journals of Lord Stanley 1849–1869* (Hassocks, 1978). For Gladstone the large-scale modern biography by R.T. Shannon still awaits its second, post-1865 volume. P. Magnus, *Gladstone* (1954) gives a good all-round portrait; E.J. Feuchtwanger, *Gladstone* (1975) is a political biography based on more recent research. J. Morley, *Life of W.E. Gladstone* (3 vols., 1903) is still important. *The Gladstone Diaries* (eds. M.R.D. Foot and H.C.G. Matthew, Oxford 1968–) are still in course of publication; the introductions by H.C.G. Matthew to volumes five: 1855–1860 (Oxford, 1978) and seven: January 1869 to June 1871 (Oxford, 1982) are well worth reading. There are four volumes devoted to Gladstone in the HMSO series *Prime Ministers' Papers*; volume I (1971) and IV (1981), both edited by John Brooke and Mary Sorensen, are particularly relevant to this period.

Other biographies of interest include J. Prest, *Lord John Russell* (1972), K. Robbins, *John Bright* (1979), James Winter, *Robert Lowe* (Toronto, 1976) and F.M. Leventhal, *Respectable Radical: George Howell and Victorian Working-Class Politics* (1971). For those who have held the office of Prime Minister H. van Thal (ed.), *The*

Prime Ministers, volume II: *From Lord John Russell to Edward Heath* (1975) can be consulted. T. Wemyss Reid, *Politicians of Today* (2 vols., 1880, reprinted in one volume, 1972) is a readable contemporary collection of sketches.

On the monarchy, see F.M. Hardie, *The Political Influence of Queen Victoria 1861–1901* (1935) and *The Political Influence of the British Monarchy 1868–1952* (1970). E. Longford, *Victoria R.I.* (1964) is a readable biography. G.H. Le May, *The Victorian Constitution* (1980) provides an up-to-date survey.

2

Many of the books listed in the previous section are also relevant here. Among printed documentary sources A. Ramm (ed.), *The Political Correspondence of Mr Gladstone and Lord Granville 1868–1876* (2 vols., 1952) and E. Drus (ed.), First Earl of Kimberley, *A Journal of Events during the Gladstone Ministry 1868–1874* (1958) are particularly important.

G.I.T. Machin, *Politics and the Churches in Great Britain 1832 to 1868* (Oxford, 1977) is a major work about the political impact of ecclesiastical questions. M.A. Crowther, *Church Embattled: Religious Controversies in Mid-Victorian England* (Newton Abbot, 1970) deals with the clash of views in the Church of England. The place of the Church in society is dealt with from different angles in K.S. Inglis, *The Churches and the Working Classes in Victorian England* (1963), G. Kitson Clark, *Churchmen and the Condition of England 1852–1885* (1973) and P.T. Marsh, *The Victorian Church in Decline. Archbishop Tait and the Church of England, 1868–1882* (Pittsburgh, 1969). For disestablishment in England and the Liberation Society, see W.H. Mackintosh, *Disestablishment and Liberation* (1972); for the disestablishment of the Irish Church, P.M.H. Bell, *Distestablishment in Ireland and Wales* (1969). Anti-Catholicism is discussed in E.R. Norman, *Anticatholicism in Victorian England* (1968) and G.F.A. Best, 'Popular Protestantism in Victorian Britain', in *Ideas and Institutions of Victorian Britain*, ed. Robert Robson (1967). For the passage of the Irish Church Disestablishment Bill see chapter I of J.D. Fair, *British Interparty Conferences. A Study of the Procedure of Conciliation in British Politics, 1867–1921* (Oxford, 1980). Among the large literature on the political impact of nonconformity, the following, incorporating recent research, are valuable: D.W. Bebbington, *The Nonconformist Conscience. Chapel and Politics, 1870–1914* (1982); Hugh McLeod, *Class and Religion in the Late Victorian City* (1974); S. Koss, *Nonconformity in Modern British Politics* (1975); C. Binfield, *So Down to Prayers: Studies in English Nonconformity, 1780–1920* (1977); and R.J. Helmstadter, 'The Nonconformist Conscience' in Peter Marsh (ed.), *The Conscience of the Victorian State* (Hassocks, 1979). On Wales two books by K.O. Morgan are indispensable: *Wales in British Politics 1868–1922* (2nd edn., Cardiff, 1970) and *Rebirth of a Nation: Wales 1880–1980* (Oxford, 1980). On the religious controversies in education Majorie Cruickshank, *Church and State in English Education* (1963) is a general account going to 1944 and beyond. An account of the campaign against the Education Act of 1870 is given in F. Adams, *History of the Elementary School Contest in England* (1882, reprinted Brighton 1972, with an introduction by A. Briggs). No modern biography has replaced T. Wemyss Reid, *Life of the Rt Hon. W.E. Forster* (2 vols., 1888). J.P. Parry, 'Religion and the Collapse of the first Gladstone Government 1870–74', *HJ* XXV (1982) discusses the political consequences of religious divisions. J.S. Hurt, *Elementary Schooling and the Working Classes 1860–1918* (1979) is useful; from a left-wing perspective there is B. Simon, *Education and the Labour Movement 1870–1920* (1965). On other aspects of education, see T.W. Bamford, *The Rise of the Public Schools* (1967); C. Dilke, *Dr Moberly's Mint-Mark. A Study of Winchester College* (1965) and J. Roach, *Public Examinations in England 1850–1900* (1971). On the trade unions of this period S. and B. Webb, *The History of Trade Unionism* (rev. edn, 1920) is the classic work, but many of its judgements are no longer tenable. H. Pelling, *A History of British Trade Unionism* (3rd edn, 1976) is the best short history. B.C. Roberts, *The Trades Union Congress 1868–1921* (1958) is a standard account; a more recent authoritative work is Ross M. Martin, *TUC: the Growth of a Pressure Group 1868–1976* (Oxford, 1980). A useful short summary will be found in Harry Browne, *The Rise of British Trade Unions 1825–1914* (1979). For later periods, see sections 3 and 6 below. On temperance and licensing B. Harrison, *Drink and the Victorians* (1971) is indispensable.

On foreign policy K. Bourne, *The Foreign Policy of Victorian England 1830–1902* is essential; it consists of commentary and documents. A.J.P. Taylor, *The Struggle for Mastery in Europe 1848–1918* (Oxford, 1952) gives a good general survey. P. Knaplund, *Gladstone's Foreign Policy* (1935) is still worth reading. On a more detailed level there is R. Millman, *British Foreign Policy and the Coming of the Franco-Prussian War* (Oxford, 1965); for the *Alabama* arbitration, see H.C. Allen, *Great Britain and the United States: a History of Anglo-American Relations 1783–1952* (1954). On imperialism in theory and practice C.C. Eldridge, *England's Mission: The Imperial Idea in the Age of Gladstone and Disraeli* (1973), by the same author, *Victorian Imperialism* (1978), a broad survey, and A.P. Thornton, *The Imperial Idea and its Enemies* (1958) are valuable. On Ireland F.S.L. Lyons, *Ireland since the Famine* (rev. edn, 1973) is an excellent and authoritative survey. For the rise of the home rule party, see D.A. Thornley, *Isaac Butt and Home Rule*; for the agrarian problem, P. Bew, *Land and the National Question in Ireland* (1979) and E.D. Steele, *Irish Land and British Politics. Tenant-Right and Nationality 1865–1870* (Cambridge, 1974); for the relations of Irish Catholicism with British Liberalism, E.R. Norman, *The Catholic Church and Ireland in the Age of Rebellion* (1965).

3

P.W. Clayden, *England under Lord Beaconsfield* (1880, reprinted 1971) is a contemporary account of these years from a Radical point of view. Two other important documents are A. Ramm (ed.), *The Political Correspondence of Mr Gladstone and Lord Granville, 1876–1886* (2 vols., Oxford, 1962) and W.E. Gladstone, *Political Speeches in Scotland, November and December 1879* (1879, reprinted as *Midlothian Speeches 1879*, with an introduction by M.R.D. Foot, Leicester, 1971). Most titles in sections 1 and 2 are relevant here. For the campaign against Ritualism, see J. Bentley, *Ritualism and Politics in Victorian Britain* (Oxford, 1978) For the Conservative social legislation see, in addition to Paul Smith's book cited in section 1, P.H.J.H. Gosden, *The Friendly Societies in England 1815–1875* (Manchester, 1961); on the trade unions, John Lovell, *British Trade Unions 1875–1933* (1977), a short survey of existing literature in the series *Studies in Economic and Social History*.

On the Eastern Question R. Millman, *Britain and the Eastern Question 1875–1878* (Oxford, 1979) is now the standard work. For a survey over a longer period, see M.S. Anderson, *The Eastern Question* (1966). R.W. Seton-Watson, *Disraeli, Gladstone and the Eastern Question* (1935) was an authoritative account from the Gladstonian point of view. R.T. Shannon, *Gladstone and the Bulgarian Agitation 1876* (2nd edn, Brighton, 1975) goes much beyond its title and gives an excellent picture of Liberalism at this time. It is supplemented by C. Harvie, *The Lights of Liberalism: University Liberals and the Challenge of Democracy* (1976) and by J.W. Barrow, *A Liberal Descent: Victorian Historians and the English Past* (Cambridge, 1981).

4

A contemporary view is given in T.H.S. Escott, *England, Its People, Polity and Pursuits* (1879). H.M.Lynd, *England in the Eighteen-Eighties: Towards a Social Basis for Freedom*

(Oxford, 1945) presents a more recent attempt at synthesis. General and authoritative surveys of economic developments are P. Mathias, *The First Industrial Nation. An Economic History of Britain 1700–1914* (1969); S.G. Checkland, *The Rise of Industrial Society in England 1815–1885* (1964); F. Crouzet, *The Victorian Economy* (1982); R. Floud and D. McCloskey (eds.), *The Economic History of Britain since 1700*, vol. 2: *1860 to the 1970s* (1981) and W. Ashworth, *An Economic History of England 1870–1939* (1960). There is much useful information in D.C. Marsh, *The Changing Social Structure of England and Wales 1871–1961* (1965) and for reference B.R. Mitchell and P. Deane (eds.), *Abstract of British Historical Statistics* (Cambridge, 1962) and P. Deane and W.A. Cole, *British Economic Growth 1688–1959* (Cambridge, 1967) are useful. A survey from a Marxist point of view is E. Hobsbawm, *Industry and Empire* (1969). Two short analyses in the series *Studies in Economic and Social History* are very valuable: R.A. Church, *The Great Victorian Boom* (1975) and S.B. Saul, *The Myth of the Great Depression* (1969). For Britain's international trade A.K. Cairncross, *Home and Foreign Investment, 1870–1913* (Cambridge, 1953) and S.B. Saul, *Studies in British Overseas Trade 1870–1914* (Liverpool, 1960) are important. On agriculture, see C.S. Orwin and E.H. Whetham, *History of British Agriculture 1846–1914* (1971); G.E. Mingay, 'The Transformation of Agriculture', in R.M. Hartwell (ed.), *The Long Debate on Poverty* (2nd edn, 1974) and G.E. Mingay (ed.), *The Victorian Countryside*, (2 vols, 1981). J. Bateman, *Great Landowners of Great Britain and Ireland* (4th edn, 1883, reprinted 1971) is an essential work of reference on landownership, while J.P.D. Dunbabin (ed.), *Rural Discontent in Nineteenth-Century Britain* (1974) and Pamela Horn, *Joseph Arch* (1971) shed light on the condition of the agricultural labourer. P.J. Perry, *British Agriculture 1815–1914* (1973) provides documents and commentary. On the philosophical shift from individualism, see M. Richter, *The Politics of Conscience: T.H. Green and his Age* (1964) and M. Freeden, *The New Liberalism* (Oxford, 1978). Original in its many-sided approach is A. Offner, *Property and Politics: Landownership, Law, Ideology and Urban Development in England* (Cambridge, 1981). Changes in economic doctrine are traced in T.W. Hutchison, *A Review of Economic Doctrines, 1870–1929* (Oxford, 1953) and E. Roll, *A History of Economic Thought* (1973). For the beginnings of socialism H. Pelling, *Origins of the Labour Party* (2nd edn, Oxford, 1965) is essential reading. On the Marxist strand in British socialism there are C. Tsuzuki, *H.M. Hyndman and British Socialism* (Oxford, 1961) and H. Collins and C. Abramsky, *Karl Marx and the British Labour Movement* (1965). For the Fabians A.M. McBriar, *Fabian Socialism and English Politics 1884–1918* (Cambridge, 1966) is the standard work. See also W. Wolfe, *From Radicalism to Socialism: men and ideas in the formation of Fabian socialist doctrines 1881–1889* (1975). For the Christian Socialists of this period, see P.D'A. Jones, *The Christian Socialist Revival 1877–1914* (1968) and C. Tsuzuki, *Edward Carpenter 1844–1929: Prophet of Human Fellowship* (Cambridge, 1980). On the link between radicalism and unbelief, see E. Royle, *Radical Politics 1790–1900, Religion and Unbelief* (1971) and S. Budd, *Varieties of Unbelief: Atheists and Agnostics in English Society 1850–1960* (1977). Many of the contributions in K.D. Brown (ed., *Essays in Anti-Labour History* (1974) deal with the individualist counterattack against collectivism.

Henry Mayhew's volumes on *London Labour and the London Poor* were a revelation to contemporaries and are still significant to historians, even though the author was occasionally misled by those whom he interviewed. G. Stedman Jones, *Outcast London* (Oxford, 1971) is the best modern work on the London poor. A.S. Wohl, 'The bitter cry of outcast London', *IRSH* XIII (1968) describes the circumstances of the outcry. H.J. Dyos and M. Wolff (eds.), *The Victorian City: Images and Realities* (1973) is a well-illustrated compendium on the subject.

G.B.A.M. Finlayson, *The Seventh Earl of Shaftesbury 1801–1885* (1981) is an excellent biography, although dealing mostly with an earlier period. C.L. Mowat, *The*

Charity Organization Society 1869-1913 (1961) covers the work of this influential body.

B. Porter, *The Lion's Share. A Short History of British Imperialism* (1975) is a good general survey; the same author's *Critics of Empire: British Attitudes to Colonialism in Africa, 1895-1914* (1968) is informative on the opposition to imperialism. R.E. Robinson and J. Gallagher, *Africa and the Victorians* (1961) has stimulated much debate amongst historians about the motivations of imperialism. P.J. Cain, *Economic Foundations of British Overseas Expansion 1815-1914* (1980), in the series *Studies in Economic and Social History*, is a short survey of this debate. Social imperialism is the theme of B. Semmel, *Imperialism and Social Reform* (1960) and other aspects of the subject are covered in C. Bolt, *Victorian Attitudes to Race* (1970) and by R.T. Shannon, 'J.R. Seeley and the Idea of a National Church' in R. Robson (ed.), *Ideas and Institutions of Victorian Britain* (1967). Benjamin H. Brown, *The Tariff Reform Movement in Great Britain 1881-1895* (New York, 1943) deals with the beginnings of protectionism.

On the structure of élites, W.L. Guttsman, *The British Political Elite* (1963) and W.L. Guttsman (ed.), *The English Ruling Class* (1969), a volume of documents, provide an introduction. W.D. Rubinstein, *Men of Property. The Very Wealthy in Britain since the Industrial Revolution* (1981) and two articles by the same author, 'Wealth, Elites and the Class Structure of Modern Britain', *Past & Present* 76 (1977), and 'The Victorian Middle Classes: Wealth, Occupation and Geography', *EconHR* XXX (1977) give much valuable information. See also D. Spring, *The English Landed Estate in the 19th Century: Its Administration* (Baltimore, 1963), M. Girouard, *The Victorian Country House* (rev. edn, New Haven, 1979) and J. Franklin, *The Gentleman's Country House and Its Plan 1835-1914* (1981). A standard work on the professions is W.J. Reader, *Professional Men: The Rise of the Professional Classes in Nineteenth Century England* (1966). For the grant of titles, see R. Pumphrey, 'The Introduction of Industrialists into the British Peerage', *AHR* LXV (1959), and H.J. Hanham, 'The Sale of Honours in Late Victorian England', *VS* III (1960). On the decline of enterprise. M.J. Wiener, *English Culture and the Decline of the Industrial Spirit 1850-1980* (Cambridge, 1981) is stimulating but speculative. See also P.L. Payne, *British Entrepeneurship in the Nineteenth Century* (1974) and A.L. Levine, *Industrial Retardation in Britain 1880-1914* (1967). On particular industries, see I.C.R. Byatt, *The British Electrical Industry 1875-1914* (Oxford, 1979), T.C. Barker and M. Robbins, *A History of London Transport* (1974), H. Pollins, *Britain's Railways* (Newton Abbot, 1971) and W.J. Reader, *Imperial Chemical Industries. A History. I: The Forerunners, 1870-1926* (Oxford, 1970).

The public school ethos is evoked in D. Newsome, *Godliness and Good Learning: Four Studies in Victorian Idealism* (1961) and in several essays in B. Simon and I. Bradley (eds.), *The Victorian Public School* (1975). On the universities, W.H.G. Armytage, *Civic Universities* (1955) provides a general survey from the end of the Middle Ages. N.A. Jepson, *The Beginnings of English University Adult Education - Policy and Problems* (1973) is a careful study of university extension. The influence of universities on industrial development is the theme of J.M. Sanderson, *The Universities and British Industry 1850-1970* (1972) and George Haines IV, 'German influence upon scientific education in England, 1867-1887', *VS* I (1958). J.M. Sanderson (ed.), *The Universities in the Nineteenth Century* (1975) is a collection of documents with commentary. There is a large literature on working-class life. E.J. Hobsbawm, *Labouring Men* (1964) was a pioneering study. S. Meacham, *A Life Apart. The English Working Class 1890-1914* (1977) draws a panoramic picture and uses oral sources. A number of scholarly regional studies illuminate local peculiarities: P. Joyce, *Work, Society and Politics. The Culture of the Factory in Later Victorian England* (Brighton, 1980) is an interesting interpretation of working-class life mainly in Lancashire and of the politics arising from it; P.J. Waller, *Democracy and Sectarianism. A Political and Social History of Liverpool 1868-1939* (Liverpool, 1981) provides not only a full account of a special situation, but offers much insight into many national social and political problems. A stimulating comparative study of Birmingham and Sheffield is Dennis Smith, *Conflict and Compromise. Class Formation in English Society 1830–1914* (1982). R. Moore, *Pitmen, Preachers and Politics. The Effects of Methodism in a Durham Mining Community* (Cambridge, 1974) illustrates the continuing influence of religion on working-class consciousness. A number of books deal with the uses of leisure in an urban environment: P. Bailey, *Leisure and Class in Victorian England. Rational Recreation and the Contest for Control 1830–1885* (1978); H.E. Meller, *Leisure and the Changing City 1870–1914* (1976); and A. Briggs, *Victorian* Cities (1963). See also Tony Mason, *Association Football and English Society, 1863–1915* (Brighton, 1980), H.S. Altham, *A History of Cricket* (1926), and T. Kelly, *History of Public Libraries in Great Britain 1845–1975* (2nd edn, 1977). For the debate on the labour aristocracy, see 'The Concept of the Labour Aristocracy' in H.M. Pelling, *Popular Politics and Society in Late Victorian Britain* (1968) and R.Q. Gray, *The Labour Aristocracy in Victorian Edinburgh* (Oxford, 1976). Another aspect is discussed in Charles More, *Skill and the English Working Class, 1870–1914* (1980).

5

There is a full-scale account for the 1880 election, T. Lloyd, *The General Election of 1880* (Oxford, 1968). T.A. Jenkins, 'Gladstone, the Whigs and the leadership of the Liberal Party, 1879–80', *HJ* XXVII (1984) discusses Gladstone's return to the premiership. Many important biographies are relevant to this and subsequent sections. For Salisbury no modern work so far replaces Lady Gwendolen Cecil's incomplete *Life of Robert, Marquis of Salisbury* (4 vols., 1921–32). Paul Smith (ed.), *Lord Salisbury on Politics* (Cambridge, 1972), a collection of Salisbury's articles in the *Quarterly*, has an excellent introduction. Essential for Salisbury as a party leader is Peter Marsh, *The Discipline of Popular Government: Lord Salisbury's Domestic Statecraft 1881–1902* (Hassocks, 1978). *The Life of Joseph Chamberlain* by J.L. Garvin (vols. 1–3, 1932–7) and Julian Amery (vols. 4–6, 1951–69) is still worth consulting. The best modern analysis is Richard Jay, *Joseph Chamberlain: a Political Study* (Oxford, 1981). See also Joseph Chamberlain, *A Political Memoir 1880–1892* (ed. C.H.D. Howard, 1953). W.L.S. Churchill, *Lord Randolph Churchill* (2 vols., 1906) is a document in its own right. R.R. James, *Lord Randolph Churchill* (1959) is a modern reassessment, but the best analysis is R.F. Foster, *Lord Randolph Churchill: A Political Life* (Oxford, 1981). For a different view see R.E. Quinault, 'Lord Randolph Churchill and Tory Democracy, 1880–85' *HJ* XXII (1979). A seminal article is J.P. Cornford, 'The Transformation of Conservatism in the late Nineteenth Century', *VS* VII (1963). There are modern biographies for a number of lesser political figures: D.A. Hamer, *John Morley* (Oxford, 1968), an important book; Roy Jenkins, *Sir Charles Dilke* (1958); Viscount Chilston, *W.H. Smith* (1965) and *Chief Whip: the Political Life and Times of Aretas Akers-Douglas, first Viscount Chilston* (1961); T.J. Spinner, *G.J. Goschen* (Cambridge, 1973). B. Holland, *The Life of Spencer Compton, 8th Duke of Devonshire* has no modern counterpart.

For foreign policy from 1880 Paul Hayes, *Modern British Foreign Policy: The Twentieth Century 1880–1939* (1978) provides a convenient summary. For some of the foreign policy problems faced by the second Gladstone government, see W.N. Medlicott, *Bismarck, Gladstone and the Concert of Europe* (1956); D.M. Schreuder, *Gladstone and Kruger* (1969); on Egypt, Part III, Chapter 1 of D.C.M. Platt, *Finance, Trade and Politics in British Foreign Policy 1815–1914*, an important work for all of this period, and A. Ramm, 'Britain and France in Egypt 1876–82', in P. Gifford and W.R. Louis, *Britain and France in Africa* (1971).

Two books are indispensable for Irish developments in the 1880s, F.S.L. Lyons,

C.S. Parnell (1977), a definitive biography, and C.C. O'Brien, *Parnell and His Party* (Oxford, 1964). J.L. Hammond, *Gladstone and the Irish Nation* (1964 edn, introduced by M.R.D. Foot) is a classic Liberal interpretation of the problem. On the links between Irish nationalism and British Radicalism, see T.W. Heyck, *The Dimensions of British Radicalism. The Case of Ireland 1874–95* (Illinois, 1974); also A. O'Day, *The English Face of Irish Nationalism* (1977).

W.L. Arnstein, *The Bradlaugh Case* (Oxford, 1965) gives a comprehensive account. See also R.E. Quinault, 'The Fourth Party and the Conservative Opposition to Bradlaugh' *EHR* XCI (1976). A revealing, if often naïve insider's view of politics comes from one of Gladstone's private secretaries, D.W.R. Bahlman (ed.), *Diary of Sir Edward Hamilton 1880–85* (2 vols., Oxford, 1972).

The passage of the third Reform Bill is analysed from the perspective of 'high politics' in Andrew Jones, *The Politics of Reform 1884* (Cambridge, 1972). An invaluable work of reference on elections under the reformed system is H.M. Pelling, *The Social Geography of British Elections, 1885–1910* (1967); also N. Blewett, 'The Franchise in the United Kingdom 1885–1918', *Past & Present* XXXII (1965). An analysis based on modern statistical methods will be found in Kenneth D. Wald, *Crosses on the Ballot* (Princeton, 1983). On the limitation of election expenses, see C.C. O'Leary, *The Elimination of Corrupt Practices in British Elections* (Oxford, 1962) and W.B. Gwyn, *Democracy and the Cost of Politics in Britain* (1962).

A.B. Cooke and J.R. Vincent, *The Governing Passion. Cabinet Government and Party Politics in Britain 1885–86* (Brighton, 1974) has revolutionized perceptions of the home rule crisis. Among valuable documents on the crisis are A.B. Cooke and J.R. Vincent (eds.), *Lord Carlingford's Journal: Reflections of a Cabinet Minister 1885* (Oxford, 1971); D.A. Hamer (ed.), Joseph Chamberlain and others, *The Radical Programme* (1885, reprinted 1971); and A.V. Dicey, *England's Case against Home Rule* (1886, reprinted 1973). The rise of the Ulster problem is traced in Peter Gibbon, *The Origins of Ulster Unionism* (Manchester, 1975).

6

There are a number of important books on the politics of this period. Michael Barker, *Gladstone and Radicalism 1885–94* (Hassocks, 1975) shows Gladstone to have been less conservative in his old age than is often made out. The emergence of new radical ideas is traced in H.V. Emy, Liberals, *Radicals and Social Politics 1892–1914* (Cambridge, 1973); H.G.G. Matthew, *The Liberal Imperialists* (Oxford, 1973) is the definitive account of another important group in the Liberal Party. M. Hurst, *Joseph Chamberlain and Liberal Reunion 1887* (1967) and P. Stansky, *Ambitions and Strategies: The Struggle for the Liberal Leadership in the 1890s* (Oxford, 1964) describe in detail phases of Liberal politics. Paul Thompson, *Socialists, Liberals and Labour. The Struggle for London 1885–1914* (1967) is indispensable on the intersection of Liberal and Labour politics. In addition to the titles given in section 4 on socialism, R. Poirier, *The Advent of the Labour Party* (1954) and Roger Moore, *The Emergence of the Labour Party 1880–1924* (1978) give useful general summaries. K.O. Morgan, *Keir Hardie: Radical and Socialist* (1975) provides the most convincing portrait of its subject. Other biographies useful for early Labour politics are L. Thompson, *Robert Blatchford* (1951) and J. Schneer, *Ben Tillett* (1982); see also J. Saville and J.M. Bellamy (eds.), *Dictionary of Labour Biography* (4 vols., 1972–77). On the trade unions, H.A. Clegg, A. Fox and A.F. Thompson, *A History of British Trade Unions since 1889* (Oxford, 1964), a standard work unfortunately incomplete, becomes relevant for this period. R. & E. Frow and M. Katanka, *Strikes* (1971) is a useful collection of documents.

On Ireland L.P. Curtis, *Coercion and Conciliation in Ireland 1880–92* (Princeton, 1963) and F.S.L. Lyons, *The Irish Parliamentary Party 1890–1910* (1951) are valuable.

There are three modern biographies of Balfour, by Kenneth Young (1963), S.H. Zebel (Cambridge, 1973) and M. Egremont (1980); see also A.J. Balfour, *Chapters of Autobiography* (1930). R.R. James, *Rosebery* (1963) is excellent. A.G. Gardiner, *Life of Sir William Harcourt* (2 vols., 1923) remains useful. There are two good modern biographies of Asquith, by Roy Jenkins (1964) and S.E. Koss (1976).

On local government see J.P.D, Dunbabin, 'The Politics of the Establishment of County Councils', *HJ* VI (1963); also E.P. Hennock, *Fit and Proper Persons* (1971) and Derek Fraser, *Urban Politics in Victorian England* (1976).

7

J.A.S. Grenville, *Lord Salisbury and Foreign Policy* (1964) is essential reading for this section. Also useful are C.J. Lowe, *The Reluctant Imperialists: British Foreign Policy 1878-1902* (2 vols., 1967) and by the same author, *Salisbury and the Mediterranean 1886-1896* (1965). The first two volumes of C.J. Lowe and M.L. Dockrill (eds.), *The Mirage of Power* (3 vols., 1972) provide documents for this period. Z.S. Steiner, *The Foreign Office and Foreign Policy 1895-1914* (Cambridge, 1969) is definitive on the machinery of foreign policy. G.W. Monger, *The End of Isolation*: British Foreign Policy 1900-1907 (1963) is a balanced survey. I. Nish, *The Anglo-Japanese Alliance* (1966) is the standard account of its subject; P.M. Kennedy, *The Rise of the Anglo-German Antagonism 1860-1914* is a wide-ranging and scholarly work covering both countries. There is a vast literature on the origins and conduct of the South African war, of which only a few can be mentioned here. On the origins: Jeffrey Butler, *The Liberal Party and the Jameson Raid* (Oxford, 1968); E. Drus, 'The Question of Imperial Complicity in the Jameson Raid', *EHR* LXVIII (1953); and A.N. Porter, *The Origins of the South African War: Joseph Chamberlain and the Diplomacy of Imperialism 1895-99* (Manchester, 1980). On the war, T. Pakenham, *The Boer War* (1979) and E.M.G. Belfield, *The Boer War* (1975). On popular support for the war, R. Price, *An Imperial War and the British Working Class* (1972). On the foreign and imperial policies of the Balfour era: Denis Judd, *Balfour and the British Empire* (1968); A.M. Gollin, *Balfour's Burden: Arthur Balfour and Imperial Preference* (1965) and Alan Sykes, *Tariff Reform in British Politics 1903-1913* deal with the impact of tariff reform; see also R.A. Rempel, *Unionists Divided. Arthur Balfour, Joseph Chamberlain and the Unionist Free Traders* (Newton Abbot, 1972). Two excellent biographies significant for this period are John Wilson, *C.B. A Life of Sir Henry Campbell-Bannerman* (1973) and David Marquand, *Ramsay MacDonald* (1977). For Milner, see A.M. Gollin, *Proconsul in Politics* (1964) and T.H. O'Brien, *Viscount Milner* (1979). J. Ramsden, *The Conservative Party: The Age of Balfour and Baldwin 1902-1940* (1978) is useful on party organization, as is Roy Douglas, *A History of the Liberal Party 1895-1970* (1971). Chris Cook, *A Short History of the Liberal Party* (1976) is brief but reliable. F. Bealey and H. Pelling, *Labour and Politics 1900-1906* is indispensable for the early years of the LRC. G.R. Searle, *The Quest for National Efficiency* (Oxford, 1971) describes a movement that cut across parties. On defence policy N. D'Ombrain, *War Machinery and High Policy* (Oxford, 1973) and J. Ehrman, *Cabinet Government and War 1890-1940* (Cambridge, 1958) trace the changes in government decision-making on defence. M.E. Howard, *The Continental Commitment* (1972) is a thoughtful appraisal of changes in British strategy. M.R. Brett and Oliver, Viscount Esher (eds.), *Journals and Letters of Reginald, Viscount Esher* (4 vols., 1934-8) illuminates many of these changes. H. Cunningham, *The Volunteer Force: A Social and Political History 1859-1908* (1975) is interesting on the social ramifications of the force. See also W.S. Hamer, *The British Army. Civil-Military Relations 1885-1905* (Oxford, 1970) and G. Harries-Jenkins, *The Army in Victorian Society* (1977). For the naval reforms see A.J. Marder, *From the Dreadnought to Scapa Flow: The Royal Navy in the Fisher Era 1904-1919* (5 vols.,

1961-1970), particularly the first volume, and R.F. Mackay, *Fisher of Kilverstone* (Oxford, 1973). See also Bryan Ranft (ed.), *Technical Change and British Naval Policy 1860-1939* (1977).

8

There are a number of interesting collections of essays on Edwardian England: A. O'Day (ed.), *The Edwardian Age: Conflict and Stability 1900-1914* (1979); D. Read (ed.), *Edwardian England* (1982); A.J.A. Morris (ed.), *Edwardian Radicalism 1900-1914* (1974); Paul Thompson, *The Edwardians* (1975), personal reminiscences with commentaries. K.O. Morgan, *The Age of Lloyd George* (1971) is a very useful survey with documents. George Dangerfield, *The Strange Death of Liberal England* (1935) presents a controversial interpretation with which many subsequent historians have taken issue, but it still makes very entertaining reading.

There is a comprehensive account of the 1906 election in A.K. Russell, *Liberal Landslide* (Newton Abbot, 1973). P.F. Clarke, *Lancashire and the New Liberalism* (Cambridge, 1971) is a seminal work, essential to an understanding of Edwardian politics; see also P.F. Clarke, 'The Electoral Position of the Liberal and Labour Parties 1910-14', *EHR* XC (1975). N. Blewett, *The Peers, the Parties and the People: The General Elections of 1910* (1972) is a major work. H.C.G. Matthew, R.I. McKibbin and J.A. Kay 'The Franchise Factor in the Rise of the Labour Party', *EHR* XCI (1976) holds the restricted franchise chiefly responsible for the failure of Labour to achieve greater electoral success before 1914. For this debate, see also M. Pugh, *The Making of Modern British Politics 1867-1939* (Oxford 1982), chapter 7 and D. Tanner, 'The Parliamentary Electoral System, The "Fourth" Reform Act and the Rise of Labour in England and Wales', *Bull. of the Inst. of Hist. Research* LVI (1983). Roy Jenkins, *Mr Balfour's Poodle* (1954) is a very readable account of the battle over the House of Lords. Among royal biographies, P. Magnus, *King Edward VII* (1964) as well as the works of Sir Harold Nicolson and K. Rose on King George V (1952 and 1983) are relevant. Bruce Murray, *The People's Budget 1909-10* (Oxford, 1980) is a comprehensive and definitive account. See also V. Bogdanor, *The People and the Party System. The Referendum and Electoral Reform in British Politics*, (Cambridge, 1981). The two fullest Lloyd George biographies are John Grigg, *The Young Lloyd George* (1973) and *Lloyd George: the People's Champion 1902-11* (1978); and Peter Rowland, *Lloyd George* (1975). The same author's *The Last Liberal Governments* (2 vols., 1968-71) provides a descriptive account for the whole of this period. For special aspects of Lloyd George, see C.J. Wrigley, *David Lloyd George and the British Labour Movement* (Hassocks, 1976); R. Scally, *the Origins of the Lloyd George Coalition: the Politics of Social Imperialism* (1975); and A.J.P. Taylor (ed.), *Lloyd George: Twelve Essays* (1971).

For the New Liberalism and the ideas behind Liberal welfare legislation there are, in addition to titles mentioned in earlier sections, two stimulating books: S. Collini, *Liberalism and Sociology: L.T. Hobhouse and political argument in England 1880-1914* (Cambridge, 1979) and P.F. Clarke, *Liberals and Social Democrats* (Cambridge, 1978). Also valuable is M.J. Wiener, *Between Two Worlds: The Political Thought of Graham Wallas* (Oxford, 1971). Among many interesting contemporary books C.F.G. Masterman, *The Condition of England* (1909) and L. Chiozza Money, *Poverty and Riches* (1905) deserve attention. Two short analytical surveys in the series *Studies in Economic History* are useful as introduction to the problems of poverty and welfare: M.E. Rose, *The Relief of Poverty, 1834-1914* (1972) and J.R. Hay, *The Origins of the Liberal Welfare Reforms* (1975). On unemployment J.F. Harris, *Unemployment and Politics 1886-1914* (Oxford, 1972) is the definitive study; the same author's biography of *Beveridge* (Oxford, 1977) is also valuable; she discusses the interplay of factors producing social policy in 'The Transition to High Politics in English Social Policy, 1880-1914' in M.

Bentley and J. Stevenson (eds.), *High and Low Politics in Modern Britain* (Oxford, 1983). Another aspect is covered in K.D. Brown, *The Labour Party and Unemployment 1900-1914* (Newton Abbot, 1971). B.B. Gilbert, *The Evolution of National Insurance in Great Britain* (1966) is is indispensable on the legislation of 1911. W.J. Mommsen (ed.), *The Emergence of the Welfare State in Britain and Germany* (1981) has valuable contributions on the interaction between the two countries. Lucy Masterman, *C.F.G. Masterman* (1939) and Trevor Wilson (ed.), *The Political Diaries of C.P. Scott* (1970) are interesting on the political background; also Beatrice Webb, *Our Partnership* (1948). For the final phase of Liberal reform before 1914, see B. B. Gilbert, 'David Lloyd George: the reform of British landholding and the budget of 1914', *HJ* XXI (1978). For Churchill, see R.S. Churchill, *W.S. Churchill, The Young Statesman 1901-14* (1967) and the companion volumes of documents.

On the Labour Party and the trade unions, in addition to works mentioned in previous sections, R.I. Mckibbin, *The Evolution of the Labour Party, 1910-1924* (Oxford, 1975) is essential: the same author offers an interesting discussion on the social context of labour politics in 'Why Was there no Marxism in Great Britain?', in *EHR* XCIX (1984). R.G. Gregory, *The Miners in Politics in England and Wales 1906-1914* (Oxford 1968) covers an important subject. An interesting local study is D. Clark, *Colne Valley – radicalism to socialism. The portrait of a northern constituency in the formative years of the Labour Party, 1890-1910* (1981). R. Holton, *British Syndicalism 1900-1914* (1976), written from a committed perspective, is a useful survey. The final phase in the development of trade unionism before 1914 is discussed by P.S. Bagwell, 'The Triple Industrial Alliance 1913-22', in A.Briggs and J. Saville, *Essays in Labour History 1886-1923* (1971). For the problem of corporatism see K. Middlemas, *Politics in Industrial Society* (1979).

The history of women's suffrage is traced in Constance Rover, *Women's Suffrage and Party Politics in Britain* (1967). The best book on the suffragettes is Andrew Rosen, *Rise Up, Women! The Militant Campaign of the Women's Social and Political Union 1903-1914* (1974). For the legislative complications of women's suffrage, see David Morgan, *Suffragists and Liberals. The Politics of Women's Suffrage in England* (Oxford, 1975). Brian Harrison, *Separate Spheres: the Opposition to Women's Suffrage in Britain* (1978) is interesting on a neglected aspect; also by the same author, 'Women's Suffrage at Westminster, 1866-1928', in M. Bentley and J. Stevenson (eds.), op. cit.

For Ulster and for the years immediately before the war Robert Blake, *The Unknown Prime Minister: The Life and Times of Andrew Bonar Law, 1858-1923* (1955) is important. Two interesting documents from the Liberal side are M. and E. Brock (eds.), *Asquith: Letters to Venetia Stanley* (Oxford, 1982) and E. David (ed.) *Inside Asquith's Cabinet: From the Diary of Charles Hobhouse* (1977). See also A.T.Q. Stewart, *The Ulster Crisis* (1967) and A.P. Ryan, *Mutiny at the Curragh* (1956). The problem is surveyed as a whole in P. Jalland, *The Liberals and Ireland: the Ulster Question in British Politics to 1914* (1980).

9

A masterly survey of British foreign policy before 1914 is provided by Zara Steiner, *Britain and the Origins of the First World War* (1977). A more detailed coverage of various aspects will be found in F.H. Hinsley (ed.), *The Foreign Policy of Sir Edward Grey* (Cambridge, 1977). Keith Robbins, *Sir Edward Grey* (1971) is the best biography and Vicount Grey, *Twenty-Five Years 1892-1916* (2 vols., 1925) is a valuable document. For the opposition to Grey's policies A.J.A. Morris, *Radicalism Against War 1906-1914* (1972) is indispensable. See also Norman Angell (R. Lane), *Europe's Optical Illusion* (1910). For the army reforms see E.M. Spiers, *The Army and Society 1815-1914* (1980) and the same author's *Haldane: An Army Reformer* (1981). For the impact of the July 1914 crisis on domestic politics C. Hazlehurst, *Politicians at War: July 1914 to May* 1915 (1971) is essential. Interesting comments on the state of the parties before 1914 will be found in D.J. Dutton 'The Unionist Pary and Social Policy', *HJ* XXIV (1981); G.R. Searle, 'The Edwardian Liberal Party and Business', *EHR* XCVIII (1983); and S. Pierson, *British Socialists: The Journey from Fanatasy to Politics* (Cambridge, Mass., 1979). S. Koss, *The Rise and Fall of the Political Press*, vol. I: *The Nineteenth Century* (1981) is authoritative and readable. A.J. Lee, *The Origins of the Popular Press 1855–1914* (1976) provides a useful general survey. There are many books on personalities in the press and in journalism, including P. Ferris, *The House of Northcliffe* (1971), A.M. Gollin, *The Observer and J.L. Garvin* (Oxford, 1960), A. Havighurst, *Radical Journalist: H.W. Massingham* (Cambridge, 1974) and S.E. Koss, *Fleet Street Radical: A.G. Gardiner and the Daily News* (1973).

On the various other aspects of British society before 1914 touched on in this chapter, see, in addition to titles mentioned under previous sections, G. Crossick (ed.), *The Lower Middle Class in Britain* (1979), Gillian Sutherland (ed.), *Studies in the Growth of Nineteenth-Century Government* (1972), A.R. Hall (ed.), *The Export of Capital from Britain 1870–1914* (1968), D.H. Aldcroft (ed.), *The Development of British Industry and Foreign Competition 1875–1914* (1968), A. Offner, 'Empire and Social Reform: British Overseas Investment and Domestic Politics, 1908–1914', *HJ* XXVI (1983), G. Jones, *Social Darwinism and English Thought: The Interaction between Biological and Social Theory* (Brighton, 1980) and S. Hynes, *The Edwardian Turn of Mind* (1968).

Table 1

Population (millions)	UK	Ireland	Germany	USA
1871	31.5	5.4	41.0	39.9
1911	45.2	4.4	64.9 (1910)	92.4 (1910)
Rural/urban ratio*	England & Wales			
1871	35:65		64:36	75:25
1911	21:79		40:60	52:48

* These figures represent orders of magnitude, as definitions of rural and urban vary widely between countries; the percentage of the British employed population in agriculture, forestry and fisheries was 15.1 in 1871 and 8.3 in 1911.

Table 2

	% of world manuf. output	% of world export trade in manuf. goods	% of world production:			% of tonnage of merchant marine
			Steel	Pig iron	Sulph. acid	
	1870	1880	1875–9	1875–9	1878	1870
UK	31.8	41.4	35.9	46.0	46.2	33.9
Germany	13.2	19.3	16.6	12.7	8.6	5.8
USA	23.3	2.8	26.6	15.6	13.8	9.1
	1913	1913	1910–13	1910–13	1913	1913
UK	14.0	29.9	10.3	13.9	13.0	33.8
Germany	15.7	26.5	22.7	21.0	20.3	8.7
USA	35.8	12.6	42.3	40.2	27.1	2.5

Table 3

Distribution of national income between families in England and Wales 1867

	% of families	% of national income	average per family
Upper class (over £1,000)	0.5	26	£6,079
Middle class (£100–£1,000)	25.0	35	£ 154
Working class	74.5	39	£ 58
	national average £111		

Distribution of landed property in England in 1873

	Number of owners	% of total land surface (excl. waste lands) held by each group
Owners of more than 10,000 acres	363	24
3,000 – 10,000 acres	1,000	17
1,000 – 3,000 acres	2,000	12.5
300 – 1,000 acres		14
1 – 300 acres		24.5

SOURCES:
D.H. Aldcroft (ed.), *The Development of British Industry and Foreign Competition 1875–1914* (1968)
F. Crouzet, *The Victorian Economy* (1982)
P. Deane and W.A. Cole, *British Economic Growth 1688–1959* (1967)
S.B. Saul, *Studies in British Overseas Trade 1870–1914* (1960)

Table 4: General Election results 1885 to December 1910

	1885	1886	1892	1895	1900	1906	Jan. 1910	Dec. 1910
Unionist percentage of poll in GB	46.5 (43.5)	52.2 (51.4)	50.2 (47.0)	53.7 (49.1)	54.3 (50.3)	43.1 (43.4)	47.4 (46.9)	48.2 (46.8)

(percentages adjusted for probable results in uncontested seats; percentages in brackets for overall UK vote)

Seats (excluding Irish Nationalists)

	1885	1886	1892	1895	1900	1906	Jan. 1910	Dec. 1910
Unionist	249	394	315	411	402	157	273	273
Liberal	335	191	274	177	186	400	275	271
LRC/Labour						30	40	42

SOURCES:
N. Blewett, *The Peers, the Parties and the People: The General Elections of 1910* (1972)
F.W.S. Craig, *British Parliamentary Election Results 1885–1918* (1974)
M. Kinnear, *The British Voter: An Atlas and Survey since 1885* (1968)

Index

Abdurrahman, ruler of Afghanistan, 151
Abraham, William, 322
Abyssinia, 227; 1867 war, 58, 108
Acland, Arthur, 203, 213, 217
Acland, Sir Thomas, 203
Acts of Parliament see individual Acts and Bills
Adam, W.P., 109
Adderley, C.B., 1st Baron Norton, 89
'Adullamites', 33, 35, 39–40, 42, 45
Affirmation Bill, 1883, 164–5
Affirmation Act, 1888, 164
Afghanistan, 108–9, 151, 178, 225
Africa, 130, 225, 226–7
Agadir crisis, 1911, 346, 348, 352–3, 355
Agricultural Holdings Bill, 1875, 89
agriculture: decline, 112, 115–16, 125; wages, 328
Agriculture, Royal Commission on, 1882, 116
Akroyd family, 144
Alabama claims, 80, 94–5
Albert, Prince Consort, 21, 53
Alden, Percy, 305
Aliens Act, 1905, 305–6
Allen, C.P., 276
Allon, Henry, 57
Amalgamated Society of Engineers, 262
Amending Bill (Irish Home Rule), 1914, 344–5
American Civil War, 1, 28, 93
Anderson, (*later* Sir) John, 316

Angell, Norman: *The Great Illusion*, 352
Anti-Slavery Society, 30
Anti-Socialist Union, 308
Applegarth, Robert, 28
Arabi, leader of Egyptian revolt, 154–5
Arch, Joseph, 74, 115
Argyll, 8th Duke of, 129, 161
aristocracy: as ruling élite, 2–3, 28, 132; schooling, 11–12; and popular suffrage, 37–8; and industrial entrepreneurship, 132–3, 141; values and status, 133; and professions, 134–5
Armenia, 226, 233
army: commissioned officers, 69–71; reform and defence organization, 259–60, 356; estimates and expenditure, 285, 356; Curragh mutiny, 343
Army Regulation Bill, 1871, 70
Arnold, Matthew, 12–13, 103, 120, 132, 134
Arnold, Thomas, 11, 136
Arnold-Forster, H.O., 259–60
Artisans Dwellings Act, 1875, 88, 126
Ashantee War, 1873, 108
Ashbourne, Edward Gibson, 1st Baron, 180
Ashley, W.J., 117
Askwith, Sir George (*later* 1st Baron), 321, 326–7
Asquith, Herbert Henry: and Eastern Question, 103; imperialism, 131, 243, 217; liberal policy, 203; as

Home Secretary, 213, 215, 217; and
Liberal leadership, 234; and Milner,
242; optimism, 250; opposes tariff
reform, 250–1; and Irish Home
Rule, 271–2, 337, 339, 341–2,
344–5; as Chancellor of Exchequer,
273–4, 346; and trade unions, 280
325–6; as Liberal leader and Prime
Minister, 282–4; taxation and financial policy, 284–8; and old-age pensions, 285; and navy estimates, 287;
and Lords, 290–1, 294, 299–300;
and first 1910 election, 291–2,
294–5; and 1910 Constitutional
Conference, 295–6; and second
1910 election, 297–8; opposes
women's suffrage, 332–3, 335; supports colleagues in Marconi scandal,
340; and Curragh mutiny, 343–4;
and outbreak of Great War, 357–9;
and press, 365
Asquith, Margot (*née* Tennant), 213
Aston Park riot, 1884, 173
Austria-Hungary: relations   with
Prussia, 34; and Balkan crisis, 97,
104, 107; and outbreak of Great
War, 354, 357–8

Baden-Powell, Col. Robert (*later* 1st
Baron), 236, 256
Bagehot, Walter, 72, 91
Baghdad railway, 350, 353, 369
Baines family, 49, 364
Baines, Edward, 63
Balcarres, David Lindsay, Earl of (*later*
27th Earl of Crawford), 300
Balfour Act, 1902 *see* Education Act,
1902
Balfour, Arthur James: in Fourth
Party, 163; as Irish Secretary,
195–6, 199; as leader of Commons,
210, 232; and Boer War, 235, 238;
in 1900 government, 241; as Party
leader, 244, 249, 279; drafts 1902
Education Bill, 138, 245, 248; and
tariff reform, 247–9, 252–3, 271,
278–9, 284, 295, 297; as Prime
Minister, 247; relations with
Chamberlain, 249, 278–9; delays
election, 252–3, 258; 1905 resigna-

tion, 253, 272; and British isolation,
254–5; and defence, 258–9; attitude
to unions and labour, 267–8; and
Ireland, 269–70; and liquor
licensing, 271; 1906 election losses,
274, 276; and Lords, 278, 280, 290,
299–300; regains seat, 278; in
Opposition, 279, 281; in first 1910
election, 292; and Constitutional
Conference, 259–6; and use of
referendum, 297; and Parliament
Bill, 298–300; and Unionist dissent,
299, 301; 1911 resignation, 315;
favours women's suffrage, 330; on
Ulster and Home Rule, 342; and
press, 365
Balfour, Gerald, 269–70
Balfour of Burleigh, 6th Baron, 249
Balkans: 1875–6   crisis,   96–104;
Turkey and, 353
Ballin, Albert, 350
Ballot Bill, 1870, 72
Bank Charter Act, 34
Baptists, 24; *see also* nonconformity
Baring family, 133
Baring, Walter, 99
Barnett, Canon Samuel Augustus, 309
Bates, Edward, 89
Bath, 4th Marquess of, 101
Baxter, Dudley, 40, 44, 115
Beale, Dorothea, 18
Beales, Edward, 36–7
Beaufort, 9th Duke of, 289
Beaverbrook, William Maxwell Ait-
ken, 1st Baron, 366
Beehive, The (newspaper), 74, 102
Beesley, E.S., 73, 76, 102
Beit, Alfred, 350
Belfast: 1886 riots, 186
Belgium, 358–9
Bell, Gertrude, 335
Bell, Richard, 266
Belloc, Hilaire, 276, 315, 340
Bennett, Arnold, 367
Bentham, Jeremy, 123
Bergson, Henri, 323
Berlin, Congress (and Treaty) of,
1878, 107, 109, 151
Berlin Memorandum, 1876, 98–9, 104
Besant, Annie, 7, 162, 206

Bessborough Commission on Irish Land, 1880, 158
Bethmann-Hollweg, Theobald von, 353
Beveridge, William, 305, 309–11
Bible, Holy, 21–2, 24
Biggar, J.G., 156
Birkenhead, F.E. Smith, 1st Earl of, 300, 327, 335
Birmingham caucus (Liberal), 48–9
Birrell, Augustine, 280, 295, 332
birth control, 6–7
birth rate, 5–7
Bismarck, Otto, Prince von, 46, 151, 155, 224
Blatchford, Robert, 208, 221, 303, 317, 366
Bloemfontein Conference, 1899, 231
Bloody Sunday (13 November, 1887), 123, 199, 202
Board of Education: formed, 245
Boers, 152–3, 228–31; *see also* South African War
Boer War *see* South African War
Boilermakers' Society, 73
Boord, Thomas William, 78
Booth, Charles, 128, 302–3
boundary commissions (electoral), 174
Boxer Rebellion, 240, 254
Bradford, Lady, 109
Bradlaugh, Charles, 7, 76, 129; case, 150, 162–5; views on Ireland, 162; career and beliefs, 162–3
Brailsford, H.N., 348
Braithwaite, W.J., 314
Bright, John: opposes aristocratic government, 2; leads Liberal left, 28, 51; supports parliamentary reform, 29–35, 37–9, 45; and cattle plague, 31; urges dissolution of parliament, 36; and Reform League, 37; as President of Board of Trade, 59; on Lords, 61; on 1870 Education Act, 66; rejoins Gladstone government, 66, 81; on balance of power, 93; and Balkan crisis, 102; Green admires, 118; in 1880 cabinet, 150; resigns over Egypt, 155; clauses in 1870 Irish Land Act, 158; supports conciliation

in Ireland, 161; jubilee celebrations, 167; 1886 abstention, 184; opposes Home Rule, 188; and New Liberalism, 277
British and Foreign Schools Society, 11
British Guiana, 226
British Medical Association, 314
British South Africa Company, 229
Broadhurst, Henry, 102, 127, 207–8
Brodrick, St John, 242, 259–60
Brontë, Charlotte, 18
Brown, Sir William, 134, 143
Bruce, H.A., 1st Baron Aberdare, 58, 73, 77–8, 81, 88
Brunel, Isambard Kingdom, 137
Brunner, Sir John, 351–2, 360
Bryant and May company, 206
Bryce, James, 139, 244, 274
Buckingham Palace Conference, 1914, 344–5
Budget Protest League, 289, 301
budgets: 1894, 217–18; 1909 ('People's'), 286–92, 351; 1914, 328–9
Bulgaria, 98–103, 105, 193, 226, 239
Buller, Sir Redvers, 235–6
Bülow, Bernhard, Prince von, 351
Bunce, J.T., 63
Burns, John: and SDF, 122–4; prominence, 206; elected at Battersea, 209; committed to Liberals, 221, 263; in Campbell-Bannerman government, 274; and Masterman, 286; and unemployed, 307; and poor relief, 308; and armaments, 352; non-interventionist in Great War, 357; resigns, 358
Burt, Thomas, 51
Buss, Frances Mary, 18
Butler, Josephine, 17–18
Butler, Samuel: *The Way of All Flesh*, 371
Butt, Isaac, 82, 156
Buxton, Sydney, 203, 326
Buxton, Noel, 352

Cadbury family, 144
Cadbury, George, 362, 366
Cairns, Hugh Calmont, 1st Earl, 52, 86

Cambon, Paul, 256

Cambridge, 2nd Duke of, 218

Campbell-Bannerman, Sir Henry, 218–19; as Liberal leader, 234, 243; on Chamberlain and Boer War, 238–9; and South African concentration camps, 242–3; and Unionist divisions, 250; and defence, 259–60, 285, 350; and Chinese labour, 268–9; and Ireland, 271–2; 1905 government, 273–4; attacks Balfour, 279; and trade unions, 281; and Lords reform, 282, 291; death, 282; foreign policy, 347, 350–1

Canada, 4, 8, 95, 339

Cardwell, Edward, Viscount, 70–1, 155, 235

Carlyle, Thomas, 24, 44, 103, 120, 132

Carnarvon, 4th Earl of; and parliamentary reform, 40–1; resigns from cabinet, 1878, 101; opposes Disraeli on foreign policy, 106; and South Africa, 109, 152; as Irish Viceroy, 180; and 1885 election, 183

Carnegie, Andrew, 143

Carson, Sir Edward, 301, 338, 341–5

Cassell, Sir Ernest, 350

cattle plague (rinderpest), 31

Cavagnari, Sir Louis, 109

Cavendish, Lord Frederick, 160

Cawdor, 3rd Earl of, 261, 295

Cecil family, 248, 302, 336

Cecil, Lord Hugh, 248, 299–300

Central Labour College, 323

Central Nonconformist Committee, 63

Chadwick, Sir Edwin, 8

Chalmers, Sir Robert, 286

Chamberlain, Austen, 249, 253, 295–6, 301, 315, 327

Chamberlain, Joseph: position, 48, 51; and Irish Home Rule, 50, 187–8; in National Education League, 63, 65–7; and slum clearance, 89; and Eastern Question, 102, 105; on housing, 127; imperialism, 131, 220, 227, 238–9, 246–7, 250; municipal socialism, 143, 176; and working-class voters, 146; on 1880 election, 148; in 1880 government, 149–50; supports Egypt policy, 154; and Parnell and Ireland, 158, 160–1, 178–9, 181, 185; relations with Gladstone, 160, 184–5, 187–8, 191; and Morley, 162; attacks Salisbury, 167; radicalism, 167, 176, 220; and franchise, 171; opposes Lords, 172–3; and Liberal Party leadership, 176, 181, 1885 programme, 176–7, 179, 201; 1885 election, 181–4; appointment and resignation under Gladstone, 184–5, 187; and Liberal Party manoeuvres, 188–91, 194; and Churchill, 193; Unionist-Tory alliance, 194–5, 199, 219–20; loses dominance of National Liberal Federation, 203; and disestablishment, 203; as Liberal Unionist leader, 211–12; and 1892 election, 211–12; relations with Salisbury, 211, 219–20, 233; as Colonial Secretary, 220, 223, 227–8; and South Africa, 229–31, 235, 237–8, 247; and domestic politics, 232, 247; and 1900 election, 240–1, 246; and 1902 Education Bill, 244–6, 248; proposes end to British isolation, 246–7, 254; South African tour, 247; urges imperial preference, 248, 250; and Balfour, 249, 278–9; and tariff reform, 249–53, 271, 278–9, 290, 303; relations with France, 255; illness, 279; and unemployment, 304; and aliens, 306

Champion, H.H., 208

Charity Commission, 12

Charity Organization Society, 127, 313

Charrington family, 133

Chelmsford, 2nd Baron, 109

Chesterton, G.K., 340

Childers, Erskine: *The Riddle of the Sands*, 350

children: mortality rates, 6–7; employment, 9–10, 15; *see also* education; family

China, 230

'Chinese slavery', 268–9, 275

Church Defence Institution (*formerly* Church Institution), 56

Churchill, Lord Randolph: on entrepreneurs, 133; in Fourth Party, 163, 166; policy and position in Conservative Party, 168–70, 189; and Aston Park riot, 173; at India Office, 180; and Ireland, 180, 193; and 1885 election, 183; in Ulster, 186; on Gladstone and Chamberlain, 188; in 1886 administration, 192–4, 223; illness, 193; resignation, 194; and Parnell case, 197

Churchill, Winston S.: on army reform, 248; and tariff reform, 250; and 'Chinese slavery', 269; in Campbell-Bannerman government, 274, 276; crosses floor to Liberals, 275; attacks Lords, 282; at Board of Trade, 283; supports Lloyd George budget, 286–7, 289–90, 302; and 1910 election, 292; and social reform, 302, 307–10, 317; and unemployed, 309–10; and Tonypandy, 322–3; and women's suffrage, 332; on Ulster and Home Rule, 337, 339, 343; and armaments, 351–2, 354; and Agadir crisis, 352; moves to Admiralty, 355; and naval mobilization, 357

Church of England (Anglicanism): organization and divisions, 20–3; worship regulation, 86–7; and Eastern Question 101; incomes, 135; and school education, 245–6, 280; disestablishment question, 363

Church of Ireland, 50, 55–6, 58, 60–1

Church of Scotland, 203

civil service, 68–9

Civil Service Commission, 68

Clarendon Commission (on public schools), 11–13, 137

Clarendon, 4th Earl of, 28, 30, 59, 93–4

Clarion, The, 209, 317, 366

Clarke, Sir George, 258

class (social): and political allegiance, 3–4, 51–3, 145–6, 275–6; and education, 9–15; and status of

women, 16–17, 20; *see also* middle class; working class

Clifford, John, 245–6, 363

Clough, Arthur Hugh, 17

Clough, Anne Jemima, 18

coal industry: eight-hour working, 307, 317, 322; unrest and strikes in, 322–3, 325–6; output, 370

Coal Mines Regulation Act, 1908, 317

Cobden treaty, 1860, 77

Cobden, Richard, 28, 51, 93, 277

Cockerton Judgement, 1901, 245

Coercion Act, 1881, 158–9, 161

Colenso, John William, Bishop of Natal, 22

collectivism, 119, 128–9

Colley, Gen. Sir George, 153

Collings, Jesse, 63, 127

Colonial Conference, 1902, 247

Committee of Imperial Defence (Cabinet Defence Committee), 237, 258, 347, 354–5

Compensation for Disturbance Bill, 1880, 158

Comte, Auguste, 117, 123

concentration camps (South Africa), 237, 242

Conciliation Act, 1896, 321

Conciliation Bills, 1911 & 1912, 332–3

Congregationalists, 22–4; *see also* nonconformity

Connaught, Prince Arthur, Duke of, 75

Connolly, James, 324

Conservative Party: and new (working-class) voters, 3, 43–4, 47, 53, 79, 91, 125, 145–6; composition, 27–8, 52, 248; and electoral reform, 31, 33, 38–42, 46–7; and coalition, 35–6; and working men's associations, 47–8; organization, 47–8, 53, 83, 148, 169–70, 211; 1868 defeat, 59; and Irish Church, 60–1; and educational reform, 63, 201; and poor relief, 79; under Disraeli, 79–80; wins 1874 election, 82–3; 1874 administration, 84–6; labour laws, 86; and trade protection, 92, 131, 182; and early socialism, 122; social reform, 128; and upper classes, 133; 1880 election defeat, 147–9; disarray, 167–9; on franchise extension and redistribution, 173–4; 1885 election and administration, 179–82; and Irish Home Rule, 181; and Liberal Unionist alliance, 188, 194, 219; in 1886 election, 189; 1886 administration, 192–3, 202; and Balfour, 210; and 1895 coalition government, 221; and 1900 election, 240–1; and protectionism, 248; and Unionist reorganization, 301; Balfour leadership succession, 301–2; on industrial relations, 322, 327; and women's suffrage, 330; attitude to Ulster and Home Rule, 336, 340, 342; position in 1914, 361; and press, 364–5; lower middle-class support, 368; *see also* Liberal Unionists

Conspiracy and Protection of Property Act, 1875, 262

Constantinople Conference, 1876, 104

Constitutional Conference, 1910, 295–6, 299

Contagious Diseases Acts, 16–17

Cook, E.T., 242

Corrupt Practices Act, 1883, 166–7, 204

Corry, Henry, 41

Corry, Montague (*later* 1st Baron Rowton), 41

County Councils Act, 1888, 330

Courtney, Leonard, 352

Cowen, Joseph, 102, 162

Cowper, Francis Thomas de Grey, 7th Earl, 195

Cowper-Temple clause (1870 Education Bill), 65, 67, 280

Craig, James, 338, 344

Cranborne, Viscount (*later* 4th Marquess of Salisbury), 241

Cranbrook, G. Gathorne-Hardy, Viscount (*later* 1st Earl) of, 200

Crewe, 1st Earl of, 295

Crimean War, 58, 68, 100, 105

Crimes Acts: 1882, 178; 1887, 196, 198

Criminal Law Amendment Act, 1871, 74, 86

Cromer, Evelyn Baring, 1st Earl of, 70, 155, 224, 335–6

Cronje, Gen. Piet, 236

Crooks, Will, 266

Cross, R.A., Viscount, 84–6, 88–90, 126, 166, 201

Crosskey, Rev. H.W., 63

Crowe, Sir Eyre, 347, 349, 359

Cuba, 226

Cunningham, W., 117

Curragh mutiny, 343–4

Curzon of Kedleston, George Nathaniel, Marquess, 255, 299–300, 335–6, 348

Cyprus, 107, 109, 151

Daily Mail, 289, 360, 365

Daily Mirror, 365

Daily News, 98–9, 126, 242, 360, 362, 366

Dale, R.W., 63

Dalkeith, Earl of (*later* 6th Duke of Buccleuch), 109–10

Dangerfield, George, 336

Dartford manifesto, 193

Darwin, Charles, 21, 117

Davidson, Randall, Archbishop of Canterbury, 280

Davies, Emily, 18

Davison, Emily Wilding, 334

Davitt, Michael, 157

death rates, 5–9

Default Act, 1902, 246

defence (military), 257–60, 285

de Grey, 2nd Earl, 64

Democratic Federation *see* Social Democratic Federation

Depression in Trade and Industry, Royal Commission on, 1885, 114, 116, 139, 182

Derby, 14th Earl of: and Tory leadership, 27, 33, 46, 55, 79; and parliamentary reform, 33, 38–9, 41; 1866 government, 35–6, 45; foreign policy, 94

Derby, 15th Earl of, 41, 62, 93–4, 96, 98, 103–4, 106–7, 339

Devonshire, Spencer Compton Cavendish, 8th Duke of (*formerly* Marquess of Hartington): in 1868 government, 59; and Liberal leadership, 87, 177; and working class, 91; and Eastern Question, 103, 105; and 1880 government, 149; and Egypt, 154; and Franchise and Redistribution Bills, 171, 174; and 1885 election, 181; votes with Tories, 184; declines 1886 government post, 184, 192, 194; opposes Home Rule, 188; position in Liberal Party, 188-90; accedes to Dukedom, 211; in 1895 government, 232; chairs Defence Committee, 237, 258; and 1902 Education Bill, 245; and free trade, 249; resigns, 249

Dewar family, 276

Dicey, A.V., 186

Dickens, Charles, 12, 120, 126, 132, 167

Dilke, Charles: and National Liberal Federation, 49; and educational reform, 67; and republicanism, 76; and Balkan crisis, 102; on Housing Commission, 1884, 127; on imperialism, 130; in 1880 government, 149-50; and Egypt, 154; and Ireland, 158, 161, 179; in 1882 government, 167; and electoral reform, 174-5; and Party programme, 176; and 1885 election, 183; divorce scandal, 184; chairs tax committee, 284; *Greater Britain*, 4, 130

Dillon, John, 344

Disraeli, Benjamin, Earl of Beaconsfield: education, 11; dislikes High Church party, 21, 86-7, 101; and Dean Stanley, 22; position as Party leader, 27, 33, 45-7, 79-80, 87; and Governor Eyre, 31; and parliamentary reform, 33-4, 38-43, 45-6, 53, 59; debates with Gladstone, 34; and coalition, 35; Cranborne and, 40; and party organization, 47-8, 51; and Liberal strength, 50; 1868 resignation, 51; and Queen Victoria, 54; Prime Minister (1868), 55; and Church in Ireland, 56-8, 60; and ecclesiastical

appointments, 57-8, 101; attacks Gladstone legislation, 62; and 1870 Education Act, 65; and army reform, 70; and Liberal decline, 78-80; and social reform, 79-80, 85-6; and Gladstone's 1873 administration, 82, 179; 1874 government, 84-91; peerage, 91; 1876 dissolution, 91; foreign policy, 91-6, 98-9, 103, 107-9, 129; on British empire, 96, 129; and Suez Canal, 96; and Balkan crisis, 98-100, 103-4, 106; 1880 election defeat, 111, 149; on Egypt, 154; and Ireland, 158; death, 168; favours women's suffrage, 330; and press, 364; *Lothair*, 79

Disraeli, Mary-Anne, 42

divorce, 16; Royal Commission on, 1910, 371

Dixon, George, 63

Donald, Robert, 365

Dreadnought, HMS, 261, 285

Dunraven, 4th Earl of, 270

Eastern Question, 91, 93, 97, 100-5, 120

economic theory, 117-18, 125

Economist, 360

education: school, 9-16; of women, 18-19; secondary, 138, 244-5; scientific and technical, 139-40; and Chamberlain's programme, 176-7; free elementary, 199-201; and child welfare, 306-7; and nonconformists, 362-3; and class improvement, 367

Education Acts (and Bills): 1870, 10-11, 14, 48, 50, 60, 62-8, 72, 364; 1876, 14, 90; 1880, 15; 1896, 232; 1902, 13, 244-6, 248, 367; 1906, 279-80, 362; 1906 (Provision of Meals), 306; 1907 (Administrative Provisions), 306-7

Education Aid Societies, 63

Edward VII, King (*formerly* Prince of Wales): Gladstone and employment for, 76; illness, 76; on Housing Commission, 127; Salisbury and, 244; accession, 244; and Kaiser,

254; and French, 255; launches
Dreadnought, 261; and Campbell-
Bannerman, 273; and Lords reform,
291, 294; death, 295
Edwards, Enoch, 318
Egypt, 153-5, 172, 177, 224-5, 227,
256
eight-hour day, 204-5, 208, 211; for
miners, 307, 317
Elcho, Francis, Lord (*later* 8th Earl of
Wemyss), 33, 128
electoral reform *see under* Parliament
Elementary Education Act, 1870 *see*
Education Acts
Elgin, 9th Earl of, 258, 274
Elibank, Alexander Murray, Master
of, 340
Eliot, George, 18, 22
Elliot, Sir Henry George, 97, 99, 106
Ellis, Tom, 203
empire *see* imperialism
Employers Federation of Engineering,
262
Employers' Liability Act, 1880, 166;
Bill, 1892, 215
Endowed Schools Act, 1869, 13
Endowed Schools Commission, 13
Engels, Friedrich, 121, 145
Ensor, R.C.K., 78
entente cordiale (Anglo-French), 256,
347-8, 352-4
entrepreneurs, 132-4
Esher, Reginald Brett, 2nd Viscount,
258-9
Essays and Reviews (book), 22
eugenics, 131
Europe, Concert of, 151, 154, 224
evangelism, 23
Evening News, 365
Exeter Hall, 30
Eyre, Edward John, Governor of
Jamaica, 30-1, 100

Fabian Society, 123-4, 131, 204, 221,
264, 267, 277; and national
insurance, 315; expansion, 317; and
social science, 371
Factories and Workshops Bill, 1895,
217
Factory Acts, 90, 114

Fair Trade League, 122, 131
family, 5-7, 9
Farmers' Alliance, 148
Farrer, Sir Thomas Henry, 1st Baron,
89
Fashoda incident, 1898, 227
Fawcett, Henry, 28-9, 71-2, 103, 129,
335
Fawcett, Millicent, 20, 335
Featherstone incident, 1893, 217
female suffrage *see* women
Fenianism, 44, 55-6, 156
Ferdinand, Archduke of Austria, 358
Fisher, Admiral John Arbuthnot, 1st
Baron, 252, 258, 260-1, 285
Fisher, Warren, 316
football, 142-3
Ford, Henry, 370
Foreign Office: recruitment, 68-9;
under Grey, 347
Forster, W.E., 30, 49; in 1868
government, 59; and 1870 Educa-
tion Act, 64-6, 364; declines Liberal
Party leadership, 87; as Chief
Secretary for Ireland, 158; resigns,
160; and Egypt, 172; founds *Leeds
Express*, 364
Fortnightly Review, 176
Forwood, A.B., 107
Fourth Party, 153-4, 166, 168
Fowler, H.H., 214
France: urbanization, 9; and Egypt,
153-5; and Russia, 225; in Africa,
227-8; improved British relations
with, 255-6, 347-8, 352-4; and
defence co-operation, 355; and out-
break of Great War, 357-9
Franchise Bills: 1884, 171-2; 1912,
333
Franco-Prussian War, 1870, 70, 94
Free Church Council *see* National Free
Church Council
Freeman, C.A., 99, 100, 103
free trade, 131, 246-53, 275-6, 284-6;
see also tariff reform
French, Gen. Sir John, 236
Frere, Sir Bartle, 109, 152
Freud, Sigmund, 371
friendly societies, 313-14
Friendly Societies Act, 1855, 73; Bill,
1875, 87-8

Froude, J.A., 24–5, 130

garden cities, 144
Gardiner, A.G., 360, 366
Garibaldi, Gen. Giuseppe, 28
Garrett, Elizabeth, 19
Garvin, J.L., 295, 350, 366
Gaskell, Elizabeth, 18
Gatacre, Sir William Forbes, 235
general elections: 1868, 58; 1874, 82–3; 1880, 111, 147–9; 1885, 179–84; 1886, 189–90, 202; 1892, 211–12; 1895, 219, 221; 1900 ('Khaki'), 240–2, 246; 1906, 274–6; 1910 (first), 291–5; (second), 297–8
George V, King, 295–7, 299, 340, 342
George, Henry, 121, 127, 284
Germany: unification of, 1; population increase, 9; and Balkan crisis, 97–8; economic rise, 113–14, 141, 251, 349–50, 369; trade protection, 131; education in, 138–9; foreign policy, 151; Salisbury and, 224–5; in southern Africa, 228–30, 254; proposed alliance with, 246, 254–5; as threat, 254–5, 259, 347–9, 352–4; naval power, 260–1, 285, 287, 349, 351, 354; national insurance in, 309, 311; refuses disarmament, 351; and Agadir crisis, 352; and Great War, 357–60; invades Belgium, 358–9; wages in, 370
Gilbert, W.S., 132
Gissing, George, 123, 367
Gladstone, Herbert, 149, 183, 243, 266–7, 274–5, 318, 362
Gladstone, William Ewart: supports parliamentary reform, 2, 29–30, 32, 34–5, 40–3, 45–6; and religion, 21–2, 87; position in Liberal Party, 28–9, 45, 50, 173, 190, 198, 202; debates with Disraeli, 34, 80; and coalition, 36; renounces leadership, 42; electioneering, 53; relations with Queen Victoria, 54, 105, 149, 215; and Irish church disestablishment, 55–7, 60–1; on curbing public expenditure, 58; 1868 government, 59–60, 62; and Irish Land Bills,

61–2, 65; and 1870 Education Act, 62, 64–5, 67; and Liberal dissensions, 67–8, 80; and army reform, 70–1; on republicanism, 76; and licensing laws, 77–8; foreign policy, 80, 91, 93–5, 99, 101, 110, 151–4, 223–4; and Irish university, 81; 1873 resignation, 81–2, 87, 179; loses 1874 election, 83; opposes Public Worship Bill, 86–7; attacks Disraeli on foreign trade and policy, 92, 108–9, 129; on Bulgarian atrocities and Balkan crisis, 100–5, 239, 360; first Midlothian campaign, 109–11, 147; Green supports, 118; on social progress, 144; 1880 election and government, 147–50; and occupation of Egypt, 153–5, 177, 224; and Ireland, 155–61, 179, 181, 183–4; and Chamberlain, 160, 167, 194, 196; and Bradlaugh case, 163–4; 1882 government changes, 167; Churchill attacks, 168; and extension of franchise, 170–1, 173; and redistribution, 174; and Gordon, 175–7; retirement question, 175–6, 178; opposes Radical Programme, 177; and Central Asia, 178; 1885 government resignation and election, 179, 181–4; forms 1886 government, 184; Home Rule Bill, 186, 197, 202, 212–15; and 1886 election, 189–90, 202; and Liberal Party defections, 190; and Parnell, 197–8; and disestablishment, 203; and revised Liberal Party policy, 203–5; and labour, 206; 1892 election and government, 212, 213–15; and Lords, 215, 278; 1894 resignation, 215–16; and 1894 budget, 218; and New Liberalism, 277; opposes women's suffrage, 330
Glasier, Bruce, 317
Goldie, Sir George, 227
Gooch, G.P., 276
Gordon, Gen. Charles George, 137, 172, 175–7
Gorst, John: and Conservative Party organization, 48, 50, 53, 79, 82, 91,

146-8, 169-70; in Fourth Party, 163; and Egypt, 172; and hungry children, 306

Goschen, George Joachim, 1st Viscount: on Housing Commission, 129; opposes parliamentary reform, 147; attacks Chamberlain programme, 176; and Liberal Party, 190; as Chancellor of Exchequer, 194; Churchill 'forgets', 195; and free elementary education, 201; and Milner, 229; and Defence Committee, 237; in 1906 election, 275; and German relations, 353

Gough, Brigadier Hubert, 343

Granville, George Leveson-Gower, 2nd Earl: Whig leadership, 28, 87; as Colonial Secretary, 59; and Foreign Office recruitment, 69; and republicanism, 76; as Foreign Secretary, 93-4, 149, 151-2, 154, 177; and Gladstone on Bulgarian atrocities, 100, 103, 105; and 1880 victory, 149; and redistribution, 174

Grayson, Victor, 281

Great Depression (1873-96), 7, 112, 115, 120

Green, T.H., 29, 118-19, 123, 276

Grey, Sir Edward: and Liberal policies, 203; as Under-Secretary in Foreign Office, 213; and Sudan, 227; and Boer War, 239; imperialism, 243, 271, 347; and Irish Home Rule, 271; as Foreign Secretary, 273-4; and Lords reform, 282; and navy estimates, 287; and first 1910 election, 292; and 1912 coal strike, 326; and women's suffrage, 331; controls foreign policy, 346-7, 352-3; and Russia, 348; and outbreak of Great War, 357-60

Gurney family, 133

Hague Conference (Second), 1907, 287, 351

Haldane, R.B.: supports imperialism, 131, 243, 273; army reforms, 137, 356; and higher education, 140; and Liberal policies, 203, 277; and Irish Home Rule, 271; at War Office, 273-4, 277, 346; and army estimates, 285; and navy estimates, 287; aids Asquith, 294; German talks, 353

Halifax, Charles Wood, 1st Viscount, 27

Hall, Norman, 57

Halsbury, 1st Earl of, 299

Hamilton, Edward, 247

Hamilton, Lord George, 249, 254

Hankey, Maurice, 355

Harcourt, Lewis, 335, 352-3, 355

Harcourt, Sir William as Liberal leader, 190, 213-14, 233; relations with Rosebery, 216, 233; 1894 budget, 217-18, 284; loses seat in 1895 election, 221; foreign policy, 223, 353; pro-Boer, 239

Hardie, James Keir: rebuffed by Liberals, 204; socialist activism, 207-10; loses seat (1895), 221; excluded from TUC, 222; and LRC, 264, 266; and trade union funds, 267; resigns from ILP Council, 317; on unions in Labour Party, 318; and women's suffrage, 331

Hardinge, Sir Charles, 347

Hardy, Thomas, 15

Harmsworth *see* Northcliffe; Rothermere

Harris, William, 63

Harrison, Frederic, 73, 76, 102

Hartington, Marquess of *see* Devonshire, Spencer Compton Cavendish, 8th Duke of

Headmasters' Conference, 13

health *see* sickness insurance

Heligoland, 225

Hemmerde, E.G., 329

Henderson, Arthur, 204, 266, 328

Herbert, Auberon, 129

Hicks Beach, Sir Michael Edward, 109, 183, 195, 233, 235, 241, 247, 249

High Church Party, 21, 86-7, 101

Hill, Octavia, 89, 127, 335

Hirst, F.W., 360

Hobhouse, Charles, 286

Hobhouse, Emily, 242
Hobhouse, L.T., 276-7, 366
Hobson, J.A., 276-7, 293
Hodgkinson, Grosvenor, 43
Hogg, Quintin, 140
Holyoake, George, 102
Home Rule Bills: 1886, 171, 185-9; 1893, 213-15; 1912-14, 337-9, 341-5
Home Rule Confederation of Great Britain, 158
Home Rule League, 156
Home Rule Party, 82
Hood, Acland, 300
Hornby v Close case, 73
hospitals, 312-13
House of Commons *see* Parliament
House of Lords *see* Lords, House of
housing, 88-9, 126-8
Housing of the Working Classes, Royal Commission on the, 1884-5, 127-8, 174
Housing of the Working Classes Act, 1885, 128
Howard, Ebenezer, 144
Howell, George, 36, 50, 74, 102
Hudson, Robert, 219
Hughes, Percival, 300
Hughes, Thomas, 28, 73, 86; *Tom Brown's Schooldays*, 136
Huxley, T.H., 22
Hyde Park: riots, 1866, 37, 39, 122; demonstrations, 1867, 42
Hyndman, H.M., 120-4, 129, 264

Iddesleigh, Sir Stafford Northcote, Earl of: background, 52; and Friendly Societies, 88; on 'bad trade', 92; and relations with USA, 95; on Gladstone and Eastern Question, 105; as leader of Tory opposition, 168-70; and Aston Park riot, 173; and redistribution, 174; Party relegation and earldom, 180; as Foreign Secretary, 193, 223; favours women's suffrage, 330
Ignatiev, Nicholas Pavlovich, Count, 104
Illingworth family, 276
Illingworth, Alfred, 205

imperialism, 129-31; Gladstone and, 153; and Salisbury government, 223; Liberals and, 242-4; and trade preference, 248, 251, 253, 249-50; as 1906 election issue, 275; and poverty, 303
income tax, 284, 288, 292, 329
incomes and wages, 115-16, 128, 135, 142, 320-23, 326, 328, 369-70
Independent Labour Party, 210, 221-2, 264, 317, 319, 322, 331, 361
India, 115, 255, 259
Indian Civil Service, 68
Industrial Council, 327-8
Industrial Revolution, 132-4
industry: development of, 132-3, 140-2; and labour, 144-5; unrest and conciliation, 320-3, 329; British decline, 369-70
infant mortality, 6-7, 9
infectious diseases, 6
Institute of Chartered Accountants, 134-5
insurance, 313-14; *see also* national insurance; sickness insurance; unemployment insurance
International Working Men's Association (First International), 75
Ireland: church disestablishment, 50, 55-6, 58, 60-1; Home Rule movement, 50, 58-9, 156-60; Fenianism in, 55-6; land tenure and reform, 61-2, 158-9, 180, 185, 195-6, 269-70, 337; Catholics and university in, 81; and Gladstone's governments, 155-6, 158-62, 184-5; and household suffrage, 171; Chamberlain's proposals for, 178-9; and 1885 election, 180-2; Gladstone's Home Rule legislation, 185-7, 202, 213-14; prominence in British politics, 192, 195-6; 'Plan of Campaign', 195, 199; in 1892 election campaign, 211-12; Balfour and, 269-70; Liberal policy on, 271-2, 292, 297; and 1910 Constitutional Conference, 295-6; labour movement in, 324; Unionist and Ulster revolt over Home Rule, 336-45

Irish Church Disestablishment Bill, 1869, 50, 60-1, 67

Irish Land Acts and Bills: 1870, 60, 61, 65, 72, 158; 1881, 129, 150, 158-61, 195; 1886, 196

Irish Land Purchase Acts: 1885 (Ashbourne's), 180, 185; 1903, 270, 337

Irish Local Government Act, 1898, 269

Irish Nationalist Party, 211, 214, 269-70, 274, 292, 294-5, 297

Irish National Land League, 157, 159-60, 197

Irish National League, 160, 196

Irish Reform Association, 270

Irish Republican Brotherhood, 55-6, 156, 341

Irish Transport and General Workers Union, 324

Irish University Bill, 1873, 50, 61, 179

Irish Volunteers, 341, 344-5

Isaacs, Rufus Daniel (*later* 1st Marquess of Reading), 314, 340

Jameson Raid, 228, 229-30, 236

Japan, 225-6, 254-6, 260-1, 348

Jevons, Stanley, 117, 123

Jex-Blake, Sophia, 19

Johnson-Webb boxing match, 363

Jones, Ernest, 36

Jones, Thomas, 316

Jowett, Benjamin, 22, 103

Kant, Immanuel, 21

Kenney, Annie, 331

Keynes, John Maynard, Baron, 277

Kimberley, John Wodehouse, 1st Earl of, 59, 149, 152, 216, 223

Kingsley, Charles, 23

Kipling, Rudyard, 137, 243, 360

Kitchener, Horatio Herbert, 1st Earl, 227, 236, 348

Kitson, Sir James, 205

Knollys, Francis, 1st Viscount, 273, 291, 296

Knowles, Thomas, 166

Knowlton, Charles: *The Fruits of Philosophy*, 7

Kruger, President Paul, 152, 228-31, 235-6, 238

Labouchere, Henry, 162, 233, 239

labour: Conservative legislation on, 85-6; industrial, 144-5; and employers' liability, 166; and Liberal Party, 204-5; exchanges, 310-11, 316; *see also* eight-hour day; trade unions; unemployment

Labour Electoral Association, 204

Labour Exchanges Bill, 1909, 310

Labour Party: class support, 4; Democratic Federation and, 121; and Liberals, 204, 207-9, 221, 317-20, 361; advance and representation, 207-10; formed, 262-3; and unemployment, 307, 316; and national insurance, 315; strength and development, 317-20; and trade union support, 317-19, 322, 328; in by-elections, 318, 320; and industrial unrest, 328; and women's suffrage, 334; and rearmament, 351; position in 1914, 361; and nonconformists, 363; *see also* Labour Representation Committee

Labour Representation Committee: formed, 262-7; in 1906 election, 274-5; in first 1910 election, 293; in second 1910 election, 297-8

Labour Representation League, 75, 121

Land and Labour League, 76

Land League *see* Irish National Land League

land: ownership, 115-16; Lloyd George's campaign, 328-9; *see also* Ireland

Land Value tax, 284-5, 287-8, 290

Lansbury, George, 205, 305, 320, 334

Lansdowne, 5th Marquess of: and Boer War, 235, 237; as Foreign Secretary, 241, 253, 347; Far East policy, 254, 348; and Lords, 280-1, 290, 297-9; and tariff reform, 295; and Constitutional Conference, 295; and Home Rule, 336, 344; resigns, 340; and Moroccan crisis, 347

Larkin, James, 324

Laurier, Sir Wilfrid, 247

Law, Andrew Bonar: background, 301–2; and industrial unrest, 327; and Home Rule, 337–45; and tariff reform, 339; resigns, 340; and George V, 340; supports Asquith in Great War, 359; as Party leader, 361; and Beaverbrook, 366

Lawson, Sir Wilfrid, 77, 162, 239–40

Layard, Sir Austen Henry, 106

Leader family, 49, 364

Leeds Express, 364

Leeds Mercury, 364

leisure and recreation, 142–4

Le Queux, William: *The Invasion of 1910*, 350

Lever, W.H., 144

Lewis, William T., 322

Liberal League, 243

Liberal Party: and new (and working-class) voters, 3–4, 44, 145–6, 268; and nonconformism, 24, 52–3; composition, 28, 51–3, 59, 276; and parliamentary reform, 30–4, 38–40, 42, 44–5, 47; organization, 48–50, 148; and Irish Church disestablishment, 56–7; 1868 government, 58–60, 72; and educational reform, 63–6; divisions and differences, 67–8, 124; Disraeli attacks, 79–80; loses 1874 election, 82; and Balkan crisis, 100, 103, 105; and radicalism, 124, 277; individualism, 129; 1880 election success and administration, 147–51; and Ireland, 155, 161–2, 165, 182–3, 187; and Bradlaugh case, 164–5; on franchise extension, 173–4; Chamberlain's programme for, 176; 1885 resignation and election, 179, 181–3; leadership, 181; and Home Rule, 187–9, 202, 211; in 1886 election, 189–90; Whigs depart, 190; and Parnell case, 197; and free elementary education, 201; Celtic dominance, 203; New Liberal policy and alignments, 203–5; and Labour Party, 204, 207–9, 221, 317–20, 361; and trade unionism, 207; 1892 election and administration, 211–13, 215, 217; Rosebery leads, 216; and 1895 election, 219, 221; foreign policy, 223–4; in opposition to Salisbury government, 233; leadership changes, 233–4; and Boer War, 234, 236, 239–40; and 1900 'Khaki' election, 240–2; divisions over imperialism, 242–4; and tariff reform, 249–50; and Chinese labour, 268; and Irish Home Rule, 272; Campbell-Bannerman government, 273–4, 276–7, 279; 1906 landslide victory, 274–6; new radicalism, 277; and Lords, 278–80, 283–4, 286, 300; and trade unions, 281; by-election results, 281, 284, 289; taxation and spending, 284–5; in first 1910 election, 292–3, 295; in second 1910 election, 297–8; social reform, 306–8, 316, 328–9; and industrial disputes, 327; and women's suffrage, 330, 335; on Ulster and Home Rule, 337; and pre-1914 foreign affairs, 352; position in 1914, 361; and nonconformist decline, 362–3; and press, 363–4, 366

Liberal Unionists: separation, 188–9; alliance with Conservatives, 188, 194, 219–22; in 1886 election, 189–90, 202; refuse coalition with Salisbury, 192; and Ireland, 199, 211; and 1892 election, 212; 1895 coalition, 219–22; and 1900 election, 240; and education, 246; and tariff reform, 246, 249–50, 271, 284; composition, 248; and 1906 election, 272, 274–5; in first 1910 election, 292–5; in second 1910 election, 297; and Lords reform, 298–300; reorganization, 300–1; and social welfare, 316; revolt over Home Rule, 336–8, 345

Liberation Society, 49, 56, 58, 101, 187

Liberty and Property Defence League, 128–9, 289, 308

libraries (public), 143–4

licensing laws (drink), 77–8, 85, 271, 284, 288

Lichfield, 7th Earl of, 73
Lichnowsky, Karl Max, Prince, 357
Liddon, Canon H.P., 99, 101, 103
Lister, Joseph, 1st Baron, 135
Lloyd George, David: Welsh interests, 203; and Welsh disestablishment, 217–18; pro-Boer, 239, 243; in 1900 election, 240; buys *Daily News*, 242, 366; attacks concentration camps, 242; popular hostility to, 243; attacks Chamberlain, 248; as President of Board of Trade, 274, 282–3; on Lords, 278, 286; as Chancellor of Exchequer, 282, 286–7; settles rail dispute, 282–3, 325, 352; qualities, 283; introduces old-age pensions, 285; 1909 budget, 286–91; and navy estimates, 287, 351–2, 354; Limehouse speech, 289–90; and first 1910 election, 292; and 1910 Constitutional Conference, 295–6; proposes party coalition, 296; and national insurance, 296, 302, 309, 311, 313–15; and social reform, 307–8; establishes MPs' salaries, 319; and proposed Labour pact, 319; and trade unions, 325–6; land campaign, 328–9; 1914 budget, 328–9; and women's suffrage, 332; on Ulster and Home Rule, 337, 344; and Marconi scandal, 340; and armaments, 351–2; and Agadir crisis, 352, 357; and outbreak of Great War, 357–8, 360; relations with press, 365–6
Local Government Bill, 1888, 199
London: population, 141; local government, 200; and Left alliance, 209; elections, 281, 284; unemployment relief, 305; as financial centre, 368–9
London Conference, 1912–13 (Anglo-German), 353
London Convention, 1884, 153, 228
Londonderry, 6th Marquess of, 232, 241
London Municipal Reform League, 200
London Protocol, 1876, 104
Long, Walter, 301, 305

Lords, House of: and Irish Church, 61; reform proposals, 61, 172–3, 177, 282, 294–300; rejects Home Rule, 214; opposes Liberals, 214, 217 278–84, 294; Rosebery and, 217, 221; rejects Lloyd George's budget, 286, 290–2; and 1910 Constitutional Conference, 295–6
Loreburn, Robert Reid, Earl, 335, 346, 352, 355
Lowe, Robert: opposes 1867 Reform Bill, 2, 30–1, 33–5; and cattle plague, 31; and education, 58; and Civil Service exams, 68–9; on trade unions, 72; as Home Secretary, 81; on political economy, 118, 194; opposes parliamentary reform, 147
Lucy, Sir Henry, 242
Lugard, Frederick, Baron, 227
Lytton, Edward Robert Bulwer, 1st Earl of, 109, 151

McColl, Malcolm, 101
MacDermott, G.H. (the Great), 106
Macdonald, Alexander, 51, 86
MacDonald, James Ramsay: and Liberals, 204, 277, 318–19, 361; and LRC, 264–5; and Liberal electoral pact, 266–7, 275; and unemployment, 307; and National Insurance Bill, 315; resigns from ILP Council, 317; and industrial relations, 328
McDonnell, Anthony, 270
MacGahan, J.A., 99
MacIver, David, 89
MacKay, Thomas, 129
McKenna, Reginald, 287, 335, 355
McMillan, Margaret, 307
McNeile, Hugh, Dean of Ripon, 57
Mafeking, 236
Magee, William Connor, Bishop of Peterborough, 101
Mahdi, the, 155, 172, 227
Majuba Hill, Battle of, 1881, 153, 236
Mallock, W.L., 129
Malthus, Thomas, 7
Manchester Examiner, 364
Manchester Guardian, 127, 277, 360

Mann, Tom, 124, 206, 324

Manning, Henry Edward, Cardinal, 56; and temperance, 77; and Irish university, 81; on Housing Commission, 127; supports Disraeli, 157; opposes Bradlaugh, 165; and Ireland, 179; opposes secular education, 182; and industrial strikes, 206

Mansion House Committee on the unemployed, 305

Marchand, Captain Jean-Baptiste, 227

Marconi scandal, 340

Markham, Violet, 335

Marlborough, John Winston Spencer Churchill, 7th Duke of, 41

Marriage and Divorce Act, 1857, 16

Married Women's Property Act, 1882, 16, 330

Marshall, Alfred, 117

Marx, Karl, 75, 121, 123, 323, 352

Massingham, H.W., 242, 285, 360, 365

Masterman, Charles F., 276, 286, 314–15; *The Condition of England*, 371

Maurice, F.D., 23

Mawdsley, John, 125, 221

Maxse, Leo, 301, 350

Mayhew, Henry, 23; *London Labour and the London Poor*, 126

Mayne, Sir Richard, 36

Maynooth, 60

Mearns, Andrew: *The Bitter Cry of Outcast London* (attrib.), 126

Mechanics Institutes, 139–40

Medical Act, 1886, 135

Mediterranean Agreements, 224

Merchant Shipping Acts: 1876, 89; 1906–7, 283

meritocracy, 69–70

Merrie England, 209

Methodism, 23–4, 145; *see also* nonconformity

Methuen, Gen. Paul Sanford, 235

Meux family, 133

Miall, Edward, 49, 65, 101

middle class, 53, 367–8

Middle Class Defence League, 308

Middleton, Captain R.W.E., 211

migration, 7–8

Mill, John Stuart: and political reform, 2; on poverty, 7; and women's rights, 16, 330; Radicalism, 28, 51; and cattle plague, 31, defeat, 51–2; and republicanism, 76; economics, 117, 123

Milner, Sir Alfred, Viscount: and Eastern Question, 103; imperialism, 131, 229; aids Harcourt's 1894 budget, 218; and South Africa, 229–31, 235–8; Selborne and, 241; conflict with Liberals, 242–3; as Governor-General of South Africa, 261; and Chinese labour, 268–9; on poverty, 303; opposes Home Rule, 342

Miners' Federation of Great Britain, 206, 317–18, 322, 325–6

Miners' Next Step, The, 323

Minimum Wages Act, 1912, 326

Mitchelstown, 199, 202

Moberly, George, 12

Mond, Ludwig, 351

Money, Chiozza, 276; *Riches and Poverty*, 369

Montenegro, 103

Moody and Sankey, 23

Morant, Sir Robert, 245, 307, 315

Morley, John: and educational reform, 67; opposes coercion in Ireland, 161–2; as Chief Secretary for Ireland, 184, 210, 213; on Salisbury and Ireland, 188; and Liberal policies, 204; and working hours, 205, 210, 217; Keir Hardie campaigns against, 209–10; and Home Rule, 213–14; supports Rosebery as Prime Minister, 216; loses seat in 1895 election, 221; and foreign policy, 223; resigns, 233; life of Gladstone, 233; pro-Boer, 239; on imperialism, 242; criticizes Balfour on tariffs, 253; in Campbell-Bannerman government, 274; and Lords reform, 299; and India, 348; and Agadir crisis, 355; non-interventionist in Great War, 357, 359

Morley, Samuel, 51, 144

Morocco, 255–6, 259, 325, 347, 355; *see also* Agadir

Morris, William, 120-2, 276
Mowatt, Sir Francis, 247
Mundella, A.J., 51
Munro-Ferguson, R.C., 203
Murphy, William, 59
Murray, Sir George, 286

Napoleon III, King of the French, 46
Nation, The (journal), 360
National Agricultural Labourers Union, 74
National Education League, 48, 63-7, 81
National Education Union, 63
National Free Church Council, 360, 362-3
National Free Labour Association, 262
national insurance, 296, 302, 309, 311-16
National Insurance Act, 1911, 311-12, 315-16, 319, 327
National League for Opposing Women's Suffrage, 335
National Liberal Federation, 49-50, 169; formed, 67; and Democratic Federation, 121; in 1880 election and government, 148-50; and Radical programme, 176; endorses Gladstone's Home Rule Bill, 187; and 1886 programme, 203; and eight-hour day, 205; criticizes Grey, 360
National Reform Union, 29, 38, 43
National Service League, 356, 360
National Society for Preventing the Education of the Poor in the Principles of the Established Church, 10-11
National Society for Women's Suffrage, 16
National Transport Workers Federation, 324-6
National Union of Conservative and Constitutional Associations, 47-8, 169-70, 271
National Union of Women's Suffrage Societies, 331, 334
Naval Defence Act, 1895, 224
Newbolt, Sir Henry, 360

Newcastle Commission on Popular Education, 10, 13
Newcastle conference (Liberal Party), 203-4; and Liberal programme, 205, 210-11, 217, 219
Newman, John Henry, Cardinal, 165
newspapers and press, 3-4, 360-6; *see also individual titles*
Nicolson, Sir Arthur, 347, 353, 359
Nigeria, 227
Nightingale, Florence, 16, 19
Nine Hour Movement, 80, 85
nonconformity (religious): and political outlook, 3, 145; and working classes, 23-4; and composition of political parties, 51-2, 362-3; and church rates, 57; and university admission, 67; and Bulgarian atrocities, 100-2; and Ulster, 211; and education bills, 245-6, 280, 362-3; and social tensions, 322; political decline, 362-3
Northcliffe, Alfred Harmsworth, Viscount, 289, 360, 365-6
Northcote, Sir Stafford *see* Iddesleigh, Earl of
Norton, Caroline, 16
Novikov, Mme, 103
Nuffield, W.R. Morris, Viscount, 370

O'Brien, William, 199, 269-70
Observer, The (newspaper), 366
Odger, George, 28, 75
old age pensions, 284-5, 306, 309
Olivier, Sydney, 123
Osborne, W.V.: judgement, 298, 318-19
O'Shea, Katharine, 160, 178, 195
O'Shea, Captain William Henry, 160, 178, 195, 197
Ottoman Empire *see* Turkey
Oundle school, 137-8
Outhwaite, R.L., 329
Overend, Gurney and Co., 34
Oxford Movement, 21

Paget, Gen. Sir Arthur, 343
Pakington, Sir John, 1st Baron Hampton, 52, 62
Palmer family, 276

Palmerston, Henry John Temple, 3rd
Viscount: death, 1, 27, 33; religious
ignorance, 21; feud with Russell, 29;
defeat, 51; defends purchase of army
commissions, 70; and foreign
affairs, 93
Pankhurst, Christabel, 330-1, 333-5
Pankhurst, Emmeline, 330-1, 334
Pankhurst, Sylvia, 330, 334
Paris Commune, 82
Paris, Treaty of, 1856, 94
Parish Councils Act, 1894, 215, 330
Parliament: electoral reform, 1-2, 10,
27-44; legislation and debate,
27-44; public interest in, 37, 39, 42,
44-5; effects of reform, 47; and
political parties, 51-4; legislative
machinery, 159; household suffrage
in counties, 165-6, 171-5; and
redistribution, 173-5; procedural
reform, 196
Parliament Act, 1910, 294-5,
297-300, 302, 315, 333, 339-40
Parnell, Charles Stewart: and
Democratic Federation, 121; leadership and career, 156-8; tactics,
159-61, 178-9; and Liberal Party,
158, 160-1, 178-9, 181-3; and Mrs
O'Shea, 160, 195; and Bradlaugh
case, 165; alliance with Tories,
170-80; and 1885 election, 182-3;
accepts Gladstone's Home Rule
Bill, 186; and 1886 election, 190;
and Plan of Campaign, 195; and
Irish Land Act, 196; *The Times*
attacks, 196-7; in divorce case,
197-8; attacks Liberals, 203; fall,
210
Passive Resistance League, 1902, 246
Patterson, Emma, 20
Pattison, Mark, 22
Peace Society, 187
Pease family, 276
Peel, Gen. Jonathan, 39-41
Peel, Sir Robert, 28, 179
Persia, 348
Pethick Lawrence, F.W. and
Emmeline, 331-2, 334
Phoenix Park murders, 160, 162, 196
Pigott, Richard, 197

Playfair Commission (on civil service),
1874, 69
Playfair, Sir Lyon, 137
Plebs League, 323
Plimsoll, Samuel, 85, 89-90
Plunkett, Sir Horace, 269
Plural Voting Bill, 1913, 333
Poland, 4, 28
polytechnics, 140
Ponsonby, Arthur, 352
Ponsonby, Sir Henry Frederick, 149
Poor Law Board, 31-2
Poor Law, 305-6, 308, 310, 312, 316;
Royal Commission on, 1905-9, 302,
308
population, 5-9, 27
Port of London Authority, 283, 325
Potter, George, 74, 102
Potter, T.B., 29
poverty and the poor, 125-9, 302-6,
308
Pratt, Tidd, 88
press *see* newspapers
Preston, Lancs., 32
Pretoria Convention, 1881, 153
prices, 321; *see also* incomes
Primrose League, 170, 301
Prince Imperial (Louis Napoleon), 109
Prisoners' Temporary Discharge for
Ill-Health Bill ('Cat and Mouse
Act'), 1913, 334
professions, 134-5
Progressive Alliance, 301, 318, 337,
361
Progressive Party, 200
Progressive Review, 277
prostitution, 16-17
Prussia, 1, 34; war with France, 70, 94
public schools, 11-13, 69, 136-8
Public Worship Regulation Bill, 1874,
86-7, 101

Quarterly Review, 5, 75

Radical Programme, The, 1885, 176-7,
182
Radicals: in Parliament, 28; and
reform, 30-1, 41, 166; and Whig-
Tory coalition, 36; relations with
Whigs, 49; social composition, 51;

and poverty, 125; and housing, 127; and Egypt, 154-5, 172; and Irish policy, 157-9, 161-2, 184-5, 187; and Chamberlain's programme, 176-7, 182; and Gladstone, 203; and Lloyd George's budget, 287; and Lloyd George's land policy, 329; and foreign affairs, 350, 352; and rearmament, 351; and outbreak of Great War, 357-8

Ragged School Union, 14

railways, 128, 141; trade disputes, 282-3, 325-6

Rainbow Circle, 277

Redistribution Bill, 1866, 32-4; 1867, 93-4; 1884, 171-2, 174

Redmond, John, 270, 292, 294, 297, 300, 337-8, 341-2, 344-5

Reform Bills: First, 1832, 2, 27; Second, 1867, 1, 2, 16, 31-43, 46, 330; Third, 1884, 2, 47, 330

Reform League, 29, 36-8, 42-4, 50

Reid, T. Wemyss, 183

religion: and schooling, 11-12; organized, 20-3; beliefs and doubts, 22-5; decline of, 371

Relugas compact, 273

Rendel, Stuart, 203

Repington, Col. Charles à Court, 360

republicanism, 75-6, 125

Revised Code (school teaching), 13-15

Rhodes, Cecil, 131, 228-9, 233

Rhondda, D.A. Thomas, Viscount, 322

Ricardo, David, 117

Richard, Henry, 58

Richmond, 6th Duke of, 41

Riddell, George, 365

Ripley family, 144

Ritchie, C.T. (*later* Baron), 247-9

Roberts, Field-Marshal Frederick Sleigh, 1st Earl, 151, 235-7, 343, 356

Roberts, Evan, 246

Robertson, J.M., 276

Rogers, Thorold, 29

Roman Catholics: in Ireland, 57, 62; and Bradlaugh case, 165; and education, 182, 202, 245, 279

Rosebery, Archibald Philip Primrose, 5th Earl of, 109-10; and imperialism, 130, 225; on national efficiency, 131; and Liberal Party, 190, 204; on Home Rule, 202; and 1892 election, 212; as Foreign Secretary, 213-14, 223, 224-4; succeeds Gladstone as Prime Minister, 216-17, 219-20; relations with Harcourt, 216, 233; and 1894 budget, 218; in 1895 election, 221; resigns, 233; and Boer War, 238-9; and Liberal Imperialism, 243; and Liberal disunity, 271-2; and Campbell-Bannerman's government, 273; and Lords reform, 297; on poverty, 303

Rothermere, Harold Sidney Harmsworth, 1st Viscount, 366

Rothschild family, 133

Rowntree, Seebohm, 302-3

Royal Institute of British Architects, 134

Royal Navy, 215, 255; reforms, 259-61; estimates, 285, 351-2, 354; and German threat, 287, 351-2; mobilization, 357

Royal Niger Company, 227

Ruskin College, Oxford, 323

Ruskin, John, 120, 127, 132, 144, 276

Russell, (Lord) John, 1st Earl, 11, 28-32, 34-6, 38-9, 45, 55

Russia: in Asia, 93-4, 254-5; and Balkan crisis, 97-8, 102-5; 1877 Turkish war, 105-7; and Afghanistan, 151, 178; and French rapprochement, 225; Salisbury and, 225-6; and Britain's China policy, 230, 254; British relations with, 254-5, 348, 353; 1904 war with Japan, 256, 348; 1904 Convention with Britain, 348; German fears of, 354; and Great War, 357-9

Sailors' Union, 324

Salisbury, Robert Cecil, 3rd Marquess of (*formerly* Lord Cranborne): career, 39; opposes parliamentary reform, 39-41; on nonconformists, 52; and Conservative Party leadership, 79; as Secretary of State for India, 84;

Disraeli criticizes, 87; and Balkans settlement, 104, 106–7; as Foreign Secretary, 107, 223–5, 227, 230; Freedom of City of London, 108; on socialism, 119; and housing, 126–8; and Party antipathies, 133; on Gladstone's European policy, 151; and Balfour, 164; Chamberlain attacks, 167; shares Tory leadership, 168–70; on Ireland, 169, 180–1, 188, 214; on franchise and redistribution, 172–4; as Conservative Party leader, 179–80, 183, 191, 194; 1885 election and administration, 183–4; 1886 defeat, 184; seeks Liberal Unionist alliance, 188–9, 195, 219; 1886 administration, 191, 192–9; and Churchill, 193–4; and Irish land reform, 196; and Parnell, 196; and free elementary education, 200–1; and fair trade, 211; and Joseph Chamberlain, 211, 219–20, 233; and 1892 election, 212; and 1895 election, 219, 222; opposed to democracy, 219–20, 222, 224; 1895 government, 223; and Africa, 227–8, 230–1; and domestic politics, 232; and Boer War, 235, 237–8; and 1900 election, 240–1; gives up Foreign Office, 241, 253; resigns, 244; and 1902 Education Bill, 245; opposes foreign alliances, 254–5; and defence, 258; favours women's suffrage, 330; on popular press, 366

Salt, Sir Titus, 144

Salter, Arthur, 316

Samuel, Herbert, 276–7, 288, 340

Sanderson, F.W., 137–8

Sandon, Viscount (*later* 3rd Earl of Harrowby), 90, 134

San Stefano, Treaty of, 1878, 107

Sarajevo, 354, 357

Schleswig-Holstein, 4

Schnadhorst, Frederick, 50, 189, 204, 211

science: and education, 139

Scientific Instruction, Royal Commission on, 1870, 139

Sclater-Booth, George, 89

Scotland, 7, 13, 203, 208–9

Scott, C.P., 277, 346, 360

Scott, J.R., 364

Seeley, J.R. 130

Seely, J.E.B., 343–4

Selborne, William Waldegrave Palmer, 2nd Earl of, 241, 255, 261

Serbia, 103, 357–8

Shackleton, David, 266–8

Shaftesbury, 7th Earl of, 21, 128

Shaw, George Bernard, 123, 131, 210, 221, 277, 371

Sheffield, 72–3

Sheffield Independent, 364

Shipping Federation, 262, 324

shops and shopping, 367–8

Shuvalov, Peter Andreivich, Count, 106

sickness insurance, 312–16

Sidgwick, Henry, 187

Simon, Sir John, 8

Skene, W.B., 147

Smillie, Robert, 318, 326

Smith, Adam, 117

Smith, Barbara Leigh, 16

Smith, Goldwin, 103, 187

Smith, Southwood, 127

Smith, Sir Hubert Llewellyn, 309, 311

Smith, W.H., 52, 166, 194, 198

Snowden, Philip, 266, 317

Social Darwinism, 119, 130, 303, 350

Social Democratic Federation, 120–4, 199, 209–10, 221, 264, 317

socialism: beginnings, 119–25; impact of, 205–7, 210; Chamberlain and, 220; and 1895 election, 221; and Labour Party, 263–4, 317; and Liberal welfarism, 317; and free love, 371

Socialist League, 121–2

social mobility, 132–5

Sorel, Georges, 323

South Africa: Disraeli and, 108; Gladstone and, 151–2; Salisbury and, 228–31; Chamberlain tours, 247; Chinese labour in, 268; and New Liberalism, 277, 351

South Africa Conciliation Committee, 239

South African War (Boer War): and army weaknesses, 71, 137; and imperialist debate, 131; outbreak and conduct of, 231, 234–7; casualties, 237; effects on domestic politics, 238–40, 264–5; German interest in, 254

South African War, Royal Commission on, 1903, 258

South Wales Miners' Federation, 322–4

Spanish-American War, 1898, 226

Spencer, John Poyntz, 5th Earl, 59, 149, 178–9, 218

Spencer, Herbert, 103, 117, 128, 130; *The Man versus the State*, 119

Spender, J.A., 360

Spofforth, Markham, 48

sport, 142–3

Spurgeon, Charles, 23

Stanhope, Edward, 170

Stanley, Arthur Penrhyn, Dean of Westminster, 22

Stanley, Lord *see* Derby, 15th Earl of

Stansfeld, James, 17

Stead, W.T., 99, 239

steel industry, 114

Steel-Maitland, Arthur, 300

Stephen, Sir James Fitzjames, 102

Stephen, Sir Leslie, 187

Strauss, D.F.: *Leben Jesu*, 22

strikes (industrial), 206, 320–1, 324–6, 328

Stuart, James, 18–19

Sudan, 155, 172, 175, 178, 227

Suez Canal, 93, 154; Company, 96

suffragettes *see* women

super tax, 288, 329

Surveyors' Institution, 135

syndicalism, 323–4

Taff Vale decision, 264–5, 267–8, 275, 280, 319

Tait, Archibald Campbell, Archbishop of Canterbury, 57, 61, 86–7

tariff reform, 246–53, 271, 275, 278, 284–5, 288–9, 295, 298–9, 339–40; in Germany, 349–50

Tariff Reform League, 249, 252, 289

Taunton Commission on Endowed Schools, 1866–8, 11–13, 18, 134

taxation, 218, 284–8; *see also* individual taxes

Taylor, Peter, 29, 51

tea-room revolt, 1867, 41–2

Technical Instruction Act, 1889, 244

Tel-el-Kebir, Battle of, 1882, 154–5

temperance movement, 76–8, 85, 207; *see also* licensing laws

Temple, Frederick, Archbishop of Canterbury, 22

Tenants Relief Bill, 1886, 195

Ten Minutes Bill, 1867, 40

textiles, 113

Thomas, J.H., 326

Thompson, Flora, 8

Thorne, Will, 206

Three Emperors' League, 97, 151

Thring, Edward, 11

Tichborne claimant, 91

Tillett, Ben, 206, 209, 265, 328

Times, The, 196–7, 365

Tirpitz, Gross-Admiral Alfred von, 353–4

Tit-Bits (journal), 365

Tonypandy, 322–3

Tooke, Thomas, 4

Torrens Act, 1868, 88, 126

Torrens, William T. McCullagh, 128

towns and cities, 8–9

Toynbee Hall, London, 119

Toynbee, Arnold, 119

Tractarians, 21, 24

trade, foreign, 113–15, 349, 368–70

Trade Boards Act, 1909, 317

trade unions: and parliamentary reform, 36; and unrest, 44, 72–3; government antagonism to, 72, 267; law and control of, 73–4; growth, 74–5, 206–7, 320–8; Conservative Party and, 80, 85–6; and fall in foreign trade, 114; membership decline, 116; Hyndman on, 124; support Liberal Party, 125; activities and effect ('new unionism'), 206–8; and ILP, 210; and Labour representation, 262–5, 317–18, 320, 328; development and legal status of, 262–3, 265, 267, 280–1; and Osborne Judgement, 298, 318–19; political allegiance,

301; and immigrant labour, 306; oppose labour exchanges, 310; and unemployment insurance, 311–12; and industrial relations, 322; in Ireland, 324; Triple Alliance, 326–7; *see also* Taff Vale decision; and individual unions

Trades Disputes, Royal Commission on, 1903, 267

Trades Disputes Act, 1906, 281, 317, 319, 327

Trades Union Congress: opposes government control, 74; and Conservative Party legislation, 86; and working hours, 204; membership growth, 206–7; Keir Hardie and, 208; 1895 standing orders, 221–2; and representation, 263; and union legislation, 267; and Irish unions, 324

Transvaal, 152–3, 228–9, 236, 240

Trevelyan, Sir George Otto, 184

Trevelyan-Northcote inquiry, 68

Triple Alliance (Germany-Austria-Italy), 224–5

Trollope, Anthony, 21

Turkey (and Ottoman Empire): and Balkans, 97–8, 100–4, 353; 1877 war with Russia, 105–7; bonds, 114; Gladstone's policy towards, 151; Salisbury and, 225–6

Tyrrell, Sir William, 347

Ulster: and Home Rule, 186, 211, 270, 336–44

Ulster Unionist Council, 270

Ulster Volunteer Force, 338, 341, 343–4

Unemployed Workmen Acts and Bills: 1905, 305; 1907, 307

unemployment: and Great Depression, 8, 112; 1886 riots, 122; and social reform, 304–7, 309–10; insurance, 310–12; fluctuations, 320–1; *see also* labour; working class

Union Defence League, 301

Unionist Free Food League, 249–50, 252

Unionists *see* Conservative Party; Liberal Unionists

United Ireland (newspaper), 181

United Kingdom Alliance, 49, 76–7, 187

United Land League, 269

United States of America: competition from, 1; border with Canada, 4; British immigrants, 8; population increase, 9; and British foreign policy, 93–5; economic rise, 113–14, 141, 251, 369; trade protection, 131; and Irish Home Rule, 156–7; Spanish War, 226; naval power, 260–1; unions in, 323–4; reciprocity with Canada, 339

universities, 18–19, 67, 139–41

Vatican Decrees, 1870, 81, 87

Venezuela, 95, 226

Vereeniging, Peace of, 1902, 237

Victoria, Queen: and ecclesiastical appointments, 21; and parliamentary reform, 38–9; widowhood, 53; political partisanship, 53–4; and church politics, 57–8; and Irish Church, 60–1; and purchase of commissions, 71; and republicanism, 75; hostility to Gladstone, 76, 105, 149, 215; as Empress of India, 96; and Eastern Question, 105; on socialism, 124; and Gladstone's 1880 victory, 149; displeasure at Chamberlain, 167; and Boer War, 235; death, 244

wages *see* incomes and wages

Wales, 7, 58–9, 203, 246; Church disestablishment, 215, 217–19, 330, 363

Walker, Sir Andrew Barclay, 134

Wallas, Graham, 123, 277

Walpole, Spencer, 37, 42, 163

War Office Reconstitution Committee (Esher), 258–9

Warburg, Max, 350

Ward, Mrs Humphry, 335

Washington, Treaty of, 1871, 94–5

Webb, Beatrice, 293, 308

Webb, Sidney, 123, 140, 205, 209, 234, 267

Webb, Sidney and Beatrice: on trade union junta, 73; imperialism, 131;

and 'new unionism', 206; and ILP, 222; Fabianism, 277; and state intervention, 303, 308, 310; and Churchill, 307; oppose national insurance, 315; and Osborne judgement, 318; and social science, 371

Webster, Sir Richard, 197

Wells, H.G., 303, 308, 367, 371

Welsh Church Disestablishment Bill, 1913, 339

Wemyss, 8th Earl of *see* Elcho, Francis, Lord

Westminster Gazette, 360

Whigs: and electoral reform, 28–33, 40, 45, 171, 173; and coalition, 35–6; and Liberal organization, 49; composition, 52; in 1868 government, 59, 68; Salisbury and, 188; 1886 defections from Liberal Party, 190; *see also* Liberal Party

Whitbread family, 133

White, Arnold, 303

Wilhelm II, Kaiser, 254

Wilkinson, Spenser, 360

Williams, E.E.: *Made in Germany*, 349

Wills family, 276

Wills, W.H., 143

Wilson, Sir Arthur, 355

Wilson, Sir Henry, 343, 355

Wilson, J. Havelock, 209, 324, 326

Wiseman, Nicholas Patrick Stephen, Cardinal, 157

Wolff, Sir Henry Drummond, 163–4

Wollstonecraft, Mary, 16

Wolseley, Sir Garnet, 154–5, 235

women: position of, 5–7, 16–19, 371; property rights, 16, 330; suffrage, 16, 329–36; employment, 18–20; education, 18–19; office work, 367

Women's National Suffrage League, 335

Women's Social and Political Union (WSPU), 331–6

Women's Trade Union League, 20

Woodard, Nathaniel, 12

Workers Educational Association, 140

Workers' Union, 327

working class: political allegiance, 3–4, 145, 190, 204, 208, 268, 298, 301, 319, 361; and family, 9; religious apathy, 23; suffrage, 31–2, 36–7, 40–1, 44, 46; Conservative Party interest in, 47–8; MPs, 51; organized movement, 74–5, 207–8; and Conservative legislation, 85; and Friendly Societies, 87–8; attitude to Bulgarian atrocities, 102; and poverty, 125; and sport, 143; living standards, 144–5, 321; and ILP, 210, 319; physical weaknesses, 303; hostility to social reform, 308; and higher education, 323

Workman's Times, 208

Workmen's Compensation Act, 1897, 232, 307

Wright, Thomas, 10

Wyndham, George, 269–70, 287, 337

Zulu War, 109